Asset Allocation Strategies for Mutual Funds

Giuseppe Galloppo

Asset Allocation Strategies for Mutual Funds

Evaluating Performance, Risk and Return

palgrave
macmillan

Giuseppe Galloppo
Department of Economics, Engineering
Society and Business
Tuscia University
Viterbo, Italy

ISBN 978-3-030-76127-1 ISBN 978-3-030-76128-8 (eBook)
https://doi.org/10.1007/978-3-030-76128-8

This Palgrave Macmillan imprint is published by the registered company Springer Nature Switzerland AG
The registered company address is: Gewerbestrasse 11, 6330 Cham, Switzerland

To Mom, Dad, Daniele, Alba and Viktoriia for their support throughout my academic career and life
Giuseppe "Pino" Galloppo

Foreword

Mutual Funds (MF) are the crucial tool for channeling the savings to firms all around the world. In 2020, the amount of assets under management by these organizations was estimated to be \$55 trillion, i.e., about \$7300 for every person.[1] MF have adopted increasingly complex strategies over time to attract a wider range of investors. This book provides readers with a detailed exposure to modern state-of-the-art MF asset allocation and portfolio management techniques. Holding a unique mix of theoretical and practical skills, the author shows new insights into different MF portfolio analysis and strategies.

The book mainly focuses on reviewing the principal tools (alpha and beta) governing the determination of risk-adjusted performance, as well as the ability of managers to create value. Why is it so relevant to correctly interpret mutual fund performances? Security markets are generally efficient, and securities are appropriately priced and free lunches can rarely be found in financial markets. Most active money managers (around 80%) underperform the market over the long term and only a few of them are able to bring any value. Actually, let's take the case of an investor who buys and holds an index fund like the S&P 500 Index (which tracks the movement of the entire market): there are only a few MF experts that can help you get better returns than you get. Thus, quoting to famous

[1] https://www.statista.com/statistics/949668/net-assets-regulated-open-end-funds-worldwide/.

investor, John Reese,[2] "*it seems professional investors have something in common with television weathermen: They are in one of the few professions in which you can make a good deal of money while still being wrong most of the time.*" There are also star-players. Peter Lynch, one of the greatest mutual fund managers, established one of the greatest track records ever at Fidelity Investments' Magellan Fund (his performance figure is a 29 percent average return on annual basis during his 13—year tenure). The historical relationship between many of the asset classes discussed in the book and their performance over various market conditions has also been detailed.

Another important feature of this book is the great emphasis put on academic research. As the famous Sir Isaac Newton quotation says "*If I have seen further, it is by standing upon the shoulders of giant*", it is crucial starting from prior research to understand what works and what doesn't work. In this perspective, this book summarizes past academic research on the mutual fund industry looking at both most widely cited academic journals in finance (as *The Journal of Finance*, *Review of Financial Studies*, *Journal of Financial Economics*, and others) and practitioner-oriented scientific journals. At the end of each single chapter, a bibliographic section offers references to the source material about many of the ideas expressed in the book. The author makes a systematic use of numerical examples to facilitate the understanding of these concepts. Reading this book requires a limited mathematical knowledge, such as basic concepts of calculus and statistics.

As a result, the book is of particular interest for students, researchers, practitioners, and professionals in banking and asset management industries.

Daniele Angelo Previati
University of Rome III, DEA Department, Rome, Italy

Franco Fiordelisi
Essex Business School, University of Essex, Colchester, UK

[2] Reese, J. P., & Forehand, J. M. (2009). *The Guru Investor: How to Beat the Market Using History's Best* Investment Strategies. Wiley.

Daniele Angelo Previati is full professor in Financial Markets and Institutions at the Department of Business Studies of the University of Rome III, and fellow of SDA Business School, Bocconi University, Milan. Nowadays he is President of the Italian Association of University Teachers of Banking and Finance, ADEIMF http://www.adeimf.it/. He has been teaching Banking and Finance topics for more than 30 years, with particular focus on bank management, strategy and organization in financial services industry, e-finance, fintech, alternative finance and crowdfunding, also with specific reference to creative and cultural industries. His main research interests relate to various perspectives on bank management: human resources management, intellectual capital, organizational change, stakeholder management, reputation and reputational risk, operational risk, internal and external communication, alternative finance, sustainability and finance, financial literacy. He has published widely, in academic and professional journals and books. He also acted as a consultant for banks and Italian Central Bank on organization design and human resources management.

Franco Fiordelisi is Professor of Banking and Finance at Essex Business School of the University of Essex. He is also the President of the Financial Intermediation Network of European Studies (FINEST). He is also part-time professor of Finance at University of Rome III and senior fellow at the Bocconi Business School in Milan. In international rankings, IDEAS/RePEc ranks his research in the top 5% in the world (last 10 years) and top 10% in the Fields of "Banking", and "Corporate Finance", as of January 2021. His work has been published in international academic journals (such as the *Journal of Financial and Quantitative Analysis*, *Review of Finance*, *Journal of Financial Intermediation*, and *Journal of Corporate Finance*) and presented to primary international financial conferences (e.g., American Finance Association, American Economic Association, European Finance Association, Financial Intermediation Research Society, and Federal Deposit Insurance Corporation).

Acknowledgments

The completion of this book could not have been possible without people who have touched my life, and I would like to acknowledge them. I owe a deep debt of gratitude to my teachers for granting me the gift of knowledge and for inculcating the joy in the learning process, especially to Prof. Daniele Angelo Previati, Prof. Franco Fiordelisi, Prof. Alessandro Carretta, Prof. Annamaria D'Arcangelis, Prof. Luigi Paganetto, and Prof. Luigi Tria, with whom I have had the privilege of working at least for a period of my professional life. First, throughout the development of this text, experienced instructors have provided critical feedback and suggestions for improvement. These individuals deserve a special thanks for their valuable insights and contributions. I would like to recognize the efforts of Prof. Franco Fiordelisi at Essex Business School, who was always willing to take the time to help me better formulate my arguments for the book, and Prof. Gianfranco Gianfrate at EDHEC Business School for his design work and consultation. A huge thank you also goes to Prof. Mauro Aliano, whose insightful advice made this book possible. I am especially honored that Prof. Daniele Angelo Previati and Prof. Franco Fiordelisi, consented to write a foreword to this edition. A special thanks goes to Dr. Davide Scutti, Professional Fund Manager at FINNAT, his encouragement has motivated me to strengthen my arguments and pursue topics that are of concern both to financial professionals and ordinary investors and the financial services industry above all for the regulatory aspects. I am particularly grateful to my colleague and, above all, my friend, Prof. Stefano Caiazza for all the support he gave me along the arduous road of econometric analyses. My deepest gratitude goes to Sara, Matteo, Paolo, Andrea, Claudia and Alessandro—my near graduate students at the second semester course a.y. 2019/2020, who took over a part of the editing project. No book comes to fruition without an editor, so I would like to thank my editor my Executive Editor Tula Weis and her colleagues Shreenidhi Natarajan; Susan Westendorf and all the staff at Palgrave Macmillan—Springer, including Lucy Kidwell for their assistance and support throughout this process. Last, but most importantly, a special thank is owed to Viktoriia for sharing the excitement of new ideas, and whose tremendous contributions to this book began the day I decided to write it and didn't end until the final draft was submitted. Simply, without her support through the many days I spent on the road lecturing to hundreds of academic papers, this book could not have been written.

I apologize for my forgetfulness. Please, accept my unspoken thanks.

There are many reasons for starting a book, but to finish it I needed the great help of the lord who put so many brothers and sisters to walk with me through my path. I have received much more than I have given. As well as in almost every experience of my life, I hope to do better in the future.

Contents

List of Figures

Chapter 2

Chapter 3

Chapter 4

Chapter 6

Chapter 7

Chapter 8

Chapter 9

List of Tables

Chapter 2

Chapter 3

Chapter 4

Chapter 5

Chapter 6

Chapter 7

Chapter 8

Chapter 9

CHAPTER 1

What Is a Mutual Fund?

1 What Is a Mutual Fund?

Mutual funds represent specific financial units. Their main activity is pooling investors' money together in order to purchase different financial securities (equities, bonds, commodities, money market instruments and other assets).

Mutual fund belongs to the category of collective investment vehicle (CIV). Investors in securities frequently hold those investments by pooling their money with other investors in a collective investment vehicle (CIV), rather than investing directly.[1] This occurs because of the economic efficiency and other advantages CIVs provide. A mutual fund is focused on a specific investment target. For example, a debt fund will have the specified objective to invest in fixed income instruments or products like bonds, government securities, etc.[2] Similarly, an equity fund will invest in stocks and other equity instruments.

The combined holdings of the mutual fund are known as its portfolio. The overall performance is usually tracked as the change in the total market capitalization of the fund—derived from the aggregate performance of the underlying investments. A portfolio manager's

[1] https://www.oecd.org/tax/treaties/45359261.pdf.

[2] https://www.hdfcfund.com/learn/beginner/mutual-funds/what-mutual-fund.

G. Galloppo, *Asset Allocation Strategies for Mutual Funds*,
https://doi.org/10.1007/978-3-030-76128-8_1

primary goal is to outperform the benchmark, which is generally a widely followed index (e.g., Standard & Poor's 500).[3] For this reason, the fastest way to see how well a fund manager is performing, is to observe fund returns relative to the benchmark.

The investment fraction within the pooled money, that is the mutual fund portfolio, belongs to each single investor and is called share. Mutual funds are, therefore, pooled investments, which let investors enjoy economies of scale and have access to well-diversified portfolios of securities. Unlike holdings representing the ownership of just one part, a share in a mutual fund includes investments in many different securities. Later in this chapter we will explore the advantages of investing into Mutual funds.

Mutual funds are created and managed by an Asset Management Company, which is registered with the SEC in the USA and the FSA in the UK, or in another local Financial Services Authority (FSA) in European Union and in the rest of the world.

Pooled money is managed together on behalf of investors by experts specialized in equity and/or debt investing—professional money managers hired by asset management company.[4]

Decisions to buy or sell securities are operated by one or more portfolio managers, supported by team of researchers. Portfolio managers allocate holdings, that are fund assets, which create fund portfolio. They attempt to produce capital gains or income for fund investors by investing according to specified investment objectives that are a part of a certain investment strategy.

Asset management company may have several mutual fund schemes with their specific investment mandates. An investor can choose, which scheme he or she wants to invest in, based on the given mandate or objective.[5] New funds are continually introduced, while less successful funds may merge with other funds (often within the same family) or may cease to exist.

Mutual fund portfolio is organized in the way it meets investment goals described in its prospectus. The regulator requires all mutual fund

[3] https://www.fidelity.com/.

[4] https://www.hdfcfund.com/learn/beginner/mutual-funds/what-mutual-fund.

[5] https://www.hdfcfund.com/learn/beginner/mutual-funds/what-mutual-fund#:~:text=An%20investor%20can%20choose%20which,Mutual%20Funds)%20Regulations%2C%201996.

schemes of Asset management company to clearly spell out the fund objectives in its prospectus that an investor must read before he/she invests in a mutual fund.

The depositary bank, that is registered with the local FSA, holds the securities of various schemes of fund in its custody and monitors the performance and compliance with the local FSA.

Mutual fund industry has been demonstrating the continuous growth since the 1980s and did not experience any interruptions in its development. At the end of 2019, mutual fund assets worldwide were $54.9 trillion, according to the Investment Company Institute.

The countries with the largest mutual fund industries are[6]:

1. United Kingdom: $26.7 trillion
2. Australia: $5.3 trillion
3. Ireland: $3.4 trillion
4. Germany: $2.5 trillion
5. Luxembourg: $2.2 trillion
6. France: $2.2 trillion
7. Japan: $2.1 trillion
8. Canada: $1.9 trillion
9. United States: $1.9 trillion
10. China: $1.4 trillion.

In the United States mutual funds play an important role in household finances. At the end of 2019, 23% of household financial assets were held in mutual funds.[7] Their role in retirement savings was even more significant since mutual funds accounted for roughly half of the assets in individual retirement accounts, 401(k)s[8] and other similar retirement plans.[9]

Luxembourg and Ireland are the primary jurisdictions for the registration of UCITS (see later for the UCITS definition) funds. These funds

[6] 2020 Investment Company Fact Book. Investment Company Institute. 2020.

[7] https://www.statista.com/statistics/255519/share-of-household-financial-assets-held-by-investment-companies-in-the-united-states/#:~:text=The%20statistic%20presents%20the%20share,ETFs%20or%20unit%20investment%20trusts.

[8] In the United States, a 401(k) plan is an employer-sponsored defined-contribution pension account.

[9] https://www.ncbi.nlm.nih.gov/pmc/articles/PMC3937807/.

may be sold throughout the European Union and in other countries that have adopted mutual recognition regimes according to the so-called passport rule.

2 Prospectus

Mutual funds use a document called a prospectus to disclose information about the fund to investors. The prospectus must be published by the fund provider annually or more often. It contains all the detailed data and information that investors may need when choosing a fund.[10] Mutual funds must provide a copy of fund prospectus to their shareholders after they purchased shares, but investors can—and should—request and read the fund prospectus before making an investment decision.[11] SEC rules require mutual funds to provide a copy of fund prospectus before or with the delivery of fund shares to investors, but an investor can—and should—also request and read a prospectus before making an investment decision.[12]

Mutual fund companies are required by law to provide investors with a prospectus before they invest. Virtually, now all fund companies make their prospectus available online as a free download (most funds provide their prospectus not just on their websites but they also have toll free numbers, where one can request a copy). Most brokers will also be able to provide a copy of the prospectus. In recent years, many of the largest online stock brokers have included a link to mutual fund prospectus in research results that are displayed when searching for the ticker symbol on the broker's site.[13] An investor can also obtain prospectuses from the SEC's Electronic Data Gathering, Analysis, and Retrieval ("EDGAR") database.[14]

The document can help investors make more informed investment decisions because it contains a host of relevant information about the investment security. Before investing in a mutual fund, an investor should

[10] https://www.merrilledge.com/article/how-to-read-a-mutual-fund-prospectus.

[11] https://www.sec.gov/fast-answers/answersmfprospectustipshtm.html.

[12] https://www.sec.gov/oiea/investor-alerts-bulletins/ib_mfprospectus1.html.

[13] https://www.sec.gov/reportspubs/investor-publications/investorpubsinwsmfhtm.html.

[14] https://www.sec.gov/oiea/investor-alerts-bulletins/ib_mfprospectus1.html

read the prospectus thoroughly, so he or she can carefully consider the fund investment objectives, risks, fees, and expenses. Make sure the fund operates in a way that's consistent with his or her own needs, investment goals, and tolerance for risk. For instance, if an investor needs to invest for income and preservation of capital, and the prospectus describes the fund investment policy as aggressive and growth oriented, then he or she hasn't found a good match.[15]

In the United States, the Securities and Exchange Commission (SEC) specifies the kinds of information that must be included in fund prospectuses and requires funds to present key data, such as fees and past performance, in a standard format, so that investors can readily compare different funds. Same regulatory scheme applies in Europe.

To be specific, the SEC and the local FSA[16] in Europe, require mutual funds to include important information in the prospectus, including[17]:

- **Minimum investments**—Mutual funds differ both in the minimum initial investment required and the minimum for subsequent investments.
- **Investment objectives**—The goal of each fund should be clearly defined—from income with preservation of principal to long-term capital appreciation, to be sure the fund objective matches investor's objective.
- **Investment strategies**—A prospectus will outline general strategies the fund managers will implement. The principal strategies of the fund show how the fund intends to achieve its investment objective. These strategies indicate the approach the fund adviser takes when deciding which securities to buy or sell. For example, the fund may choose to concentrate in one or more industries, geographic regions or types of securities. In addition, some funds may be actively managed, while others seek to replicate the performance of a specified index. Although a fund's name often suggests that the fund focuses on a particular type of investment, you should not rely upon the fund's name without examining the prospectus further.

[15] https://equitable.com/products/investment-strategies/questions/what-is-mutual-fund-prospectus.

[16] https://www.sec.gov/oiea/investor-alerts-bulletins/ib_mfprospectus1.html.

[17] https://www.merrilledge.com/article/how-to-read-a-mutual-fund-prospectus.

- **Risk factors**—All investments in funds involve risk of financial loss. The reward for taking on risk is the potential for a greater investment return. An investor with a high-risk tolerance is generally willing to risk losing money in order to seek larger investment gains than those typically achieved by a lower-risk investment. On the other hand, an investor with a low-risk tolerance may favor investments in funds that are generally more stable in value. When reading a fund prospectus, it is important to determine if the fund satisfies your investment objective and matches your risk tolerance, as well as the risks in your overall portfolio. The investor risk tolerance depends upon several factors, including financial situation, age, and family obligations. The types of risks to which a fund is subject, vary considerably with the nature of its investments. Some of the most common risks for funds include:
- **Market risk**. The fund may incur losses due to declines in the markets in which it invests.
- **Business or Issuer risk**. The fund may invest in a company that goes out of business, suffers financial problems, or otherwise does not perform as expected, especially, if the fund primarily invests in companies without an established record.
- **Credit risk**. The fund may invest in bonds or other debt instruments from an issuer who is unable to pay interest payments as scheduled or repay the principal.
- **Interest rate risk**. The value of the fund's investments in bonds or other debt instruments may decrease if interest rates rise.
- **Inflation risk**. The value of the fund's investments in bonds or other debt instruments also may not keep track with price increases from inflation.
- **Concentration risk**. The fund may concentrate its investments in a particular industry, sector or geographical area, which can result in a less diversified portfolio that may be subject to greater volatility in performance than a fund that does not concentrate its investments.

Other Major risks that households and financial intermediaries are likely to face, when investing in a particular mutual fund, will be included in the prospectus.[18] For example, a global or international mutual fund

[18] https://www.thebalance.com/what-is-a-mutual-fund-prospectus-357947.

prospectus is probably going to spend time explaining currency risks, the possibility of companies implementing capital restrictions, the dangers of war, and other considerations that are less relevant (under most circumstances) to a purely domestic mutual fund. If the fund employs leverage it will be explained where and when they do this. Leverage is the use of borrowing to increase returns. The prospectus will tell if the mutual fund lends its own securities out to others, such as short sellers, in exchange for income. The portfolio turnover rate will be also shown.

- **Performance data**—This section shows the fund track record. Remember that past results do not guarantee future performance. Investor will find selected per-share data including net asset value (NAV) and total return for different time periods as prescribed by SEC guidelines. Performance data listed in a prospectus are based on standard formulas established by the SEC and enable you to make comparisons with other funds. When evaluating performance, look at the track record of a fund over a time period that matches your own investment goals. At the same, be careful choosing the right benchmark. For instance, Treasury bills selected as a benchmark for equity is not relevant, because one must use S&P 500 as commonly recognized benchmark for equity asset class.
- **Fees and expenses**—Sales and management fees associated with a mutual fund must be clearly listed. The prospectus includes a breakdown of the historical expenses paid by the mutual fund shareholders over the past few years. The prospectus will also display the impact these fees and expenses, would have on a hypothetical investment over time.
- **Distribution policy and Tax information**—A fund pays its investors income from realized capital gains, dividends, interest, or other income stemming from the securities and investing activities of the fund. The distribution policy tells an investor how these payments are made. Some funds distribute returns directly to unitholders (Income Funds), while others reinvest the distributions back into the fund, buying more units for fundholders (Capitalization Funds). A prospectus will include information on the tax status and implications of a fund's distributions—whether they will be treated as dividend income or capital gains.
- **Investor services**—Shareholders may have access to certain services, such as automatic investment of dividends and systematic withdrawal

plans. This section of the prospectus, usually near the back of the publication, will describe these services and how investors can take advantage of them.

- **Fund Management**—Here shareholders can discover how long the fund manager has been managing the fund. One must watch out for the fund that has been in operation significantly longer than the fund manager has been managing it. The performance of such funds can be credited not to the present manager but to the previous ones. If the current manager has been managing the fund for only a short period of time, one should look into his or her past performance with other funds with similar investment goals and strategies. A better gauge can be received of manager talent and investment style. Names of the directors or trustees who represent the mutual fund shareholders, including the range of their investment in the fund (e.g., \$10,0001–\$50,000 or \$100,000 +) must be provided. The amount the directors are paid for their service and the control persons and principal owners of the fund will be listed. The range of investment, when people making the decision about the fund's investment strategy is disclosed. This includes the portfolio manager or members of the investment committee and will show if they have money in the fund itself. So, an investor can decide whether they are sufficiently exposed to the risks of their decisions.[19] Investors can also find detailed information relating to the fund's investment advisers and details on how to purchase and redeem shares.

A full prospectus may run 20 pages or more and it can be difficult to tease out answers to common investor questions.[20] The Securities and Exchange Commission permits fund companies to issue simplified summary prospectuses to help investors better understand their funds' key characteristics. The Summary Prospectus, which is used by many funds, is just a few pages long and contains key information about a fund.[21] The SEC requires mutual funds to present the information in a standard format so that investors can readily compare different mutual funds. The summary prospectus appears in the following standardized

[19] https://www.thebalance.com/what–is–a–mutual–fund–prospectus–357947.

[20] https://www.merrilledge.com/article/how–to–read–a–mutual–fund–prospectus.

[21] https://www.sec.gov/fast–answers/answersmfprospectustipshtm.html.

order: (1) investment objectives/goals; (2) fee table; (3) investments, risks, and performance; (4) management—investment advisers and portfolio managers; (5) purchase and sale of fund shares; (6) tax information; and (7) financial intermediary compensation.

In Europe, the UCITS IV Directive goes in the same direction of the SEC Summary Prospectus, and it sets out the framework for the KIID, a stand-alone, pre-contractual, 2-page document containing the essential features of the fund.

3 Time Value of Mutual Fund Investment

The time value of the investment in mutual fund involves that investors buy shares that rise or fall in value based on the performance of the fund's underlying securities. These investors may be retail or institutional in nature. Mutual fund investors do not actually own the securities in the companies the fund purchases, but share in the profits or losses of the fund's total holdings—hence the "mutual" in "mutual funds." Investors gain or lose from the fund activity proportionally to the part they own—shares, therefore, such type of investing differs from the one in stock shares, because shares in mutual fund do not give any voting rights to its holders.

The purchase of mutual fund' share means buying the portfolio performance, which defines the value of mutual fund. That's why the price of the mutual fund, also known as its net asset value (NAV) is determined by the total value of the securities in the portfolio (minus the fund's liabilities), divided by the total amount (number) of the fund's outstanding shares.

Unlike stock prices, the NAV of mutual fund shares usually is not trading hourly on the market and is defined at the end of the trading day, therefore, mutual fund shares are bought or redeemed at the current NAV. To be specific, funds must compute their net asset value according to the rules set forth in their prospectuses. Most compute their NAV at the end of each business day (in a nutshell this is true for all open-end funds).

Investors typically earn a return from a mutual fund in three ways:

1. **Dividend and interest payments**. Income is earned from dividends on stocks and interest on bonds held in the fund's portfolio. Owners are funded in the form of distribution, because a fund pays off

the received return over the year.[22] Nevertheless, funds often give investors a choice either to receive distributions directly, or have them reinvested in the fund.

2. **Capital Gains Distributions**. The price of the securities in a fund changes over time. When a fund sells a security that has gone up in price, this is a capital gain. On the contrary, when a fund sells a security that has gone down in price, this is a capital loss. When a fund sells a security that has increased in price, the fund has a capital gain. At the end of the year, according to the same rationale exposed just below, the fund distributes these capital gains to investors, minus any capital losses.
3. **Increased NAV**. If price of fund holdings increases and they are not sold, then the price of the fund share will increase too. If the market value of a fund portfolio increases, after deducting expenses, then the value of the fund and its shares increases.[23] The higher NAV reflects the higher value of the investment.

4 Mutual Funds Advantages and Disadvantages

There are advantages and disadvantages of mutual funds in their comparison with direct investing. The advantages of mutual funds include economies of scale, diversification, liquidity, and professional management. However, these come with mutual fund fees and expenses.

[22] Once dividends and distributions are disbursed, the fund's share price declines by the total of the per—share distribution to the fund's shareholders. The price falls because the distribution is withdrawn from the fund's assets, which decreases the net asset value (NAV). Distribution means the portion of capital gains, dividends or interest income from the fund that investors receive periodically. Net capital gain distribution is common for all investors and are received as result of selling of mutual fund holdings. The capital gains are calculated as the difference between the sell price of the stock and its buy price minus operating expenses to get the exact amount of distribution. After paying out the dividends and distributions, the share price of the fund reduces by the total distribution per share among the fund shareholders. Distribution is taken from fund's assets, so the price falls and the NAV go down.

[23] https://www.investor.gov/introduction-investing/investing-basics/investment-products/mutual-funds-and-exchange-traded-1#:~:text=If%20the%20market%20value%20of,higher%20value%20of%20your%20investment.

4.1 Mutual Fund Benefits

Diversification

There is no need to buy and screen for huge amount of assets by one single person when dealing with mutual funds, because they allow easily access the diversified portfolio. Mutual funds typically invest in a range of companies and industries. This helps to lower the investor portfolio risk if one company fails.[24] It would be very difficult for an investor to create a diversified portfolio of investments on his own with a small amount of money. This is one of the most important principles of investing.

Professional Management

One of the key advantages of investing in a mutual fund is that each investor (even with a small investment) gets access to professional money management and expertise.[25] The reason to buy a mutual fund is explained by lack of time or knowledge to manage a portfolio on one's own and restricted access to information that have professionals only. Professional portfolio managers and analysts have the expertise and technology resources needed to research companies and analyze market information before making investment decisions. Fund managers identify which securities to buy and sell through individual security evaluation, sector allocation, and analysis of technical factors.[26] Moreover, company management also provides monitoring of performance. Therefore, a mutual fund allows to receive professional assistance from the side of money managers for small individual investors and at a relatively small cost.

Easy Access and Liquidity

Mutual funds are highly liquid investments, because they are a part of all major stock exchanges and can be quite easily bought or sold. The majority of mutual funds allow investors to buy or sell their fund shares once a day at the close of the market at the fund's NAV. Mutual funds become the most often way for individual investors to deal with specific asset types, such as foreign equities or exotic commodities. Moreover, mutual funds allow to take larger positions and invest in various assets

[24] https://www.investor.gov/introduction-investing/investing-basics/investment-products/mutual-funds-and-exchange-traded-1.

[25] https://www.hdfcfund.com/learn/beginner/mutual-funds/what-mutual-fund.

[26] https://www.fidelity.com/learning-center/investment-products/mutual-funds/what-are-mutual-funds.

by pooling investments from many small investors. The fund might have access to certain products available only to institutional investors.[27] In addition, investors have wide variety of offers from managers to choose with respect to their investing preferences and styles. With respect to liquidity constraints, we should underline how for majority of stock funds the required minimum initial investment may be substantially less than what an investor would have had to invest to build a diversified portfolio of individual stocks or bonds. Furthermore, mutual fund investors can easily redeem their shares at any time, for the current net asset value (NAV) plus any redemption fees.[28]

Economies of Scale

Since a mutual fund buys and sells large amounts of securities at a time, its transaction costs are lower than what an individual would pay for securities transactions.[29]

Transparency

Regulation authorities of mutual fund industry require mutual funds to ensure fairness and accountability to investors.

4.2 *Mutual Fund Disadvantages*

Cash Drag

Mutual funds represent a vehicle of money pooled together, where there is always someone who puts money into it and someone that takes it out. To maintain the capacity to satisfy share redemptions each day, funds typically have to keep a large portion of their portfolios in cash. Cash is necessary to maintain good liquidity, however, money must be working. For that matter, unlike a typical investor, mutual funds have to keep a large part of their portfolio in cash to keep their liquidity and ability to support withdrawals.

[27] Institutional investors aim to invest money on behalf of others and can be represented in the form of a company or organization, with the most common types: mutual funds, pension and insurance companies. Their purpose is to buy and sell huge number of various securities that made them become the whales of Wall Street. They are more sophisticated than individual investors and might be a subject to less restriction in respect to regulation.

[28] https://www.investor.gov/introduction-investing/investing-basics/investment-products/mutual-funds-and-exchange-traded-1.

[29] https://smfs.co/Login/MutualFund.aspx#:~:text=A%20mutual%20fund%20is%20a,to%20make%20and%20monitor%20investments.&text=Economies%20of%20Scale%20%2D%20Because%20a,would%20pay%20for%20securities%20transactions.

High Costs

The main disadvantage of mutual funds is that, because the fund is managed, an investor will incur fees no matter how the fund performs.

Maintaining a mutual fund is an expensive process, because every single step from manager's salary to investor statements requires expenses that must be carried by investors. It is very important to pay attention to the fees to be paid, because they are very various among funds. Fund investors pay the fees annually in the form of expense ratio (fees for running the fund typically range from 1 to 3%), that reduce the overall payout of the fund and are to be paid by mutual fund investors regardless fund performance, making them only losses in years, when mutual fund does not bring any returns. Later in this chapter we investigate the topic of the fees associated with Mutual funds.

Dilution

Dilution is also the result of a successful fund growing too big. New money in funds with strong performance create challenges for fund managers to find right investment opportunities for a new capital. We come back on this point in the chapter devoted to the relationship between size and performance.

Lack of Liquidity

A mutual fund allows investors to request their shares to be converted into cash at any time, however, unlike stock that trades throughout the day, many mutual fund redemptions take place only at the end of each trading day except when mutual fund investing in illiquid assets.

5 How to Buy and Sell Mutual Funds

In the US and UK funds are sold by two main methods. The first involves sales by brokers or dealers in the US or by independent financial advisers IFA's in the UK and in EU. Funds sold in this way usually involve a front-end or back-end load fee, with the fund determining the load but it is retained by selling broker (or IFA) as compensation to the investment advice provided. The second sales method is direct marketing of funds via newspapers and 'fund supermarkets' such as Charles Schwab's One Source.[30] A fund supermarket is a program offered by a broker-dealer or other financial institution through which its customers may purchase- and

[30] https://www.schwab.com/mutual-funds/no-load-mutual-funds/onesource-select-list.

redeem a variety of funds, with or without paying transaction fees.[31] In Europe investors buy the most of mutual fund shares from the fund itself, or more often through a financial intermediary. The price that investors pay for the mutual fund is the fund's per share net asset value plus any fees charged at the time of purchase, such as sales loads.[32] Mutual fund shares are "redeemable," meaning investors can sell the shares back to the fund at any time. The fund usually must send the payment to investors within a very short number of days (for an open-end fund: 7 or less).

6 Depositary Bank

A depository bank is a specialist financial entity which, depending on jurisdiction, facilitates investment in securities markets.

In the United States, a depository is a bank providing various agency services in connection with a depositary receipt program. The depositary bank issues and cancels the receipts which represent ownership of the underlying shares, distributes dividend payments and shareholder information, maintains the register of holders and arranges a custodian to hold the ordinary shares in the foreign jurisdiction.[33]

In the EU, a depository is represented by a financial institution, that provides services to Investment Funds. Such funds are organized in the form of UCITS or Alternative Investment Fund with authorization to trade in any EU jurisdiction. Under UCITS (2009/65/EC) and AIFMD (2011/61/EU) Directives, authorized investment funds must have a depository that safekeeps the fund assets and controls whether fund activity meet the relevant regulatory requirements and constitutional documents of the fund. Under this scheme a depositary bank (matching also the role of a custodian) would be to:

- arrange settlement of any purchases and sales
- collect information on and income from such assets (dividends in the case of stocks/equities and coupons—interest payments—in the

[31] https://www.sec.gov/divisions/investment/noaction/1998/ici103098.pdf.

[32] https://www.investor.gov/introduction-investing/investing-basics/investment-products/mutual-funds-and-exchange-traded-1.

[33] https://www.adr.db.com/drwebrebrand/resources/glossary-of-terms#glossaryD.

case of bonds) and administer related tax withholding documents and foreign tax reclamation
- administer voluntary and involuntary corporate actions on securities held such as stock dividends, stock splits, business combinations (mergers), tender offers, bond calls, etc.
- maintain currency/cash bank accounts, effect deposits and withdrawals and manage other cash transactions
- other services like: fund accounting, administration, legal, compliance and tax support services.

Depositaries receive great attention from the side of EU regulation, where in particular, the recent "UCITS V" directive imposed a "strict[34]" standard of depositary liability that covers fund assets' failure due to different reasons.

7 Fund Structures

There are three primary structures of mutual funds: open-end funds, unit investment trusts, and closed-end funds. There is also a very common category called ETF and which has been remarkably successful in the last twenty years. ETFs can belong to the category of both open-end and unit investment trusts.

Open-end funds
In an open-ended mutual fund, an investor can invest or enter and redeem or exit at the time when investors decide to buy or redeem their shares.[35] This scheme allows, therefore, investors to buy or sell units at any point in time. It does not have a fixed maturity period. The number of shares in issue varies according to demand, hence, the term "open ended". When talking about mutual funds, investors and professionals often mean "open-end" funds, that redeem the shares based on a daily net asset value—NAV, that drives from prices of fund securities. Every jurisdiction has their own set of regulations regarding mutual funds. For example, in

[34] Strict liability is a definition from criminal and civil law area and means legal responsibility of a person for consequences of their activity even with absence of fault or criminal intentions.

[35] https://www.hdfcfund.com/learn/beginner/mutual-funds/different-types-mutual-funds.

the USA, open-end funds buy back shares daily at the end of the day, but in EU the UCITS funds are obliged to accept redemptions only twice a month, however, most of them are working on the daily basis. An open-ended fund can also decide to stop taking in new investors if they do not want to, or cannot manage significant (very large in terms of assets under management) funds.

Unit investment trusts

Unit investment trusts (UITs) are issued to the public only once when they are created. Once created, the duration of UIT is agreed. Therefore, investors have a right, whether to redeem shares any time like in open-end fund, or wait until the end of the UIT life time. The specificity of unit investment trusts is that their portfolio of securities is set up at the moment of its creation and they do not have professional investment managers.

Closed-end funds

Closed-end funds, differently from open-end funds, generally do not continuously offer their shares for sale and they generally issue and sell shares to the public only once, when they are created through an initial public offering. In closed-ended funds, the unit capital to invest is then pre-defined. That means that fund company does not have a right to sell more units that were initially defined. This case the maturity date is usually fixed and investors can invest during the New Fund Offer (NFO) period. His/her investment will automatically be redeemed on the maturity date.[36] According to this rationale, during the standard investment life closed-end fund shares generally are not redeemable. That is, a closed-end fund is not required to buy its shares back from investors upon request. Therefore, those investors who are willing to sell their shares, can do it only to other investors and have no right to sell the shares back to the fund.

There are some types of close end mutual funds that allow investors to sell their units directly to mutual funds by repurchasing at NAV related prices on the periodical basis. However, it may happen that investor shares are listed for trading on a secondary market. At the same time, investors might receive a price for their shares which is strongly different from the

[36] https://www.hdfcfund.com/learn/beginner/mutual-funds/different-types-mutual-funds.

actual NAV, which can be higher ("premium" to NAV) or lower ("discount" to NAV). Closed-end funds are permitted to invest in a greater number of "illiquid" securities than are mutual funds.[37] Due to this feature, funds that seek to invest in markets, where the securities tend to be more illiquid, are typically organized as closed-end funds.[38] Closed-end funds come in many varieties. They can have different investment objectives, strategies, and investment portfolios.

Index Funds and Exchange-traded funds (ETFs)

Another group, which has become extremely popular in the last few years, falls under the moniker "index funds". A very popular type of index funds are the ETFs (Exchange-traded funds). Unlike other types of mutual funds, ETFs are traded like individual stocks on stock exchanges, charge lower fees and can be bought or sold anytime during the trading day. ETFs can also be sold short or purchased on margin.[39] Exchange-traded funds (ETFs) combine characteristics of both closed-end funds and open-end funds. ETFs are traded throughout the day on a stock exchange. Standard ETFs are shaped as index funds, but financial innovation has hugely impacted this product and, nowadays it is common to find several smart beta ETFs in the market, investing in complex risk factors.

Their investment strategy is based on the belief that it is very hard, and often expensive, to try to beat the market consistently. An index fund, according to this rationale, is a type of mutual fund with holdings that match or track a particular market index, such as the S&P 500. These funds include stocks tracking a specific index, therefore, they reflect the risk and return of the market. From the point of view of the asset mix, therefore, an index fund identifies stocks and their corresponding ratio in the market index and put the money in similar proportion and in similar stocks, aiming to replicate the underlying market index. Index funds can be distinguished by their focus on company size, geographical focus or industry sector.

[37] https://www.sec.gov/fast-answers/answersmfclosehtm.html#: ~ :text = Closed%2Dend%20funds%20are%20permitted,the%20fund%20in%20determining%20NAV).

[38] https://www.sec.gov/fast-answers/answersmfclosehtm.html.

[39] https://www.thestreet.com/personal-finance/education/can-mutual-funds-be-purchased-on-margin-15186673#:%E2%80%89~%E2%80%89:text%E2%80%89=%E2%80%89ETFs%20are%20essentially%20mutual%20funds,stock%20throughout%20the%20trading%20day.&text%E2%80%89=%E2%80%89Their%20pricing%20and%20structure%20allow,same%20fashion%20as%20individual%20stocks.

In addition, ETFs are more cost effective and liquid than mutual funds. Their strategy is characterized by less expenses on research from analysts and advisors. These funds are often designed with cost-sensitive investors in mind.[40]

Index funds are ideal for investors who want to invest in equity mutual funds but at the same time don't want to depend on the fund manager discretionary power.
Unlike traditional index funds, which track a market index, ***non-traditional index funds*** use custom-built indexes to select the fund's investments. By tracking a custom-built index, a non-traditional index fund may seek to achieve performance greater than a particular market or sector. Or, such a fund may seek exposure to securities based on factors like financial strength, or environmental, social and governance concerns.[41] Under the non-traditional index funds an emerging class of very popular strategies is represented by **Smart Beta**. The custom-built indexes for these funds often use "factors" to select the fund's investments. A factor is a characteristic or feature that is believed to cause certain types of securities to outperform or underperform the market as a whole.[42] Examples of common factors are value, dividends or quality. The Quant Funds are also included within the Smart Beta category. The custom-built indexes for these funds use numerical methods like quantitative analysis or algorithms to select the fund's investments.[43]

On the opposite side of Index Funds or ETF, we have actively managed funds seeking to outperform market indices, and carry the potential for greater return than passively managed funds. They also carry higher potential rewards as well as risks.

Interval
It operates as a combination of open and closed ended scheme. Such type of funds opens only for purchases or redemptions in a time period agreed by the fund house but they are closed all other time. They may be traded

[40] http://wealthtrustcap.com/Wealthtrust/mutual-fund-partners.aspx.

[41] https://www.sec.gov/oiea/investor-alerts-and-bulletins/ib_smartbeta.

[42] https://www.investor.gov/introduction-investing/investing-basics/investment-products/mutual-funds-and-exchange-traded-3.

[43] https://www.sec.gov/oiea/investor-alerts-and-bulletins/ib_smartbeta.

on the stock exchange or they may even be open for sale or redemption during pre-determined intervals at NAV related prices.[44]

8 Classification of Funds by Types of Asset Class or Underlying Investments

Depending on portfolio targets (security types), investment objectives and seeking returns, mutual funds are divided into several categories. Their principal investments are described in the prospectus. The fund prospectus as described above, is, a legal document that describes the fund investment objective, investment approach and permitted investments. According to the European Fund and Asset Management Association (EFAMA) classification, each fund is assigned one of four categories according to the assets in which the fund invests:

- Equity: an equity fund should invest at least 85% of its assets in stocks.
- Bond: a bond fund should invest at least 90% in fixed income transferable securities. No exposure to equity is normally allowed.
- Money market: money market funds are categorized along duration (usually from an average maturity of 30 days until a weighted average modified duration of one year maximum) and investment possibility (from investment grade money market instruments to transferable debt instruments).
- Mixed: a mixed fund invests in stocks, bonds and cash.

8.1 Equity Funds

Equity mutual funds buy stocks of a collection of publicly traded companies. Equity funds have a higher potential for growth but more potential volatility in value. A rule of thumb is that the younger you are, the more your portfolio should include equity funds, as you have more time to weather inevitable ups and downs in market value. Equity funds are one of the most popular type of mutual fund, accounting for 24.5% of all mutual funds owned in 2019, according to the Investment Company Institute (ICI).

[44] https://economictimes.indiatimes.com/definition/interval-schemes.

The performance of invested shares in the stock market defines whether investors loose or win from such funds. Another gain component is associated with the generation of dividends by the companies owned by the fund. Equity funds have the potential to generate significant returns over a period. Hence, the risk associated with these funds also tends to be comparatively higher.

Equity mutual funds can be sliced and diced in several ways depending on the goals of the fund. Each of these groups tries to maintain a portfolio of stocks with certain characteristics. Some equity funds are named for the size of the companies they invest in: small-, mid-, or large-cap. Others, for example, get their name from the chosen investment approach and can be related to income, value or growth.

Funds based on Company Size

Some funds focus only on "large cap" or "small cap" companies, which refer to market capitalization of companies. Market capitalization is derived by multiplying the share price by number of shares outstanding. Large-cap companies have high market capitalizations. The discrimination threshold, in terms of market capitalization, is not fixed standard, but depends on the threshold value chosen by the individual asset management company. Large-cap stocks are typically blue chip firms that are often recognizable by name. The market value of large-cap companies ranges from 5 to 10 billion USD or even greater, while small-cap companies have a market cap from 200 million to 2 billion USD. These smaller companies tend to be riskier investments. Mid-cap stocks fill in the gap between small- and large-cap, that are companies worth from $2 billion to $5 or to $10 billion.

Industry or Sector Funds

These types of mutual funds forgo broad diversification to focus on a particular industry. Sector funds are indeed targeted strategy funds aimed at specific sectors of the economy, such as technology, oil and gas, aviation or health care, and so on. For example, investors who wish to exposure to gains from companies like Google and Apple could put money in a technology fund. In case of crash of one industry sector, the losses can be covered by gains from other sectors, that is why it is important for investors to have ownership in funds from different sectors, so to diversify their portfolio. If we do not consider a portfolio logic, or if we consider a single bet investment, as these funds invest only in specific sectors with only a few stocks, the risk factor is on the higher side.

Growth and Value Funds
The investment style of the fund is another mutual fund differentiator. Value funds look for companies those stock is undervalued by the market. Value asset managers employ a style of investing that looks for high-quality, low-growth companies. Such companies have low price-to-earnings (P/E) and price-to-book (P/B) ratios, high dividend yields. For the growth funds the main interest is in stocks that are expected to bring returns higher than average. Growth funds, look to companies that have had (and are expected to have) strong growth in earnings, sales, and cash flows. These companies typically have high P/E ratios and do not pay dividends. Another investment type is called "blend" and it includes mix of strict value and growth investments, including companies that are somewhere between value and growth types of stocks.

Regional, Global and Emerging Market Funds
Mutual funds can be organized depending on geographical location, that allow investors to focus on certain areas. This can mean focusing on a broader region (say Latin America) or an individual country (for example, only Brazil). The main interest in this fund from investor side is that they make it easier to buy stocks in foreign countries, which can otherwise be difficult or expensive. Emerging market funds invest in stock markets of countries with growing economies.

8.2 Fixed-Income or Bond Funds

Rather than buy stocks, a fixed-income mutual fund focuses on investments that pay a set rate of return, such as government bonds, corporate bonds, or other debt instruments. Considered a safer and less risky investment than stocks, bond funds have less potential for growth than equity funds. In 2019, about 21% of all U.S. mutual funds are bond funds, as Investment Company Institute (ICI) stats show.[45]

Bond funds are characterized by low risk-return profile and are a good choice for low-risk style investors looking for stable income. Unlike equity funds preferred mostly by younger investors, bond funds are mostly desirable among those near retirement age to protect their savings. However, they are subject to credit risk. Bond funds can be sub-classified according to:

[45] https://www.icifactbook.org/ch1/20_fb_ch1.

- The maturity of the bonds held (i.e., short-, intermediate- or long-term)
- The country of issuance of the bonds (such as the European market, U.S., emerging market or global)
- Issuer entity. Corporate or Government. With respect to the latter, Gilt or government funds, invest only in government securities, and they are preferred by investors who are risk averse and want no or limited credit risk associated with their investment. However, they are subject to high interest rate risk.

8.3 *Money Market Funds*

Money market mutual funds are fixed-income mutual funds that invest in money market instruments, which are fixed income securities with a very short time to maturity and high credit quality. These high-quality debt securities could be issued by governments, banks or corporations. Examples of assets held by these funds include U.S. Treasury's, certificates of deposit and commercial paper. Money market funds usually have the lowest returns because they carry the lowest risk. These funds are suitable for investors with a low-risk appetite, who are looking at parking their surplus funds over a short-term.[46] Investors often use money market funds as an alternative to putting money in a savings bank account. They make up 13% (2019 data) of the mutual fund market, according to the Investment Company Institute (ICI).

8.4 *Mixed or Balanced Funds*

Also known as hybrid funds, balanced funds as the name suggests, represent investments that are a combination of equity and fixed-income. Balanced funds invest in a mix of stocks, bonds and other securities. The allocation may keep changing based on market risks. Indeed, the ratio can either be variable or fixed. In short, it takes the best of two mutual funds by distributing, say, 70% of assets in stocks and the rest in bonds or vice

[46] https://www.hdfcfund.com/learn/beginner/mutual-funds/different-types-mutual-funds#:~:text=Money%20market%20funds%20or%20liquid%20funds%3A&text=These%20funds%20are%20suitable%20for,in%20a%20savings%20bank%20account.

versa.[47] They also be structured in the form of "fund of funds," investing in a group of other mutual funds. Funds of funds target either affiliated funds managed by the same sponsor or unaffiliated funds, managed by other fund sponsor, or a mix of both. For diversification reasons and lower cost at the same time, some investors prefer choosing one fund that invests in many funds rather than invest in several funds. Balanced funds make up 21% of the mutual fund market in 2019, according to the ICI. They are more suitable for investors who are looking at a combination of moderate returns with comparatively low risk.[48]

8.5 Alternative Funds and Socially Responsible Funds

This catch-all category of funds includes open-end and hedge funds, ETFs and managed futures, and it includes also real estate investment trusts. There is a growing investor interest in corporate socially responsible mutual funds, which invest only in companies that meet the criteria of certain guidelines. Socially-responsible funds avoid investing in controversial industries like tobacco or firearms and instead focus on funding companies with strong environmental and labor practices. The idea is to get competitive performance while still maintaining a healthy conscience. Other such funds invest primarily in green technology, such as solar and wind power or recycling. A Smart Beta category is also relevant for this type of funds, in the form of Environmental, Social and Governance (ESG) Funds. The custom-built indexes for these funds use environmental, social and governance factors to select the fund's investments.[49] These factors are subjective and could include concerns like avoiding the use of toxic chemicals (environmental), using certain approaches to executive compensation (governance), or achieving diversity on the Board (social).[50] ESG investing is sometimes referred to as socially responsible investing.

[47] https://kuvera.in/blog/mutual-funds-101-all-you-need-to-know/.

[48] https://www.hdfcfund.com/learn/beginner/mutual-funds/different-types-mutual-funds#:~:text=Balanced%20funds%3A&text=They%20are%20more%20suitable%20for,returns%20with%20comparatively%20low%20risk.

[49] https://www.sec.gov/oiea/investor-alerts-and-bulletins/ib_smartbeta.

[50] https://www.investor.gov/introduction-investing/investing-basics/investment-products/mutual-funds-and-exchange-traded-3.

8.6 Pension Funds

Pension Funds represent a typical investment fund based on Investment Goal. Here the scheme is in putting away a portion of the household income in a chosen pension fund to accrue over a long period to secure an investor and his or her family's financial future after retiring from regular employment aiming to take care of most contingencies (like a medical emergency or child wedding).

9 Fund Fees

It costs money to run a mutual fund and investors in a mutual fund pay the fund expenses. Some funds cost more to operate than others. Some of these expenses reduce the value of an investor's account; others are paid by the fund and reduce the net asset value. There are a variety of fees that may be associated with mutual funds. Some funds come with transaction charges for buys and sells or commissions known as loads. And there are funds that charge a redemption fee if you sell shares you've only owned for a short time. Investors also pay ongoing expenses to cover the cost of operating the fund; this includes investment advisory fees (paying the fund manager and the research staff), as well as transaction costs associated with buying and selling securities within the fund. When evaluating a fund, remember that fees play a factor and may potentially detract from a fund's performance over time.[51] Investors should also compare fees against industry benchmarks and averages. Also, to understand the difference between funds, their total expense ratios must be compared.

Mutual fund fees generally fall into two big buckets:

- **Shareholder fees**: Sales commissions and other one-time costs when you buy or sell mutual fund shares.
- **Annual fund operating expenses** representing the cost of ongoing expenses: ongoing fees toward the cost of paying managers, accountants, legal fees, marketing and the like.

The details on these can be found in a mutual fund's prospectus.

[51] https://www.fidelity.com/learning-center/investment-products/mutual-funds/what-are-mutual-funds.

Shareholder fees

Shareholder fees include sales charges, redemption fees, commissions and they are paid at the time of buying or selling funds by investors directly. These expenses may include:

Sales Loads[52]

Funds that use brokers to sell their shares typically compensate the brokers. Funds may do this by imposing a fee on investors, known as a sales load (or sales charge), which is paid to the selling brokers. In this respect, a sales load is like a commission investor pay when they purchase any type of security from a broker. Although sales load most frequently are used to compensate outside brokers that distribute fund shares, some funds that do not use outside brokers still charge sales loads. There are two general types of sales loads—a front-end sales load investors pay when they purchase fund shares and a back-end or deferred sales load investors pay when they redeem their shares.

Front-end Load or sales loads

A front-end load or sales loads are compensation paid to financial professionals, such as a broker or investment advisor, to buy mutual fund shares. This compensation is the percentage of total amount invested, found from the sum of net asset value and the front-end load per share, which can decline with increased amount of investments. The key point to keep in mind about a front-end sales load is it reduces the amount available to purchase fund shares. For example, if an investor writes a $10,000 check to a fund for the purchase of fund shares, and the fund has a 5% front-end sales load, the total amount of the sales load will be $500. The $500 sales load is first deducted from the $10,000 check (and typically paid to a selling broker), and assuming no other front-end fees, the remaining $9500 is used to purchase fund shares for the investor.[53] The Maximum sales load under the Investment Company Act of 1940 is 9%. The maximum sales load under NASD Rules is $8^{1}/_{2}$%.[54]

[52] https://www.investor.gov/introduction-investing/investing-basics/glossary/mutual-fund-fees-and-expenses.

[53] https://www.sec.gov/fast-answers/answersmffeeshtm.html#:~:text=The%20key%20point%20to%20keep,sales%20load%20will%20be%20%24500.

[54] "Invest Wisely: An Introduction to Mutual Funds". U.S. Securities and Exchange Commission. Retrieved October 28, 2014.

Breakpoints

Some mutual funds that charge front-end sales loads will charge lower sales loads for larger investments. The investment levels required to obtain a reduced sales load are commonly referred to as "breakpoints".[55] There is no requirement for funds to offer breakpoints in the fund sales load but there is an obligation to disclose the breakpoints if they exist.

Deferred Sales Charge (Load)—Back-End Loads

Some mutual funds include a specific fee, called a back-end load, to be paid by investors when redeeming the shares. This fee typically goes to the brokers that sell fund shares and are often associated with class "B" mutual fund shares. Some funds may charge this fee if the investor sell shares within a short period of time after purchasing them, or for early withdrawals. It is also called a 'short-term trading fee' when investor sell a fund before a certain amount of time. This is a fee designed to discourage investors from trying to make a quick profit by 'timing' the market.

The notion of short period could include "anywhere from a few days to over a year" depending on the fund, usually defined as within 30, 60, or 90 days of purchase. Back-end loads are paid by investor and are deducted from the redemption. Shareholder transaction fees are not part of the expense ratio. To compute the amount of back-end sales the lesser of the shareholder's initial investment or the redemption value of shareholder's investment are to be considered. For example, if the shareholder initially invests $10,000, and at redemption the investment has appreciated to $12,000, a back-end sales load calculated in this manner would be based on the value of the initial investment—$10,000—not on the value of the investment at redemption. Investors should carefully read a fund's prospectus to determine whether the fund calculates its back-end sales load in this manner.[56]

The most common type of back-end sales load is the "contingent deferred sales load", also referred to as a "CDSC", or "CDSL".[57] Usually, the amount of this type of load will depend on how long the investor holds his

[55] https://www.sec.gov/fast-answers/answersbreakpthtm.html#:~:text=The%20investment%20levels%20required%20to,set%20them%20at.%20their%20discretion.

[56] https://www.investor.gov/introduction-investing/investing-basics/glossary/mutual-fund-fees-and-expenses.

[57] https://www.sec.gov/fast-answers/answersmffeeshtm.html#:~:text=The%20most%20common%20type%20of,or%20her%20shares%20long%20enough.

or her shares and typically decreases to zero if the investor holds his or her shares long enough. For example, a contingent deferred sales load might be 5% if an investor holds his or her shares for one year, 4% if the investor holds his or her shares for two years, and so on until the load goes away completely. If the back-end load declines the longer the investor holds shares, it is called a contingent deferred sales charge (CDSC). The rate at which this fee will decline will be disclosed in the fund's prospectus. If you own your B share funds for the required amount of time, according to that fund's schedule, then investors will not incur a surrender charge,[58] when they sell them.[59]

Load funds vs. no-load funds

As the name implies, load funds impose commissions. Sometimes, however, an investment company offers a no-load mutual fund, which doesn't carry any commission or sales charge. These funds are distributed directly by an investment company, rather than through a secondary party. However, not every type of shareholder fee is a sales load, and a no-load fund may charge fees that are not sales loads.[60] For example, a no-load fund is permitted to charge purchase fees, redemption fees, exchange fees, and account fees, none of which is considered to be a sales load. In the US, the no-load funds have no right to charge front or back-end loads, as well as distribution and services fee greater than 0.25% of fund assets.

Redemption Fee

A redemption fee is another type of fee that some funds charge their shareholders when the shareholders redeem their shares.[61] Although a redemption fee is deducted from redemption proceeds just like a deferred sales load, it is not considered to be a sales load. Unlike a sales load, which is used to pay brokers, a redemption fee is typically used to defray fund costs associated with a shareholder's redemption and is paid directly to the fund, not to a broker.[62] The SEC limits redemption fees to 2%.

[58] A surrender charge is a fee levied on a life insurance policyholder upon cancellation of their life insurance policy (from Investopedia).

[59] https://www.thebalance.com/mutual-fund-fees-to-ask-about-2388528.

[60] https://www.sec.gov/fast-answers/answersmffeeshtm.html.

[61] https://www.sec.gov/fast-answers/answersmffeeshtm.html.

[62] https://www.investor.gov/introduction-investing/investing-basics/glossary/mutual-fund-fees-and-expenses.

Exchange Fee
This fee is charged by some funds in case their shares are exchanged or transferred to another fund from the same investment company
Purchase Fee
This fee is taken from shareholders for buying the shares of certain funds. Unlike a front-end sales load, a purchase fee is paid to the fund (not to a broker) and is typically imposed to defray some of the fund's costs associated with the purchase.[63] Often it is associated with class 'A' shares of a mutual fund.
Transaction costs
These costs are incurred in the trading of the fund's assets. Transaction costs are usually high for funds with a high turnover ratio,[64] or those that invest in illiquid and exotic markets. Usually, such costs are reported similarly to the case of the total expense ratio.

Annual Fund Operating Expenses
Management Fees

Management fees are fees that are drawn from fund assets to the asset management company or to the fund's investment adviser (or its affiliates) for managing the fund's investment portfolio and for administrative fees payable to the investment adviser that are not included in the "Other Expenses" category.[65]
Distribution [and/or Service] (12b-1) Fees

Distribution and service fees are fees paid out of fund assets to cover the costs of marketing and selling fund shares, such as compensating brokers

[63] https://www.sec.gov/fast-answers/answersmffeeshtm.html#: ~ :text = Unlike%20a%20sales%20load%2C%20which,fund%2C%20not%20to%20a%.

[64] The asset turnover ratio measures the value of a company's sales or revenues relative to the value of its assets. The asset turnover ratio can be used as an indicator of the efficiency with which a company is using its assets to generate revenue. The higher the asset turnover ratio, the more efficient a company is at generating revenue from its assets. Conversely, if a company has a low asset turnover ratio, it indicates it is not efficiently using its assets to generate sales (https://www.investopedia.com/terms/a/assetturnover.asp).

$$\text{Asset Turnover Ratio} = \frac{\text{Total Sales}}{(\text{Beginning Assets} + \text{Ending Assets})}$$

where: Total Sales = Annual sales totalBeginning Assets = Assets at start of yearEnding Assets = Assets at end of year.

[65] https://www.investor.gov/introduction-investing/investing-basics/glossary/mutual-fund-fees-and-expenses.

and others who sell fund shares, and paying for advertising, the printing and mailing of prospectuses to new investors, and the printing and mailing of sales literature and sometimes to cover the costs of providing shareholder services.[66] With this regard, "Shareholder Service Fees" are fees paid to persons to respond to investor inquiries and provide investors with information about their investments[67] (see also next paragraph).
In the United States, this fee is sometimes called 12b-1 fees after section 12 of the Investment Company Act of 1940.[68] 12b-1 fees get their name from the SEC rule that authorizes a fund to pay them. The rule permits a fund to pay distribution fees out of fund assets only if the fund has adopted a plan (12b-1 plan) authorizing their payment.[69] A 12(b)1 fee, is paid to a financial advisor or financial services company as compensation for marketing the fund. The distribution and services fee are paid by the fund and reduces net asset value. Some 12b-1 plans also authorize and include "shareholder service fees", which are fees paid to persons to respond to investor inquiries and provide investors with information about their investments.[70] A fund may pay shareholder service fees without adopting a 12b-1 plan. If shareholder service fees are part of a fund's 12b-1 plan, these fees will be included in this category of the fee table. If shareholder service fees are paid outside a 12b-1 plan, then they will be included in the "Other Expenses" category. If you purchase a "C share" mutual fund, it will typically have an extra 1% 12(b)1 fee, in addition to an expense ratio. Just like the expense ratio, this service fee will be deducted out of the total fund assets before your share price is determined.[71]

Other Expenses
This group covers expenses not included in previous categories: custodial expenses; legal expenses; accounting expenses; transfer agent expenses; and other administrative expenses. **Custody fee**: paid to a custodian bank for holding the fund's portfolio in safekeeping and collecting income

[66] https://www.sec.gov/files/ib_mutualfundfees.pdf.

[67] https://www.investor.gov/introduction-investing/investing-basics/glossary/distribution-andor-service-12b-1-fees.

[68] See the section later in this chapter entitled, "Regulation and Operation".

[69] https://www.sec.gov/fast-answers/answers12b-1feeshtm.html.

[70] https://www.sec.gov/fast-answers/answersmffeeshtm.html.

[71] https://www.thebalance.com/mutual-fund-fees-to-ask-about-2388528.

owed on the securities. Account fees are periodic fees that some funds separately impose on investors in connection with the maintenance of their accounts.[72] Often account fees arise when the account balance falls below a specified minimum investment amount. For example, some funds impose an account maintenance fee on accounts whose value is less than a certain dollar amount.

Total Annual Fund Operating Expenses

This line of the fee table is the total of a fund's annual fund operating expenses, expressed as a percentage of the fund's average net assets.[73]

Expense ratio or MER

The expense ratio (ER) is often called the management expense ratio (MER) and it reflects the amount of fund assets used to cover administrative and operating expenses. The expense ratio can be found as the relation of current fees and expenses charged during the year (operating expenses) to average net assets (average value of fund assets under management in USD or in any other currency). Normally, the expense ratio includes management fee and charges for fund services, but it does not include front and back-end loads, securities and shareholder transaction fees.

One notable component of the expense ratio of U.S. funds is the "12b-1 fee", which represents expenses used for advertising and promotion of the fund. 12b-1 fees are paid by the fund out of mutual fund assets and are generally limited to a maximum of 1.00% per year (.75% distribution and .25% shareholder servicing) Under FINRA[74] Rules,[75] the US funds include the "12b-1 fee" (a fee for advertising and promotion), which is paid from mutual fund assets by the fund itself and cannot be higher than 1% per year.

[72] https://www.sec.gov/fast-answers/answersmffeeshtm.html.

[73] https://www.investor.gov/introduction-investing/investing-basics/glossary//mutual-fund-fees-and-expenses.

[74] FINRA is a not-for-profit organization that—working under the supervision of the SEC—actively engages with and provides essential tools for investors, member firms and policymakers. FINRA provides oversight for the brokerage industry and enables investors and firms to participate in the market with confidence by safeguarding its integrity. https://www.finra.org/rules-guidance/rulebooks/finra-rules.

[75] Rushinek, A., & Rushinek, S. (1995). Forecasting sales, expenses and stock market values by quarterly financial statement ratio analysis: A microcomputer software development model. *Managerial Auditing Journal, 10*(2), 7–33.

The ER is shown as a percentage of the fund assets. They can range from less than 1% for money market funds, to more than 3% for some specialty funds. The rate for MER depends on fund complexity and management team, where such type as index fund, for example, will have very low MER because it does not require much research and trading from management. In order to be able to compare the expenses of different funds, the latter are required to use the same formula for the expense ratio and disclosure their results.

This fee is deducted from the total assets of the fund before investor share price is determined.[76]

From the above we can highlight some general rules about expense ratios:

- When comparing fund fees, keep the items above in mind. It doesn't make sense to compare the fund fee on a U.S. large-cap fund to one on an international fund. That is not an apples-to-apples comparison.
- Fund complexity defines the necessity in more sophisticated managements and, thus, explains the high MER. Actively managed funds have higher operating expenses than passive funds or index funds. This is because an actively managed fund is conducting ongoing research trying to determine the best securities to own.
- International funds have higher fees than domestic funds. It costs more to purchase investments that are traded outside of the U.S. This higher cost is passed along in the form of higher expense ratios.[77]
- Small-cap funds have higher fees than large-cap funds. It costs more to buy and sell small stocks than large ones. This higher cost is passed along in the form of higher expense ratios.
- Index funds or passively managed funds typically have the lowest fees.
- To summarize, expenses matter relative to investment type. For the sake of simplicity, let's assume that there are three broad investment categories for mutual funds (equity, bond, and money market—in declining order of historical returns). Investors need to understand

[76] https://www.thebalance.com/mutual-fund-fees-to-ask-about-2388528#:~:text=Regardless%20of%20the%20cost%2C%20all,your%20share%20price%20is%20determined.

[77] https://www.thebalance.com/mutual-fund-fees-to-ask-about-2388528.

that the fund expense ratio lessens the gross return depending on the type of investments the fund holds. In equity funds with historical gross return of 10%, an expense ratio of 1% will need 10% of investor's return, in bond funds with historical gross return at 8% level, an expense ratio of 1% will require 12.5% of investor's return, while in money market fund with historical gross return at 5%, the expense ratio of 1% will consume 20% of investor's historical total return.

Changes in expense ratio
Fund expenses can be predicted, as high expense funds result in high expense ratios, so financial reports and fund prospectus can be analyzed by investors to see the fund expense ratio in the last five years. For funds it is very difficult to get much lower expense ratio once it has been already operating for some years. This is because funds have both fixed and variable expenses, but most expenses are variable, while the same variable costs are fixed on a percentage basis. It is very hard for a fund to reduce its expense ratio level because most fund expenses have a variable nature, but these expenses are a constant fixed percentage of fund assets. For example, 0.75% management fee will consume 0.75% of fund assets. Where the total management fee depends on the level of the Asset Under Management (AUM), fixed costs depend on total amount of assets acquired by a fund.

10 Regulation and Operation

A commonality among mutual funds throughout the world is that every major economy has specific rules pertaining to the registration, marketing and sale of funds. The mutual fund industry is a highly regulated space, but those regulations differ by country or region. The regulation of mutual fund industry is very strict worldwide, however, it might differ significantly in specificity of rules about registration, marketing and selling in every major economy. Regulations are in place to protect the consumer; this helps to ensure that asset managers are keeping the interests of investors above their own, and that investors are not getting taken advantage of. For investors it is crucial to have a high trust level in the asset management companies, thus, be confident that the mutual fund industry is properly controlled by the relevant authority.

The availability of mutual funds for investments depends on the domicile country of investors. Let's look at some of the regulators and the related regulations to see how the rules shape the funds.

10.1 The U.S. Market

All mutual funds sell to U.S. retail investors must be registered with the SEC Securities and Exchange Commission and must abide by the rules set forth under the Investment Company Act of 1940, commonly referred to as the '40s Act. Some of the rules under the '40s Act deal with diversification issues. Specifically, section12 limits the amount of fund assets that can be invested in other investment companies. In other words, the rule prohibits a mutual fund from concentrating too many of its holdings in the stock of an investment company. This acts as a protection for U.S. investors, as a fund that is registered with the SEC is regulated according to U.S. securities law.

The Investment Company Act of 1940 is regulated by the Securities and Exchange Commission (SEC) and it sets some standards to regulate the organization and activities of investment companies. This legislation applies to any publicly-traded investment products, including open and close-end mutual funds, unit investment trusts.

Primarily, the Investment Company Act was adopted in 1940 with its main goal to benefit the financial market stability by means of regulations after the stock market crash in 1929. Also, there was the Securities Act of 1933 to respond to that stock market crash, however, it focused more on transparency for investors, while the Investment Company Act of 1940 paid great attention to the regulatory issues for retail investment products. Its provisions include definition of the qualities for "investment company" and the requirements regarding financial disclosure, charge of services, fiduciary duties, filings. The Investment Company Act of 1940 defines also the registration procedure for investment companies to be done within the SEC before offering their securities on public. On March 2001, The Securities and Exchange Commission adopted a new rule under the Investment Company Act of 1940 to address certain broad categories of investment company names that are likely to mislead investors about an investment company's investments and risks. The rule requires a registered investment company with a name suggesting that the company focuses on a particular type of investment (*e.g.*, an investment company that calls itself the ABC Stock Fund, the XYZ Bond Fund, or the QRS U.S. Government Fund) to invest at least 80% of its assets in the type of investment suggested by its name. The rule also would address:

- names suggesting that an investment company focuses its investments in a particular country or geographic region;
- names indicating that a company's distributions are exempt from income tax;
- and names suggesting that a company or its shares are guaranteed or approved by the United States government.[78]

The US laws governing the mutual funds are the following:

- The Securities Act of 1933 provides obligation for all public investments to be registered with the SEC and to disclose their investment processes.
- The Securities and Exchange Act of 1934 controls regular reporting of issuers of securities to their investors, and created the Securities and Exchange Commission as a principal regulator of mutual funds.
- The Revenue Act of 1936 includes taxation procedure for mutual funds, where they cannot be taxed on their income and profit if they answer certain requirement of the US Internal Revenue Code, where tax liabilities are related to their investors. Funds must diversify their investment, have limited ownership of voting securities and distribute their income in the form of dividends, interests and capital gains net of losses to their investors.
- The Investment Advisers Act of 1940 set up regulation of investment advisors, that must be registered with SEC and follow the requirements set to protect investors.
- The National Securities Markets Improvement Act of 1996 defines the federal government as the main authority, where states regulators have the authority to investigate and prosecute fraud actions towards mutual funds.

[78] https://www.sec.gov/rules/final/ic-24828.htm.

10.2 European Union

In the European Union, funds are governed by laws and regulations established by their home country. At the same time, there is a mutual recognition mechanism set by the EU, that allows funds regulated in one country to be sold in another country under some certain regulatory obligations. The directive establishing this regime is the Undertakings for Collective Investment in Transferable Securities Directive (UCITS), and funds that comply with its requirements are known as UCITS funds. "UCITS compliant" is a favorite expression of many mutual fund providers in their marketing strategies.
UCITS cover many regulation processes controlling that funds do not concentrate their holdings to guarantee the diversification. To market mutual funds across all member countries of the European Union, an asset management companies needs only register its fund in one EU country under the authority of that country's financial regulator. This local authority, like in Ireland it would be Irish financial Services Regulatory Authority (IFSRA) for example, are included into the Committee of European Securities Regulators—the main body to coordinate the security regulators in the EU. This represents the so-called passport scheme.[79] The EU passporting system for banks and financial services companies enables financial firms that are authorized in any EU state to trade freely in any other with minimal additional authorization. These passports are the foundation of the EU single market for financial services.

Due to their image of being safe and well-regulated, UCITS funds got popularity among investors. According to the European Commission, they account for around 75% of all collective investments by small investors in Europe. While in everyday usage, a UCITS is a mutual fund based in the European Union, such funds are guaranteed to be safe and well-regulated, that makes them popular in EU, South America and Asia and among investors that prefer investing into unit trusts. While the funds are regulated in Europe, buyers from all over the world can invest in UCITS funds.[80]

[79] https://www.bba.org.uk/wp-content/uploads/2016/12/webversion-BQB-3-1.pdf.

[80] https://ec.europa.eu/info/business-economy-euro/growth-and-investment/investment-funds_it.

History of UCITS

The original UCITS Directive was adopted in 1985 and was aimed to help open-ended funds to facilitate their operations with transferable securities. It promoted the idea of the unite regulation of funds in all the Europe giving an opportunity to funds from one European country to be sold to the public in any other country in Europe without authorization.

However, due to specificity of individual marketing goals in every European country, the idea of such single regulation created many challenges. Therefore, in early 1990's the Directive was updated to better harmonize the regulation systems in European countries, that, hence, brought to the draft of the UCITS II directive, however, the agreement among Council of Ministers was not found anyway. Finally, a new proposal was published in 1998 with two parts: a product and a service provider proposal. In 2001 UCITS III Directives (Directive 2001/107/EC "Management Directive" & Directive 2001/108/EC "Product Directive") were introduced enabling wider range of eligible assets, extended use of derivatives as well as improved regulation of investment fund management companies (Directive 2001/107/EC, 2001; Directive 2001/108/EC, 2001).[81]

Under the Management Directive 2001/107/EC,[82] management companies are provided with the possibility to operate in all the European Union with allowed activities, which demonstrates the simplified prospectus to assist the cross-border marketing of UCITS.

Product Directive 2001/108/EC allows cross-border marketing by given the funds an opportunity to invest in various financial instruments under the same regulation in every EU country. This UCITS funds must answer the same investment limits.

To get the permission for EU wide marketing, a collective investment fund must apply for UCITS, so the idea of single fund market in the EU will be supported. In addition, such a large market will allow reduction of costs for investment managers.

[81] Grima, S., Romanova, I., Bezzina, F., & Chetcuti Dimech, F. (2016). Alternative investment fund managers directive and its impact on Malta's financial service industry.

[82] https://eur-ex.europa.eu/LexUriServ/LexUriServ.do?uri=CELEX:32001L0107:EN:HTML.

The proposal of UCITS IV[83] Directive was approved by the European Parliament on 13 January 2009 and also by the Council of the European Union as the Directive 2009/65/EC, to be implemented on 1 July 2011. UCITS IV The Undertakings for Collective Investment in Transferable Securities Directive (UCITS) 2009/65/EC is a consolidated EU Directive, that allows free operation of collective investment funds across EU with just a single authorization at one member state.

UCITS IV updated the UCITS III Directives by introducing the following changes:

- Notification Procedure. The UCITS IV Directive requires a UCITS intending to be registered in a host EU Member State to submit a notification letter to the host Member State regulator, this document having to be submitted together with a UCITS compliance attestation provided by the home country regulator.[84]
- Key Investor Information Document (KIID). The UCITS IV Directive sets out the framework for the KIID, a stand-alone, pre-contractual, 2-page document containing the essential features of the fund and is to be systematically provided to investors before they decide to invest.[85]
- Adapted Framework for Mergers that is a new legal framework to facilitate cross-border UCITS mergers.
- Master-feeder Structures. In a master-feeder structure, the feeder is the "collection fund" in the target distribution country in which retail and/or institutional investors may be allowed to invest. The feeder invests the cash received from its own investors in the master, becoming its unitholder.[86]
- Cooperation between Member State Supervisory Authorities by introducing a more effective mechanisms and increased efficiency in

[83] https://eur-lex.europa.eu/LexUriServ/LexUriServ.do?uri=OJ:L:2009:302:0032:0096:en:PDF.

[84] https://www.pwc.lu/en/ucits4/docs/pwc–flyer–notification.pdf.

[85] https://www2.deloitte.com/lu/en/pages/kiid/articles/key–investor–information–document–kiid.html.

[86] https://www.pwc.lu/en/asset–management/docs/pwc–amprofile–ucits–master–feeder.pdf.

cooperation between institutions supervising the operation of funds in different member states
- Management Company Passport. The availability of the UCITS management company passport means that a management company located in one-member state is permitted to manage UCITS established in other member states.

On 23 July 2014 the European Union adopted directive 2014/91/EU (UCITS V) on the co-ordination of laws, regulations and administrative provisions relating to undertakings for collective investment in transferable securities as regards depositary functions, remuneration policies and sanctions.[87]

UCITS V can be compared with the Alternative Investment Fund Managers Directive (AIFMD)[88] (European Union Directive 2011/61/EU), which is a parallel regulation for hedge funds and alternative investments.
UCITS V includes new rules on UCITS for fund managers, covering different arrangements and depositaries' liability with general remuneration principles.

The depositary as a specific function under UCITS legislation (rather as it does under AIFMD), may delegate its safekeeping functions (but not other depositary functions to a third-party custodian.
In order to further improve regulation on financial markets The European Commission has in 2017 published a consultation document on UCITS entitled "Product Rules, Liquidity Management, Depositary, Money Market Funds, Long Term Investments" (the "Consultation Paper").[89]

This "Consultation Paper" defines eight topics set by Commission that form the basis of UCITS VI. It includes proposal on UCITS depositary, remuneration and administrative sanctions related to UCITS V. The eight topics covered are:

- Eligible assets and the use of derivatives

[87] https://eur-lex.europa.eu/legal-content/EN/ALL/?uri=celex:32014L0091.

[88] The Alternative Investment Fund Managers Directive (AIFMD) is a European Union (EU) regulation that applies to hedge funds, private equity funds, and real estate funds.

[89] https://ec.europa.eu/finance/consultations/2012/ucits/index_en.htm.

- Efficient portfolio management techniques
- Over-the-counter (OTC) derivatives
- Extraordinary liquidity management tools
- Depositary passport

- Money Market Funds
- Long term investments
- Addressing UCITS IV.

11 Share Classes

Mutual funds also differ by a series of classes they belong to and that is identified by letters, for example "Series A", "Series D" etc., in order to signal about the fee structure and other specificities. Therefore, a mutual fund offers different combinations of front and back-end loads, services, fees, by selling different share types. All of them invest in the same portfolio of securities, but each has different expenses and, therefore, different net asset values and different performance results. Some of these share classes may be available only to certain types of investors.

Sales loads are assessed depending on what "class" of shares investors buy[90]:

- **A-class shares** have a front-end sales load, together with a small distribution and services fee. They also tend to have a lower 12b-1 fee and lower annual expenses than other mutual fund share classes. Some mutual funds reduce the front-end load as the size of the investment increases.
- **B-class shares** typically do not have a front-end sales load. Instead, they may impose a contingent deferred sales load and a 12b-1 fee (along with other annual expenses). A "contingent deferred sales charge," or CDSC), is a fee according to which an investor doesn't pay unless he or she sell his or hers shares before a specified time period, usually up to five or seven years after the original purchase. Investors are charged on a sliding scale depending on how soon they

[90] It is widely used to put these codes, but nothing detracts from the fact that asset management companies can define other classes. There is nothing to suggest that certain classes not classified as institutional, due to the fact that commissions are not downgraded (rebates), are in reality aimed at institutional investors.

redeem shares after original purchases, so it pays to stay invested. B-class share funds typically charge higher ongoing annual fees than A-class share funds. Class B shares usually convert automatically to Class A shares with a lower 12b-1 fee if they have been held for a certain period.

- **C-class shares** may carry commissions charged every year like a 12b-1 fee, other annual expenses, and either a front- or back-end sales load. They could also have a modest contingent deferred sales charge that is discontinued after one or two years. Class C shares usually do not convert to another class. Class C shares tend to have higher annual expenses than either Class A or Class B shares.
- **Class I** are usually subject to very high minimum investment requirements and are, therefore, known as "institutional" shares. They are no-load shares.
- **Class N** is nearly to be a No-Load FUND share. This class charge a distribution and services fee very low in level (e.g. no more than 0.25% of fund assets).
- **Class R** are usually for use in retirement plans such as 401(k)[91] plans. They typically do not charge loads but do charge a small distribution and services fee.

12 Tax Considerations

The securities held within the portfolio often pay dividends or interest. Securities can also be sold by the fund manager after rising in value. These types of events can help generate income for the fund, which by law must be paid out to investors in the form of periodic distributions. For the most part, investors who own shares in the mutual fund at the time these distributions are made are responsible for the taxes on that money.

[91] In the United States, a 401(k) plan is an employer-sponsored defined-contribution pension account defined in subsection 401(k) of the Internal Revenue Code. There are different types of employee funding: traditional and Roth, or tax-deferred and tax exempt, or EET and TEE. Profits are never taxed in the account, but for tax exempt accounts contributions and withdrawals do not impact on income tax, and for tax deferred accounts contributions are taken from taxable income and withdrawals are added to taxable income.

Investors who own mutual funds that are not held within an IRA[92] or another tax-advantaged account may be subject to two different types of taxes:

- Dividend income, which is generally taxed at investor ordinary income tax rate
- Capital gains from the sale of securities or exchange shares of the fund at a profit; those capital gains could also be taxed at ordinary income tax rate or the more favorable long-term capital gains rate, depending on how long the investor held those shares.[93]

In the US, mutual funds are pass-through entities for tax purposes and the fund does not pay any taxes on its holdings—dividend and capital gains realizations are passed on equally to all the fund's shareholders (regardless of when the shares were created). In the US, investors, who purchase shares in a fund, which have accrued but unrealized gains, face the prospect of distributions of realized gains even if they have only held the fund for a short time—this is the 'capital gain overhang' (Bergstresser & Poterba, 2002).

In Europe, the income (profits) of mutual funds and SICAVs of the EU countries constitute capital income and are subject to tax. The tax is applied at the time of realization of the income, or on the actual divestment or periodic payment of the proceeds (any periodic coupons). Any losses from divestment or trading costs (fixed rights, entry and exit commissions, switches) constitute capital losses deductible from the taxable base of all income other than financial one. Therefore, they cannot be offset against capital gains deriving from mutual funds, or other collective investment fund, because such capital gains are exactly considered as

[92] An IRA is an account set up at a financial institution that allows an individual to save for retirement with tax-free growth or on a tax-deferred basis.

https://www.fidelity.com/building-savings/learn-about-iras/what-is-an-ira#:%E2%80%89~%E2%80%89:text%E2%80%89=%E2%80%89An%20individual%20retirement%20account%20(IRA,in%20a%20tax%2Dadvantaged%20way.&text%E2%80%89=%E2%80%89Traditional%20IRA%20%2D%20You%20make%20contributions,you%20withdraw%20them%20in%20retirement.

[93] https://www.fidelity.com/learning-center/investment-products/mutual-funds/what-are-mutual-funds.

all others capital gains. Therefore, they may be offset against capital gains generated by other Securities which generate different income.

References

Bergstresser, D., & Poterba, J. (2002). Do after-tax returns affect mutual fund inflows? *Journal of Financial Economics, 63*(3), 381–414.

Grima, S., Romanova, I., Bezzina, F., & Chetcuti Dimech, F. (2016). *Alternative investment fund managers directive and its impact on Malta's financial service industry*.

Rushinek, A., & Rushinek, S. F. (1995). Forecasting sales, expenses and stock market values by quarterly financial statement ratio analysis. *Managerial Auditing Journal, 10*(2), 7–33.

CHAPTER 2

Performance

1 Introduction

Mutual funds have played a dramatically increased role in financial markets in recent decades. In this regard, mutual fund performance has received a great deal of attention from both practitioners and academics.

Investors are increasingly interested in mutual fund selection, demanding detailed mutual fund information, and investment advice.

With an aggregate investment of quite fifty-five trillion dollars[1] at the end of 2019, and a wide diffusion in the portfolio of standard household investors all over the world, the investing public's interest in identifying successful fund managers is understandable.

Most authors conclude that returns of most actively managed funds are lower than index fund returns, but some others find that managers display some skills.

From an academic perspective, the goal of identifying superior fund managers is interesting, because it challenges the efficient market hypothesis (EMH).[2]

[1] https://www.icifactbook.org/ch1/20_fb_ch1.

[2] Pandow, B. A., & Butt, K. A. (2017). Risk and return analysis of mutual fund industry in India. *Journal of Banking and Financial Dynamics, 1*, 54–65. Bollen, N. P., & Busse, J. A. (2001). On the timing ability of mutual fund managers. *The Journal of Finance, 56*(3), 1075–1094.

G. Galloppo, *Asset Allocation Strategies for Mutual Funds*, https://doi.org/10.1007/978-3-030-76128-8_2

Under this rationale, two key issues on fund performance have been central to recent academic and policy debates. The first is whether active funds have an (ex-post) abnormal fund performance in terms of gross returns (but after adjustments for risk), which is positive. A second major issue is whether abnormal fund performance can be identified ex-ante and for how long it persists in the future.[3] The above two issues (especially the second one) are usually interpreted as a direct test of EMH in a market with low entry barriers. There are many professional traders operating in a competitive environment, and the information is provided at a relatively low cost. Precisely, they anticipate the conditions under which EMH is effective. Therefore, mutual funds provide a way to test investor behavior based on the classic financial theory paradigm, where people assume that individuals make rational decisions in a relatively stable market with low information costs. Competition leads to the elimination of low-quality financial products and to the growth of high-quality financial products. In this fashion, Gil-Bazo and Ruiz-Verdù (2008)[4] provide a model of the market for mutual funds, in which competition among high-performance funds for the money of sophisticated (performance-sensitive) investors pushes their fees down and drives the low-performance funds out of the market.

Also, the popular press pays much attention to the performance of mutual fund managers. There is even the notion of "star managers" with public domain reputation for their stock-picking skills. In this regard, the media often focuses on the investment results of this small group of mutual funds "star managers", such as Scott Schoelzel of the Janus 20 Fund during the late 1990s, or Bill Miller of the Legg-Mason Value Trust Fund during the early 2000s (Ding & Wermers, 2012).[5] In this line, one of the most striking examples in the mutual fund industry is

[3] Cuthbertson, K., Nitzsche, D., & O'Sullivan, N. (2010). Mutual fund performance: Measurement and evidence 1. *Financial Markets, Institutions & Instruments, 19*(2), 95–187.

[4] Gil-Bazo, J., & Ruiz-Verdù, P. (2008). When cheaper is better: Fee determination in the market for equity mutual funds. *Journal of Economic Behavior and Organization, 67*, 871–885.

[5] https://www.researchgate.net/publication/228169647_Mutual_Fund_Performance_and_Governance_Structure_The_Role_of_Portfolio_Managers_and_Boards_of_Directors.

Peter Lynch who ran the Fidelity Magellan Fund from 1977 to 1990, earning his investors 2700% over thirteen years (Backs, 2002).[6]

The implication of the media spotlight on some managers with long records of outperformance is that portfolio managers matter in generating portfolio performance, that is experienced managers, or managers with a good track record, outperform other managers, in addition to passively managed funds (Ding & Wermers, 2012).

It should also be noted that the growth in assets under management has been quite impressive in the last 25 years. The growth trend of the last 15 years, between the period before the start of the global financial crisis, say 2007 and the end of 2019, was equal to about 30 trillion of new assets under management and equal to a rate of over 100%. As of the end of 2007 (Ferreira et al., 2013),[7] the world mutual fund industry managed financial assets exceeding $26 trillion (including over $12 trillion in stocks), more than four times the $6 trillion of assets managed at the end of 1996 (Investment Company Institute, 2008). The number of mutual funds has also grown dramatically to more than 120,000 funds worldwide at the end of 2019 (including nearly 55,000 equity funds). Although the growth of the mutual fund industry started in the USA, where the industry plays an extremely important role in financial markets, this trend has spread more recently to other countries around the world (Ferreira et al., 2013; Khorana et al., 2005).

Previous scholars have tried to explain the performance of mutual funds, which is a critical aspect in investor fund selection. Several fund characteristics have been analyzed as potential determinants of future fund performance, including fund size (there is evidence that fund performance worsens with fund size, see among others: Chen et al., 2004), age, fees and expenses (fund performance tend to lower fees and expenses, Gil-Bazo and Ruiz-Verdù, 2009), loads, turnover, flows, and returns. In particular, there is evidence of short-term persistence in fund performance, and that money flows to past good performers. The so called "smart money" effect predicts that investors display some fund selection ability as they tend to invest in funds with subsequent good performance.

[6] https://www.semanticscholar.org/paper/On-the-performance-of-mutual-fund-managers-Baks/3a3cd7097b462df59f2a17dca1ab2d52c47ea60a?p2df.

[7] Ferreira, M. A., Keswani, A., Miguel, A. F., & Ramos, S. B. (2013). The determinants of mutual fund performance: A cross-country study. *Review of Finance, 17*(2), 483–525.

Later in the book we will go into deep on the aspect of the persistence (see Chapter 6).

2 Previous Findings in Academic Literature

In this section of literature review, we are going to analyze the empirical works that focus on other issues than mutual fund flows, as well as rating, persistence, size, diversification, active management and volatility, because there are dedicated chapters on these themes along the text.

One of the great themes of mutual fund investing is the fee issue. Another way to see how fees affect a fund's risk-performance profile is to focus on a portion of those fees that is fund manager incentives. Massa and Patgiri (2009)[8] test how incentives affect performance and risk taking in the US mutual fund industry. Authors hypothesize that incentives increase risk taking as well as performance and provide evidence to support the hypothesis. Fund managers, with higher incentives improving performance by increasing the return gap. By affecting performance and risk taking, incentives also affect the survival probability of the fund. When past performance is controlled for, an increase in incentives reduces the survival probability of the funds.

These findings have implications in terms of the debate on mutual fund fees and managers' compensation. Indeed, if higher incentives cannot sustain higher performance, thereby increasing performance and risk, then higher incentives may be neutral to investors. On the contrary, if they improve risk-adjusted performance (which seems to be the case), then incentives will become a useful tool to motivate fund managers and increase benefits.

The expense ratio is one of the few reliable predictors of mutual fund return performance,[9] and the increasing market share of low-cost index and exchange-traded funds suggests that investors use this information when making investment decisions.

Mutual fund fees pay for the services provided to investors by the fund. Since the main service provided by mutual funds is portfolio management,

[8] Massa, M., & Patgiri, R. (2009). Incentives and mutual fund performance: Higher performance or just higher risk taking? *The Review of Financial Studies, 22*(5), 1777–1815.

[9] Leisher, T. K. (2019). Exchange-traded funds: The unknown investment opportunity. *Undergraduate Economic Review, 15*(1), 15.

the fees should reflect the risk-adjusted performance of the fund.[10] As a consequence, a positive correlation between the risk-adjusted expected income and expenses before charging should occur. One of the economic assumptions at the bottom of this finding could be a Cost-based Explanation postulating that fund performance could be positively associated with fund costs, if higher costs reflect higher salaries to attract more talented managers or larger investments in research tools.

In contrast to this prediction, Gil-Bazo and Ruiz Verdù (2009) find a puzzling negative relation between before-fee risk-adjusted performance and fees in a sample of U.S. equity mutual funds: funds with worse before-fee risk-adjusted performance charge higher fees.

Christoffersen and Musto (2002)[11] propose that mutual funds' fees are set taking into account the elasticity of the demand for their shares, so that funds facing less elastic demand charge higher fees. These authors argue that funds with worse past performance face less elastic demand, since performance-sensitive investors leave funds following bad performance. If performance is persistent at least for the worst-performing funds (as indicated by Carhart, 1997), Christoffersen and Musto's hypothesis could explain Gil-Bazo and Ruiz Verdù (2009) finding of a negative relation between fees and before-fee performance.

Arguments for a negative correlation between costs and performance rely on a couple of assumptions, such as first, the existence of economies of scale that lower operating costs for larger funds; and second, the fact that larger size may be associated with better performance and performance is persistent.

Similarly, older funds might benefit from learning economies, which could be passed on to investors in the form of lower fees.

In a certain way, complementary explanation of the relationship between fee and performance argues that funds with a greater proportion of performance-insensitive investors (as somehow are the investors in ethic and sustainability mutual funds) will charge higher fees, since for these funds the reduction in after-fee performance, caused by an increase in fees, will not translate into a large flow of money out of the fund. This would explain an inverse relationship between fee and performance.

[10] Gil-Bazo, J., & Ruiz-Verdú, P. (2009). The relation between price and performance in the mutual fund industry. *The Journal of Finance, 64*(5), 2153–2183.

[11] Christoffersen, S. E., & Musto, D. K. (2002). Demand curves and the pricing of money management. *The Review of Financial Studies, 15*(5), 1499–1524.

Another explanation, that is a strategic marketing explanation for this negative relationship, is that low-performance funds incur higher marketing costs and those costs are passed on to investors in the form of higher fees.

In the body of literature, addressing the impact of board structure on ongoing fund performance, Chen et al. (2004)[12] and Ferreira et al. (2013) test the hypothesis that organizational diseconomies, in particular hierarchy costs (Stein, 2002), erode fund performance. Large organizations with hierarchies are particularly inefficient in processing soft information, which is pivotal in the case of mutual funds, as managers may find it hard to convince other members of the investment committee to implement their ideas (Ferreira et al., 2013). Consistent with this view, authors find evidence that funds managed by a single asset manager perform better than team-managed funds in a worldwide sample of funds.

In this research stream, one of the main points at issue is whether certain governance structures, such as predominantly independent mutual fund boards, are more capable in providing the discipline to protect shareholders from performance-reducing actions, such as late-trading or market-timing detrimental to value creation.

According to Ding and Wermers (2012),[13] we should consider that portfolio managers are employees of management companies and not of the mutual funds themselves. Therefore, fund management companies through inside and independent (outside) directors may provide effective governance for a mutual fund. There is a difference between the information effectiveness of the two types of inside and independent (outside) directors, where inside executives at fund management company likely know more about the skills and effort exerted by their mutual fund managers. Authors also provide fund managers with research analyst resources, so the management company understands the strategies implemented by its portfolio managers better than outsiders.

The same authors also underline how effective governance can lose effectiveness and negatively affect performance, if complexity increases.

[12] Chen, J., Hong, H., Huang, M., & Kubik, J. D. (2004). Does fund size Erode mutual fund performance? The role of liquidity and organization. *American Economic Review, 94*(5), 1276–1302.

[13] Ding, B., & Wermers, R. (2012). Mutual fund performance and governance structure: The role of portfolio managers and boards of directors. Available at *SSRN* 2207229.

They provide the Managerial Entrenchment Hypothesis, according to which funds that are members of larger management companies and funds with a large number of inside directors will exhibit worse performance and will less frequently replace underperforming managers. Also, portfolio managers may become powerful in the internal management company organization, and this can lead to their replacement being more difficult.

Other authors investigate the effect of country characteristics on fund performance. A group of authors (Ferreira et al., 2013; Khorana et al., 2005, 2009) find country characteristics to have predictive power beyond fund characteristics. There is a strong positive relation between the performance of mutual funds and a country's level of investor protection and financial development.[14] In particular, funds perform better in countries with high trading activity and low trading costs, and funds domiciled in countries of common law tradition perform better (Ferreira et al., 2013).

In relation to other fund characteristics, the fund age could be also considered as a proxy of management skills.[15] This can be due to consideration that a fund that has been on the market for many years is probably performing better than its peer competitors, however, previous scholars find mixed evidence in this issue.

3 Baseline Metrics of Fund Performance

This section measures investment fund performance using a number of approaches.

3.1 Equilibrium Models[16]

In the first part of this section, we discuss theoretical models of mutual fund industry. Is it reasonable to expect certain funds to fall below or exceed their benchmarks for a long period of time, or is it reasonable

[14] Ferreira, M. A., Keswani, A., Miguel, A. F., & Ramos, S. B. (2013). The determinants of mutual fund performance: A cross-country study. *Review of Finance, 17*(2), 483–525.

[15] See also Sect. 7.2.

[16] For more details see: Cuthbertson, K., Nitzsche, D., & O'sullivan, N. (2010). Mutual Fund performance: Measurement and evidence. *Financial Markets, Institutions & Instruments, 19*(2), 95–187. https://doi.org/10.1111/j.1468-0416.2010.00156.x.

for investors to use prior trading rules to generate positive and continuous abnormal returns? In short, are there any models that can provide a theoretical basis for the behavior of "smart money", so that investors can "beat the market"? In their seminal article, Grossman and Stiglitz (1980) pointed out that in equilibrium, the expected abnormal return should not be zero, otherwise there would be no incentive to collect and process expensive information by the different types of market operators. Berk and Green (2004) accepted the idea of high information processing costs, and used a general equilibrium competition model (without moral hazard or asymmetric information) to analyze capital flows, ex post benefits, and performance persistence. This model is very similar to the company's standard perfect competition model. The latter has reduced returns to scale and low barriers to entry, ensuring that any short-term abnormal profits (for example, due to reduced costs or stock selection skills) are quickly offset. In this model, fund managers do have different skills in total return levels (stock selection ability), and investors can learn this skill based on past returns-investors and then chase the nearest "past winner". This performance-flow relationship is endogenous in the model and is non-linear (convex), because the cost function of non-linear-past winners' funds attract disproportionate cash inflows (Cuthbertson et al., 2010). However, net cash inflows will be affected by diminishing returns, so successful funds find it even more difficult to obtain abnormal net returns, thus, any profit is therefore short-lived, and zero abnormal returns are obtained on average in equilibrium. Essentially, a skilled manager will adopt an aggressive strategy until the expected net return of the marginal dollar inflow equals the return of the passive index fund (with similar risk characteristics), after which any additional cash inflow will flow into the index. The model of Lynch and Musto (2003) shares some assumptions with Berk and Green (2004) because investors can understand the manager's ability based on past returns. However, in the Lynch and Musto models, external differences in capabilities lead to differences in performance persistence, because the return of funds experiencing cash inflows will not decrease[17] This model is not an attempt to explain persistence itself, but the result of the persistence of differences between past

[17] Bessler, W., Blake, D. P., Lückoff, P., & Tonks, I. (2010, March). Why does mutual fund performance not persist? The impact and interaction of fund flows and manager changes. In *The Impact and Interaction of Fund Flows and Manager Changes (March 12, 2010). Paris December 2010 Finance Meeting* EUROFIDAI-AFFI.

winners and losers, which leads to a prominent performance-flow relationship. The decision to change strategy is a key feature of the model, and it is assumed that past losers are more open for the change than past winners. If past winners persist (because their successful strategy will not change), then we expect that past performance will cause a large amount of money to flow into winners' funds. Similarly, if past losers continue to exist, then we expect to see cash outflows. But why do severe past losers barely experience lower future outflows than moderate past losers? It is the latter that the model focuses on.

Lynch and Musto use a two-period model, and when the first-period fund returns are low, managers may switch strategies, which will reduce the ability of past returns to predict future returns, so this decreases the predictive power of past returns for future returns. On the contrary, when the first-period fund returns are high, managers will retain the same successful strategy, so the past "winners" will continue to exist. The convex flow-performance relationship is derived from the prediction of the persistence difference in returns. Since past winners continue with their winning strategy, they experience strong cash inflows. The worse the performance of "bad" funds, the greater the likelihood that investors believe in successful strategic changes. Therefore, they tend not to move their money from underperforming funds in a disproportionate manner. These two key models of the flow-performance relationship give clear but different predictions. In both models, managers have differential skill, which investors infer from past performance. However, in Berk and Green model, the average fund performance (after deducting costs) is zero in the wake of anomalies, and the performance persistence (of past winners and losers) is weak or uneven. In the Lynch and Musto model, the performance of past winners persists (because they have not changed their strategy due to the fact that they belong to successful manager group), but the performance of past losers will change according to the management decision to change the fund strategy.

3.2 Return Base Measures

Raw returns of the mutual funds are calculated using the standard formula:

$$R_p = \frac{NAV_t - NAV_{t-1}}{NAV_{t-1}} \tag{1}$$

where NAV_t is the Net Asset Value at time t.

The second metric (Eq. 2) evaluates the return in excess of the benchmark (or active return) of an investment manager.[18] This approach measures the return differential between the portfolio (R_p) and underlying benchmark index (R_b) in a manner that does not account for the risk exhibited by the fund. The excess return (ER) is expressed as:

$$ERp = R_p - R_b \tag{2}$$

3.3 Descriptive Statistics of the Sample

Below, there are an average summary statistics of mutual funds from our sample. The sample period is from January 2006 to December 2019, a total of 168 months. The mean (μ) and standard deviation (σ) are sample estimates and Skewness ($\mathcal{S}$) is computed as

$$\mathcal{S} = \frac{1}{\sigma^3 T} \sum_{t=1}^{T} (r_t - \mu)^3 \tag{3}$$

and excess kurtosis (K) is computed as

$$\mathrm{K} = \frac{1}{\sigma^4 T} \sum_{t=1}^{T} (\mathcal{R}_t - \mu)^4 - 3 \tag{4}$$

The Jarque-Bera ($\mathcal{JB}$) test for normality is distributed $\mathcal{X}_2^2$ under the null and is given by

$$\mathcal{JB} = \frac{T}{6} \left[\mathcal{S}^2 + \frac{\mathrm{K}^2}{4} \right] \tag{5}$$

Standard Deviation: Measure of Total Risk

Financial analysts and statisticians prefer to use a quantitative risk measure called the variance of returns, denoted by

$$\mathcal{V}ar(r) = \frac{1}{n} \sum_{t=1}^{n} [r_i - r_{am}]^2 \tag{6}$$

[18] Gallagher, D. R. (2003). Investment manager characteristics, strategy, top management changes and fund performance. *Accounting & Finance, 43*(3), 283–309.

where:

r_i = return on individual mutual fund unit.

r_{am} = mean rate of return.

The square root of the variance is called the standard deviation $\sigma = \sqrt{Var(r)}$.

Table 1 reports summary statistics of mutual fund alphas. We estimate alphas for EU and US funds across equity and bond asset classes. We report alpha CAPM, Carhart and Fama–French. We winsorized alphas at the bottom and top 1% level. We observe that EU equity funds perform better than US equity funds. EU equity funds are positive with the highest average alpha of 0.23% in the most extended model of Carhat with a standard deviation of 1.05%. US equity funds evidence underperformance in mutual fund industry, with average alpha of −0.02% and standard deviation of 0.99% in Carhart model. We also observe that EU bond funds perform better than US bond funds. The average EU bond alpha is 6.41% with standard deviation 17.20%, while the average US bond alpha is 1.99% with standard deviation of 9.01%.

3.4 *Risk Adjusted Performance Measures*[19]

Treynor's Ratio

One of the most common measures is the Treynor's Ratio. Jack Treynor (1965) conceived an index of portfolio performance measure called as reward to volatility ratio, based on systematic risk defined in Eq. (9). He assumes that the investor can eliminate unsystematic risk by holding a diversified portfolio. Hence his performance measure denoted as T_p is the excess return over the risk-free rate per unit of systematic risk, in other words it indicates risk premium per unit of systematic risk (Sapar & Madava, 2003).

$$T_p = \frac{Risk\ premium}{Systamatic\ Risk\ Index} = \frac{r_{p-}r_f}{\beta_p} \tag{7}$$

[19] Sapar, N. R., & Madava, R. (2003). Performance evaluation of Indian mutual funds. *SSRN Electronic Journal*. https://doi.org/10.2139/ssrn.433100.

Table 1 Summary statistics

Equity EU					
Variable	*Number of observations*	*Mean*	*Standard deviation*	*Min*	*Max*
Alpha CAPM	78.78	0.13%	1.24%	−10.33%	88.13%
Alpha Carhart	78.78	0.23%	1.05%	−45.12%	130.19%
Alpha Fama–French	78.78	0.13%	1.18%	−58.57%	135.27%
Equity US					
Variable	*Number of observations*	*Mean*	*Standard deviation*	*Min*	*Max*
Alpha CAPM	100.776	−0.01%	1.21%	−8.68%	132.37%
Alpha Carhart	100.776	−0.02%	0.99%	−12.08%	123.42%
Alpha Fama–French	100.776	−0.02%	1.00%	−11.69%	123.72%
Bond EU					
Variable	*Number of observations*	*Mean*	*Standard deviation*	*Min*	*Max*
Alpha BOND	37.284	6.41%	17.20%	−21.14%	61.92%
Bond US					
Variable	*Number of observations*	*Mean*	*Standard deviation*	*Min*	*Max*
Alpha BOND	28.08	1.99%	9.01%	−161.77%	120.82%

Notes Alpha CAPM comes by running the following time-series regression: $R_{i,t} - R_{f,t} = \alpha_i + \beta_i (R_{m.t} - R_{f,t}) + \mu_{i,t}$, where the $R_{m.t}$ and R_f are the market return and the risk-free rate respectively. Alpha Fama–French is calculated according to the following model: $R_{it} - R_{ft} = \alpha_i + b_i\ (R_{Mt} - R_{ft}) + s_i SMB_t + h_i HML_t + e_{it}$, *where* R_{it} is the return on fund i for month t, R_{ft} is the risk-free rate and R_{Mt} is the market return over the same period, SMB_t and HML_t are the Fama–French (1993) size and book-to-market factors. SMB_t = the realization on the capitalization factor (small-cap return minus large-cap return) for month t; HML_t = the realization on the value factor (value return minus growth return) for month t, e_{it} = an error term corresponding to the regression residuals. Alpha Carhart is calculated according to the following four-factor model given by: $R_{it} - R_{ft} = \alpha_i + b_i\ (R_{Mt} - R_{ft}) + s_i SMB_t + h_i HML_t + m_i MOM_t + e_{it}$. MOM_t is the risk factor mimicking portfolio for capturing Jegadeesh and Titman (1993) one-year momentum anomaly in the stock holdings of the mutual funds. Alpha Bond is computed according to the following model: $r_{p,t} = \alpha_p^{BOND} + \beta_{1,p} MKTRF_t^{Bond} + \beta_{2,t} MKTRF_t^{Equity} + \beta_{3,p} DEFAULT_t + \beta_{4,p} TERM_t + \varepsilon_{p,t}$; where $r_{p,t}$ is the monthly return on a portfolio of funds in excess of the one-month T-bill rate; $MKTRF_t^{Bond}$ is the Local (European or US) Total Bond Market Index return in excess of the one-month T-bill rate. $MKTRF_t^{Equity}$ is the (European) U.S. equity market return in excess of the one-month T-bill rate and is included to control for potential equity market bias $DEFAULT$ is the difference in return between investment grade corporate bonds and government bonds (10-year Treasury Constant Maturity Yield); $TERM_t$ is the difference in return between long-term (30-year Treasury Constant Maturity Yield) and short-term goverment bonds (one-year Treasury Constant Maturity Yield) (Figs. 1, 2, 3, and 4)

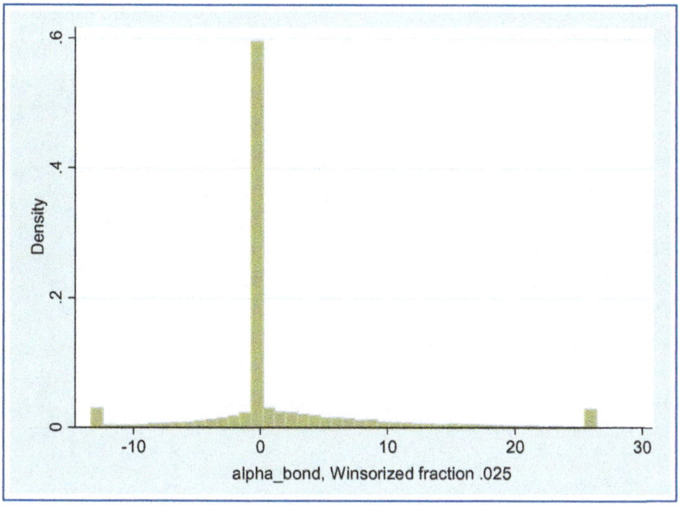

Fig. 1 Histogram of US BOND alpha

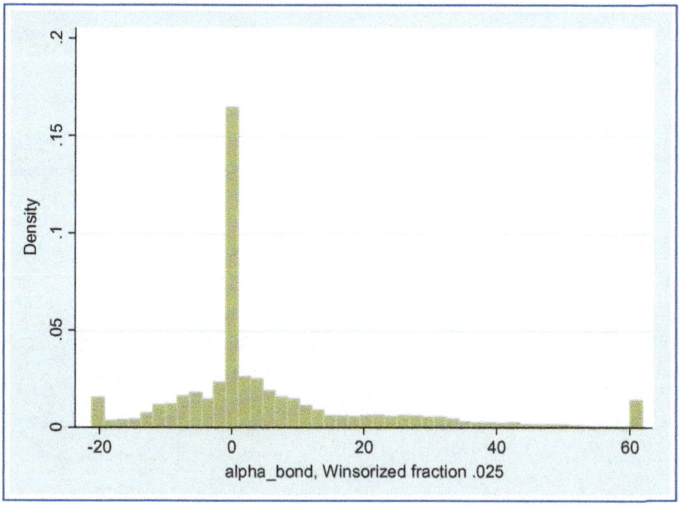

Fig. 2 Histogram of EUROPE BOND alpha

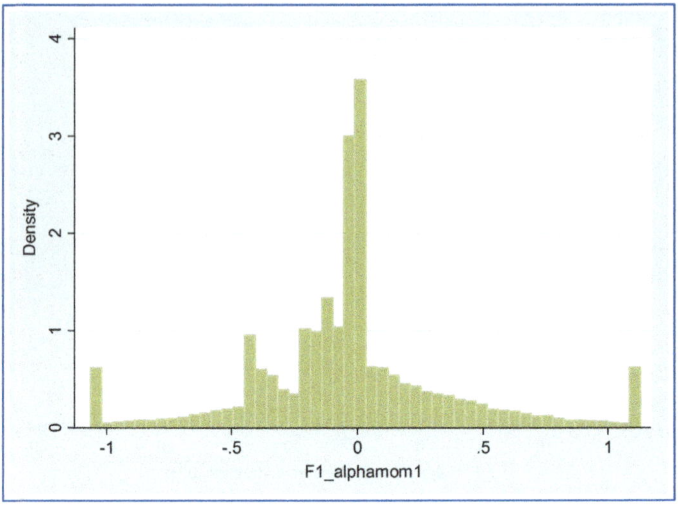

Fig. 3 Histogram of US EQUITY Carhart alpha

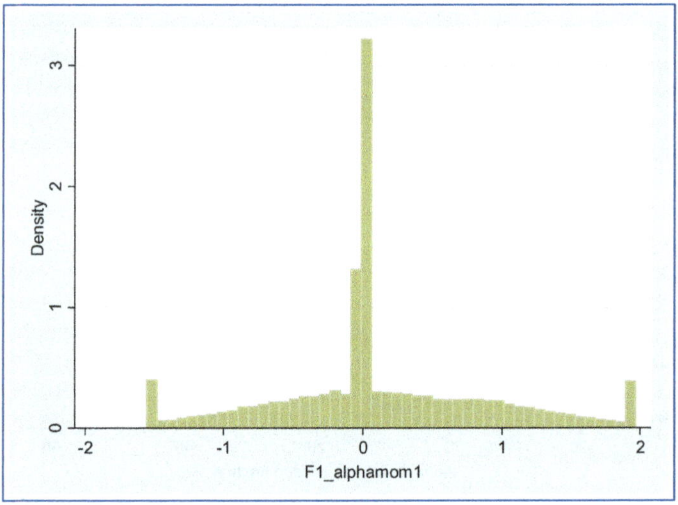

Fig. 4 Histogram of EUROPE EQUITY Carhart alpha

where T_p = Treynor's Ratio, r_p = portfolio return, r_f = risk free return and β_p = Beta coefficient for portfolio. As the market beta is 1, Treynor's index T_p for benchmark portfolio is $(r_m - r_f)$ where r_m = market return. If T_p of mutual fund scheme is greater than $(r_m - r_f)$, then the scheme has outperformed the market.

The main limitation of the Treynor index is that it can be applied to schemes that have a positive beta during the bull market. The results will mislead if applied during bear phase of the market to the schemes with negative betas. The second limitation is it ignores the reward for unsystematic or unique risk.

Sharpe's Ratio

William F. Sharpe (1966) designed an index to measure portfolio performance, which is called the ratio of return to variability expressed by S_P defined in Eq. (9). He assumes that a small investor fully invests in mutual funds and does not hold any investment portfolio to eliminate unsystematic risks, and therefore requires a total risk premium. In this way, the Sharpe ratio uses the variance of the returns to adjust the returns, just like in the world of mean-variance by Markowitz (1952).

$$S_P = \frac{Risk\ Premium}{Total\ Risk} = \frac{r_p - r_f}{\sigma_P} \tag{8}$$

where S_P = Sharpe's Ratio, r_p = portfolio return, r_f = risk free return and σ_P = standard deviation of portfolio returns.

The S_P for benchmark portfolio is $\frac{r_m - r_f}{\sigma_m}$, where σ_{m} = standard deviation of market returns. If S_P of the mutual fund scheme is greater than that of the market portfolio, the fund has outperformed the market.

The advantage of the Sharpe ratio over the Treynor index is that it considers whether investors should obtain a reasonable return for the total risk relative to the market. Mutual fund plans with greater unique risks may outperform the Treynor index and may underperform in the Sharpe ratio. Mutual fund plans with a large Treynor ratio and a low Sharpe ratio can be attributed to greater unique risks. Thus, the two indices rank the mutual fund performance differently. The major limitation of the Sharpe ratio is that it is based on the Capital Market Line (CML). The main feature of the capital market line is that only valid portfolios can be drawn on CML without inefficiency. Hence, it assumes that a managed portfolio (mutual fund scheme) is an efficient portfolio.

Beta: Measure of Systematic Risk

To obtain the measure of systematic risk (Beta) of the mutual fund scheme, Market Model is applied. The mathematical form of the model is:

$$r_P = \alpha + \beta * r_m + e_p \tag{9}$$

where r_P is the return on the mutual fund scheme, r_m is the return on the market, α is the intercept, β is the slope or the beta coefficient, e_p is the error term.

The higher the value of β, the higher the sensitivity of fund returns to market returns; the lower the value, the lower the sensitivity. In the bull market phase, mutual funds need a higher β value, while in the downward phase, they need a lower β value to beat the market. By regressing monthly market returns and monthly mutual fund returns, the constants α and β are calculated through regression analysis. The regression also provides the value of R^2 (coefficient of determination), which gives the strength of the relationship between the market and fund returns and indicates the degree of dispersion in return observations.

Coefficient of Determination: Measure of Diversification[20]

The potential advantage of mutual fund investment is the diversification of portfolio (see the Chapter 8 for a more detailed analysis on this topic).

Diversification reduces unique, unsystematic or diversified risks, thereby improving performance. The diversification extent can be measured by the value of coefficient of determination(R^2). A low R^2 value indicates the fund has large scope for diversification.

[20] Coefficient of determination, in statistics, R^2, is a measure that establishes the ability of an econometric model to predict or explain an outcome in the linear regression setting. More specifically, R^2 indicates the proportion of the overall variance in the dependent variable (Υ) that is predicted or explained in a linear regression framework by the predictor variable (X, also known as the independent variable).

In general, a high R^2 value indicates that the model is a good fit for the data (in a linear setting). An R^2 of 0.15, for example, indicates that the 15% of the variation in the outcome (that is the Υ variable) has been explained just by predicting the outcome using the set of covariates included in the model. In a linear but multivariate setting, that is where more than one explanatory variable acts in the linear relationship with dependent variable (Υ), R^2 turn out to be Adjusted R^2. The adjusted R-squared is a modified version of R^2 that has been adjusted for the number of predictors in the model while maintaining its role in assessing the ability of an econometric model to predict or explain an outcome in the linear regression setting.

Sharpe Measure

Sharpe (1963) suggested that, it is possible to consider the return for each security to be represented by the following equation:

$$r_P = \alpha + \beta * r_m + e \tag{10}$$

where r_P = expected return, α = intercept, β = beta coefficient, r_m = expected market return, e = error term with a zero mean and constant standard deviation.

Sharpe pointed out that the variance explained by the index can be called systematic risk, while the unexplained variance is called residual risk or non-systematic risk. Sharpe suggests that systematic risk and unsystematic risk for a security can be quantified as:

$$Systematic\ Risk = \beta^2\ x\ Var(r_m) \tag{11}$$

$$Unsystematic\ Risk\ (Unique\ Risk) = Var(r_i) - \beta^2\ x\ Var(r_m) \tag{12}$$

where:

$Var(r_i)$ = Variance of mutual fund scheme return,

$Var(r_m)$ = Variance of market return,

β = beta coefficient of the mutual fund strategy.

A well-diversified fund is expected to have a low level of unsystematic risk.

4 Risk Factor Performance Measures

Risk adjusted mutual fund performance is usually measured using either factor models or characteristic based performance measures. The factor model is parametric, while the latter is semi-parametric and matches the fund's stock holdings with specific stocks with similar characteristics (Cuthbertson et al., 2010). Moreover, as high raw returns may be associated with higher risk, evaluating and comparing securities investment fund performance only based on raw returns fails to consider the levels of risk borne. To address this issue this section implements a wide range of risk-adjusted performance measures which are divided into three broad classes, (i) unconditional models (Carhart, 1997; Fama & French, 1993; Jensen, 1968), (ii) conditional-beta models, in which factor loadings are allowed to vary conditional upon publicly available information (Ferson

& Schadt, 1996) and (iii) conditional alpha-beta models where alphas are also time-varying conditional on economic information (Christopherson et al., 1998).

4.1 Unconditional Factor Models[21]

The most commonly cited unconditional factor models to measure risk-adjusted fund performance such as the Capital Asset Pricing Model (CAPM), the Fama and French (1993) three-factor model and the Carhart (1997) four-factor model are described here.

In a general framework, an m-factor model of a stock-*j*'s excess return $r_{j,t} = R_{j,t} - R_{f,t}$ is:

$$r_{j,t} = \beta_j' F_t + \varepsilon_{j,t} \tag{13}$$

where $R_{f,t}$ = risk free rate, $F_t = \{F_{1,t}, F_{2,t}, \ldots, F_{m,t}\}$' are the m-factors and $\beta_j' = \{\beta_{j,1}, \beta_{j,2}, \ldots \beta_{j,m}\}$ are the *m*-factors loadings.

A robust factor model should explain the cross-section of *average* returns on any set of assets or portfolios and in practice the *m*-factors are often chosen to maximize the power of the tests in addressing the significance of the relationship between Mutual Fund returns (both as single asset or fund portfolio) and Risk Factors (Cuthbertson et al., 2010). For example, CAPM beta cannot explain the cross-section of the average return of a stock portfolio based on double ranking, book market value BMV and size (divided into 25 quintiles), while Fama-French (1992) can fully explain this cross-section section (1993). The Three-factor model (3F), which includes market returns, "size" and "market value" risk factors. The "market value" risk factor may be due to the higher sensitivity of firms to economic conditions, leading to a higher probability of getting into trouble during the economic downturn. Similarly, compared with large companies, small companies may exhibit greater information asymmetry to investors.

A mutual fund-*i* at time *t*, with asset proportions $w_{k,t}$ $(k = 1, 2, \ldots, N)$ has a required return (to compensate for factor risk) equal to $\beta_{i,t}' \sum F_t$ and the fund abnormal performance is given by $\alpha_{i,t}$ in the regression

[21] Cuthbertson, K., Nitzsche, D., & O'sullivan, N. (2010). Mutual fund performance: Measurement and evidence. *Financial Markets, Institutions & Instruments, 19*(2), 95–187. https://doi.org/10.1111/j.1468-0416.2010.00156.x.

(Admirati et al., 1986; Lehmann & Modest, 1987):

$$r_{i,t} = \sum_{j=1}^{N}(w_{j,t}\alpha_k + w_{j,t}\beta_j')F_t + \sum_{j=1}^{N} w_{j,t}\varepsilon_{j,t} = \alpha_{i,t} + \beta_{i,t}'F_t + \varepsilon_{i,t} \tag{14}$$

where $\varepsilon_{i,t} = \sum_{j=1}^{N} w_{j,t}\varepsilon_{j,t}$,

$$\alpha_{i,t} = \sum_{j=1}^{N}(w_{j,t}\alpha_k) \quad \text{and} \quad \beta_{i,t}' = \sum_{j=1}^{N}(w_{j,t}\beta_{j,i}).$$

Note that the fund's parameters will be time varying if either the factor betas or the fund weights are time varying, but in practical applications these parameters are often assumed to be constant over the investment horizon considered. If one believes that the factors represent risk (systematic) components, then alpha represents the stock picking skill of fund managers.[22] The logic is that after considering over time all systematic influences on fund returns, a positive estimated alpha $\hat{\alpha}_{i,t} = \bar{r}_{i,t} - \widehat{\beta'}_i \bar{F}_t$ indicates that the fund has an average return which exceeds that from following 'mechanical' investment strategies (Cuthbertson et al., 2010). One can think of mechanical investment strategies, such as an index fund that replicates some common risk factors and therefore systematically invests in momentum, or value stocks, for example.

Jensen's Measure

Michael C. Jensen (1968) measures the performance as the excess return provided by the portfolio over the expected (CAPM) returns. The performance measure (Jensen alpha) is defined as the intercept in Eq. (17). He assumes that the investor expects at least CAPM returns.

Jensen's alpha measures the ability of the mutual fund manager to add value over and above the return which would be justified by the systematic risk of his portfolio.

[22] For those who are agnostic about the factors acting as proxy variables for 'risk', these regressions are usually referred to as performance attribution models (Cuthbertson et al., 2010).

Let R_i be the return of the ith asset and R_f be the risk-free rate. In the Capital Asset Pricing Model (CAPM) of Sharpe (1964) and Lintner (1965), we have[23]:

$$E[R_i] = R_f + \beta_i\big(E[R_M] - R_f\big) \tag{15}$$

where R_m is the return of the market portfolio and β_i is the measure of the systematic risk, defined by:

$$\beta_i = \frac{cov(R_i, R_m)}{var(R_m)} \tag{16}$$

This model is also called the one-factor pricing model, because the stock return is entirely explained by one risk factor represented by the market. According to Fama and French (2004), this model is the centerpiece of MBA investment courses and is widely used in finance by practitioners despite a large body of evidence in the academic literature of the invalidation of this model:

> The attraction of the CAPM is that it offers powerful and intuitively pleasing predictions about how to measure risk and the relation between expected return and risk. Unfortunately, the empirical record of the model is poor- poor enough to invalidate the way it is used in applications. (Fama & French, 2004, p. 25)

The CAPM is certainly the most used model to measure the performance of mutual funds. Jensen (1968) proposes to estimate the CAPM by running the following time-series regression:

$$R_{i,t} - R_{f,t} = \alpha_i + \beta_i\big(R_{m.t} - R_{f,t}\big) + \mu_{i,t} \tag{17}$$

where the $R_{m.t}$ and R_f are the market return and the risk-free rate respectively. Error term $\mu_{i,t}$ is serially independent and verifies $E[\mu_{i,t}] = 0$ and $\mathrm{var}(\mu_{i,t}) = \sigma_i^2$.

Jensen (1968) uses the estimate α_i (the famous Jensen Alpha) to measure abnormal performance of the mutual funds. In particular, Jensen considers that a significantly and positive α_i shows that the fund manager

[23] Hereil, P., Mitaine, P., Moussavi, N., & Roncalli, T. (2010). Mutual fund ratings and performance persistence. https://doi.org/10.2139/ssrn.1749414.

has an ability to forecast stock prices or more simply that he exhibits stock picking ability. Jensen alpha continues to be used today even if it is largely criticized by the academic literature.

The intercept of this single-factor model has also been used to infer the stock picking ability or selectivity of the manager. This model can be augmented to include additional risk factors.[24]

A positive value of Jensen alpha (α_i) indicates that the fund manager provides a return higher than the CAPM return and is above the securities market line (SML); a negative value indicates that the return provided by the fund is lower than the expected return and lower than the SML. The Jensen model assumes that the portfolio is fully invested and is subjected to the limitations of CAPM.[25]

The CAPM is, in principle, a static representation of capital markets, which ignores their dynamic component. Therefore, it is an incomplete framework in the presence of stochastically evolving risk factors (see Merton, 1973). In fact, Size and Value strategies could yield positive returns without any CAPM beta exposure (see Fama and French, 1993, 1996), and the same applies to momentum strategies (see Jegadeesh & Titman, 1993).[26]

Fama's Measure[27]

Jensen's measure computes excess returns over expected returns based on premium for systematic risk. Eugene F. Fama (1972) goes a step ahead, he suggests to measure fund performance in terms of excess returns over expected returns based on premium for total risk (Sapar & Madava, 2003). In other words, the excess returns are computed based on Capital Market Line (CML).

[24] Elton et al. (1996) and Gruber (1996) suggest that the excess bond return should be included in order to allow for fund returns from bond holdings. Hence, the augmented model is given by:

$$R_P - R_f = \alpha_{jensen} + \beta_M(R_M - R_f) + \beta_B(R_B - R_f) + e_t. \tag{18}$$

[25] Sapar, N. R., & Madava, R. (2003). Performance evaluation of Indian mutual funds. Available at *SSRN* 433100.

[26] Babalos, V., Caporale, G. M., Kostakis, A., & Philippas, N. (2008). Testing for persistence in mutual fund performance and the ex-post verification problem: Evidence from the Greek market. *The European Journal of Finance, 14*(8), 735–753.

[27] See reference show at Footnote 8.

Fama breaks down the observed return into four components:

(i) Risk-free return r_f.
(ii) Compensation for systematic risk $\beta(r_m - r_f)$.
(iii) Compensation for inadequate diversification $(r_m - r_f)\{(\sigma_p/\sigma_m) - (\beta)\}$.
(iv) Net superior returns due to selectivity $(r_p - r_f) - (\sigma_p/\sigma_m)(r_m - r_f)$.

The second and third measures indicate the impact of diversification and market risk. By altering systematic and unique risk a portfolio can be reshuffled to get the desired return.

Fama says the portfolio performance can be judged by the net superior returns due to selectivity. His performance measure denoted by Fp is defined in Eq. (19).

$$Fp = (Portfolio\ Return - Riskfree\ return) - Return\ due\ to\ all\ risks$$

$$\ldots = (r_p - r_f) - \left({}^{\sigma p}/_{\sigma_m}\right)[r_m - r_f] \tag{19}$$

where F_p = Fama's measure for portfolio, r_p = porftfolio return, r_f = risk free return, σ_p = standard deviation of the portfolio return, σ_m = standard deviation of the market returns.

A positive value for Fp indicates that the fund earned returns higher than expected returns and lies above CML, and a negative value indicates that the fund earned returns less than expected returns and lies below CML.

Three and Four Factor Models

A single factor model, as for Jensen's measure (alpha), however, assumes that a fund's investment behaviour can be approximated using only a single market index, for instance the S&P 500 for the USA.[28] It does not, however, account for non-S&P 500 holdings, for instance small cap stocks. For this reason, Elton et al. (1993) proposes adding a small cap benchmark to the previous one-factor CAPM. In addition to that, in 1992, Fama and French studied several factors to explain average

[28] Otten, R., & Bams, D. (2004). How to measure mutual fund performance: Economic versus statistical relevance. *Accounting & Finance, 44*(2), 203–222.

returns (size, EPS, leverage and book-to-market equity).[29] They (Fama & French, 1992, 1993, 1996) provide strong evidence for the relevance of yet another factor (HML), besides a small cap index. Based on their work on the cross-sectional variation of stock returns, Fama and French (1993, 1996) propose a three-factor model. Besides a value-weighted market proxy, two additional risk factors are used, size and book-to-market. The Fama French model reads:

$$R_{it} - R_{ft} = \alpha_{i,t} + b_i \left(R_{Mt} - R_{ft}\right) + s_i SMB_t + h_i HML_t + e_{it} \quad (20)$$

where R_{it} is the return on fund i for month t, R_{ft} is the risk-free rate and R_{Mt} is the market return over the same period, SMBt and HMLt are the Fama–French (1993) size and book-to-market factors. $SMBt =$ the realization on the capitalization factor (small-cap return minus large cap return) for month t; $HMLt$ = the realization on the value factor (value return minus growth return) for month t e_{it} = an error term corresponding to the regression residuals. Small-company stocks tend to have a positive loading on *SMB* (a positive slope, s_i) and big-company stocks tend to have a negative loading. Similarly, a positive estimate of h_i indicates sensitivity to the value factor and a negative estimate indicates a growth tilt.[30] Thus, funds were identified as small cap or large cap on the basis of their estimated *SMB* slopes, and funds were sorted into value and growth on the basis of their *HML* slopes.

The intercept, sometimes referred to as Fama-French alpha, is a measure of performance relative to the three-factor benchmark (Davis, 2001). Following this approach, we are able to capture excess returns generated by tactical asset allocation strategies exploiting the inconsistencies of the CAPM. More specifically, excess fund returns are decomposed into excess market returns, returns generated by buying small size stocks and selling big size stocks (Small Minus BigSMB), and returns generated by buying stocks with high book-to-market ratios and selling stocks with low book-to-market ratios (High Minus LowHML). The intercept

[29] On US data, Fama and French (1993) find that the three-factor model provides significantly greater explanatory power than the CAPM.

[30] Davis, J. L. (2001). Mutual fund performance and manager style. *Financial Analysts Journal*, *57*(1), 19–27.

of this regression represents the value the manager has added to his portfolio over and above what could be justified by market risk and generated by these known strategies.[31]

Although the three factor Fama French model improves average CAPM pricing errors, it is not able to explain the cross-sectional variation in momentum-sorted portfolio returns.[32] Therefore, Carhart (1997) extends the Fama–French model by adding a fourth factor that captures the Jegadeesh and Titman (1993) momentum anomaly[33] The resulting model is consistent with a market equilibrium model with four risk factors, which can also be interpreted as a performance attribution model, where the coefficients and premia on the factor-mimicking portfolios indicate the proportion of mean return attributable to four elementary strategies[34]:

Carhart model use the $MOMt$ equals to the period t value of the Carhart (1997) momentum return measure. In this way, Carhart model (1997) builds on the Fama and French model but also captures returns generated by the momentum effect (as analyzed in Jegadeesh & Titman, 1993). This strategy (MOM) implies buying and selling stocks with high and low past years returns respectively. The four-factor model is given by:

$$R_{it} - R_{ft} = \alpha_{i,t} + b_i \left(R_{Mt} - R_{ft}\right) + s_i SMB_t + h_i HML_t + m_i MOM_t + e_{it} \tag{21}$$

The risk factors of Carhart's (1997) model are included in order not to reward fund managers for taking advantage of stock market systematic anomalies.[35] The momentum factor, MOM_t, is a measure of difference between the returns on past high-performing versus past poor-performing

[31] Babalos, V., Caporale, G. M., Kostakis, A., & Philippas, N. (2008). Testing for persistence in mutual fund performance and the ex-post verification problem: Evidence from the Greek market. *The European Journal of Finance, 14*(8), 735–753.

[32] Bauer, R., Otten, R., & Rad, A. T. (2006). Ethical investing in Australia: Is there a financial penalty? *Pacific-Basin Finance Journal, 14*(1), 33–48.

[33] Bauer, R., Koedijk, K., & Otten, R. (2005). International evidence on ethical mutual fund performance and investment style. *Journal of Banking & Finance, 29*(7), 1751–1767.

[34] Otten, R., & Bams, D. (2002). European mutual fund performance. *European Financial Management, 8*(1), 75–101.

[35] Carhart (1997) indicates that performance persistence mainly can be explained by including a momentum factor. Zheng (1999) suggests that the "smart-money" effect is closely related to momentum in stock returns regression.

stocks and hence MOM_t reflects a fund's sensitivity to pursuing a zero-investment strategy of purchasing past outperforming 'momentum' stocks and short-selling stocks with low historical returns. Carhart (1997) finds evidence that the momentum factor is statistically well-identified where it explains almost 50% of the spread in returns between the top and bottom decile portfolios of funds based on raw return. As such, the momentum risk factor mimics a risk factor which accounts for variation in fund returns.[36] However, the momentum variable is comparatively less significant in studies on the UK mutual fund industry (e.g., Blake & Timmermann, 1998; Quigley & Sinquefield, 2000; Tonks, 2004; Cuthbertson et al., 2008).

The intercept of this regression Carhart' α_i can be used as a performance measure and it takes into account not only market risk but also excess returns generated by risk factors well-documented strategies.

Finally, according to Otten and Bams (2004), Elton et al. (1993) and Elton and Gruber (1999) and Bollen and Busse (2004),[37] the four-factor model could be augmented to include a bond index in mutual fund performance assessment. They argue that some funds invest in higher yielding and risky bonds, which is not picked up by the risk-free rate (R_f). Although in their analysis, Elton et al. (1993) and Elton and Gruber (1999), state that the bond index only shows up significantly for less than 50% of all funds, Bollen and Busse (2004) find a more powerful results in considering the sensitivity of funds returns to a government bond index (Otten & Bams, 2004):

$$\begin{aligned} R_P - R_f = & \alpha_{AC} + \beta_M (R_M - R_f) + \beta_1 SMB + \beta_2 HML \\ & + \beta_3 MOM + \beta_B (R_B - R_f) + e_t \end{aligned} \tag{22}$$

where R_{Bt} is the return on a government bond index at time t.

4.2 Empirical Results

Tables 2 and 3 report averages of mutual fund returns and alphas for funds by investment target, US Equity and European Equity respectively.

[36] Gao, J., O'Sullivan, N., & Sherman, M. (2020). An evaluation of Chinese securities investment fund performance. *The Quarterly Review of Economics and Finance, 76*, 249–259.

[37] Otten, R., & Bams, D. (2004). How to measure mutual fund performance: Economic versus statistical relevance. *Accounting & Finance, 44*(2), 203–222.

Table 2 Unconditional models US sample—RISK factor loadings

	Alpha CAPM	*Beta CAPM*	*R-quad*			
US_LARGE	0.0002	0.5477	0.4568			
US_BLEND	−0.0003	0.4901	0.4486			
US_SMALL	0.0003	0.6207	0.4193			
US_VALUE	−0.0006	0.6556	0.5540			
US_Growth	0.0008	0.4916	0.4137			
	Alpha Fama–French	*Beta FF*	*SMB FF*	*HMLFF*	*R-quad*	
US_LARGE	0.0001	0.5334	0.0685	−0.0385	0.5781	
US_BLEND	−0.0006	0.4896	0.0155	−0.0131	0.5497	
US_SMALL	0.0009	0.5506	0.4187	0.0045	0.5946	
US_VALUE	−0.0002	0.6473	0.0732	0.1180	0.6550	
US_Growth	0.0005	0.4776	0.0287	−0.1103	0.5448	
	Alpha Carhart	*Beta Carhart*	*SMB Carhart*	*HML Carhart*	*Momentum*	*R-quad*
US_LARGE	0.0002	0.5153	0.0252	−0.0763	−0.0425	0.6421
US_BLEND	−0.0005	0.4821	−0.0135	−0.0327	−0.0282	0.6169
US_SMALL	0.0009	0.5371	0.3853	−0.0263	−0.0231	0.6554
US_VALUE	−0.0001	0.6267	0.0226	0.0562	−0.0615	0.7088
US_Growth	0.0006	0.4614	−0.0164	−0.1320	−0.0288	0.6119

CORRELATION MATRIX

Beta_Fama French	1.00			
Smb	0.37	1.00		
Hml	−0.37	−0.67	1.00	
Beta_Momentum	1.00			
Smb	0.27	1.00		
Hml	−0.11	−0.48	1.00	
Mom	0.09	−0.10	0.63	1.00

Notes CAPM comes by running the following time-series regression: $R_{i,t} - R_{f,t} = \alpha_i + \beta_i (R_{m,t} - R_{f,t}) + \mu_{i,t}$, where the $R_{m,t}$ and R_f are the market return and the risk-free rate respectively. The Fama French model reads: $R_{it} - R_{ft} = \alpha_i + b_i\ (R_{Mt} - R_{ft}) + s_i SMB_t + h_i HML_t + e_{it}$, *where* R_{it} is the return on fund i for month t, R_{ft} is the risk-free rate and R_{Mt} is the market return over the same period, SMB_t and $HML_t$are the Fama–French (1993) size and book-to-market factors. SMB_t = the realization on the capitalization factor (small-cap return minus large cap return) for month t; HML_t = the realization on the value factor (value return minus growth return) for month t e_{it} = an error term corresponding to the regression residuals. The four-factor model is given by: $R_{it} - R_{ft} = \alpha_i + b_i\ (R_{Mt} - R_{ft}) + s_i SMB_t + h_i HML_t + m_i MOM_t + e_{it}$. MOM_t is the risk factor mimicking portfolio for capturing Jegadeesh and Titman (1993) one-year momentum anomaly in the stock holdings of the mutual funds. The momentum factor, MOM_t, is a measure of difference between the returns on past high-performing versus past poor-performing stocks and hence MOM_t reflects a fund's sensitivity to pursuing a zero-investment strategy of purchasing past outperforming 'momentum' stocks and short-selling stocks with low historical returns.

Table 3 Unconditional models EUROPE sample—RISK factor loadings

	Alpha CAPM	*Beta CAPM*	*R-quad*			
EU_LARGE	0.0010	0.6819	0.4645			
EU_BLEND	0.0008	0.6677	0.4629			
EU_SMALL	0.0030	0.7088	0.4077			
EU_VALUE	0.0000	0.8252	0.4940			
EU_Growth	0.0037	0.7164	0.4566			
	Alpha Fama–French	*Beta FF*	*SMB FF*	*HML FF*	*R-quad*	
EU_LARGE	0.0023	0.6449	0.1929	0.1686	0.5967	
EU_BLEND	0.0021	0.6326	0.1867	0.1632	0.5962	
EU_SMALL	0.0034	0.7487	0.7510	0.1214	0.6018	
EU_VALUE	0.0019	0.7585	0.2200	0.4160	0.6375	
EU_Growth	0.0033	0.7258	0.3010	−0.0906	0.5879	
	Alpha Carhart	*Beta Carhart*	*SMB Carhart*	*HML Carhart*	*Momentum*	*R-quad*
US_LARGE	0.0012	0.6532	0.1666	0.1471	0.0245	0.6609
US_BLEND	0.0011	0.6388	0.1614	0.1387	0.0172	0.6612
US_SMALL	0.0020	0.7488	0.7192	0.1250	0.0588	0.6653
US_VALUE	0.0011	0.7572	0.1916	0.3565	−0.0314	0.6963
US_Growth	0.0016	0.7329	0.3018	−0.1927	−0.0197	0.6550

Beta_Fama French	*1.00*			
Smb	0.43	1.00		
Hml	−0.27	−0.18	1.00	
Beta_Momentum	1.00			
Smb	0.44	1.00		
Hml	−0.28	−0.48	1.00	
Mom	−0.19	−0.51	0.76	1.00

Notes CAPM comes by running the following time-series regression: $R_{i,t}-R_{f,t}=\alpha_i+\beta_i\left(R_{m.t}-R_{f,t}\right)+\mu_{i,t}$, where the $R_{m.t}$ and R_f are the market return and the risk-free rate respectively. The Fama French model reads: $R_{it}-R_{ft}=\alpha_i+b_i\ \left(R_{Mt}-R_{ft}\right)+s_i SMB_t+h_i HML_t+e_{it}$, *where* R_{it} is the return on fund i for month t, Rft is the risk-free rate and R_{Mt} is the market return over the same period, SMB_t and HML_t are the Fama–French (1993) size and book-to-market factors. SMB_t = the realization on the capitalization factor (small-cap return minus large cap return) for month t; HML_t = the realization on the value factor (value return minus growth return) for month t e_{it} = an error term corresponding to the regression residuals. The four-factor model is given by: $R_{it}-R_{ft}=\alpha_i+b_i\ \left(R_{Mt}-R_{ft}\right)+s_i SMB_t+h_i HML_t+m_i MOM_t+e_{it}$. MOM_t is the risk factor mimicking portfolio for capturing Jegadeesh and Titman (1993) one-year momentum anomaly in the stock holdings of the mutual funds. The momentum factor, MOM_t, is a measure of difference between the returns on past high-performing versus past poor-performing stocks and hence MOM_t reflects a fund's sensitivity to pursuing a zero-investment strategy of purchasing past outperforming 'momentum' stocks and short-selling stocks with low historical returns.

We winsorize returns and alphas at the bottom and top 1% level. We estimate alphas for every investment style portfolio in the two geographical areas.

Tables report the estimation results of the unconditional models which include the CAPM (model 1), the Fama and French three-factor model (model 2) and Carhart four-factor model (model 3). Alpha from all the unconditional models is a performance measure adjusted by unconditional risk factor loadings (e.g., market, size value and momentum risks) for US and EU equity asset class and for investment styles: blend, value and growth and asset sizes large and small caps.

We start our testing sequence by introducing the single factor unconditional CAPM, model 1 for the US Equity Sample. In a single factor model CAPM, there is the highest alpha estimate of 0.0008 for US growth, with market beta of 0.49 and an adjusted R^2 of 0.41. When considering the US VALUE Investment Style using a single factor model only, it leads to a monthly alpha estimate of −0.0006, an average market beta of 0.65 and an adjusted R^2 of 0.55. Based on these results we could argue that mutual funds based on US VALUE Strategy follow the market not quite closely, and under-perform the index by 0.06% per month. The cross-sectional average alpha of the CAPM for US SMALL strategy is 0.03% monthly (0.4% p.a.) which suggests the average outperformance of US SMALL securities investment funds by this amount.

The next model we consider is the Fama French three-factor model, which introduces two additional risk factors, size and book-to-market (model 2). When examining the betas, we are able to comment on funds' average investment strategies. The *SMB* factor, on average is positive that makes us believe that all funds portfolio is relatively more driven by small cap returns than large cap returns (for US small $\beta = 0.5506$ and alpha $= 0.0009$). *HML* factor is negative for US LARGE, BLEND and GROWTH, that indicates a sensitivity to low book-to-market stocks (growth) rather than to high book-to-market stocks (value). After adding SMB and HML alpha estimates drops slightly for US LARGE, US BLEND and US GROWTH, but increases a little for US SMALL and VALUE. When the *HML* factor loading on the other hand is significantly negative, indicating a sensitivity to low book-to-market stocks (growth) instead of high book-to-market stocks (value). Furthermore, the exposure to the market drops very little. On average, we observe a decrease of few points in the Market Beta, after adding *SMB* and *HML*. Controlling for the market risk, size and book-to-market exposures, the alpha estimate rises from 0.03 to 0.09% for the US Small sample.

Model 3 emerges by adding the momentum factor *MOM*, resulting in the Carhart model. The significantly positive *MOM* coefficient signals the sensitivity of the all-fund's portfolio for high momentum stocks. *MOM* is negative for all investment styles that is a sign of negative effect of momentum factor in the next month, thus, assumes that investors demonstrate their contrarian behaviour. In spite of the fact that, when more risk factors are employed to adjust fund performance, a lower value of alpha may be expected. The inclusion of the momentum factor makes alpha estimates slightly increase by 0.0001 for all investment styles, except US SMALL that remains at the same level (0.0009), which is the highest coefficient among other funds in portfolio. The Fama and French and Carhart multi-factor models indicate broadly similar performance findings. In general, factor model demonstrates that US mutual funds follow the market quite closely, there is no dramatic difference in coefficients when getting from one model to another, however, we observe US blend and US value underperform the index in all models. In terms of Carhart Alpha, the Investment Styles with the best performance are US SMALL and US GROWTH, while the Investment Styles with the worst performance are US VALUE and US BLEND. US LARGE are in the middle of the pack with an average alpha of 0.02% per month, which is consistent with the average alpha in Chen et al. (2004) for US funds.

Lastly, as was expected, as the risk factors increase, which represent nothing but regressors of the market portfolio model estimation equation, the level of *R*-squared increases.

In Table 3 we report averages of mutual fund returns and alphas for funds by investment target in European Equity market. We find that EU mutual funds, in their turn, outperform on average the index in all models. In a single factor model CAPM, we observe the highest coefficient of 0.0037 for EU GROWTH investment style, with market beta of 0.7164 and an adjusted R^2 of 0.4566. In Fama-French three factor model we examine betas to be able to comment on funds' average investment strategies. The *SMB* factor is positive that means all funds portfolio is relatively more driven by small cap returns than large cap returns (for EU small we observe $SMB = 0.7510$, $\beta = 0.7487$ and alpha $= 0.0034$). *HML* factor is mostly positive for observed investment styles that indicates a sensitivity to high book-to-market stocks rather than to low book-to-market stocks, however, the coefficient is negative for EU

GROWTH. Therefore, we observe an increase of alpha estimates except EU growth, after adding SMB and HML factors, and a decrease of all the coefficients when including momentum factor *MOM*, that is Carhart model. *MOM* is negative for EU VALUE and EU GROWTH investment styles, but *MOM* is positive for EU LARGE, EU BLEND, EU SMALL signals the sensitivity of this fund portfolios for high momentum stocks. Controlling for momentum, therefore alpha estimates are slightly more negative relative to the Fama–French model. Carhart (1997) points out that momentum has also an important role in performance persistence. From a statistical viewpoint most of previous academics conclude that in an unconditional setting the four-factor Carhart model (21) is best suited to measure mutual fund performance.

Starting with the CAPM (model 1), the Fama and French three-factor model (model 2) and Carhart four-factor model (model 3), we move over to conditional performance measurement. This model introduces time-variation in the risk factor parameters (regression betas).

4.3 Conditional Factor Models[38]

Traditionally, performance is measured using unconditional expected returns[39] assuming that both the investor and manager use no information about the state of the economy to form expectations. However, if managers trade on publicly available information, and employ dynamic strategies, unconditional models may produce inferior results (Otten & Bahms, 2004). Therefore, if the expected benefits and risks change over time, calculating the average alpha value using a fixed beta estimate throughout the performance period will lead to unreliable results. In this fashion, Ferson and Schadt (1996) argue that the traditional unconditional measures of abnormal performance might be unreliable, because common variation in risk levels and risk premia will be confounded with average performance.[40] They argue that a managed portfolio strategy that

[38] Cuthbertson, K., Nitzsche, D., & O'sullivan, N. 2010. Mutual fund performance: Measurement and evidence. *Financial Markets, Institutions & Instruments, 19*(2), 95–187. https://doi.org/10.1111/j.1468-0416.2010.00156.x.

[39] Otten, R., & Bams, D. (2004). How to measure mutual fund performance: Economic versus statistical relevance. *Accounting & Finance, 44*(2), 203–222.

[40] Kacperczyk, M., Sialm, C., & Zheng, L. (2005). On the industry concentration of actively managed equity mutual funds. *The Journal of Finance, 60*(4), 1983–2011.

can be replicated using readily available public information should not be judged as having superior performance (Kacperczyk et al., 2005). They advocate a conditional performance-based model that uses predetermined tools to capture factor loads over time.

To address these concerns on unconditional performance models, Chen and Knez (1996) and Ferson and Schadt (1996) advocate conditional performance measurement. According to Otten and Bahms (2004), this is performed by considering both time-varying conditional expected returns and conditional betas instead of the usual, unconditional betas. By allowing the factor loading on the market risk factor at time t to be linearly related to a vector of instruments for the economic information set Z_t, and where Z_{t-1} is a vector of lagged predetermined instruments.

Assuming that the beta for a fund varies over time, and that this variation can be captured by a linear relation to the conditional instruments, then $\beta_{it} = \beta_{i0} + B_i^{'} Z_{t-1}$, where $B_i^{'}$ is a vector of response coefficients of the conditional beta with respect to the instruments in Z_{t-1}. For a single index model, the equation to be estimated reads:

$$R_{it} - Rf_t = \alpha_{it} + \beta_{i0}(Rm_t - Rf_t) + B_i^{'} Z_{t-1}(Rm_t - Rf_t) + e_{it} \quad (23)$$

Here, α_{it} measures abnormal performance after controlling for (i) publicly available information, Z_{t-1} which may influence abnormal return and (ii) adjustment of the factor loadings based on publicly available information.[41]

According to this rationale, the CAPM market beta varies over time. Subsequently time-variation also could be added to *SMB* and *HML* (Fama French model), Momentum (Carhart model) and the bond beta[42] Equation (5) can easily be extended to incorporate multiple factors, which results in a conditional model with time-varying betas. For example, the model can be extended to the Fama and French three-factor model and

[41] To estimate the equation, several authors consider (z_t) the vector of deviations of the economic information set *Zt* from unconditional means, and hence β_{i0} is the unconditional mean of the conditional beta. The mean value of *zt* is zero as (z_t) is deviations from mean. As such, its effect on α_{0i} is not as a risk factor bur rather is due only to the time varying nature of systematic risk.

[42] Christopherson et al. (1998, 1999) argue that in the same way beta can be dynamic, alphas may also be dynamic. Introducing time-variation in alpha makes it possible to examine whether managerial performance is indeed constant, or whether it varies over time as a function of the conditioning information. To be specific.

the Carhart four-factor model, in which the additional factor loadings are each specified as linear functions of an economic information set Z_t, and as conditional betas. In the information set Z_t, for L instruments, the conditional three-factor factor model and the conditional four-factor model would involve estimating $(L + 1)*3 + 1$ and $(L + 1)*4 + 1$ parameters respectively.

With respect to the instruments, most studies (see for example: Cuthbertson et al.,[43] 2010; Kacperczyk et al., 2005[44]; Otten & Bams, 2004[45]) follow Ferson and Schadt (1996) and Christopherson et al. (1998) using the Z_t variables which are publicly available and proven to be useful for predicting stock returns by several previous studies. To be specific, in this section, and according to the most of previous scholars in this context, we consider: (i) the 1-month T-bill rate; (ii) dividend yield on the market index; (iii) the slope of the term structure; and finally (iv) the quality spread, by comparing the yield on government and corporate bonds. All instruments are lagged 1 month.

We formally tested six model specifications, which will be evaluated based on statistical and economical relevance (Table 4).

A representative selection of the estimation results of the conditional beta models are reported in Table 4. The performance measure from these conditional beta models is the alpha of a managed fund, which controls for unconditional risk factor loadings (e.g., market, size, value and momentum risks) and for investment strategies, where fund managers dynamically alter portfolio weights and adjust the fund's risk factor sensitivities (betas) using publicly available economic information introduced

Christopherson et al. (1998) assume that alpha (as well as the beta's) may depend linearly on z_t so that $\alpha_{i,t} = \alpha_{oi} + A_t'(z_t)$ and the performance model is:

$$r_{i,t+1} = \alpha_{0i} + A_i(z_t) + b_{0i}(r_{b,t+1}) + B_i'(z_t * r_{b,t+1}) + \varepsilon_{i,t+1}. \quad (24)$$

[43] Cuthbertson, K., Nitzsche, D., & O'sullivan, N. 2010. Mutual fund performance: Measurement and evidence. *Financial Markets, Institutions & Instruments, 19*(2), 95–187. https://doi.org/10.1111/j.1468-0416.2010.00156.x.

Cuthbertson et al. (2010).

[44] Kacperczyk, M., Sialm, C., & Zheng, L. (2005). On the industry concentration of actively managed equity mutual funds. *The Journal of Finance, 60*(4), 1983–2011.

[45] Otten, R., & Bams, D. (2004). How to measure mutual fund performance: Economic versus statistical relevance. *Accounting & Finance, 44*(2), 203–222.

Table 4 Six multifactor conditional and unconditional models

Model		*Number of factors*
1	Unconditional CAPM	1
2	Unconditional Fama and French	3
3	Unconditional Fama and French + momentum	4
4	Conditional CAPM	5
5	Conditional Fama and French	15
6	Conditional Fama and French + momentum	20

above, as follows: (i) the lagged level of the risk-free interest rate, (ii) the lagged level of dividend yield on the market factor, (iii) a lagged measure of the slope of the term structure (TERM), and (iv) a lagged measure of default spread in the corporate bond market (QUAL). Model 4 is the CAPM (1964) model where the market risk factor loading is conditioned on the full set of public information variables as indicated. Model 5 is Fama and French based factor models, where the market risk factor loading is conditioned on the full set of public information variables. Model 6 is conditional versions of the Carhart four-factor model where all four-risk factor loading in the Carhart specification are conditioning on the set of public information variables.

4.4 *Empirical Results*

To determine the explanatory power of a range of performance models, discussed in the previous paragraph, we use the following benchmarks. From Kenneth French library[46] we obtain returns on the aggregate US market index and the factor mimicking portfolios for size (*SMB*) and book-to-market (*HML*). The factor-mimicking portfolio for the 1-year momentum in stock returns (*MOM*) is provided by same data provider. Finally, we examine the marginal explanatory power of introducing time-variation in betas and alpha. In line with, for instance Gao et al. (2020), Cuthbertson et al. (2010), Otten and Bams (2004), Ferson and Schadt (1996), we use a collection of public information variables that have been proven to predict returns and risks over time. They are: (i) the 1-month T-bill rate; (ii) dividend yield on the market index; (iii) the slope of the term structure; and finally (iv) the quality spread, by comparing the yield

[46] https://mba.tuck.dartmouth.edu/pages/faculty/ken.french/data_library.html.

of government and corporate bonds. All instruments are lagged 1 month to be predictive.

The estimation results of the conditional alpha-beta measures are shown in Table 5 for the US Sample and in Table 6 for the European Sample. For each of the six models we report alpha, beta(s), adjusted R^2. In this class of models, the performance measure is the alpha adjusted by controlling for investment strategies, which use publicly available economic information by (i) conditioning stocks when high abnormal excess returns are expected conditional on the economic information and (ii) dynamically altering the portfolio risk factor sensitivities (betas) conditional on the information.

Table 5 represents conditional performance measurement for US sample. In this table and in the next one (Table 6) we do not report the statistically significant evidence (that is *, ** or ***), because all estimation coefficients, both for the alpha measures and the risk factor loadings are statistically significant at least at 5% level. In the first line of the Table (alpha_CAPMCOND) we report the performance measure that is alpha adjusted by factor loadings on the risk factors for the economic information set (the 1-month T-bill rate, dividend yield on the market index, the slope of term structure, the quality spread), and the findings indicate that fund managers adjust the risk factors loadings in response to the full set of economic information set. For all US sample, irrespective to the specific Investment Style, we observe the results from all conditional models from the CAPM, indicate investment fund managers outperform. When adding *SMB* and *HML*, we observe slight decrease of alpha coefficient for US BLEND and VALUE investment styles. The coefficient of alpha remains almost the same when introducing the *MOM* in Carhart model for all funds.

The findings in relation to the significance of risk factor loadings are broadly similar to those from unconditional models. All conditional beta models consistently show the market and size risk factors as statistically significant determinants of the cross-sectional variation in fund returns, together with value and momentum risk factors. Among all conditional beta models, the public economic information instruments are also statistically significant at the 5% significance level. To be specific, while on average the Term Structure show both positive and negative influence over the alpha, depending over different Investment Styles, the 1-month T-bill rate and the quality spread exhibit a negative meaning. When we compare conditional (Tables 2 and 3) with conditional models (Tables 5

Table 5 Conditional models US sample

Baseline model	*Alpha and factor*	*US_LARGE*	*US_BLEND*	*US_SMALL*	*US_VALUE*	*US_GROWTH*
CAPM	alpha_CAPMCOND	0.000	0.000	0.001	0.000	0.001
CAPM	beta_CAPMCOND	1.573	1.262	1.052	0.987	2.405
CAPM	beta*r1month	151.471	−250.599	−104.776	−111.221	148.852
CAPM	beta*rdivy	−0.229	−0.222	−1.082	−1.145	0.005
CAPM	beta*rtermstr	−15.236	−8.200	4.246	13.320	−44.543
CAPM	beta*qualspread	−27.683	−19.197	−34.936	−27.200	−39.596
Fama–French	alpha_FFCOND	0.000	−0.001	0.001	−0.001	0.002
Fama–French	beta_FFCOND	1.362	0.758	1.043	0.511	1.787
Fama–French	smb_FFCOND	−0.913	−1.388	1.149	−1.721	−1.287
Fama–French	hml_FFCOND	0.987	1.193	2.335	2.692	0.598
Fama–French	beta_r1month_FFC	16.873	20.824	6.476	45.667	−2.245
Fama–French	beta_rdivy_FFC	−3.081	−1.198	−1.391	−1.608	−4.092
Fama–French	beta_rtermstr_FFC	4.314	3.204	−2.797	−3.060	7.661
Fama–French	beta_qualspread_FFC	−28.098	−11.947	−16.841	−3.203	−41.735
Fama–French	betaSMB_r1month	0.000	0.000	0.000	0.000	0.000
Fama–French	betaSMB_rdivy	2.283	1.338	1.511	−0.982	4.429
Fama–French	betaSMB_rtermstr	34.718	43.682	3.372	38.244	59.870
Fama–French	betaSMB_qualspread	23.516	38.197	−9.505	57.695	18.739
Fama–French	hml_r1month	4.775	1.958	−0.098	5.017	5.725
Fama–French	hml_rdivy	−2.635	−1.514	−6.619	−4.613	−2.094
Fama–French	hml_rtermstr	−64.098	−63.525	−69.746	−99.832	−59.597
Fama–French	hml_qualspread	−14.041	−25.692	−51.512	−43.291	−7.892
Carhart	alpha_FIVECOND	0.001	−0.001	0.001	−0.001	0.003
Carhart	beta_FIVECOND	1.097	0.852	1.130	1.374	1.114
Carhart	smb_FIVECOND	0.364	0.235	0.694	0.249	0.418
Carhart	hlm_FIVECOND	0.078	0.053	0.327	0.444	−0.146

(continued)

Table 5 (continued)

Baseline model	*Alpha and factor*	*US_LARGE*	*US_BLEND*	*US_SMALL*	*US_VALUE*	*US_GROWTH*
Carhart	mom_FIVECOND	−0.081	−0.138	0.300	−0.374	−0.018
Carhart	beta_r1month_fivecond	0.000	0.000	0.000	0.000	0.000
Carhart	beta_rdivy_fivecond	−1.783	0.330	−1.464	1.499	−4.647
Carhart	beta_rtermstr_fivecond	−15.879	−15.907	−12.526	−32.932	−11.236
Carhart	beta_qualspread_fivecond	−16.679	−11.201	−17.265	−16.914	−19.926
Carhart	SMB_r1month_fivecond	0.000	0.000	0.000	0.000	0.000
Carhart	SMB_rdivy_fivecond	−1.158	−0.475	1.552	−1.602	−0.891
Carhart	SMB_rtermstr_fivecond	0.741	3.580	4.670	4.913	−2.540
Carhart	SMB_qualspread_fivecond	−12.735	−11.248	−15.617	−12.509	−14.873
Carhart	hml_r1month_fivecond	0.000	0.000	0.000	0.000	0.000
Carhart	hml_rdivy_fivecond	0.472	−1.201	−4.906	−4.768	3.699
Carhart	hml_rtermstr_fivecond	−13.845	−7.940	−2.174	−11.477	−16.414
Carhart	hml_qualspread_fivecond	−2.475	−2.533	−8.069	−9.897	2.972
Carhart	mom_r1month_fivecond	0.000	0.000	0.000	0.000	0.000
Carhart	mom_rdivy_fivecond	−1.771	0.011	0.723	−1.671	−2.652
Carhart	mom_rtermstr_fivecond	15.091	16.135	29.453	25.346	9.008
Carhart	mom_qualspread_fivecond	−5.034	−3.261	−20.720	−0.484	−4.477

Notes Conditional Models allow the factor loading on the risk factors at time t to be linearly related to a vector of instruments for the economic information set Zt: (i) the 1-month T-bill rate; (ii) dividend yield on the market index; (iii) the slope of the term structure; and finally (iv) the quality spread, by comparing the yield on government and corporate bonds. All instruments are lagged 1 month. All estimates are statistically significant at least at 5% level

Table 6 Conditional models EUROPE sample

Baseline model	*Alpha and factor*	*US_LARGE*	*US_BLEND*	*US_SMALL*	*US_VALUE*	*US_GROWTH*
CAPM	alpha_CAPMCOND	0.000	0.000	0.003	−0.001	0.004
CAPM	beta_CAPMCOND	0.302	0.353	0.488	−0.362	1.468
CAPM	beta*r1month	−5101.681	−4927.873	−2260.231	−1350.092	−16,836.069
CAPM	beta*rdivy	3.595	3.404	3.330	4.765	2.308
CAPM	beta*rtermstr	30.723	28.672	9.569	29.111	10.283
CAPM	beta*qualspread	−28.882	−27.785	−16.266	6.972	−45.992
Fama–French	alpha_FFCOND	−0.006	−0.007	−0.006	−0.008	−0.011
Fama–French	beta_FFCOND	1.176	1.206	1.258	0.900	1.224
Fama–French	smb_FFCOND	0.752	0.561	−0.080	2.162	−2.577
Fama–French	hml_FFCOND	−2.341	−2.236	−1.978	−3.124	−2.501
Fama–French	beta_r1month_FFC	0.000	0.000	0.000	0.000	0.000
Fama–French	beta_rdivy_FFC	1.337	1.703	−0.584	1.374	2.494
Fama–French	beta_rtermstr_FFC	−24.329	−24.764	−19.326	−11.549	−52.033
Fama–French	beta_qualspread_FFC	33.133	21.567	48.417	−12.346	15.001
Fama–French	betaSMB_r1month	0.000	0.000	0.000	0.000	0.000
Fama–French	betaSMB_rdivy	11.821	11.381	10.269	8.434	17.756
Fama–French	betaSMB_rtermstr	−24.595	−19.396	−10.047	−14.816	−11.764
Fama–French	betaSMB_qualspread	64.228	55.850	94.855	−5.246	154.968
Fama–French	hml_r1month	0.000	0.000	0.000	0.000	0.000
Fama–French	hml_rdivy	−11.101	−11.928	−10.378	−15.577	2.989
Fama–French	hml_rtermstr	216.758	204.345	214.299	190.144	243.397
Fama–French	hml_qualspread	−71.165	−54.423	−106.759	−31.999	−82.211
Carhart	alpha_FIVECOND	0.003	0.003	0.003	0.002	0.020
Carhart	beta_FIVECOND	−0.117	−0.105	0.155	0.054	−2.496
Carhart	smb_FIVECOND	−0.365	−0.317	−0.081	0.047	−1.435
Carhart	hlm_FIVECOND	0.118	0.096	0.409	−0.049	−0.578

(continued)

Table 6 (continued)

Baseline model	*Alpha and factor*	*US_LARGE*	*US_BLEND*	*US_SMALL*	*US_VALUE*	*US_GROWTH*
Carhart	mom_FIVECOND	−0.789	−0.839	−0.777	−1.069	−3.276
Carhart	beta_r1month_fivecond	0.000	0.000	0.000	0.000	0.000
Carhart	beta_rdivy_fivecond	0.228	0.517	−1.210	0.931	3.801
Carhart	beta_rtermstr_fivecond	5.131	3.637	7.592	4.519	15.407
Carhart	beta_qualspread_fivecond	16.407	16.430	13.884	13.488	96.983
Carhart	SMB_r1month_fivecond	0.000	0.000	0.000	0.000	0.000
Carhart	SMB_rdivy_fivecond	12.768	12.903	12.386	15.079	27.200
Carhart	SMB_rtermstr_fivecond	1.443	1.427	3.808	−5.781	−11.083
Carhart	SMB_qualspread_fivecond	−7.778	−8.563	−1.546	−11.361	35.361
Carhart	hml_r1month_fivecond	0.000	0.000	0.000	0.000	0.000
Carhart	hml_rdivy_fivecond	−2.325	−2.018	−2.657	−1.623	3.365
Carhart	hml_rtermstr_fivecond	8.042	7.735	5.805	14.774	15.806
Carhart	hml_qualspread_fivecond	−1.597	−1.211	−9.867	5.709	5.716
Carhart	mom_r1month_fivecond	0.000	0.000	0.000	0.000	0.000
Carhart	mom_rdivy_fivecond	−3.291	−3.491	−3.084	−4.411	20.251
Carhart	mom_rtermstr_fivecond	24.306	25.820	28.714	29.767	−3.632
Carhart	mom_qualspread_fivecond	18.442	16.968	16.450	22.417	110.261

Notes Conditional Models allow the factor loading on the risk factors at time t to be linearly related to a vector of instruments for the economic information set Zt; (i) the 1-month T-bill rate; (ii) dividend yield on the market index; (iii) the slope of the term structure; and finally (iv) the quality spread, by comparing the yield on government and corporate bonds. All instruments are lagged 1 month. All estimates are statistically significant at least at 5% level and 6), we conclude that not taking into account time-variation, led to a bias in the estimation of managerial performance.

Table 6 represents conditional performance measurement for EU sample in conditional models introducing time-variation in the CAPM, Fama–French and Carhart beta. The performance measure is alpha adjusted by factor loadings on the risk factors for the economic information set (the 1-month T-bill rate, dividend yield on the market index, the slope of term structure, the quality spread). In CAPM model we observe negative sign for US VALUE. When adding *SMB* and *HML*, we observe decrease of alpha coefficient for all investment styles, thus, there is an evidence of underperformance. When introducing the *MOM* in Carhart model, the coefficients of alpha in all funds become positive. That means that there is outperformance when applying the most extended Carhart model.

We now graphically reflect the time-varying nature of the alpha and betas discussed before. Figure 5 represents US equity sample for the time-varying alpha CAPM, alpha Fama–French, alpha Carhart, Market beta, SMB, HML, and Momentum for the all-fund's portfolio. After adding time-variation to the market beta, we allow SMB and HML to vary too. The alpha of the all-fund's portfolio seems to demonstrate on average only weak time-variation, nevertheless along the time axis several volatility spikes do emerge. We observe that during the period December 2006–December 2019, the average fund increased its exposure to the market index, while decreased the proportion of small caps in portfolio (*SMB*) and demonstrated significant value exposure (*HML*). Figure 6 represents EU equity sample for the time-varying alpha CAPM, alpha Fama-French, alpha Carhart, Market beta, SMB, HML, and Momentum for the all-funds portfolio. Beta market shows a tendency for increase. After introducing time-variation to the market beta, *SMB* and *HML* demonstrate significant variations (ups and downs). During the period December 2006–December 2019 the average fund increased its exposure to the market index, the proportion of small caps in portfolio (*SMB*) has a tendency to decrease and there is a significant value exposure (*HML*).

Furthermore, in untabulated results, we find that the average *R*-square presents a modest improvement from unconditional models, which motivates the use of conditional models to research performance. The incremental explanatory power of the conditioning variables that is: (i) the 1-month T-bill rate; (ii) dividend yield on the market index; (iii) the slope of the term structure; and finally (iv) the quality spread, by comparing

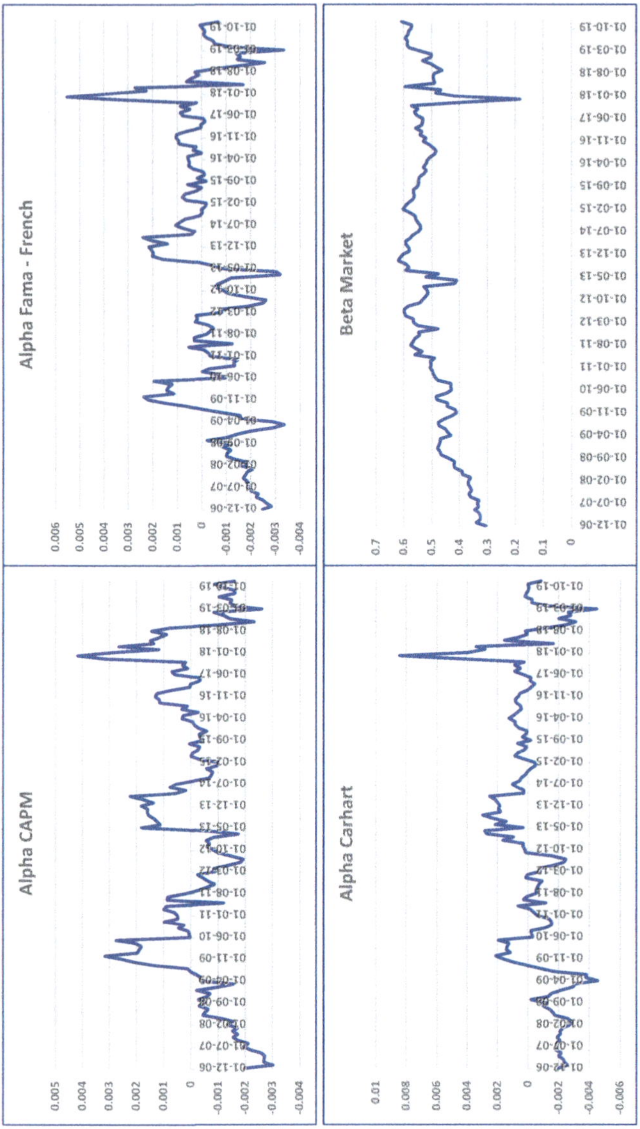

Fig. 5 US equity sample

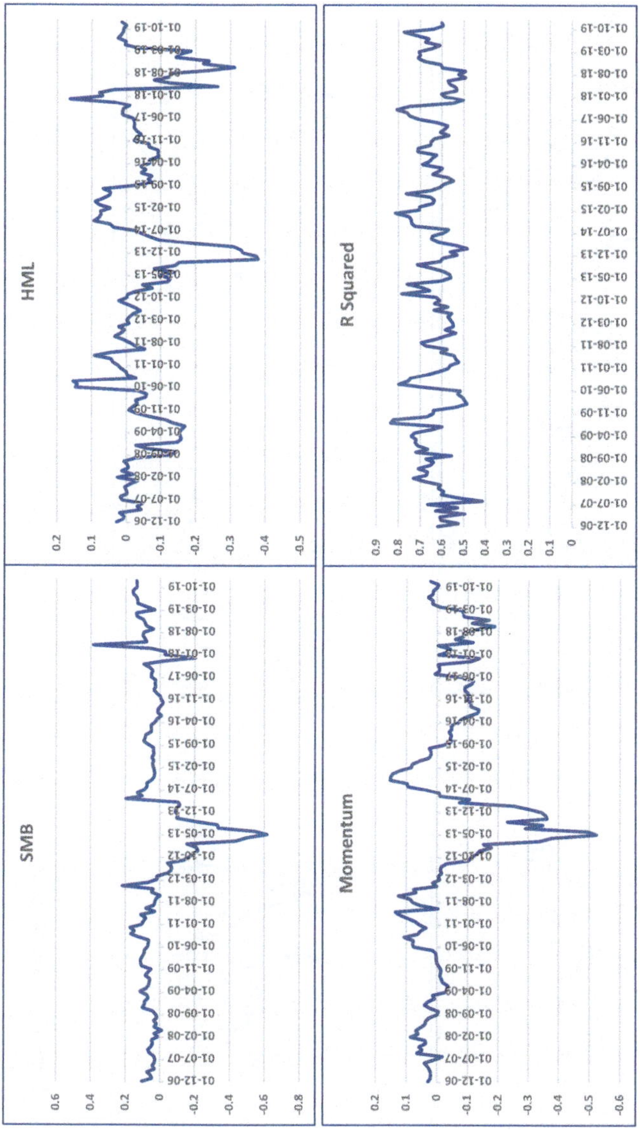

Fig. 5 (continued)

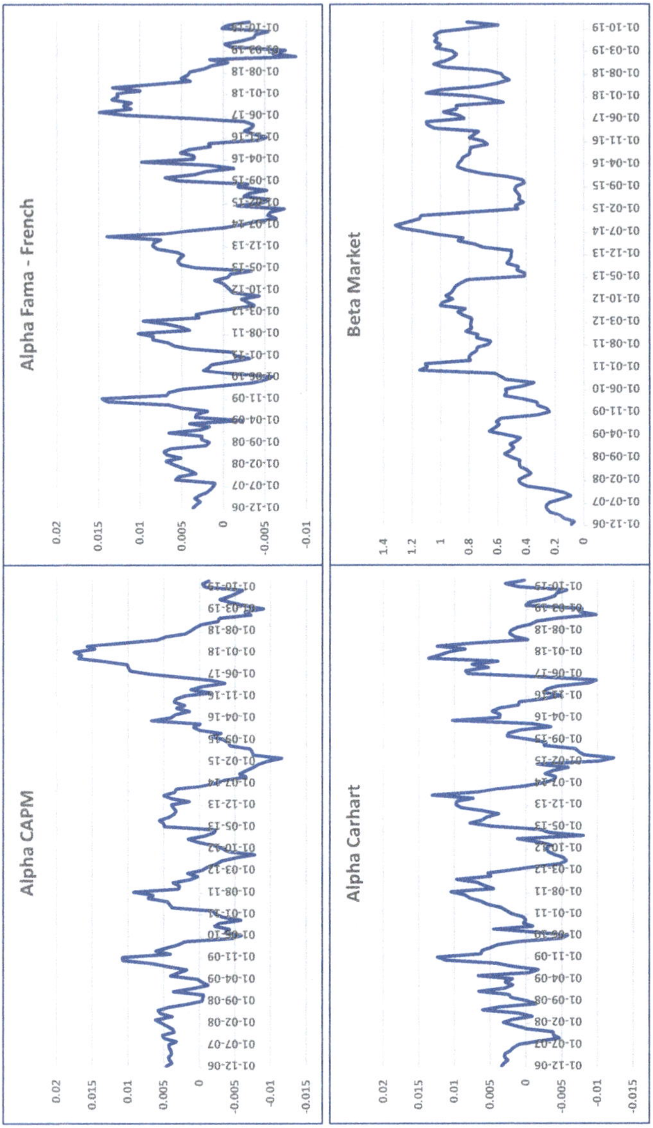

Fig. 6 Europe equity sample

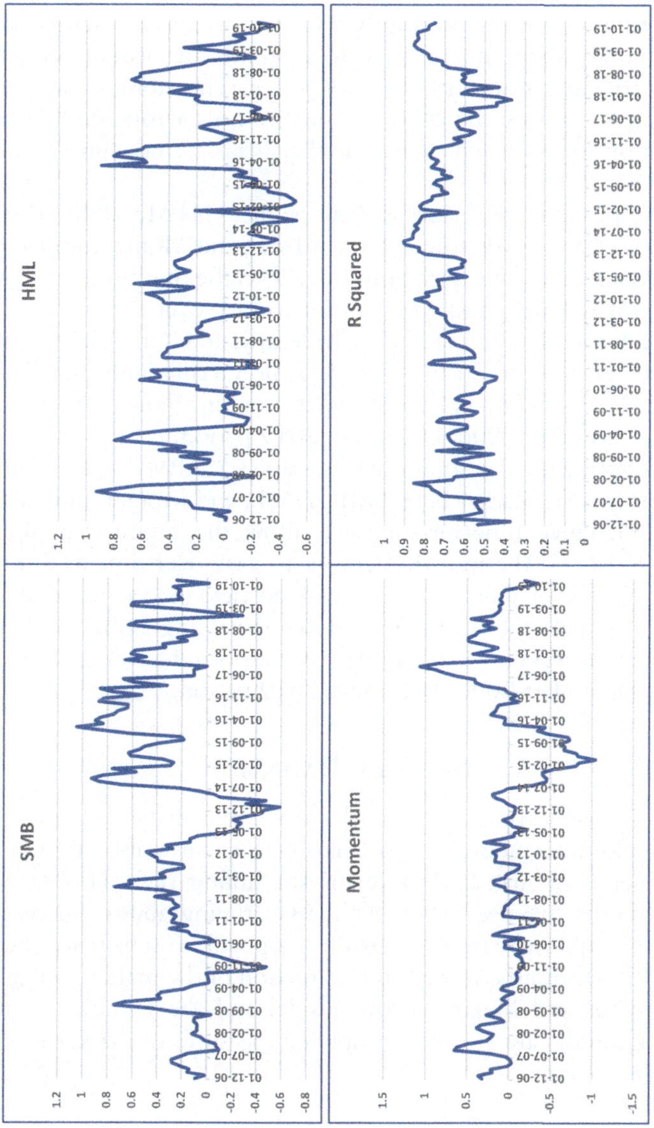

Fig. 6 (continued)

the yield on government and corporate bonds; is significant for all investment style portfolios. Thus, according to Vidal-García (2013),[47] we can observe that time-varying betas jointly with the additional factors used in the conditional model are relevant to establish an evident relationship between past and future fund performance. Therefore, conditional models are able to capture the cross-sectional returns across funds better than unconditional models which assume that betas are not time-varying but constant.

This figure presents the time-varying alpha CAPM, alpha Fama-French, alpha Carhart, Market beta, SMB, HML, and Momentum factor. In order to introduce time-variation we allow the multifactor alpha, Market beta, SMB, HML, and Momentum to vary over time as a function of (1) the 1-month T-bill rate, (2) dividend yield (3) the slope of the term structure and (4) the quality spread. Time-varying alpha and betas for the US Equity Sample: alpha and risk factors in figures are average level over the December 2006–December 2019 period.

This figure presents the time-varying alpha CAPM, alpha Fama-French, alpha Carhart, Market beta, SMB, HML, and Momentum factor. In order to introduce time-variation we allow the multifactor alpha, Market beta, SMB, HML, and Momentum to vary over time as a function of (1) the 1-month T-bill rate, (2) dividend yield (3) the slope of the term structure and (4) the quality spread. Time-varying alpha and betas for the Europe Equity Sample: alpha and risk factors in figures are average level over the December 2006–December 2019 period.

5 Market Timing

The models discussed above evaluate the stock selectivity skills of fund managers. In addition, models of portfolio performance also attempt to identify whether fund managers have market timing skill. This section discusses the models we use to test for market timing ability. Successful market timers should increase or decrease the portfolio sensitivity (beta) according to their forecasts of the future direction of the market in aggregate. The Treynor and Mazuy (1966) model and the Henriksson and Merton (1981) model are two widely applied measures of market timing ability in the literature.

[47] Vidal-García, J. (2013). The persistence of European mutual fund performance. *Research in International Business and Finance, 28*, 45–67.

Market timing refers to the dynamic allocation of capital among broad classes of investments, often restricted to equities and Long or Short-term government debt.[48] A successful market timer increases the weight of the stock portfolio before the market rises and reduces the weight of the stock before the market falls.

Treynor and Mazuy (1966) explain that a positive value for gamma is indicative of market-timing ability. The authors argue that market-timers will benefit when returns are large and positive (negative) if they increase (decrease) betas, when they expect positive (negative) excess market returns.[49] They point out that modifying the Jensen (1968) regression to include squared benchmark returns can effectively measure both market timing and security selection ability.

Treynor and Mazuy (1966) extend the CAPM into a quadratic model by specifying a linear function between β_i in (17) at time t and the expected future market excess return:

$$\beta_{i,t} = \theta_i + \gamma_{iu}\left[r_{m,t+1}\right] \tag{25}$$

using (25) to modify (17) yields:

$$r_{i,t+1} = \alpha_i + \theta_i\left(r_{m,t+1}\right) + \gamma_{iu}\left[r_{m,t+1}\right]^2 + \varepsilon_{i,t+1} \tag{26}$$

where $r_{i,t+1}$ and $r_{m,t+1}$ are the expected excess fund and market returns over the risk-free interest rate. γ_{iu} measures the unconditional market timing ability, and a positive value of γ_{iu} implies that the fund manager successfully times the market and increases (decreases) fund beta during a bull (bear) market. At time t Treynor and Mazuy (1966) use same regression as in (26) to test for market timing:

$$r_{p,t} = \alpha_p + \beta_p\, r_{m,t} + \gamma_p r_{m,t}^2 + \varepsilon_{p,t} \tag{27}$$

where $r_{p,t}$ is the excess return on a portfolio at time t, $r_{m,t}$ is the excess return on the market, and γ_p measures timing ability. If a mutual fund manager increases (decreases) the portfolio's market exposure prior to a

[48] Bollen, N. P., & Busse, J. A. (2001). On the timing ability of mutual fund managers. *The Journal of Finance, 56*(3), 1075–1094.

[49] Vidal-García, J., Vidal, M., Boubaker, S., & Uddin, G. S. (2016). The short-term persistence of international mutual fund performance. *Economic Modelling, 52,* 926–938.

market increase (decrease) then the portfolio's return will be a convex function of the market's return, and γ_p will be positive.

In this Section, we also use the Henriksson and Merton (1981) model of market timing (Vidal-Garcia et al., 2016). Henriksson and Merton (1981) indeed develop a slightly different test of market timing.

In their model, the mutual fund manager allocates capital between cash and equities based on forecasts of the future market return, as before, the manager decides between a small number of market exposure levels. It involves to test a model with two target betas via the following regression:

$$r_{p,t} = \alpha_p + \beta_p \, r_{m,t} + \gamma_p r^*_{m,t} + \varepsilon_{p,t} \tag{28}$$

where:

$$r^*_{m,t} = I\{r_{m,t} > 0\} r_{m,t} \tag{29}$$

and $I\{r_{m,t} > 0\} r_{m,t}$ is an indicator function that equals one if $r_{m,t}$ is positive and zero otherwise. The magnitude of γ_p in Eq. (28) measures the difference between the target betas, and it is positive for a manager that successfully times the market.

Grinblatt and Titman (1994) show that tests of performance are quite sensitive to the chosen benchmark. For this reason, they run four-factor model analogues of Eqs. (20) and (21) in which the three additional factors are the Fama and French (1993) size and book-to-market factors and Carhart's (1997) momentum factor. The additional factors have been shown to capture the major anomalies of Sharpe's (1964) single-factor CAPM, and are included so as not to reward managers for simply exploiting these anomalies. The three additional factors appear only as linear terms; they do not estimate "factor timing" except for the market factor. We express the four-factor TM regression as:

$$r_{p,t} = \alpha_p + \sum_{i=1}^{4} \beta_{p,i} \, r_{i,t} + \gamma_p r^2_{m,t} + \varepsilon_{p,t} \tag{30}$$

and the four-factor HM regression as

$$r_{p,t} = \alpha_p + \sum_{i=1}^{4} \beta_{p,i} \, r_{i,t} + \gamma_p r^*_{m,t} + \varepsilon_{p,t} \tag{31}$$

Ferson and Schadt (1996) estimate conditional versions of the Treynor and Mazuy (1966) model They permit β_i in (17) at time t to be a linear specification of both the expected market excess return at time $t + 1$ and the publicly available economic information set, Z_t:

$$\beta_{i,t} = \theta_i + C_i^{\cdot *} Z_t + \gamma_{ic}\left[r_{m,t+1}\right] \tag{32}$$

substituting (32) into (17) yields:

$$r_{i,t+1} = \alpha_i + \theta_i\left(r_{m,t+1}\right) + C_i^{\cdot}\left(z_t\,{}^{*}r_{m,t+1}\right) + \gamma_{ic}\left[r_{m,t+1}\right]^2 + \varepsilon_{i,t+1} \tag{33}$$

The conditional market timing model in (33) captures both the part of timing ability attributable to a manager's private market timing skills (measured by γ_{ic}) and the part of timing ability attributable to publicly available information (the term $C_i^{\cdot}\left(z_t\,{}^{*}r_{m,t+1}\right)$). We may wish to only consider the former measure to reflect 'private' market timing ability.

6 The Style-Based Analysis[50]

For the first time, the style-based analysis was introduced by Sharpe (1992) in order to provide a better understanding of mutual fund performance, trying to disentangle the contribution to performance of different risk factors. Indeed, the comparison with the fund benchmark can often be misleading if the manager develops investment biases in favor of certain sectors or geographical areas (Hereil et al., 2010). In order to evaluate the true performance of the fund, it is important to determine the components of its effective exposure and return. The style-based analysis is one solution to address this problem.

First of all, the style factors or market exposures have to be selected. To do so, a qualitative study of the manager's effective investment universe is necessary. The selected factors should cover the entire universe, mutually exclusive and have low correlation.

To illustrate these factors, according to Hereil et al. (2010), here is a list of popular indices/portfolios used, when dealing with equity mutual funds:

[50] See for details: Hereil, P., Mitaine, P., Moussavi, N., & Roncalli, T. (2010). Mutual fund ratings and performance persistence. Available at *SSRN* 1749414.

- Style indices—they are used to distinguish if the manager follows, for example, a GROWTH or VALUE investment philosophy.
- Capitalization indices—they can be LARGE, MID or SMALL and provide information on the size of the companies held in the fund.
- Sector indices—they allow us to know if the fund implements particular bets on specific industries.
- Geographical indices—they are used to split the fund exposures by country or regions.

The return $R_{i,t}$ of the fund i at date t can be explained by the returns $R_{j,t}$ of the style factor according to the following equation:

$$R_{i,t} = \sum_{j=1}^{n} \omega_{i,j} R_{j,t} + u_{i,t} \tag{34}$$

$$\text{u.c.} \quad \omega_{i,j} \geq 0 \text{ and } \sum_{j=1}^{n} \omega_{i,j} = 1 \tag{35}$$

The coefficients $\omega_{i,j}$ are the weights attributed to the jth style factor. They must be positive and sum to one in order to reflect the constraints faced by the manager (no short selling, 100% fully invested). The residual terms $u_{i,t}$ are assumed to be uncorrelated among each other and across time. Looking at the above formula, the fund performance can be broken down into two distinct components:

- The component $\sum_{j=1}^{n} \omega_{i,j} R_{j,t}$.
  This first term captures the part of the fund returns explained by the style factors. It can be seen as the performance of the asset allocation. Furthermore, the style weights are useful to know if the manager is consistent with his stated investment strategy as showed in the fund prospectus. As it well established that the performance is mainly determined by asset allocation, so this information is valuable to investors.
- The component $u_{i,t}$.
  This second term is the residual performance explained by the active management of the fund. It means that $\mathbb{E}[u_{i,t}]$ is not necessarily equal to 0. It can be further decomposed into the manager's skill

in performing the stock-picking, the tactical asset allocation and the performance linked to factors absent from the model.

By looking at the R^2 of the regression, it is, therefore, possible to get an indication of the percentage returns explained by the factors included in the analysis, that is the asset allocation and by the active management. For instance, a high R^2 will imply a passive management. On the contrary, a low R^2 will not necessarily indicate an active management as it can be a consequence of a model misspecification meaning that the model suffers due to omitted variables.

Let us consider the example of two equity mutual funds. The first one is focused over USA stock market (label as USA Style Analysis in Figs. 7 and 9), while the second over the European stock market (label as European Style Analysis in Figs. 8 and 10). We apply a style-based analysis using the MSCI indices for the four reference styles LARGE Cap/SMALL Cap and GROWTH/VALUE, therefore, we consider 2 sets of factors:

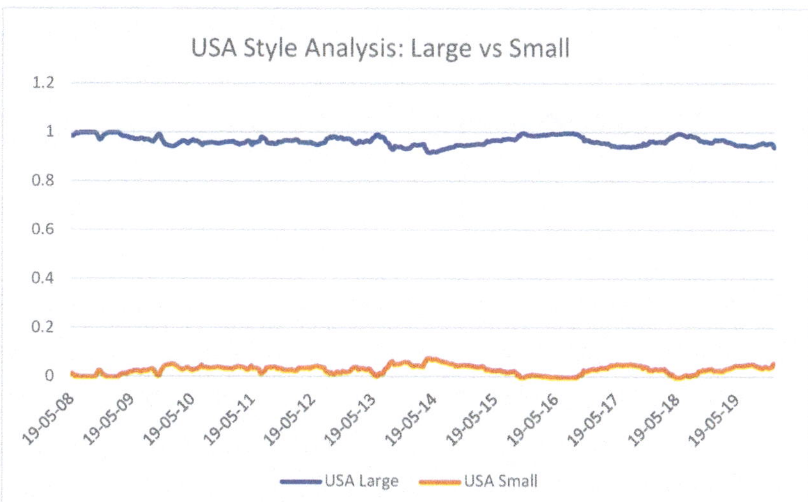

Fig. 7 Style analysis of mutual funds focused on S&P 500—large vs small

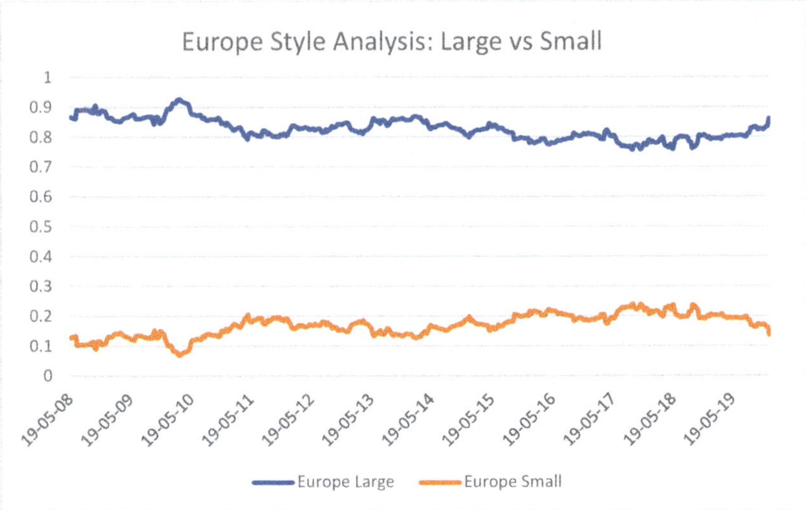

Fig. 8 Style analysis of mutual funds focused on EX600—large vs small

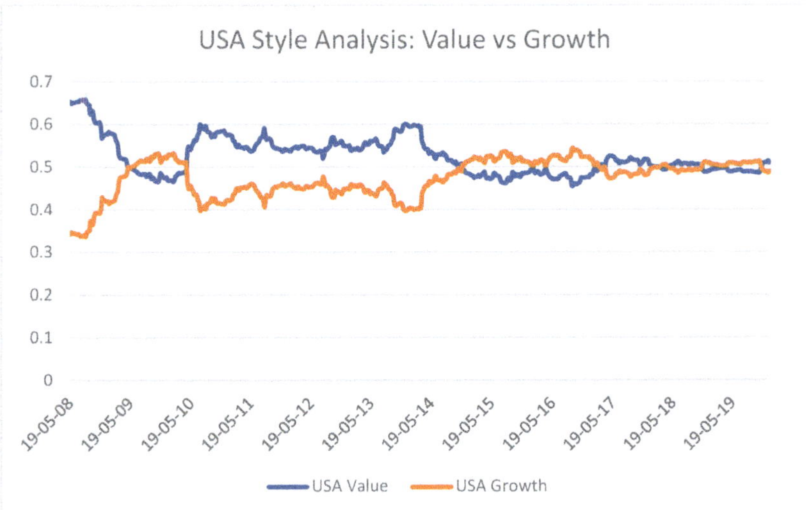

Fig. 9 Style analysis of mutual funds focused on S&P500—value vs growth

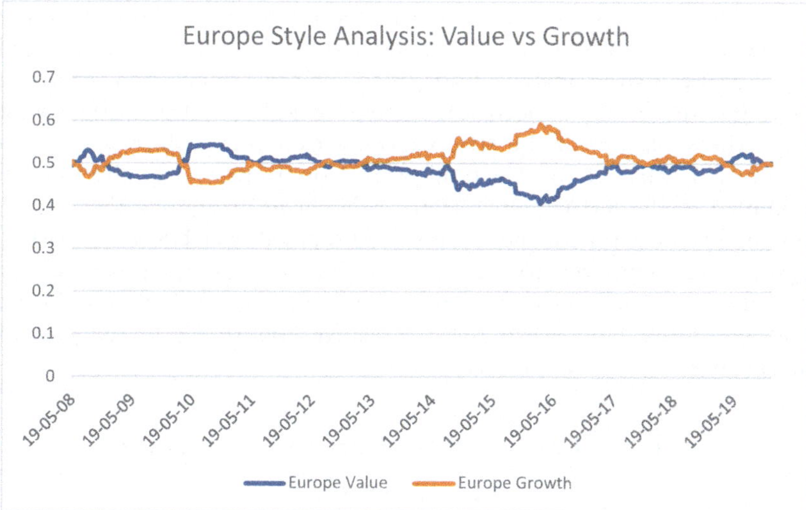

Fig. 10 Style analysis of mutual funds focused on EX600—value vs growth

(a) LARGE/SMALL.
(b) VALUE/GROWTH.

The style-based analysis is performed with weekly returns and a rolling-period of 52 weeks.

Results for the entire time sample (that is 2007–2019) are presented in Figs. 7 and 9 for the mutual fund focused over USA stock market and in Figs. 8 and 10 for the mutual fund focused over European stock market. The USA equity based mutual fund, considering only LARGE cap indices—model (a)—leads us to an implicit allocation, on average along the sample period, of over the 90% on the LARGE factor and 10% on the SMALL factor. Introducing VALUE-GROWTH style factors in the regression according to model (b), we now obtain (Fig. 9) an allocation very similar between the value and growth risk factors, of 50% even if there are periods (2008 and 2009, and between 2010 and 2014) in which the allocations on the two factors diverge significantly, with a predominance, on average, of the VALUE factor over the GROWTH factor. These results are in accordance with the fund's self-reported investment strategy. This example shows the importance of appropriately selecting factors consistent with the manager's investment universe. Looking at the rolling regression results in Fig. 8, concerning the mutual fund focused over European stock market, leads us to the same conclusion regarding the importance of the LARGE-cap factors. In addition, it provides insight about the evolution of the style exposure over time, which appears to be similar to that of the US fund even if on average, $\omega_{i,j}$, the weights attributed to the SMALL style factor is larger in magnitude than corresponding style factor for the mutual fund focused over US stock market. It is however important to keep in mind that weights represent one-year estimation window exposures rather than an instantaneous picture of the fund allocation. Here we observe a relative consistence in the growth management style in 2014–2017 years.

7 Determinants of Fund Performance

7.1 *Fund Size*

Mutual fund sizehas been one of the most studied variables in mutual fund research, and the relation between fund size and performance still puzzles academics and practitioners.[51] Several studies try to answer questions such as: does fund size affect investors fund selection ability? Is management skill more pronounced when a fund is small? In this book there is a chapter dedicated to the analysis of the relationship between fund size and performance. In this section, therefore, we do not go into depth on the subject but we report only some scientific evidence extracted from previous empirical works.

Large mutual funds present several advantages over small ones. First, a larger fund can spread fixed expenses on a larger asset base and have more research resources. Managers of large funds can benefit from investment opportunities not available to smaller funds. Large funds are able to negotiate better spreads, as they have larger positions and trading volumes. In addition, brokerage commissions decline with the decline in transaction size (Brennan & Hughes, 1991). However, large funds face some problems and management challenges. The scale of investment is one of the determinants of performance persistence (Berk & Green, 2004;

[51] See for a good review of this literature: Ferreira, M. A., Keswani, A., Miguel, A. F., & Ramos, S. B. (2013). The determinants of mutual fund performance: A cross-country study. *Review of Finance, 17*(2), 483–525.

Gruber, 1996). Although, small funds can be concentrated in a few investment positions, when the funds become larger, managers must continue to look for good investment opportunities, and the effect of management skills weakens, which means that scale is not economic. Cremers and Petajisto (2009) discover that small funds are more active, while a significant fraction of large active funds are close to indexing funds. In addition, larger mutual fund managers must trade a larger number of stocks, which arouses the attention of other market participants and therefore bears higher price-affected costs. Chen et al. (2004) name this effect the liquidity constraints hypothesis.

Grinblatt and Titman (1989, 1994) on the relationship between fund returns and fund size find mixed evidence. More recently, Chen et al. (2004) find that fund returns decline with lagged fund size. Result is most obvious in funds that invest in less liquid and smaller stocks, indicating that the adverse effects of scale are related to liquidity. They also suggest that because of organizational diseconomies, in addition to liquidity, fund size erodes performance. Pollet and Wilson (2008) found that the reason for the diminishing returns of mutual fund scale returns is that as the fund grows, it is impossible to scale investment strategies due to liquidity constraints. They found that when the fund receives capital inflows, it tends to expand its position rather than diversify its investment in new assets. A group of scholars (Edelen et al., 2007; Yan, 2008) point out trading costs and liquidity as the primary source of diseconomies of scale for US funds. Outside the United States, Dahlquist et al. (2000) found that large equity funds tend to perform worse than small equity funds in Sweden. Overall, the evidence on the relationship between scale and performance is not strongly consistent, but recent work seems to support the existence of diseconomies of scale.

7.2 Age

Fund age provides a measure of a fund's longevity and its manager's ability (Ferreira et al., 2013). The effect of age on performance can run in both directions. One might argue that young mutual funds will be more agile and committed to achieving better performance in order to survive. On the other hand, youth may be disadvantaged. Newer funds usually face higher costs and lack experience during startup. Because of their smaller size, the returns and ratings of newer mutual funds are also more susceptible to manipulation. When we consider the manager experience, according to Ding and Wermers (2012),[52] we should consider that the total career experience may have two different effects for the impact of the portfolio manager on fund performance. First, over time, managers may develop skills in analyzing stocks, or establish contacts with sell-side analysts or the CEO of the company that is about to invest. Under this rationale, Cohen et al. (2008) find evidence consistent with fund managers developing networks with CEOs, who are same-school alumni. Thus, experience may be a proxy for the ability to gather private information about stock valuations and, this way, to perform good deals. Secondly, experienced managers may gain power in mutual fund management companies, which may lead to deep-rooted incompetent managers, especially in small management companies, where fund managers are more likely to hold senior management positions.

7.3 Fees[53]

The relationship between mutual fund income and expenses (including management fees) can test the value of active management. Indeed, mutual fund fees can be seen as the price that uninformed investors pay to managers to invest their money by catching good opportunities in the market. Expenses vary considerably around the world. Khorana et al. (2009) found that large funds and mutual fund families charge lower fees, while funds distributed in more countries charge higher fees. Furthermore, they find that fees are negatively related to investor protection. All in all, the empirical evidence on the relation between mutual fund performance and fees is mixed. In a sample of American mutual funds, some authors found that fees and net fee performance (Carhart, 1997) and even pre-charge performance (Gil-Bazo & Ruiz-Verdù, 2009) were negatively correlated, while others found that there is no negative correlation (Chen et al., 2004). Empirical evidences for European funds also seem to support a negative relation between fees and performance (Dahlquist et al., 2000; Otten & Bams, 2002). They find a negative relation between

[52] Ding, B., & Wermers, R. (2012). Mutual fund performance and governance structure: The role of portfolio managers and boards of directors. https://doi.org/10.2139/ssrn.2207229.

[53] See for more details Ding, B., & Wermers, R. (2012).

the expense ratio and net-of-fees performance. This relation, however, is statistically insignificant for US funds and only significant in some specifications for non-US funds. Thus, there is not consistent evidence of a statistically significant negative relation between fees and performance.

Other authors find no relation between performance and loads (Chen et al., 2004) or a negative relation (Carhart, 1997; Pollet & Wilson, 2008).

7.4 *Flows*[54]

As mentioned previously in the case of the size, in this book we have a chapter dedicated to the analysis of the relationship between flows and performance. Here, we report just a very small group of previous academic evidences from seminal papers. According to Gruber's (1996) smart money hypothesis, investors can find skilled managers and invest their money in them. Therefore, fund flows should have a positive correlation with future returns. Some authors (Gruber, 1996; Zheng, 1999) pointed out that the performance of funds that experienced net inflows (in the last 3 months) was significantly better than that of funds that experienced net inflows.

However, Sapp and Tiwari (2004) argue that the smart money effect is explained by momentum.

7.5 *Past Performance*

The relevance in considering past returns as determinants of fund performance is to refer to the fact that there is ample evidence of performance persistence in US mutual funds (Brown & Goetzmann, 1995; Carhart, 1997; Grinblatt & Titman, 1994; Hendricks et al., 1993; Kosowski,[55] 2011). This persistence seems to be stronger among the most poorly performing funds. Outside the USA, we have some mixed

[54] See for more details Ding, B., & Wermers, R. (2012). Mutual fund performance and governance structure: The role of portfolio managers and boards of directors. https://doi.org/10.2139/ssrn.2207229.

[55] Kosowski, R. (2011). Do mutual funds perform when it matters most to investors? US mutual fund performance and risk in recessions and expansions. *The Quarterly Journal of Finance, 1*(3), 607–664.

evidences. Dahlquist et al. (2000) do not find any performance persistence for a sample of Swedish funds, however, Otten and Bams (2002) find performance persistence for UK funds and Abdel-Kader and Qing (2007)[56]—for Chinese funds.

7.6 *Empirical Analysis*

In order to investigate the determinants of equity mutual fund performance, we run separate regressions using US and European funds, that allows us to compare the determinants of the performance of funds in the USA versus the European side. Specifically, for each month t, we estimate the following regression:

$$\begin{aligned}\hat{\alpha}_{i,t}^{4F}\left(\alpha_p^{BOND}\right) =& Intercept_{i,t} + \beta_1 flow_{i,t-1} + \beta_2 \log(TNA)_{i,t-1} \\ &+ \beta_3 \hat{\alpha}_{i,t-1}^{4F}\ \beta_4 ExpenseRatio_{i,t-1} + \beta_5 Age_{i,t-1} \\ &+ \beta_6 ActiveShare_{i,t-1} + \beta_7 Volatility_{j,t} \\ &+ \beta_8 R - square_{j,t-1} + \varepsilon_{i,t} \qquad (36)\end{aligned}$$

where $\hat{\alpha}_{i,t}^{4F}$ is the 52-weeks rolling window estimation of the conditional four-factor Carhart alpha for fund i in month t. $\hat{\alpha}_{i,t}^{4F}$ *and* α_p^{BOND} are described at Eqs. (44) and (45) respectively. In the multivariate approach, the time sample analyzed spans from December 2006 to December 2019. We focus over a host of fund characteristics in our analysis of performance. The 1st characteristic is fund age ($Age_{i,t-1}$) as given by the number of months since fund launch date.[57] The 2nd characteristic is the total expense ratio ($ExpenseRatio_{i,t-1}$), defined as total annual expenses as a fraction of TNA. The 3th characteristic of interest is flows defined as the

[56] Abdel-Kader, M., & Qing, K. Y. (2007). Risk-adjusted performance, selectivity, timing ability, and performance persistence of Hong Kong mutual funds. *Journal of Asia-Pacific Business, 8*(2), 25–58.

[57] When fund lauch date is prior to the first date (in terms of month) included in our time sample, we consider the first date as lauch date, i.e. the first month/year included in our time sample.

normalized monthly net flow ($flow_{i,t-1}$) of fund i in month $t-1$ corresponding to the percentage growth in total assets under management (in local currency) between the beginning and the end of month t, net of internal growth (assuming reinvestment of dividends and distributions):

$$Flow_{it} = \frac{TNA_{it} - TNA_{i,t-1}(1 + R_{it})}{TNA_{i,t-1}},$$

where TNA_{it} is the TNA in local currency of fund i, and $R_{i,t}$ is fund i return in local currency. The 4nd characteristic is the Fund size measured by $\log(TNA)_{i,t-1}$ corresponding to the natural logarithm of the total net assets of fund i in period $t-1$ in US dollars.

We also include three additional control variables namely Volatility, R-squared and Active measure. $Volatility_{j,t}$ is the volatility of monthly returns (Standard Deviation over 52 weeks rolling estimation). According to Bliss et al. (2008), we also added the CAPM $Rsquare_{j,t-1}$ measure as a control variable. $ActiveShare_{i,t-1}$ is a measure of active management by the fund as defined by Cremers and Petajisto (2009) and Miller et al. (2007). These variables have been included in regression analysis in previous studies (e.g., Bergstresser et al., 2009; Chen et al., 2004, 2007; Friesen & Sapp, 2007; Huang et al., 2011; Jiang & Yuksel, 2017; Keswani & Stolin, 2008; Sialm et al, 2015).

Miller et al.'s (2007) active share measure, captures the proportion of fund's holdings different from its benchmark[58] When fund holdings largely match benchmark holdings, investors benefit from the beta part of return expressed by benchmark-like raw performance. Investors could

[58] According to Miller et al.'s (2007) procedure, we can define w_A as the proportion of the portfolio P that we consider to be actively managed, so the returns of the portfolio P' can be written as the weighted sum of its passive return $r_{I'}$ and of its active return $r_{A'}$ as follows:

$$r_{P'} = (1 - w_A)r_{I'} + w_A r_{A'} \tag{37}$$

By construction, the returns of the active component of the portfolio ($r_{A'}$) are uncorrelated with those of the passive component ($r_{I'}$). Taking this into account, to compute the variance from (3) we obtain:

$$\sigma_{P'}^2 = (1 - w_A)^2\sigma_{I'}^2 + w_A^2\sigma_{A'}^2 \tag{38}$$

where $\sigma_{I'}^2$ is the passive variance, and $\sigma_{A'}^2$ is the active variance.

also obtain the benefit at lower fees by investing in a number of financial instruments such as ETFs, certificates, indexed funds and some derivative contracts.

However, there is a robust literature (see among others: Amihud & Goyenko, 2013; Huij & Derwall, 2011) that establish how active management helps improve the performance. This evidence benefits investors, who are willing to pay performance fees to the fund manager with successful ability to make an extra-return due to the active management component.

We want the proportion of variance that is explained by passive and active components to be the same for P' as it was for P, for the passive component we have:

$$\frac{(1-w_A)^2\sigma_{I'}^2}{\sigma_{P'}^2} = R^2, \tag{39}$$

whereas for the active component we have:

$$\frac{W_A^2\sigma_{A'}^2}{\sigma_{P'}^2} = 1 - R^2 \tag{40}$$

Rearranging both (3) and (4), we have:

$$\frac{W_A^2\sigma_{A'}^2}{(1-w_A)^2\sigma_{I'}^2} = \frac{1-R^2}{R^2} \tag{41}$$

In the absence of any specific information about the two components of a portfolio, the natural assumption is that the active and passive components have the same variance. Taking the square root of each side, we obtain:

$$\frac{w_A}{(1-w_A)} = \frac{\sqrt{1-R^2}}{R} \tag{42}$$

Solving (6) for the value of the w_A, the weight of the active share in the portfolio yields:

$$w_A = \frac{\sqrt{1-R^2}}{R+\sqrt{1-R^2}} \tag{43}$$

Pooled panel regressions exhibit significant residual correlations within a year, due to active share and many independent variables that are persistent over time, so the model includes time fixed effects and standard errors are clustered by fund. Therefore, the effect is hopefully to be truly cross-sectional and cannot be explained by an overall market reaction. All explanatory variables are lagged one-period.

Fund performance is evaluated based on fund alpha. To catch the difference in risk return trade off between equity and fixed income strategies, we run two separate conditional market models. To compute the equity preformance, we consider $\hat{\alpha}_{i,t}^{4F}$. The four-factor alpha $\hat{\alpha}_{i,t}^{4F}$ is the intercept of four-factor model:

$$r_{p,t} = \alpha_p + \beta_{1,p} MKTRF_t + \beta_{2,p} SMB_t + \beta_{3,p} HML_t + \beta_{4,p} MOM_t + \varepsilon_{pt} \quad (44)$$

where $r_{p,t}$ is the monthly return on a funds in excess of the one-month Treasury bill (T-bill) rate. $MKTRF_t$ is the stock market return in excess of the one-month T-bill rate. *SMB, HML,* and *MOM* are, respectively, returns on zero-investment factor-mimicking international portfolios for size, book-to-market, and momentum. Multifactor attributes are drawn from Kenneth R. French—Data Library.

When we take into account Fixed Income Mutual Funds, we follow previous studies (Ayadi & Kryzanowski, 2011; Boney et al., 2009), we refer to (α^{BOND}) that is the intercept of the following model:

$$r_{p,t} = \alpha_p^{BOND} + \beta_{1,p} MKTRF_t^{Bond} + \beta_{2,p} DEFAULT_t + \beta_{3,p} TERM_t + \varepsilon_{pt} \quad (45)$$

which includes the excess market return (RMRF), default risk (DEFAULT), and term risk (TERM). The excess return on the bond market ($MKTRF_t^{Bond}$) is the 10 Year Government rate, DEFAULT denotes the difference in return between investment grade corporate and government bonds (10-year Treasury Constant Maturity Yield); TERM is defined as the difference in return between long-term (10-year Treasury Constant Maturity Yield) and short-term government bonds (1-year Treasury Constant Maturity Yield).

Tables 7 and 8 reports the results of performance regressions using the Carhart four-factor model alphas as a measure of risk-adjusted performance for the Mutual fund with Asset type focus corresponding to Equity, while we use alpha from the model described at Eq. (45), when considering the Mutual fund sample with Asset type focus over fixed income (Bond) assets. For the latter groups results are reported in Tables 9 and 10. Later, we consider the Financial Crisis Impact over our results. Column (2) and Column (4) in Panel A, and Column (2), Column (4) and Column (6) in Panel B present estimates for Crisis Period, with respect to the Equity Side. Column (2) and Column (4) present estimates for Crisis Period, with respect to the Bond Side.

Table 7 reports the results of panel regression of mutual fund performance on fund characteristics for US equity funds. Panel A shows estimates for SMALL and LARGE caps. We found negative statistically significant relation between Age and performance for LARGE caps at 5% while it reverses during Crisis period for the SMALL group. There is no statistically significant reaction for net expense ratio. We observe flows to have positive and statistically significant coefficient for LARGE caps and for SMALL caps at 1% level in no crisis time, indicating a smart money effect. However, Sapp and Tiwari (2004) argue that the smart money effect is explained by momentum. Size is positively related to fund performance in the sample of LARGE caps (we observe positive statistically significant 5% reaction), but the relation is negative but not statistically significant for SMALL caps. Carhart alpha in $t-1$ is positive and statistically significant at 1% level for all equity sample in Panel A. The effect of volatility of monthly returns on performance is positive with strong statistically significant reaction at 1% level for US LARGE caps in no crisis time and 5% level in crisis time, while the reaction of SMALL caps is negative at 5% level of statistical significance in no crisis period. CAPM Rsquare$_{j,t-1}$ and Active share are positive at 1% statistically significant level for LARGE caps in crisis period. Panel B shows estimates for investment styles in crisis and no crisis time. The relationship between age of the fund and fund performance does not demonstrate any statistically significant reaction, which is consistent with the evidence in Chen et al. (2004). The net expense ratio is negative at 1% statistically significant level for BLEND style in all periods and for VALUE style in no crisis. Flows analysis reveals positive statistically significant reaction for BLEND style in all periods (1%), and for VALUE styles (5 and 1% level of statistical significance in no crisis and crisis time respectively), signaling of the presence of smart

Table 7 Determinants of performance—EQUITY US

PANEL A: SMALL & LARGE				
	LARGE_NO CRISIS	*LARGE_CRISIS*	*SMALL_NO CRISIS*	*SMALL_CRISIS*
AGE	0.0186	−0.4473**	−0.0474	2.1392***
	(0.0400)	(0.2099)	(0.0574)	(0.6215)
EXPENSE	0.0002	−0.0046	0.0106	−0.0309
	(0.0194)	(0.0380)	(0.0455)	(0.0820)
FLOWS	3.4762***	0.3920	5.4254***	4.4590**
	(1.0821)	(2.2152)	(1.0590)	(1.6613)
SIZE	0.0071**	0.0057	−0.0000	−0.0182
	(0.0030)	(0.0063)	(0.0066)	(0.0147)
Alpha_MOM T-1	0.5323***	0.6061***	0.5366***	0.4224***
	(0.0198)	(0.0357)	(0.0252)	(0.0534)
VOLATILITY	1.5497***	3.1285**	−4.4956**	5.5302
	(0.4415)	(1.3968)	(1.9905)	(3.6613)
RSQUAREDCAPM	0.0721	1.6334***	−0.4697	−0.4431

(continued)

Table 7 (continued)

PANEL A: SMALL & LARGE

	LARGE_NO CRISIS	*LARGE_CRISIS*	*SMALL_NO CRISIS*	*SMALL_CRISIS*
	(0.1141)	(0.3895)	(0.2937)	(1.0495)
ACTIVE	0.2126	2.0297***	−0.5158	0.1784
	(0.1469)	(0.5368)	(0.4802)	(1.5030)
CONS	−0.2965**	−1.8252***	0.7091	0.2267
	(0.1347)	(0.4950)	(0.4468)	(1.3257)
N	13.350	2010	3973	493

Standard errors in parentheses
* $p < 0.10$, ** $p < 0.05$, *** $p < 0.01$

PANEL B: MANAGEMENT STYLES

	BLEND_NO CRISIS	*BLEND_CRISIS*	*VALUE_NO CRISIS*	*VALUE_CRISIS*	*GROWTH_NO CRISIS*	*GROWTH_CRISIS*
AGE	−0.0184	−0.0173	−0.1675	−0.0075	−0.9960	−0.0930
	(0.0132)	(0.0143)	(0.1440)	(0.0379)	(0.5852)	(0.0560)
EXPENSE	−0.0340***	−0.0439***	−0.0525***	−0.0487	−0.0316	−0.0045
	(0.0069)	(0.0148)	(0.0184)	(0.0403)	(0.0890)	(0.0315)
FLOWS	1.1841***	1.2730***	2.0444**	3.5528***	5.8941	1.0090
	(0.4408)	(0.3397)	(0.8873)	(1.0131)	(3.5844)	(1.7502)
SIZE	0.0047***	0.0065***	−0.0029	0.0055	−0.0145	0.0130***
	(0.0018)	(0.0027)	(0.0048)	(0.0055)	(0.0149)	(0.0040)
Alpha_MOM T-1	0.5160***	0.4259**	0.5415***	0.4371***	0.4846***	0.5286***
	(0.0119)	(0.0208)	(0.0230)	(0.0357)	(0.0625)	(0.0266)
VOLATILITY	0.2050***	0.1949***	1.6377**	−3.6293*	9.1757**	1.7296***

PANEL B: MANAGEMENT STYLES

	BLEND_NO CRISIS	*BLEND_CRISIS*	*VALUE_NO CRISIS*	*VALUE_CRISIS*	*GROWTH_NO CRISIS*	*GROWTH_CRISIS*
	(0.0400)	(0.0599)	(0.7306)	(2.0429)	(3.8389)	(0.6031)
RSQUAREDCAPM	−0.2245***	−0.1134*	0.9503***	−0.3905	2.4649***	0.0016
	(0.0511)	(0.0622)	(0.1596)	(0.2414)	(0.8278)	(0.2059)
ACTIVE	−0.2138***	−0.1027**	1.1696***	−0.3720	3.0556**	−0.0164
	(0.0629)	(0.0518)	(0.1925)	(0.3566)	(1.1281)	(0.2624)
CONS	0.1915***	0.3804**	−0.9274***	0.4499	−2.6991**	−0.0978
	(0.0645)	(0.1534)	(0.1976)	(0.3278)	(1.1731)	(0.2440)
N	37,815	37,815	6482	4271	516	4708

Standard errors in parentheses

$^{*}p < 0.10$, $^{**}p < 0.05$, $^{***}p < 0.01$

Notes This table reports the results of the panel regressions of mutual fund performance on fund characteristics. Portfolio performance is evaluated based on simple Return and portfolio alpha according to the following model: $r_{p,t} = \alpha_p^{BOND} + \beta_{1,t} MKTRF_t^{Bond} + \beta_{2,p} DEFAULT_t + \beta_{3,p} TERM_t + \varepsilon_{p,t}$; where $r_{p,t}$ is the monthly return on a portfolio of funds in excess of the one-month T-bill rate; $MKTRF_t^{Bond}$ is the Local (European or US) Total Bond Market Index return in excess of the one-month T-bill rate. $DEFAULT$ is the difference in return between investment grade corporate bonds and government bonds (10-year Treasury Constant Maturity Yield); $TERM_t$ is the difference in return between long-term (30-year Treasury Constant Maturity Yield) and short-term government bonds (one-year Treasury Constant Maturity Yield). AGE is defined as the number of months from the fund's inception. $\text{Flow}_{i,t-1}$ is the normalized monthly net flow of fund i in month $t-1$. SIZE is the logarithm of the total net assets of fund i in period $t-1$ $\log(\text{TNA})_{i,t-1}$; $\text{ExpenseRatio}_{i,t-1}$, is the net expense ratio. $\text{Volatility}_{j,t}$ is the volatility of monthly returns (Standard Deviation over a 52 weeks rolling estimation). According to Bliss et al. (2008) we also added the CAPM $\text{Rsquare}_{j,t-1}$ measure as a control variable. $\text{ActiveShare}_{i,t-1}$ is a measure of active management by the fund as defined by Cremers and Petajisto (2009) and Miller et al. (2007). The sample period is from December 2006 to December 2019. The crisis period range between June 2007 to December 2010. The *t*-statistics are based on standard errors clustered by both fund and time. *, **, and ***, respectively, denote significance at the 10, 5, and 1% levels

Table 8 Determinants of performance—EQUITY EUROPE

PANEL A: SMALL & LARGE

	LARGE_NO CRISIS	*LARGE_CRISIS*	*SMALL_NO CRISIS*	*SMALL_CRISIS*
AGE	−0.0349	−0.4635	0.0453	−0.1647
	(0.0233)	(0.3573)	(0.0377)	(0.3693)
EXPENSE	−0.0504***	−0.0211	0.0028	0.0043
	(0.0159)	(0.0291)	(0.0284)	(0.0608)
FLOWS	2.2338***	0.0586	2.2007***	−2.3355
	(0.3901)	(1.0365)	(0.6282)	(2.8750)
SIZE	0.0029	0.0012	−0.0001	−0.0233
	(0.0036)	(0.0083)	(0.0063)	(0.0163)
Alpha_MOM T-1	0.3622***	0.3711***	0.4489***	0.4335***
	(0.0150)	(0.0378)	(0.0204)	(0.0452)
VOLATILITY	−0.6734	2.5998	0.0922	1.6674
	(1.1202)	(1.7351)	(2.0781)	(1.2302)
RSQUAREDCAPM	−0.0250	−0.9233	−0.6759*	0.5772

PANEL A: SMALL & LARGE

	LARGE_NO CRISIS	*LARGE_CRISIS*	*SMALL_NO CRISIS*	*SMALL_CRISIS*
	(0.2158)	(0.6809)	(0.3405)	(0.7853)
ACTIVE	−0.2321	−1.6936**	−1.2235**	0.2733
	(0.3656)	(0.8201)	(0.5519)	(1.1577)
CONS	0.2399	1.3673*	1.1489**	0.1418
	(0.3106)	(0.7276)	(0.5038)	(1.0662)
N	18.582	3052	7998	1344

Standard errors in parentheses
* $p < 0.10$, ** $p < 0.05$, *** $p < 0.01$

PANEL B: MANAGEMENT STYLES

	BLEND_NO CRISIS	*BLEND_CRISIS*	*VALUE_NO CRISIS*	*VALUE_CRISIS*	*GROWTH_NO CRISIS*	*GROWTH_CRISIS*
AGE	−0.0453*	−0.5549	0.0226	−0.5638	−0.0124	0.4564
	(0.0240)	(0.3551)	(0.0565)	(0.3757)	(0.0579)	(0.8320)
EXPENSE	−0.0427***	−0.0192	−0.0860*	−0.0617	−0.0603	−0.0703
	(0.0150)	(0.0286)	(0.0462)	(0.0731)	(0.0785)	(0.1314)
FLOWS	2.5404***	−0.1838	3.1606***	1.9756	2.8341***	−4.0238

(continued)

Table 8 (continued)

PANEL B: MANAGEMENT STYLES

	BLEND_NO CRISIS	*BLEND_CRISIS*	*VALUE_NO CRISIS*	*VALUE_CRISIS*	*GROWTH_NO CRISIS*	*GROWTH_CRISIS*
	(0.4445)	(0.9838)	(0.9996)	(2.6352)	(0.9955)	(4.2457)
SIZE	0.0036	−0.0022	−0.0091	0.0164	0.0122*	0.0353*
	(0.0039)	(0.0103)	(0.0101)	(0.0097)	(0.0067)	(0.0182)
Alpha_MOM T-1	0.3587***	0.3709***	0.2887***	0.4067***	0.4350***	0.6174***
	(0.0145)	(0.0389)	(0.0421)	(0.0676)	(0.0446)	(0.1324)
VOLATILITY	−1.4876	3.2619*	0.4210	7.0949***	0.6589***	0.9476
	(1.3315)	(1.9189)	(2.2917)	(1.7080)	(0.0221)	(4.3367)
RSQUAREDCAPM	0.0379	−0.4948	−0.8142**	−1.0720	−0.1614	−2.1991
	(0.2500)	(0.7814)	(0.3335)	(1.0514)	(0.4042)	(1.5557)
ACTIVE	−0.0710	−0.9829	−1.1561**	−1.9972	−0.3121	−3.7067*
	(0.4297)	(0.9535)	(0.5190)	(1.5579)	(0.5175)	(1.9449)
CONS	0.1458	0.8089	1.2026**	0.9841	0.2136	2.4024
	(0.3737)	(0.8531)	(0.5089)	(1.3026)	(0.4918)	(1.5795)
N	18.085	2926	4003	691	3815	493

Standard errors in parentheses
$^{*}p < 0.10$, $^{**}p < 0.05$, $^{***}p < 0.01$

Notes This table reports the results of the panel regressions of mutual fund performance on fund characteristics. Portfolio performance is evaluated based on Carhart or Momentum Four Factor alpha. AGE is defined as the number of months from the fund's inception. $\text{Flow}_{i,t-1}$ is the normalized monthly net flow of fund i in month $t-1$. SIZE is the logarithm of the total net assets of fund i in period $t-1$ $\log(\text{TNA})_{i,t-1}$. $\text{ExpenseRatio}_{i,t-1}$, is the net expense ratio. $\text{Volatility}_{j,t}$ is the volatility of monthly returns (Standard Deviation over a 52 weeks rolling estimation). According to Bliss et al. (2008) we also added the CAPM $\text{Rsquare}_{j,t-1}$ measure as a control variable. $\text{ActiveShare}_{i,t-1}$ is a measure of active management by the fund as defined by Cremers and Petajisto (2009) and Miller et al. (2007). The sample period is from December 2006 to December 2019. The crisis period range between June 2007 and December 2010. The t-statistics are based on standard errors clustered by both fund and time. *, **, and ***, respectively, denote significance at the 10, 5, and 1% levels.

Table 9 Determinants of performance—BOND US

	CORPORATE NO CRISIS	*CORPORATE CRISIS*	*GOVERNMENT NO CRISIS*	*GOVERNMENT CRISIS*
AGE	3.0369	26.2606	17.1455*	−46.3240
	(13.2175)	(152.2089)	(9.8335)	(85.7895)
EXPENSE	23.3056*	−6.1849	6.5064	−7.7076
	(13.5551)	(59.4407)	(8.9455)	(21.1889)
FLOWS	54.0256	146.8075	174.4160	656.1800**
	(97.7428)	(306.2686)	(142.8650)	(295.5436)
SIZE	2.6603	3.4066	1.1628	4.6228
	(2.0881)	(8.3527)	(1.8813)	(3.7145)
Alpha_BOND T-1	74.2397***	72.3128***	78.6596***	80.8304***
	(1.1003)	(3.7521)	(0.7251)	(1.8072)
VOLATILITY	30.1535***	15.4473	27.2120***	6.9019
	(4.1202)	(27.8554)	(8.5110)	(15.3392)
RSQUARED	102.5521	106.1044	−89.3725	252.7921***
	(293.5413)	(83.9697)	(380.8048)	(86.0389)
ACTIVE	57.2103***	26.7293	10.6669	22.5575
	(13.7435)	(59.0488)	(11.6177)	(30.0047)
CONS	−491.8218***	−297.6519	−108.5286	−266.8682
	(125.4871)	(543.3177)	(105.6710)	(264.3569)
N	8394	846	7785	1328

Standard errors in parentheses
$^{*}p < 0.10$, $^{**}p < 0.05$, $^{***}p < 0.01$

Notes This table reports the results of the panel regressions of mutual fund performance on fund characteristics. Portfolio performance is evaluated based on simple Return and portfolio alpha according to the following model: $r_{p,t} = \alpha_p^{BOND} + \beta_{1,t} MKTRF_t^{Bond} + \beta_{2,p} DEFAULT_t + \beta_{3,p} TERM_t + \varepsilon_{p,t}$; where $r_{p,t}$ is the monthly return on a portfolio of funds in excess of the one-month T-bill rate; $MKTRF_t^{Bond}$ is the Local (European or Us) Total Bond Market Index return in excess of the one-month T-bill rate. $DEFAULT$ is the difference in return between investment grade corporate bonds and government bonds (10-year Treasury Constant Maturity Yield); $TERM_t$ is the difference in return between long-term (30-year Treasury Constant Maturity Yield) and short-term government bonds (one-year Treasury Constant Maturity Yield). AGE is defined as the number of months from the fund's inception. $\text{Flow}_{i,t-1}$ is the normalized monthly net flow of fund i in month t−1. SIZE is the logarithm of the total net assets of fund i in period t−1 $\log(\text{TNA})_{i,t-1}$; $\text{ExpenseRatio}_{i,t-1}$, is the net expense ratio. $\text{Volatility}_{j,t}$ is the volatility of monthly returns (Standard Deviation over a 52 weeks rolling estimation). According to Bliss et al. (2008) we also added the CAPM $\text{Rsquare}_{j,t-1}$ measure as a control variable. $\text{ActiveShare}_{i,t-1}$ is a measure of active management by the fund as defined by Cremers and Petajisto (2009) and Miller et al. (2007). The sample period is from December 2006 to December 2019. The crisis period range between June 2007 and December 2010. The t-statistics are based on standard errors clustered by both fund and time. *, **, and ***, respectively, denote significance at the 10, 5, and 1% levels.

Table 10 Determinants of performance—BOND EUROPE

	CORPORATE NO CRISIS	*CORPORATE CRISIS*	*GOVERNMENT NO CRISIS*	*GOVERNMENT CRISIS*
AGE	−2.8006	387.1309	−25.5052*	−62.6641***
	(11.8690)	(266.1589)	(13.4997)	(20.0434)
EXPENSE	−5.6470	−102.1091*	18.4778	64.0918
	(16.7103)	(52.9216)	(14.8865)	(61.9757)
FLOWS	−30.1064	−200.2436*	27.6786*	−49.5453
	(21.5122)	(105.9304)	(16.5707)	(45.4488)
SIZE	−2.2814	−4.6522	−1.2180	−11.7391
	(2.3517)	(10.0044)	(2.1071)	(8.1632)
Alpha_BOND T-1	74.7726***	76.6449***	77.0288***	74.6602***
	(3.2259)	(3.1174)	(2.0586)	(4.8248)
VOLATILITY	54.5249	35.6647	110.6172***	255.7197***
	(47.5773)	(40.1230)	(30.2351)	(91.1517)
RSQUARED	−7.2049***	−31.1590***	−4.0672*	−16.5188**
	(1.6775)	(5.0596)	(2.0727)	(6.7072)
ACTIVE	−90.1689***	−36.6123***	−6.6962	−70.6555
	(21.1480)	(6.6610)	(19.8001)	(69.6335)
CONS	875.7152***	3814.1751***	46.3038	1091.0913*
	(212.5794)	(577.9676)	(172.8891)	(599.8775)
N	17.052	2574	9354	1619

Standard errors in parentheses

* $p < 0.10$, ** $p < 0.05$, *** $p < 0.01$

Notes This table reports the results of the panel regressions of mutual fund performance on fund characteristics. Portfolio performance is evaluated based on Carhart or Momentum Four Factor alpha. AGE is defined as the number of months from the fund's inception. $\text{Flow}_{i,t-1}$ is the normalized monthly net flow of fund i in month −1. SIZE is the logarithm of the total net assets of fund i in period $t-1$ $\log(\text{TNA})_{i,t-1}$. $\text{ExpenseRatio}_{i,t-1}$, is the net expense ratio. $\text{Volatility}_{j,t}$ is the volatility of monthly returns (Standard Deviation over a 52 weeks rolling estimation). According to Bliss et al. (2008) we also added the CAPM $\text{Rsquare}_{j,t-1}$ measure as a control variable. $\text{ActiveShare}_{i,t-1}$ is a measure of active management by the fund as defined by Cremers and Petajisto (2009) and Miller et al. (2007). The sample period is from December 2006 to December 2019. The crisis period range between June 2007 and December 2010. The t-statistics are based on standard errors clustered by both fund and time. *, **, and ***, respectively, denote significance at the 10, 5, and 1% levels.

money affect. Fund size has a positive and statistically significant effect at 1% for BLEND style funds in all periods, and for GROWTH style during the crisis. Carhart alpha in $t-1$ (Alpha_MOM T-1) is strongly statistically significant with positive sign in all funds. Volatility effects on fund performance are positive and statistically significant in all styles, except the negative sign in VALUE style during the crisis (−3.6293 at 10% statistically significant level). CAPM $\text{Rsquare}_{j,t-1}$ and Active share are negative and statistically significant at 1% level for BLEND style in all periods, and are positive and statistically significant for VALUE and GROWTH styles in no crisis period.

Table 8 reports the results of panel regression of mutual fund performance on fund characteristics for EU equity funds. Panel A shows estimates for SMALL and LARGE caps. We observe no statistically significant relation between Age and performance for both LARGE and SMALL caps in line with Chen et al. (2004). Net expense ratio is negatively statistically significant at 1% level only for LARGE caps sample in no crisis time. Flows are positively related to returns at 1% statistically significant level for LARGE caps and SMALL caps in no crisis time. We do not observe any statistically significant reaction in relation of size to fund performance for EU equity funds. Carhart alpha in $t-1$ is positive and statistically significant at 1% level for all equity samples. The effect of volatility of monthly returns on performance is not statistically significant. CAPM $\text{Rsquare}_{j,t-1}$ is negative with very weak statistically significant reaction of 10% only for small caps in no crisis. Active share is negative at 5% statistically significant level for large caps crisis and small caps no crisis. Panel B shows estimates for investment styles in crisis and no crisis time for EU equity funds. The relationship between age of the fund and fund performance is negative with weak statistically significant reaction at 10% for blend style in no crisis period. The net expense ratio is negative at 1% statistically significant level for BLEND style and at 10% statistically significant level for VALUE style in no crisis period.

Flows demonstrate their positive statistically significant effect on performance in no crisis periods with positive statistically significant reaction at 1% for all styles in our sample analyzed. Fund size has a positive and statistically significant effect at 10% only for GROWTH style in both periods.

Carhart alpha in $t-1$ is strongly statistically significant with positive sign in all funds. Volatility effects on fund performance are positive and statistically significant for BLEND and VALUE styles in crisis time, and for GROWTH in no crisis. CAPM $\text{Rsquare}_{j,t-1}$ and Active share are negative and statistically significant at 5% level for VALUE style in no crisis period and active share demonstrates weak negative statistically significant reaction at 10% for GROWTH style in crisis.

Table 9 reports the results of panel regression of mutual fund performance on fund characteristics for US bond funds. There is statistically significant reaction between Age and performance only for US government bonds in no crisis period. Net expense ratio has weak positive statistically significant reaction at 10% level for corporate bonds in no crisis period. Flows are positively related to returns at 5% statistically significant level for government bonds during the crisis. There is no statistically significant reaction in relation of size to fund performance. Relation between volatility and fund performance is positive and statistically significant at 1% for corporate and government bond funds in no crisis period. CAPM Rsquare$_{j,t-1}$ is positive with strong statistically significant reaction at 1% level for government bonds during the crisis. Active share is positive at 1% statistically significant level for corporate bonds in no crisis period.

Table 10 reports the results of panel regression of mutual fund performance on fund characteristics for EU bond funds. We observe negative statistically significant reaction between Age and performance for government bonds at 10% level in no crisis time and at 1% level during the crisis. Net expense ratio has weak negative statistically significant reaction at 10% level for corporate bonds in crisis period. Flows are positively related to returns at 10% statistically significant level for government bonds in no crisis period, and this relation is statistically significant with negative sign at 10% level for corporate bonds sample in crisis period. There is no statistically significant reaction in relation of size to fund performance. Alpha bond in $t-1$ is strongly statistically significant with positive sign in all measures. Relation between volatility and fund performance is positive and statistically significant at 1% for government bonds in all periods. CAPM Rsquare$_{j,t-1}$ is negative at 1% statistically significant level for corporate bonds sample in all periods, and negative at 10 and 5%—for government bonds in no crisis and in crisis period, respectively. Active share is strongly negative at 1% statistically significant level for corporate bonds in both periods.

8 Performance-Decomposition Methodology[59]

Thus, to understand and to benchmark the performance of an actively managed fund, following Wermers (2003) and Ding and Wermers (2012), we report several measures that quantify the ability of the manager to choose stocks and to generate superior performance at the net return level. These measures divide the income of the stocks held by mutual funds into several parts to benchmark the stock portfolio and understand how mutual fund managers generate the net income level of the fund. The measures that we employ to decompose the return of a mutual fund include the following[60]:

1. the portfolio-weighted return on stocks currently held by the fund, in excess of returns (during the same time period) on matched control portfolios having the same style characteristics (selectivity),
2. the portfolio-weighted return on control portfolios having the same characteristics as stocks currently held by the fund, in excess of time-series average returns on those control portfolios (style timing).

A. The Characteristic Selectivity (CS) Measure

The first component of performance measures the stock-picking ability of the fund manager, controlling for the particular style used by that manager.[61] This measure of stock-picking ability, which is called the "Characteristic-Selectivity" measure (*CS*), is developed in Daniel et al. (1997), where mutual fund holdings are benchmarked with characteristic-matched portfolio of stocks. Specifically, the CS measure for fund i during

[59] Wermers, R. (2003). Is money really 'smart'? New evidence on the relation between mutual fund flows, manager behavior, and performance persistence. https://doi.org/10.2139/ssrn.414420.

[60] These measures are developed in Daniel et al. (1997) and are more fully described there. In that paper, the authors argue that decomposing performance with the use of benchmark portfolios matched to stocks on the basis of the size, book-to-market, and prior-year return characteristics of the stocks is a more precise method of controlling for style-based returns than the method of decomposing performance with factor-based regressions used by Carhart (1997).

[61] Wermers, R. (2000). Mutual fund performance: An empirical decomposition into stock-picking talent, style, transactions costs, and expenses. *The Journal of Finance*, 55(4), 1655–1695.

quarter (or month) r is calculated as

$$CS_t = \sum_{j=1}^{N} \tilde{\omega}_{j,t-1}(\tilde{R}_{j,t} - \tilde{R}_t^{b_{j,t-1}}) \tag{46}$$

where $\tilde{\omega}_{j,t-1}$ is the portfolio weight on stock j at the end of quarter (or month) $t-1$,

$\tilde{R}_{j,t}$ is the quarter t buy-and-hold return of stock j, and $\tilde{R}_t^{b_{j,t-1}}$ is the quarter t buy-and-hold return of the characteristic-based benchmark portfolio that is matched to stock j at the end of quarter (or month[62]) $t-1$.

$$CS_{i,r} = \sum_{j=1}^{j_{r-1}} w_{i,j,r-1}\left(R_{j,r} - R_r^{b_{j,r}}\right) \tag{47}$$

To construct the characteristic-based benchmark portfolio for a given stock during a given quarter, we characterize that stock over three dimensions the size, book value of equity to market value of equity ratio, and prior-year return of that stock.[63] According to Wermers (2003)[64] and Ding and Wermers (2012), first, all stocks (listed on NYSE, AMEX, or Nasdaq) having book value of equity information, and stock return and market capitalization of equity data, are ranked, at the end of each June, by their market capitalization. Quintile portfolios are formed (using NYSE size quintile breakpoints), and each quintile portfolio is further subdivided into book-to-market quintiles, based on their book-to-market data as of the end of the December immediately prior to the ranking

[62] When we consider monthly observation $w_{i,j,r-1}$ is the portfolio weight of stock j held by manager i at the end of the month $r-1$; $R_{j,r}$ is the month r return on stock j, $R_r^{b_{j,r}}$ is the month return on stock j's characteristic-matched portfolio (matched, at the previous June 30, on market capitalization, the ratio of book-equity to market-equity, and prior one-year return); and J_r indicates the number of stocks held by the fund at the end of month $r-1$.

[63] Benchmarking a stock follows procedure based on Daniel et al. (1997) and is described in more detail in that paper. Here we follow Ding, B., & Wermers, R. (2012). Mutual fund performance and governance structure: The role of portfolio managers and boards of directors. https://doi.org/10.2139/ssrn.2207229.

[64] Wermers, R. (2003). Is money really 'smart'? New evidence on the relation between mutual fund flows, manager behavior, and performance persistence (May 2003).

year. Finally, each of the resulting 25 fractile portfolios is further subdivided into quintiles based on the 12-month past return of stocks through the end of May of the ranking year. This three-way ranking procedure results in 125 fractile portfolios, each having a distinct combination of size, book-to-market, and momentum characteristics. The three-way ranking procedure is repeated at the end of June of each year, and the 125 portfolios are reconstituted at that date. Value-weighted returns are computed for each of the 125 fractile portfolios, and the benchmark for each stock during a given quarter is the buy and-hold return of the fractile portfolio of which that stock is a member during that quarter. Therefore, the characteristic-adjusted return for a given stock is computed as the buy-and-hold stock return minus the buy-and-hold value-weighted benchmark return during the same quarter (or month, if data with much time granularity are available).

A caveat is in order regarding the interpretation of the CS measure, because it controls for only three characteristic dimensions of stocks-size, book-to-market, and past returns. Empirical research has shown that mutual funds show a distinct preference for other stock characteristics that are related to average returns-for example, stocks with greater liquidity (see Chen et al., 2000).

B. The Characteristic Timing (CT) Measure

The above-mentioned stock selective measures do not reflect the ability of fund managers to time various stock characteristics according to specific risk factors. Fund managers can generate additional performance if size, book-to-market, or momentum strategies have time-varying expected returns that the manager can exploit by "tilting" portfolio weights toward stocks having these characteristics when the returns on the characteristics are highest. Therefore, the second part of our performance measures the success of fund managers in selecting different stock characteristics; this component is called "Characteristics Timing":

The quarter t component of this measure is

$$CT_t = \sum_{j-1}^{N} \left(\tilde{\omega}_{j,t-1} \tilde{R}_t^{b_{j,t-1}} - \tilde{\omega}_{j,t-5} \tilde{R}_t^{b_{j,t-5}} \right) \tag{48}$$

Note that this expression deducts the quarter t return of the quarter $t-5$ matching characteristic portfolio for stock j from the quarter t return of the quarter $t-1$ matching characteristic portfolio for stock j.

9 Estimating Bond Fund Alphas

Similar to what happens for equity funds, the academic literature has proposed models for estimating the performance of fixed income funds. Following Clare et al. (2019),[65] we begin by estimating our baseline single index model for the full sample of Fixed Income (Bond) funds. The model is of the following form.

$$R_{pt} - R_{ft} = \alpha_{1p} + \beta_{1p} \times ERM_t + \varepsilon_{pt} \tag{49}$$

where R_{pt} is the monthly return at time t on mutual fund p and R_{ft} is the monthly risk-free rate, ERM_t is the excess return (over R_{ft}) in month t on the Bloomberg Barclays Global-Aggregate Total Return Index, α_{1p} represents Jensen's alpha alike for mutual fund p, β_{1p} is the market risk of fund p and ε_{pt} is a white noise error term.

A Multi-Factor Model for Bond Funds

In this section, we extend the previous analysis by extending the one-factor model with other bond market-specific factors. These models allow us to calculate multi-factor alpha, but also provide more information about the drivers of returns generated by bond fund managers. In line with Clare et al. (2019), Choi and Kronlund (2018), and Chen et al. (2010) among others, we add a factor to capture the impact of changes in the steepness of the yield curve (TS) and a factor designed to capture the reward for taking on credit risk (CS). As described previously, we calculate TS as the 10 year US Treasury yield minus the one-month TBill yield. We calculate CS as the yield on Baa rated corporate bonds minus the yield on Aaa rated corporate bonds. In addition, we specify the fund's self-declared benchmark in the multi-factor model. This allows us to estimate a benchmark-bias adjusted alpha (i.e., where the fund's benchmark may have a non-zero alpha against the market factor).

[65] Clare, A., O'Sullivan, N., Sherman, M., & Zhu, S. (2019). The performance of US bond mutual funds. *International Review of Financial Analysis, 61,* 1–8.

Augmenting Model described in Eq. (49) gets a multi-factor model of the form

$$R_{pt} - R_{ft} = \alpha_p + \beta_{1p} \times \left(R_{bt} - R_{ft}\right) + \beta_{2p} \times ERM_t + \beta_{3p} \times TS_t + \beta_{4p} \times CS_t + \varepsilon_{pt} \quad (50)$$

where[66] R_{bt} is the return on the benchmark of fund p at time t, TS_t and CS_t are the term spread and credit spread at time t. Our market factor is ERM_t, the excess return over month t on the Bloomberg Barclays Global-Aggregate Total Return Index.

Table 11 presents results for US bond mutual fund performance and market-timing. Panel A stands for multifactor alpha and betas. For each category of funds, we present summary statistics, which is the cross-sectional average values of alphas and betas (market government index, default, term structure), standard deviation across funds, the proportion of funds with positive or negative OLS coefficient estimates. The average alpha is positive, but it is smaller in US government sample (alpha = 1.65 with standard deviation 7.45) rather than in US corporate sample (alpha = 2.16, with standard deviation 7.27). In US corporate, 52.22% of funds have positive alpha coefficient estimates and in US government sample this coefficient is 47.40%. We observe that market Beta is positive in US corporate sample but negative in US government sample. Beta default and Beta term structure loadings are negative in US corporate sample but positive and negative respectively, for US government bonds. The excess returns in terms of multifactor alpha, of those funds that have a positive β_{3p} coefficient are positively correlated with a steepening of the yield curve, while those with a positive β_{4p} coefficient are positively correlated with a widening of credit spreads. For the US corporate group, there is some evidence that the term spread factor has a stronger role to play in bond fund returns compared to the credit spread, where 54.41% of these funds have a positive and significant loading on term spread, while, 16.88% of Corporate funds have a positive and significant loading on the credit spread factor. Overall, even after controlling for the additional explanatory risk factors of term spread and credit spread, a notable percentage of funds continue to achieve a positive and significant alpha.

Table 12 presents results for EU bond mutual fund performance and market-timing ability. Panel A stands for multifactor alpha and betas with

[66] The term $\left(R_{bt} - R_{ft}\right)$ is similar to the $MKTRF_t^{Bond}$ in Eq. (7).

Table 11 Bond mutual fund performance and market-timing ability. US bond mutual funds

PANEL A: MULTIFACTOR ALPHA AND BETAS					
US CORPORATE					
Variable	*Mean*	*Standard deviation*	*Min*	*Max*	*% Pos*
Alpha	2.16	7.27	−13.30	26.37	52.22
Beta Market Gov. Index	0.03	0.09	−0.24	0.28	59.99
Beta Default	−0.05	1.21	−3.81	3.16	16.88
Beta Term Strructure	−7.05	49.31	−177.97	132.24	54.41
US GOVERNMENT					
Variable	*Mean*	*Standard deviation*	*Min*	*Max*	*% Pos*
Alpha	1.65	7.45	−13.30	26.37	47.40
Beta Market Gov. Index	−0.02	0.09	−0.24	0.28	44.68
Beta Default	0.12	1.19	−3.81	3.16	18.36
Beta Term Strructure	−11.97	52.53	−177.97	132.24	60.85
PANEL B: MARKET TIMING					
US CORPORATE					
Variable	*Mean*	*Standard deviation*	*Min*	*Max*	*% Pos*
Beta Market Timing	0.04	0.10	−0.23	0.34	66.31
Beta Market Timing Quad	−0.06	2.60	−8.90	7.05	54.63
US GOVERNMENT					
Variable	*Mean*	*Standard deviation*	*Min*	*Max*	*% Pos*
Beta Market Timing	−0.02	0.10	−0.21	0.45	45.36
Beta Market Timing Quad	0.09	2.51	−9.91	7.13	54.54

Notes This table presents the average of an OLS parameter; "Standard Deviation" represents the standard deviation of an OLS parameter; "% +" represents the proportion of funds with a positive or negative OLS coefficient estimates. Augmenting Model described in Eq. (50) gets a multi-factor model of the form

the cross-sectional average values of alphas and betas (market government index, default, term structure), standard deviation across funds, the proportion of funds with positive or negative OLS coefficient estimates. The average alphas of EU bonds are positive and significantly higher than those of US. Average alpha in EU government sample (alpha = 7.46) with standard deviation 18.51) is higher than in EU corporate sample (alpha = 5.87 with standard deviation 16.43). About 52.34% of funds

Table 12 Bond mutual fund performance and market-timing ability. EUROPE bond mutual funds

PANEL A: MULTIFACTOR ALPHA AND BETAS					
EU CORPORATE					
Variable	*Mean*	*Standard deviation*	*Min*	*Max*	*% Pos*
Alpha	5.87	16.43	−21.14	61.92	52.34
Beta market gov. index	0.13	0.28	−0.48	0.78	72.68
Beta default	−0.75	3.10	−10.09	8.09	37.52
Beta term Structure	25.23	85.49	−56.24	127.35	37.18
EU GOVERNMENT					
Variable	*Mean*	*Standard deviation*	*Min*	*Max*	*% Pos*
Alpha	7.46	18.51	−21.14	61.92	54.66
Beta market gov. index	0.10	0.29	−0.48	0.78	68.91
Beta default	−0.53	3.32	−11.19	9.20	42.29
Beta term structure	29.77	89.37	−65.13	136.24	42.31

PANEL B: MARKET TIMING					
EU CORPORATE					
Variable	*Mean*	*Standard deviation*	*Min*	*Max*	*% Pos*
Beta market timing	0.15	0.32	−0.46	0.99	59.34
Beta market timing quad	−1.00	6.20	−19.58	12.55	52.82
EU GOVERNMENT					
Variable	*Mean*	*Standard deviation*	*Min*	*Max*	*% Pos*
Beta market timing	0.12	0.32	−0.57	1.10	52.65
Beta market timing quad	−0.65	6.43	−20.09	13.67	51.65

Notes This table presents the average of an OLS parameter; "Standard Deviation" represents the standard deviation of an OLS parameter; "% + " represents the proportion of funds with a positive or negative OLS coefficient estimates. Augmenting Model described in Eq. (50) gets a multi-factor model of the form

have positive alpha coefficient estimates in EU corporate sample, while 54.66%—in EU government. Market Beta and Beta Term structure loadings are positive for both types of EU bonds, while Beta Default loading is negative.

A competitive model to evaluate the performance α_p^{BOND}, is the Jiang and Yuksel (2017) model, using a slightly different version of the multifactor model described in Eq. (50) as follows:

$$r_{p,t} = \alpha_p^{BOND} + \beta_{1,p} MKTRF_t^{Bond} + \beta_{2,t} MKTRF_t^{Equity}$$

$$+ \beta_{3,p} DEFAULT_t + \beta_{4,p} TERM_t + \varepsilon_{p,t} \quad (51)$$

where $r_{p,t}$ is the monthly return on a portfolio of funds in excess of the one-month T-bill rate; $MKTRF_t^{Bond}$ is the Local (European or US) Total Bond Market Index return in excess of the one-month T-bill rate. $MKTRF_t^{Equity}$ is the (European) U.S. equity market returns in excess of the one-month T-bill rate and is included to control for potential equity market bias[67] $DEFAULT$ is the difference in return between investment grade corporate bonds and government bonds (10-year Treasury Constant Maturity Yield); $TERM_t$ is the difference in return between long-term (30-year Treasury Constant Maturity Yield) and short-term government bonds (one-year Treasury Constant Maturity Yield). The rates for investment grade corporate bonds and for long- and short-term government bond rates are from the Federal Reserve's website.[68] A reduced version of the Jiang and Yuksel (2017) model, involves to not consider the $MKTRF_t^{Equity}$ risk factor and we use this version to run all the regression getting the results showed in Tables 11 and 12.

Market Timing for Bond Funds

In this section, in line with Clare et al. (2019), we turn our attention to the market timing ability of bond mutual funds. In particular, we explore the ability of bond fund managers to anticipate fluctuations in the aggregate bond market, as measured by the Barclays Global-Aggregate Total Return Index, and increase (decrease) the fund's market exposure in advance of higher (lower) market returns. Here we follow the testing method originally proposed by Treynor and Mazuy (1966), which tests whether a fund's sensitivity to the market is greater in up-markets compared to down markets. The Treynor-Mazuy model is estimated as follows.

$$R_{pt} - R_{ft} = \alpha_{2p} + \beta_{2p} \times ERM_t + \gamma_p \times \left[ERM^2\right]_t + \varepsilon_{pt} \quad (52)$$

A positive and significant value for γ_p may be interpreted, in the Treynor and Mazuy model, as indicating that the manager has timing ability, that is increasing (reducing) exposure to market risk as the market rises (falls).

[67] Untabulated tests show that Including $MKTRF_t^{Equity}$ clearly improves the explanatory powers of the factor model.

[68] http://www.federalreserve.gov/releases/h15/data.htm.

Our findings with respect to market timing ability are presented for the US Fixed Income Mutual Fund Sample in Table 11. Panel B demonstrates market timing ability. In US corporate sample Beta market is positive with average value of 0.04, while on average the timing statistics, γ_p, for US Corporate group, are negative (−0.06), indicating that on average the market timing decisions of managers tend to subtract rather than add value for investors, while for the US Government group presents contrary evidence. However, there is evidence that both Corporate and Government funds demonstrate their ability to time aggregate bond market fluctuations, where in US corporate category 66.31% and 54.63% of funds within Beta market timing and beta market timing squared respectively, have positive timing coefficients (higher percentages than in US government sample with beta market timing of 45.36% and beta market timing squared of 54.54%). These percentages are higher than would be expected under a true null hypothesis. Nevertheless, when we couple the average γ_p coefficient with its standard deviation, we should conclude for a non-significant meaning of the market timing ability term.

Our findings with respect to market timing ability are presented for the European Fixed Income Mutual Fund Sample in Table 12, Panel B. Beta market timing is positive and the coefficient is higher in EU corporate sample (0.15) than in EU government sample (0.12). Beta market timing squared is negative in both samples, indicating that on average the market timing decisions of managers tend to subtract rather than add value for investors. Despite this evidence in Both EU bond market types of funds there are fund managers who are able to time aggregate bond market fluctuations, where we observe positive timing coefficients of 52.65 and 51.65% for EU government beta market timing and beta market timing squared. Looking at the relatively higher level of coefficient standard deviation, with respect to the magnitude of the market timing coefficient γ_p we should conclude, as it happens for US sample, for a not statistically significant evidence in terms of market timing ability for Fixed Income Mutual Fund Managers.

$$R_{pt} - R_{ft} = \alpha_p + \beta_{1p} \times (R_{bt} - R_{ft}) + \beta_{2p} \times TS_t + \beta_{3p} \times CS_t + \varepsilon_{pt}$$

where R_{bt} is the return on the benchmark of fund p at time t, TS_t and CS_t are the term spread and credit spread at time t. Our market factor is ERM_t, the excess return over month t on the Bloomberg Barclays Global-Aggregate Total Return Index. Market timing figures come out from the Treynor-Mazuy model as follows.

$$R_{pt} - R_{ft} = \alpha_{2p} + \beta_{2p} \times ERM_t + \gamma_p \times \left[ERM^2\right]_t + \varepsilon_{pt}$$

A positive and significant value for γ_p may be interpreted, in the Treynor and Mazuy model, as indicating that the manager has timing ability, that is increasing (reducing) exposure to market risk as the market rises (falls).

$$R_{pt} - R_{ft} = \alpha_p + \beta_{1p} \times (R_{bt} - R_{ft}) + \beta_{2p} \times TS_t + \beta_{3p} \times CS_t + \varepsilon_{pt}$$

where R_{bt} is the return on the benchmark of fund p at time t, TS_t and CS_t are the term spread and credit spread at time t. Our market factor is ERM_t, the excess return over month t on the Bloomberg Barclays Global-Aggregate Total Return Index. Market timing figures come out from the Treynor-Mazuy model as follows.

$$R_{pt} - R_{ft} = \alpha_{2p} + \beta_{2p} \times ERM_t + \gamma_p \times \left[ERM^2\right]_t + \varepsilon_{pt}$$

A positive and significant value for γ_p may be interpreted, in the Treynor and Mazuy model, as indicating that the manager has timing ability, that is increasing (reducing) exposure to market risk as the market rises (falls).

10 Correlation Analysis Across Various Performance Measures[69]

Due to the fact that mutual funds usually provide past performance based on different evaluation windows, investors may combine multiple performance-based signals to make investment decisions. In the spirit of Jeon et al. (2017), we use eight different performance measures and five different evaluation periods. Thus, for each fund i in month t, we consider investors having 40 distinct performance-based signals. For each month t, we rank all funds using each of the 40 performance measures. Tables from 13 to 16 present the Spearman rank correlation coefficients

[69] Jeon, H., Kang, J., & Lee, C. (2017). Precision about manager skill, mutual fund flows, and performance persistence. *The North American Journal of Economics and Finance, 40,* 222–237.

across different estimation windows when we use the same performance measure. The overall pattern shows that, for the Risk-Adjusted Performance measures (e.g., Sharpe Ratio, Treynor, Sortino and Information Ratio), the correlation coefficient rises as the overlapping period increases. For example, in Table 1 BOND US SAMPLE, Panel B, we calculate a correlation coefficient of 0.93 between the performance ranks based on the present period and one month ahead. On the other hand, the correlation coefficient between performance ranks based reference period (month T0) and four months is only 0.75.

Table 13 presents the Spearman rank correlation across different performance evaluation periods for US bond sample. We apply eight performance measures (Sharpe ratio, Simple Return, Treynor ratio, Information ratio, Sortino Index, CAPM, Fama-French alpha and Carhart's four-factor alpha) and each panel reports the rank correlation coefficients for each different performance measure.

Panel A demonstrates Simple return measure for US bond sample. The overall pattern shows that the correlation coefficient rises with increase of the overlapping period. For example, a correlation coefficient is 0.069 between the performance ranks based on one month and on two months, then it gets 0.073 between the performance ranks based on two months and on three months, and 0.078—on three and four months. However, the correlation coefficient between performance ranks based on base and four months is only 0.039. Panel B reports Sharpe Ratio performance measure for US bond sample. The overall pattern shows the decrease of correlation coefficient with the increasing overlapping period quite systemically by 0.1. For example, a correlation coefficient is 0.930 between the performance ranks based on reference period (month T0) and on one month ahead. However, the correlation coefficient between performance ranks based on base month and four months is 0.660. Panel C describes Treynor ratio performance measure US bond sample. We observe a clear decrease in the correlation coefficient between performance ranks with increase of the overlapping period from base to two months, then increase in the correlation coefficient between performance ranks with increase of the overlapping period from two to three months (by + 0.024) with respect to T + 1 and T + 2 period, and then, again, drop of the coefficient in the period from three to four months (by − 0.002). However, the correlation coefficient between performance ranks based on reference period (month T0) and on four months ahead is 0.141. Panel D reports Sortino ratio performance measure for US bond

Table 13 Bond US sample

Panel A: Return

	T0	*T + 1*	*T + 2*	*T + 3*	*T + 4*
T0	1.000				
T + 1	0.075	1.000			
T + 2	0.070	0.069	1.000		
T + 3	0.092	0.074	0.073	1.000	
T + 4	0.039	0.090	0.075	0.078	1.000

Panel B: Sharpe Ratio

	T0	*T + 1*	*T + 2*	*T + 3*	*T + 4*
T0	1.000				
T + 1	0.930	1.000			
T + 2	0.844	0.931	1.000		
T + 3	0.753	0.846	0.932	1.000	
T + 4	0.660	0.756	0.848	0.933	1.000

Panel C: Treynor

	T0	*T + 1*	*T + 2*	*T + 3*	*T + 4*
T0	1.000				
T + 1	0.473	1.000			
T + 2	0.297	0.470	1.000		
T + 3	0.246	0.318	0.494	1.000	
T + 4	0.141	0.268	0.343	0.492	1.000

Panel D: Sortino

	T0	*T + 1*	*T + 2*	*T + 3*	*T + 4*
T0	1.000				
T + 1	0.924	1.000			
T + 2	0.828	0.924	1.000		
T + 3	0.727	0.830	0.926	1.000	
T + 4	0.628	0.730	0.832	0.926	1.000

(continued)

Table 13 (continued)

Panel E: Information ratio

	T0	*T+ 1*	*T+ 2*	*T+ 3*	*T+ 4*
T0	1.000				
T + 1	0.878	1.000			
T + 2	0.776	0.875	1.000		
T + 3	0.701	0.773	0.876	1.000	
T + 4	0.619	0.688	0.768	0.872	1.000

Panel F: CAPM Alpha

	T0	*T+ 1*	*T+ 2*	*T+ 3*	*T+ 4*
T0	0.000				
T + 1	0.924	1.000			
T + 2	0.861	0.924	1.000		
T + 3	0.796	0.862	0.925	1.000	
T + 4	0.732	0.797	0.863	0.925	1.000

Panel G: Fama–French alpha

	T0	*T+ 1*	*T+ 2*	*T+ 3*	*T+ 4*
T0	1.000				
T + 1	0.899	1.000			
T + 2	0.828	0.900	1.000		
T + 3	0.757	0.827	0.901	1.000	
T + 4	0.680	0.756	0.828	0.901	1.000

Panel H: Carhart alpha

	T0	*T+ 1*	*T+ 2*	*T+ 3*	*T+ 4*
T0	0.000				
T + 1	0.886	1.000			
T + 2	0.805	0.886	1.000		
T + 3	0.733	0.805	0.887	1.000	
T + 4	0.653	0.734	0.806	0.887	1.000

Notes Rank correlation across different performance evaluation periods. This table shows the Spearman rank correlation coefficients across performance evaluation periods for a fixed performance measure. We use eight performance measures (Sharpe ratio, Simple Return, Treynor ratio, Information ratio, Sortino Index, Jensen's alpha, Fama-French alpha and Carhart's four-factor alpha) and each panel reports the rank correlation coefficients for each different performance measure. The sample period is from January 2006 to December 2019. The time interval is one month (so T + 1 corresponds to one Month ahead, T + 2 two months ahead and so on)

sample. The overall pattern demonstrates almost no change in correlation coefficients, with only slight increase of the correlation coefficient by 0.002 with increase of the overlapping period from two months to three months with respect to T + 1 and T + 2 period, On the other hand, the correlation coefficient between performance ranks based on base month and four months is only 0.628. In Panel E we analyze Information Ratio performance measure for US bond sample. The overall pattern shows decrease of correlation coefficient with increasing overlapping period. The correlation coefficient between performance ranks based on reference period (month T0) and four months patterns is 0.619.

Panel F reports CAPM alpha performance measure for US bond sample. The correlation coefficient remains almost at the same level as the overlapping period increases. The correlation coefficient between performance ranks based on reference period (month T0) and four months is 0.732, while there is only slight increase of the correlation coefficient by 0.06 when considering correlation between one to four months. Panel G demonstrates Fama-French alpha performance measure for US bond sample. In overall, there is a decrease of correlation coefficient with the raise of the overlapping period. For example, we calculated a correlation coefficient of 0.899 between performance ranks based on reference period (month T0) and one month, then it gets 0.900—between one month and two months. However, the correlation coefficient between performance ranks based on base month and four months is 0.680. Panel H presents Carhart Alpha performance model for US bond sample. The correlation coefficient remains almost the same during the whole period and raises only by 0.08 with increase of the overlapping period from two to three months, with respect to T + 1 and T + 3 period. The correlation coefficient between performance ranks based on base month and four months is 0.653.

Table 14 presents the Spearman rank correlation across different performance evaluation periods for EU bond sample. We apply eight performance measures (Sharpe ratio, Simple Return, Treynor ratio, Information ratio, Sortino Index, CAPM, Fama-French alpha and Carhart's four-factor alpha) and each panel reports the rank correlation coefficients for each different performance measure. Panel A reports Simple Return measure for EU bond sample. The overall pattern shows decrease of the correlation coefficient with rise of the overlapping period. For example, the correlation coefficient is 0.044 between the performance ranks based on reference period (month T0) and one month and it is

Table 14 Bond Europe sample

Panel A: Return

	T0	*T + 1*	*T + 2*	*T + 3*	*T + 4*
T0	1.000				
T + 1	0.044	1.000			
T + 2	0.076	0.034	1.000		
T + 3	0.038	0.087	0.029	1.000	
T + 4	0.072	0.034	0.095	0.022	1.000

Panel B: Sharpe Ratio

	T0	*T + 1*	*T + 2*	*T + 3*	*T + 4*
T0	1.000				
T + 1	0.909	1.000			
T + 2	0.806	0.908	1.000		
T + 3	0.687	0.805	0.908	1.000	
T + 4	0.557	0.685	0.805	0.908	1.000

Panel C: Treynor

	T0	*T + 1*	*T + 2*	*T + 3*	*T + 4*
T0	1.000				
T + 1	0.715	1.000			
T + 2	0.551	0.711	1.000		
T + 3	0.462	0.545	0.708	1.000	
T + 4	0.391	0.475	0.557	0.721	1.000

Panel D: Sortino

	T0	*T + 1*	*T + 2*	*T + 3*	*T + 4*
T0	1.000				
T + 1	0.911	1.000			
T + 2	0.808	0.906	1.000		
T + 3	0.690	0.805	0.907	1.000	
T + 4	0.562	0.685	0.805	0.906	1.000

(continued)

Table 14 (continued)

Panel E: Information ratio

	T0	*T+ 1*	*T+ 2*	*T+ 3*	*T+ 4*
T0	1.000				
T + 1	0.894	1.000			
T + 2	0.747	0.893	1.000		
T + 3	0.613	0.747	0.895	1.000	
T + 4	0.492	0.612	0.749	0.895	1.000

Panel F: CAPM Alpha

	T0	*T+ 1*	*T+ 2*	*T+ 3*	*T+ 4*
T0	1.000				
T + 1	0.862	1.000			
T + 2	0.730	0.859	1.000		
T + 3	0.604	0.727	0.858	1.000	
T + 4	0.493	0.602	0.725	0.857	1.000

Panel G: Fama–French Alpha

	T0	*T+ 1*	*T+ 2*	*T+ 3*	*T+ 4*
T0	1.000				
T + 1	0.798	1.000			
T + 2	0.658	0.794	1.000		
T + 3	0.528	0.657	0.793	1.000	
T + 4	0.431	0.528	0.654	0.792	1.000

Panel H: Carhart Alpha

	T0	*T+ 1*	*T+ 2*	*T+ 3*	*T+ 4*
T0	1.000				
T + 1	0.767	1.000			
T + 2	0.603	0.762	1.000		
T + 3	0.472	0.596	0.761	1.000	
T + 4	0.378	0.472	0.592	0.757	1.000

Notes Rank correlation across different performance evaluation periods. This table shows the Spearman rank correlation coefficients across performance evaluation periods for a fixed performance measure. We use eight performance measures (Sharpe ratio, Simple Return, Treynor ratio, Information ratio, Sortino Index, Jensen's alpha, Fama-French alpha and Carhart's four-factor alpha) and each panel reports the rank correlation coefficients for each different performance measure. The sample period is from January 2006 to December 2019. The one month (so T + 1 corresponds to one Month ahead, T + 2 two months ahead and so on)

only 0.022 between third and fourth months. However, the correlation coefficient between performance ranks based on base month and four months is 0.072. Panel B reports results for Sharpe Ratio measure for EU bond sample. The correlation coefficient drops when moving from the first to the second month and then remains the same (0.908) with increasing overlapping period. The correlation coefficient between performance ranks in reference period (month T0) and fourth months ahead is only 0.557. Panel C presents Treynor performance measure for EU bond sample. The correlation coefficient drops with increase of the overlapping period but rises by 0.16 between third and fourth months, with respect to T + 2 and T + 4 period. The correlation coefficient between performance ranks in reference period (month T0) and four months ahead ranks at 0.391 level. Panel D demonstrates results for Sortino performance measure for EU bond sample. The overall pattern shows the decrease of the correlation coefficient in general, with its very slight rise by 0.1 between performance ranks based on the period between two and three months, with respect to T + 1 and T + 2 period. The correlation coefficient between reference period (month T0) and four months estimation window is 0.562. Panel E shows Information Ratio results for EU bond sample. The correlation coefficient drops with increasing overlapping period from reference period (month T0) to the second month, and then remains the same (0.895) in the period from the second to fourth months. The correlation between performance based on reference period (month T0) and four months is 0.492. Panel F stands for CAPM alpha measure of performance for EU bond sample. The overall pattern shows the correlation coefficient drops as the overlapping period increases. The correlation between performance results on reference period (month T0) and fourth months is 0.493. Panel G reports Fama-French alpha performance measure for EU bond sample. In general, the correlation coefficient drops with the rise of the overlapping period from 0.798 between reference period (month T0) and first month to 0.792 between third and fourth months. The correlation between performance results on base and fourth month is 0.431. Panel H demonstrates results for Carhart alpha performance measure for EU bond sample, where we observe drop in the correlation coefficient as the overlapping period increases, from 0.767 between the base and first month to 0.757 between the third and fourth month. The correlation between performance results on reference period (month T0) and four months is 0.378.

Table 15 presents the Spearman rank correlation across different

Table 15 Equity US sample

Panel A: Return

	T0	*T + 1*	*T + 2*	*T + 3*	*T + 4*
T0	1.000				
T + 1	0.015	1.000			
T + 2	0.045	0.016	1.000		
T + 3	0.067	0.050	0.023	1.000	
T + 4	0.022	0.068	0.052	0.030	1.000

Panel B: Sharpe ratio

	T0	*T + 1*	*T + 2*	*T + 3*	*T + 4*
T0	1.000				
T + 1	0.908	1.000			
T + 2	0.818	0.907	1.000		
T + 3	0.725	0.817	0.907	1.000	
T + 4	0.637	0.716	0.811	0.903	1.000

Panel C: Treynor

	T0	*T + 1*	*T + 2*	*T + 3*	*T + 4*
T0	1.000				
T + 1	0.572	1.000			
T + 2	0.399	0.571	1.000		
T + 3	0.337	0.417	0.591	1.000	
T + 4	0.222	0.355	0.437	0.589	1.000

Panel D: Sortino

	T0	*T + 1*	*T + 2*	*T + 3*	*T + 4*
T0	1.000				
T + 1	0.906	1.000			
T + 2	0.810	0.905	1.000		
T + 3	0.717	0.808	0.904	1.000	
T + 4	0.632	0.710	0.804	0.901	1.000

(continued)

Table 15 (continued)

Panel E: Information ratio

	T0	*T + 1*	*T + 2*	*T + 3*	*T + 4*
T0	1.000				
T + 1	0.846	1.000			
T + 2	0.759	0.847	1.000		
T + 3	0.680	0.758	0.845	1.000	
T + 4	0.608	0.678	0.756	0.843	1.000

Panel F: CAPM Alpha

	T0	*T + 1*	*T + 2*	*T + 3*	*T + 4*
T0	1.000				
T + 1	0.854	1.000			
T + 2	0.769	0.854	1.000		
T + 3	0.696	0.767	0.853	1.000	
T + 4	0.639	0.694	0.765	0.850	1.000

Panel G: Fama-French Alpha

	T0	*T + 1*	*T + 2*	*T + 3*	*T + 4*
T0	1.000				
T + 1	0.822	1.000			
T + 2	0.715	0.821	1.000		
T + 3	0.623	0.713	0.821	1.000	
T + 4	0.545	0.621	0.710	0.817	1.000

Panel H: Carhart Alpha

	T0	*T + 1*	*T + 2*	*T + 3*	*T + 4*
T0	1.000				
T + 1	0.806	1.000			
T + 2	0.703	0.806	1.000		
T + 3	0.606	0.702	0.806	1.000	
T + 4	0.523	0.604	0.700	0.804	1.000

Notes Rank correlation across different performance evaluation periods. This table shows the Spearman rank correlation coefficients across performance evaluation periods for a fixed performance measure. We use eight performance measures (Sharpe ratio, Simple Return, Treynor ratio, Information ratio, Sortino Index, Jensen's alpha, Fama-French alpha and Carhart's four-factor alpha) and each panel reports the rank correlation coefficients for each different performance measure. The sample period is from January 2006 to December 2019. The one month (so T + 1 corresponds to one Month ahead, T + 2 two months ahead and so on)

performance evaluation periods for US Equity sample. We apply eight performance measures (Sharpe ratio, Simple Return, Treynor ratio, Information ratio, Sortino Index, CAPM, Fama-French alpha and Carhart's four-factor alpha) and each panel reports the rank correlation coefficients for each different performance measure. Panel A demonstrates results for Simple Return measure of performance for US Equity sample. We observe raise in correlation coefficient with increasing overlapping period. We calculated the correlation coefficient of 0.015 between performance ranks based on the reference period (month T0) and first month, for example, and 0.030—between the third and fourth month. However, the correlation coefficient between performance ranks based on base month and four months is only 0.022. Panel B shows results for Sharpe Ratio measure of performance for US Equity sample, where the correlation coefficient drops as the overlapping period increases, from 0.908 between reference period (month T0) and one month to 0.903 between third and fourth months. The correlation coefficient between performance ranks based on reference period (month T0) and four months is 0.637. Panel C stands for Treynor performance measure for US Equity sample, where the correlation coefficient drops by only 0.001 between first and second month, with respect to T + 1 and T0 period, while it increases by 0.020 between second and third month with respect to T + 1 and T + 2 period. It drops again by 0.002 when passing from the correlation between T + 2 and T + 3 period to third and fourth month. The correlation coefficient between performance ranks based on reference period (month T0) and four months is 0.222. Panel D demonstrates results for Sortino performance measure for US Equity sample. The overall patterns show that correlation coefficient drops with increase of the overlapping period from 0.906 between the reference period (month T0) and first month to 0.901 between third and fourth months. The correlation coefficient between performance ranks based on reference period (month T0) and four months is 0.632. Panel E reports Information Ratio performance measure for US Equity sample. In general, the correlation coefficient tends to drop 0.846 between reference period (month T0) and first month to 0.843 between third and fourth month. The correlation coefficient between performance ranks based on base and four months is 0.608. Panel F demonstrates CAPM alpha performance measure for US Equity sample. The overall pattern shows the decrease of correlation coefficient with increase of overlapping period, from 0.854 between reference period (month T0) and first month period to 0.850 between third- and four-months period. The correlation coefficient between performance ranks based on base and four months is 0.639. Panel G shows Fama-French alpha performance measure for US Equity sample. In general, the correlation coefficient decreases as the overlapping period increases from 0.822 between the base and first month to 0.817 between the third and fourth month. The correlation coefficient between performance ranks between reference period (month T0) and four months is 0.545. Panel H shows results for Carhart alpha performance measure for US Equity sample. The correlation coefficient remains at the same level with increase of the overlapping periods and drops by 0.002 between the third and fourth month with respect to T + 2 and T + 3 period. The correlation coefficient between performance ranks in reference period (month T0) and four months period is 0.523.

Table 16 presents the Spearman rank correlation across different performance evaluation periods for EU Equity sample. We apply eight performance measures (Sharpe ratio, Simple Return, Treynor ratio, Information ratio, Sortino Index, CAPM, Fama-French alpha and Carhart's four-factor alpha) and each panel reports the rank correlation coefficients for each different performance measure.

Panel A reports results for Simple return measure for EU Equity sample. The correlation coefficient is increasing with increase of overlapping period from −0.009 between performance ranks based on reference period (month T0) and first month, to 0.005 between performance ranks on third and fourth month. However, the correlation coefficient between performance ranks based on base month and four months is 0.016. Panel B reports results for Sharpe Ratio measure for EU Equity sample. The overall pattern shows decrease of the correlation coefficient from 0.921 between the reference period (month T0) and first month to 0.919 between third and fourth month, while the overlapping period is increasing. The correlation coefficient between performance ranks based on reference period (month T0) and four months is 0.643. Panel C shows results for Treynor Ratio performance measure for EU Equity sample. We observe decrease of the correlation coefficient up to the performance ranks based on the last period, where the decrease in terms of coefficient magnitude raise up to nearly 0.52 (that is 1.000 − 0.485) when passing from the reference period (month T0) base time to four periods ahead (T + 4). The correlation coefficient between performance ranks based on

Table 16 Equity Europe sample

Panel A: Return

	T0	*T + 1*	*T + 2*	*T + 3*	*T + 4*
T0	1.000				
T + 1	−0.009	1.000			
T + 2	0.021	−0.006	1.000		
T + 3	0.104	0.025	−0.001	1.000	
T + 4	0.016	0.104	0.029	0.005	1.000

Panel B: Sharpe ratio

	T0	*T + 1*	*T + 2*	*T + 3*	*T + 4*
T0	1.000				
T + 1	0.921	1.000			
T + 2	0.837	0.919	1.000		
T + 3	0.748	0.833	0.920	1.000	
T + 4	0.643	0.738	0.831	0.919	1.000

Panel C: Treynor

	T0	*T + 1*	*T + 2*	*T + 3*	*T + 4*
T0	1.000				
T + 1	0.831	1.000			
T + 2	0.707	0.829	1.000		
T + 3	0.592	0.702	0.826	1.000	
T + 4	0.485	0.600	0.713	0.841	1.000

Panel D: Sortino

	T0	*T + 1*	*T + 2*	*T + 3*	*T + 4*
T0	1.000				
T + 1	0.914	1.000			
T + 2	0.822	0.910	1.000		
T + 3	0.729	0.817	0.910	1.000	
T + 4	0.618	0.719	0.816	0.910	1.000

(continued)

Table 16 (continued)

Panel E: Information ratio

	T0	*T+ 1*	*T+ 2*	*T+ 3*	*T+ 4*
T0	1.000				
T + 1	0.912	1.000			
T + 2	0.817	0.910	1.000		
T + 3	0.715	0.814	0.910	1.000	
T + 4	0.606	0.713	0.813	0.909	1.000

Panel F: CAPM Alpha

	T0	*T+ 1*	*T+ 2*	*T+ 3*	*T+ 4*
T0	1.000				
T + 1	0.859	1.000			
T + 2	0.756	0.856	1.000		
T + 3	0.659	0.752	0.855	1.000	
T + 4	0.565	0.656	0.750	0.854	1.000

Panel G: Fama–French Alpha

	T0	*T+ 1*	*T+ 2*	*T+ 3*	*T+ 4*
T0	1.000				
T + 1	0.827	1.000			
T + 2	0.693	0.823	1.000		
T + 3	0.561	0.690	0.822	1.000	
T + 4	0.446	0.561	0.688	0.820	1.000

Panel H: Carhart Alpha

	T0	*T+ 1*	*T+ 2*	*T+ 3*	*T+ 4*
T0	1.000				
T + 1	0.782	1.000			
T + 2	0.604	0.777	1.000		
T + 3	0.470	0.596	0.776	1.000	
T + 4	0.371	0.465	0.595	0.774	1.000

Notes Rank correlation across different performance evaluation periods. This table shows the Spearman rank correlation coefficients across performance evaluation periods for a fixed performance measure. We use eight performance measures (Sharpe ratio, Simple Return, Treynor ratio, Information ratio, Sortino Index, Jensen's alpha, Fama-French alpha and Carhart's four-factor alpha) and each panel reports the rank correlation coefficients for each different performance measure. The sample period is from January 2006 to December 2019. The one month (so T + 1 corresponds to one Month ahead, T + 2 two months ahead and so on)

reference period (month T0) and four months 0.485. Panel D demonstrates Sortino performance measure for EU Equity sample. We observe decrease of the correlation coefficient between first and second month and then it remains the same as of 0.910 as the overlapping period increases. The correlation coefficient between performance ranks based on reference period (month T0) and four months is 0.618. Panel E shows results for Information Ratio EU Equity sample. The correlation coefficient is decreasing with increasing overlapping period from 0.912 to 0.909, however is 0.606 between performance ranks based on reference period (month T0) and four months. Panel E reports CAPM alpha results EU Equity sample. The correlation coefficient is decreasing with increase of the overlapping period from 0.859 between the reference period (month T0) and first month to 0.854 between the third and fourth month. The correlation coefficient between performance ranks based on the reference period (month T0) and fourth year is 0.565. Panel G reports results for Fama-French alpha performance measure EU Equity sample.

The correlation coefficient shows its decreasing value with increase of the overlapping period, from 0.827 between the reference period (month T0) and first month to 0.820 between the third and four months, while it takes the value of 0.446 between performance ranks based on base month and four months. Panel H demonstrates results for Carhart Alpha performance measure EU Equity sample. The correlation coefficient is decreasing with increase of the overlapping period from 0.782 between the reference period (month T0) and first month to 0.774 between the third and fourth month, however, it takes a value of 0.371 between performance ranks based on base and four months.

Our empirical evidences show that if we use different evaluation periods, the information contained in the same performance indicator will be different. We have shown that how mutual fund managers (and asset management companies) describe the past performance of mutual funds, depends on the choice of performance indicators and evaluation period. The rank correlation analysis proves the necessity for mutual fund investors to combine a lot of information from different performance models and time periods in order to make the right decision.

11 Style-Based Portfolio Formation

Cuthbertson et al. (2010) report that when sorting funds by their loading on the momentum factor, funds with high past $\beta\ MOM_t$ tend to outperform in the post-ranking period, using Fama–French alpha $\alpha_{i,\ 4ff}$. Empirical results show also, that funds which have high momentum factor loadings are not actively pursuing a momentum strategy but, "luckily" happen that they hold last year's winning stocks, and enjoy a high average (raw) return over the next year, however, with a negative risk adjusted return.

Regardless of one's beliefs about what High minus Low and Small minus Big measure, the premiums associated with the factors can be earned by a passive strategy of buying a diversified portfolio of stocks with a desired level of sensitivity to the factors (Davis, 2001).

Following the style rank procedure of Davis (2001), we placed funds in style portfolios at the beginning of each year from 2007 through 2019. At the beginning of 2007, for example, returns for the previous 12 months were used to estimate preformation slopes on the *HML*, *MOM* and *SMB* factors.

Based on these preformation slopes, funds with similar styles were allocated into portfolios, and returns for these equally weighted portfolios were calculated for each month of 2006 through 2019. The portfolios were reformed each month. We used univariate *SMB*, *HML* and *MOM* sorts to form decile portfolios and repeated this process for each year yielded a time series of 156 equally weighted monthly returns for each portfolio.

11.1 Results for Style-Based Portfolios

In this section we reported the results for the portfolios formed by univariate sorts, that is the portfolios formed by independent *HML* and *SMB* sorts, and the portfolios formed by *MOM* sorts.

Portfolios Formed by Univariate Sorts

Table 17 reports Four-Factor Results for Deciles of Mutual Funds formed from Risk Factor Sorts for US SAMPLE. Panel A shows regression results for funds sorted by pre-formation and post-formation SMB slopes. The pre-formation intercepts are positive only starting from the sixth SMB decile to the tenth decile. According to our results, when sorting funds by SMB decile, fund managers should expect the highest coefficient of intercept alpha in the seventh decile. The post formation alphas, at time T + 4, are positive in the first decile and from the sixth to tenth decile,

Table 17 Four-factor results for deciles of mutual funds formed from risk factor sorts

PANEL A: SMB Pre-formation averages by decile					
SMB Decile	*SMB*	*HML*	*Mom*	*R squared*	*Intercept Alpha*
1	36.76%	−4.45%	−3.35%	73.90%	0.00%
2	7.69%	−2.34%	−0.25%	62.07%	−0.11%
3	3.33%	−2.02%	−0.67%	45.51%	−0.05%
4	2.62%	−1.57%	−1.57%	42.17%	−0.04%
5	−0.17%	−0.05%	0.34%	35.88%	−0.41%
6	−2.42%	−5.96%	−10.32%	46.17%	0.04%
7	−13.05%	−12.17%	−20.38%	72.29%	0.13%
8	−17.23%	−9.24%	−12.96%	80.45%	0.06%
9	−29.51%	−8.02%	−8.32%	79.80%	0.06%
10	−41.79%	−6.80%	−3.68%	79.14%	0.06%

	Post formation Alpha (averages by decile)			
	T + 1	*T + 2*	*T + 3*	*T + 4*
1	0.00%	0.01%	0.01%	0.01%
2	−0.11%	−0.11%	−0.11%	−0.11%
3	−0.43%	−0.42%	−0.44%	−0.42%
4	−0.06%	−0.05%	−0.05%	−0.05%
5	−0.04%	−0.04%	−0.04%	−0.04%
6	0.04%	0.04%	0.05%	0.04%
7	0.14%	0.13%	0.15%	0.14%
8	0.06%	0.05%	0.06%	0.07%
9	0.03%	0.03%	0.03%	0.03%
10	0.01%	0.00%	0.00%	0.00%

(continued)

where the coefficient of alpha takes the biggest value in the seventh decile with increasing time periods.

Panel B shows regression results for funds sorted by pre-formation and post-formation HML slopes. The pre-formation intercepts are a mix of positive and negative coefficients. We find that when sorting funds by HML decile, the highest coefficient of the intercept alpha is very low and is 0.04% in the seventh decile, while intercept gets its worst meaning of −0.27% in the fifth decile. The post formation alphas, at time T + 4, get a positive value of the coefficient from sixth to last (10th) decile, where alpha coefficient is the highest (0.06%) in the seventh decile with

Table 17 (continued)

PANEL B: HML Pre-formation averages by decile

HML decile	*HML*	*SMB*	*Mom*	*R squared*	*Intercept Alpha*
1	22.87%	2.43%	3.78%	60.33%	0.03%
2	2.74%	2.17%	0.68%	43.27%	−0.07%
3	1.87%	2.14%	0.38%	45.57%	−0.05%
4	0.53%	3.45%	−1.69%	55.59%	0.01%
5	0.34%	0.03%	0.06%	40.92%	−0.27%
6	−8.90%	2.05%	−13.16%	72.08%	0.03%
7	−15.19%	0.26%	−13.71%	84.01%	0.04%
8	−19.22%	2.26%	−10.06%	87.05%	0.02%
9	−34.84%	2.88%	−12.24%	84.26%	−0.02%
10	−50.45%	3.50%	−14.42%	81.47%	−0.05%

Post formation Alpha (averages by decile)

	T + 1	*T + 2*	*T + 3*	*T + 4*
1	−0.03%	−0.02%	−0.02%	−0.03%
2	−0.07%	−0.06%	−0.06%	−0.06%
3	−0.27%	−0.28%	−0.28%	−0.28%
4	−0.05%	−0.05%	−0.05%	−0.05%
5	0.01%	0.00%	0.00%	−0.01%
6	0.03%	0.02%	0.03%	0.01%
7	0.06%	0.06%	0.07%	0.06%
8	0.02%	0.03%	0.03%	0.04%
9	0.00%	0.01%	0.01%	0.02%
10	−0.02%	−0.01%	−0.01%	0.00%

PANEL C: MOM Pre-formation averages by decile

MOM Decile	*Mom*	*SMB*	*HML*	*R squared*	*Intercept Alpha*
1	18.12%	4.48%	4.81%	59.43%	−0.04%
2	3.05%	3.75%	0.05%	50.18%	−0.10%
3	0.83%	1.67%	0.51%	45.01%	−0.10%
4	0.01%	0.23%	0.52%	22.36%	−0.06%
5	−2.90%	0.78%	0.24%	57.39%	0.01%
6	−13.07%	−5.42%	−9.64%	71.73%	0.05%
7	−17.70%	−2.62%	−14.06%	84.42%	0.09%
8	−17.98%	0.42%	−15.47%	87.01%	0.05%
9	−27.17%	1.42%	−17.78%	84.90%	0.07%

(continued)

Table 17 (continued)

PANEL C: MOM Pre-formation averages by decile

MOM Decile	*Mom*	*SMB*	*HML*	*R squared*	*Intercept Alpha*
10	−36.36%	2.42%	−20.08%	82.79%	0.10%

Post formation Alpha (averages by decile)

	T + 1	*T + 2*	*T + 3*	*T + 4*
1	−0.05%	−0.04%	−0.04%	−0.04%
2	−0.10%	−0.09%	−0.10%	−0.09%
3	−0.06%	−0.06%	−0.08%	−0.07%
4	−0.10%	−0.09%	−0.09%	−0.08%
5	0.01%	0.00%	0.01%	0.01%
6	0.05%	0.05%	0.06%	0.05%
7	0.09%	0.08%	0.09%	0.09%
8	0.05%	0.06%	0.07%	0.07%
9	0.05%	0.05%	0.06%	0.06%
10	0.06%	0.05%	0.05%	0.04%

Notes **US SAMPLE**
We build fund portfolios by considering risk factor decile sort according to the Carhart model (1997). The four-factor model is given by: $R_{it}-R_{ft}=\alpha_i+b_i\ (R_{Mt}-R_{ft})+s_i SMB_t+h_i HML_t+m_i MOM_t+e_{it}$. The risk factors of Carhart's (1997) model are included in order not to reward fund managers for taking advantage of stock market systematic anomalies. MOM_t is the risk factor mimicking portfolio for capturing Jegadeesh and Titman (1993) one-year momentum anomaly in the stock holdings of the mutual funds. The momentum factor, MOM_t, is a measure of difference between the returns on past high-performing versus past poor-performing stocks and hence MOM_t reflects a fund's sensitivity to pursuing a zero-investment strategy of purchasing past outperforming 'momentum' stocks and short-selling stocks with low historical returns. The Carhart model nests the Fama–French Model where risk factors are: SMB_t = the realization on the capitalization factor (small-cap return minus large cap return) for month t; HML_t = the realization on the value factor (value return minus growth return) for month t e_{it} = an error term corresponding to the regression residuals.

increasing time periods, and the worst value of alpha is caught in the third decile along with the increase of the time period.

Panel C demonstrates regression results for funds sorted by pre-formation and post-formation MOM slopes. The pre-formation intercepts are positive starting from the fifth decile. Our results prove that fund managers should probably consider the seventh (0.09%) and the tenth deciles (0.10), when sorting funds by MOM decile. The post formation intercept, at time T + 4, is positive only starting from the fifth decile, where we observe the highest values of the coefficient in the seventh decile. Interestingly enough on average the *R*-squared values are higher corresponding to the deciles from 7 to 10 irrespective the specific factor (SMB, HML or MOM) we used to sort the fund portfolios. *R* squared values ranges between quite 70 and 90%.

Table 18 reports Four-Factor Results for Deciles of Mutual Funds formed from Risk Factor Sorts for Europe SAMPLE. Panel A shows regression results for EU funds sorted by pre-formation and post-formation SMB slopes. The pre-formation intercepts are mostly positive with a tendency to increase in the next decile, however, the intercept coefficient is negative (−0.01%) and zero in the seventh and eighth deciles, respectively. The results demonstrate that fund managers must consider the tenth decile, where alpha intercept gets 0.34%. The post formation alphas, at time T + 4, are mostly positive and are increasing with the next decile, where the best option will be the tenth decile.

Panel B shows regression results for EU funds sorted by pre-formation and post-formation HML slopes. Alpha return is positive in all deciles and takes the highest value of the coefficient in the first decile (0.21%), when it drops across deciles and increasing only in the tenth decile (0.16%). The post formation alphas, at time T + 4, are positive except the ninth decile of the whole post-formation periods. The intercept takes the highest value of the coefficient in the first decile.

Panel C shows regression results for funds sorted by pre-formation and post-formation MOM slopes. The pre-formation intercepts are positive in all deciles, where we observe the dramatic growth in the coefficient value from eight to tenth deciles. The highest coefficient of intercept alpha is 0.42% in the tenth decile. In post formation period, at time T + 4, the intercept is mostly positive and demonstrates a tendency for increase when moving to the next decile and with increasing time period. The intercept coefficient is the highest in the tenth decile along with increasing time period. With respect to the *R*-squared values, unlike what we observed with respect to the US sample, there is no evidence that the higher *R*-squared values are combined with the deciles from seventh to tenth, although higher *R*-squared are on average coupled to the last two deciles (ninth and tenth).

Table 18 Four-factor results for deciles of mutual funds formed from risk factor sorts

PANEL A: SMB Pre-formation averages by decile

SMB Decile	*SMB*	*HML*	*Mom*	*R squared*	*Intercept Alpha*
1	67.16%	7.03%	−1.30%	67.10%	0.09%
2	50.48%	18.30%	1.05%	68.80%	0.07%
3	35.15%	14.83%	−0.16%	66.15%	0.06%
4	25.27%	11.95%	−0.62%	64.30%	0.07%
5	17.35%	7.30%	−1.81%	64.99%	0.09%
6	8.96%	9.67%	1.16%	66.71%	0.13%
7	0.09%	0.04%	−0.03%	40.65%	−0.01%
8	0.00%	−0.02%	0.00%	65.95%	0.00%
9	−1.65%	14.19%	7.01%	69.37%	0.21%
10	−37.26%	25.43%	12.81%	65.63%	0.34%

Post formation Alpha (averages by decile)

	T + 1	*T + 2*	*T + 3*	*T + 4*
1	0.10%	0.10%	0.10%	0.10%
2	0.05%	0.05%	0.06%	0.06%
3	−0.01%	0.00%	−0.01%	0.02%
4	0.06%	0.08%	0.07%	0.06%
5	0.07%	0.06%	0.06%	0.06%
6	0.07%	0.06%	0.05%	0.03%
7	0.14%	0.14%	0.13%	0.11%
8	0.22%	0.22%	0.20%	0.21%
9	−0.05%	−0.11%	−0.04%	−0.05%
10	0.34%	0.34%	0.36%	0.37%

PANEL B: HML Pre-formation averages by decile

HML Decile	*HML*	*SMB*	*Mom*	*R squared*	*Intercept Alpha*
1	61.44%	22.77%	18.65%	66.90%	0.21%
2	39.32%	26.24%	10.91%	69.60%	0.16%
3	23.87%	26.84%	4.73%	65.70%	0.12%

(continued)

Table 18 (continued)

PANEL B: HML Pre-formation averages by decile

HML Decile	*HML*	*SMB*	*Mom*	*R squared*	*Intercept Alpha*
4	13.31%	26.06%	0.23%	64.66%	0.10%
5	3.08%	20.24%	−3.00%	58.98%	0.05%
6	0.00%	0.00%	0.00%	52.11%	0.00%
7	0.00%	0.00%	0.01%	47.40%	0.00%
8	−4.87%	22.53%	−7.24%	64.31%	0.05%
9	−18.98%	32.28%	−10.73%	71.84%	0.05%
10	−64.02%	34.87%	−18.29%	69.89%	0.16%

	Post formation Alpha (averages by decile)			
	T + 1	*T + 2*	*T + 3*	*T + 4*
1	0.21%	0.21%	0.20%	0.19%
2	0.16%	0.16%	0.16%	0.15%
3	0.00%	0.01%	0.00%	0.00%
4	0.12%	0.13%	0.13%	0.12%
5	0.10%	0.10%	0.11%	0.11%
6	0.04%	0.06%	0.06%	0.06%
7	0.04%	0.04%	0.05%	0.06%
8	0.05%	0.04%	0.02%	0.04%
9	−0.01%	−0.02%	−0.03%	−0.04%
10	0.16%	0.14%	0.15%	0.16%

PANEL C: MOM Pre-formation averages by decile

MOM decile	*Mom*	*SMB*	*HML*	*R squared*	*Intercept Alpha*
1	37.06%	21.05%	37.17%	63.55%	0.03%
2	20.30%	26.19%	27.12%	65.32%	0.09%
3	7.71%	21.23%	13.63%	61.78%	0.04%
4	0.88%	25.18%	9.44%	61.88%	0.03%
5	0.00%	0.00%	0.00%	28.12%	0.00%
6	0.00%	0.00%	−0.02%	69.77%	0.00%
7	−6.02%	23.97%	2.95%	65.91%	0.08%
8	−14.83%	26.12%	0.89%	72.52%	0.15%
9	−22.25%	29.33%	−0.05%	74.18%	0.24%
10	−44.02%	37.31%	−13.33%	72.31%	0.42%

(continued)

Table 18 (continued)

	Post formation Alpha (averages by decile)			
	T + 1	*T + 2*	*T + 3*	*T + 4*
1	0.05%	0.08%	0.10%	0.11%
2	0.11%	0.10%	0.13%	0.14%
3	−0.03%	0.00%	0.00%	−0.01%
4	0.05%	0.05%	0.07%	0.07%
5	0.04%	0.04%	0.03%	0.04%
6	0.10%	0.11%	0.09%	0.10%
7	0.14%	0.18%	0.16%	0.17%
8	0.22%	0.23%	0.19%	0.18%
9	0.00%	0.00%	0.02%	−0.12%
10	0.36%	0.29%	0.26%	0.22%

EUROPE SAMPLE

Notes We build fund portfolios by considering risk factor decile sort according to the Carhart model (1997). The four-factor model is given by: $R_{it} - R_{ft} = \alpha_i + b_i\ (R_{Mt} - R_{ft}) + s_i SMB_t + h_i HML_t + m_i MOM_t + e_{it}$. The risk factors of Carhart's (1997) model are included in order not to reward fund managers for taking advantage of stock market systematic anomalies. MOM_t is the risk factor mimicking portfolio for capturing Jegadeesh and Titman (1993) one-year momentum anomaly in the stock holdings of the mutual funds. The momentum factor, MOM_t, is a measure of difference between the returns on past high-performing versus past poor-performing stocks and hence MOM_t reflects a fund's sensitivity to pursuing a zero-investment strategy of purchasing past outperforming 'momentum' stocks and short-selling stocks with low historical returns. The Carhart model nests the Fama-French Model where risk factors are: SMB_t = the realization on the capitalization factor (small-cap return minus large cap return) for month t; HML_t = the realization on the value factor (value return minus growth return) for month t e_{it} = an error term corresponding to the regression residuals.

References

Abdel-Kader, M., & Qing, K. Y. (2007). Risk-adjusted performance, selectivity, timing ability, and performance persistence of Hong Kong mutual funds. *Journal of Asia-Pacific Business, 8*(2), 25–58.

Admati, A. R., Bhattacharya, S., Pfleiderer, P., & Ross, S. A. (1986). On timing and selectivity. *The Journal of Finance, 41*(3), 715–730.

Amihud, Y., & Goyenko, R. (2013). Mutual fund's R^2 as predictor of performance. *The Review of Financial Studies, 26*(3), 667–694.

Ayadi, M. A., & Kryzanowski, L. (2011). Fixed-income fund performance: Role of luck and ability in tail membership. *Journal of Empirical Finance, 18*(3), 379–392.

Babalos, V., Caporale, G. M., Kostakis, A., & Philippas, N. (2008). Testing for persistence in mutual fund performance and the ex-post verification problem:

Evidence from the Greek market. *The European Journal of Finance, 14*(8), 735–753.

Baks, K. P. (2002). *On the performance of mutual fund managers*. https://repository.upenn.edu/dissertations/AAI3072967/.

Bauer, R., Koedijk, K., & Otten, R. (2005). International evidence on ethical mutual fund performance and investment style. *Journal of Banking & Finance, 29*(7), 1751–1767.

Bauer, R., Otten, R., & Rad, A. T. (2006). Ethical investing in Australia: Is there a financial penalty? *Pacific-Basin Finance Journal, 14*(1), 33–48.

Bergstresser, D., Chalmers, J. M., & Tufano, P. (2009). Assessing the costs and benefits of brokers in the mutual fund industry. *The Review of Financial Studies, 22*(10), 4129–4156.

Berk, J. B., & Green, R. (2004). Mutual fund flows and performance in rational markets. *Journal of Political Economy, 112*, 1269–1295.

Bessler, W., Blake, D. P., Lückoff, P., & Tonks, I. (2010, March). Why does mutual fund performance not persist? The impact and interaction of fund flows and manager changes. In *The impact and interaction of fund flows and manager changes (March 12, 2010). Paris December 2010 finance meeting EUROFIDAI-AFFI*.

Blake, D., & Timmermann, A. (1998). Mutual fund performance: Evidence from the UK. *Review of Finance, 2*(1), 57–77.

Bliss, R. T., Potter, M. E., & Schwarz, C. (2008). Performance characteristics of individually-managed versus team-managed mutual funds. *The Journal of Portfolio Management, 34*(3), 110–119.

Bollen, N. P., & Busse, J. A. (2001). On the timing ability of mutual fund managers. *The Journal of Finance, 56*(3), 1075–1094.

Bollen, N. P., & Busse, J. A. (2004). Short-term persistence in mutual fund performance. *The Review of Financial Studies, 18*(2), 569–597.

Boney, V., Comer, G., & Kelly, L. (2009). Timing the investment grade securities market: Evidence from high quality bond funds. *Journal of Empirical Finance, 16*(1), 55–69.

Brennan, M. J., & Hughes, P. J. (1991). Stock prices and the supply of information. *The Journal of Finance, 46*(5), 1665–1691.

Brown, S. J., & Goetzmann, W. N. (1995). Performance persistence. *The Journal of Finance, 50*(2), 679–698.

Carhart , M. (1997). On persistence in mutual fund performance. *The Journal of Finance, 52*(1), 57–82.

Chen, H. L., Jegadeesh, N., & Wermers, R. (2000). The value of active mutual fund management: An examination of the stockholdings and trades of fund managers. *Journal of Financial and quantitative Analysis, 35*(3), 343–368.

Chen, Y., Ferson, W., & Peters, H. (2010). Measuring the timing ability and performance of bond mutual funds. *Journal of Financial Economics, 98*(1), 72–89.

Chen, Z., & Knez, P. J. (1996). Portfolio performance measurement: Theory and applications. *The Review of Financial Studies, 9*(2), 511–555.

Chen, J., Hong, H., Huang, M., & Kubik, J. D. (2004). Does fund size erode mutual fund performance? The role of liquidity and organization. *American Economic Review, 94*(5), 1276–1302.

Chen, X., Yao, T., & Yu, T. (2007). Prudent man or agency problem? On the performance of insurance mutual funds. *Journal of Financial Intermediation, 16*(2), 175–203.

Christopherson, J. A., Ferson, W. E., & Turner, A. L. (1999). Performance evaluation using conditional alphas and betas. *The Journal of Portfolio Management, 26*(1), 59–72.

Christopherson, J. A., Ferson, W. E., & Glassman, D. A. (1998). Conditioning manager alphas on economic information: Another look at the persistence of performance. *The Review of Financial Studies, 11*(1), 111–142.

Christoffersen, S. E., & Musto, D. K. (2002). Demand curves and the pricing of money management. *The Review of Financial Studies, 15*(5), 1499–1524.

Choi, J., & Kronlund, M. (2018). Reaching for yield in corporate bond mutual funds. *The Review of Financial Studies, 31*(5), 1930–1965

Clare, A., O'Sullivan, N., Sherman, M., & Zhu, S. (2019). The performance of US bond mutual funds. *International Review of Financial Analysis, 61*, 1–8.

Cohen, L., Frazzini, A., & Malloy, C. (2008). The small world of investing: Board connections and mutual fund returns. *Journal of Political Economy, 116*(5), 951–979.

Cremers, K. M., & Petajisto, A. (2009). How active is your fund manager? A new measure that predicts performance. *The Review of Financial Studies, 22*(9), 3329–3365.

Cuthbertson, K., Nitzsche, D., & O'Sullivan, N. (2008). UK mutual fund performance: Skill or luck? *Journal of Empirical Finance, 15*(4), 613–634.

Cuthbertson, K., Nitzsche, D., & O'Sullivan, N. (2010). Mutual fund performance: Measurement and evidence. *Financial Markets, Institutions & Instruments, 19*(2), 95–187.

Dahlquist, M., Engström, S., & Söderlind, P. (2000). Performance and characteristics of Swedish mutual funds. *Journal of Financial and Quantitative Analysis, 35*, 409–423.

Daniel, K., Grinblatt, M., Titman, S., & Wermers, R. (1997). Measuring mutual fund performance with characteristic-based benchmarks. *The Journal of Finance, 52*(3), 1035–1058.

Davis, J. L. (2001). Mutual fund performance and manager style. *Financial Analysts Journal, 57*(1), 19–27.

Ding, B., & Wermers, R. (2012). Mutual fund performance and governance structure: The role of portfolio managers and boards of directors. Available at *SSRN* 2207229.

Edelen, R. M., Evans, R. B., & Kadlec, G. B. (2007). Scale effects in mutual fund performance: The role of trading costs. Available at *SSRN* 951367.

Elton, E., & Gruber, M. (1999). Common factors in active and passive portfolios. *European Finance Review, 3,* 53–78.

Elton, E. J., Gruber, M. J., Das, S., & Hlavka, M. (1993). Efficiency with costly information: A reinterpretation of evidence from managed portfolios. *The Review of Financial Studies, 6*(1), 1–22.

Elton, E. J., Gruber, M. J., & Blake, C. R. (1996). The persistence of risk-adjusted mutual fund performance. *Journal of Business, 69,* 133–157.

Fama, E. F. (1972). Components of investment performance. *The Journal of Finance, 27*(3), 551–567.

Fama, E., & French, K. R. (1992). The cross-section of expected stock returns. *Journal of Finance, 47*, 427–465.

Fama, E. F., & French, K. R. (1993). Common risk factors in the returns on stocks and bonds. *Journal of Financial Economics, 33*(1), 3–56.

Fama, E., & French, K. R. (1996). Multifactor explanations of asset pricing anomalies. *Journal of Finance, 51,* 55–84.

Fama, E. F., & French, K. R. (2004). The capital asset pricing model: Theory and evidence. *Journal of Economic Perspectives, 18*(3), 25–46.

Ferreira, M. A., Keswani, A., Miguel, A. F., & Ramos, S. B. (2013). The determinants of mutual fund performance: A cross-country study. *Review of Finance, 17*(2), 483–525.

Ferson, W. E., & Schadt, R. W. (1996). Measuring fund strategy and performance in changing economic conditions. *The Journal of Finance, 51*(2), 425–461.

Friesen, G. C., & Sapp, T. R. (2007). Mutual fund flows and investor returns: An empirical examination of fund investor timing ability. *Journal of Banking & Finance, 31*(9), 2796–2816.

Gallagher, D. R. (2003). Investment manager characteristics, strategy, top management changes and fund performance. *Accounting & Finance, 43*(3), 283–309.

Gao, J., O'Sullivan, N., & Sherman, M. (2020). An evaluation of Chinese securities investment fund performance. *The Quarterly Review of Economics and Finance, 76,* 249–259.

Gil-Bazo, J., & Ruiz-Verdú, P. (2008). When cheaper is better: Fee determination in the market for equity mutual funds. *Journal of Economic Behavior & Organization, 67*(3–4), 871–885.

Gil-Bazo, J., & Ruiz-Verdú, P. (2009). The relation between price and performance in the mutual fund industry. *The Journal of Finance, 64*(5), 2153–2183.
Grinblatt, M., & Titman, S. (1989). Mutual fund performance: An analysis of quarterly portfolio holdings. *Journal of Business, 62,* 393–416.
Grinblatt, M., & Titman, S. (1994). A study of monthly mutual fund returns and performance evaluation techniques. *Journal of Financial and Quantitative Analysis, 29,* 419–444.
Grossman, S. J., & Stiglitz, J. E. (1980). On the impossibility of informationally efficient markets. *The American Economic Review, 70*(3), 393–408.
Gruber, M. J. (1996). Another puzzle: The growth in actively managed mutual funds. *The Journal of Finance, 51,* 783–791.
Hendricks, D., Patel, J., & Zeckhauser, R. (1993). Hot hands in mutual funds: Short-run persistence of relative performance, 1974–1988. *The Journal of Finance, 48*(1), 93–130.
Henriksson, R. D., & Merton, R. C. (1981). On market timing and investment performance: II. Statistical procedures for evaluating forecasting skills. *Journal of Business, 54,* 513–533.
Hereil, P., Mitaine, P., Moussavi, N., & Roncalli, T. (2010). Mutual fund ratings and performance persistence. Available at *SSRN* 1749414.
Huang, J., Sialm, C., & Zhang, H. (2011). Risk shifting and mutual fund performance. *The Review of Financial Studies, 24*(8), 2575–2616.
Huij, J., & Derwall, J. (2011). Global equity fund performance, portfolio concentration, and the fundamental law of active management. *Journal of Banking & Finance, 35*(1), 155–165.
Jegadeesh, N., & Titman, S. (1993). Returns to buying winners and selling losers: Implications for stock market efficiency. *The Journal of Finance, 48*(1), 65–91.
Jensen, M. C. (1968). The performance of mutual funds in the period 1945–1964. *The Journal of Finance, 23*(2), 389–416.
Jeon, H., Kang, J., & Lee, C. (2017). Precision about manager skill, mutual fund flows, and performance persistence. *The North American Journal of Economics and Finance, 40*, 222–237.
Jiang, G. J., & Yuksel, H. Z. (2017). What drives the "Smart-Money" effect? Evidence from investors' money flow to mutual fund classes. *Journal of Empirical Finance, 40*, 39–58.
Kacperczyk, M., Sialm, C., & Zheng, L. (2005). On the industry concentration of actively managed equity mutual funds. *The Journal of Finance, 60*(4), 1983–2011.
Keswani, A., & Stolin, D. (2008). Which money is smart? Mutual fund buys and sells of individual and institutional investors. *The Journal of Finance, 63*(1), 85–118.

Khorana, A., Servaes, H., & Tufano, P. (2005). Explaining the size of the mutual fund industry around the world. *Journal of Financial Economics, 78*(1), 145–185.

Khorana, A., Servaes, H., & Tufano, P. (2009). Mutual fund fees around the world. *The Review of Financial Studies, 22*(3), 1279–1310.

Kosowski, R. (2011). Do mutual funds perform when it matters most to investors? US mutual fund performance and risk in recessions and expansions. *The Quarterly Journal of Finance, 1*(3), 607–664.

Lehmann, B. N., & Modest, D. M. (1987). Mutual fund performance evaluation: A comparison of benchmarks and benchmark comparisons. *The Journal of Finance, 42*(2), 233–265.

Leisher, T. K. (2019). Exchange-traded funds: The unknown investment opportunity. *Undergraduate Economic Review, 15*(1), 15.

Lintner, J. (1965). The valuation of risk assets and the selection of risky investments in stock portfolios and capital budgets. *Review of Economics and Statistics, 47*(1), 13–37.

Lynch, A. W., & Musto, D. K. (2003). How investors interpret past fund returns. *The Journal of Finance, 58*(5), 2033–2058.

Markowitz, H. (1952). Portfolio selection. *The Journal of Finance, 7*(1), 77–91. https://doi.org/10.2307/2975974.

Massa, M., & Patgiri, R. (2009). Incentives and mutual fund performance: Higher performance or just higher risk taking? *The Review of Financial Studies, 22*(5), 1777–1815.

Merton, R. C. (1973). An intertemporal capital asset pricing model. *Econometrica: Journal of the Econometric Society, 41*, 867–887.

Miller, D. A, Goldfarb, B., & Kirsch, D. (2007). Was there too little entry during the Dot Com Era? *Journal of Financial Economics, 86*(1), 100–144.

Otten, R., & Bams, D. (2002). European mutual fund performance. *European Financial Management, 8*(1), 75–101.

Otten, R., & Bams, D. (2004). How to measure mutual fund performance: Economic versus statistical relevance. *Accounting & Finance, 44*(2), 203–222.

Pandow, B. A., & Butt, K. A. (2017). Risk and return analysis of mutual fund industry in India. *Journal of Banking and Financial Dynamics, 1*, 54–65.

Pollet, J. M., & Wilson, M. (2008). How does size affect mutual fund behavior? *The Journal of Finance, 63*(6), 2941–2969.

Quigley, G., & Sinquefield, R. A. (2000). Performance of UK equity unit trusts. *Journal of Asset Management, 1*(1), 72–92.

Sapar, N. R., & Madava, R. (2003). Performance evaluation of Indian mutual funds. Available at *SSRN* 433100.

Sapp, T., & Tiwari, A. (2004). Does stock return momentum explain the "smart money" effect? *The Journal of Finance, 59*(6), 2605–2622.

Sharpe, W. F. (1963). A simplified model for portfolio analysis. *Management Science, 9*(2), 277–293.

Sharpe, W. F. (1964). Capital asset prices: A theory of market equilibrium under conditions of risk. *Journal of Finance, 19*(3), 425–442.

Sharpe, W. F. (1966). Mutual fund performance. *The Journal of Business, 39*(1), 119–138.

Sharpe, W. F. (1992). Asset allocation: Management style and performance measurement. *Journal of Portfolio Management, 18*(2), 7–19.

Sialm, C., Starks, L. T., & Zhang, H. (2015). Defined contribution pension plans: Sticky or discerning money? *The Journal of Finance, 70*(2), 805–838.

Stein, J. C. (2002). Information production and capital allocation: Decentralized versus hierarchical firms. *The Journal of Finance, 57*(5), 1891–1921.

Tonks, I. (2004). Performance persistence of pension-fund managers. *The Journal of Business, 78*(5), 1917–1942.

Treynor, J. (1965). How to rate management of investment funds. *Harvard Business Review, 41*, 63–75.

Treynor, J., & Mazuy, K. (1966). Can mutual funds outguess the market. *Harvard Business Review, 44*(4), 131–136.

Vidal-García, J. (2013). The persistence of European mutual fund performance. *Research in International Business and Finance, 28*, 45–67.

Vidal-García, J., Vidal, M., Boubaker, S., & Uddin, G. S. (2016). The short-term persistence of international mutual fund performance. *Economic Modelling, 52*, 926–938.

Wermers, R. (2000). Mutual fund performance: An empirical decomposition into stock-picking talent, style, transactions costs, and expenses. *The Journal of Finance, 55*(4), 1655–1695.

Wermers, R. (2003). Is money really "smart"? New evidence on the relation between mutual fund flows, manager behavior, and performance persistence. *SSRN*.

Yan, X. (2008). Liquidity, investment style, and the relation between fund size and fund performance. *Journal of Financial and Quantitative Analysis, 43*, 741–767.

Zheng, L. (1999). Is money smart? A study of mutual fund investors' fund selection ability. *The Journal of Finance, 54*(3), 901–933.

CHAPTER 3

Size

1 Introduction

The performance of active mutual funds has been of long-standing interest to financial economists but is also relevant to financial practitioners. The extent to which an active fund can outperform its passive benchmark depends not only on the fund manager ability to detect good investment opportunities but also on various constraints faced by the fund.[1] According to Pástor et al. (2015), one constraint discussed prominently in recent literature is decreasing returns to scale. If scale impacts performance, skill and scale could interact: a more skilled large fund can underperform a less skilled small fund. Therefore, to learn about skills, we must understand the effects of scale. On the relationship between Size and Performance, the literature has advanced two hypotheses. Pástor et al. (2015) provides a theoretical framework of these hypotheses. The first one is fund-level decreasing returns to scale: as the size of an active fund increases, the fund's ability to outperform its benchmark declines (e.g., Berk & Green, 2004; Perold & Salomon, 1991). The second hypothesis is industry-level decreasing returns to scale: as the size of the active mutual fund industry increases, the ability of any given fund to outperform declines (Pástor & Stambaugh, 2012). Both hypotheses have been

[1] Pástor, Ľ., Stambaugh, R. F., & Taylor, L. A. (2015). Scale and skill in active management. *Journal of Financial Economics, 116*(1), 23–45.

G. Galloppo, *Asset Allocation Strategies for Mutual Funds*, https://doi.org/10.1007/978-3-030-76128-8_3

motivated by liquidity constraints. When considering the fund level, a larger fund's trades have a larger impact on asset prices of the asset under management, eroding the fund's performance. Edelen et al. (2007) report that trading costs are a major source of diseconomies of scale for mutual funds. At the industry level, as more and more money chases opportunities to outperform the market, rising prices make this opportunity even more elusive. In accordance with such liquidity constraints, and due to the fact that mutual funds have the highest amount of total assets traded worldwide, more and more evidence shows that mutual fund transactions can impose meaningful prices on the stock market pressure. Edelen and Warner (2001) discover that aggregate flow into equity mutual funds has an aggregate impact on market returns. Khan et al. (2012), Lou (2012), Coval and Stafford (2007), and Wermers (2003) also find significant price impact associated with mutual fund trading.

Understanding the nature of the economies of scale in the mutual fund industry is also central to the long-standing debate over the value of active fund management. As a matter of fact, the level of diseconomies of scale in asset management has important implications for tests of manager skill and the expected level of performance persistence (Reuter & Zitzewitz, 2010).[2]

The traditional analytic framework of skill in active management builds on the assumption of constant returns to scale (Zhu, 2018).[3] That is to say, management skill for a fund with $1 million of assets under management is indistinguishable from a fund with $1 billion of assets under management as long as they both achieve the same risk-adjusted return. The manager's chosen portfolio weights for the fund's investments are independent of fund size. This hypothesis is defined as "perfect scaling," or "scaling" for short.

Under this framework, skill and scale are independent, and fund size is regarded as uninformative and randomly paired with funds. If the nature of the returns to scale is not constant, fund size then is informative, and unobserved skill is reflected in two observable measures, return and size. Consequently, the traditional framework that studies managerial skill

[2] Reuter, J., & Zitzewitz, E. (2010). *How much does size erode mutual fund performance? A regression discontinuity approach* (No. w16329). National Bureau of Economic Research.

[3] Zhu, M. (2018). Informative fund size, managerial skill, and investor rationality. *Journal of Financial Economics, 130*(1), 114–134.

and ignores size fails to fully utilize the available information, which can have biased previous studies against finding differential ability in active management (Zhu, 2018).

Berk and Green (2004) provide an intriguing potential answer based on diseconomies of scale. In their model rational investors chase performance to the point that expected future returns are equalized across funds (Reuter & Zitzewitz, 2010). Funds managed by skilled managers attract greater portfolio flows than funds managed by unskilled managers (Phillips et al., 2018).[4] The crucial assumption in Berk and Green's model is indeed the existence of diseconomies of scale in mutual fund performance.

In equilibrium, more-skilled managers manage more assets but precisely because of the diseconomies of scale associated with managing more assets—earn the same expected future return as their less-skilled peers (Reuter & Zitzewitz, 2010). Authors suggest that diminishing returns to scale in the mutual fund industry can reconcile the lack of persistence in fund return performance with the presence of managerial skill at picking stocks. If actively managed mutual funds suffer from diminishing returns to scale, funds should alter investment behavior as assets under management increase (Pollet & Wilson, 2008).[5] In this model, managers are assumed to face costs that are positive, increasing, and convex in fund Total Net assets. These assumptions are intended to capture the idea that "with a sufficiently large fund, a manager will spread his information gathering activities too thin or that large trades will be associated with a larger price impact and higher execution costs".[6] Authors emphasize that if the acquisition of a large holding does not increase price impact, then there is no need for a particular manager to alter information gathering activities at all. The manager can simply scale up his or her few best investment ideas.

[4] Phillips, B., Pukthuanthong, K., & Rau, P. R. (2018). Size does not matter: Diseconomies of scale in the mutual fund industry revisited. *Journal of Banking and Finance, 88,* 357–365.

[5] Pollet, J. M., & Wilson, M. (2008). How does size affect mutual fund behavior? *The Journal of Finance, 63*(6), 2941–2969.

[6] Berk, J. B., & Green, R. C. (2004). Mutual fund flows and performance in rational markets. *Journal of Political Economy, 112*(6), 1269–1295.

Despite the important theoretical and practical implications, the answer to the nature of returns to scale in active management is inconclusive (Zhu, 2018).

Some researchers argue that growth in fund size provides cost advantages because brokerage commissions and research costs, as well as administrative and overhead expenses, do not increase in direct proportion to fund size. Other researchers, however, contend that a large asset base might erode fund performance because of liquidity (Yan, 2008).[7]

Some authors (Chen et al., 2004; Yan, 2008) claim for a "liquidity hypothesis": the effect of size on performance is stronger among small-cap funds due to the fact that small-cap stocks are less liquid, then size ought to erode performance much more for funds that have to invest in small stocks, which tend to be illiquid.

Chen et al. (2004)[8] present evidence that fund size erodes performance. They find that the adverse effect of size on performance is stronger among small-cap funds. To the extent that small-cap stocks are less liquid, they argue that their evidence provides support for the hypothesis that fund size erodes performance because of liquidity.[9] Similarly, Beckers and Vaughan (2001) argue that as a fund grows larger, "the portfolio manager loses flexibility: it becomes harder to switch in and out of positions. Executing a desired trade will take longer or create adverse market impact price moves. The resulting reduction in the speed and nature of the portfolio adjustment will ultimately impair fund performance".[10]

When the size increases, it could be observed as "Price impact" issue, that requires managers to deviate from perfect scaling by increasing the number of distinct holdings as fund TNA grows.[11] Pollet and Wilson (2008) consider two basic propositions. First, in the presence of liquidity costs, managers will slowly increase the number of different holdings in their portfolios based on the inflow of new money from investors. This

[7] Yan, X. (2008). Liquidity, investment style, and the relation between fund size and fund performance. *Journal of Financial and Quantitative Analysis*, 741–767.

[8] Chen, J., Hong, H., Huang, M., & Kubik, J. D. (2004). Does fund size erode mutual fund performance? The role of liquidity and organization. *American Economic Review, 94*(5), 1276–1302.

[9] See footnote 7.

[10] Beckers, S. E., & Vaughan, G. (2001). Small is beautiful. *The Journal of Portfolio Management, 27*(4), 9–17.

[11] See footnote 5.

response will be greater when liquidity costs are more severe. Second, as funds grow, managers will increase the ownership share at a reduced rate to cope with new capital flows. The apparently limited skill of fund managers to generate additional good investment ideas given the imperfect scalability of their fund's size could be related to the difficulty to hire additional money managers or research staff to augment the number of investment ideas. Both the costs of organizational diseconomies described by Chen et al. (2004), and the benefits of product proliferation as part of marketing strategies for fund families described by Massa (1998)[12] would be consistent with this explanation. Berk and Green (2004) argue that the need to add poorer-performing investments, that is the acceptance of less profitable investments, make the excess returns disappear and eliminate predictability.

Another possible response to liquidity constraints is to close the fund to new investors. Bris et al. (2007) investigates fund closures in detail. Results are entirely consistent with the hypothesis that closure is primarily a response to higher liquidity costs.

Of course, the process of growing a fund that impairs the manager's ability to create excess returns is a process that can take time. If Berk and Green (2004) are correct but investors need time to perform a new allocation funds or even to receive and process data, then growth in size takes place over time. Thus, diseconomies of scale, to the extent they exist, will impact fund performance slowly over time. In this case, predictability can exist, although it should disappear over longer time periods (Elton et al., 2012).[13]

2 Previous Findings in Academic Literature

The predictability of mutual fund performance became a very popular investigation by various scholars, where the understanding the development of mutual fund performance from mutual fund size became a very valuable issue for investment decisions. Due to investment decisions taken, mutual funds play a crucial role in capital allocation and are drivers

[12] Massa, M. (1998). *Why so many mutual funds? Mutual fund families, market segmentation and financial performance* (Working Paper, INSEAD).

[13] Elton, E. J., Gruber, M. J., & Blake, C. R. (2012). Does mutual fund size matter? The relationship between size and performance. *The Review of Asset Pricing Studies, 2*(1), 31–55.

of economy. Many studies investigate fund performance but very few of them focus on fund characteristics, such as size, flows, transaction costs to performance specifically. Those studies demonstrate quite mixed empirical evidences on the fund characteristics that affect performance. Jeon et al. (2017) showed that future fund flows react to past performance more strongly if the precision is high, by including attention to cross-sectional evidence on relationship between fund performance and fund characteristics, including fund size. Recent works of Basso and Funari (2017), El Ghoul and Karoui (2017), Berkowitz et al. (2017) proved that fund characteristics serve as an important benchmark that affects fund performance and it varies according to fund category.[14]

Early empirical studies provide evidence that is consistent with decreasing returns to scale. Chen et al. (2004) first document a negative relation between fund size and performance. They investigate the effect of scale on performance in the active money management industry. Authors first document that fund returns, both before and after fees and expenses, decline with lagged fund size, even after accounting for various performance benchmarks. They then explore a number of potential explanations for this relationship. This association is most pronounced among funds that have to invest in small and illiquid stocks, suggesting that these adverse scale effects are related to liquidity.[15] They argue that increased inflow to funds with illiquid holdings increases trading costs and price pressure on the stocks held by the fund and thus impedes fund performance.[16] Controlling for its size, a fund's return does not deteriorate with the size of the family that it belongs to, indicating that scale need not be bad for performance depending on how the fund is organized (Chen et al., 2004). A two-standard deviation shock to the size of the other funds in the family leads to about a 4–6-basis-point movement in the fund's performance the following month (or about 48–72-basis-points

[14] See also Shari, A., & Mahat, F. (2019). Mutual fund characteristics, risk governance and fund performance in ASEAN market: A conceptual framework. *International Journal of Accounting, 4*(24), 42–52.

[15] Chen, J., Hong, H., Huang, M., & Kubik, J. D. (2004). Does fund size erode mutual fund performance? The role of liquidity and organization. *American Economic Review, 94*(5), 1276–1302.

[16] Phillips, B., Pukthuanthong, K., & Rau, P. R. (2018). Size does not matter: Diseconomies of scale in the mutual fund industry revisited. *Journal of Banking and Finance, 88*, 357–365.

movement annually) depending on the performance measure used. The most plausible interpretation of this finding is that there are economies associated with trading commissions and lending fees at the family level, that is belonging to a large family helps a lot in saving trading and fees.

Yan (2008) measures liquidity using bid-ask spread and market impact and documents similar results. He finds that funds which hold fewer liquid portfolios and which have high liquidity demand, such as growth funds and high-turnover funds, have a stronger negative relation between size and performance.

Edelen et al. (2007)[17] examine the role of trading costs as a source of decreasing returns to scale. They regress fund returns on both relative trade size and fund size, finding that relative trade size subsumes fund size in the regression. The authors conclude that trading costs are the primary source of diseconomies of scale for funds.

Gutierrez et al. (2009)[18] find no evidence of a size-return correlation for bond funds, and suggest that differences in size return correlation between stock funds and bond funds reflect differences in economies of scale in trading costs for stocks and bonds.

Petajisto (2013) shows that larger funds are more likely to be closet indexers who earn inferior returns, implying that the indexation strategies employed by larger funds drives the poor returns earned by these funds.[19] The evidence of fund-level decreasing returns to scale is not pervasive across funds. Ferreira et al. (2013)[20] analyze the relation between size and performance across 27 countries. They find diseconomies of scale for U.S. funds but not for non-U.S. funds; in fact, the latter funds seem to exhibit increasing returns to scale.

[17] Edelen, R. M., Evans, R. B., & Kadlec, G. B. (2007). *Scale effects in mutual fund performance: The role of trading costs*. https://doi.org/10.2139/ssrn.951367.

[18] Gutierrez, R. C., Maxwell, W. F., & Xu, D. (2009). *On economies of scale and persistent performance in corporate-bond mutual funds*. https://doi.org/10.2139/ssrn.1133959.

[19] Petajisto, A. (2013). Active share and mutual fund performance. *Financial Analysts Journal, 69*(4), 73–93.

[20] Ferreira, M. A., Keswani, A., Miguel, A. F., & Ramos, S. B. (2013). The determinants of mutual fund performance: A cross-country study. *Review of Finance, 17*(2), 483–525.

Tang et al. (2012) document an inverted U-shape relationship between fund size and performance for Chinese mutual funds.[21] They show that "the initial positive relationship between fund size and performance is likely caused by the economy of scale. In other words, growth in fund size provides cost advantages, namely, brokerage commissions, and research and marketing costs do not increase in direct proportion to fund size. However, as the fund grows, the negative relationship between fund size and performance contradicts the theory of economy of scale and liquidity constraints erode fund performance".

To understand the U-shape relationship between fund size and performance, we should consider that the economy of scale and liquidity constraints might exist simultaneously. Therefore, for small funds, liquidity might not be an important issue due to their lack of large stock positions. However, the economy of scale would play an important role at this level due to the fact that, when size increases, funds can save their broker fees, marketing fees and so on. On the contrary, as funds do increase and tend to become very large, the economy of scale effect might not improve and the liquidity issue might be more important instead. Thus, there can be an inverted U-shape relationship between fund size and performance (Tang et al., 2012).

Authors like Chen et al. (2004), Yan (2008) and Tang et al. (2012) affirm that "large funds tend to hold a large portion of portfolios that are not easily bought or sold at an ideal price; thus, large funds pay more in trading costs than do small funds. In the meantime, when facing a liquidity problem, large funds tend to liquefy their portfolio, for example, by adding some unfavorable but liquid stocks to the portfolio, thus eroding fund performance."

More recent literature documented negative relation between fund size and performance. Elton et al. (2012) show a positive (though insignificant) relation between size and performance by examining samples of increasingly larger funds. They speculate that the reduction in expense ratios for larger funds outweighs possible diseconomies of scale when the funds increase in size (see also, Phillips et al., 2018).

Reuter and Zitzewitz (2013) use a regression discontinuity approach to address the endogeneity of fund size. Specifically, they use a reduced-form

[21] Tang, K., Wang, W., & Xu, R. (2012). Size and performance of Chinese mutual funds: The role of economy of scale and liquidity. *Pacific-Basin Finance Journal, 20*(2), 228–246.

regression model, in which the dependent variable is fund return in period $t + 1$ and the independent variable of interest is a dummy variable that indicates whether fund return is above the threshold in period t. Reuter and Zitzewitz (2013) argue that in order to examine whether size erodes performance, we need to identify the variation in fund size that is uncorrelated with manager skill.[22] To this end, they[23] study the difference in performance between funds that have differing numbers of Morningstar stars but have almost identical Morningstar numerical rankings. First, they observe that funds with past returns above a Morningstar rating threshold are more likely to receive inflows than funds with past returns immediately below the threshold. For the next six months, they find on average that the funds with greater inflows have slightly better performance, but they have slightly worse performance over 12, 18, and 24 months (see also, Elton et al., 2012). Authors conclude that the magnitude of diseconomies of scale is not strong enough to be significant. Pástor et al. (2015)[24] address the endogeneity of fund size by including fund fixed effects to account for heterogeneity in managerial skills. They find an insignificant but negative relation between size and performance

Furthermore, Pástor et al. (2015) find strong evidence of decreasing returns at the industry level: as the size of the active mutual fund industry increases, a fund's ability to outperform passive benchmarks declines. Authors affirm that "at the fund level, all methods considered indicate decreasing returns, though estimates that avoid econometric biases are insignificant". They also find that the active management industry has become more skilled over time and that performance deteriorates over an average fund's lifetime.

Bhojraj et al. (2012) attribute the positive relation between size and performance to private information. They show that the positive relation between family size and performance is limited to the time-frame before 2000, prior to the SEC establishing fair disclosure regulations. They argue that large fund families received material, non-public information from

[22] McLemore, P. (2019). Do mutual funds have decreasing returns to scale? Evidence from fund mergers. *Journal of Financial and Quantitative Analysis, 54*(4), 1683–1711.

[23] Reuter, J., & Zitzewitz, E. (2010). *How much does size erode mutual fund performance? A regression discontinuity approach* (No. w16329). National Bureau of Economic Research.

[24] Pástor, Ľ., Stambaugh, R. F., & Taylor, L. A. (2015). Scale and skill in active management. *Journal of Financial Economics, 116*(1), 23–45.

investment banks giving them an unfair advantage over smaller fund families. When fair disclosure regulations were established, this advantage was eliminated (see also, Phillips et al., 2018).

With respect to mutual fund family, Elton et al. (2012) affirm that large funds might offset any increase in transaction costs and the need to take a larger number of investments by commanding a larger share of the resources of the fund's family. Large funds may have an informational advantage in the form of a greater access to the best analysts or traders. Since fund family flows depend on the performance of the best-performing funds (see Nanda et al., 2004[25]), they may get the pick of or early access to the best investment opportunities that the fund family discovers. Gaspar et al. (2006)[26] provide evidence that would support fund families favoring well-performing funds.

One literature strand believes that increase of fund size reduces its ability to outperform the benchmark due to liquidity constraints. Pástor et al. (2020) outline that when choosing such fund characteristics as size, expense ratio and turnover, a fund considers that lower liquidity and higher turnover increase expected profits together with transaction costs, where such costs increase in the fund's size as well. Investor recognize this role of the fund size when making their decisions on the amount of capital to allocate in a fund. A larger fund trades larger amounts that requires higher transaction costs. Additionally, Pástor et al. (2020) underlines that larger funds tend to have lower turnover and higher liquidity of portfolio, while funds with smaller size and higher expense ratios have lower turnover and hold fewer liquid portfolios. In addition, Pástor et al. (2017) proves that fund size helps proxy for the liquidity of the fund's holdings. In line with previous findings, Casavecchia and Ge (2019) proves that fund performance declines with fund's own size but increases with the size of the other funds in the fund family, where lagged fund performance affects positively both net and gross current risk-adjusted returns, unlike the number of investment objectives by fund family that affects fund performance negatively. Chua and Tam (2020) believes that fund managers tend to maximize the size of compensation by manipulating

[25] Nanda, V., Wang, Z. J., & Zheng, L. (2004). Family values and the star phenomenon: Strategies of mutual fund families. *The Review of Financial Studies, 17*(3), 667–698.

[26] Gaspar, J. M., Massa, M., & Matos, P. (2006). Favoritism in mutual fund families? Evidence on strategic cross-fund subsidization. *The Journal of Finance, 61*(1), 73–104.

with relative performance ranking, in order to increase the size of assets under management and therefore earn more management fees. Manager actions are seen in the style drift that leads to increase in fund flows. When assets grow in size together with the growth of the size of the fund industry, fund managers feel difficulties to compete and their interest is to deviate from their investment strategies for performance improvement. Cao et al. (2017) believes that small cap funds that have higher allocations to large stocks do not demonstrate performance persistence over time. He finds the same evidence in relation to small cap funds with lower allocations to larger stocks. Novy-Marx (2014) finds that the volatility can be explained by controlling for size, profitability and other fund characteristics. In addition, funds considering the low volatility portfolio strategy have different levels of risk (systematic and unsystematic) in relation to funds with high volatility portfolio. In addition, low volatility funds have lower market risk, less small cap and growth exposure, less momentum than high volatility funds. Jordan and Riley (2015) also underlines that such fund characteristics such as fund size, age, expense ratio and turnover are all predictive of future abnormal returns, where total return volatility is driving this effect, not idiosyncratic volatility. Small size, low turnover and expense ratio and old mutual fund age affect alpha positively.

Pollet and Wilson (2008)[27] describe the limits to the scalability of fund portfolios, such as price impact or liquidity constraints, as the proximate cause of the diminishing returns to scale assumed by Berk and Green (2004), in terms of ownership costs. It exists at least two ways in which liquidity constraints can affect fund performance. In the first case, managers have no ability to generate additional investment ideas when existing opportunities have been fully exploited. All they can do is "go down their list" to the next-best investment opportunity (Pollet & Wilson, 2008).

Management overwhelmingly reacts to an increase in size by increasing their ownership share in stocks already held in the portfolio rather than by increasing the number of investments (see also, Elton et al., 2012). Pollet and Wilson (2008) find that a doubling of fund size increases the number of stocks in the fund by less than 10%. Under this empirical evidence, managers diversify only because they are prevented by their

[27] Pollet, J. M., & Wilson, M. (2008). How does size affect mutual fund behavior? *The Journal of Finance, 63*(6), 2941–2969.

size from increasing their existing holdings. Provided some managers are able to add superior stocks with greater ease because they have a better list, liquidity constraints will not lower returns as much for these managers.[28] In the second case, some managers are overconfident about their ability to select superior stocks and in this case the overconfident managers are not diversifying optimally. Moreover, since management does not react to increasing size by adding a large number of new investments, if performance deteriorates with size, it has to be due to increased transaction costs[29] due to a larger position in the securities they hold or organizational diseconomies (see Elton et al., 2012).

3 Methodology and Empirical Results

In this section, we study the relationship between fund size and performance through the portfolio approach and regressions.

Descriptive statistics

Tables 1 and 2 report summary statistics for our sample. We report the means and standard deviations for the variables of interest for each fund size quintile for European and US Equity Sample. Chen et al. (2004) and Elton et al. (2000) claim that it must pay attention in making inferences regarding the performances of funds that have less than 15 million dollars in total net assets under management, because the reported returns of the smallest funds might be upward biased. For the usual reasons related to scaling, the proxy of fund size that we will use in our analysis is the log of a fund's TNA (LOGTNA).

When we disaggregate statistics by fund size quintiles, we find that the average expense ratios range between about 1.14 and 0.49%. FLOW in month t is defined as the fund's TNA in month t minus the product of the fund's TNA at month $t - 1$ with the net fund return between months $t - 1$ and t, all divided by the fund's TNA at month $t - 1$. The funds in the sample for the highest size quintile have an average fund flow of about 0.006 and 0.035% a month, for the US and European sample

[28] Pollet, J. M., & Wilson, M. (2008). How does size affect mutual fund behavior. *The Journal of Finance, 63*(6), 2941–2969.

[29] Christoffersen et al. (2006), who studied Canadian mutual funds, measure trading costs as the difference between a fund's net price and the value-weighted average price. They find that larger mutual funds have lower trading costs (both transaction costs and price impact) than smaller funds.

Table 1 Descriptive statistics European equity sample

Variable	*Mutual Fund Size Quintile*				
	1	*2*	*3*	*4*	*5*
ALPHA	0.002	0.002	0.001	0.000	0.001
AGE	0.676	0.496	0.369	0.461	0.522
EXPENSE	1.145	0.738	0.492	0.605	0.643
FLOWS	0.035	0.014	0.013	0.010	−0.009
SIZE	19.815	18.032	16.475	15.374	13.033
VOLATILITY	0.048	0.038	0.026	0.025	0.030
R SQUARED	0.593	0.484	0.370	0.432	0.392
ACTIVE	0.451	0.523	0.600	0.560	0.584

Correlation matrix

ALPHA	1.000							
AGE	−0.014	1.000						
EXPENSE	0.002	0.492	1.000					
FLOWS	0.010	−0.016	−0.017	1.000				
SIZE	0.026	0.177	0.138	−0.010	1.000			
VOLATILITY	0.148	0.258	0.324	0.002	0.014	1.000		
R SQUARED	−0.006	0.433	0.416	−0.006	0.088	0.458	1.000	
ACTIVE	0.001	−0.449	−0.424	0.006	−0.092	−0.448	−0.983	1.000

Portfolio performance is evaluated based on Carhart or Momentum Four Factor alpha. AGE is defined as the number of months from the fund's inception. FLOW in month t is defined as the fund's TNA in month t minus the product of the fund's TNA at month $t-1$ with the net fund return between months $t-1$ and t, all divided by the fund's TNA at month $t-1$. SIZE is the logarithm of the total net assets of fund i in period $t-1$ $\log(\text{TNA})_{i,t-1}$. $\text{ExpenseRatio}_{i,t-1}$, is the net expense ratio. $\text{Volatility}_{j,t}$ is the volatility of monthly returns (Standard Deviation over a 52 weeks rolling estimation). According to Bliss et al. (2008) we also added the CAPM $R\text{square}_{j,t-1}$ measure as a control variable. $\text{ActiveShare}_{i,t-1}$ is a measure of active management by the fund as defined by Cremers and Petajisto (2009) and Miller et al. (2007). The sample period is from December 2006 to December 2019. The t-statistics are based on standard errors clustered by both fund and time. First Size Quintile (1) is the highest

respectively. These summary statistics are similar to those obtained for the sub-sample of funds in fund size quintiles two to five. We also report the cross-sectional correlations between the various fund characteristics. A number of patterns emerge. First, LOGTNA (SIZE) exhibits on average a low correlation with respect to other variables both in US and European Sample. Second, FLOWS varies inversely with AGE and Expense. Lastly, as we should have expected, we observe a strong and negative correlation

Table 2 Descriptive statistics US equity sample

Variable	*Mutual fund size quintile*				
	1	*2*	*3*	*4*	*5*
ALPHA	0.001	−0.001	0.000	0.000	0.000
AGE	0.655	0.444	0.390	0.463	0.510
EXPENSE	0.982	0.792	0.563	0.515	0.490
FLOWS	0.006	0.023	0.012	0.001	0.003
SIZE	19.184	17.142	15.378	13.670	10.691
VOLATILITY	0.038	0.028	0.020	0.013	0.014
R SQUARED	0.704	0.507	0.378	0.257	0.272
ACTIVE	0.361	0.509	0.603	0.697	0.690

Correlation matrix

ALPHA	1							
AGE	0.054	1						
EXPENSE	−0.006	0.503	1					
FLOWS	−0.001	−0.021	−0.008	1				
SIZE	0.029	0.187	0.08	0.007	1			
VOLATILITY	0.468	0.163	0.205	−0.005	0.076	1		
R SQUARED	0.002	0.315	0.356	−0.012	0.196	0.454	1	
ACTIVE	−0.005	−0.301	−0.344	0.011	−0.645	−0.447	−0.988	1

Portfolio performance is evaluated based on Carhart or Momentum Four Factor alpha. AGE is defined as the number of months from the fund's inception. FLOW in month t is defined as the fund's TNA in month t minus the product of the fund's TNA at month $t-1$ with the net fund return between months $t-1$ and t, all divided by the fund's TNA at month $t-1$. SIZE is the logarithm of the total net assets of fund i in period $t-1$ $\log(\text{TNA})_{i,t-1}$. $\text{ExpenseRatio}_{i,t-1}$, is the net expense ratio. $\text{Volatility}_{j,t}$ is the volatility of monthly returns (Standard Deviation over a 52 weeks rolling estimation). According to Bliss et al. (2008) we also added the CAPM $\text{Rsquare}_{j,t-1}$ measure as a control variable. $\text{ActiveShare}_{i,t-1}$ is a measure of active management by the fund as defined by Cremers and Petajisto (2009) and Miller et al. (2007). The sample period is from December 2006 to December 2019. First Size Quintile (1) is the highest

between EXPENSE and ACTIVE, as measured in terms of Miller et al. (2007) measure.

In line with Tang et al. (2012) we first estimate the approximate relationship between fund size and performance using a portfolio approach.

3.1 Time-Series Portfolio Approach

Since we are interested in the relationship between fund size and performance, we sort mutual funds at the beginning of each month based on the quintile rankings of their previous-month TNA. At the end of each quarter, we divide all sample funds into quintiles based on their TNA of the previous quarter. Then, we rebalance these portfolios each quarter and we compute equal-weighted monthly returns for each quintile.

We then track these five portfolios for one month and use the entire time series of their past twelve-monthly net returns to calculate the loadings to the various risk factors (Beta Market,[30] SMB, HML, MOM) for each of these five portfolios. For each month, each mutual fund inherits the loadings of the one of these five portfolios that it belongs to.[31] Indeed, a very conservative way to deal with the first worry about heterogeneity in fund styles is to adjust for fund performance by various benchmarks (Chen et al., 2004). Since funds may have different styles, we adjust for such heterogeneity by utilizing various performance benchmarks that account for the possibility that they load differently on small cap stock, value stock, and price momentum strategies Therefore, we evaluate the performance of these portfolios by using several models, to be specific, we run the tests by considering both one- and multi-factor models. Specifically, we use the Capital Asset Pricing Model (CAPM) of Sharpe (1964).

$$R_{it} - R_{ft} = \alpha_i + b_i(R_{Mt} - R_{ft}) + e_{it} \tag{1}$$

where $R_{i,t}$ is the (net fund) return on one of our five fund-size sorted mutual fund portfolios in month t in excess of the one-month T-bill return, α_i is the excess return of that portfolio, β_i is the loading on the market portfolio, and $\varepsilon_{i,t}$ stands for a generic error term that is uncorrelated with all other independent variables.

Moreover, we also consider returns adjusted using the Fama and French (1993) three-factor model and this model augmented with the momentum factor of Jegadeesh and Titman (1993), which has been shown in various contexts to provide explanatory power for the observed cross-sectional variation in fund performance (see, e.g., Carhart, 1997).

[30] Beta Market here represents the Beta coefficient in the four factor Model (BETA MOM).

[31] https://www.jstor.org/stable/3592823?seq=1#metadata_info_tab_contents.

In a similar manner as we consider for CAPM model above, we use alpha, the intercept term in the regression of fund portfolio returns on risk factors, as the performance measure. Note that the CAPM model and the Fama-French three-factor model are both nested in the Carhart four-factor model.

$$R_{it} - R_{ft} = \alpha_i + b_i(R_{Mt} - R_{ft}) + s_i SMB_t + h_i HML_t + e_{it} \tag{2}$$

$$R_{it} - R_{ft} = \alpha_i + b_i(R_{Mt} - R_{ft}) + s_i SMB_t + h_i HML_t + m_i MOM_t + e_{it} \tag{3}$$

where R_{it} is the (net fund) return on one of our five size-sorted mutual fund portfolios in month t in excess of the one-month T-bill return, α_i is the excess return, b_i's are loadings on the various portfolios, and e_{it} stands for a generic error term that is uncorrelated with all other independent variables. Returns to SMB (small stocks minus large stocks) and HML (high book-to market stocks minus low book-to-market stocks) portfolios, and the returns to price momentum portfolio MOM (a portfolio that is long stocks that are past twelve-month winners and short stocks that are past twelve-month losers and hold for one month) are considered.

Table 3 shows loadings calculated using the 4-Factor Model for Europe Equity sample according to each size quintile. We see that Beta Mom takes the highest value in the first fund size quintile in every sample, except GROWTH style funds with the highest coefficient of Beta Mom in fifth fund size quintile (1.125). In general, all funds tend to have higher loadings on SMB Mom and HML Mom, where VALUE style funds tend to load a bit more on HML (the loading on HML in first quintile is 0.465 while the corresponding loading for these funds in fifth quintile is 0.338). The loading on SMB is the highest for SMALL caps funds (1.039 in first quintile and 0.464 in fifth quintile) and GROWTH style funds (0.314 in first quintile and 0.845 in fifth quintile). LARGE, BLEND and SMALL funds tend to load more on Momentum in fifth quintile.

Table 4 shows loadings calculated using the 4-Factor Model for US Equity sample. We see that Beta Mom takes the highest value in the first fund size quintile. Funds of all equity samples tend to have negative loadings on HML Mom, except positive values of the coefficient for VALUE style from first to fourth fund size quintiles. The loading on SMB is the highest in the fifth quintile for all samples of equities, except SMALL cap sample (0.616 in first quintile and 0.514 in fifth quintile). All samples

Table 3 Loadings calculated using the 4-factor model. EUROPE EQUITY

Fund Size Quintile	*Beta MOM*	*HML MOM*	*Momentum*	*SMB MOM*	R *quad*
Large					
1.	0.917	0.305	0.076	0.183	0.749
2.	0.731	0.157	0.021	0.176	0.706
3.	0.495	0.099	−0.016	0.130	0.593
4.	0.518	0.040	−0.011	0.176	0.630
5.	0.601	0.106	0.158	0.236	0.583
Blend					
1.	0.901	0.285	0.074	0.165	0.750
2.	0.722	0.146	0.015	0.181	0.705
3.	0.470	0.084	−0.029	0.114	0.593
4.	0.526	0.047	−0.008	0.209	0.645
5.	0.592	0.133	0.148	0.219	0.574
Small					
1.	1.076	0.238	0.081	1.039	0.759
2.	0.836	0.181	0.104	0.795	0.713
3.	0.611	0.058	0.018	0.578	0.605
4.	0.603	0.039	0.007	0.608	0.644
5.	0.498	0.112	0.139	0.464	0.538
Value					
1.	0.981	0.465	−0.027	0.261	0.761
2.	0.931	0.469	−0.052	0.178	0.771
3.	0.559	0.267	−0.023	0.115	0.632
4.	0.700	0.283	−0.048	0.179	0.669
5.	0.725	0.338	0.009	0.396	0.670
Growth					
1.	0.900	0.039	0.090	0.314	0.708
2.	0.525	0.084	0.078	0.165	0.632
3.	0.724	−0.026	0.020	0.211	0.617
4.	0.758	−0.414	−0.113	0.419	0.688
5.	1.125	−1.845	−0.586	0.845	0.675

The four-factor model is given by: $R_{it} - R_{ft} = \alpha_i + b_i(R_{Mt} - R_{ft}) + s_i SMB_t + h_i HML_t + m_i MOM_t + e_{it}$. Returns to SMB (small stocks minus large stocks) and HML (high book-to market stocks minus low book-to-market stocks) portfolios, and the returns to price momentum portfolio MOM (a portfolio that is long stocks that are past twelve-month winners and short stocks that are past twelve-month losers and hold for one month) are considered. MOM_t is the risk factor mimicking portfolio for capturing Jegadeesh and Titman (1993) one-year momentum anomaly in the stock holdings of the mutual funds. The momentum factor, MOM_t, is a measure of difference between the returns on past high-performing versus past poor-performing stocks and hence MOM_t reflects a fund's sensitivity to pursuing a zero-investment strategy of purchasing past outperforming 'momentum' stocks and short-selling stocks with low historical returns

Table 4 Loadings calculated using the 4-factor model. US EQUITY

Fund Size Quintile	*Beta MOM*	*HML MOM*	*Momentum*	*SMB MOM*	*R quad*
Large					
1.	0.768	−0.159	−0.059	0.041	0.787
2.	0.547	−0.058	−0.032	0.015	0.685
3.	0.437	−0.038	−0.031	0.027	0.586
4.	0.368	−0.070	−0.058	0.001	0.546
5.	0.305	−0.088	−0.051	0.065	0.494
Blend					
1.	0.850	−0.070	−0.028	−0.021	0.831
2.	0.642	−0.046	−0.027	−0.011	0.712
3.	0.342	−0.037	−0.038	0.001	0.538
4.	0.185	0.033	−0.015	−0.045	0.434
5.	0.197	−0.031	−0.014	0.033	0.453
Small					
1.	0.899	−0.045	−0.054	0.616	0.873
2.	0.409	−0.014	−0.004	0.297	0.615
3.	0.534	−0.052	−0.059	0.353	0.599
4.	0.374	0.002	0.003	0.319	0.541
5.	0.646	−0.037	0.012	0.514	0.684
Value					
1.	0.894	0.043	−0.050	0.027	0.869
2.	0.511	0.058	−0.034	0.017	0.674
3.	0.540	0.082	−0.067	−0.009	0.604
4.	0.701	0.056	−0.091	0.035	0.749
5.	0.608	−0.002	−0.178	0.123	0.685
Growth					
1.	0.562	−0.212	−0.045	0.000	0.660
2.	0.565	−0.125	−0.006	−0.073	0.693
3.	0.434	−0.091	−0.026	0.012	0.601
4.	0.328	−0.118	−0.059	−0.038	0.502
5.	0.230	−0.117	−0.016	0.062	0.479

The four-factor model is given by: $R_{it} - R_{ft} = \alpha_i + b_i(R_{Mt} - R_{ft}) + s_i SMB_t + h_i HML_t + m_i MOM_t + e_{it}$. Returns to SMB (small stocks minus large stocks) and HML (high book-to market stocks minus low book-to-market stocks) portfolios, and the returns to price momentum portfolio MOM (a portfolio that is long stocks that are past twelve-month winners and short stocks that are past twelve-month losers and hold for one month) are considered. MOM_t is the risk factor mimicking portfolio for capturing Jegadeesh and Titman (1993) one-year momentum anomaly in the stock holdings of the mutual funds. The momentum factor, MOM_t, is a measure of difference between the returns on past high-performing versus past poor-performing stocks and hence MOM_t reflects a fund's sensitivity to pursuing a zero-investment strategy of purchasing past outperforming 'momentum' stocks and short-selling stocks with low historical returns of US equities tend to load negatively on Momentum in the majority of fund size quintiles.

In line with Yan (2008), in each panel of Tables 5 and 6,[32] single and multifactor alphas, the CAPM alpha, the Fama French three-factor alpha, the Carhart four-factor alpha are reported.

Table 5 demonstrates results for performance measure according to fund size for US sample. When using the CAPM model, we find that funds in first quintile outperform funds in the fifth quintile. There is a mix of positive and negative alphas across quintile for all equity samples, except the growth style funds that seem to outperform the market across all the quintiles. In Fama-French model, all equity funds outperform in the first quintile, however, we observe the highest positive alphas across all quintiles for small cap funds. In Carhart alpha model, funds in first quintile continue to outperform, and we do not observe any dramatic change of the alpha coefficient, when adding factors from Carhart model. Small cap funds continue to show outperformance over the market in all fund size quintiles.

Figure 1 shows performance measure according to fund size for US sample, where alpha takes the highest value of the coefficient in the first fund size quintile and funds underperform dramatically in the second fund size quintile.

Table 6 shows results for performance measure according to fund size for EU sample. In CAPM model, we find alpha to be positive almost in all equity samples. All funds tend to outperform in the first fund size quintile, except GROWTH style that shows dramatic increase of alpha in fifth quintile. We observe the highest values of alpha coefficients for SMALL caps and for GROWTH style funds across all funds size quintiles. When using Fama-French model, funds in first and second quintiles outperform funds from the largest quintiles. In this model, the alpha coefficients are the highest among alphas from all the performance models, especially in first quintile for SMALL caps (0.0050) and for GROWTH style funds (0.0045). In Carhart model, the majority of funds tend to outperform in the first fund size quintile (with the highest value of alpha 0.0032 for SMALL caps and 0.0027 for GROWTH style funds), however, for VALUE style funds we observe the highest alphas in the second fund size

[32] Yan, X. (2008). Liquidity, investment style, and the relation between fund size and fund performance. *Journal of Financial and Quantitative Analysis*, 741–767.

Table 5 US sample—performance measure according to fund size

Fund Size Quintile	*CAPM ALPHA*	*FAMA FRENCH ALPHA*	*CARHART ALPHA*
Large			
1.	0.0017	0.0011	0.0011
2.	−0.0003	−0.0003	−0.0002
3.	0.0000	−0.0001	0.0000
4.	−0.0004	−0.0003	−0.0001
5.	0.0000	0.0001	0.0001
Blend			
1.	0.0003	0.0000	0.0001
2.	−0.0010	−0.0013	−0.0012
3.	−0.0006	−0.0008	−0.0007
4.	0.0008	0.0004	0.0003
5.	−0.0009	−0.0011	−0.0012
Small			
1.	0.0019	0.0021	0.0021
2.	−0.0001	0.0002	0.0002
3.	0.0004	0.0015	0.0016
4.	−0.0007	0.0008	0.0007
5.	−0.0005	0.0006	0.0003
Value			
1.	0.0003	0.0005	0.0005
2.	−0.0005	−0.0006	−0.0007
3.	−0.0008	−0.0002	0.0001
4.	−0.0011	−0.0001	0.0001
5.	−0.0014	0.0000	0.0004
Growth			
1.	0.0023	0.0019	0.0021
2.	0.0006	0.0003	0.0003
3.	0.0005	0.0002	0.0004
4.	0.0001	−0.0002	0.0001
5.	0.0004	0.0001	−0.0001

CAPM comes by running the following time-series regression: $R_{i,t} - R_{f,t} = \alpha_i + \beta_i (R_{m.t} - R_{f,t}) + \mu_{i,t}$, where the $R_{m.t}$ and R_f are the market return and the risk-free rate respectively. The Fama French model reads: $R_{it} - R_{ft} = \alpha_i + b_i (R_{Mt} - R_{ft}) + s_i SMB_t + h_i HML_t + e_{it}$, *where* R_{it} is the return on fund i for month t, R_{ft} is the risk-free rate and R_{Mt} is the market return over the same period, *SMBt* and *HMLt* are the Fama and French (1993) size and book-to-market factors. *SMBt* = the realization on the capitalization factor (small-cap return minus large cap return) for month t; *HMLt* = the realization on the value factor (value return minus growth return) for month t e_{it}= an error term corresponding to the regression residuals. The four-factor model is given by: $R_{it} - R_{ft} = \alpha_i + b_i (R_{Mt} - R_{ft}) + s_i SMB_t + h_i HML_t + m_i MOM_t + e_{it}$. MOM_t is the risk factor mimicking portfolio for capturing Jegadeesh and Titman (1993) one-year momentum anomaly in the stock holdings of the mutual funds. The momentum factor, MOM_t, is a measure of difference between the returns on past high-performing versus past poor-performing stocks and hence MOM_t reflects a fund's sensitivity to pursuing a zero-investment strategy of purchasing past outperforming 'momentum' stocks and short-selling stocks with low historical returns

Table 6 Europe sample—performance measure according to fund size

Fund Size Quintile	*CAPM ALPHA*	*FAMA FRENCH ALPHA*	*CARHART ALPHA*
Large			
1.	0.0019	0.0038	0.0020
2.	0.0013	0.0027	0.0017
3.	0.0005	0.0016	0.0011
4.	0.0001	0.0010	0.0001
5.	0.0013	0.0016	0.0005
Blend			
1.	0.0017	0.0036	0.0018
2.	0.0013	0.0027	0.0017
3.	0.0003	0.0013	0.0008
4.	0.0001	0.0010	0.0000
5.	0.0009	0.0012	0.0002
Small			
1.	0.0045	0.0050	0.0032
2.	0.0042	0.0048	0.0026
3.	0.0024	0.0028	0.0019
4.	0.0011	0.0014	0.0003
5.	0.0011	0.0018	0.0008
Value			
1.	0.0004	0.0025	0.0017
2.	0.0007	0.0032	0.0021
3.	−0.0002	0.0013	0.0007
4.	−0.0004	0.0018	0.0011
5.	−0.0004	0.0004	−0.0008
Growth			
1.	0.0035	0.0045	0.0027
2.	0.0027	0.0031	0.0017
3.	0.0012	0.0021	0.0010
4.	0.0036	0.0011	−0.0009
5.	0.0153	0.0083	0.0044

CAPM comes by running the following time-series regression: $R_{i,t} - R_{f,t} = \alpha_i + \beta_i (R_{m.t} - R_{f,t}) + \mu_{i,t}$, where the $R_{m.t}$ and R_f are the market return and the risk-free rate respectively. The Fama French model reads: $R_{it} - R_{ft} = \alpha_i + b_i (R_{Mt} - R_{ft}) + s_i SMB_t + h_i HML_t + e_{it}$, *where* R_{it} is the return on fund i for month t, *Rft* is the risk-free rate and *RMt* is the market return over the same period, SMBt and HMLt are the Fama and French (1993) size and book-to-market factors. *SMBt* = the realization on the capitalization factor (small-cap return minus large cap return) for month t; *HMLt* = the realization on the value factor (value return minus growth return) for month t e_{it}= an error term corresponding to the regression residuals. The four-factor model is given by: $R_{it} - R_{ft} = \alpha_i + b_i (R_{Mt} - R_{ft}) + s_i SMB_t + h_i HML_t + m_i MOM_t + e_{it}$. MOM_t is the risk factor mimicking portfolio for capturing Jegadeesh and Titman (1993) one-year momentum anomaly in the stock holdings of the mutual funds. The momentum factor, MOM_t, is a measure of difference between the returns on past high-performing versus past poor-performing stocks and hence MOM_t reflects a fund's sensitivity to pursuing a zero-investment strategy of purchasing past outperforming 'momentum' stocks and short-selling stocks with low historical returns

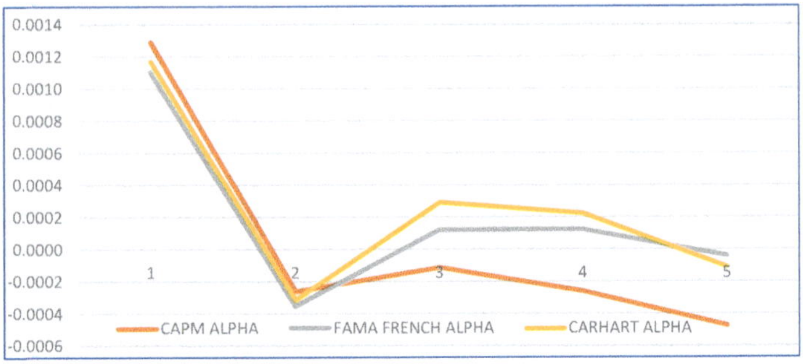

Fig. 1 US sample—performance measure according to fund size (CAPM comes by running the following time-series regression: $R_{i,t} - R_{f,t} = \alpha_i + \beta_i(R_{m.t} - R_{f,t}) + \mu_{i,t}$, where the $R_{m.t}$ and R_f are the market return and the risk-free rate respectively. The Fama French model reads: $R_{it} - R_{ft} = \alpha_i + b_i(R_{Mt} - R_{ft}) + s_i SMB_t + h_i HML_t + e_{it}$, *where Rit* is the return on fund i for month t, Rft is the risk-free rate and RMt is the market return over the same period, SMBt and HMLt are the Fama and French (1993) size and book-to-market factors. *SMBt* = the realization on the capitalization factor (small-cap return minus large cap return) for month t; *HMLt* = the realization on the value factor (value return minus growth return) for month t e_{it}= an error term corresponding to the regression residuals. The four-factor model is given by: $R_{it} - R_{ft} = \alpha_i + b_i(R_{Mt} - R_{ft}) + s_i SMB_t + h_i HML_t + m_i MOM_t + e_{it}$. MOM_t is the risk factor mimicking portfolio for capturing Jegadeesh and Titman (1993) one-year momentum anomaly in the stock holdings of the mutual funds. The momentum factor, MOM_t, is a measure of difference between the returns on past high-performing versus past poor-performing stocks and hence MOM_t reflects a fund's sensitivity to pursuing a zero-investment strategy of purchasing past outperforming 'momentum' stocks and short-selling stocks with low historical returns)

quintile (0.0021) and for GROWTH style funds—in the fifth fund size quintile (0.0044).

Figure 2 shows performance measure according to fund size for EU sample, where alpha takes the highest value of the coefficient in the first fund size quintile in Fama-French and Carhart model, but the highest in fifth fund size quintile, when considering the CAPM model. Even though it is still positive, we observe decrease in fund performance in fourth quintile with the worst alpha coefficient related to Carhart model.

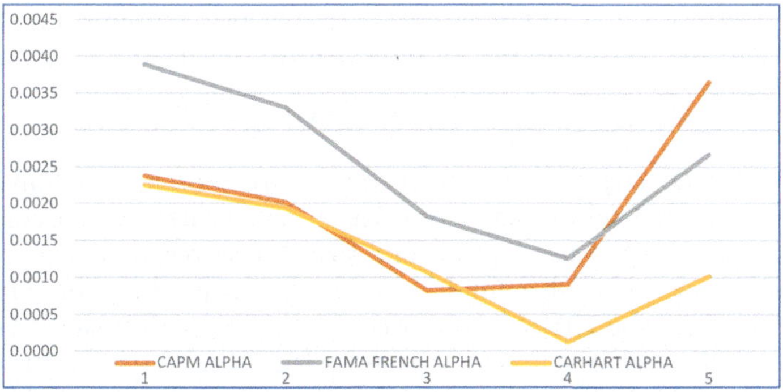

Fig. 2 EUROPE sample—performance measure according to fund size (CAPM comes by running the following time-series regression: $R_{i,t} - R_{f,t} = \alpha_i + \beta_i(R_{m.t} - R_{f,t}) + \mu_{i,t}$, where the $R_{m.t}$ and R_f are the market return and the risk-free rate respectively. The Fama French model reads: $R_{it} - R_{ft} = \alpha_i + b_i(R_{Mt} - R_{ft}) + s_i SMB_t + h_i HML_t + e_{it}$, *where Rit* is the return on fund i for month t, *Rft* is the risk-free rate and *RMt* is the market return over the same period, *SMBt* and *HMLt* are the Fama and French (1993) size and book-to-market factors. *SM t* = the realization on the capitalization factor (small-cap return minus large cap return) for month t; *HMLt* = the realization on the value factor (value return minus growth return) for month t e_{it}= an error term corresponding to the regression residuals. The four-factor model is given by: $R_{it} - R_{ft} = \alpha_i + b_i(R_{Mt} - R_{ft}) + s_i SMB_t + h_i HML_t + m_i MOM_t + e_{it}$. MOM_t is the risk factor mimicking portfolio for capturing Jegadeesh and Titman (1993) one-year momentum anomaly in the stock holdings of the mutual funds. The momentum factor, MOM_t, is a measure of difference between the returns on past high-performing versus past poor-performing stocks and hence MOM_t reflects a fund's sensitivity to pursuing a zero-investment strategy of purchasing past outperforming 'momentum' stocks and short-selling stocks with low historical returns)

3.2 *Relationship Between Fund Size and Performance: Model Specification in Regression Analysis*

To deal with the concern related to firm specific effect about the correlation of fund size with other fund characteristics, we analyze the effect of past fund size on performance in the regression framework proposed by Chen et al. (2004), where we can control for the effects of other fund characteristics on performance. As argued by Yan (2008) and Carhart (1997), one of the advantages of the portfolio regression approach is that it does not suffer too much from survivor bias and look-ahead bias. Specifically, the regression specification that we utilize is:

$$FUNDRET_{i,t} = \mu + \phi LOGTNA_{i,t-1} + \gamma X_{i,t-1} + \varepsilon_{i,t} \quad (4)$$

where $FUNDRET_{i,t}$ is the return (either gross or net) of fund i in month t adjusted by various performance benchmarks, μ is a constant, $LOGTNA_{i,t-1}$ is the measure of fund size. Moreover, fund size may be correlated with such other fund characteristics as fund age or turnover, and it may be these characteristics that are driving performance. Hence, we regress the various adjusted returns on lagged fund size (as measured by the log of total net assets under management), and also include in the regressions a host of other observable fund characteristics. To be specific we consider $X_{i,t-1}$ representing a set of control variables (in month $t-1$) that includes: Volatility, R-Squared, Active measure, Age, Expense ratio, past-month fund flows, and past-month returns in terms of Multifactor Alpha.[33] Here, $\varepsilon_{i,t}$ again stands for a generic error term that is uncorrelated with all other independent variables. The coefficient of interest is φ, which captures the relationship between fund size and fund performance, controlling for other fund characteristics. γ is the vector of loadings on the control variables.

$FUNDRET_{i,t}$ measures the fund performance as computed by several multifactor models. We use the Carhart factor model. The Carhart (1997) four-factor model regression is given by:

$$\begin{aligned} R_{it} - R_{ft} = a_i + \beta_i(R_{mt} - R_{ft}) + s_i(SMB_t) + h_i(HML_t) \\ + p_i(MOM_t) + \varepsilon_{it} \quad (5) \end{aligned}$$

where:

R_{it} is the expected return on an investment;
R_{ft} is the expected return on risk-free assets;
R_{mt} is the expected return on the market;
$R_{it} - R_{ft}$ is the expected risk premium of the investment.
$R_{mt} - R_{ft}$ is the expected market risk premium;

In this model, SMB, small minus big, represents variances in stock returns that are due to the size factor or factors systematically related to

[33] Chen, J., Hong, H., Huang, M., & Kubik, J. D. (2004). Does fund size erode mutual fund performance? The role of liquidity and organization. *American Economic Review, 94*(5), 1276–1302.

size. HML, high minus low, captures variances in stock returns that are due to the difference in return between the portfolio with high book-to-market stocks and the portfolio with low book-to-market stocks. β_i is the investment's sensitivity to the market factor, and a_i is the intercept or the Jensen index interpreted as estimated excess return on the investment (i.e. risk-adjusted performance of the investment). In the Carhart (1997) four factor model, (MOM_t) is the difference in return between the portfolio with the past 12-month winners and the portfolio with the past 12-month losers (momentum anomaly).

When we deal with fixed Income funds, we consider the following model:

$$\begin{aligned} r_{p,t} = \alpha_p^{BOND} &+ \beta_{1,p} MKTRF_t^{Bond} + \beta_{2,t} MKTRF_t^{Equity} \\ &+ \beta_{3,p} DEFAULT_t + \beta_{4,p} TERM_t + \varepsilon_{p,t} \end{aligned} \tag{6}$$

where $r_{p,t}$ is the monthly return on a portfolio of funds in excess of the one-month T-bill rate; $MKTRF_t^{Bond}$ is the Local (European or Us) Total Bond Market Index return in excess of the one-month T-bill rate. $MKTRF_t^{Equity}$ is the (European) U.S. equity market returns in excess of the one-month T-bill rate and is included to control for potential equity market bias.[34] $DEFAULT$ is the difference in return between investment grade corporate bonds and government bonds (10-year Treasury Constant Maturity Yield); $TERM_t$ is the difference in return between long-term (30-year Treasury Constant Maturity Yield) and short-term government bonds (one-year Treasury Constant Maturity Yield). The rates for investment grade corporate bonds and for long- and short-term government bond rates are from the Federal Reserve's website.[35] All of the alphas are estimated on a rolling basis by using weekly returns within the window of 12 months.

[34] Untabulated tests show that Including $MKTRF_t^{Equity}$ clearly improves the explanatory powers of the factor model.

[35] http://www.federalreserve.gov/releases/h15/data.htm.

3.3 *Relationship Between Fund Size and Performance: Empirical Results*

Table 7 shows determinants of performance according to fund size for US bond sample. The sample consists of funds from fund size quintiles to one to five. Size is 10% statistically significant and positive in first fund size quintile. Coefficients coupled to the rest of quintiles are all not statistically significant. This result shows that the relationship between performance and size is valid only for larger funds.

With respect to the other control variables, we found statistically significant reaction with negative sign and at 10% level for expense ratio in fourth fund size quintile. There is no statistically significant reaction for age and flows variables. Alpha bond in $t - 1$ is strongly statistically significant at 1% level with positive sign in all fund size quintiles. Volatility effects performance across all fund size quintiles with positive statistically significant sign, except no effect in fifth fund size quintile. R Squared is positive and statistically significant at 10% level in third and fifth fund size quintile. Active share causes positive statistically significant reaction in first and third fund size quintiles.

Table 8 shows determinants of performance according to fund size for EU bond sample. The size variable shows positive and 5% statistically significant reaction in first quintile. Coefficients coupled to the rest of quintiles are all not statistically significant. This result shows, as we already observed for the US bond fund sample, that the relationship between performance and size is valid only for larger funds.

With respect to the other control variables, we found negative statistically significant reaction of performance to fund age in third and fifth fund size quintiles (10 and 5% respectively). However, the net expense ratio demonstrates positive statistically significant effect on performance in third and fourth fund size quintiles. The reaction to fund flows is negative at 5% statistically significant level. Alpha bond in $t - 1$ is strongly statistically significant at 1% level with positive sign in all fund size quintiles. The effect of volatility on fund performance is positive with 1 and 10% statistically significant level in first and third fund size quintiles. R Squared is negative at 1% statistically significant level in first, second and third fund size quintiles. Active share is negative and statistically significant in first, second and fourth fund size quintiles.

Table 9 shows determinants of performance according to fund size for US Equity sample. Size is positive and statistically significant at 1%

Table 7 Determinants of performance according to fund size—BOND US

	QUINTILE 1	*QUINTILE 2*	*QUINTILE 3*	*QUINTILE 4*	*QUINTILE 5*
AGE	−0.6163	−0.9022	10.0432	−13.9747	−9.2495
	(18.4186)	(16.0351)	(15.8886)	(19.1863)	(30.3252)
EXPENSE	25.3047	15.8087	16.5951	−31.6556*	33.3147
	(16.2662)	(13.9466)	(13.9684)	(16.8990)	(41.0328)
FLOWS	134.3060	−124.8738	−83.7145	−413.3394	872.8452
	(96.3275)	(222.6829)	(441.0465)	(1102.7284)	(932.5130)
SIZE	11.1828*	2.6293	−3.2968	6.1737	0.8463
	(6.1046)	(6.0672)	(6.7213)	(7.4852)	(9.3390)
$\alpha_p^{BOND}t-1$	75.0587***	76.3967***	78.2653***	77.8715***	73.0075***
	(1.2918)	(1.1935)	(1.4759)	(2.1057)	(4.1558)
VOLATILITY	33.7474***	23.2420**	48.9942***	38.4153***	−56.1984
	(9.4307)	(10.9471)	(12.3458)	(5.1294)	(34.0600)
R SQUARED	1.9728	0.9138	2.4975*	3.9984	10.0427*
	(1.4064)	(1.2708)	(1.4358)	(3.0704)	(5.4515)
ACTIVE	31.6287**	11.3433	27.7623*	35.5650	78.2724
	(15.2859)	(14.3061)	(16.0518)	(26.1108)	(50.4819)
CONS	−436.4693**	−104.3009	−187.7688	−378.8212	−691.9362
	(171.7757)	(148.3368)	(178.1577)	(248.1826)	(472.2133)
N	7546	7522	7316	7009	7781

Standard errors in parentheses $^{*}p < 0.10$, $^{**}p < 0.05$, $^{***}p < 0.01$

This table reports the results of the panel regressions of mutual fund performance on fund characteristics. Portfolio performance is evaluated based on simple Return and portfolio alpha according to the following model: $r_{p,t} = \alpha_p^{BOND} + \beta_{1,p}MKTRF_t^{Bond} + \beta_{2,t}MKTRF_t^{Equity} + \beta_{3,p}DEFAULT_t + \beta_{4,p}TERM_t + \varepsilon_{p,t}$; where $r_{p,t}$ is the monthly return on a portfolio of funds in excess of the one-month T-bill rate; $MKTRF_t^{Bond}$ is the Local (European or Us) Total Bond Market Index return in excess of the one-month T-bill rate. $MKTRF_t^{Equity}$ is the (European) U.S. equity market return in excess of the one-month T-bill rate and is included to control for potential equity market bias $DEFAULT$ is the difference in return between investment grade corporate bonds and government bonds (10-year Treasury Constant Maturity Yield); $TERM_t$ is the difference in return between long-term (30-year Treasury Constant Maturity Yield) and short-term goverment bonds (one-year Treasury Constant Maturity Yield). AGE is defined as the number of months from the fund's inception. $Flow_{i,t-1}$ is the normalized monthly net flow of fund i in month $t-1$. SIZE is the logarithm of the total net assets of fund i in period $t-1$ $\log(TNA)_{i,t-1}$. $ExpenseRatio_{i,t-1}$, is the net expense ratio. $Volatility_{j,t}$ is the volatility of monthly returns (Standard Deviation over a 52 weeks rolling estimation). According to Bliss et al. (2008) we also added the CAPM $Rsquare_{j,t-1}$ measure as a control variable. $ActiveShare_{i,t-1}$ is a measure of active management by the fund as defined by Cremers and Petajisto (2009) and Miller et al. (2007). The sample period is from December 2006 to December 2019. The t-statistics are based on standard errors clustered by both fund and time. *, **, and ***, respectively, denote significance at the 10, 5, and 1% levels

Table 8 Determinants of performance according to fund size—BOND EUROPE

	QUINTILE 1	*QUINTILE 2*	*QUINTILE 3*	*QUINTILE 4*	*QUINTILE 5*
AGE	14.7250	12.2131	−34.1853*	−19.1817*	−32.7525**
	(31.6634)	(22.2562)	(18.0787)	(11.4418)	(12.6232)
EXPENSE	−36.0191	18.7060	44.0317*	29.6804**	26.9319
	(22.3427)	(20.9317)	(22.3386)	(13.0573)	(18.1101)
FLOWS	−51.6435**	−21.5719	24.9257	−26.5586	168.9363
	(19.8743)	(30.3225)	(68.0713)	(120.8113)	(282.6469)
SIZE	32.8777**	4.1749	6.1340	−3.9125	0.6771
	(13.5465)	(6.3582)	(12.2410)	(6.7908)	(4.1531)
$\alpha_p^{BOND}{}_{t} - 1$	75.6756***	78.5196***	70.2792***	73.1418***	73.1854***
	(2.8975)	(2.0186)	(4.6069)	(2.7586)	(2.5953)
VOLATILITY	151.7240***	26.1402	79.1824*	11.2865	31.6620
	(36.8433)	(36.7611)	(42.3292)	(28.2374)	(30.2527)
R SQUARED	−10.4455***	−11.7676***	−2.0536	−4.4571***	0.1500
	(2.1708)	(2.2823)	(1.9243)	(1.3837)	(2.2676)
ACTIVE	−92.4482***	−131.6790***	5.1201	−39.2517*	6.2705

	QUINTILE 1	*QUINTILE 2*	*QUINTILE 3*	*QUINTILE 4*	*QUINTILE 5*
	(24.2264)	(28.8838)	(20.7294)	(20.3836)	(26.8774)
CONS	44.7682	1,246.5828***	−143.8374	438.0637**	−78.7816
	(352.6242)	(320.2693)	(274.0449)	(191.2737)	(238.4907)
N	6546	6522	6316	6009	6781

Standard errors in parentheses $^{*}p < 0.10$, $^{**}p < 0.05$, $^{***}p < 0.01$
This table reports the results of the panel regressions of mutual fund performance on fund characteristics. Portfolio performance is evaluated based on simple Return and portfolio alpha according to the following model: $r_{p,t} = \alpha_p^{BOND} + \beta_{1,p} MKTRF_t^{Bond} + \beta_{2,t} MKTRF_t^{Equity} + \beta_{3,p} DEFAULT_t + \beta_{4,p} TERM_t + \varepsilon_{p,t}$; where $r_{p,t}$ is the monthly return on a portfolio of funds in excess of the one-month T-bill rate; $MKTRF_t^{Bond}$ is the Local (European or Us) Total Bond Market Index return in excess of the one-month T-bill rate. $MKTRF_t^{Equity}$ is the (European) U.S. equity market return in excess of the one-month T-bill rate and is included to control for potential equity market bias $DEFAULT$ is the difference in return between investment grade corporate bonds and government bonds (10-year Treasury Constant Maturity Yield); $TERM_t$ is the difference in return between long-term (30-year Treasury Constant Maturity Yield) and short-term goverment bonds (one-year Treasury Constant Maturity Yield). AGE is defined as the number of months from the fund's inception. $\text{Flow}_{i,t-1}$ is the normalized monthly net flow of fund i in month $t - 1$. SIZE is the logarithm of the total net assets of fund i in period $t - 1$ $\log(\text{TNA})_{i,t-1}$. $\text{ExpenseRatio}_{i,t-1}$, is the net expense ratio. $\text{Volatility}_{j,t}$ is the volatility of monthly returns (Standard Deviation over a 52 weeks rolling estimation). According to Bliss et al. (2008) we also added the CAPM $\text{Rsquare}_{j,t-1}$ measure as a control variable. $\text{ActiveShare}_{i,t-1}$ is a measure of active management by the fund as defined by Cremers and Petajisto (2009) and Miller et al. (2007). The sample period is from December 2006 to December 2019. The t-statistics are based on standard errors clustered by both fund and time. *, **, and ***, respectively, denote significance at the 10, 5, and 1% levels

Table 9 Determinants of performance according to fund size—EQUITY US

	Quintile 1	*Quintile 2*	*Quintile 3*	*Quintile 4*	*Quintile 5*
AGE	−0.0177**	−0.0161**	−0.0162**	0.0080	0.0075
	(0.0086)	(0.0079)	(0.0074)	(0.0077)	(0.0105)
EXPENSE	−0.0145***	−0.0110***	−0.0101**	−0.0032	−0.0086
	(0.0040)	(0.0032)	(0.0043)	(0.0048)	(0.0085)
FLOWS	1.1548***	0.8894*	3.8787***	−1.8315	9.7646
	(0.2159)	(0.4602)	(1.0122)	(2.3518)	(6.6308)
SIZE	0.0019	0.0059***	−0.0015	0.0002	0.0010
	(0.0022)	(0.0020)	(0.0016)	(0.0014)	(0.0021)
$\alpha_p^{CAR}{}_{t} - 1$	79.3965***	79.8636***	80.0717***	80.9624***	77.6568***
	(0.6107)	(0.6848)	(0.7526)	(1.0737)	(2.1074)
VOLATILITY	0.4953**	0.2842**	0.3848	0.0434***	0.0320
	(0.2262)	(0.1343)	(0.2417)	(0.0068)	(0.7002)
R SQUARED	−0.0554	−0.0441	−0.0335	0.1147**	0.1809
	(0.0351)	(0.0371)	(0.0434)	(0.0444)	(0.1123)
ACTIVE	−0.0724*	−0.0694	−0.0245	0.1285**	0.1734
	(0.0419)	(0.0457)	(0.0557)	(0.0583)	(0.1196)
CONS	0.0449	−0.0353	0.0671	−0.1347**	−0.2105**
	(0.0548)	(0.0557)	(0.0576)	(0.0549)	(0.1035)

	Quintile 1	*Quintile 2*	*Quintile 3*	*Quintile 4*	*Quintile 5*
N	16,646	16,422	16,417	16,111	16,872

Standard errors in parentheses $^{*}p < 0.10$, $^{**}p < 0.05$, $^{***}p < 0.01$

This table reports the results of the panel regressions of mutual fund performance on fund characteristics. Portfolio performance is evaluated based on Carhart or Momentum Four Factor alpha. AGE is defined as the number of months from the fund's inception. $\text{Flow}_{i,t-1}$ is the normalized monthly net flow of fund i in month $t - 1$. SIZE is the logarithm of the total net assets of fund i in period $t - 1$ $\log(\text{TNA})_{i,t-1}$; $\text{ExpenseRatio}_{i,t-1}$, is the net expense ratio. $\text{Volatility}_{j,t}$ is the volatility of monthly returns (Standard Deviation over a 52 weeks rolling estimation). According to Bliss et al. (2008) we also added the CAPM $\text{Rsquare}_{j,t-1}$ measure as a control variable. $\text{ActiveShare}_{i,t-1}$ is a measure of active management by the fund as defined by Cremers and Petajisto (2009) and Miller et al. (2007). The sample period is from December 2006 to December 2019. The crisis period range between June 2007 and December 2010. The t-statistics are based on standard errors clustered by both fund and time. *, **, and ***, respectively, denote significance at the 10, 5, and 1% levels level in the second fund size quintile. This evidence confirms our pervious findings that is the relationship between performance and size is valid on average, only for funds with above median size (that is for funds with size coupled to the first three quintiles).

We found negative statistically significant reaction at 5% level for Age in first, second and third fund size quintiles. Net expense ratio is negative and statistically significant at 1% level in first, second and third fund size quintile. Flows are positive and statistically significant from one to three fund size quintiles. Alpha for equity sample in $t - 1$ is positive with strong statistically significant reaction at 1% level in all fund size quintiles. Volatility effect on performance is positive and statistically significant in first, second and fourth fund size quintiles. R Squared is positive at 5% statistically significant level in fourth fund size quintile. Active share is negative at 10% statistically significant level in first fund size quintile and negative at 5% statistically significant level in fourth fund size quintile.

Table 10 shows determinants of performance according to fund size for Europe Equity sample. There is no statistically significant reaction for Age variable. Size variable is 10% statistically significant with positive sign only in third fund size quintile. For this group we could conclude that, on average, there is no statistically significant association between fund size and performance.

Expense ratio is strongly negative and statistically significant at 1% level in all fund size quintiles except the fifth. Flows demonstrate positive statistically significant reaction in first and third fund size quintiles. Alpha for equity sample in $t - 1$ is, once again positive with strong statistically significant reaction at 1% level in all fund size quintiles. Volatility shows positive statistically significant reaction in first, third and fifth quintiles, and 1% negative statistically significant reaction in fourth fund size quintile. R Squared is negative at 1% statistically significant level in first and third fund size quintiles. Active share is negative at 1% statistically significant level in first and third fund size quintiles.

If fund managers expect a negative relationship between fund size and fund performance when a fund size is over an optimal value, then fund managers often start a new fund when new money comes in.

Figure 3 shows the average fund size of mutual funds by year for EU bonds. Even though being rather fluctuating, in general, the fund size demonstrates the tendency to decrease in the time period from 2013 (18.5) to 2019 (18.00).

Figure 4 shows the average fund size of mutual funds by year for US

Table 10 Determinants of performance according to fund size—EQUITY EUROPE

	QUINTILE 1	*QUINTILE 2*	*QUINTILE 3*	*QUINTILE 4*	*QUINTILE 5*
AGE	−0.0126	−0.0135	−0.0131	−0.0047	0.0001
	(0.0128)	(0.0127)	(0.0101)	(0.0080)	(0.0124)
EXPENSE	−0.0246***	−0.0268***	−0.0166***	−0.0268***	−0.0065
	(0.0049)	(0.0054)	(0.0064)	(0.0094)	(0.0119)
FLOWS	0.3214**	0.4228	1.3903*	−0.9665	1.9418
	(0.1580)	(0.2989)	(0.7347)	(1.2026)	(3.0098)
SIZE	−0.0051	−0.0021	0.0054*	0.0017	0.0004
	(0.0044)	(0.0039)	(0.0031)	(0.0033)	(0.0029)
$\alpha_p^{CAR}{}_t - 1$	75.7546***	77.8947***	78.9075***	80.4480***	81.7282***
	(0.9511)	(0.7365)	(0.9141)	(0.9310)	(1.5707)
VOLATILITY	0.8875***	0.7746	0.6560**	−0.0835***	0.1788***
	(0.2289)	(0.6519)	(0.2766)	(0.0289)	(0.0161)
R SQUARED	−0.6788***	0.2095	−0.4010***	0.0493	−0.0207
	(0.2092)	(0.1816)	(0.1345)	(0.1375)	(0.1708)
ACTIVE	−0.9621***	0.4575	−0.6332***	0.1207	−0.0413
	(0.3490)	(0.2963)	(0.2211)	(0.2176)	(0.2824)
CONS	0.9709***	−0.2482	0.4587**	−0.0723	0.0331
	(0.2628)	(0.2574)	(0.1892)	(0.1809)	(0.2319)

(continued)

Table 10 (continued)

	QUINTILE 1	*QUINTILE 2*	*QUINTILE 3*	*QUINTILE 4*	*QUINTILE 5*
N	19,546	19,522	19,316	19,009	19,781

Standard errors in parentheses $^{*}p < 0.10$, $^{**}p < 0.05$, $^{***}p < 0.01$

This table reports the results of the panel regressions of mutual fund performance on fund characteristics. Portfolio performance is evaluated based on Carhart or Momentum Four Factor alpha. AGE is defined as the number of months from the fund's inception. $\text{Flow}_{i,t-1}$ is the normalized monthly net flow of fund i in month $t - 1$. SIZE is the logarithm of the total net assets of fund i in period $t - 1$ $\log(\text{TNA})_{i,t-1}$; $\text{ExpenseRatio}_{i,t-1}$, is the net expense ratio. $\text{Volatility}_{j,t}$ is the volatility of monthly returns (Standard Deviation over a 52 weeks rolling estimation). According to Bliss et al. (2008) we also added the CAPM $\text{Rsquare}_{j,t-1}$ measure as a control variable. $\text{ActiveShare}_{i,t-1}$ is a measure of active management by the fund as defined by Cremers and Petajisto (2009) and Miller et al. (2007). The sample period is from December 2006 to December 2019. The crisis period range between June 2007 and December 2010. The t-statistics are based on standard errors clustered by both fund and time. *, **, and ***, respectively, denote significance at the 10, 5, and 1% levels

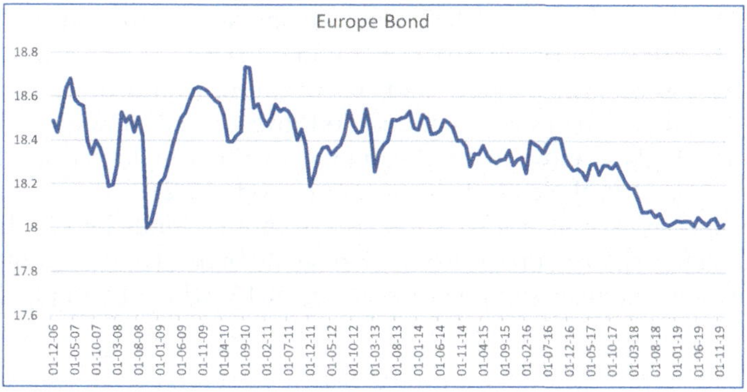

Fig. 3 The average fund size of the mutual funds by year. Europe bond (The average fund size of the mutual funds by year. This figure plots the averaged fund size of the mutual funds. The sample period is from 2006 to 2019. The sample includes all European mutual funds. Fund Size is measured in terms of natural Logarithm of Total Assets)

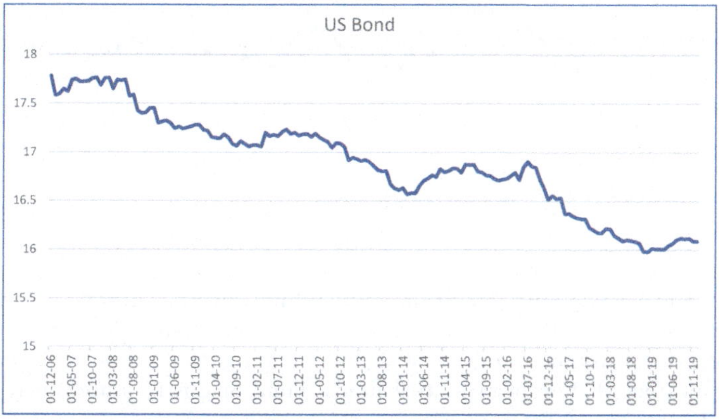

Fig. 4 The average fund size of the mutual funds by year. US bond (The average fund size of the mutual funds by year. This figure plots the averaged fund size of the mutual funds. The sample period is from 2006 to 2019. The sample includes all US mutual funds. Fund Size is measured in terms of natural Logarithm of Total Assets)

bonds, that is systematically falling across all investigated period from 17.8 to 16.00, with slight rise in 2010, 2014 and 2016.

Figure 5 shows the average fund size of mutual funds by year for EU equity, which fluctuates across the period investigated, however demonstrates the highest value in the beginning of the sample period (18.5), that depreciates in the end of the sample period (17.2).

Figure 6 shows the average fund size of mutual funds by year for US equity, which sharply drops from 17.6 in 2016 to 16.5 in 2009, and demonstrates the fluctuating nature before 2015, when it steadily drops.

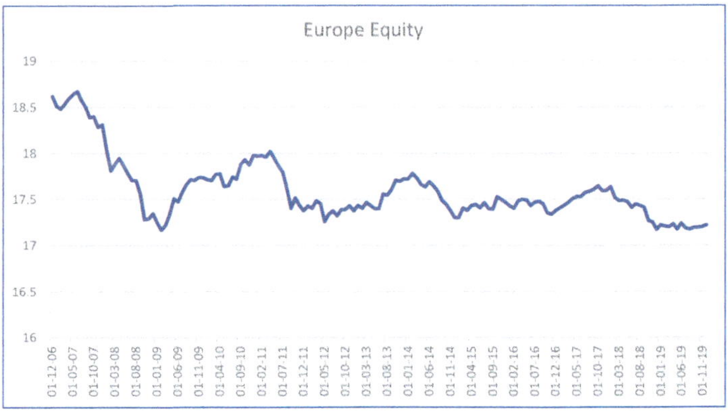

Fig. 5 The average fund size of the mutual funds by year. Europe equity (The average fund size of the mutual funds by year. This figure plots the averaged fund size of the mutual funds. The sample period is from 2006 to 2019. The sample includes all European mutual funds. Fund Size is measured in terms of natural Logarithm of Total Assets)

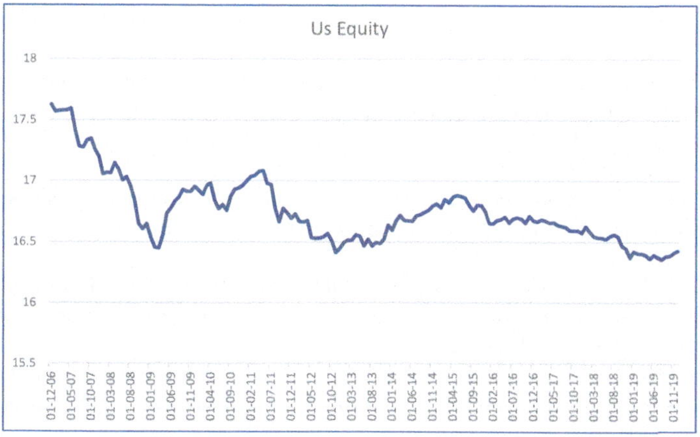

Fig. 6 The average fund size of the mutual funds by year. US equity (The average fund size of the mutual funds by year. This figure plots the averaged fund size of the mutual funds. The sample period is from 2006 to 2019. The sample includes all US mutual funds. Fund Size is measured in terms of natural Logarithm of Total Assets)

References

Basso, A., & Funari, S. (2017). The role of fund size in the performance of mutual funds assessed with DEA models. *The European Journal of Finance, 23*(6), 457–473.

Beckers, S. E., & Vaughan, G. (2001). Small is beautiful. *The Journal of Portfolio Management, 27*(4), 9–17.

Berk, J. B., & Green, R. C. (2004). Mutual fund flows and performance in rational markets. *Journal of Political Economy, 112*(6), 1269–1295.

Berkowitz, J. P., Schorno, P. J., & Shapiro, D. A. (2017). Characteristics of mutual funds with extreme performance. *Review of Financial Economics, 34*, 50–60.

Bhojraj, S., Cho, Y. J., & Yehuda, N. (2012). Mutual fund family size and mutual fund performance: The role of regulatory changes. *Journal of Accounting Research, 50*(3), 647–684.

Bliss, R. T., Potter, M. E., & Schwarz, C. (2008). Performance characteristics of individually-managed versus team-managed mutual funds. *The Journal of Portfolio Management, 34*(3), 110–119.

Bris, A., Gulen, H., Kadiyala, P., & Rau, P. R. (2007). Good stewards, cheap talkers, or family men? The impact of mutual fund closures on fund managers, flows, fees, and performance. *The Review of Financial Studies, 20*(3), 953–982.

Cao, C., Iliev, P., & Velthuis, R. (2017). Style drift: Evidence from small-cap mutual funds. *Journal of Banking and Finance, 78,* 42–57.

Carhart, M. M. (1997). On persistence in mutual fund performance. *The Journal of Finance, 52*(1), 57–82.

Casavecchia, L., & Ge, C. (2019). Jack of all trades versus specialists: Fund family specialization and mutual fund performance. *International Review of Financial Analysis, 63,* 69–85.

Chen, J., Hong, H., Huang, M., & Kubik, J. D. (2004). Does fund size erode mutual fund performance? The role of liquidity and organization. *American Economic Review, 94*(5), 1276–1302.

Christoffersen, S. K., Keim, D. B., & Musto, D. K. (2006). *Valuable information and costly liquidity: Evidence from individual mutual fund trades*. Available at SSRN 951501.

Chua, A. K. P., & Tam, O. K. (2020). The shrouded business of style drift in active mutual funds. *Journal of Corporate Finance, 64,* 101667.

Coval, J., & Stafford, E. (2007). Asset fire sales (and purchases) in equity markets. *Journal of Financial Economics, 86*(2), 479–512.

Cremers, K. M., & Petajisto, A. (2009). How active is your fund manager? A new measure that predicts performance. *The Review of Financial Studies, 22*(9), 3329–3365.

Edelen, R. M., Evans, R. B., & Kadlec, G. B. (2007). *Scale effects in mutual fund performance: The role of trading costs*. Available at SSRN 951367.

Edelen, R. M., & Warner, J. B. (2001). Aggregate price effects of institutional trading: A study of mutual fund flow and market returns. *Journal of Financial Economics, 59*(2), 195–220.

El Ghoul, S., & Karoui, A. (2017). Does corporate social responsibility affect mutual fund performance and flows? *Journal of Banking and Finance, 77,* 53–63.

Elton, E. J., Gruber, M. J., & Blake, C. R. (2012). Does mutual fund size matter? The relationship between size and performance. *The Review of Asset Pricing Studies, 2*(1), 31–55.

Elton, E. J., Gruber, M. J., Commer, G., & Li, K. (2000). *Spiders: Where are the bugs*. Available at SSRN 307136.

Fama, E. F., & French, K. R. (1993). Common risk factors in the returns on stocks and bonds. *Journal of Financial Economics, 33*(1), 3–56.

Ferreira, M. A., Keswani, A., Miguel, A. F., & Ramos, S. B. (2013). The determinants of mutual fund performance: A cross-country study. *Review of Finance, 17*(2), 483–525.

Gaspar, J. M., Massa, M., & Matos, P. (2006). Favoritism in mutual fund families? Evidence on strategic cross-fund subsidization. *The Journal of Finance, 61*(1), 73–104.

Gutierrez, R. C., Maxwell, W. F., & Xu, D. (2009). *On economies of scale and persistent performance in corporate-bond mutual funds*. Available at SSRN 1133959.

Jegadeesh, N., & Titman, S. (1993). Returns to buying winners and selling losers: Implications for stock market efficiency. *The Journal of Finance, 48*(1), 65–91.

Jeon, H., Kang, J., & Lee, C. (2017). Precision about manager skill, mutual fund flows, and performance persistence. *The North American Journal of Economics and Finance, 40,* 222–237.

Jordan, B. D., & Riley, T. B. (2015). Volatility and mutual fund manager skill. *Journal of Financial Economics, 118*(2), 289–298.

Khan, M., Kogan, L., & Serafeim, G. (2012). Mutual fund trading pressure: Firm-level stock price impact and timing of SEOs. *The Journal of Finance, 67*(4), 1371–1395.

Lou, D. (2012). A flow-based explanation for return predictability. *The Review of Financial Studies, 25*(12), 3457–3489.

Massa, M. (1998). *Why so many mutual funds? Mutual fund families, market segmentation and financial performance*. Mutual Fund Families, Market Segmentation and Financial Performance (Working Paper INSEAD).

McLemore, P. (2019). Do mutual funds have decreasing returns to scale? Evidence from fund mergers. *Journal of Financial and Quantitative Analysis, 54*(4), 1683–1711.

Miller, D. A., Goldfarb, B., & Kirsch, D. (2007). Was there too little entry during the Dot Com Era? *Journal of Financial Economics, 86*(1), 100–144.

Nanda, V., Wang, Z. J., & Zheng, L. (2004). Family values and the star phenomenon: Strategies of mutual fund families. *The Review of Financial Studies, 17*(3), 667–698.

Novy-Marx, R. (2014). *Understanding defensive equity* (No. w20591). National Bureau of Economic Research.

Pástor, L., & Stambaugh, R. F. (2012). On the size of the active management industry. *Journal of Political Economy, 120*(4), 740–781.

Pástor, Ľ., Stambaugh, R. F., & Taylor, L. A. (2015). Scale and skill in active management. *Journal of Financial Economics, 116*(1), 23–45.

Pástor, Ľ., Stambaugh, R. F., & Taylor, L. A. (2017). Do funds make more when they trade more? *The Journal of Finance, 72*(4), 1483–1528.

Pástor, Ľ., Stambaugh, R. F., & Taylor, L. A. (2020). Fund tradeoffs. *Journal of Financial Economics, 138*(3), 614–634.

Perold, A. F., & Salomon, R. S., Jr. (1991). The right amount of assets under management. *Financial Analysts Journal, 47*(3), 31–39.

Petajisto, A. (2013). Active share and mutual fund performance. *Financial Analysts Journal, 69*(4), 73–93.

Phillips, B., Pukthuanthong, K., & Rau, P. R. (2018). Size does not matter: Diseconomies of scale in the mutual fund industry revisited. *Journal of Banking and Finance, 88*, 357–365.

Pollet, J. M., & Wilson, M. (2008). How does size affect mutual fund behavior? *The Journal of Finance, 63*(6), 2941–2969.

Reuter, J., & Zitzewitz, E. (2013). *How much does size Erode fund performance? A regression discontinuity approach* (Dartmouth University Working Paper).

Reuter, J., & Zitzewitz, E. (2010). *How much does size erode mutual fund performance? A regression discontinuity approach* (No. w16329). National Bureau of Economic Research.

Shari, A., & Mahat, F. (2019). Mutual fund characteristics, risk governance and fund performance is ASEAN market: A conceptual framework. *International Journal of Accounting, 4*(24), 42–52.

Tang, K., Wang, W., & Xu, R. (2012). Size and performance of Chinese mutual funds: The role of economy of scale and liquidity. *Pacific-Basin Finance Journal, 20*(2), 228–246.

Wermers, R. (2003). *Are mutual fund shareholders compensated for active management "Bets"*? (Working Study). University of Maryland.

Yan, X. (2008). Liquidity, investment style, and the relation between fund size and fund performance. *Journal of Financial and Quantitative Analysis, 43*, 741–767.

Zhu, M. (2018). Informative fund size, managerial skill, and investor rationality. *Journal of Financial Economics, 130*(1), 114–134.

CHAPTER 4

Active Management

1 Introduction

Actively managed mutual funds are an important constituent of the financial sector.[1] Passive management of a portfolio is easy to define: it consists of replicating the return on an index with a strategy of buying and holding all (or almost all) index stocks in the official index proportions. Active management can then be defined as any deviation from passive management.

For this reason, an active equity fund manager can attempt to outperform the fund's benchmark only by taking positions that are different from the benchmark. According to Cremers and Petajisto (2009) fund holdings can differ from the benchmark holdings in two general ways: either stock selection or factor timing (or both).[2] Stock selection involves picking individual stocks that the manager expects to outperform their peers. Factor timing involves time-varying bets on systematic risk factors such as sectors of the economy, or group of stocks belonging to style factors (e.g., Value or Momentum Stocks/Index) or more generally by considering any systematic risk relative to the benchmark index.

[1] Kacperczyk, M., Sialm, C., & Zheng, L. (2005). On the industry concentration of actively managed equity mutual funds. *The Journal of Finance, 60*(4), 1983–2011.

[2] Cremers, K. M., & Petajisto, A. (2009). How active is your fund manager? A new measure that predicts performance. *The Review of Financial Studies, 22*(9), 3329–3365.

G. Galloppo, *Asset Allocation Strategies for Mutual Funds*,
https://doi.org/10.1007/978-3-030-76128-8_4

2 Previous Findings in Academic Literature

In the academic literature related to influence of active management scheme on performance of mutual funds, there are different and mixed empirical evidences from the previous scholars. The hypothesis relating to the fact that high Active Share funds outperform low Active Share funds also depends on the period and the geographical sample investigated by the various empirical works.

Kacperczyk et al. (2005) examine whether some fund managers create value by concentrating their portfolios in industries where they have informational advantages. To this end, using U.S. mutual fund data from 1984 to 1999, authors construct portfolios of funds with different industry concentration levels. The traditional view is that investors should widely diversify their holdings in the industry to reduce the idiosyncratic risks of their investment portfolios. However, if fund managers believe that certain industries will outperform the overall market, or if they have a wealth of information to select profitable stocks in specific industries, they may wish to hold a concentrated portfolio. Consistent with this hypothesis, authors would expect funds with skilled managers to hold more concentrated portfolios. As a consequence of this, there should be observed a positive relation between fund performance and industry concentration. This could be the case; indeed, empirical results in Kacperczyk et al. (2005) show that more concentrated funds perform better after adjusting for risk and style differences using the four-factor model of Carhart (1997). When considering mutual funds with above-median industry concentration, the results show an average abnormal return of 1.58% per year before deducting expenses and 0.33% per year after deducting expenses, whereas mutual funds with below-median industry concentration yield an average abnormal return of 0.36% before and –0.77% after expenses.

Several studies Del Guercio and Tkac (2002), and Nanda et al. (2004) affirm that mutual fund investors reward outstanding risk adjusted performance with disproportionately high money inflows but do not penalize poor performance in a similar manner. This behavior results in a convex option-like payoff profile for mutual funds. Therefore, some managers, especially those with low investment capabilities, may have an incentive to adopt volatile investment strategies to increase their chances of achieving extreme performance. Consistent with this assumption, funds pursuing this game strategy will hold a more concentrated investment portfolio.

In this case, we should not observe a positive correlation between fund performance and industry or risk factor concentration.

Cremers and Petajisto (2009) introduce a measure of active portfolio management, the Active Share, which represents the share of portfolio holdings that differ from the benchmark index holdings. They compute Active Share for domestic equity mutual funds from 1980 to 2003, finding that active Share predicts fund performance: funds with the highest Active Share significantly outperform their benchmarks, both before and after expenses, and they exhibit strong performance persistence. When considering a two-dimensional sort of non-index funds by Active Share and tracking error, it comes out that fund performance in excess of the benchmark is significantly related to the driver of the active management. Cremers and Petajisto (2009) in their empirical results show that funds with the highest Active Share exhibit some skill. High-active share portfolios, outperform their benchmarks by 1.51–2.40% per year. On the opposite side, funds with the lowest Active Share have poor benchmark-adjusted returns in terms of alphas before expenses (between 0.11% and −0.63%) and do even worse after expenses, underperforming by −1.42 to −1.83% per year. When considering the statistical significance of the difference in performance, between the top and bottom Active Share groups, the test rejects the null hypothesis of statistically insignificant. Interestingly, tracking error by itself is not related to fund returns. This means that not all dimensions of active management are rewarded in the market, but the dimension captured by Active Share is. From an economic point of view, these empirical results suggest that the most active stock pickers have enough skill to outperform their benchmarks even after considering fees and transaction costs. On the contrary, funds focusing on factor bets (that is funds investing in risk factor themes, e.g., Value stocks) seem to have zero to negative skill, which leads to particularly bad performance after fees. From these results, interesting considerations emerge also from the point of view of the information efficiency of the financial markets, given the existence of some mispricing in individual stocks that active managers can exploit. On the other hand, broader factor portfolios may either be too efficiently priced or too difficult for the managers to predict.

When looking at stock returns directly,[3] Cohen et al. (2010) find that the largest active positions of fund managers outperform, suggesting that managers should hold less diversified portfolios. Considering a different

[3] An interesting literature review on the issue of active share, is reported by Petajisto (2013).

set of assets, that is hedge funds, Sun et al. (2012) find that funds aggressively deviating from their peers outperform the more conservative funds. Petajisto (2013), while finding that the average actively managed mutual fund has underperformed its benchmark index, shows that the degree and type of active management matters considerably for performance. In a similar fashion of what performed previously in a seminal paper (Cremers & Petajisto, 2009), the scholars use Active Share and tracking error to sort domestic equity mutual funds into five categories based on the type of active management they practice. They find that the most active stock pickers were able to add value to their investors, beating their benchmark indices by about 1.26% per year after all fees and expenses. Economically, this means that there are some inefficiencies in the market that can be exploited by active stock selection. Furthermore, authors find that active stock selection is most successful at times of high cross-sectional dispersion in stock returns. However, fund managers are not able to add value by betting on broader factor portfolios, indicating that they are more efficiently priced than individual stocks. For mutual fund investors, these findings suggest that they need to pay attention to measures of active management when selecting fund to invest in.

Ferreira et al. (2013) show that active management—measured by the divergence of the fund portfolio composition (the portfolio weights of the stocks that it holds) from the composition of the fund's benchmark index—enhances fund performance.[4]

Wahal and Wang (2011) show that the entry of new active funds that are close substitutes to incumbent funds creates competitive pressure for the incumbent funds to decrease their fees.[5]

Cremers et al. (2016) report that active fund managers care about their relative performance compared to benchmark indices (Basak & Pavlova, 2013). An increased fear of losing more assets could lead fund managers to adopt a defensive strategy or to increase the fraction of stocks in the portfolio that belong to their benchmark indices to avoid underperformance relative to their own benchmark. Cremers et al. (2016) find that a fund's active share predicts its future risk-adjusted performance. The effect is economically significant: a one standard deviation increase in active share is associated with an increase of about 1% per year in benchmark-adjusted returns and 0.7% per year in four-factor alpha.

[4] Amihud, Y., & Goyenko, R. (2013). Mutual fund's R^2 as predictor of performance. *The Review of Financial Studies, 26*(3), 667–694.

[5] Cremers, M., Ferreira, M. A., Matos, P., & Starks, L. (2016). Indexing and active fund management: International evidence. *Journal of Financial Economics, 120*(3), 539–560.

Some scholars in the academic literature, on the other hand, expresses caution on the evidence of better performance connected to the active management. Schlanger et al. (2012) look at five different measures of active management and they find no evidence that they predict performance. Frazzini et al. (2016) closely replicate the findings produced in Cremers and Petajisto (2009) and in Petajisto (2013), believing that their conclusions are subject to misinterpretation because results are largely dependent by a bias towards the small-cap sector (in the same line we have the evidences reported in Cremers et al., 2013; and also in Cohen et al., 2014; which also shows and discusses the underperformance of small-cap benchmarks over the same sample period). They find no reliable statistical evidence that high and low Active Share funds have returns that are different from each other, neither that high Active Share funds outperform low Active Share funds.

3 Active Management Measures

In this section we present various active management measures, based both on the difference between holdings of the fund and that of the benchmark, and on the different composition of the fund and benchmark with reference to the sectoral distribution of the underlying portfolios.

An active manager can only add value by deviating from his benchmark index. A manager can do this in two different ways: by stock selection or factor timing (Petajisto, 2013). Stock selection involves active bets on individual stocks, for example, selecting only one stock from a particular industry. Factor timing involves time-varying bets on broader factor portfolios, for example, overweighting particular sectors of the economy, or having a temporary preference for value stocks, or even choosing to keep some assets in cash rather than investing in equities. Factor timing is proxied by tracking error, as reported along the text in this section.

3.1 Active Share

Cremers and Petajisto (2009)[6] introduce a straightforward approach to quantify active management by comparing the holdings of a mutual fund with the holdings of its benchmark index. They label this measure the

[6] Cremers, K. M., & Petajisto, A. (2009). How active is your fund manager? A new measure that predicts performance. *The Review of Financial Studies, 22*(9), 3329–3365.

Active Share of a fund, and define it as:

$$\text{Active Share} = \frac{1}{2}\sum_{i=1}^{N} |\omega_{fund,i} - \omega_{index,i}| \tag{1}$$

where $\omega_{fund,i}$ and $\omega_{index,i}$ are the portfolio weights of asset i in the fund and in the index, and the sum is taken over the universe of all assets.[7]

To say simply, Active Share represents the percentage of the fund's portfolio that differs from the fund's benchmark index. For an all-equity mutual fund that has no leveraged or short positions, the Active Share of the fund will always be between zero and 100%. For a mutual fund that never shorts a stock and never buys on margin, Active Share will always be between zero and 100%. In other words, the short side of the long-short portfolio never exceeds the long index position. In contrast, the Active Share of a hedge fund can significantly exceed 100% due to its leverage and net short positions in individual stocks.[8]

Active Share has an intuitive economic interpretation. In particular, it is possible to decompose any portfolio into a 100% position in its benchmark index plus a zero-net-investment long-short portfolio on top of that.[9] This long-short portfolio represents all the active bets the fund has taken. The measure of Active Share represents the size of that long-short portfolio as a fraction of the total portfolio of the fund. In the original specification, authors divide the sum of portfolio weight differences by two so that a fund that has zero overlap with its benchmark index gets a 100% Active Share (i.e., according to this rationale it does not count the long side and the short side of the positions separately).

For example, a fund might have 100% in the S&P 500 plus 30% in active long positions and 30% in active short positions. In this example, 30% stands for the size of this active long-short portfolio and correspond to the Active Share of the portfolio. Let's introduce a different example,

[7] Cremers and Petajisto (2009) compute the sum across stock positions only, as in their original framework they apply the measure exclusively to all-equity portfolios. However, in general one should sum up across all positions, including cash and bonds, which may also be part of the portfolio (and obviously of the index).

[8] Cremers, K. M., & Petajisto, A. (2009). How active is your fund manager? A new measure that predicts performance. *The Review of Financial Studies, 22*(9), 3329–3365.

[9] Asness (2004) discusses the same decomposition, albeit from the point of view of tracking error alone.

by considering the value of asset under management of the portfolio. Say, we have a fund with a \$200 million portfolio benchmarked against the S&P 500. Imagine that the manager starts by investing \$200 million in the benchmark (S&P 500), thus the portfolio represents a pure index fund with 500 stocks. Now let's assume that the fund manager only likes half of the stocks, so say 250 out of 500. Then he eliminates the other half from his portfolio, generating \$100 million in cash, and then he invests that \$100 million in the other (250) stocks he likes. This results in an Active Share value of 50% (i.e., 50% overlap with the index). As reported previously Active Share can be easily interpreted as the fraction of the portfolio that is different from the benchmark index. If the asset manager invests in only 50 stocks out of 500 (assuming no size bias), his Active Share will be 90% (i.e., 10% overlap with the index). According to this measure, it is therefore perfectly equally to pick just 50 stocks out of a relevant investment universe of 500 or 10 stocks out of 100. In either case, the asset manager chooses to exclude 90% of the candidate stocks from the portfolio.

According to Cremers and Petajisto (2009) the Active Share measure is useful for two main reasons. First, it provides information about a fund's potential for beating its benchmark index. In a certain way, we can say that an active manager can only add value relative to the index by deviating from it. Some positive (in absolute value) level of Active Share is therefore a necessary (albeit not sufficient) condition for outperforming the benchmark. Secondly, although Active Share is a convenient independent measure of active management, as we will see later, it can also be used with tracking error to gain a more comprehensive understanding of active management, allowing us to distinguish stock selection and factor timing.

3.2 *Tracking Error*

The other measure of active management, which is used by fund managers the most, is tracking error volatility, often simply called tracking error.

Tracking error (or more formally, tracking error volatility) is commonly defined (see e.g., Grinold & Kahn, 1999) as the time-series standard deviation of the difference between a fund return ($R_{fund,t}$) and its benchmark index return ($R_{index,t}$):

$$\text{Tracking error} = Stdev\left[R_{fund,t} - R_{index,t}\right] \quad (2)$$

Intuitively, tracking error measures the volatility of the fund that is not explained by movements in the fund's benchmark index.

A typical active manager aims to reach an expected return higher than the benchmark index, but at the same time, they want to have a low tracking error (volatility) to minimize the risk of significant underperformance of the index (Cremers & Petajisto, 2009). Mean-variance analysis in this excess-return framework is a standard tool of active managers (e.g., Roll, 1992 or Jorion, 2003).

A general definition of tracking error effectively assumes that the beta relative to the benchmark index is equal to one, so any beta that deviates from the beta equal to one, will produce tracking error.

Cremers, and Petajisto (2009[10]) also adopt a slightly modified definition of tracking error, obtained by regressing excess fund returns on excess index returns:

$$R_{fund,t} - R_{f,t} = \alpha_{fund} + \beta_{fund}\left(R_{index,t} - R_{f,t}\right) + \varepsilon_{fund,t} \tag{3}$$

$$\text{Tracking error} = Stdev\left[\varepsilon_{fund,t}\right] \tag{4}$$

Now that we have introduced the two commonly known measures of active management, let's understand what are the differences between those two measures: the tracking error and the active share. To see that, we start from considering a portfolio with 50 stocks—in other words, a potentially well-diversified portfolio. In these two active management measures, the way active management appears depends on a key question: do we observe exposure to systemic risks in active positions? Following Petajisto (2013), we can say that when, for example, all the overweight positions are in technology stocks, which tend to move together, even small active positions will generate a high tracking error. In addition, suppose there are 50 industries, each industry has 20 stocks, and the fund selects only one stock from 20 stocks in each industry, while maintaining the same industry weight as the benchmark index. Therefore, the fund has a high selectivity in various industries, generating a high active share of about 95%, but since it does not hold any positions in various industries, most of the risks in its active positions will be diversified, resulting

[10] Cremers, K. M., & Petajisto, A. (2009). How active is your fund manager? A new measure that predicts performance. *The Review of Financial Studies, 22*(9), 3329–3365.

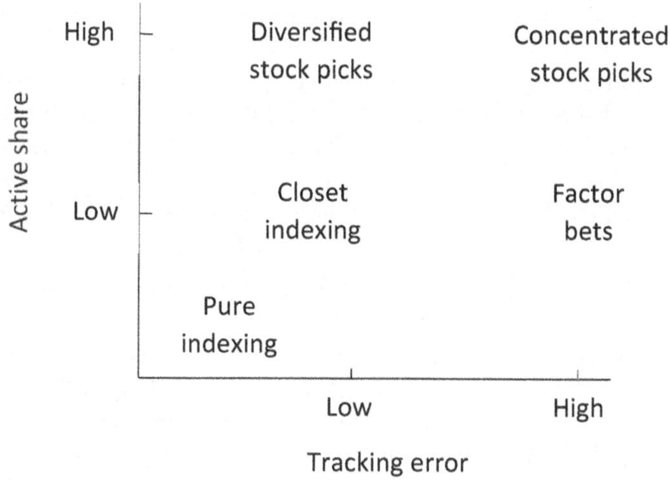

Fig. 1 Different types of active and passive management. Active Share represents the fraction of portfolio holdings that differ from the benchmark index, thus emphasizing stock selection. Tracking error is the volatility of fund return in excess of the benchmark, so it emphasizes bets on systematic risk

in lower tracking error. Hence, Active Share and tracking error emphasize different aspects of active management. Active Share is a reasonable proxy for stock selection, whereas tracking error is a proxy for systematic factor risk. To get a complete picture of active management, we need both measures.

Figure 1[11] illustrates how these two dimensions act and how they can be linked to different types of active management. Diversified stock pickers have a high Active Share and low tracking error, while the opposite approach is taken by funds focusing on factor bets. Concentrated funds combine stock selection with factor bets, thus, scoring high on both measures. Closet indexers score low on both measures.

Say differently, the main conceptual difference between the measures is that tracking error incorporates the covariance matrix of returns and thus

[11] We draw the figure from Cremers, K. M., & Petajisto, A. (2009). How active is your fund manager? A new measure that predicts performance. *The Review of Financial Studies, 22*(9), 3329–3365.

puts significantly more weight on correlated active bets, whereas Active Share puts equal weight on all active bets regardless of diversification.

To understand the relationship between tracking error and covariance matrix that drives the correlation effect among the assets in portfolio, we should remind the definition of the Variance of the sum or difference of two correlated random variables.

For example, the Variance of the difference of two correlated random variables is:

$$Var(X - Y) = \sigma_X^2 + \sigma_Y^2 - 2 * \sigma_{X,Y} \tag{5}$$

With the Eq. (5) in mind, we immediately see how the $\sigma_{X,Y}$ acts within the relationship between the two variables X and Υ which in our case represent the return of the fund and that of the benchmark.

Lastly, a diversified stock picker can be very active despite its low tracking error, because its stock selection across different industries can result in large deviations from the benchmark portfolio. On the contrary, a fund betting on systematic factors can generate a large tracking error even without large deviations from index holdings.[12]

3.3 Measure of Active Management Based on R^2

According to Miller (2007),[13] a fund's reported R^2 does not directly give us the share of funds being passively managed; rather, it gives the share of variance in returns that can be explained by the benchmark. However, starting from the R^2 it could be possible to explicitly model the sources of variance in the portfolio, and, therefore, succeed in deriving a formula for the active share of funds.

Without knowing well, the composition of the portfolio in terms of single asset holding, it is not possible to literally divide the fund's portfolio into passive and active parts; however, this does not mean that people cannot break it down to achieve the required separation. In fact, we do not need to define the decomposition on an asset-by-asset basis, but we need only ascertain the statistical properties that this decomposition must

[12] Cremers, K. M., & Petajisto, A. (2009). How active is your fund manager? A new measure that predicts performance. *The Review of Financial Studies, 22*(9), 3329–3365.

[13] Miller, R. M. (2007). Measuring the true cost of active management by mutual funds. *Journal of Investment Management, 5*(1), 29–49.

satisfy (Miller, 2007). Considering that few mutual funds can provide timely information about their holdings, this is an ideal choice. Starting from a single assumption about how the variance is distributed across the fund's portfolio, we can specify the attributes of the decomposition without knowing the fund's holdings. The only necessary information is the R^2 derived from regressing the return of the fund over the return of the benchmark, which is equal to the ratio of the return variance explained by the index. The standard linear regression equation for portfolio returns can be written as:

$$r_p = \alpha_p + \beta_p r_I + \varepsilon_p \tag{6}$$

where r_p is the return of the portfolio and r_I is the return of the index. Equation (6) is commonly estimated by data providers, by using weekly returns over a rolling period of 52 weeks or using monthly returns over a period of three to five years. If the returns are taken to be the returns in excess of the risk-free rate of return, beta β is the amount of index-related risk contained in the portfolio and alpha α, also known as Jensen's alpha, is an index-adjusted measure of the portfolio's performance. Lastly, ε_p is the residual return, the return not explained by the index that is usually taken to be normally distributed with zero mean and a constant variance.

A standard property of least-squares regression makes the residual returns uncorrelated with the returns of the index (Miller, 2007). The usual caveats for linear regressions apply here. In particular, a standard assumption is that we deal with constant regression parameters by considering a portfolio with constant risk/return characteristics over the entire period of the analysis.

While this is an innocuous assumption for most funds, it precludes the possibility of substantial shifts in portfolio make-up that could result from a fund manager who practices market timing or asset rotation.[14] In addition, since the past statistical attributes of the fund are intended to be used to make decisions about fund asset allocation, the risk profile of the fund during the estimation period should continue in present and hopefully into the nearest future. With those caveats in mind, Miller (2007) convert Eq. (3) into a variance decomposition equation by taking the

[14] Dybvig (2003) explore the limitations of static performance measures when applied to a dynamic setting such as a fund manager who engages in information-based asset selection strategies.

variance of both sides of it, while taking into account that alpha and beta are constants and that the covariance between r_I and ε_p is zero to get:

$$\sigma_p^2 = \beta_p^2\sigma_I^2 + \sigma^2(\varepsilon_p) \tag{7}$$

Equation (7) has the effect of decomposing the portfolio variance, σ_p^2, into two parts. The first part, $\beta_p^2\sigma_I^2$ is the variance explained by the index. The R^2 for the regression Eq. (6) is, by definition, the variance explained by the index divided by the overall portfolio variance. The second part, $\sigma^2(\varepsilon_p)$ is the variance not explained by the index, i.e., the residual variance. The residual variance divided by the overall portfolio variance is then seen to be $1 - R^2$.

The index component can be regarded as a purely passive component because it can be achieved by investing in the index and using or deleveraging the investment according to the beta. On the other hand, the remaining component represents the largest amount of variance that can be attributed to the active side of the fund manager allocation.

One possible source of difference that cannot be attributed to the manager's behavior is the "noise" associated with the manager's inability to completely drop the idiosyncratic risk elements associated with the manager's active betting.

The coefficient β_p in regression Eq. (6) captures the degree of influence that the index has on the portfolio. This becomes β_p^2 when expressed in terms of variance. However, the effect of the active component has not been separated, and there is no coefficient of active portfolio in Eq. (3), only the residual error term, ε_p. In order to achieve the ideal separation between the passive and active components of the portfolio P, we will imagine what this decomposition will bring if possible. Let's start by assuming that the only metric we know about the portfolio are the index (I) used to estimate regression (6), the estimated coefficients in that regression, and its R^2. We will assume that we do not know the actual holdings in the portfolio.

We should consider how to construct a synthetic portfolio P' that has the same risk and return characteristics (alpha, beta, variance and its decomposition, etc.) as portfolio P but with a clear separation between the assets invested in its passive and active parts. We will construct the passive part of P', which we will call I', so that it is a leveraged version of the index I. This passive component is called the fund's tracking portfolio, which is nothing more than the portfolio holding replicating the index.

On the other hand, the active component (we call it A') is not directly constructed. Instead, its attributes are inferred from the attributes of the fund's portfolio.

According to Miller's (2007) procedure, we can define w_A as the proportion of the portfolio P that we consider to be actively managed, so the returns of the portfolio P' can be written as the weighted sum of its passive return $r_{I'}$ and of its active return $r_{A'}$ as follows:

$$r_{P'} = (1 - w_A)r_{I'} + w_A r_{A'} \tag{8}$$

By construction, the returns of the active component of the portfolio ($r_{A'}$) are uncorrelated with those of the passive component ($r_{I'}$). Taking this into account, to compute the variance from (7) we obtain:

$$\sigma_{P'}^2 = (1 - w_A)^2 \sigma_{I'}^2 + w_A^2 \sigma_{A'}^2 \tag{9}$$

where $\sigma_{I'}^2$ is the passive variance, and $\sigma_{A'}^2$ is the active variance.

We want the proportion of variance that is explained by passive and active components to be the same for P' as it was for P, for the passive component we have:

$$\frac{(1 - w_A)^2 \sigma_{I'}^2}{\sigma_{P'}^2} = R^2, \tag{10}$$

whereas for the active component we have:

$$\frac{W_A^2 \sigma_{A'}^2}{\sigma_{P'}^2} = 1 - R^2 \tag{11}$$

Rearranging both (8) and (9), we have:

$$\frac{W_A^2 \sigma_{A'}^2}{(1 - w_A)^2 \sigma_{I'}^2} = \frac{1 - R^2}{R^2} \tag{12}$$

In the absence of any specific information about the two components of a portfolio, the natural assumption is that the active and passive components have the same variance. Taking the square root of each side, we obtain:

$$\frac{w_A}{(1 - w_A)} = \frac{\sqrt{1 - R^2}}{R} \tag{13}$$

Solving (13) for the value of the w_A, the weight of the active share in the portfolio yields:

$$w_A = \frac{\sqrt{1 - R^2}}{R + \sqrt{1 - R^2}} \tag{14}$$

3.4 *Industry Concentration Index*[15]

Kacperczyk et al. (2005) develop a measure, the Industry Concentration Index (ICI), to quantify the extent of portfolio concentration in 10 broadly defined industries. In a similar manner of what happens in the case of the Active Share metric, this index is based on the difference between the industry weights of a mutual fund and the industry weights of the total market portfolio.

Authors define the Industry Concentration Index, on the basis of the fund holdings. Specifically, authors assign each stock held by a mutual fund to one of 10 industries. The choice relating to the 10 Industries is due to the fact that a standard representation used by the global financial community, connected to the belonging of a single stock to a specific sector is considering the GICS 10 standard. The GICS 10 (Global Industry Classification Standard)[16] is a sector taxonomy developed in 1999 by MSCI and Standard & Poor's (S&P).

The Industry Concentration Index at time t for a mutual fund is defined as the sum of the squared deviations of the value weights for each of the 10 different industries held by the mutual fund, $\omega_{j,t}$, relative to the industry weights of the total stock market, $\overline{\omega}_{j,t}$:

$$ICI_t = \sum_{j=1}^{10} \left(\omega_{j,t} - \overline{\omega}_{j,t}\right)^2 \tag{15}$$

In a similar approach of Active Share, the Industry Concentration Index measures how much a mutual fund portfolio deviates from the market portfolio. If mutual funds and market portfolios have exactly

[15] Kacperczyk, M., Sialm, C., & Zheng, L. (2005). on the industry Concentration of actively managed Equity mutual funds. *the Journal of Finance, 60*(4), 1983–2011.

[16] https://www.msci.com/gics.

the same industry composition, the index equals zero and increases as mutual funds become more concentrated in a few industries. The industry concentration index is related to the Herfindahl index, which is usually used in industry organizations to measure the level of concentration in a specific industry. The Industry Concentration Index can be thought of as a market-adjusted Herfindahl Index.

The Herfindahl Index is defined as $HI_t = \sum_{i=1}^{N} \left(\omega_{i,t}\right)^2$.

4 Portfolio Sorted by the Two Dimensions of Active Management: Active Share vs. Tracking Error

In this section, we investigate the relation between concentration and fund performance using a portfolio approach. To gauge the relative performance of funds with different concentration levels, we sort all mutual funds into 5 × 5 portfolios according to their concentration at the beginning of each month accounting both for the Tracking Error and the Miller (2007)' active share measure. For each quintile portfolio, we compute the equally weighted average return for each month.

The sample consists of monthly returns for each fund. We compute the equal-weighted benchmark-adjusted return within each of the fund portfolios, and then take the time series average of these returns over the entire sample period.

The first sample we analyze is the European Equity Mutual Fund Sample. When we regress the monthly benchmark-adjusted returns on the three-factor model of Fama and French (1993) and the four-factor model of Carhart (1997), thus, controlling for exposure to the market, size, value, and momentum, we obtain the alphas shown in Panel A and B. First, we focus on Fama-French Alpha, by looking at Panel A. Looking at last column in Table 1 (High–Low), both for Alpha Fama-French and Carhart, it seems that Active Share does not help us much when picking funds: the marginal distribution across all tracking error quintiles shows zero or consistently negative alphas. Going from low to high Active Share may even hurt performance, which is statistically significant for all the groups. In contrast, Tracking Error may improve fund performance. Looking at last row in Panel A, the difference in alphas between the highest and lowest Tracking Error quintiles ranges between −0.10 and

Table 1 Net equal-weighted alphas for mutual funds in 2006–2019, sorted by the two dimensions of active management

EUROPE EQUITY SAMPLE						
Panel A: Alpha Fama-French						
Active Share Quintile						
Track Error Quintile	1	2	3	4	5	High–Low
1. (High)	0.01%***	0.06%***	0.67%***	0.30%***	0.07%***	−0.06%***
2.	0.05%***	0.10%***	0.23%***	0.14%***	0.12%***	−0.07%***
3.	0.08%***	0.08%***	0.23%***	0.19%***	0.08%***	0.00%***
4.	0.03%***	0.22%***	0.14%***	0.20%***	0.16%***	−0.13%***
5. (Low)	0.02%***	−0.12%***	0.10%***	0.17%***	0.17%***	−0.16%***
High–Low	−0.01%***	0.18%***	0.57%**	0.13%**	−0.10%***	
Panel B: Alpha Carhart						
Active Share Quintile						
Track Error Quintile	1	2	3	4	5	High–Low
1.	0.06%***	0.18%***	0.68%***	0.53%***	0.24%***	−0.18%***
2.	0.09%***	0.26%***	0.36%***	0.18%***	0.15%***	−0.06%***
3.	0.10%***	0.24%***	0.32%***	0.33%***	0.14%***	−0.04%***
4.	0.02%***	0.31%***	0.28%***	0.46%***	0.31%***	0.29%***
5.	0.01%***	−0.10%***	0.17%***	0.30%***	0.38%***	0.37%***
High–Low	0.06%***	0.28%***	0.51%***	0.23%***	−0.14%***	

The measures of active management are computed as follows: Active Share is calculated as $w_A = \frac{\sqrt{1-R^2}}{R+\sqrt{1-R^2}}$. Track errors is calculated as follows: $Tracking\ error = Stdev[R_{fund,t} - R_{index,t}]$. The table shows Alpha are based on FFC (Fama and French [1993] and Carhart [1997]) factor model. ***, **, * denotes significance at the 1, 5 or 10% level

0.57% per month (1% statistically significant). The difference in alphas is positive and economically significant within quite all tracking error quintiles. An investor should clearly avoid the lowest Tracking Error quintiles and instead pick from the Tracking Error quintiles from second to fourth. When we focus over Alpha Carhart, we observe on average a similar picture. With respect to the sorting performed by Tracking Error quintiles, on average we have a confirmation of previous results. An investor should clearly avoid the lowest Tracking Error quintiles and instead pick from the Tracking Error quintiles from second to fourth. When focusing on Active Share, evidences of Panel A still hold here.

All in all, the evidence in these two panels suggests that the funds with low Active Share and low Tracking Error tend to do worst, both in terms of Fama-French and Carhart alpha. This evidence implies that closet indexers (low Active Share, low tracking error) exhibit no ability and tend to lose money, while Funds with low Active Share and high tracking error tend to perform well, which implies that diversified stock picks (Fig. 1) tend to create value for fund investors.

In the second sample we consider the US Equity Mutual Funds. First, we focus on Fama-French Alpha, by looking at Panel A. Looking at last column in Table 1 (High–Low), both for Alpha Fam-French and Carhart, it seems that Active Share does not help us much when picking funds: the marginal distribution across all tracking error quintiles shows low in magnitude or consistently negative alphas. Going from low to high Active Share may even hurt performance, which is statistically significant for all the groups, in a similar manner as we observed for the European Fund Sample. In contrast, Tracking Error may improve fund performance, but just when picking from the highest Tracking Error quintile and when the picking is coupled also with thew highest quintile of the Active Share.

Looking at last row in Panel A, and Panel B the difference in alphas between the highest and lowest Tracking Error quintiles, when coupled together with the highest quintile of the Active Share, ranges between 0.29 and 0.23% per month (1% statistically significant), when considering Alpha Fama-French and Carhart respectively. An investor should focus over the highest tracking Error and Active Share quintiles. This evidence implies that concentrated stock pickers (High Active Share, High tracking error) exhibit managerial skill and tend to gain money for fund investors (Table 2).

5 Mutual Fund's R^2 as Predictor of Performance

Recent studies have shown that active management will have a positive impact on the performance of the fund. Active management can be measured by the deviation of the fund held from the diversified benchmark portfolio (see review above). This active management measure requires information about the composition of the mutual fund's portfolio and its benchmark index, which is difficult to obtain and calculate for many investors. In addition, the benchmark portfolio is not always accurately defined. Furthermore, as mentioned above, mutual funds communicate their holdings only at certain times during the year.

Table 2 Net equal-weighted alphas for mutual funds in 2006–2019, sorted by the two dimensions of active management

US EQUITY SAMPLE

Panel A: Alpha Fama-French						
Active Share Quintile						
Track Error Quintile	1	2	3	4	5	High–Low
1. (High)	−0.06%***	0.03%***	0.22%***	−0.02%***	0.28%***	−0.34%***
2.	−0.04%***	0.05%***	0.19%***	0.30%***	0.08%***	−0.12%***
3.	0.01%***	0.07%***	−0.02%***	−0.19%***	−0.08%***	0.09%***
4.	−0.32%***	0.33%***	0.04%***	−0.03%***	−0.05%***	−0.26%***
5. (Low)	−0.35%***	0.02%***	0.30%***	0.07%***	0.04%***	−0.39%***
High−Low	0.29%***	0.01%***	−0.08%***	−0.09%***	0.24%***	
Panel B: Alpha Carhart						
Active Share Quintile						
Track Error Quintile	1	2	3	4	5	High–Low
1.	−0.06%***	0.02%***	0.30%***	−0.11%***	−0.13%***	0.07%***
2.	−0.04%***	0.03%***	0.16%***	0.23%***	0.02%***	−0.07%***
3.	−0.03%***	0.06%***	−0.06%***	−0.24%***	−0.12%***	0.09%***
4.	−0.30%***	0.27%***	0.00%***	−0.02%***	−0.07%***	−0.23%***
5.	−0.29%***	0.03%***	0.22%***	0.06%***	0.03%***	−0.32%***
High−Low	0.23%***	−0.01%***	0.08%***	−0.17%***	−0.16%***	

The measures of active management are computed as follows: Active Share is calculated as $w_A = \frac{\sqrt{1-R^2}}{R+\sqrt{1-R^2}}$. Track errors is calculated as follows: $Tracking\ error = Stdev[R_{fund,t} - R_{index,t}]$. The table shows Alpha are based on FFC (Fama and French [1993] and Carhart [1997]) factor model. ***, **, * denotes significance at the 1, 5 or 10% level

Amihud and Goyenko (2013) propose an alternative, intuitive and easily calculable measure of the active management in a mutual fund, which authors term *selectivity*. They propose that fund performance can be predicted starting by its R^2, obtained from a regression of its returns on a multi-factor benchmark model. Authors find that R^2 is a significant predictor - even after controlling for fund characteristics, past performance and style - with a negative coefficient, of fund ***alpha*** (the excess return from a multi-factor model).

Amihud and Goyenko (2013) employ the benchmark model of factor-mimicking portfolios proposed by Fama and French (1993) and Carhart (1997) (denoted FFC) with return vectors RM−Rf (the market excess return), SMB (small minus big size stocks), HML (high minus low book-to-market ratio stocks) and UMD (winner minus loser stocks).

A regression of fund j returns on the benchmark factor returns produces R_j^2, which Amihud and Goyenko (2013) propose as a predictor of fund performance.

R^2 is the proportion of the fund return variance that is explained by the variation in these factors, thus lower R^2 means that the fund tracks them less closely. Lower R^2 indicates greater *selectivity* and it significantly predicts better performance.

Selectivity is thus measured by $1 - R^2$, the proportion of the fund's variance that is due to idiosyncratic risk or multi-factor tracking error, as it follows:

$$1 - R^2 = \frac{RMSE^2}{VARIANCE} = \frac{RMSE^2}{SystematicRisk^2 + RMSE^2} \tag{16}$$

RMSE is the idiosyncratic volatility—the volatility of the residual from the return-over-index regression—and *SystematicRisk*^{2} is the return variance that is due to the benchmark indexes 'risk. If the fund's idiosyncratic volatility is higher relative to its total variance, the *selectivity* is greater, which means that the fund's volatility is less driven by factor-based (systematic) volatility.

If *selectivity* enhances mutual fund performance, it should be negatively related to R^2.

Fund performance is measured by $alpha_j$, the risk-adjusted excess fund return based on a multifactor model, either the Fama-French (or Carhart Four Factor) or more simply the Jensen alpha.

6 Fund Portfolio Performance Based on Sorting by Lagged R^2

Amihud and Goyenko (2013) also identify an R^2-based strategy that earns a significant positive risk-adjusted excess return. Sorting funds periodically into quintiles by their R^2 and *alpha*, they find that the portfolio with the lowest R^2 and highest *alpha* generates in the subsequent period a significant *alpha* of 3.804% or higher, depending on the benchmark factor model used.

In the same fashion of Amihud and Goyenko (2013), we examine a strategy that predicts fund performance based on the fund's lagged R^2

(that is R^2_{t-1}). R^2_{t-1} is estimated by regressing monthly excess fund returns (over the T-bill rate) on the monthly CAPM, Fama French and FFC (Four Factor Carhart Model) factor returns over 12 months preceding month t.[17] In the estimation period we regress monthly fund excess return (over the one-month T-bill rate) on the CAPM, Fama French and FFC factor returns, moving this window a month at a time. We consider both conditional and unconditional specification of Multifactor Models. This regression produces estimates of R^2 and ***alpha*** (the regression intercept) that are used to predict the fund's excess return in the test month that follows. In each month t, we sort funds into deciles by their R^2_{t-1}.

This procedure produces 10 portfolios with equal number of funds in each. Then Portfolios are formed by sorting all funds every month into deciles by R-squared. We present for each portfolio the regression ***alpha*** (the regression intercept) and its t-statistic, using robust standard errors (following White, 1980).

Firstly, we focus over the US Equity Mutual fund Sample (Panel A). The results in Table 3 show that ***alpha*** declines when moving from high R^2_{t-1} to low R^2_{t-1}. That is, greater selectivity, measured by lower R^2, produces higher ***alpha***. The monthly ***alpha*** ranges between 1.55% (Conditional Alpha Carhart) and 0.26% (Conditional Alpha CAPM) for the portfolio of funds in the lowest quintile R^2_{t-1}. For the portfolio with the highest R^2_{t-1} (R-squared decile 1), the monthly ***alpha*** ranges between −0.02% (Conditional Alpha Carhart) and 0.05% (Conditional Alpha CAPM).

On average, all results are highly statistically significant. We replicate this analysis using European Equity Mutual fund Sample. The results, presented in Panel B, show again that on average performance is significantly better for low-R^2_{t-1}. funds. The monthly ***alpha*** ranges between 1.96% (Conditional Alpha Carhart) and 0.11% (Unconditional Alpha Carhart) for the portfolio of funds in the lowest quintile R^2_{t-1} while the monthly ***alpha*** performance ranges between −1.08% (Conditional Alpha Fama-French) and 0.31% (Conditional Alpha Carhart) when sorting portfolio of funds in the highest quintile R^2_{t-1}.

[17] The short estimation period accommodates Bollen and Busse's (2005) observation that funds' stock selection ability persists over a short period. Berk and Green (2004) propose that superior performance in mutual funds cannot persist even if it is a result of skill because it induces an inflow of funds which makes the fund grow in size and its performance to worsen because of decreasing returns to scale in fund management.

Table 3 Fund portfolio alpha, based on sorting on lagged R-squared

R-Squared Decile	*Panel A: US Equity*					
	Alpha CAPM		*Alpha Fama-French*		*Alpha Carhart*	
	Unconditional	*Conditional*	*Unconditional*	*Conditional*	*Unconditional*	*Conditional*
1.	0.03%***	0.05%***	0.02%***	0.03%***	0.03%***	−0.02%***
2.	0.00%	0.00%***	−0.03%***	−0.02%	−0.03%***	−0.10%***
3.	−0.04%***	−0.05%***	−0.07%***	−0.11%***	−0.07%***	−0.16%***
4.	−0.07%***	−0.11%***	−0.11%***	−0.20%***	−0.11%***	−0.22%***
5.	−0.12%***	−0.15%***	−0.14%***	−0.23%***	−0.12%***	−0.05%***
6.	0.05%***	0.02%***	0.02%**	−0.03%***	0.01%***	0.04%***
7.	−0.04%***	−0.02%***	−0.02%***	−0.07%***	−0.02%***	−0.05%***
8.	0.03%***	0.09%***	0.14%***	0.12%***	0.15%***	0.04%***
9.	0.18%***	0.17%***	0.28%***	0.76%***	0.33%***	0.80%***
10.	0.33%***	0.26%***	0.43%***	1.39%***	0.51%***	1.55%***

R-Squared Decile	*Panel B: EUROPE Equity*					
	Alpha CAPM		*Alpha Fama-French*		*Alpha Carhart*	
	Unconditional	*Conditional*	*Unconditional*	*Conditional*	*Unconditional*	*Conditional*
1.	0.17%***	0.15%***	0.27%***	−1.08%***	0.13%***	0.31%***
2.	0.23%***	0.20%***	0.35%***	−1.24%***	0.17%***	0.39%***
3.	0.19%***	0.18%***	0.32%***	−1.11%***	0.16%***	0.37%***
4.	0.15%***	0.16%***	0.29%***	−0.98%***	0.15%***	0.36%***

(continued)

Table 3 (continued)

R-Squared Decile	*Panel B: EUROPE Equity*					
	Alpha CAPM		*Alpha Fama-French*		*Alpha Carhart*	
	Unconditional	*Conditional*	*Unconditional*	*Conditional*	*Unconditional*	*Conditional*
5.	0.10%***	0.07%***	0.26%***	−1.06%***	0.19%***	0.32%***
6.	0.06%***	−0.02%***	0.14%***	−0.29%***	0.11%***	0.08%***
7.	0.06%***	−0.04%***	0.14%***	−0.64%***	0.05%***	0.04%***
8.	0.08%***	0.01%***	0.26%***	−0.75%***	0.10%***	−0.10%***
9.	0.15%***	0.08%***	0.25%***	−0.01%***	0.10%	0.93%***
10.	0.22%***	0.15%***	0.25%***	0.73%***	0.11%***	1.96%***

The table presents the portfolio alphas using monthly returns. Portfolios are formed by sorting all funds every month into deciles by R-squared. Then, for the following month test period (t) we calculate the monthly average alphas for each portfolio of funds. The process repeats by moving the estimation and test period one month at a time. Alphas and R-squared are obtained for the 12-month estimation period ($t - 1$) by regressing each fund's monthly excess returns (over the short-term Treasury rate) on the factors returns, using the CAPM, the FFC (Fama and French [1993] and Carhart [1997]) factor model. We also include conditional models by taking account: (i) the 1-month T-bill rate; (ii) dividend yield on the market index; (iii) the slope of the term structure; and finally (iv) the quality spread, by comparing the yield on government and corporate bonds. All instruments are lagged 1 month. For each portfolio we present alphas, the intercept from the above regression. The statistical significance level according to t-statistic is obtained by clustering the errors at fund level. The sample period of the test months is from 12/2006 to 12/2019 (156 months). ***, **, * denotes significance at the 1, 5 or 10% level

7 Predicting Fund Performance Measured by Alpha with *R*-Squared

To deal with the concern related to firm specific effect about the correlation of fund size with other fund characteristics, we analyze the effect of past R-squared on performance in the regression framework proposed by Cremers et al. (2011) and Chen et al. (2004); among others, where we can control for the effects of other fund characteristics on performance. Specifically, the regression specification that we utilize is:

$$FUNDRET_{i,t} = \mu + \gamma_1 R^2_{j,t-1} + \gamma_2 X_{i,t-1} + \sum_{n=1}^{10} \lambda_{nt} StyleDummy_{j,n} + \varepsilon_{i,t} \quad (17)$$

where $FUNDRET_{i,t}$ is the return (in terms of Multifactor Alpha, $\alpha_{i,t}$) of fund i in month t. and also include in the regressions a host of other observable fund characteristics. To be specific we consider $X_{i,t-1}$ representing a set of control variables (in month $t - 1$) that includes: fund size (as measured by the log of total net assets under management), Age, Expense ratio, past-month fund flows. The explanatory variables include also past-month returns in terms of Multifactor Alpha,[18] which may reflect managerial skill and persistence in performance (see Brown & Goetzmann, 1995; Gruber, 1996). Here, $\varepsilon_{i,t}$ again stands for a generic error term that is uncorrelated with all other independent variables. The coefficient of interest is γ_1, which captures the relationship between R-squared and fund performance, controlling for other fund characteristics. γ_2 is the vector of loadings on the control variables. In separate specifications, we consider also the effect of the Global Financial Crisis. The crisis period range between June 2007 and December 2010.

Firstly, we focus over the US Equity Mutual fund Sample. The results in Table 4 show that, on average *alpha* is negatively influenced by R-squared whatever the multifactor models we used for its estimation. Results are statistically significant when we consider the Three-factors Fama-French model and the Four-factors Carhart model. Once again

[18] Chen, J., Hong, H., Huang, M., & Kubik, J. D. (2004). Does fund size erode mutual fund performance? The role of liquidity and organization. *American Economic Review, 94*(5), 1276–1302.

Table 4 The effect of R^2 on stock fund alpha—cross-section regressions. US SAMPLE

	Alpha CAPM	*Alpha CAPM CRISIS*	*Alpha Fama-French*	*Alpha Fama-French CRISIS*	*Alpha Carhart*	*Alpha Carhart CRISIS*
R^2 CAPM	−0.0026	0.0220**				
	(0.0029)	(0.0092)				
R^2 Fam-Fren			−0.0104***	0.0285		
			(0.0040)	(0.0177)		
R^2 MOM					−0.0166***	0.0133
					(0.0048)	(0.0191)
$\alpha_p^{CAPM}i, t-1$	86.2813***	85.5798***				
	(0.3048)	(0.5615)				
$\alpha_p^{FF}i, t-1$			82.6106***	80.8845***		
			(0.3430)	(0.7154)		
$\alpha_p^{CAR}i, t\text{-}1$					79.9145***	80.5296***
					(0.3809)	(0.6972)
AGE	−0.0064**	−0.0829***	−0.0091***	−0.0683*	−0.0083**	−0.0867**
	(0.0031)	(0.0316)	(0.0034)	(0.0365)	(0.0040)	(0.0389)
EXPENSE	−0.0069***	−0.0098**	−0.0104***	−0.0057	−0.0119***	−0.0050
	(0.0017)	(0.0040)	(0.0019)	(0.0039)	(0.0022)	(0.0041)
FLOWS	1.0225***	0.8717*	1.2423***	1.5701***	1.3076***	1.7249***
	(0.1663)	(0.4691)	(0.1865)	(0.4662)	(0.1835)	(0.4610)
SIZE	0.0010***	−0.0001	0.0017***	0.0023**	0.0020***	0.0030***
	(0.0003)	(0.0010)	(0.0004)	(0.0009)	(0.0004)	(0.0010)
CONS	−0.0039	0.0346**	−0.0215***	−0.0469**	−0.0265***	−0.0528**
	(0.0058)	(0.0175)	(0.0065)	(0.0196)	(0.0076)	(0.0215)

	Alpha CAPM	*Alpha CAPM CRISIS*	*Alpha Fama-French*	*Alpha Fama-French CRISIS*	*Alpha Carhart*	*Alpha Carhart CRISIS*
N	64,117	10,201	64,117	10,201	64,117	10,201

Standard errors in parentheses $^{*}p < 0.10$, $^{**}p < 0.05$, $^{***}p < 0.01$

Dependent variable are multifactor model $\boldsymbol{alpha}_{j,t}$, using monthly returns. $R^2_{j,t-1}$ and $\boldsymbol{alpha}_{j,t,-1}$ are obtained from regressions of fund-j monthly return (in excess of the free risk rate) on the base of the CAPM, the Fama-French and the Carhart factor model. The estimation period is of 12 months. Fund Controls include the natural log of assets, natural log of age, and expense ratio, all measured as of the end of calendar year t. Flows represents the Net fund flow of each fund during the previous month The crisis period range between June 2007 and December 2010. The t-statistics are based on standard errors clustered by both fund and time. *, **, and ***, respectively, denote significance at the 10, 5, and 1% levels greater selectivity, measured by lower R^2, produces higher *alpha*. Interestingly enough when we account for the Global Financial crisis period, we obtain a positive association, when we consider CAPM Alpha or no statistically significant results.

When, we focus over the European Equity Mutual fund Sample, regression results in Table 5 show that, on average *alpha* is again negatively influenced by R-squared whatever the multifactor models we used for its estimation. Unlike the previous evidence, relating to American Equity Mutual funds, results here are never statistically significant whatever the multifactor models we considered.

8 Fund Performance in a Multivariate Regression Over the Two Dimensions of Active Management

In this section, we further extend our analysis using multivariate regressions. This approach differs from the portfolio approach in two major respects. One first concern relies in the aspect that, decile portfolio analysis cannot control mutual fund characteristics related to fund performance. For example, on average, a well-diversified mutual fund is larger than a more concentrated fund. It may be that small funds perform better than large funds, and the degree of concentration is important only because it is related to scale. A multivariate regression framework simultaneously controls for these different factors. Second, the portfolio approach aggregates mutual funds of similar concentration levels into different groups. Here, we take advantage of the rich panel of individual mutual funds. To directly isolate the effect of different fund characteristics in terms of portfolio concentration on fund performance, we run fixed effects panel regressions of fund performance on all the explanatory variables (Tables 6 and 7). We use three different performance metrics: CAPM alphas, three-factor alphas of returns (Fama and French, 1993), four-factor alphas of returns (Carhart, 1997). We use 1 year of past monthly returns to estimate the coefficients of the unconditional factor models.

Next, we regress the abnormal return of each mutual fund in each month on the concentration variables and on other fund characteristics. We focus on two concentration variables different from the R-squared: Tracking Error and Active Share (Miller, 2007).

Table 5 The effect of R^2 on stock fund alpha—cross-section regressions. EUROPE SAMPLE

	Alpha CAPM	*Alpha CAPM CRISIS*	*Alpha Fama-French*	*Alpha Fama-French CRISIS*	*Alpha Carhart*	*Alpha Carhart CRISIS*
R^2 CAPM	0.0087	−0.0023				
	(0.0087)	(0.0242)				
R^2 Fam-Fre			−0.0029	−0.0506		
			(0.0142)	(0.0469)		
R^2 MOM					−0.0057	−0.0870
					(0.0191)	(0.0587)
$\alpha_p^{CAPM} i, t-1$	85.6307***	83.2508***				
	(0.3573)	(0.7126)				
$\alpha_p^{FF} i, t-1$			83.0960***	82.9032***		
			(0.3135)	(0.5718)		
$\alpha_p^{CAR} i, t\text{-}1$					78.5288***	72.4912***
					(0.4150)	(1.0745)
AGE	−0.0071**	−0.0750	−0.0096**	−0.0052	−0.0038	0.0893
	(0.0033)	(0.0519)	(0.0038)	(0.0569)	(0.0049)	(0.0803)
EXPENSE	−0.0133***	−0.0154**	−0.0178***	−0.0232***	−0.0239***	−0.0343***
	(0.0024)	(0.0061)	(0.0026)	(0.0070)	(0.0031)	(0.0095)
FLOWS	0.8558***	0.7345**	0.5673***	0.5222*	0.3723***	0.9627**
	(0.0888)	(0.3156)	(0.0935)	(0.2999)	(0.1249)	(0.3912)
SIZE	−0.0009	−0.0034*	−0.0001	−0.0001	0.0007	−0.0038
	(0.0006)	(0.0020)	(0.0006)	(0.0019)	(0.0008)	(0.0029)
CONS	0.0461***	0.1133***	0.0755***	0.1227***	0.0514***	0.2415***
	(0.0104)	(0.0320)	(0.0142)	(0.0368)	(0.0181)	(0.0559)
N	52,483	8506	52,483	8506	52,483	8506

Standard errors in parentheses $^{*}p < 0.10$, $^{**}p < 0.05$, $^{***}p < 0.01$

Dependent variable are multifactor model ***alpha***$_{j,t}$, using monthly returns. $R^2_{j,t-1}$ and ***alpha***$_{j,t,\text{-}1}$ are obtained from regressions of fund-j monthly return (in excess of the free risk rate) on the base of the CAPM, the Fama-French and the Carhart factor model. The estimation period is of 12 months. Fund Controls include the natural log of assets, natural log of age, and expense ratio, all measured as of the end of calendar year t. Flows represents the Net fund flow of each fund during the previous month The crisis period range between June **2007** and December **2010**. The t-statistics are based on standard errors clustered by both fund and time. *, **, and ***, respectively, denote significance at the 10, 5, and 1% levels

Table 6 The effect of active share and Track Error on stock fund alpha. US SAMPLE

	Alpha CAPM	*Alpha CAPM CRISIS*	*Alpha Fama-French*	*Alpha FF CRISIS*	*Alpha Carhart*	*Alpha Carhart CRISIS*
ACTIVE	0.0009	0.1176***	0.0102**	0.1496***	0.0182***	0.1341***
	(0.0038)	(0.0202)	(0.0041)	(0.0281)	(0.0049)	(0.0304)
TRACK	0.0531**	1.0472***	0.0636**	1.2194***	0.0728**	1.0616***
	(0.0261)	(0.1945)	(0.0281)	(0.2198)	(0.0299)	(0.2650)
$\alpha_p^{CAPM}{}_{i,t}$	86.2587***	85.6350***				
	(0.3050)	(0.5646)				
$\alpha_p^{FF}{}_{i,t}$			82.5746***	80.8399***		
			(0.3434)	(0.7123)		
$\alpha_p^{CAR}{}_{i,t}$					79.8856***	80.5121***
					(0.3808)	(0.6902)
AGE	−0.0065**	−0.0948***	−0.0093***	−0.1041***	−0.0085**	−0.1312***
	(0.0031)	(0.0312)	(0.0034)	(0.0375)	(0.0040)	(0.0391)
EXPENSE	−0.0068***	−0.0106***	−0.0104***	−0.0068*	−0.0119***	−0.0060
	(0.0017)	(0.0039)	(0.0019)	(0.0038)	(0.0022)	(0.0040)
FLOWS	1.0244***	0.8343*	1.2374***	1.5362***	1.3044***	1.6956***
	(0.1663)	(0.4667)	(0.1866)	(0.4662)	(0.1835)	(0.4620)
SIZE	0.0010***	−0.0002	0.0018***	0.0020**	0.0020***	0.0027***
	(0.0003)	(0.0009)	(0.0004)	(0.0009)	(0.0004)	(0.0010)
CONS	−0.0074	0.0666***	−0.0122	0.0087	−0.0087	−0.0073
	(0.0070)	(0.0197)	(0.0077)	(0.0198)	(0.0090)	(0.0202)
N	64,117	10,201	64,117	10,201	64,117	10,201

Standard errors in parentheses $^{*}p < 0.10$, $^{**}p < 0.05$, $^{***}p < 0.01$

This table report the cross-section regressions results of the effect of active share and Track Error on stock fund alpha. Active Share is calculated as $w_A = \frac{\sqrt{1-R^2}}{R+\sqrt{1-R^2}}$. Track errors is calculated as follows: $Trackingerror = Stdev[R_{fund,t} - R_{index,t}]$. Fund Controls include the natural log of assets, natural log of age, and expense ratio, all measured as of the end of calendar year t. Flows represents the Net fund flow of each fund during the previous month. The crisis period range between June 2007 and December 2010. The *t*-statistics are based on standard errors clustered by both fund and time. *, **, and ***, respectively, denote significance at the 10, 5, and 1% levels

Table 7 The effect of active share and Track Error on stock fund alpha. EUROPE SAMPLE

	Alpha CAPM	*Alpha CAPM CRISIS*	*Alpha Fama-French*	*Alpha FF CRISIS*	*Alpha Carhart*	*Alpha Carhart CRISIS*
ACTIVE	−0.0168	−0.0358	0.0094	−0.0045	0.0197	0.0564
	(0.0140)	(0.0472)	(0.0170)	(0.0625)	(0.0235)	(0.0811)
TRACK	0.0527***	0.5835	0.1429***	1.0838***	0.1636***	1.0303
	(0.0172)	(0.4274)	(0.0215)	(0.2937)	(0.0447)	(0.6768)
$\alpha_p^{CAPM}{}_{i,t}$	85.6042***	83.1843***				
	(0.3584)	(0.7326)				
$\alpha_p^{FF}{}_{i,t}$			83.0636***	82.7437***		
			(0.3155)	(0.5745)		
$\alpha_p^{CAR}{}_{i,t}$					78.4951***	72.3462***
					(0.4171)	(1.1034)
AGE	−0.0074**	−0.0891*	−0.0095**	−0.0151	−0.0033	0.0970
	(0.0033)	(0.0534)	(0.0038)	(0.0634)	(0.0049)	(0.0872)
EXPENSE	−0.0133***	−0.0150**	−0.0179***	−0.0229***	−0.0240***	−0.0343***
	(0.0025)	(0.0060)	(0.0026)	(0.0070)	(0.0030)	(0.0095)
FLOWS	0.8583***	0.7345**	0.5664***	0.5049*	0.3689***	0.9321**
	(0.0889)	(0.3174)	(0.0939)	(0.3014)	(0.1246)	(0.3874)
SIZE	−0.0008	−0.0030	−0.0000	0.0007	0.0008	−0.0029
	(0.0006)	(0.0020)	(0.0006)	(0.0019)	(0.0008)	(0.0028)
CONS	0.0571***	0.0981**	0.0626***	0.0270	0.0300	0.0886
	(0.0125)	(0.0390)	(0.0141)	(0.0449)	(0.0185)	(0.0622)
N	52,483	8506	52,483	8506	52,483	8506

Standard errors in parentheses * $p < 0.10$, ** $p < 0.05$, *** $p < 0.01$

This table report the cross-section regressions results of the effect of active share and Track Error on stock fund alpha. Active Share is calculated as $w_A = \frac{\sqrt{1-R^2}}{R+\sqrt{1-R^2}}$. Track errors is calculated as follows: $Trackingerror = Stdev[R_{fund,t} - R_{index,t}]$. Fund Controls include the natural log of assets, natural log of age, and expense ratio, all measured as of the end of calendar year t. Flows represents the Net fund flow of each fund during the previous month. The crisis period range between June 2007 and December 2010. The t-statistics are based on standard errors clustered by both fund and time. *, **, and ***, respectively, denote significance at the 10, 5, and 1% levels

To be specific, we investigate the relation between fund concentration and fund performance using a regression approach and to gauge with different concentration levels, we consider the Miller (2007)'s Active Share and the Tracking Error at the beginning of each month. In this way, we perform an analysis, accounting for the same concentration measures we used in the Sect. 4, but in a cross-sectional setting. Specifically, the regression specification that we utilize is:

$$FUNDRET_{i,t} = \mu + \gamma_1 Active_{i,t-1} + \gamma_2 TRACK_{i,t-1} + \gamma_3 X_{i,t-1} + \sum_{n=1}^{10} \lambda_{nt} StyleDummy_{j,n} + \varepsilon_{i,t} \quad (18)$$

where $FUNDRET_{i,t}$ is the return (in terms of Multifactor Alpha, $\alpha_{i,t}$) of fund i in month t. and also include in the regressions a host of other observable fund characteristics. To this end, we consider $X_{i,t-1}$ representing a set of control variables (in month $t - 1$). The list of other explanatory variables includes a set of control variables we considered in previous analysis. We take the natural logarithms of the age and the size variables because both variables are skewed to the right. Wermers (2003) shows that flows of mutual fund investors can have an impact on asset prices. To control for the effect of lagged inflows, we include the lagged-month flows into each mutual fund as an additional explanatory variable. We lag all explanatory variables by one month. Using the lagged explanatory variables mitigates potential endogeneity problems. Since the pooled panel regressions exhibit significant residual correlations within a year, we also include year dummies and cluster standard errors by year and fund in each regression.

The explanatory variables include also Expense ratio and the past-month returns in terms of Multifactor Alpha,[19] which may reflect managerial skill and persistence in performance (see Brown & Goetzmann, 1995; Gruber, 1996). Here, $\varepsilon_{i,t}$ again stands for a generic error term that is uncorrelated with all other independent variables. The coefficients of interest are γ_1 and γ_2, which captures the relationship between concentration measures and fund performance, controlling for other fund

[19] Chen, J., Hong, H., Huang, M., & Kubik, J. D. (2004). Does fund size erode mutual fund performance? The role of liquidity and organization. *American Economic Review, 94*(5), 1276–1302.

characteristics. γ_3 is the vector of loadings on the control variables. In separate specifications, we consider also the effect of the Global Financial Crisis. The crisis period range between June 2007 and December 2010.

Table 6 summarizes the results of the unconditional CAPM, three and four factor models for the US Equity Mutual Fund Sample. We also considered the effect of the Global Financial Crisis period (The crisis period range between June 2007 and December 2010). Interestingly enough, when we focus just on the two concentration variables (e.g. The Tracking Error and the Active Share), the results indicate that on average a diversified fund portfolio earn more money in terms of multifactor alpha. This evidence holds when considering different a set of multifactor alphas. Even more interesting is how this result holds also when we consider the effect of the period of the Global Financial Crisis. The column next to the multifactor alpha summarizes the coefficient using the crisis period as estimation sample. The magnitude of the Active Coefficient difference increases further if we compare the Crisis Period with respect to the all-time period.

In general, the results of the multifactor models are stronger and statistically more significant than the results using the simple CAPM model. Thus, the relationship between the performance and the portfolio concentration is partly driven by the set of risk factors we used as performance model.

When we consider the second concentration variable, that is the Tracking Error, we find again that the most concentrated fund portfolios tend to outperform the least concentrated portfolios.

Specifically, an increase in the Concentration Level, as measured in terms of Tracking Error, by 10 percentage points (corresponding approximately to one standard deviation of the Tracking Error on yearly basis) increases, during the Crisis period, the monthly Fama-French alpha of a mutual fund by 12 basis points ($= 1.21 \times 10 = 12.1$), or by approximately 144 percentage points on an annual basis. This effect is economically and statistically significant.

A trading strategy of going long in the most concentrated portfolios and going short in the most diversified portfolios could generate a positive risk-adjusted returns.

Concentrated funds appear to outperform diversified funds even after taking into account different Portfolio Model and Risk Factors.

On average, Active Share comes up as a highly significant predictor of future alphas (First row in Table), with a coefficient of 0.1341 in the model accounting for the Carhart 4-factors, during Global Financial Crisis times (Column six). This means that, controlling for the other variables, a 30% increase in Active Share is associated with an increase of 0.40% in Carhart alpha over the following month.

This may appear to be a small increase, but if we consider a valuation on an annual basis, we should conclude that the same increase in Active Share (e.g., 30%) could be associated with an increase of quite 5% the following year.

With respect to the control variables on average, expenses have a statistically significant negative effect on the abnormal return of the mutual fund. Fund age is negatively related to fund performance, and lagged flow is positively related to fund performance. The findings on control variables, even if they are not central to the purposes of this analysis, are consistent with previous findings (Cremers et al., 2016).[20]

In the Table 7, we use the European Sample. Again, here we examine the relation between portfolio concentration and fund performance for two sample periods: 2006–2019 and 2007–2010. The results of this analysis, show a similar positive relation between portfolio concentration and fund performance in both sample periods (All period and Crisis Period) than that found for the sample of the American (US) Funds, but only when the portfolio concentration level is measured in terms of Tracking Error. The coefficient remains similar and is statistically significant at the 1% level.

The sign and magnitude of the coefficient on the Portfolio Concentration, in terms of Tracking Error, are consistent with our previous analysis using the US Equity Sample. Specifically, an increase in the Concentration Level, as measured in terms of Tracking Error, by 10 percentage points (corresponding approximately to one standard deviation of the Tracking Error on yearly basis) increases, during the Crisis period, the monthly Fama-French alpha of a mutual fund by 11 basis points ($= 1.08 \times 10 = 10.8$), or by approximately 132 percentage points on an annual basis. This effect is economically and statistically significant.

Interestingly enough, for the US Equity Sample, unlike Tracking Error, Active Share does not come up as a highly significant predictor of future multifactor alphas (column 1, 3 and 5), with a coefficient both

[20] Cremers, M., Ferreira, M. A., Matos, P., & Starks, L. (2016). Indexing and active fund management: International evidence. *Journal of Financial Economics, 120*(3), 539–560.

positive and negative, depending the sample period and the multifactor model we use to estimate the Active Share, and a *t*-statistic exhibiting no statistically significant reaction at standard level.

References

Amihud, Y., & Goyenko, R. (2013). Mutual fund's R^2 as predictor of performance. *The Review of Financial Studies, 26*(3), 667–694.

Asness, C. S. (2004). An alternative future. *The Journal of Portfolio Management, 30*(5), 94–103.

Basak, S., & Pavlova, A. (2013). Asset prices and institutional investors. *American Economic Analysts Journal, 59*(5), 70–82.

Berk, J. B., & Green, R. (2004). Mutual fund flows and performance in rational markets. *Journal of Political Economy, 112,* 1269–1295.

Bollen, N. P. B., & Busse, J. A. (2005). Short-term persistence in mutual fund performance. *Review of Financial Studies, 18,* 569–597.

Brown, S., & Goetzmann, W. (1995). Attrition and mutual fund performance. *Journal of Finance, 50,* 679–698.

Carhart., M. (1997). On persistence in mutual fund performance. *Journal of Finance, 52*(1), 57–82.

Chen, J., Hong, H., Huang, M., & Kubik, J. D. (2004). Does fund size erode mutual fund performance? The role of liquidity and organization. *American Economic Review, 94*(5), 1276–1302.

Cohen, R. B., Polk, C., & Silli, B. (2010). *Best ideas.* Available at SSRN 1364827.

Cohen, T., Leite, B., Nielson, D., & Browder, A. (2014, February). Active share: A misunderstood measure in manager selection. *Fidelity Leadership Series Investment Insights.*

Cremers, K. M., & Petajisto, A. (2009). How active is your fund manager? A new measure that predicts performance. *The Review of Financial Studies, 22*(9), 3329–3365.

Cremers, M., Ferreira, M., Matos, P., & Starks, L. (2011). *The mutual fund industry worldwide: Explicit and closet indexing, fees, and performance* (Unpublished Working Paper). Yale School of Management.

Cremers, M., Ferreira, M. A., Matos, P., & Starks, L. (2016). Indexing and active fund management: International evidence. *Journal of Financial Economics, 120*(3), 539–560.

Cremers, M., Petajisto, A., & Zitzewitz, E. (2013). Should benchmark indices have alpha? *Revisiting Performance Evaluation, Critical Finance Review, 2,* 1–48.

Del Guercio, D., & Tkac, P. A. (2002). The determinants of the flow of funds of managed portfolios: Mutual funds versus pension funds. *Journal of Financial and Quantitative Analysis, 37,* 523–557.

Dybvig, P. H. (2003). *The fallacy of large numbers and a defense of diversified active managers* (Washington University in Saint Louis Working Paper).

Fama, E. F., & French, K. R. (1993). Common risk factors in the returns on stocks and bonds. *Journal of financial economics, 33*(1), 3–56.

Ferreira, M. A., Keswani, A., Miguel, A. F., & Ramos, S. B. (2013). The determinants of mutual fund performance: A cross-country study. *Review of Finance, 17*(2), 483–525.

Frazzini, A., Friedman, J., & Pomorski, L. (2016). Deactivating active share. *Financial Analysts Journal, 72*(2), 14–21.

Grinold, R. C., & Kahn, R. N. (1999). *Active portfolio management* (2nd ed.). McGraw-Hill.

Gruber, M. (1996). Another puzzle: The growth in actively managed mutual funds. *Journal of Finance, 51*, 783–810.

Jorion, P. (2003). Portfolio optimization with tracking-error constraints. *Financial Management, 18*(4), 13–22.

Kacperczyk, M., Sialm, C., & Zheng, L. (2005). On the industry concentration of actively managed equity mutual funds. *The Journal of Finance, 60*(4), 1983–2011.

Miller, R. M. (2007). Measuring the true cost of active management by mutual funds. *Journal of Investment Management, 5*(1), 29–49.

Nanda, V., Wang, Z., & Zheng, L. (2004). Family values and the star phenomenon. *Review of Financial Studies, 17*(3), 667–698.

Petajisto, A. (2013). Active share and mutual fund performance. *Financial Analysts Journal, 69*(4), 73–93.

Roll, R. (1992). A mean/variance analysis of tracking error. *The Journal of Portfolio Management, 18*(4), 13–22.

Schlanger, T., Philips, C. B., & LaBarge, K. P. (2012, May). The search for outperformance: Evaluating 'active share.' *Vanguard*.

Sun, Z., Wang, A., & Zheng, L. (2012). The road less traveled: Strategy distinctiveness and hedge fund performance. *The Review of Financial Studies, 25*(1), 96–143.

Wahal, S., & Wang, A. Y. (2011). Competition among mutual funds. *Journal of Financial Economics, 99*, 40–59.

Wermers, R. (2003). *Are mutual fund shareholders compensated for active management "Bets"*? (Working Study). University of Maryland.

White, H. (1980). A heteroscedasticity-consistent covariance matrix estimator and a direct test for heteroscedasticity. *Econometrica, 48*, 817–838.

CHAPTER 5

Flows

1 Introduction

Understanding the behavior of fund investors has been a central research question for a long time. From the perspective of investors, one of the most important factors for investment decisions is the past performance of mutual funds (Jeon et al., 2017).[1] Since the investment decisions of mutual funds investors are reflected in fund flows, numerous researchers have investigated the relationship between fund performance and future fund flows.[2] The question here is whether investors can identify superior mutual funds?

According to the "smart money" hypothesis of Gruber (1996) and Zheng (1999), money is "smart" enough to flow to funds that will outperform in the future, that is, that investors have genuine fund selection ability. Some fund managers have skills and some individual investors can detect that skills, and send their money to skilled managers.

The first studies to address this question (Gruber, 1996; Zheng, 1999) find that, indeed, stock market returns and flows into equity

[1] Jeon, H., Kang, J., & Lee, C. (2017). Precision about manager skill, mutual fund flows, and performance persistence. *The North American Journal of Economics and Finance, 40*, 222–237.

[2] Frazzini, A., & Lamont, O. A. (2008). Dumb money: Mutual fund flows and the cross-section of stock returns. *Journal of Financial Economics, 88*(2), 299–322.

G. Galloppo, *Asset Allocation Strategies for Mutual Funds*,
https://doi.org/10.1007/978-3-030-76128-8_5

funds are contemporaneously correlated: positive returns are accompanied by inflows into equity funds, and negative returns are accompanied by outflows or diminished inflows (Jank, 2012).[3]

Gruber (1996) aims to understand the continued expansion of the actively managed mutual fund sector despite the widespread evidence that on average active fund managers do not add value.[4] To test whether investors are more sophisticated than simple chasers of past performance, he examines whether investors' money tends to flow to funds that subsequently outperform (Yu, 2012).[5] Working with a subset of U.S. equity funds, he finds evidence that the weighted average performance of funds that receive net inflows is positive on a risk-adjusted basis (Keswani & Stolin, 2008). Thus, money appears to be smart. Zheng (1999) further develops the analyses of Gruber (1996), expanding the data set to cover the universe of all equity funds between 1970 and 1993. He finds that funds that enjoy positive net flows subsequently perform better on a risk-adjusted basis than funds that experience negative net flows. He also examines whether a trading strategy could be devised based on the predictive ability of net flows and find evidence that information on net flows into small funds could be used to make risk-adjusted profits.[6]

Several competing theories provide explanations for this co-movement (Warther, 1995). The so-called feedback-trader hypothesis affirms that observed market returns cause fund flows. Investors buy fund shares as a response to rising prices and, conversely, they sell when prices fall, hereby causing the positive co-movement. But causality could also run the opposite way. Mutual fund investors may represent sentiment unrelated to fundamentals. Through this uninformed demand from fund investors, stock prices may temporarily diverge from their fundamental values (Jank, 2012). This hypothesis, which claims that flows cause returns, is known as the price-pressure hypothesis.

Sapp and Tiwari (2004), however, argue that the smart money effect documented in prior studies is an artifact of these studies' failure to

[3] Jank, S. (2012). Mutual fund flows, expected returns, and the real economy. *Journal of Banking & Finance, 36*(11), 3060–3070.

[4] See also Keswani, A., & Stolin, D. (2008). Which money is smart? Mutual fund buys and sells of individual and institutional investors. *The Journal of Finance, 63*(1), 85–118.

[5] Yu, H. Y. (2012). Where are the smart investors? New evidence of the smart money effect. *Journal of Empirical Finance, 19*(1), 51–64.

[6] See Footnote 2.

account for the momentum factor in stock returns. Authors calculate abnormal performance following money flows with and without accounting for the momentum factor, and find that inclusion of the momentum factor in the performance evaluation procedure eliminates outperformance of high flow funds (see also on the same topic Keswani & Stolin, 2008).

At the opposite side of the smart money hypothesis, we have "the dumb money" effect (Frazzini & Lamont, 2008), when mutual fund investors have poor market timing ability and they seem to make just the "wrong" decisions: earning lower returns than the market (Ben-Rephael et al., 2012).

The current literature on mutual fund flows can be grouped either in the direction of specific fund characteristics (asset class, style, size) or in the line of relationship between mutual fund flows and performance, with focus on market characteristics and investor behaviour (market volatility, performance persistence, fees, different market stages, smart-money effects and management skills).

2 Flows and Fund Characteristics (Other Than Performance) in Academic Literature

Style. Teo and Woo (2004) investigate that flows into funds within a style category are correlated with the past returns of that style category. Consistent with Teo and Woo (2004), Barber et al. (2016) confirm that flows chase style category returns. However, in contrast with the style-investing story, they find that flows are as, responsive to the fund's size category exposure in a lower meaning than that associated with the fund's deviation from this category average.

Retail and institutional funds. The difference in behavior between retail and institutional funds is investigated in the paper of Jiang and Yuksel (2017). Actively managed mutual funds serve different investor clientele, including both institutional and retail investors. As documented in previous studies, institutional investors are sophisticated and have better understanding of fund characteristics (Akbas et al., 2016; Del Guercio & Tkac, 2002; Evans & Fahlenbrach, 2012; Jiang & Yuksel,

2017; Keswani & Stolin, 2008).[7] In contrast, retail investors are more likely to show behavioral biases, such as the disposition effect (Odean, 1998), or chasing funds based on past performance (Bailey et al., 2011). As such, if the positive flow-performance relation is driven by smart money, Jiang and Yuksel (2017) expect (and find) it to be more pronounced among institutional funds.

So, finally, authors while finding a significantly positive relation between fund flows and subsequent fund performance, also proved that fund with net inflows outperform those with net outflows over the next month. They also find that although institutional fund investors show an ability to pick active funds, there is no evidence of such ability among retail fund investors.

Macroeconomic and microeconomic information. Macroeconomic and microeconomic information is related to mutual fund flows too. Barber et al. (2016) find that mutual fund flows are indeed related to predictive variables, and in particular to dividend yield. According to Jank (2012), in line with the information-response hypothesis, mutual fund flows are related to other variables that predict the equity premium and the real economy. An increase in default spread (consumption-wealth ratio) indicating riskier times, is associated with outflows; while an increase in relative T-Bill rate, indicating less risky times, is associated with inflows into equity funds. Overall, the predictive variables describe fund flows considerably better than stock market returns alone. While stock market return explains about 40.8% of the variation of unexpected mutual fund flows, predictive variables explain up to 51.7%. Jank (2012) shows that (unexpected) changes in predictive variables (proxying for macroeconomic news), rather than the level of these variables, are an important determinant of mutual fund flows.

Taxes. Ivković and Weisbenner (2009) revealed that consistent with tax motivations, individual investors are reluctant to sell mutual funds that have appreciated in value and are willing to sell losing funds. In the U.S., capital gains are taxed on a realization basis, which provides investors with an incentive to hold mutual fund shares, whose net asset value per share (NAV) have appreciated since purchase (thus delaying the payment of taxes) and redeem mutual fund shares whose NAV have

[7] Jiang, G. J., & Yuksel, H. Z. (2017). What drives the "Smart-Money" effect? Evidence from investors' money flow to mutual fund classes. *Journal of Empirical Finance, 40*, 39–58.

fallen in value since purchase (thus, using those losses to reduce taxes right away).[8] In addition, individuals pay attention to investment costs as redemption decisions are sensitive to both expense ratios and loads. In the same fashion, Goldstein et al. (2017) affirm that investors, holding mutual funds in taxable accounts, are reluctant to sell funds appreciated in value and willing to sell funds that have fallen in price. In further support of tax-motivated trading, (see Footnote 1) Ivkovich and Weisbenner (2006), find that taxable investors' redemption decisions are sensitive to proxies for future distribution behavior of the fund.[9] In a related paper, same authors claim that "in taxable accounts, the fund turnover ratio, the historical share of total fund returns distributed to the fund investors over the preceding five years, and the fund capital-gains overhang—three proxies for future fund distribution behavior—are all positively related to redemption probability. By contrast, in tax-deferred accounts turnover does not play a role in redemption decisions and the relation between redemption probability and past fund distribution policy is significantly weaker than it is in taxable accounts".[10]

Fees and participation costs. Barber et al. (2005) analyze mutual fund flows over the last 30 years and find negative relations between flows and front-end-load fees. In contrast, they find no relation between operating expenses and flows. However, using Fama-McBeth (quarterly and monthly) rolling cross-regressions approach, Barber et al. (2005) re-examine the impact of past returns and different types of fees on future fund flows. They find that (quarterly) flows into individual funds are positively related to past (excess) fund returns, R-squared and 12b-1 (advertising) fees but are negatively related to front-end loads—however, funds with high operating expenses do not lead to reduced inflows. They argue that this demonstrates greater sensitivity of flows to advertising and load fees which are "visible", rather than to operating expenses, which are less "visible" (see also Del Guercio & Tkac, 2002; Wilcox, 2003). Investors face participation costs when investing in mutual funds. Huang

[8] Ivković, Z., & Weisbenner, S. (2009). Individual investor mutual fund flows. *Journal of Financial Economics, 92*(2), 223–237.

[9] Ivkovich, Z., & Weisbenner, S. J. (2006, May). 'Old' money matters: The sensitivity of mutual fund redemption decisions to past performance. In EFA 2006 Zurich Meetings Paper.

[10] Ivković, Z., & Weisbenner, S. (2009). Individual investor mutual fund flows. *Journal of Financial Economics, 92*(2), 223–237.

et al. (2007) gauge perfectly the effect of the participation costs over the fund flows. Participation costs affect fund flows through three channels.[11] First, for a given fund, there are cross-sectional differences in participation costs due to investors' various levels of financial sophistication. As past performance has to exceed a threshold value for an individual investor to realize a utility gain from investigating and potentially investing in the fund, better past performance attracts investors with higher costs to overcome their participation barriers. Hence, fund flows are increasingly more sensitive to higher past performance. Second, for an individual investor, the cost of active information collection limits the number of funds he investigates. Since past performance provides a signal of managerial ability, the investor considers both the ranking of past performance and his participation costs in each fund, when deciding about which funds to learn more. The higher his participation costs, the fewer funds he investigates, and the more likely he concentrates his investment in a few funds with superior past performance. Third, transaction costs make it more costly for investors to trade in mutual funds. As a result, investors do not purchase (sell) funds unless their past performance is sufficiently good (bad). This *no-trading effect* makes flows less sensitive to medium levels of performance for higher transaction-costs funds. Ivković and Weisbenner (2009) consider the role that investment costs play in the context of fund-level flows. The most striking finding is that individuals' fund-level inflows and outflows are *each* positively related to expense ratios—whereas higher expenses may attract more "new" money through advertising or a perception that higher expenses reflect better managerial talent or fund family services, they also prompt "old" money to leave the fund sooner than it otherwise would. According to Huang et al. (2007) information cost of collecting and analyzing information about a new fund before investing in it, is relevant in analyzing mutual fund performance. Huang et al. (2007) model the information cost as a fixed cost faced by new investors. Although investors can freely observe past performance of all funds, in accordance to their level of skill and to their information set available at the moment of the investment decision, investors have varied degrees of familiarity with different funds. To make an informed choice, investors can act either by *actively* seeking out the relevant information about the fund or by *passively* accumulating knowledge as it comes to

[11] Huang, J., Wei, K. D., & Yan, H. (2007). Participation costs and the sensitivity of fund flows to past performance. *The Journal of Finance, 62*(3), 1273–1311.

them through advertising or broker recommendations. The more funds expend in resources to lower information barriers; the less investors have to bear the active cost. A second type of cost is related to the ***transaction cost*** of purchasing or redeeming fund shares and it acts jointly to participation cost related to catch the relevant information in order to make a rationale investment decision.

Volatility. Cao et al. (2008) estimated the dynamic relation between market volatility and flows by using a vector autoregression (VAR) approach. They found that daily market volatility was negatively related to concurrent and lagged flows. In addition, the inflow shock induces lower market volatility, while an outflow induces higher volatility. Further, daily flow is negatively related to lag-1 volatility, providing evidence that mutual fund investors time market volatility. In support of these findings. Rakowski (2010) documents that funds with more volatile flows underperform those with less volatile flows. Oh and Parwada (2007) found that equity fund managers would increase stock purchases in times of rising market volatility, disregarding fundamental information, and sell stock assets in times of wide dispersion in investors belief. Raddatz and Schmukler (2012) showed the return-chasing trading behaviour and proved that fund managers and investors would reduce their exposure at the world level during market downturn and increase it during market upturn, where the resulting effect would be pro-cyclical, which accelerates price movements and increases volatility. In line with this, Li et al. (2015) find that fund flows are pro-cyclical ahead of the business cycle and counter-cyclical after the business cycle. Therefore, better (worse) economic prospects are strongly associated with more (less) fund flows but lower (higher) market volatility (Qureshi et al., 2017).

Other fund characteristics. According to, among others, Huang et al. (2007), fund characteristics such as age, volatility of past performance, affiliation with a large or "star family" affect both the level of fund flows and the sensitivity of flows to past performance.[12]

[12] See, for example, Chevalier and Ellison (1997) for the impact of fund age; Sirri and Tufano (1998), Jain and Wu (2000), and Gallaher et al. (2005) for the effect of marketing and advertising expenses; Sirri and Tufano (1998) and Huang et al. (2004) for the importance of performance volatility; and Sirri and Tufano (1998), Massa (2003), Khorana and Servaes (2004), and Nanda et al. (2004) for the significance of the affiliation with large or star producing fund families.

3 Mutual Fund Flows and Performance in Academic Literature

Many researchers document asymmetric relationship between mutual fund flows and past performance: funds with superior recent performance enjoy disproportionately large new money inflows, while funds with poor performance suffer smaller outflows.[13] The two influential works in this research stream are those of Renneboog et al., (2008, 2011), investigating the relationship between future excess returns and average past fund flows. Jeon et al. (2017), by using seven performance measures proposed in both the academic and practice-oriented literature (performance relative to the market benchmark, Sharpe's ratio, Jensen's alpha, Treynor's ratio, information ratio, appraisal ratio, and Carhart's four-factor alpha) over multiple past performance evaluation windows of one, two, three, four, and five years, respectively, define a measure of the imprecision of multiple performance-based signals, and they find that future fund flows respond more (less) strongly to past performance measured with high (low) precision.

In the equity fund literature, there is a generally well-established positive but convex relation between performance and fund flow: inflows are more sensitive to past good performance than outflows are to past poor performance, that is outflows are overall not that sensitive to bad past performance (see Cuthbertson et al., 2010 for a review).

Goldstein et al. (2017) explore flow patterns in corporate bond mutual funds. They show that corporate bond funds exhibit a concave flow-to-performance relationship: their outflows are sensitive to bad performance more than their inflows are sensitive to good performance. Puy (2016) finds strong evidence of global contagion in both equity and bond flows. Periods of high (low) financial stress and poor (good) macroeconomic outlooks in advanced markets are being associated with equity and bond outflows (inflows) at the world level. He finds that the level of political risk, as well as the distance between the location of the fund and the recipient country, are the best predictors of contagion sensitivity. In other

[13] Fong, T. P. W., Sze, A. K. W., & Ho, E. H. C. (2018). Determinants of equity mutual fund flows–Evidence from the fund flow dynamics between Hong Kong and global markets. *Journal of International Financial Markets, Institutions and Money, 57*, 231–247.

words, when facing a shock at home, investors tend to cut (or increase) their exposure to risky countries to a greater extent.

Ivković and Weisbenner (2009) find that inflows are related only to funds' relative performance measures, that is, funds' one-year performance relative to other funds pursuing the same investment objective. On the other hand, outflows are related only to funds' one-year "absolute" returns.

Berk and van Binsbergen (2015) examine mutual fund performance and flow relationships at various horizons by measuring the percent of time that the direction of a fund's flow is the same as the sign of its alpha as estimated using a variety of asset pricing models. At each horizon that they analyze, the sign of flows is more likely to have the same sign as the alpha from the CAPM model than from the alpha calculated using competing asset pricing models.[14] It means that fund flows are best explained by CAPM alphas than by competing models. In the same line, Barber et al. (2016) find that CAPM alphas are the best predictor of flows among competing performance evaluation models. Investors differ in their response to performance; more sophisticated investors use more sophisticated benchmarks. Since investors should use all available information, when assessing fund performance, these results suggest that investors with limited training or financial expertise are less equipped to evaluate fund managers. Del Guercio and Reuter (2014) document that broker-sold mutual funds, which tend to have a less sophisticated investors clientele, experience flows that are more responsive to a fund's market-adjusted return than to its four-factor alpha.

Smart money effect. The literature documents a significantly positive relation between mutual fund flow and future fund performance. Academic scholars attribute this relation to the "smart-money" effect, namely, the ability of mutual fund investors to predict short-term fund performance and invest accordingly by moving money from poor performers to good ones.[15] The seminal papers on the topic of the smart money effect are those of Gruber (1996) and Zheng (1999). Using a sample of 227 stock mutual funds during the period of 1985–1994,

[14] Barber, B. M., Huang, X., & Odean, T. (2016). Which factors matter to investors? Evidence from mutual fund flows. *The Review of Financial Studies, 29*(10), 2600–2642.

[15] Jiang, G. J., & Yuksel, H. Z. (2017). What drives the "Smart-Money" effect? Evidence from investors' money flow to mutual fund classes. *Journal of Empirical Finance, 40*, 39–58.

Gruber (1996) shows that, in the US market, the risk-adjusted returns obtained by new cash flows are higher than the returns achieved by the average investor, both in actively managed and index funds. Again, for the US market, Zheng (1999) found that funds with net cash inflows show better financial performance than funds that suffer net cash outflows. Sapp and Tiwari (2004) present evidence that the results documented in Gruber (1996) and Zheng (1999) are driven by stock return momentum (Jiang & Yuksel, 2017). They consider that the key aspect is the way in which financial performance is measured. Neither Gruber (1996) nor Zheng (1999) use the four-factor Carhart model (1997) (which controls for the momentum style) as a financial performance measure. For the US market, Sapp and Tiwari (2004) found that when financial performance is measured without controlling for momentum style, there is evidence of the smart money effect, but this positive evidence disappears after controlling for it. Meanwhile, Keswani and Stolin (2008), with a sample of British mutual funds and with monthly data in the case of the US market over a more recent sample period of 1991–2004, contradict the empirical evidence of Sapp and Tiwari (2004) and get results for a positive smart money effect, even after controlling for momentum style. In the same line, Ghargori et al. (2007) obtained positive evidence of smart money effect after controlling for momentum style. On the contrary, Frazzini and Lamont (2008) analysed the portfolio holdings of the funds receiving inflows and suffering outflows in the US market. They found empirical evidence of the "dumb money" effect among individual investors. Thus, these investors put their money in funds that hold stocks showing poor financial behaviour in subsequent periods.

Other works that study the smart money effect for conventional mutual fund investors are those of Vicente et al. (2011) (Spanish market), Yu (2012) (US market), Feng et al. (2014) (Chinese market), and Laborda and Muñoz (2016) (US market—government bond funds). Vicente et al. (2011) obtained empirical evidence of a smart money effect that is mainly relevant for the purchasing decisions. Yu (2012) found that the smart money effect occurs among investors in top-performing small funds, even after controlling for momentum style. Feng et al. (2014) found smart money effect among institutional mutual fund investors but dumb money effect among individual investors. Laborda and Muñoz (2016), in the case of investors in US sovereign bond funds, obtained almost no significant evidence of positive selection skills. More recently, Jiang and Yuksel (2017) analysed the smart money effect for conventional mutual fund investors in the US market, distinguishing between institutional and noninstitutional investors. They obtained empirical evidence about a positive relationship between fund flows and subsequent financial performance. They observed that this empirical evidence is mainly conducted by bad performance of funds suffering net outflows, not by the good performance of funds experiencing net inflows. Moreover, they found that this effect is more relevant for noninstitutional/ no-load fund investors than for institutional/load fund ones.

Persistence and management skills. A number of studies have proposed an alternative explanation for the positive flow-performance relation based on the persistence of fund flows, which refers to "persistent-flow" hypothesis.[16] This hypothesis is reflected in works of Jiang and Yuksel (2017), Wermers (2003) and Lou (2012), and suggests that the positive relationship between fund flows and subsequent financial performance is due to the persistence of fund flows. Authors argue that due to high persistence of fund flows, mutual funds with past inflows (outflows) are expected to receive additional capital (redemptions), expand (liquidate) their existing holdings, and drive up (down) their own performance in subsequent periods.[17] Unlike the smart-money hypothesis, which attributes to positive relation between fund flow and future fund performance to investors' ability to identify skilled fund managers, the persistent-flow hypothesis suggests a simple mechanism of price pressure—investors' flows to mutual funds drive this positive relation (Jiang & Yuksel, 2017)). Many scholars believe that positive relationship between capital flow and subsequent financial performance is also driven by skills of investors in selecting senior managers. To investigate further whether fund managers' skill may contribute to the positive flow-performance relation, Jiang and Yuksel (2017) examine the relation between fund flow and active fund management. The main premise is that in response to net inflows, skilled managers are more likely to expand investment opportunities through active trading rather than passive trading of existing positions. A growing literature shows that active style is indicative of fund managers' superior skills. Using fund

[16] Jiang, G. J., & Yuksel, H. Z. (2017). What drives the "Smart-Money" effect? Evidence from investors' money flow to mutual fund classes. *Journal of Empirical Finance, 40*, 39–58.

[17] Lou, D. (2012). A flow-based explanation for return predictability. *The Review of Financial Studies, 25*(12), 3457–3489.

return R^2 (Amihud & Goyenko, 2013), active share (Cremers & Petajisto, 2009; Petajisto, 2013), and Tracking Errors as proxies for active style, Jiang and Yuksel (2017) show that fund flows are positively related to active style for institutional funds but not for retail funds. Finally, they explore the alternative explanation of the positive flow-performance relation, namely, the persistent-flow hypothesis. Consistent with prior studies, authors find that mutual fund flows are highly persistent. Moreover, retail funds exhibit stronger persistence in net outflow than institutional funds and retail investors tend to redeem their positions from mutual funds in a more persistent manner.

Different market stages. In the academic literature, dealing with the correspondence between fund flows and returns under different market stages, a literature on surge flows is getting attention, where a surge refers to exceptionally large capital inflows (Ghosh et al., 2014). Fund flows play an important role in the transmission of shocks (Jinjarak et al., 2011; Raddatz & Schmukler, 2012). Furthermore, Tillmann (2013) establishes that surges of international fund flows may trigger and prolong asset price bubbles and amplify financial fragility. Ghosh et al. (2014) report that global factors, including US interest rates, and global risk aversion, are key factors associated with large net capital flows in EMEs.[18] Ghosh et al. (2014) argue that higher risk aversion is likely to be associated with lower surges since most emerging countries receiving capital inflows aren't safe havens in times of increased uncertainty. Higher commodity prices may be positively correlated with inflows in as much as they indicate a boom in demand for receiving countries' exports (Ghosh et al., 2014). Forbes and Warnock (2012) report that domestic economic growth is the key pull factor explaining gross inflow surges. As argued by Ghosh et al. (2014), if capital flows respond to interest rate and return differentials, they will be larger when expected returns in receiving countries are higher. Li et al. (2018) based their analysis on monthly data for 55 countries and suggested that although most global factors were significant, they could only explain a small part of the surges in fund flows. They found that notably domestic factors affected the magnitude of surges. Chalmers et al. (2010) also document a flight to- quality among mutual fund investors during economic crises.

[18] EMEA is a shorthand designation meaning Europe, the Middle East and Africa.

4 Methodology and Empirical Results

4.1 Flow Computation

Our consideration of monthly observations is explained by the absence of consistent day-end TNA of funds (consistent with Ferreira et al., 2012; Huang et al., 2007; Jeon et al, 2017; Jiang & Yuksel, 2017; Keswani & Stolin, 2008; Rakowski & Wang, 2009, who outline strong flow-performance relationship monthly). Moreover, we observed that most of mutual funds reported their daily flows of current days, but others included daily flows only partially. We do not provide a more detailed granularity in this study also due to the fact that investments into funds analyzed here demonstrate less problems of high frequency trading than other financial assets.

First of all, we calculate *Net Flow* on date *t* for a single fund in the way, supported by previous studies (Cao et al., 2008; Rakowski & Wang, 2009). To go further, we calculate the *Differential Flow* from one period to another in the following Eq. (1):

$$Flow_t = TNA_t - NAV_t \frac{\text{TNA}_{t-1}}{NAV_{t-1}} \tag{1}$$

Then, we compute percentage flows Eq. (2):

$$\%Flow_t = \frac{Flow_t}{\left(\frac{TNA_t}{1+r_t}\right)} \tag{2}$$

4.2 Flow and Return: Multivariate Approach

In this section, we perform panel regressions of fund returns on investors' flows and other fund characteristics. We grouped funds by investment target representing the fund style, as follows: EUR Corporate Bond, EUR Government Bond, Europe Large-Cap Equity, Europe Small and Mid-Cap Equity, Europe Growth Equity, Europe Value Equity, Europe Blend Equity, US Corporate Bond, US Government Bond, US Large-Cap Equity, US Small and Mid-Cap Equity, US Growth Equity, US Value Equity, US Blend Equity.

For our sample, we have chosen only funds with at least 12 months observations. First of all, a five-standard-deviation filter was used to avoid the outliers in the result of recording errors. Second, we applied a three-standard-deviation filter to catch false reversals or continuations. After these filters, we eliminated extreme observations (top and bottom 1% of flows) and calculated the net flows and percentage flows from Eqs. (1) and (2).

We employ the research design of previous scholars (Akbas et al., 2016; Clare et al., 2019; Fong et al., 2018; Jiang & Yuksel, 2017) by taking fund returns (measured in terms of multifactor alphas) and fund flows. Following the literature (see among others: Jiang & Yuksel, 2017), we also control for various fund characteristics that are potential determinants of subsequent fund performance.

To be specific, by using a multivariate approach, we regress the conditional four-factor Carhart alpha for each fund, computed using a rolling window of 52 weeks, on flows in the previous month and other mutual fund characteristics. We also control for time (month) fixed effects. The standard errors are clustered at mutual fund level.

Specifically, for each month t, we estimate the following regression:

$$\begin{aligned}\hat{\alpha}_{i,t}^{MF}\left(\alpha_{p}^{BOND}\right) =& Intercept_{i,t} + \beta_1 Flow_{i,t-1} + \beta_2 \log(TNA)_{i,t-1} \\ &+ \beta_3 \hat{\alpha}_{i,t-1}^{MF} + \beta_4 ExpenseRatio_{i,t-1} + \beta_5 ActiveShare_{i,t-1} \\ &+ \beta_6 Volatility_{j,t-1} + \beta_7 R - square_{j,t-1} + \varepsilon_{i,t}\end{aligned} \quad (3)$$

where $\widehat{\alpha}_{i,t}^{MF}$ is the 52-weeks rolling window estimation of the multi-factor alpha (CAPM, Fama-French or Carhart alpha), for fund i in month t. $\hat{\alpha}_{i,t}^{4F}$ *and* α_{p}^{BOND} are described in Eqs. (4) and (5), respectively. In this way, in the multivariate approach, the time sample analysed spans from December 2006 to December 2019. $Flow_{i,t-1}$ is the normalized monthly net flow of fund i in month $t-1$. $\log(TNA)_{i,t-1}$ is the logarithm of the total net assets of fund i in period $t-1$ representing the Mutual Fund *SIZE*; $ExpenseRatio_{i,t-1}$, is the net expense ratio. These variables have been included in regression analysis in previous studies (e.g., Bergstresser et al., 2009; Chen et al., 2004, 2007; Friesen & Sapp, 2007; Huang et al., 2011; Jiang & Yuksel, 2017; Keswani & Stolin, 2008; Sialm et al, 2015).

Fund performance is evaluated based on fund alpha. To catch the difference in risk return trade off between equity and fixed income strategies, we run two separate conditional market models. To compute the equity perfromance we account for a set of multi-factor models. In the more extensive specification we consider t he four-factor alpha $\widehat{\alpha}_{i,t}^{4F}$

representing the intercept of four-factor model, as follows:

$$r_{p,t} = \alpha_p + \beta_{1,p}MKTRF_t + \beta_{2,p}SMB_t + \beta_{3,p}HML_t + \beta_{4,p}UMD_t + \varepsilon_{pt} \quad (4)$$

where $r_{p,t}$ is the monthly return on a funds in excess of the one-month Treasury bill (T-bill) rate.[19] $MKTRF_t$ is the stock market return in excess of the one-month T-bill rate. *SMB, HML, and UMD* (MOM) are, respectively, returns on factor-mimicking portfolios for size, book-to-market, and momentum. Multifactor attributes are drawn from Kenneth R. French—Data Library.

When we take into account Fixed Income Mutual Funds, we follow previous studies (Ayadi & Kryzanowski, 2011; Boney et al., 2009), and we refer to (α^{BOND}) that is the intercept of the following model:

$$r_{p,t} = \alpha_p^{BOND} + \beta_{1,p}MKTRF_t^{Bond} + \beta_{2,p}DEFAULT_t + \beta_{3,p}TERM_t + \varepsilon_{pt} \quad (5)$$

which includes the excess market return $MKTRF_t^{Bond}$ is the Local (European or Us) Total Bond Market Index return in excess of the one-month T-bill rate, default risk (DEFAULT), and term risk (TERM). DEFAULT denotes the difference in return between investment grade corporate and government bonds (10-year Treasury Constant Maturity Yield); TERM is defined as the difference in return between long-term (10-year Treasury Constant Maturity Yield) and short-term government bonds (1-year Treasury Constant Maturity Yield).

In order to verify whether the relationship between flows and returns is time dependent, we examine the relation between mutual fund flows and future fund performance in different time periods and provide an evidence that flow-performance relationship is changing according to market conditions. All tables report the regression results for the fund sample grouped by asset types and management styles according to All sample period and global crisis market conditions.

Our main interest is not to make inferences regarding the entire set of control variables but to focus primarily over the coefficient coupled with past flows (FLOWS).

Tables 1, 2, 3, and 4, report the regression results for the different

[19] We consider one-month treasury bill at local market level both for European and US Fixed Income mutual funds.

Table 1 Multivariate tests: regressions of fund performance on fund flows and other attributes—EUROPEAN FIXED INCOME FUNDS

Panel A—ALL Sample Period

	Simple return CORPORATE	*Alpha CORPORATE*	*Simple return GOVERNMENT*	*Alpha GOVERNMENT*
AGE	0.0001	0.1938	−0.0002	−45.0406
	(0.0003)	(36.6572)	(0.0005)	(38.5697)
EXPENSE	−0.0005	-72.6388^{**}	-0.0008^{*}	−7.5626
	(0.0003)	(31.8651)	(0.0005)	(51.2729)
FLOWS	-0.0278^{***}	903.6459	0.0188^{***}	149.0404
	(0.0061)	(678.9371)	(0.0046)	(744.6085)
SIZE	0.0001	1.3600	0.0001	6.5049
	(0.0001)	(6.7227)	(0.0001)	(5.7961)
RETURN	-0.1205^{***}		-0.1833^{***}	
	(0.0290)		(0.0204)	
ALPHA		−132.5246		−852.7172
		(294.7319)		(647.4790)
CONS	0.0005	11.7043	0.0010	−51.1912
	(0.0012)	(119.5399)	(0.0012)	(117.8488)
N	17,087	17,087	9359	9359

Standard errors in parentheses $^{*}p < 0.10$, $^{**}p < 0.05$, $^{***}p < 0.01$

Panel B—Crisis Time

	Simple return CORPORATE	*Alpha CORPORATE*	*Simple return GOVERNMENT*	*Alpha GOVERNMENT*
AGE	0.0097^{***}	9.8115^{**}	0.0016	−2.5864
	(0.0029)	(4.5961)	(0.0026)	(4.0846)
EXPENSE	0.0000	0.9909	−0.0011	0.9063
	(0.0007)	(2.0885)	(0.0007)	(0.8433)
FLOWS	-0.0672^{***}	−19.0200	0.0207^{**}	2.3847
	(0.0170)	(14.1578)	(0.0098)	(5.3979)
SIZE	0.0000	0.0107	0.0001	−0.0574
	(0.0002)	(0.1763)	(0.0001)	(0.1614)
RETURN	-0.0934^{**}		-0.2901^{***}	
	(0.0439)		(0.0323)	
ALPHA		109.8772^{***}		95.6281^{***}
		(20.7181)		(3.2507)
CONS	0.0008	−5.0860	0.0009	5.5159^{*}
	(0.0030)	(11.3573)	(0.0021)	(3.1378)

(continued)

Table 1 (continued)

Panel B—Crisis Time

	Simple return CORPORATE	*Alpha CORPORATE*	*Simple return GOVERNMENT*	*Alpha GOVERNMENT*
N	2892	2892	1819	1819

Standard errors in parentheses $^{*}p < 0.10$, $^{**}p < 0.05$, $^{***}p < 0.01$

Notes This table reports the results of the panel regressions of mutual fund performance on the previous month's fund flows and other fund characteristics (all one period lagged). AGE is defined as the number of months from the fund's inception.$Flow_{i,t-1}$ is the normalized monthly net flow of fund i in month $t-1$. SIZE is the logarithm of the total net assets of fund i in period $t-1$ $\log(TNA)_{i,t-1}$; $ExpenseRatio_{i,t-1}$, is the net expense ratio. Portfolio performance is evaluated based on simple Return and portfolio alpha according to the following model: $r_{p,t} = \alpha_p^{BOND} + \beta_{1,p}MKTRF_t^{Bond} + \beta_{2,t}MKTRF_t^{Equity} + \beta_{3,p}DEFAULT_t + \beta_{4,p}TERM_t + \varepsilon_{p,t}$; where $r_{p,t}$ is the monthly return on a portfolio of funds in excess of the one-month T-bill rate; $MKTRF_t^{Bond}$ is the Local (European or Us) Total Bond Market Index return in excess of the one-month T-bill rate. $MKTRF_t{}^{Equity}$ is the (European) U.S. equity market return in excess of the one-month T-bill rate and is included to control for potential equity market bias$DEFAULT$ is the difference in return between investment grade corporate bonds and government bonds (10-year Treasury Constant Maturity Yield); $TERM_t$ is the difference in return between long-term (30-year Treasury Constant Maturity Yield) and short-term government bonds (one-year Treasury Constant Maturity Yield). The ALL Sample Period is from December 2006 to December 2019. The crisis period range betweeh June 2007 to December 2010.

sample of funds according to the specific investment target. The coefficients of other fund characteristics are similar to those reported in the literature. For example, funds with lower expenses tend to have higher returns.

Table 1 reports multivariate tests: regression results of fund performance on the previous months' fund flows and other fund characteristics for European fixed income funds (corporate and government bonds) both for the all-sample period (2006–2019) and financial crisis time (2007–2010). The coefficients of other fund characteristics correspond to those from the existing literature. We confirm that the relation between fund flows and future fund performance is not univocal, thus, it can be positive or negative. The coefficient of fund flows is negative and strongly significant for corporate bonds in both all-sample period and crisis times, but it is strongly positive for government bonds at 1% level in all-sample period and 5% level in crisis time. Therefore, the coefficient is higher in crisis time, signifying the increase of sensitivity of fund flows.

Table 2 Multivariate tests: regressions of fund performance on fund flows and other attributes—US FIXED INCOME FUNDS

Panel A—ALL Sample Period

	Simple return CORPORATE	*Alpha CORPORATE*	*Simple return GOVERNMENT*	*Alpha GOVERNMENT*
AGE	−0.0007**	−0.2434*	−0.0000	0.0700
	(0.0003)	(0.1416)	(0.0003)	(0.2153)
EXPENSE	−0.0001	0.2251	−0.0001	0.1967
	(0.0004)	(0.1582)	(0.0002)	(0.1451)
FLOWS	−0.0053	8.7165	0.0179	31.2920
	(0.0138)	(17.0481)	(0.0192)	(18.7897)
SIZE	0.0002***	0.0291	0.0001**	0.0872
	(0.0000)	(0.0248)	(0.0000)	(0.0628)
RETURN	0.0446**		−0.0268	
	(0.0207)		(0.0185)	
ALPHA		91.8200***		95.9156***
		(2.6084)		(3.4280)
CONS	−0.0002	−0.0509	−0.0006	−1.5376
	(0.0007)	(0.4334)	(0.0008)	(1.0408)
N	8394	8394	7785	7785

Standard errors in parentheses $^{*}p < 0.10$, $^{**}p < 0.05$, $^{***}p < 0.01$

Panel B—Crisis Time

	Simple return CORPORATE	*Alpha CORPORATE*	*Simple return GOVERNMENT*	*Alpha GOVERNMENT*
AGE	0.0033	2.0439	0.0031	−3.5287**
	(0.0039)	(2.7389)	(0.0027)	(1.4784)
EXPENSE	−0.0020**	0.3695	−0.0005	0.3318
	(0.0009)	(1.4063)	(0.0004)	(0.2397)
FLOWS	−0.0271	41.7519	0.0339	62.8908**
	(0.0305)	(30.5195)	(0.0385)	(29.6724)
SIZE	0.0001	−0.0074	0.0002*	0.1477**
	(0.0002)	(0.1284)	(0.0001)	(0.0715)
RETURN	0.0282		0.0243	
	(0.0474)		(0.0402)	
ALPHA		85.8636***		99.1976***
		(4.6202)		(4.9713)
CONS	0.0029	−0.2383	−0.0016	−2.2225*
	(0.0026)	(1.8591)	(0.0017)	(1.2176)

(continued)

Table 2 (continued)

Panel B—Crisis Time

	Simple return CORPORATE	*Alpha* CORPORATE	*Simple return* GOVERNMENT	*Alpha* GOVERNMENT
N	956	956	1480	1480

Standard errors in parentheses $^{*}p < 0.10$, $^{**}p < 0.05$, $^{***}p < 0.01$.

Notes This table reports the results of the panel regressions of mutual fund performance on the previous month's fund flows and other fund characteristics (all one period lagged). AGE is defined as the number of months from the fund's inception.$Flow_{i,t-1}$ is the normalized monthly net flow of fund i in month $t-1$. SIZE is the logarithm of the total net assets of fund i in period $t-1$ $\log(TNA)_{i,t-1}$; $ExpenseRatio_{i,t-1}$, is the net expense ratio. Portfolio performance is evaluated based on simple Return and portfolio alpha according to the following model: $r_{p,t} = \alpha_p^{BOND} + \beta_{1,p}MKTRF_t^{Bond} + \beta_{2,t}MKTRF_t^{Equity} + \beta_{3,p}DEFAULT_t + \beta_{4,p}TERM_t + \varepsilon_{p,t}$; where $r_{p,t}$ is the monthly return on a portfolio of funds in excess of the one-month T-bill rate; $MKTRF_t^{Bond}$ is the Local (European or Us) Total Bond Market Index return in excess of the one-month T-bill rate. $MKTRF_t^{Equity}$ is the (European) U.S. equity market return in excess of the one-month T-bill rate and is included to control for potential equity market bias$DEFAULT$ is the difference in return between investment grade corporate bonds and government bonds (10-year Treasury Constant Maturity Yield); $TERM_t$ is the difference in return between long-term (30-year Treasury Constant Maturity Yield) and short-term government bonds (one-year Treasury Constant Maturity Yield). The ALL Sample Period is from December 2006 to December 2019. The crisis period range between June 2007 to December 2010

Table 2 reports multivariate tests: regression results of fund performance on the previous months' fund flows and other fund characteristics for US fixed income funds (corporate and government bonds) both for the all-sample period (2006–2019) and financial crisis time (2007–2010). Other fund characteristics are similar to previous literature. We confirm that the coefficient for fund flows is positive and statistically significant at 5% level only when measured with alpha regression model for government bond type.

Table 3 reports Multivariate tests: regressions of fund performance on fund flows and other attributes for US equity mutual funds for the all-sample period (2006–2019) and crisis period (2007–2010), and for blend, value, growth asset styles and large and small cap size assets, which is measured by means of different alphas, such as CAPM or Jensen Alpha, Fama-French Alpha and Carhart or Momentum Four Factor alpha. In general, we catch a better reaction in terms of significance in all-sample period. For blend asset style, the coefficient of fund flows is positive 1% statistically significant for all multifactor performance measures in both

Table 3 Multivariate tests: regressions of fund performance on fund flows and other attributes—US EQUITY FUNDS

Panel A—ALL SAMPLE PERIOD (BLEND, VALUE and GROWTH MUTUAL FUNDS)

	CAPM alpha_ BLEND	*Fama–French alpha_BLEND*	*Carhart alpha_ BLEND*	*CAPM alpha_ VALUE*	*Fama–French alpha_ VALUE*	*Carhart (MOM) alpha_ VALUE*	*CAPM alpha_GROWTH*	*Fama–French alpha_ GROWTH*	*Carhart (MOM) alpha_ GROWTH*
AGE	−0.0055	−0.0078*	−0.0055	−0.0119	−0.0114	−0.0140	−0.0320**	−0.0345**	– 0.0329**
	(0.0036)	(0.0041)	(0.0049)	(0.0105)	(0.0131)	(0.0149)	(0.0120)	(0.0146)	(0.0145)
EXPENSE	−0.0105***	−0.0119***	−0.0133***	−0.0182*	−0.0203**	−0.0251***	0.0017	0.0002	0.0007
	(0.0019)	(0.0021)	(0.0024)	(0.0101)	(0.0090)	(0.0091)	(0.0077)	(0.0085)	(0.0087)
FLOWS	1.0319***	1.4049***	1.3650***	0.9005**	0.7121	0.4015	0.6037	1.6098	1.6388*
	(0.2214)	(0.2470)	(0.2369)	(0.3905)	(0.4915)	(0.4838)	(0.7368)	(1.0500)	(0.8912)
SIZE	0.0006	0.0013**	0.0016**	0.0020	0.0016	0.0027	0.0032***	0.0035***	0.0035***

Panel A—ALL SAMPLE PERIOD (BLEND, VALUE and GROWTH MUTUAL FUNDS)

	CAPM alpha_ BLEND	*Fama–French alpha_BLEND*	*Carhart alpha_ BLEND*	*CAPM alpha_ VALUE*	*Fama–French alpha_ VALUE*	*Carhart (MOM) alpha_ VALUE*	*CAPM alpha_GROWTH*	*Fama–French alpha_ GROWTH*	*Carhart (MOM) alpha_ GROWTH*
	(0.0005)	(0.0005)	(0.0006)	(0.0014)	(0.0015)	(0.0018)	(0.0009)	(0.0010)	(0.0012)
Alpha_ CAPM	85.0392***			82.2992***			86.8415***		
	(0.4713)			(1.2403)			(1.0153)		
Alpha_FF		82.1688***			80.7082***			81.7487***	
		(0.4557)			(1.2960)			(1.3693)	
Alpha_MOM			79.6771***			77.1042***			79.9730***
			(0.5107)			(1.1177)			(1.4180)
CONS	0.0028	−0.0100	−0.0132	−0.0218	−0.0020	−0.0126	−0.0148	−0.0251	−0.0247
	(0.0079)	(0.0094)	(0.0107)	(0.0296)	(0.0316)	(0.0347)	(0.0182)	(0.0221)	(0.0255)
N	37,815	37,815	37,815	4271	4271	4271	4708	4708	4708

Standard errors in parentheses $^{*}p < 0.10$, $^{**}p < 0.05$, $^{***}p < 0.01$

(continued)

Table 3 (continued)

Panel B—CRISIS TIME (BLEND, VALUE and GROWTH MUTUAL FUNDS)

	CAPM alpha_ BLEND	*Fama–French alpha_ BLEND*	*Carhart alpha_ BLEND*	*CAPM alpha_ VALUE*	*Fama–French alpha_ VALUE*	*Carhart (MOM) alpha_ VALUE*	*CAPM alpha_ GROWTH*	*Fama–French alpha_ GROWTH*	*Carhart (MOM) alpha_ GROWTH*
AGE	−0.0404	−0.0322	−0.0674	−0.2574	−0.1624	−0.1412	0.0009	−0.0214	−0.0953
	(0.0343)	(0.0421)	(0.0424)	(0.2117)	(0.2796)	(0.3242)	(0.0945)	(0.1239)	(0.1231)
EXPENSE	− 0.0094**	−0.0047	−0.0026	−0.0102	−0.0160	−0.0312	0.0071	0.0042	0.0079
	(0.0043)	(0.0043)	(0.0042)	(0.0337)	(0.0284)	(0.0283)	(0.0098)	(0.0134)	(0.0171)
FLOWS	0.8250*	1.6688***	1.7457***	2.2615	2.1626	1.7493*	0.6171	0.9242	2.3648
	(0.4777)	(0.5403)	(0.5538)	(1.3314)	(1.4442)	(0.8621)	(2.5556)	(2.8339)	(3.1792)
SIZE	−0.0002	0.0018	0.0028**	−0.0035	0.0033	0.0097***	−0.0001	0.0020	0.0015
	(0.0011)	(0.0013)	(0.0012)	(0.0032)	(0.0024)	(0.0034)	(0.0027)	(0.0031)	(0.0030)
Alpha_ CAPM	84.9950***			81.4209***			86.2722***		
	(0.7300)			(3.1711)			(1.4947)		
Alpha_FF		80.3150***			76.9252***			80.7259***	
		(0.8701)			(3.6190)			(2.3155)	
Alpha_MOM			80.8236***			75.5860***			79.0764***
			(0.8285)			(4.0175)			(3.0021)
CONS	0.0312*	−0.0263	−0.0449**	0.1559	−0.0094	−0.1314	0.0130	−0.0471	−0.0444
	(0.0184)	(0.0209)	(0.0205)	(0.0941)	(0.0777)	(0.0887)	(0.0412)	(0.0525)	(0.0517)
N	7362	7362	7362	586	586	586	784	784	784

Standard errors in parentheses $^{*}p < 0.10$, $^{**}p < 0.05$, $^{***}p < 0.01$.

Panel C—ALL SAMPLE PERIOD (SMALL and LARGE MUTUAL FUNDS)

	CAPM alpha LARGE	*Fama–French alpha_ LARGE*	*Carhart alpha LARGE*	*CAPM alpha SMALL*	*Fama–French alpha SMALL*	*Carhart alpha SMALL*
AGE	−0.0000	−0.0031	−0.0018	−0.0147	0.0006	−0.0076
	(0.0082)	(0.0084)	(0.0094)	(0.0117)	(0.0119)	(0.0141)
EXPENSE	0.0002	−0.0045	−0.0059	−0.0004	−0.0091	−0.0161
	(0.0046)	(0.0050)	(0.0057)	(0.0093)	(0.0100)	(0.0132)
FLOWS	0.5090	1.0328**	1.0811***	1.2062***	1.1389**	1.5399***
	(0.3939)	(0.3990)	(0.4000)	(0.3495)	(0.4742)	(0.5044)
SIZE	0.0014**	0.0024***	0.0027***	−0.0005	0.0020	0.0023
	(0.0006)	(0.0006)	(0.0007)	(0.0014)	(0.0017)	(0.0021)
Alpha_CAPM	87.5672***			86.8465***		
	(0.6232)			(0.7474)		
Alpha_FF		83.0195***			84.2332***	
		(0.7346)			(0.8990)	
Alpha_MOM			80.2042***			81.5843***
			(0.7979)			(1.1995)
CONS	−0.0196	−0.0308**	−0.0330**	0.0245	0.0029	0.0158
	(0.0121)	(0.0129)	(0.0152)	(0.0239)	(0.0276)	(0.0344)
N	13,350	13,350	13,350	3973	3973	3973

(continued)

Table 3 (continued)

Panel D—CRISIS TIME (SMALL and LARGE MUTUAL FUNDS)

	Alpha_CAPM LARGE	*Fama–French alpha LARGE*	*Carhart alpha LARGE*	*Alpha_CAPM SMALL*	*Fama–French alpha SMALL*	*Carhart alpha SMALL*
AGE	−0.0724	−0.0670	−0.0913	0.3783*	0.2554	0.2668
	(0.0510)	(0.0605)	(0.0685)	(0.2102)	(0.1635)	(0.1735)
EXPENSE	−0.0003	−0.0116	−0.0106	−0.0077	−0.0051	−0.0173
	(0.0072)	(0.0082)	(0.0100)	(0.0153)	(0.0259)	(0.0345)
FLOWS	0.1027	0.8342	1.0761	−0.0418	−0.1295	−0.3655
	(1.0927)	(0.9797)	(0.9279)	(1.3634)	(0.9668)	(1.4054)
SIZE	0.0018	0.0022	0.0019	−0.0093*	0.0024	0.0005
	(0.0013)	(0.0015)	(0.0018)	(0.0047)	(0.0060)	(0.0066)
Alpha_CAPM	87.3136***			86.4934***		
	(0.9428)			(1.5914)		
Alpha_FF		84.5153***			84.1060***	
		(1.2919)			(2.1631)	
Alpha_MOM			83.4538***			83.7173***
			(1.3329)			(1.7321)
CONS	0.0097	−0.0187	−0.0167	0.1571***	−0.0879	−0.0627
	(0.0261)	(0.0318)	(0.0362)	(0.0407)	(0.0608)	(0.0678)
N	2254	2254	2254	553	553	553

Notes This table reports the results of the panel regressions of mutual fund performance on the previous month's fund flows and other fund characteristics (all one period lagged). Portfolio performance is evaluated based on simple Return and portfolio alphas (CAPM or Jensen Alpha, Fama–French Alpha and Carhart or Momentum Four Factor alpha). AGE is defined as the number of months from the fund's inception. $Flow_{i,t-1}$ is the normalized monthly net flow of fund i in month $t-1$. SIZE is the logarithm of the total net assets of fund i in period $t-1$ $\log(TNA)_{i,t1}$; $ExpenseRatio_{i,t-1}$, is the net expense ratio. The ALL Sample Period is from December 2006 to December 2019. The crisis period range beteeh June 2007 to December 2010. The t-statistics are based on standard errors clustered at mutual fund level. *, **, and ***, respectively, denote significance at the 10%, 5%, and 1% levels. We considered Time and Country fixed effects. We consider several management style. To be specific we account for Blend, Value, Growth, Large and Small CAP Mutual funds

Table 4 Multivariate tests: regressions of fund performance on fund flows and other attributes—EUROPEAN EQUITY FUNDS

Panel A—ALL SAMPLE PERIOD (BLEND, VALUE and GROWTH MUTUAL FUNDS)

	CAPM alpha_ BLEND	*Fama–French alpha_BLEND*	*Carhart alpha_ BLEND*	*CAPM alpha_ VALUE*	*Fama–French alpha_ VALUE*	*Carhart alpha_ VALUE*	*CAPM alpha_ GROWTH*	*Fama–French alpha_ GROWTH*	*Carhart alpha_ GROWTH*
AGE	−0.0122**	−0.0152**	−0.0109	0.0052	−0.0136	−0.0253	−0.0054	−0.0069	−0.0048
	(0.0051)	(0.0059)	(0.0076)	(0.0141)	(0.0172)	(0.0216)	(0.0111)	(0.0141)	(0.0174)
EXPENSE	−0.0152***	−0.0194***	−0.0257***	−0.0209**	−0.0240***	−0.0261**	−0.0160	−0.0091	−0.0235
	(0.0032)	(0.0037)	(0.0045)	(0.0089)	(0.0081)	(0.0103)	(0.0126)	(0.0139)	(0.0151)
FLOWS	0.4115***	0.2583***	0.1758	0.3256*	0.0429	−0.0839	0.2860**	0.3108**	0.1401
	(0.0709)	(0.0774)	(0.1091)	(0.1638)	(0.2143)	(0.2481)	(0.1320)	(0.1472)	(0.2169)
SIZE	0.0001	0.0009	0.0021*	−0.0029	−0.0029	−0.0011	0.0003	0.0007	0.0006
	(0.0009)	(0.0009)	(0.0012)	(0.0025)	(0.0026)	(0.0032)	(0.0011)	(0.0012)	(0.0016)
Alpha_CAPM	84.1968***			81.4959***			88.1034***		
	(0.6771)			(1.1558)			(1.4777)		
Alpha_FF		82.6591***			81.2945***			84.3132***	
		(0.5492)			(1.1279)			(1.4682)	
Alpha_MOM			78.4085***			77.0615***			81.0665***
			(0.7321)			(1.5829)			(1.4227)
CONS	0.0353**	0.0578***	0.0238	0.0665	0.1261**	0.0963	0.0408	0.0493*	0.0422
	(0.0144)	(0.0162)	(0.0212)	(0.0461)	(0.0487)	(0.0584)	(0.0251)	(0.0279)	(0.0361)
N	18,124	18,124	18,124	4008	4008	4008	3852	3852	3852

Standard errors in parentheses. $^{*}p < 0.10$, $^{**}p < 0.05$, $^{***}p < 0.01$

(continued)

Table 4 (continued)

Panel B—CRISIS TIME (BLEND, VALUE and GROWTH MUTUAL FUNDS)

	CAPM alpha_ BLEND	*Fama–French alpha_ BLEND*	*Carhart alpha_ BLEND*	*CAPM alpha_ VALUE*	*Fama–French alpha_ VALUE*	*Carhart alpha_ VALUE*	*CAPM alpha_ GROWTH*	*Fama–French alpha_GROWTH*	*Carhart alpha_GROWTH*
AGE	−0.1724**	−0.1713*	−0.1492	0.1213	0.0835	0.0247	0.0869	0.1925	0.4560*
	(0.0791)	(0.0955)	(0.1419)	(0.1695)	(0.1869)	(0.2127)	(0.1619)	(0.1575)	(0.2395)
EXPENSE	−0.0158**	−0.0217**	−0.0307***	−0.0467**	−0.0508**	−0.0652***	0.0006	0.0708	0.0660
	(0.0073)	(0.0093)	(0.0116)	(0.0189)	(0.0212)	(0.0211)	(0.0295)	(0.0500)	(0.0437)
FLOWS	0.2779	0.2017	0.3557	0.4901	0.3162	0.4935	0.0479	0.1129	−0.8136
	(0.2041)	(0.2228)	(0.2990)	(0.4654)	(0.5124)	(0.4502)	(0.6351)	(0.6594)	(0.9207)
SIZE	0.0007	0.0036	0.0006	0.0040	0.0041	0.0017	−0.0032	−0.0068	−0.0147*
	(0.0027)	(0.0033)	(0.0053)	(0.0046)	(0.0039)	(0.0050)	(0.0043)	(0.0049)	(0.0079)
Alpha_CAPM	82.3598***			81.6543***			89.9553***		
	(1.2170)			(1.5609)			(2.4025)		
Alpha_FF		82.4134***			83.3176***			85.5708***	
		(0.9856)			(1.6304)			(2.8347)	
Alpha_MOM			73.5154***			75.7922***			77.8430***
			(1.6367)			(2.2231)			(3.0402)
CONS	0.0733*	0.0781	0.1207	−0.0460	0.0197	0.0686	0.0521	0.0782	0.1672
	(0.0397)	(0.0525)	(0.0861)	(0.1119)	(0.1145)	(0.1331)	(0.0556)	(0.0654)	(0.1158)
N	3285	3285	3285	786	786	786	549	549	549

Standard errors in parentheses * $p < 0.10$, ** $p < 0.05$, *** $p < 0.01$

Panel C—ALL SAMPLE PERIOD (SMALL and LARGE MUTUAL FUNDS)						
	CAPM alpha LARGE	*Fama–French alpha_ LARGE*	*Carhart alpha LARGE*	*CAPM alpha SMALL*	*Fama–French alpha SMALL*	*Carhart alpha SMALL*
AGE	−0.0088*	−0.0094	−0.0007	−0.0005	−0.0006	0.0042
	(0.0050)	(0.0062)	(0.0077)	(0.0098)	(0.0126)	(0.0166)
EXPENSE	−0.0166***	−0.0228***	−0.0303***	−0.0047	−0.0036	−0.0054
	(0.0031)	(0.0039)	(0.0046)	(0.0076)	(0.0090)	(0.0109)
FLOWS	0.4126***	0.2837***	0.1935**	0.4036***	0.6017***	0.5166**
	(0.0701)	(0.0684)	(0.0949)	(0.1384)	(0.1614)	(0.2214)
SIZE	0.0000	0.0009	0.0013	−0.0007	−0.0016	−0.0002
	(0.0008)	(0.0009)	(0.0011)	(0.0017)	(0.0018)	(0.0024)
Alpha_CAPM	83.8564***			85.9639***		
	(0.7156)			(0.8237)		
Alpha_FF		82.4528***			83.8332***	
		(0.5392)			(0.5780)	
Alpha_MOM			77.8976***			78.7494***
			(0.7202)			(0.9336)
CONS	0.0378***	0.0594***	0.0383*	0.0604**	0.0922***	0.0562
	(0.0137)	(0.0166)	(0.0203)	(0.0276)	(0.0293)	(0.0389)
N	18,673	18,673	18,673	8005	8005	8005

(continued)

Table 4 (continued)

Panel D—CRISIS TIME (SMALL and LARGE MUTUAL FUNDS)

	CAPM alpha LARGE	*Fama–French alpha_ LARGE*	*Carhart alpha LARGE*	*CAPM alpha SMALL*	*Fama–French alpha SMALL*	*Carhart alpha SMALL*
AGE	−0.0932	−0.0378	0.0914	−0.0042	0.0750	0.0082
	(0.0696)	(0.0830)	(0.1204)	(0.1158)	(0.0760)	(0.1881)
EXPENSE	−0.0201***	−0.0325***	−0.0488***	0.0014	−0.0029	−0.0023
	(0.0072)	(0.0094)	(0.0118)	(0.0188)	(0.0191)	(0.0262)
FLOWS	0.3542*	0.3356	0.5118*	0.1784	0.8943*	1.6295**
	(0.1992)	(0.2129)	(0.2767)	(0.4542)	(0.4476)	(0.8017)
SIZE	0.0028	0.0062*	−0.0013	−0.0085*	−0.0066	−0.0112*
	(0.0026)	(0.0033)	(0.0040)	(0.0047)	(0.0040)	(0.0065)
Alpha_CAPM	82.2118***			82.4410***		
	(1.2390)			(1.8307)		
Alpha_FF		82.3619***			81.1376***	
		(0.9482)			(1.3952)	
Alpha_MOM			72.1612***			68.2003***
			(1.7089)			(2.3489)
CONS	0.0234	0.0105	0.1213**	0.2246***	0.2248***	0.3461***
	(0.0381)	(0.0514)	(0.0587)	(0.0693)	(0.0639)	(0.0992)
N	3415	3415	3415	1490	1490	1490

Notes This table reports the results of the panel regressions of mutual fund performance on the previous month's fund flows and other fund characteristics (all one period lagged). Portfolio performance is evaluated based on simple Return and portfolio alphas (CAPM or Jensen Alpha, Fama–French Alpha and Carhart or Momentum Four Factor alpha). AGE is defined as the number of months from the fund's inception. $Flow_{it}1$ is the normalized monthly net flow of fund i in month $t-1$. SIZE is the logarithm of the total net assets of fund i in period $t-1$ $\log(TNA)_{i,t-1}$; $ExpenseRatio_{i,t-1}$ is the net expense ratio. The ALL Sample Period is from December 2006 to December 2019. The crisis period range betweeh June 2007 to December 2010. The t-statistics are based on standard errors clustered at mutual fund level. *, **, and ***, respectively, denote significance at the 10%, 5%, and 1% levels. We considered Time and Country fixed effects. We consider several management style. To be specific we account for Blend, Value, Growth, Large and Small CAP Mutual funds.

all-sample period and crisis times, except 10% statistically significant reaction in CAPM model in crisis time. For value asset type, the coefficient of fund flows is only positive at 5% level in CAPM model in all-sample period and at 10% level in Carhart (MOM) model in crisis times. As for growth asset style, the coefficient reacted positively at 10% statistically significant level only in Carhart (MOM) alpha model in all-sample period, while there is no significant reaction in times of crisis. Panel C and Panel D of Table 3 show our analyses for US large and small cap mutual funds. The coefficient of mutual fund flows for large cap is positive and statistically significant for Fama–French and Carhart alpha model, while it is positive at high statistically significant level for all models of small cap scheme measure. There is no statistically significant reaction for all size schemes analyzed in crisis time (Panel D).

Table 4 report multivariate tests: regressions of fund performance on fund flows and other attributes for European equity mutual funds for the all-sample period (2006–2019) and crisis period (2007–2010), and for blend, value, growth asset styles and large and small cap size assets, which is again measured by means of different alphas, such as CAPM or Jensen Alpha, Fama-French Alpha and Carhart or Momentum Four Factor alpha. A better statistically significant reaction is seen in all-sample period rather than crises times. The coefficient of fund flows is positive and statistically significant for blend (1% level in CAPM and Fama–French models), value (10% level only in CAPM model), growth (5% level in CAPM and Fama-French models) asset styles, while there is no reaction for these assets in financial crisis time. As for the size scheme, we catch strong positive statistically significant reaction of the coefficient in all models for large and small cap mutual funds, while for financial crisis time coefficient caused positive statistically significant reaction for both large caps (10% in CAPM and Carhart models) and small caps (10% in Fama–French and 5% in Carhart models) measures.

Overall, the results are consistent with the rationale that the positive flow-performance relation could be driven by smart money effect, and, therefore, bond fund investors being considered less sophisticated than equity fund investors, exhibit a lower relation when considering the dynamic between past flows and return. To be specific, the results in Tables 1 and 2, for fixed income, and in Tables 3 and 4, for the equity side, show that when the performance is measured in terms of Alpha, the flow coefficient is almost always lower in magnitude then the corresponding equity mutual fund coefficients (the only statistically significant result is coupled with government fund type during crisis times).

4.3 Performance of Flow Portfolios

Examining quarterly investors' money flows, most of academic literature show that on average investors are able to earn superior returns based on their investment decisions. That is, funds that receive greater investor flow subsequently outperform their less popular peers. In this section, we examine the fund flow and performance relation for the full sample of mutual funds during the period of 2006–2019. The evidence presented in Keswani and Stolin (2008) and Clifford et al. (2014) suggests that the flow-performance relation is stronger at monthly frequency. Based on a monthly fund flow for each fund, in line with the approach performed by Jiang and Yuksel (2017), we form positive and negative flow portfolios based on the net flow of a fund during the previous month. To evaluate the performance of positive and negative flow portfolios, we consider the following performance measures: Simple Return, Standard Deviation, Alpha CAPM, Alpha Fama French, the Sharpe ratio and Alpha Momentum or Carhart Alpha. The latter, is according to the same specification of Eq. (4).[20]

Tables 5, 6, 7 and 8 report the performance of positive and negative fund flow portfolios for all funds and the differences in alphas between positive and negative flow portfolios.

Sapp and Tiwari (2004) believe that if investors can indeed identify skilled managers, new capital flows should continue to receive positive abnormal returns even after controlling for momentum factors. On the other hand, if fund investors only chase funds based on past performance, then funds that happen to hold a high concentration of stocks of the latest winner (High MOM), will receive more investor capital inflows on average. It also could be the case that these funds would benefit on average more than other funds from the effect of stock return momentum. In turn, this could lead to the discovering of a positive flow-performance relation despite the absence of any ability by investors to

[20] We obtain the Fama/French international three factors and international momentum factor from Kenneth R. French's website.

Table 5 Performance of fund portfolios formed on past flows—EUROPEAN EQUITY FUNDS

	Return	*St. Dev*	*Alpha CAPM*	*Alpha_FF*	*Alpha_Mom*	*Sharpe*	*Return*	*St. Dev*	*Alpha CAPM*	*Alpha_FF*	*Alpha_Mom*	*Sharpe*
LARGE	*All Sample Period*						*Crisis Period*					
Positive Flows	0.46%	3.94%	0.09%	0.27%	0.14%	17.31%	−0.67%	6.66%	0.29%	0.52%	0.29%	−2.10%
Negative Flows	0.58%	4.18%	0.04%	0.20%	0.11%	14.66%	0.19%	6.42%	0.40%	0.61%	0.26%	4.34%
Positive–Negative	−0.12%	−0.24%	0.05%	0.07%	0.03%	2.65%	−0.86%	0.24%	−0.11%	−0.09%	0.03%	−6.44%
BLEND	*All Sample Period*						*Crisis Period*					
Positive Flows	0.46%	3.93%	0.09%	0.27%	0.14%	16.97%	−0.72%	6.77%	0.27%	0.50%	0.27%	−1.36%
Negative Flows	0.54%	4.17%	0.02%	0.18%	0.09%	14.06%	0.19%	6.39%	0.38%	0.59%	0.21%	3.22%
Positive–Negative	−0.08%	−0.24%	0.07%	0.09%	0.05%	2.90%	−0.91%	0.38%	−0.11%	−0.09%	0.05%	−4.57%
SMALL	*All Sample Period*						*Crisis Period*					
Positive Flows	0.97%	4.47%	0.41%	0.44%	0.25%	24.67%	0.96%	0.34%	7.72%	0.72%	0.89%	0.64%
Negative Flows	0.35%	4.70%	0.19%	0.24%	0.13%	15.99%	−0.30%	7.25%	0.62%	0.81%	0.29%	6.18%
Positive–Negative	0.62%	−0.22%	0.22%	0.19%	0.12%	8.68%	1.25%	−6.91%	7.10%	−0.10%	0.60%	−5.54%
VALUE	*All Sample Period*						*Crisis Period*					
Positive Flows	0.53%	4.42%	0.03%	0.27%	0.23%	18.78%	−0.81%	7.11%	0.21%	0.46%	0.22%	−4.58%
Negative Flows	0.38%	4.60%	−0.10%	0.14%	0.09%	10.56%	0.17%	6.34%	0.20%	037%	0.03%	1.67%
Positive–Negative	0.15%	−0.18%	0.13%	0.13%	0.14%	8.22%	−0.98%	0.77%	0.02%	0.08%	0.19%	−6.25%

(continued)

Table 5 (continued)

	Return	*St. Dev*	*Alpha CAPM*	*Alpha_FF*	*Alpha_Mom*	*Sharpe*	*Return*	*St. Dev*	*Alpha CAPM*	*Alpha_FF*	*Alpha_Mom*	*Sharpe*
GROWTH	*All Sample Period*						*Crisis Period*					
Positive Flows	0.53%	4.73%	0.51%	0.51%	0.29%	20.62%	−0.34%	6.15%	0.49%	0.63%	0.39%	1.76%
Negative Flows	1.34%	5.06%	0.49%	0.22%	0.00%	15.79%	0.62%	5.69%	0.55%	0.62%	0.26%	12.23%
Positive–Negative	−0.81%	−0.33%	0.02%	0.29%	0.29%	4.83%	−0.97%	0.46%	−0.05%	0.01%	0.13%	−10.47%

Notes Performance of Fund Portfolios Formed on Past Flows. This table reports the average performance of positive and negative flow portfolios formed within the sample of funds according to the managemnt style. Each month, funds in each sample are grouped to form a positive and a negative fund flow portfolio based on the sign of the net fund flow of each fund during the previous month. Portfolio performance is evaluated based on simple Return and portfolio alphas (CAPM or Jensen Alpha, Fama-French Alpha and Carhart or Momentum Four Factor alpha). The table reports estimates of alphas for equal-weighted portfolios and the corresponding Simple return and Sharpe ratios of the portfolios. The differences in alphas between the positive and the negative fund flow portfolios are also reported. Alphas are expressed in percentage per month. The All Sample Period is from December 2006 to December 2019. The crisis period range betweeh June 2007 to December 2010

Table 6 Performance of fund portfolios formed on past flows—US EQUITY FUNDS

	Return	*St. Dev*	*Alpha CAPM*	*Alpha_FF*	*Alpha_MOM*	*Sharpe*	*Return*	*St. Dev*	*Alpha CAPM*	*Alpha_FF*	*Alpha_Mom*	*Sharpe*
LARGE	*All Sample Period*						*Crisis Period*					
Positive Flows	0.92%	3.67%	0.10%	0.10%	0.14%	29.0%	−0.31%	5.16%	0.19%	0.00%	−0.07%	2.70%
Negative Flows	0.92%	3.79%	0.05%	0.11%	0.15%	26.6%	0.79%	5.20%	0.23%	0.03%	−0.06%	0.36%
Positive–Negative	0.00%	−0.12%	0.04%	−0.02%	−0.01%	2.94%	−1.10%	−0.04%	−0.04%	−0.04%	−0.01%	2.34%
BLEND	*All Sample Period*						*Crisis Period*					
Positive Flows	0.75%	3.60%	0.05%	0.00%	0.02%	28.46%	−0.66%	5.33%	0.06%	−0.05%	−0.10%	−4.01%
Negative Flows	1.03%	3.64%	−0.01%	−0.02%	0.02%	28.46%	0.57%	5.03%	0.06%	−0.04%	−0.10%	0.35%
Positive–Negative	−0.27%	−0.05%	0.05%	0.02%	0.00%	0.00%	−1.24%	0.29%	0.00%	−0.01%	0.00%	−4.36%
SMALL	*All Sample Period*						*Crisis Period*					
Positive Flows	1.15%	4.07%	0.09%	0.25%	0.28%	30.77%	0.96%	6.44%	0.67%	0.13%	−0.03%	4.72%
Negative Flows	0.67%	4.30%	−0.08%	0.17%	0.20%	24.24%	−0.33%	6.38%	0,.74%	0.28%	0.18%	4.94%
Positive–Negative	0.48%	−0.22%	0.17%	0.07%	0.07%	6.53%	1.28%	0.06%	−0.07%	−0.14%	−0.21%	−0.22%
VALUE	*All Sample Period*						*Crisis Period*					
Positive Flows	0.85%	3.39%	−0.03%	0.04%	0.07%	28.68%	−0.92%	5.42%	0.13%	−0.01%	−0.16%	−0.31%
Negative Flows	0.71%	3.52%	−0.12%	0,.00%	0.02%	23.86%	0.93%	5.54%	0.11%	−0.02%	−0.08%	−0.05%
Positive–Negative	0.14%	−0.13%	0.09%	0.04%	0.05%	4.82%	−1.85%	−0.12%	0.02%	0.01%	−0.07%	−0.27%

(continued)

Table 6 (continued)

	Return	*St. Dev*	*Alpha CAPM*	*Alpha_FF*	*Alpha_MOM*	*Sharpe*	*Return*	*St. Dev*	*Alpha CAPM*	*Alpha_FF*	*Alpha_Mom*	*Sharpe*
GROWTH	*All Sample Period*						*Crisis Period*					
Positive Flows	0.98%	3,.80%	0.23%	0.19%	0.26%	30.95%	−0.21%	4.97%	0.11%	−0.08%	−0.19%	3.29%
Negative Flows	1.07%	3.99%	0.25%	0.29%	0.33%	27.99%	0.80%	4.82%	0.18%	−0.05%	−0.12%	0.73%
Positive–Negative	−0.09%	−0.20%	−0.02%	−0.10%	−0.07%	2.95%	−1.01%	0.15%	−0.08%	−0.04%	−0.07%	2.56%

Notes Performance of Fund Portfolios Formed on Past Flows. This table reports the average performance of positive and negative flow portfolios formed within the sample of funds according to the managemnt style. Each month, funds in each sample are grouped to form a positive and a negative fund flow portfolio based on the sign of the net fund flow of each fund during the previous month. Portfolio performance is evaluated based on simple Return and portfolio alphas (CAPM or Jensen Alpha, Fama-French Alpha and Carhart or Momentum Four Factor alpha). The table reports estimates of alphas for equal-weighted portfolios and the corresponding Simple return and Sharpe ratios of the portfolios. The differences in alphas between the positive and the negative fund flow portfolios are also reported. Alphas are expressed in percentage per month. The All Sample Period is from December 2006 to December 2019. The crisis period range betweeh June 2007 to December 2010

Table 7 Performance of fund portfolios formed on past flows—EUROPEAN FIXED INCOME FUNDS

	Return	*St. Dev*	*Alpha*	*Sharpe*
CORPORATE FIXED INCOME—All Sample Period				
Positive Flows	1.12%	2.70%	0.15%	10.99%
Negative Flows	−0.89%	2.67%	0.02%	3.38%
Positive–Negative	2.01%	0.03%	0.13%	7.62%
CORPORATE FIXED INCOME—Crisis Period				
Positive Flows	1.57%	3.98%	0.54%	20.76%
Negative Flows	−1.16%	3.78%	0.24%	11.46%
Positive–Negative	2.73%	0.19%	0.31%	9.30%
GOVERNMENT FIXED INCOME—All Sample Period				
Positive Flows	−0.01%	2.38%	0.00%	5.50%
Negative Flows	0.17%	2.53%	−0.01%	4.67%
Positive–Negative	−0.17%	−0.15%	0.01%	0.83%
GOVERNMENT FIXED INCOME—Crisis Period				
Positive Flows	0.10%	3.43%	0.25%	14.05%
Negative Flows	0.43%	3.59%	0.31%	15.61%
Positive–Negative	−0.33%	−0.15%	−0.07%	−1.56%

Notes Performance of Fund Portfolios Formed on Past Flows. This table reports the average performance of positive and negative flow portfolios formed within the sample of funds according to the managemnt style. Each month, funds in each sample are grouped to form a positive and a negative fund flow portfolio based on the sign of the net fund flow of each fund during the previous month. Portfolio performance is evaluated based on simple Return and portfolio alpha according to the following model: $r_{p,t} = \alpha_p^{BOND} + \beta_{1,p} MKTRF_t^{Bond} + \beta_{2,t} MKTRF_t^{Equity} + \beta_{3,p} DEFAULT_t + \beta_{4,p} TERM_t + \varepsilon_{p,t}$ where $r_{p,t}$ is the monthly return on a portfolio of funds in excess of the one-month T-bill rate; $MKTRF_t^{Bond}$ is the Local (European or Us) Total Bond Market Index return in excess of the one-month T-bill rate. $MKTRF_t^{Equity}$ is the (European) U.S. equity market return in excess of the one-month T-bill rate and is included to control for potential equity market bias $DEFAULT$ is the difference in return between investment grade corporate bonds and government bonds (10-year Treasury Constant Maturity Yield); $TERM_t$ is the difference in return between long-term (30-year Treasury Constant Maturity Yield) and short-term government bonds (one-year Treasury Constant Maturity Yield).The table reports estimates of alphas for equal-weighted portfolios and the corresponding Simple return and Sharpe ratios of the portfolios. The differences in alphas between the positive and the negative fund flow portfolios are also reported. Alphas are expressed in percentage per month. The All Sample Period is from December 2006 to December 2019. The crisis period range betweeh June 2007 to December 2010

Table 8 Performance of fund portfolios formed on past flows—US FIXED INCOME FUNDS

	Return	*St. Dev*	*Alpha*	*Sharpe*
CORPORATE FIXED INCOME—All Sample Period				
Positive Flows	0.25%	1.08%	0.11%	20.66%
Negative Flows	0.24%	1.01%	0.07%	13.62%
Positive–Negative	0.01%	0.07%	0.04%	7.04%
CORPORATE FIXED INCOME—Crisis period				
Positive Flows	0.27%	1.86%	0.33%	19.93%
Negative Flows	0.46%	1.79%	0.35%	17.59%
Positive–Negative	−0.19%	0.07%	−0.02%	2.34%
GOVERNMENT FIXED INCOME—All Sample Period				
Positive Flows	0.07%	1.01%	0.07%	2.68%
Negative Flows	0.14%	0.89%	0.08%	0.92%
Positive–Negative	−0.07%	0.13%	−0.01%	1.76%
GOVERNMENT FIXED INCOME—Crisis Period				
Positive Flows	0.15%	1.63%	0.19%	14.99%
Negative Flows	0.52%	1.53%	0.22%	16.46%
Positive–Negative	−0.37%	0.10%	−0.03%	−1.47%

Notes Performance of Fund Portfolios Formed on Past Flows. This table reports the average performance of positive and negative flow portfolios formed within the sample of funds according to the managemnt style. Each month, funds in each sample are grouped to form a positive and a negative fund flow portfolio based on the sign of the net fund flow of each fund during the previous month. Portfolio performance is evaluated based on simple Return and portfolio alpha according to the following model $r_{p,t} = \alpha_p^{BOND} + \beta_{1,p} MKTRF_t^{Bond} + \beta_{2,t} MKTRF_t^{Equity} + \beta_{3,p} DEFAULT_t + \beta_{4,p} TERM_t + \varepsilon_{p,t}$; where $r_{p,t}$ is the monthly return on a portfolio of funds in excess of the one-month T-bill rate; $MKTRF_t^{Bond}$ is the Local (European or Us) Total Bond Market Index return in excess of the one-month T-bill rate. $MKTRF_t^{Equity}$ is the (European) U.S. equity market return in excess of the one-month T-bill rate and is included to control for potential equity market bias$DEFAULT$ is the difference in return between investment grade corporate bonds and government bonds (10-year Treasury Constant Maturity Yield); $TERM_t$ is the difference in return between long-term (30-year Treasury Constant Maturity Yield) and short-term government bonds (one-year Treasury Constant Maturity Yield).The table reports estimates of alphas for equal-weighted portfolios and the corresponding Simple return and Sharpe ratios of the portfolios. The differences in alphas between the positive and the negative fund flow portfolios are also reported. Alphas are expressed in percentage per month. The All Sample Period is from December 2006 to December 2019. The crisis period range between June 2007 to December 2010

select skilled fund managers gaining superior performance with respect to their peers.

Table 5 reports the performance of fund equally weighted portfolios formed on positive and negative past flows for European equity mutual funds and the difference between positive and negative flow portfolios. Portfolio performance is evaluated based on simple return and portfolio alphas (CAPM or Jensen Alpha, Fama–French Alpha and Carhart or Momentum Four Factor Alpha and Sharpe ratio) and for different asset styles: blend, value, growth and asset size large and small caps. The full sample period is from December 2006 to December 2019. The crisis period range between June 2007 to December 2010. The results in Table 5 show that for large cap mutual funds sample, in all-sample period the difference between positive and negative flow portfolios is negative for simple return (−0.12%), however, the biggest positive difference at 2.65% is seen when checking for Sharpe ratio. In crisis time, there is a negative difference in flow portfolios in Alpha CAPM and Fama-French models, as well as Sharpe ratio (−6.44%). The results for blend asset style demonstrate negative difference between positive and negative flow portfolios based on Simple return model, but positive for Alphas and Sharpe ratio in all-sample period, while in crisis times there is only the positive difference (0.05%), when Momentum Four Factor Alpha is applied. Checking for small cap size, we find positive difference between positive and negative flows for Simple return model (0.62%) and Sharpe ratio (8.68%) in all-sample period, while the highest positive difference in CAPM model (7.10%) with the negative Sharpe ratio (−5.54%). Value asset style demonstrate all positive results for the analyzed difference in all-sample period, however, in crisis the Simple return model brings negative difference results (−0.98%) just as Sharpe Ratio (−6.25%). Analyzing for growth asset style mainly shows negative simple return (−0.81%) in all-sample period and negative results in crisis times (Simple return (−0.97%), CAPM (−0.05%), Sharpe Ratio (−10.47%).

Table 6 reports the performance of fund equally weighted portfolios formed on positive and negative past flows for US equity mutual funds and the difference between positive and negative flow portfolios. Portfolio performance is evaluated based on simple return and portfolio alphas (CAPM or Jensen Alpha, Fama-French Alpha and Carhart or Momentum Four Factor Alpha and Sharpe ratio) and for different asset styles: blend, value, growth and asset size large and small caps. The results in Table 6 show that for large cap mutual funds sample, in all-sample period the difference between positive and negative flow portfolios is both positive or negative depending on a model, however, the coefficient is very little, like 0% for Simple Return, however it is slightly increased when testing for CAPM (0.04%), and Sharpe ratio is pretty high (2.94%); in crisis times the picture is pretty similar, however, the difference coefficient for Simple return model reduces down to −1.10%. For blend style, the difference between positive and negative flow portfolios in all-sample period is negative only for simple return (−0.27%), while it ranges at 0% level when testing for Momentum Four Factor Alpha and Sharpe Ratio; in crisis times the coefficient drops down to (−1.24%) in Simple Return model and remains at almost zero level for all other measures, except the Sharpe ratio (−4.36%). When checking the reaction for small cap mutual fund sample, full sample analysis shows positive difference between positive and negative flow portfolios for all models, that gets negative in crisis time, except the Simple return (1.28%). The results for value style are all positive in all-sample period, however, in crisis time the difference in Simple return model drops a lot comparing to all-sample period (−1.85%). Our test for growth asset style revealed all negative difference results both in all-sample period and crisis times, except the positive Sharpe ratio at 2.95% and 2.56% levels, respectively.

We next investigate the flow-performance relation for bond funds. We focus on funds that invest in corporate bonds. Bond fund investors are generally considered less sophisticated than equity fund investors. According to this rationale, if the positive flow-performance relation is driven by smart money, we expect the relation to be stronger for bond funds. To evaluate the performance α_p^{BOND}, of positive and negative flow portfolios, we follow Jiang and Yuksel (2017) and use a slightly different version of the multifactor model described in Eq. (5) as follows:

$$\begin{aligned} r_{p,t} =& \alpha_p^{BOND} + \beta_{1,p} MKTRF_t^{Bond} + \beta_{2,t} MKTRF_t^{Equity} \\ &+ \beta_{3,p} DEFAULT_t + \beta_{4,p} TERM_t + \varepsilon_{p,t} \end{aligned} \tag{7}$$

where $r_{p,t}$ is the monthly return on a portfolio of funds in excess of the one-month T-bill rate; $MKTRF_t^{Bond}$ is the Local (European or Us) Total Bond Market Index return in excess of the one-month T-bill rate. $MKTRF_t{}^{Equity}$ is the (European) U.S. equity market return in excess of the one-month T-bill rate and is included to control for potential equity market bias.[21] $DEFAULT$ is the difference in return between investment grade corporate bonds and government bonds (10-year Treasury Constant Maturity Yield); $TERM_t$ is the difference in return between long-term (30-year Treasury Constant Maturity Yield) and short-term government bonds (one-year Treasury Constant Maturity Yield). The rates for investment grade corporate bonds and for long- and short-term government bond rates are from the Federal Reserve's website.[22]

Table 7 reports the performance of fund portfolios formed on past flows—positive and negative for European fixed income funds (corporate and government), tested in Simple return model, Single and Multi-factor Alphas and Sharpe Ratio. In general, we found that the difference between the positive and the negative fund flows portfolios gets higher in crisis time, therefore, it slightly increases in Simple return model from 2.01% (all-sample period) up to 2.73% (crisis time), as well as for other measures Alpha model (from 0.13 to 0.31%), and the Sharpe ratio (from 7.62 to 9.30%). The results are different when checking for government fixed income instruments. The difference between the positive and the negative fund flows portfolios in Simple return model is negative (−0.17%) in all-sample period and gets negatively higher (−0.33%) in crisis, however, testing for Alpha and Sharpe Ratio demonstrates change of the sign from positive in all-sample period to negative in crisis period.

Table 8 reports the performance of fund portfolios formed on past flows–positive and negative for US fixed income funds (corporate and government), tested in Simple return model, Alphas and Sharpe Ratio. Analysis for corporate bond type demonstrates change of sign from positive to negative for difference between the positive and the negative fund flows portfolios in Simple return and Alpha models, however, for Sharpe ratio it remains positive but drops its value from 7.04% in all-sample period to 2.34% in crisis. As for the government type of fixed income instruments, there is a negative sign in Simple return and Alpha models in all-sample period, and this difference gets slightly negatively higher in crisis period, unlike testing for Sharpe ratio, where we observe the change of difference from positive (1.76%) all-sample period to negative (−1.47%) in crisis.

[21] Untabulated tests show that Including $MKTRF_t^{Equity}$ clearly improves the explanatory powers of the factor model.

[22] http://www.federalreserve.gov/releases/h15/data.htm.

The positive relation, with respect to the European and US (blend, small and value), and when measured in all-sample period, between fund flows and future fund performance for the full sample of funds equity side in line with previous literature (Keswani & Stolin, 2008; Sapp & Tiwari, 2004). On the contrary, we observe a negative coefficient for the fixed income funds government Europe, during crisis period, and for all the US fixed income funds (but corporate in all-sample period acts differently). This evidence is coherent with Jiang and Yuksel (2017), who got similar results for a sample of U.S. domestic bond mutual funds.

References

Akbas, F., Armstrong, W. J., Sorescu, S., & Subrahmanyam, A. (2016). Capital market efficiency and arbitrage efficacy. *Journal of Financial and Quantitative Analysis, 51*, 387–413.

Amihud, Y., & Goyenko, R. (2013). Mutual fund's R 2 as predictor of performance. *The Review of Financial Studies, 26*(3), 667–694.

Ayadi, M. A., & Kryzanowski, L. (2011). Fixed-income fund performance: Role of luck and ability in tail membership. *Journal of Empirical Finance, 18*(3), 379–392.

Bailey, W., Kumar, A., & Ng, D. (2011). Behavioral biases of mutual fund investors. *Journal of Financial Economics, 102*(1), 1–27.

Barber, B. M., Huang, X., & Odean, T. (2016). Which factors matter to investors? Evidence from mutual fund flows. *The Review of Financial Studies, 29*(10), 2600–2642.

Barber, B. M., Odean, T., & Zheng, L. (2005). Out of sight, out of mind: The effects of expenses on mutual fund flows. *The Journal of Business, 78*(6), 2095–2120.

Ben-Rephael, A., Kandel, S., & Wohl, A. (2012). Measuring investor sentiment with mutual fund flows. *Journal of Financial Economics, 104*(2), 363–382.

Bergstresser, D., Chalmers, J. M., & Tufano, P. (2008). Assessing the costs and benefits of brokers in the mutual fund industry. *The Review of Financial Studies, 22*(10), 4129–4156.

Berk, J. B., & Van Binsbergen, J. H. (2015). Measuring skill in the mutual fund industry. *Journal of Financial Economics, 118*(1), 1–20.

Boney, V., Comer, G., & Kelly, L. (2009). Timing the investment grade securities market: Evidence from high quality bond funds. *Journal of Empirical Finance, 16*(1), 55–69.

Cao, C., Chang, E. C., & Wang, Y. (2008). An empirical analysis of the dynamic relationship between mutual fund flow and market return volatility. *Journal of Banking & Finance, 32*(10), 2111–2123.

Carhart., M. (1997). On persistence in mutual fund performance. *Journal of Finance, 52*(1), 57–82.

Chalmers, J., Kaul, A., & Phillips, B. (2010). *Economic conditions, flight to quality and mutual fund flows*. Working Paper, University of Alberta.

Chen, J., Hong, H., Huang, M., & Kubik, J. D. (2004). Does fund size erode mutual fund performance? The role of liquidity and organization. *American Economic Review, 94*(5), 1276–1302.

Chen, X., Yao, T., & Yu, T. (2007). Prudent man or agency problem? On the performance of insurance mutual funds. *Journal of Financial Intermediation, 16*(2), 175–203.

Chevalier, J., & Ellison, G. (1997). Risk taking by mutual funds as a response to incentives. *Journal of Political Economy, 105*(6), 1167–1200.

Clare, A., O'Sullivan, N., Sherman, M., & Zhu, S. (2019). The performance of US bond mutual funds. *International Review of Financial Analysis, 61*, 1–8.

Clifford, C. P., Jordan, B. D., & Riley, T. B. (2014). Average funds versus average dollars: Implications for mutual fund research. *Journal of Empirical Finance, 28*, 249–260.

Cremers, K. M., & Petajisto, A. (2009). How active is your fund manager? A new measure that predicts performance. *The Review of Financial Studies, 22*(9), 3329–3365.

Cuthbertson, K., Nitzsche, D., & O'Sullivan, N. (2010). Mutual fund performance: Measurement and evidence. *Journal of Financial Markets, Instruments and Institutions, 19*(2), 95–187.

Del Guercio, D., & Reuter, J. (2014). Mutual fund performance and the incentive to generate alpha. *The Journal of Finance, 69*(4), 1673–1704.

Del Guercio, D., & Tkac, P. A. (2002). The determinants of the flow of funds of managed portfolios: Mutual funds versus pension funds. *Journal of Financial and Quantitative Analysis, 37*, 523–557.

Evans, R. B., & Fahlenbrach, R. (2012). Institutional investors and mutual fund governance: Evidence from retail–institutional fund twins. *The Review of Financial Studies, 25*(12), 3530–3571.

Feng, X., Zhou, M., & Chan, K. C. (2014). Smart money or dumb money? A study on the selection ability of mutual fund investors in China. *The North American Journal of Economics and Finance, 30*, 154–170.

Ferreira, M. A., Keswani, A., Miguel, A. F., & Ramos, S. B. (2012). The flow-performance relationship around the world. *Journal of Banking & Finance, 36*(6), 1759–1780.

Fong, T. P. W., Sze, A. K. W., & Ho, E. H. C. (2018). Determinants of equity mutual fund flows–Evidence from the fund flow dynamics between Hong Kong and global markets. *Journal of International Financial Markets, Institutions and Money, 57*, 231–247.

Forbes, K. J., & Warnock, F. E. (2012). Capital flow waves: Surges, stops, flight, and retrenchment. *Journal of International Economics, 88*(2), 235–251.

Frazzini, A., & Lamont, O. A. (2008). Dumb money: Mutual fund flows and the cross-section of stock returns. *Journal of Financial Economics, 88*(2), 299–322.

Friesen, G. C., & Sapp, T. R. (2007). Mutual fund flows and investor returns: An empirical examination of fund investor timing ability. *Journal of Banking & Finance, 31*(9), 2796–2816.

Gallaher, S., Kaniel, R., & Starks, L. T. (2006, January). Madison avenue meets Wall Street: Mutual fund families, competition and advertising. *Competition and Advertising*.

Ghargori, P., Chan, H., & Faff, R. (2007). Investigating the performance of alternative default-risk models: Option based versus accounting-based approaches. *Australian Journal of Management, 31*, 207–234.

Ghosh, A. R., Qureshi, M. S., Kim, J. I., & Zalduendo, J. (2014). Surges. *Journal of International Economics, 92*(2), 266–285.

Goldstein, I., Jiang, H., & Ng, D. T. (2017). Investor flows and fragility in corporate bond funds. *Journal of Financial Economics, 126*(3), 592–613.

Gruber, M. (1996). Another puzzle: The growth in actively managed mutual funds. *Journal of Finance, 51*, 783–810.

Huang, J., Kelsey D. W., & Yan, H. (2004). *Volatility of performance and mutual fund flows*. Working Paper, University of Texas at Austin.

Huang, J., Sialm, C., & Zhang, H. (2011). Risk shifting and mutual fund performance. *The Review of Financial Studies, 24*(8), 2575–2616.

Huang, J., Wei, K. D., & Yan, H. (2007). Participation costs and the sensitivity of fund flows to past performance. *The Journal of Finance, 62*(3), 1273–1311.

Ivković, Z., & Weisbenner, S. (2009). Individual investor mutual fund flows. *Journal of Financial Economics, 92*(2), 223–237.

Ivkovich, Z., & Weisbenner, S. J. (2006, May). 'Old' money matters: The sensitivity of mutual fund redemption decisions to past performance. *In* EFA 2006 Zurich Meetings Paper.

Jain, P. C., & Wu, J. S. (2000). Truth in mutual fund advertising: Evidence on future performance and fund flows. *The Journal of Finance, 55*(2), 937–958.

Jank, S. (2012). Mutual fund flows, expected returns, and the real economy. *Journal of Banking & Finance, 36*(11), 3060–3070.

Jeon, H., Kang, J., & Lee, C. (2017). Precision about manager skill, mutual fund flows, and performance persistence. *The North American Journal of Economics and Finance, 40*, 222–237.

Jiang, G. J., & Yuksel, H. Z. (2017). What drives the "Smart-Money" effect? Evidence from investors' money flow to mutual fund classes. *Journal of Empirical Finance, 40*, 39–58.

Jinjarak, Y., Wongswan, J., & Zheng, H. (2011). International fund investment and local market returns. *Journal of Banking & Finance, 35*(3), 572–587.

Keswani, A., & Stolin, D. (2008). Which money is smart? Mutual fund buys and sells of individual and institutional investors. *The Journal of Finance, 63*(1), 85–118.

Khorana, A., & Servaes, H. (2004). *Conflicts of interest and competition in the mutual fund industry.* Working Paper, London Business School.

Laborda, R., & Muñoz, F. (2016). Optimal allocation of government bond funds through the business cycle. Is money smart? *International Review of Economics & Finance, 45*, 46–67.

Li, S., de Haan, J., Scholtens, B., & Yang, H. (2015). Are international fund flows pro-or counter-cyclical? *Applied Economics Letters, 22*(5), 378–384.

Li, S., de Haan, J., & Scholtens, B. (2018). Surges of international fund flows. *Journal of International Money and Finance, 82*, 97–119.

Lou, D. (2012). A flow-based explanation for return predictability. *The Review of Financial Studies, 25*(12), 3457–3489.

Massa, M. (2003). How do family strategies affect fund performance? When performance-maximization is not the only game in town. *Journal of Financial Economics, 67*(2), 249–304.

Nanda, V., Wang, Z., & Zheng, Lu. (2004). Family values and the star phenomenon. *Review of Financial Studies, 17*, 667–698.

Odean, T. (1998). Are investors reluctant to realize their losses? *Journal of Finance, 53*, 1775–1798.

Oh, N. Y., & Parwada, J. T. (2007). Relations between mutual fund flows and stock market returns in Korea. *Journal of International Financial Markets, Institutions and Money, 17*(2), 140–151.

Petajisto, A. (2013). Active share and mutual fund performance. *Financial Analysts Journal, 69*(4), 73–93.

Puy, D. (2016). Mutual funds flows and the geography of contagion. *Journal of International Money and Finance, 60*, 73–93.

Qureshi, F., Kutan, A. M., Ismail, I., & Gee, C. S. (2017). Mutual funds and stock market volatility: An empirical analysis of Asian emerging markets. *Emerging Markets Review, 31*, 176–192.

Raddatz, C., & Schmukler, S. L. (2012). On the international transmission of shocks: Micro-evidence from mutual fund portfolios. *Journal of International Economics, 88*(2), 357–374.

Rakowski, D. (2010). Fund flow volatility and performance. *Journal of Financial and Quantitative Analysis*, 223–237.

Rakowski, D., & Wang, X. (2009). The dynamics of short-term mutual fund flows and returns: A time-series and cross-sectional investigation. *Journal of Banking & Finance, 33*(11), 2102–2109.

Renneboog, L., Ter Horst, J., & Zhang, C. (2008). The price of ethics and stakeholder governance: The performance of socially responsible mutual funds. *Journal of Corporate Finance, 14*(3), 302–322.
Renneboog, L., Ter Horst, J., & Zhang, C. (2011). Is ethical money financially smart? Nonfinancial attributes and money flows of socially responsible investment funds. *Journal of Financial Intermediation, 20*(4), 562–588.
Sapp, T., & Tiwari, A. (2004). Does stock return momentum explain the "smart money" effect? *The Journal of Finance, 59*(6), 2605–2622.
Sialm, C., Starks, L. T., & Zhang, H. (2015). Defined contribution pension plans: Sticky or discerning money? *The Journal of Finance, 70*(2), 805–838.
Sirri, E. R., & Tufano, P. (1998). Costly search and mutual fund flows. *The Journal of Finance, 53*(5), 1589–1622.
Teo, M., & Woo, S. J. (2004). Style effects in the cross-section of stock returns. *Journal of Financial Economics, 74*(2), 367–398.
Tillmann, P. (2013). Capital inflows and asset prices: Evidence from emerging Asia. *Journal of Banking & Finance, 37*(3), 717–729.
Vicente, L., Ortiz, C., & Andreu, L. (2011). Is the average investor smarter than the average euro? *Journal of Financial Services Research, 40*(3), 143–161.
Warther, V. A. (1995). Aggregate mutual fund flows and security returns. *Journal of Financial Economics, 39*(2–3), 209–235.
Wermers, R. (2003). *Are mutual fund shareholders compensated for active management "Bets"*? University of Maryland.
Wilcox, R. T. (2003). Bargain hunting or star gazing? Investors' preferences for stock mutual funds. *The Journal of Business, 76*(4), 645–663.
Yu, H. Y. (2012). Where are the smart investors? New evidence of the smart money effect. *Journal of Empirical Finance, 19*(1), 51–64.
Zheng, L. (1999). Is money smart? A study of mutual fund investors' fund selection ability. *the Journal of Finance*, *54*(3), 901–933.

CHAPTER 6

Persistence

1 Introduction

For decades, the development of mutual fund industries has motivated a large body of literature that attempts to further understand mutual fund performance, an important issue for both investors and managers because of its undeniable impact on wealth.[1] Both individual and institutional investors have an interest in performance methods that can help them select mutual funds providing the best future results. Like investors in other retail financial markets, mutual fund investors face non-negligible costs of gathering and processing information as well as financial constraints, which can affect both their decision to participate in the market and their fund choices (Dumitrescu & Gil-Bazo, 2018).

Two key issues on fund performance have been central to recent academic and policy debates. The first is whether average risk adjusted abnormal fund performance (after expenses) is positive, negative or zero.[2] This correspond to the question: can mutual fund managers generate

[1] Matallín-Sáez, J. C., Soler-Domínguez, A., & Tortosa-Ausina, E. (2016). On the robustness of persistence in mutual fund performance. *The North American Journal of Economics and Finance, 36,* 192–231.

[2] Cuthbertson, K., Nitzsche, D., & O'Sullivan, N. (2008). UK mutual fund performance: Skill or luck? *Journal of Empirical Finance, 15*(4), 613–634.

G. Galloppo, *Asset Allocation Strategies for Mutual Funds*,
https://doi.org/10.1007/978-3-030-76128-8_6

positive alpha? Active fund management is often justified by assuming that mutual funds are able to create value for investors.[3] Under this perspective, consistent with the model of Berk and Green (2004), empirical studies have traditionally found little evidence that active mutual fund managers have the ability to consistently outperform the market after fees, expenses, and transaction costs.

Berk and Green (2004) articulate perhaps the most influential line of thought on this question. In their model, investors learn about managerial ability from past returns and demand shares of all funds with positive expected risk-adjusted returns net of fees and other costs.[4] They emphasize diseconomies of scale and believe that due to the shortage of fund managers, talented managers will attract new funds and manage more capital (Gruber, 1996). However, as funds increase, they will encounter diseconomies of scale, and alpha will decrease to zero in equilibrium. Evidence on fund-specific scale diseconomies is mixed, but Pástor and Stambaugh (2012) and Pástor et al. (2015) find that scale diseconomies operate at the aggregate industry level (Hoberg et al., 2018).

Research on whether active fund management generates positive alpha questions dates back at least to Jensen (1968), finding that neither funds in aggregate nor individual funds perform better than what would be expected by random chance (Hoberg et al., 2018). Cuthbertson et al. (2008) affirm that on balance, US studies of mutual (and pension) funds suggest little or no superior performance but somewhat stronger evidence of underperformance (e.g. Baks, 2004; Carhart, 1997; Chevalier & Ellison, 1999; Daniel et al., 1997; Grinblatt et al., 1995; Lakonishok et al., 1992; Pástor & Stambaugh, 2002; Wermers, 2000). In addition, other authors find that using UK data on mutual and pension funds give similar results (e.g. Blake & Timmermann, 1998; Blake et al., 1999; Thomas & Tonks, 2001).

However, this consensus has been challenged by studies that consider time-variation in managerial skill (Glode, 2011; Kacperczyk et al., 2014;

[3] Herrmann, U., & Scholz, H. (2013). Short-term persistence in hybrid mutual fund performance: The role of style-shifting abilities. *Journal of Banking & Finance, 37*(7), 2314–2328.

[4] Hoberg, G., Kumar, N., & Prabhala, N. (2018). Mutual fund competition, managerial skill, and alpha persistence. *The Review of Financial Studies, 31*(5), 1896–1929.

Kosowski, 2011) or identify observable fund characteristics that predict outperformance (Cremers & Petajisto, 2009).[5]

A second major issue is whether abnormal performance can be identified ex-ante and for how long it persists. This correspond to the question: can fund managers generate positive alpha persistently? If this ability persists, investors can predict future performance of funds based on their current performance (Herrmann & Scholz, 2013). The mutual fund industry itself defends the idea that some mutual fund managers have superior ability that persists over time, suggesting to investors that it is possible to predict future performance based on past returns. The possibility of persistent performance is quite important from an economic perspective. If current performance could be used to predict future performance, this would be a serious challenge for market efficiency (Herrmann & Scholz, 2013). Most of previous scholars investigated persistence by using either a contingency table approach or performance ranked portfolio strategies or by observing actual trades of mutual funds. Using the first two techniques the evidence is rather mixed. For US funds, selecting funds with outstanding future performance seems to be quite difficult, and it may be impossible, unless portfolio rebalancing is frequently carried out (for example, at least once a year) and the performance period does not exceed about one year (for example, Blake & Morey, 2000; Bollen & Busse, 2005; Brown & Goetzmann, 1995; Carhart, 1997; Grinblatt & Titman, 1992; Hendricks et al., 1993; Mamaysky et al., 2004; Wermers, 2003).[6]

From an academic perspective, the goal of identifying superior fund managers and the persistency of performance is interesting because it challenges the efficient market hypothesis (Bollen & Busse, 2001), if fund returns persist then it may be possible for investors to re-allocate their savings towards "winner funds" and make "money be smart" (Cuthbertson et al., 2010). Under this rationale the study of performance persistency becomes a direct test of the EMH[7] in financial markets. On the other side, by keeping markets efficient, active management provides

[5] Dumitrescu, A., & Gil-Bazo, J. (2018). Market frictions, investor sophistication, and persistence in mutual fund performance. *Journal of Financial Markets*, *40*, 40–59.

[6] Cuthbertson, K., Nitzsche, D., & O'Sullivan, N. (2008). UK mutual fund performance: Skill or luck? *Journal of Empirical Finance, 15*(4), 613–634.

[7] Efficient Market Hypothesis (EMH).

a critical function in modern capitalist economies. Making efficient, rational capital allocation contributes to foster both the economy and the wealth for society as a whole (Jones & Wermers, 2011).

2 Previous Findings in Literature

The analysis of mutual fund performance persistence is important in order to find whether return can be predicted. Previous papers discovered an evidence of positive mutual fund performance persistence (Chen et al., 2010; Ferreira et al., 2012) by looking at the return-chasing nature of mutual funds, where higher performance was connected with larger inflows, thus, future money inflows were expected after good past performance. Also, there is a huge discussion on whether performance persistence is seen over short-term periods (Jeon et al., 2017; Rakowski & Wang, 2009) by analyzing behavioral aspects and past performance as a signal for investment decisions, or in the long term (Bessler et al., 2018) by observing whether fund flows can explain actually the absence of persistence in mutual fund performance. Authors found that among actively managed US mutual funds, winners tend to outperform losers, and tried to prove whether fund flows and manager changes can explain the absence of persistence in mutual fund performance. Their findings suggest that both out and underperformance of equity mutual funds result in no persistence, if financial market functions well.

Over the last 20 years, a relatively high number of studies have dealt with analyzing persistence in mutual funds' performance (Abdelsalam et al., 2014). The importance of this topic is related to the relevance of past performance as a key criterion for choosing mutual funds. Given the importance of this question, i.e., whether good past performance is followed by good subsequent performance (and likewise for bad performance), for both academics and practitioners, the related literature has grown remarkably over the last two decades.[8]

Nevertheless, Abdelsalam et al. (2014), state that the literature on mutual fund persistence have not reached a consensus as to the lack or existence of persistence, as well as its potential explanations. On the one hand, we have the academic papers affirming no evidence of persistence.

[8] Abdelsalam, O., Duygun, M., Matallín-Sáez, J. C., & Tortosa-Ausina, E. (2014). Do ethics imply persistence? The case of Islamic and socially responsible funds. *Journal of Banking & Finance, 40*, 182–194.

Fletcher and Forbes (2002) found no persistence using the Carhart measure. Dahlquist et al. (2000) provided evidence of no persistence in their study of Swedish equity funds. Droms and Walker (2001) found no evidence of persistence over long-horizons, while Bollen and Busse (2005) suggested that persistence is by its nature a short-term phenomenon, to be found over short-term horizons such as quarterly periods.[9] Christensen (2005) investigating Denmark found no predictive ability of past performance measures. Quigley and Sinquefield (2000), Cuthbertson et al. (2008) and Massa and Patgiri (2009) found similar conclusions to those by Carhart (1997) in terms of no significant evidence of persistence in the analysis of investment strategies based on past performance.[10] Finally, Otten and Bams (2002) found that, with the exception of the United Kingdom, none of the equity funds in Europe's largest market has continued to exist.

From the opposite side, the literature presents numerous evidences that report the existence of the persistence of mutual fund returns.[11] A number of studies have documented indeed performance persistence in U.S. mutual funds include Teo and Woo (2001), Ibbotson and Patel (2002) and Wermers (2003). Other relevant literature found evidence of the existence of persistence effect in European funds (Banegas et al., 2013; Vidal-García, 2013); and American equity funds (Herrmann & Scholz, 2013). Lynch and Musto (2003), Cohen et al. (2005) and Kosowski et al. (2006) found that there is persistence in winners' funds, but there is no persistence in losers.

Several studies show evidence in support of the performance persistence in U.S. equity funds after considering fund investment styles. By examining managers' momentum, Wermers (2003) finds evidence of persistence in superior growth funds. Meier and Rombouts (2009) investigate the relation between performance persistence and changes in

[9] Droms, W. G., & Walker, D. A. (2001). Persistence of mutual fund operating characteristics: Returns, turnover rates, and expense ratios. *Applied Financial Economics, 11*(4), 457–466.

[10] Quigley, G., & Sinquefield, R. A. (2000). Performance of UK equity unit trusts. *Journal of Asset Management, 1*(1), 72–92.

[11] Babalos, V., Caporale, G. M., Kostakis, A., & Philippas, N. (2008). Testing for persistence in mutual fund performance and the ex-post verification problem: Evidence from the Greek market. *The European Journal of Finance, 14*(8), 735–753.

style.[12] The authors use a new holdings-based measure of style rotation for a large sample of US equity mutual funds, and find that top and bottom performing decile portfolios experience a higher degree of style rotation than middle deciles. They argue that there is a higher degree of performance persistence among style consistent funds. Their results imply that an investor needs to consider style rotation when choosing mutual funds based on past performance, otherwise future returns might exhibit big shifts in performance rankings. Moreover, authors find a significant negative relation between abnormal performance and management expenses, turnover, and maximum load for most countries.[13]

Several papers report that the persistence phenomenon is only short living. Many factors cause the lack of persistence over long time horizons. One is the decreasing investment opportunities (Berk & Green, 2004). A fund manager can only invest in each investment in a limited way; otherwise, they create a market impact and this investment opportunity will be arbitraged away (Vidal-García et al., 2016b). Investors allocate their money to best performers making superior funds grow to the point, where outperformance is no longer possible. An option is that top performing fund managers, who have built a strong reputation, may decide to find better paid jobs (Nain & Yao, 2013).

In Casarin et al. (2002), persistence was reported in the risk-adjusted returns of Italian equity funds, but only on a short-term basis. Deaves (2004) found persistence only over short horizons in Canada. Vidal-García et al. (2016b) examine the short-term persistence in performance of equity mutual funds around the world between 1990 and 2013. They used a large number of unbiased survival samples from 35 countries, and these strong evidences proved the continued existence of mutual fund returns every day during the quarterly evaluation period. They rank countries by abnormal returns and estimate how each country will perform in the next quarter. The authors found that from a statistical and economic perspective, performance persistence is particularly evident in the top and bottom countries. The top country is Brazil with a daily abnormal return from stock selection of 0.0921%, and the bottom country is Sweden with an abnormal return from stock selection of −0.0842% per day, both are

[12] Vidal-García, J., Vidal, M., Boubaker, S., & Uddin, G. S. (2016). The short-term persistence of international mutual fund performance. *Economic Modelling, 52*, 926–938.

[13] Meier, I., & Rombouts, J. V. (2009). *Style rotation and performance persistence of mutual funds*. Available at SSRN 1313242.

quite robust across the different performance models. Interestingly, the country with the highest durability is New Zealand, and the country with the lowest persistence is Malaysia. When checking performance over a longer period of time, the abnormal returns disappeared. This way, results confirm that superior performance is a short-lived phenomenon. Herrmann and Scholz (2013)[14] apply cross-sectional regressions to indicate short-term performance persistence for total performance and alpha. Sorting funds into decile portfolios, they further show the economic relevance of performance persistence. The spread between the average performance of the best and the worst deciles of funds in the second quarter is positive.

A good review of the literature, prior to the period of the Global Financial Crisis, is provided by Droms (2006), who highlights, above all, that: (i) poor past performance counts more than good past performance; (ii) within-category performance is more persistent than performance relative to overall market; (iii) short term performance persistence is much stronger than long-term persistence; (iv) international equity funds show very strong short-term performance persistence but no longer-term persistence; (v) findings of persistence may be sensitive to the period tested; and that (vi) Morningstar within category ratings, provide useful information for selecting mutual funds based on past performance.

In the specific case of the literature analyzing ethical funds and SRI performance persistence, the number of available studies is low (compared with the literature focusing on conventional funds) and results provide mixed empirical evidence.[15] Many other studies have found that the performance of ethics or SRI funds is durable (Gregory & Whittaker, 2007; Renneboog et al., 2011). Gregory and Whittaker (2007) studied the UK SRI fund and provided empirical evidence supporting the continuity of performance, especially over a longer time frame. However, they find that performance appears to be time and model-varying. Bauer et al. (2005) found that compared with traditional funds, ethical mutual funds are generally less affected by market return fluctuations, which may lead

[14] Herrmann, U., & Scholz, H. (2013). Short-term persistence in hybrid mutual fund performance: The role of style-shifting abilities. *Journal of Banking & Finance, 37*(7), 2314–2328.

[15] Abdelsalam, O., Duygun, M., Matallín-Sáez, J. C., & Tortosa-Ausina, E. (2014). Do ethics imply persistence? The case of Islamic and socially responsible funds. *Journal of Banking & Finance, 40,* 182–194.

to persistence. Renneboog et al. (2011) found that ethical funds are not so sensitive to past negative funds, and that SRI funds that perform better than "losses" are far better than their controlled portfolios. In study of Abdelsalam et al. (2014) persistence is found for several deciles of distributions, but only for the best and the worst funds (especially in the case of SRI funds) it results statistically significant.

From the point of view of the econometric approaches, nevertheless most of the studies employ return-based approaches to measure fund performance, two strands of literature stand in contrast to each other.

Firstly, a group of methodologies involve the use of contingency tables, transition matrices and cross-sectional regressions of fund performance on its lagged value to analyze if current performance predicts future performance. The application of statistical measures such as contingency tables by Droms and Walker (2001), Silva et al. (2005), Babalos et al. (2008) and Elyasiani and Jia (2011), has reinforced the persistence evidence mainly over short time horizons. Evidence of persistence is also found when the transition probability matrix approach is used, as in Brown and Goetzmann (1997) and Malkiel (1995).[16] However, Cuthbertson et al. (2010) point out some limitations of contingency tables, such as the fact that they are not easy for investors to interpret.[17] Secondly, another method for measuring performance continuity in the literature is the recursive portfolio method, proposed originally by Grinblatt and Titman (1993), Hendricks et al. (1993) and Carhart (1997). This method evaluates durability by estimating the performance of a recursive portfolio that follows investment recommendations based on the past performance of mutual funds. If there is persistence, one can expect that investing in the worst (best) mutual fund in the past will lead to worse (better) performance in the future. In the last two decades, Bollen and Busse (2005), Cohen et al. (2005), Busse and Irvine (2006), Kacperczyk et al. (2008), Busse et al. (2010), Fama and French (2010), and Benos and Jochec (2011) have adopted similar approaches in different markets.

[16] Babalos, V., Caporale, G. M., Kostakis, A., & Philippas, N. (2008). Testing for persistence in mutual fund performance and the ex-post verification problem: Evidence from the Greek market. *The European Journal of Finance, 14*(8), 735–753.

[17] Matallín-Sáez, J. C., Soler-Domínguez, A., & Tortosa-Ausina, E. (2016). On the robustness of persistence in mutual fund performance. *The North American Journal of Economics and Finance, 36,* 192–231.

Matallín-Sáez et al. (2016) apply contingency tables and transition matrices to measure mutual fund persistence, where results indicate generalized evidence supporting persistence. However, when the analysis is carried out for different subperiods, the evidence of persistence does not hold for all them. Thus, for the 1990–2007 subperiod persistence is found, and is more significant for the case of funds that add positive value for investors; however, for the 2008–2015 subperiod they find no evidence of persistence. Indeed, in this most recent subperiod some evidence of reversal persistence is even found: investing in past losers results in better future performance than investing in past winners. The existence of mutual fund persistence seems to be conditioned by the sample period considered, a result that could explain the varied and inconclusive evidence found in the literature. Mixed evidence is also presented by Agudo and Magallón (2005) for the Spain market. Kosowski et al. (2006), using net returns after trading costs and fees, find evidence of persistence in growth-oriented funds, but find no evidence for the managerial skills of income-oriented funds.

With regard to different econometric approaches, other articles concentrate on assessing the market timing abilities of fund managers. Here, the two most popular return-based approaches examining market timing abilities are Treynor and Mazuy (1966; hereafter referred to as TM) and Henriksson and Merton (1981; HM). Both approaches suppose that market timing decisions depend on a fund manager's opinion on the future size of the market's excess return.[18] TM assumes that fund managers increase (decrease) the market risk of their investment portfolio based on the degree of positive (negative) forecasted excess market returns. As a result, there is a convex relationship between fund returns and market returns. The basic assumption of the HM method is that fund managers can invest their portfolios in markets or risk-free assets. Their decision depends on whether they expect positive or negative market excess returns. Bollen and Busse (2001, 2005) and others used TM and HM methods to test the market timing capabilities of stock funds. They use daily capital returns and quarterly measurement periods instead of the usual monthly returns and measurement periods of several months. However, because the TM and HM methods use specific forms of market

[18] Herrmann, U., & Scholz, H. (2013). Short-term persistence in hybrid mutual fund performance: The role of style-shifting abilities. *Journal of Banking & Finance, 37*(7), 2314–2328.

timing, if fund managers time the market in different ways, using different approaches, may lead to bias in performance estimates (for example, see Coles et al., 2006; Krimm et al., 2011). In addition, the nonlinear relationship between fund and market returns, implied by these two methods, may be caused by factors other than the timing of active markets (Goetzmann et al., 2007). To overcome these problems, recent studies apply holding based approaches. Among other things, Jiang et al. (2007), Elton et al. (2012) and Wermers (2012) use mutual fund assets to assess market timing ability. However, implementing a holding-based approach will bring potential challenges. First, according to laws and regulations, funds are allowed to conduct quarterly disclosure of portfolio holdings (US Securities and Exchange Commission, 2004). When using stocks held in a portfolio, it is difficult to determine the fund's performance in time. Second, in the holding-based method, window decoration is a major issue. This means that the fund holdings reported afterwards may not reflect the actual portfolio characteristics of each period (for example, see Carhart et al., 2002; Elton et al., 2010; He et al., 2004; Morey & O'Neal, 2006; Ortiz et al., 2012; Sias, 2007). Finally, irregular and infrequent portfolio holding reports can lead to incomplete time series, which greatly reduces the data sample.

Kosowski et al. (2006) studied the distribution of fund Alpha and found that many funds produce consistent positive Alpha, and this does not depend solely on luck. They found that skilled funds add approximately \$1.2 billion in wealth to the mutual fund industry each year, but funds that seem to lack skills also lose approximately \$1.5 billion each year. Barras et al. (2010) control skill "false discovery" by adjusting funds with significant estimated alpha values finding zero true alpha values. They show that about 76% of funds do have stock picking capabilities, but almost all funds draw rent from them through fees. If certain mutual fund managers do have skills, then being able to identify them is a valuable exercise. Cremers and Petajisto (2009) show that funds that deviate the farthest from the benchmark tend to outperform "closet index" funds, that is, funds that claim to be active but hold portfolios similar to the baseline. In similar work, Amihud and Goyenko (2013) found that fund performance can be predicted by the selectivity of the fund. They used R^2 (R-squared) to measure the—level to stay close—to a declared benchmark by regressing fund returns on a multi-factor benchmark model. Funds with low R^2 (high selectivity) outperform funds with high R^2 (low selectivity).

Lastly, several papers focus their intention on measuring whether investors are just wasting their time and money or a better performance is explained by the fact that the money is "smart". Recent studies on the topic (Akbas et al., 2015; Fong et al., 2018; Jiang & Yuksel, 2017) agree that money is smart by examining mutual fund persistence by the dynamic of investor inflows and fund manager skill.

3 Methodology and Empirical Results

3.1 Ranked Portfolios Approach

There are many tests for fund performance persistence, including contingency table tests, rank correlation test and Carhart (1997) recursive portfolio formation test. A key advantage of the latter over the former is that it is a test of the economic significance of the persistence of funds, not just a test of statistical significance. Therefore, following convention in the mutual fund literature, we start by using performance-ranked portfolio strategies. Performance-ranked portfolio tests classify funds each period into portfolios according to past performance (Vidal-García, 2013). After an initial ranking period, the performance of funds is compared and ranked.

This empirical strategy is, therefore, based on a recursive estimation methodology, similar to that initially proposed by Carhart (1997)—although several refinements were proposed afterwards by Busse et al. (2010) and Fama and French (2010), among others. The main purpose of this method is to ascertain whether performance persistence exists based on the evaluation of portfolios which are built following a past performance investment strategy.[19] If there is persistence, the performance investment strategy of the past will be successful, that is, the best funds still exist the next year and vice versa.

According to Matallín-Sáez et al. (2019)[20] persistence is then calculated for monthly windows. The first of these windows estimates past

[19] Abdelsalam, O., Duygun, M., Matallín-Sáez, J. C., & Tortosa-Ausina, E. (2014). Do ethics imply persistence? The case of Islamic and socially responsible funds. *Journal of Banking & Finance, 40,* 182–194.

[20] Matallín-Sáez, J. C., Soler-Domínguez, A., Tortosa-Ausina, E., & de Mingo-López, D. V. (2019). Ethical strategy focus and mutual fund management: Performance and persistence. *Journal of Cleaner Production, 213,* 618–633.

performance, while the second window rebalances recursively the portfolio combinations. In addition, when estimating performance of a non-overlapping rolling window, we will be allowing the model parameters to vary over time. This is an interesting feature, due to the substantial amount of literature on time varying systematic risk. According to above explanation and similarly to Abdelsalam et al. (2017), we apply the recursive portfolio approach by means of the following algorithm:

1. In the first step, the performance of the funds is estimated by means of Eq. (1) for the first sample period. Our primary approach to measuring performance is to calculate factor models with time-series regressions.
2. Funds are ranked in increasing order according to the performance achieved in the period in order to form quintiles within each group of funds according to investment area.

   Specifically, funds will be ranked based on the average return during the ranking period, and the style portfolio will be classified based on this ranking while considering specific style benchmark (e.g. USA mid-small cap funds will be ranked by considering appropriate mid-small cap US index).
3. At the start of the following period we form five equally weighted portfolios according to quintile past performance, Q1; ...; Q5, where the first portfolio (Q1) invests in the worst performing funds in the previous period and, conversely, the last portfolio (Q5) invests in the previous period's best funds. The same investment strategy is followed for the other quintiles.

   Each 1st of month, we create equal-weighted portfolios of mutual funds for each investment style, we hold these portfolios for one calendar month, and then portfolios are created again the next month (Vidal-García, 2013), therefore, by using monthly intervals, we rank mutual funds based on the average rate of return over the past month, then create a value-weighted style portfolio that we hold next month and then calculate their monthly returns.

   The number of funds in each portfolio might be slightly different. The highest-ranked portfolio includes the fund with the highest average abnormal return during the ranking period, and the lowest-ranked portfolio includes the fund with the lowest average abnormal return.

Repeating this process at the end of each month, we obtain a time series of monthly returns for each style combination from January 2007 to December 2019. Then, we calculate the equal-weighted return for each portfolio in the next year.

4. This process is repeated at the beginning of each period (i.e., we would restart in step 2). Therefore, each portfolio would represent a dynamic investment strategy that rebalances selected funds according to their previous performance. Acting this way, we focus on persistence in 1-month period.
5. We form aggregate measures of performance using equal-weighted portfolio returns of all mutual funds for that month. We roll forward, creating a set of post-ranking month returns. We obtain a time-series of post ranking returns for each portfolio.

Our hypothesis is, therefore, that should persistence in mutual fund performance exist, a portfolio with an investment strategy based on a poor (good) past performance will show a negative (positive) abnormal performance. In other words, we measure the persistence of fund performance by examining whether funds that have performed well in the past can repeat this in the following periods.[21]

We measure the performance across all the funds within that investment style, by considering the equal-weighted return of all mutual funds in the category. In some previous studies (see among others, Dumitrescu & Gil-Bazo, 2018; Vidal-García, 2013),[22] academicians prefer to weight by the size of the fund, because fund managers will provide better services and will increase efforts to manage larger funds, because the fee is determined based on the value of the assets under management, then the larger mutual fund pays the fund manager higher income. In this approach, at the beginning of each month, funds will be weighted according to the assets under management.

We considered as aggregate measure of post-ranked performance the Jensen Alpha, and the three factor and four factor Alpha, while as measure

[21] Agarwal, V., & Naik, N. Y. (2000). Multi-period performance persistence analysis of hedge funds. *Journal of Financial and quantitative Analysis,* 327–342.

[22] Vidal-García, J. (2013). The persistence of European mutual fund performance. *Research in International Business and Finance, 28,* 45–67.

Dumitrescu, A., & Gil-Bazo, J. (2018). Market frictions, investor sophistication, and persistence in mutual fund performance. *Journal of Financial Markets, 40,* 40–59.

of performance persistence in the ranking month we use benchmark-adjusted returns, by subtracting a benchmark return from the annual raw return:

$$R_{x,t} = R_{i,t} - R_{b,t} \tag{1}$$

where $R_{i,t}$ is the return on fund i for month t, $R_{b,t}$ is the benchmark return, and $R_{x,t}$ is the excess return.

Most investors and fund managers focus on benchmark-adjusted returns as performance measure, since the investment alternative is an index fund which replicates the stock index return, and beating this index is their investment objective. We use MSCI style indices as benchmarks based on the investment style of each portfolio to adjust raw returns. Thus, we include individual country style indices among the benchmarks, allowing for partial market segmentation.

We show the results of performance persistence tests for the US equity sample in Table 1, in first Column we report performance from a CAPM model, while the second and third column exhibit 3 and 4-factor model alpha. The first panel (Rank (1)—Best Quintile) contains the best-performing funds, taking into account their previous month's benchmark-adjusted return and Rank (5) contains the worst-performing funds. From our results, we can state that, on average, performance persistence is greater when the Rank is the highest. Looking at the alphas reported in the Panel corresponding to the first quintile (Rank (1)—Best Quintile), we can observe that on average all the alphas are greater than other Rank groups, regardless of the specific investment style. On the other hand, when Mutual fund portfolios are sorted taking into account their previous month's benchmark-adjusted return, corresponding to Rank (5) containing the worst-performing funds, we obtain on average the worst alpha performance. This evidence indicates that there are signs of persistence for the extreme quintiles of the distribution of past returns. In line with Vidal-García (2013), funds in the top and bottom ranks maintain their positions more frequently than the other fund portfolios. Furthermore, results show that the information content of the performance history does not vary across the different fund investment styles, and is not influenced by the measurement methodology used. In other words, this results on average holds, regardless of the specific portfolio model we consider to get the alpha, that is, past top-performing bond funds go on to perform relatively poor in the following period.

Table 1 Performance persistence. US EQUITY

1 Month Rank (1)—Best Quintile

Investment Styles	*Alpha CAPM*	*Alpha Fama-French*	*Alpha Carhart*
Large Cap	0.08***	0.01*	0.02***
Blend	−0.02***	−0.05***	−0.03***
Small Cap	0.09***	0.10***	0.11***
Value	−0.02*	−0.02**	−0.01
Growth	0.09***	0.02*	0.03***

1 Month Rank (2)

Investment Styles	*Alpha CAPM*	*Alpha Fama-French*	*Alpha Carhart*
Large Cap	−0.02***	−0.04***	−0.04***
Blend	−0.04***	−0.06***	−0.05***
Small Cap	0.01	0.04***	0.03***
Value	0.00	0.05***	0.05***
Growth	0.06***	−0.02*	−0.01

1 Month Rank (3)

Investment Styles	*Alpha CAPM*	*Alpha Fama-French*	*Alpha Carhart*
Large Cap	0.01	0.00	0.01
Blend	−0.04***	−0.05***	−0.04***
Small Cap	−0.01	0.12***	0.13***
Value	−0.06***	−0.02*	−0.01
Growth	0.01	−0.03***	−0.02**

1 Month Rank (4)

Investment Styles	*Alpha CAPM*	*Alpha Fama-French*	*Alpha Carhart*
Large Cap	0.01*	−0.01**	0.00
Blend	0.02***	−0.01***	−0.02***
Small Cap	0.00	0.12***	0.11***
Value	−0.06***	0.00	0.01
Growth	0.12***	0.02*	0.00

(continued)

Table 1 (continued)

1 Month Rank (5)—Worst Quintile

Investment Styles	*Alpha CAPM*	*Alpha Fama-French*	*Alpha Carhart*
Large Cap	−0.12***	−0.08***	−0.07***
Blend	−0.14***	−0.16***	−0.16***
Small Cap	−0.05***	0.10***	0.12***
Value	−0.18***	−0.10***	−0.08***
Growth	0.03***	−0.05***	−0.05***

Mutual funds are sorted on first day of each month from 2006 to 2019 into investment styles portfolios taking into account their previous month's benchmark-adjusted return. The portfolios are equal-weighted monthly. Rank (1) contains the best-performing funds, taking into account their previous month's benchmark-adjusted return and Rank (5) contains the worst-performing funds. Ranks are calculated taking into account the quintiles of their previous month's benchmark-adjusted return. Alpha is the intercept of the Multifactor Model. The table shows average simulated alphas and their t-statistics. *, **, and ***, respectively, denote significance at the 10, 5, and 1% levels

There is positive persistence at the bottom end of the performance distribution—past poor performing funds remain relatively poor performing in the future. Finally, funds in the middle of the performance distribution over the previous months remain in the middle of the distribution over the following three months.

In Table 2 we report the results of performance persistence tests for the European equity sample, where in first column we report performance from a CAPM model, while the second and third column exhibit 3 and 4-factor model alpha. The first panel (Rank (1)—Best Quintile) contains the best-performing funds, taking into account their previous month's benchmark-adjusted return and Rank (5) contains the worst-performing funds. In a similar fashion of the results presented in the previous table, we observe that on average, performance persistence is greater when the Rank is the highest. Looking at the alphas reported in the Panel corresponding to the first quintile (Rank (1)—Best Quintile), we can observe that on average all the alphas are greater than other Rank groups, regardless of the specific investment style. The evidence relating to the persistence of the performance of the top quintile is even clearer in the European sample than in the US sample. Indeed, observing the results relating to the alpha CAPM (first column) and partly to the Carhart Alpha (Last Column), we find that the returns calculated in terms of alpha tend to decline uniformly, passing from a best to a worse quintile ranking

Table 2 Performance persistence. EUROPE EQUITY

1 Month Rank (1)—Best Quintile			
Investment Styles	*Alpha CAPM*	*Alpha Fama-French*	*Alpha Carhart*
Large Cap	0.15***	0.23***	0.14***
Blend	0.14***	0.21***	0.13***
Small Cap	0.38***	0.39***	0.26***
Value	0.10***	0.2***	0.16***
Growth	0.31***	0.34***	0.20***
1 Month Rank (2)			
Investment Styles	*Alpha CAPM*	*Alpha Fama-French*	*Alpha Carhart*
Large Cap	0.13***	0.27 ***	0.15***
Blend	0.12***	0.26 ***	0.15***
Small Cap	0.36***	0.37 ***	0.21***
Value	0.09***	0.26 ***	0.16***
Growth	0.25***	0.32 ***	0.19***
1 Month Rank (3)			
Investment Styles	*Alpha CAPM*	*Alpha Fama-French*	*Alpha Carhart*
Large Cap	0.05***	0.18***	0.11***
Blend	0.04***	0.17***	0.11***
Small Cap	0.25***	0.29***	0.19***
Value	−0.04*	0.15***	0.11***
Growth	0.14***	0.24***	0.14***
1 Month Rank (4)			
Investment Styles	*Alpha CAPM*	*Alpha Fama-French*	*Alpha Carhart*
Large Cap	0.05***	0.20***	0.07***
Blend	0.04***	0.19***	0.06***
Small Cap	0.19***	0.30***	0.13***
Value	−0.07***	0.15***	0.07***
Growth	0.17***	0.30***	0.14***

(continued)

Table 2 (continued)

1 Month Rank (5)—Worst Quintile			
Investment Styles	*Alpha CAPM*	*Alpha Fama-French*	*Alpha Carhart*
Large Cap	0.03***	0.23***	0.05***
Blend	0.01	0.21***	0.02***
Small Cap	0.17***	0.32***	0.11***
Value	−0.07***	0.19***	0.04*
Growth	0.14***	0.25***	0.01

Mutual funds are sorted on first day of each month from 2006 to 2019 into investment styles portfolios taking into account their previous month's benchmark-adjusted return. The portfolios are equal-weighted monthly. Rank (1) contains the best-performing funds, taking into account their previous month's benchmark-adjusted return and Rank (5) contains the worst-performing funds. Ranks are calculated taking into account the quintiles of their previous month's benchmark-adjusted return. Alpha is the intercept of the Multifactor Model. The table shows average simulated alphas and their t-statistics. *, **, and ***, respectively, denote significance at the 10, 5, and 1% levels

group. On the other hand, when Mutual fund portfolios are sorted taking into account their previous month's benchmark-adjusted return, corresponding to Rank (5) containing the worst-performing funds, we obtain mixed evidence particularly with respect to the Fama-French Alpha.

Persistence is important from a practical and economic perspective, as it implies a violation of market efficiency and a value-increasing opportunity for investors. All in all, performance estimates from the CAPM present significantly different sizeable abnormal returns for the previous month's top-ranked and bottom-ranked portfolios of funds. The difference in terms of annual percentage in each category for the US group is: Large-Cap (0.20), Blend (0.12), Small Cap (0.14), Value (0.16) and Growth (0.06). The difference in terms of annual percentage in each category for the European group is: Large-Cap (0.12), Blend (0.13), Small Cap (0.21), Value (0.17) and Growth (0.17).

In a similar fashion performance estimates from the Fama-French present significantly different sizeable abnormal returns for the previous month's top-ranked and bottom-ranked portfolios of funds. The difference in terms of annual percentage in each category for the US group is: Large-Cap (0.09), Blend (0.11), Small Cap (0.01), Value (0.08) and Growth (0.03). The difference in terms of annual percentage in each category for the European group is: Large-Cap (0.01), Blend (0.01), Small Cap (0.07), Value (0.04) and Growth (0.09).

In a similar way, the performance estimates of the Carhart model show that the highest-ranked and lowest-ranked fund portfolios have on average significantly different abnormal returns in the post-rank month. The difference in terms of annual percentage in each category for the US group is: Large-Cap (0.09), Blend (0.19), Small Cap (−0.01), Value (0.09) and Growth (0.08). The difference in terms of annual percentage in each category for the European group is: Large-Cap (0.09), Blend (0.11), Small Cap (0.15), Value (0.12) and Growth (0.19).

3.2 Longer-Term Persistence in Mutual Fund Portfolios

As we find some evidence of performance persistence, we would like to know whether the results hold when persistence is measured over a longer period.[23] Following Vidal-García (2013), we repeat our regression analysis with longer-term measures of persistence and investigate time horizons from 1 to 3 years. The knowledge of longer-term performance persistence will add a great deal of value for investors. Carhart (1997) argues that if manager skill exists, a 1-month return is probably a noisy measure. In order to reduce the noise in past-performance rankings, he creates portfolios of mutual funds on lagged 2- to 5-year returns. He then repeats his previous analysis to evaluate how much cross-sectional variation in mean return can be explained by the 4-factor model. To this end, in our empirical tests, on January 1 of each year, funds are ranked into equal-weighted portfolios based on their Carhart model alphas estimated over the previous 1-year period.

Figures from one to 4 demonstrate that the dynamics of mutual fund returns over time are consistent with the earlier conclusions of Carhart (1997), who reported a lack of performance persistence and a strong tendency for performance to mean revert.

Specifically, in the BOND US group, the top 20% of funds (winner funds) generate average raw returns in the formation year of 0.47% per month which decline to 0.10% per month in the subsequent evaluation year and at 0.11% at time $T + 3$ (that is 3 years ahead). The bottom 20% of funds (loser funds), in contrast, experience a mean reversion in raw returns from -1.21 to 0.14% per month at $T + 1$ interval, and at 0.15% at time $T + 3$. In other words, a raw return spread between winner and

[23] Vidal-García, J. (2013). The persistence of European mutual fund performance. *Research in International Business and Finance, 28,* 45–67.

loser funds of 1.33% per month (15.96% per annum) in the formation year declines to −0.01% per month (−0.12% per annum) in the first evaluation year (Figs. 1, 2, 3 and 4).

In the BOND Europe group, the top 20% of funds (winner funds) generate average raw returns in the formation year of 1.16% per month which decline to 0.14% per month in the subsequent evaluation year and at 0.20% at time $T + 3$. The bottom 20% of funds (loser funds), in contrast, experience a mean reversion in raw returns from –1.87 to 0.01% per month at $T + 1$ interval, and at 0.20% at time $T + 3$. In other words, a raw return spread between winner and loser funds of 3.03% per month (36.36% per annum) in the formation year declines to 0.13% per month (1.56% per annum) in the first evaluation year.

In the Equity US group, the top 20% of funds (winner funds) generate average raw returns in the formation year of 2.04% per month, which decline to 0.24% per month in the subsequent evaluation year and at 0.50% at time $T + 3$. The bottom 20% of funds (loser funds), in contrast, experience a mean reversion in raw returns from –3.83 to 0.78% per month at $T + 1$ interval, and at 0.47% at time $T + 3$. In other words, a raw return spread between winner and loser funds of 5.87% per month

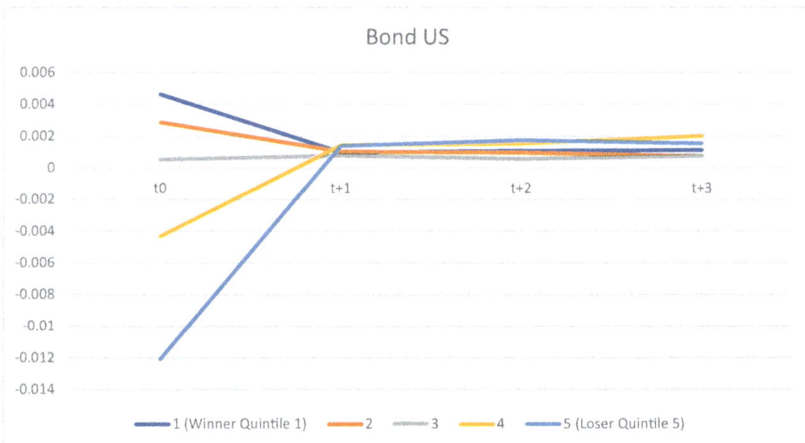

Fig. 1 US Bond. This figure presents the average monthly raw returns of the quintile portfolios relative to the evaluation year ($t0$). Portfolios are formed based on previous year alphas

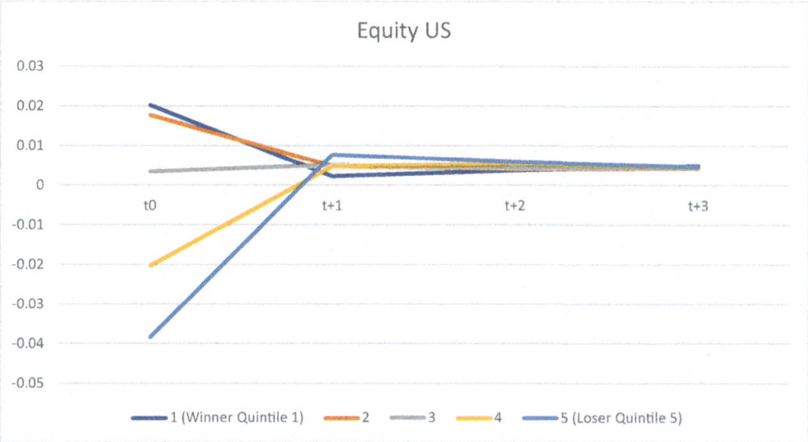

Fig. 2 US Equity. This figure presents the average monthly raw returns of the quintile portfolios relative to the evaluation year ($t0$). Portfolios are formed based on previous year four factor alphas

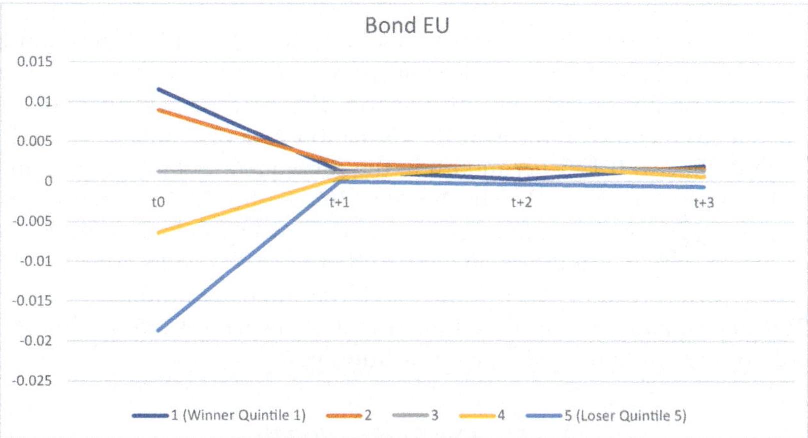

Fig. 3 Europe Bond. This figure presents the average monthly raw returns of the quintile portfolios relative to the evaluation year ($t0$). Portfolios are formed based on previous year alphas

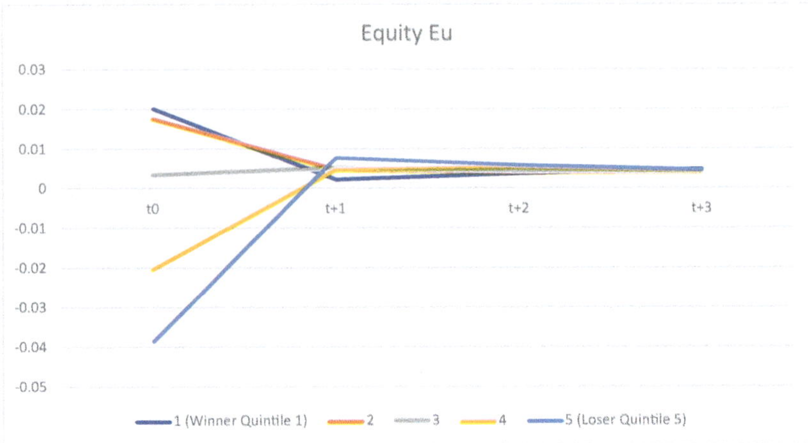

Fig. 4 Europe Equity. This figure presents the average monthly raw returns of the quintile portfolios relative to the evaluation year ($t0$). Portfolios are formed based on previous year four factor alphas

(70.44% per annum) in the formation year declines to −0.54% per month (−6.48% per annum) in the first evaluation year.

In the Equity Europe group, the top 20% of funds (winner funds) generate average raw returns in the formation year of 2.36% per month, which decline to 0.17% per month in the subsequent evaluation year and at 0.39% at time $T + 3$. The bottom 20% of funds (loser funds), in contrast, experience a mean reversion in raw returns from -3.64 to 0.35% per month at $T + 1$ interval, and at 0.39% at time $T + 3$. In other words, a raw return spread between winner and loser funds of 6.00% per month (72% per annum) in the formation year declines to −0.18% per month (−2.16% per annum) in the first evaluation year.

3.3 *Contingency Tables*

We also analyzed the persistence of mutual funds investment style performance through contingency tables.

The contingency tables methodology is a non-parametric analysis of persistence to test the frequency with which winner or loser funds maintained that position over subsequent time periods.

To test for independence in the results from year to year, the contingency table estimates were examined by the use of the repeat winner approach (Malkiel, 1995), the odds ratio (Brown & Goetzmann, 1995), and the Chi-square statistic (Kahn & Rudd, 1995). The first test is the repeat winner strategy proposed by Malkiel (1995).

The null hypothesis for these three non-parametric tests is that of no persistence.

To construct these test statistics, in the same fashion of Babalos et al. (2008),[24] and Vidal-García (2013), we classify the mutual funds as winners (W) or losers (L) depending on whether their performance measure was above or below the median value for each time period.

Winning and losing funds are classified according to the median fund return for each year. Contingency tables sort funds as winners or losers in each time period, and the different combinations are counted: winner–winner (WW), winner–loser (WL), loser–winner (LW), and loser–loser (LL). Winner-winner (WW) refers to funds with abnormal returns whose returns in each period are higher than the median return.[25] Winner-loser refers to funds whose returns are higher than the median return in the previous (testing) period while the return in the next period is lower than the median return and vice versa for the loser–winner (LW), combinations. Thus, contingency tables present the frequency with which winners and losers repeat.

The contingency tables show the probability of a fund in a ranking position being in the same rank in the following period. If the performance is completely random, then investors will expect the highest-ranked fund in the next investment period to have an equal chance of appearing in any ranking position, because the past evaluation period has no effect on subsequent periods.

If we find statistical evidence that the winner in one year is still the winner in the second year, the null hypothesis of no persistence will be rejected. If the statistical evidence shows that the number of observations in the WW/LL category is significantly more than the other two

[24] Babalos, V., Caporale, G. M., Kostakis, A., & Philippas, N. (2008). Testing for persistence in mutual fund performance and the ex-post verification problem: Evidence from the Greek market. *The European Journal of Finance, 14*(8), 735–753.

[25] Vidal-García, J. (2013). The persistence of European mutual fund performance. *Research in International Business and Finance, 28,* 45–67.

categories, there is performance persistence. The advantage of the contingency table method is the way to track the fluctuation of a single fund and evaluate its transition probability. When the sample of funds is limited, tabulation is preferable to other methods.

In the Malkiel (1995) test, no persistence means that a past winner will be either winner or loser in the next period with equal probability $p = 0.5$.

He uses a binomial test of $p > 1/2$ to check the significance of the proportion of *WW* to (*WW* + *WL*):

The test statistic is calculated as follows:

$$M = \frac{(WW - (ww + WL) * 0.5)}{\sqrt{(WW + WL) * 0.5 * 0.5}} \tag{2}$$

and it follows a standard normal distribution. A *M*-statistic above zero show performance persistence.[26]

In the test of Brown and Goetzmann (1995), the null hypothesis is that the number of funds changing category next period is equal to the number of funds remaining in the same category. The hypothesis is tested using the cross-product ratio (CPR)[27]:

$$CPR = \frac{WW * LL}{WL * LW} \tag{3}$$

The CPR is calculated as $(WW \times LL)/(LW \times WL)$, the ratio of the product of repeat winners (*WW*) and repeat losers (*LL*) divided by the product of winner–losers (*WL*) and loser–winners (*LW*). Under the null hypothesis of no persistence the CPR equals 1. A CPR greater than one indicates persistence, and a value below one shows a reversal in performance. The statistical significance of the CPR can be determined by a

[26] Some authors, to examine the significance of the proportion of *WW* to (*WW* + *WL*), while keeping the rationale of the test unchanged, adopt a different notation, as it follows:

$$Z = \frac{(y - np)}{\sqrt{np(1-p)}}$$

where Z is a statistical variable with a normal distribution (0,1), y is the number of repeat winners (*WW*), and n is the number of repeat winners and winners/losers (*WW* + *WL*).

[27] Babalos, V., Caporale, G. M., Kostakis, A., & Philippas, N. (2008). Testing for persistence in mutual fund performance and the ex-post verification problem: Evidence from the Greek market. *The European Journal of Finance, 14*(8), 735–753.

Z-statistic, which equals the ratio of the natural logarithm of the CPR and the standard error of the natural logarithm of the CPR. Using large samples, it is normally distributed with mean log CPR, while for small sample sizes results about CPRs may be misleading.

For the statistical significance of the test values, the following Z-test is constructed:

$$Z = \frac{lnCPR}{\sigma_{lnCPR}} \tag{4}$$

where:

$$\sigma_{lnCPR} = \sqrt{\frac{1}{WW} + \frac{1}{LL} + \frac{1}{WL} + \frac{1}{LW}} \tag{5}$$

Finally, Kahn and Rudd (1995) used a chi-square test to compare the frequency of observed events with expected events. In the absence of persistence, the expected number of current winners remaining to be winners is equal to the expected number of winners who become losers, as well as the number of current losers remaining losers and the number of losers who become winners. Cortez et al. (1999) specify this chi-square statistic as:

$$\chi^2 = \frac{\left(WW - \frac{N}{4}\right)^2}{\frac{N}{4}} + \frac{\left(WL - \frac{N}{4}\right)^2}{\frac{N}{4}} + \frac{\left(LW - \frac{N}{4}\right)^2}{\frac{N}{4}} + \frac{\left(LL - \frac{N}{4}\right)^2}{\frac{N}{4}} \tag{6}$$

which follows a chi-square distribution with one degree of freedom. Some authors[28] rearrange Eq. (6) as follows:

$$\chi = \frac{(WW - D1)^2}{D1} + \frac{(WL - D2)^2}{D2} + \frac{(LW - D3)^2}{D3} + \frac{(LL - D4)^2}{D4} \tag{7}$$

where:

$$D1 = \frac{(WW + WL) * (WW + LW)}{N} \tag{8}$$

$$D2 = \frac{(WW + WL) * (WL + LL)}{N} \tag{9}$$

[28] See for example Vidal-García, J. (2013). The persistence of European mutual fund performance. *Research in International Business and Finance, 28,* 45–67.

$$D3 = \frac{(LW + LL) * (WW + LW)}{N} \tag{10}$$

$$D4 = \frac{(LW + LL) * (WL + LL)}{N} \tag{11}$$

where N is the number of funds.

Carpenter and Lynch (1999) explained that the Chi-squared test is well specified and more robust to the presence of survivorship bias in comparison to other tests of performance.[29]

Performance Measures

According to Babalos et al. (2008) we consider several performance measures. Raw returns of the mutual funds were calculated using the standard formula:

$$\mathcal{R}_p = \frac{NAV_t - NAV_{t-1}}{NAV_{t-1}} \tag{12}$$

Raw returns are employed as our first performance measure. Next, we use the three-factor model of Fama and French (1996) employed here is the following:

$$R_{it} - R_{ft} = \alpha_i + b_i(R_{Mt} - R_{ft}) + s_i SMB_t + h_i HML_t + e_{it} \tag{13}$$

The intercept of this regression is interpreted as a performance measure. According to this method, we can use the inconsistency of CAPM to capture the excess revenue generated by the tactical asset allocation strategy. More specifically, excess fund returns are decomposed into excess market returns, returns generated by buying small size stocks and selling big size stocks (Small Minus Big—SMB), and returns generated by buying stocks with high book-to-market ratios and selling stocks with low book-to-market ratios (High Minus Low—HML). The intercept of this regression represents that the manager has increased the value of his portfolio, beyond the value proven by market risk and the value generated by these known strategies. Similar to CAPM, R_{Mt} is the stock market return.

[29] Vidal-García, J., Vidal, M., Boubaker, S., & Uddin, G. S. (2016). The short-term persistence of international mutual fund performance. *Economic Modelling*, *52*, 926–938.

Empirical Results

Table 3 reports a non-parametric contingency table of the performance persistence of mutual fund winners and losers from 2006 to 2019. The results show repeat wining and repeat losing observations as well as its significance, and those that are winning fund portfolios in one of the two (the first is the evaluation) periods and loser fund portfolios in the other period.

The contingency table results, as summarized in the tests figures, are not very different from what academic's scholars find previously (see among others: Clare et al., 2019; Matallín-Sáez et al., 2019; Vidal-García et al., 2016a) and reveal that persistence is universally significant (look at Zeta statistic in the last column) for all mutual fund investment style portfolios.

Fama-French Measure

The first measure used is the Fama-French model (see regression 12) to adjust for known sources of risk. This regression incorporates a portfolio strategy that takes advantage of the size and mark-to-market anomalies recorded in Fama and French (1993, 1996). Using this regression, we can adjust the returns generated by the strategy of investing in small and valuable stocks. Therefore, for the period when the return of small stocks clearly exceeds the return of large capital stocks, the single-factor model will allocate these excess returns to positive performance. Therefore, funds that follow a small-cap strategy will show positive or negative performance, and this performance will persist over time, even if it is entirely due to investment strategy. Table 3 reports the results for persistence using regression intercept as a performance metric. For fund portfolios of all investment styles, there is some evidence of persistence in the 2006–2019 period. Thus, when we consider the Fama-French Alpha (Panel A) it is clear that in the ALL sample (first row in Table 1) winners will possibly remain winners, but losers will possibly not remain losers and change their status, as the number of funds repeating as winners is larger than the number of funds that change their status. On the contrary, the number of funds repeating as losers is lower than the number of funds that become next period 'winners (78,297 vs. 91,650). The test shows a probability above 50% for most funds in a rank position being in the same raking in the following period. Looking at the different investment style fund portfolios, on average the ranks of all of the top and bottom mutual

Table 3 Fund persistence—non parametric test 2006–2019

Panel A: Fama-French Alpha

Investment styles	*Number of.*				*Stat-Test*		
	WW	*LL*	*LW*	*WL*	*CPR*	*Sigma CPR*	*Zeta*
ALL Sample	39884	78297	91650	5883	5.79	0.01	118.76
Europe Large	5203	9635	11506	646	6.74	0.04	43.44
Europe Small	2007	4407	5337	2118	0.78	0.04	−6.59
Europe Blend	5215	9374	11257	668	6.50	0.04	43.12
Europe Value	1123	2071	2434	127	7.52	0.10	20.53
Europe Growth	1103	2199	2576	112	8.41	0.10	20.60
US Large	3519	6019	6863	634	4.87	0.05	33.95
US Small	1194	2228	2556	146	7.13	0.09	21.27
US Blend	9528	14768	16860	1894	4.41	0.03	53.80
US Value	1431	2574	2911	188	6.73	0.08	23.21
US Growth	853	2004	2293	182	4.10	0.09	16.17
Europe Corporate	4737	9085	11225	470	8.16	0.05	41.66
Europe Government	2521	4757	5866	254	8.05	0.07	30.37
US Corporate	1427	4125	4882	240	5.02	0.07	22.14
US Government	23	5051	5084	37	0.62	0.27	−1.81

Panel B: Raw Returns

Investment styles	*Number of.*				*Stat-Test*		
	WW	*LL*	*LW*	*WL*	*CPR*	*Sigma CPR*	*Zeta*
ALL Sample	18500	62074	91082	26201	0.48	0.01	−66.97
Europe Large	2676	7487	11152	3379	0.53	0.03	−21.14
Europe Small	1068	3590	5135	1326	0.56	0.05	−12.35
Europe Blend	2718	7276	10978	3335	0.54	0.03	−20.57
Europe Value	573	1633	2403	677	0.58	0.07	−8.48
Europe Growth	584	1725	2484	683	0.59	0.06	−8.08
US Large	1081	5342	7618	2104	0.36	0.04	−24.62
US Small	487	1812	2606	772	0.44	0.07	−12.59
US Blend	2787	13340	19479	5614	0.34	0.03	−41.89
US Value	586	2132	3011	872	0.48	0.06	−12.29
US Growth	358	1567	2271	649	0.38	0.07	−13.13
Europe Corporate	2651	7498	10836	2747	0.67	0.03	−12.99
Europe Government	1230	3945	5700	1588	0.54	0.04	−14.41
US Corporate	732	2974	4461	1293	0.38	0.05	−18.75
US Government	969	1753	2948	1162	0.50	0.05	−13.25

Contingency tables sort funds as winners or losers in each time period, and the different combinations are counted: winner–winner (WW), winner–loser (WL), loser–winner (LW), and loser–loser (LL). Winner-winner (WW) refers to funds with abnormal returns whose returns in each period are higher than the median return. The Raw Return is the annual arithmetic mean return of the funds, while the Fama-French Alpha indicates the intercept of the Fama-French Model (1993)

fund portfolios persist. This means that the results obtained by mutual funds during the second period are dependent on those obtained in the previous period. As can be observed, we reject the hypothesis of no persistence, at the 1% level, for all fund portfolios (the only two exceptions are the results reported with respect to the analysis of US Government fund portfolio and with respect to the analysis of Equity Europe Small group). This result is a strong evidence, suggesting that investors could benefit from past performance information. The fund portfolios with the highest persistence are the Equity Europe Growth group and the one with the lowest persistence is Equity Europe Small group. In line with previous studies, when analyzing the Fama-French performance, we show that persistence is present across fund portfolios with different styles, and not mainly concentrated in the top or in the bottom fund portfolios.

Raw Returns

Next, we use raw returns (Panel B). The classification of the funds across time and the statistics of the non-parametric tests are given in Table 3. There is no significant evidence of persistence in all examined fund portfolios during the sample periods (2006–2019). In the overall sample (first row of Panel B), differently from the evidence we find with respect to the Fama-French Alpha, past winners have significantly lower probability to remain winners than to turn losers next period (18,500 vs. 26,201). The same evidence holds for the past losers having significantly lower probability to remain losers than to turn winners next period (62,074 vs. 91,082).

Regarding the puzzling evidence of the persistence with respect to different performance measures, that is Raw returns and Fama-French Alpha, Babalos et al. (2008)[30] reports that "persistence could be mainly not explained by the investment strategy of the funds. Since raw returns are not adjusted for risk, equity funds which invest in highly volatile stocks are more likely to be characterized as winners in periods with positive market returns and as losers in periods with negative market returns. Therefore, persistence is observed more often in years with the same sign for market returns. On the other hand, when the stock

[30] Babalos, V., Caporale, G. M., Kostakis, A., & Philippas, N. (2008). Testing for persistence in mutual fund performance and the ex-post verification problem: Evidence from the Greek market. *The European Journal of Finance, 14*(8), 735–753.

market trend is reversed, past winners are more likely to become losers". Authors conclude that Raw returns as a performance measure is inefficient and it can lead to spurious results, because persistence could be due mainly to market returns, rather than managerial ability. In the European Sample the ranking of fund portfolios does not persist, so that the percentage of funds repeating as winners or losers is lower than the amount of funds changing their status. We cannot conclude that winners will most likely remain winners and losers will possibly remain losers or might disappear. Differently from this evidence, we find with respect to the Fama-French Alpha, mutual fund performance during the second period does not depend on the performance in the previous one. Our repeat winners and losers test presents a probability lower 50% being in the same ranking position in the following period. We, hence, reject the hypothesis of persistence for all fund portfolios. The statistical tests indeed are not indicative of performance persistence for fund portfolios. According to Vidal-García et al. (2016a) these tests are robust under the assumption that fund return distribution is non-normal, while might need some adjustment for potential small sample bias, as this test is only valid asymptotically.[31]

Our results are in line with the findings of Vidal-García et al. (2016a), Matallín-Sáez et al. (2019) and Clare et al. (2019), who state that, in general, contingency tests are robust and powerful. We can conclude that there is a quite strong phenomenon of performance persistence, when considering performance as measured in terms of Fama-French Alphas. Consequently, previous fund performance information is useful for potential investment strategies in order to achieve higher returns.

According to Vidal-García et al. (2016a), it might seem puzzling that investors still invest in underperforming funds. In this sense, Gruber (1996) explained that this fact may be due to the existence of two types of investors, namely a mature customer base and a disadvantaged customer base. He pointed out that the first type of investors will consider fund performance information when making investment decisions, while the second type will not. The latter group includes unsuspecting investors, usually influenced by marketing and broker recommendations.

[31] To take this into account, Vidal-García et al. (2016a) presents also the Chi-square test.

3.4 Cross-Sectional Regression

Following Bollen and Busse (2005), Baks (2004)[32] and Vidal-García et al. (2016b),[33] we provide additional evidence regarding the persistence of fund performance, by applying a simple regression framework that relates past and current manager performance to investigate persistence.

We thus estimate a regression of fund performance during the post-month *m* on the performance during the preceding month for each pair of successive monthly periods

$$Perf_{i,m} = a_m + b_m Perf_{i,m-1} + \gamma_1 X_{i,t-1} + e_{i,m} \tag{14}$$

where $Perf_{i,m}$ denotes the performance of fund *i* in month *m*. The independent variable in each regression, $Perf_{i,m}$ is estimated using the Carhart factor model. The four-factor Carhart model is given by:

$$R_{it} - R_{ft} = \alpha_i + b_i\left(R_{Mt} - R_{ft}\right) + s_i SMB_t + h_i HML_t + m_i MOM_t + e_{it} \tag{15}$$

where:

R_{it} is the expected return on an investment;

R_{ft} is the expected return on risk-free assets;

R_{mt} is the expected return on the market;

$R_{it} - R_{ft}$ is the expected risk premium of the investment;

$R_{mt} - R_{ft}$ is the expected market risk premium;

SMB_t is the return on the mimicking portfolio for size factor; and

HML_t is the return on the mimicking portfolio for book-to-market factors.

In this model, SMB (small minus big) represents variances in stock returns that are due to the size factor or factors systematically related to size. HML (high minus low) captures variances in stock returns that are due to the difference in return between the portfolio with high book-to-market stocks and the portfolio with low book-to-market stocks. β_i is the investment's sensitivity to the market factor, and a_i is the intercept interpreted as estimated excess return on the investment (i.e. risk factor-adjusted performance of the investment). In the Carhart (1997)

[32] See footnote 34.

[33] Vidal-García, J., Vidal, M., Boubaker, S., & Uddin, G. S. (2016). The short-term persistence of international mutual fund performance. *Economic Modelling, 52,* 926–938.

four factor model (MOM_t), is the difference in return between the portfolio with the past 12-month winners and the portfolio with the past 12-month losers. This factor aims to capture the Jegadeesh and Titman (1993) momentum anomaly.

The independent variable $Perf_{i,m-1}$, is similarly defined to $Perf_{i,m}$, except for the fact that it refers to the previous month's manager returns. We include in the regressions a host of other observable fund characteristics. To be specific we consider $X_{i,t-1}$ representing a set of control variables (in month t-1) that includes: fund size (as measured by the log of total net assets under management), Age, Expense ratio, past-month fund flows. Finally, we assume that the error term of the factor model in Eq. (15), used to estimate the various $Perf_{i,m}$ in Eq. (14), is independent of the error term of the regression in Eq. (14).[34]

We estimate the regression each month for every category of mutual funds. A positive slope coefficient would be an indication that previous performance is a predictor of the next period's performance.

Tables 4 and 5 presents the results for the cross-sectional regressions. The average slope is insignificant when we rank by Carhart Alpha measures, similar to the results obtained by Bollen and Busse (2005) for US mutual funds. We can observe that only in two cases do we find a statistically significant coefficient coupled to $Perf_{i,m-1}$. Firstly, in the US Equity Small Sample, we observe a positive coefficient of lagged performance ($Perf_{i,m-1}$) at 10% level.

Secondly and interestingly enough in the European Equity Large Sample, we observe a negative coefficient of lagged performance ($Perf_{i,m-1}$) at 5% level. The latter evidence is indicative of a contrary strategy, consisting of buying mutual funds that have been losers and selling mutual funds that have been winners.

3.5 BOND Mutual Fund

In addition to the performance analysis above, it is also important to check whether past relative performance can help predict the future relative performance of the bond mutual fund industry (i.e., the issue of persistence in the context of bond). This is a particularly under-explored question in the bond fund industry. To measure Bond performance, we

[34] Baks, K. P. (2004). *On the performance of mutual fund managers*. Manuscript, Emory University. https://repository.upenn.edu/dissertations/AAI3072967/.

Table 4 Annual regressions of multifactor alpha on past alpha—US EQUITY

	Large	*Large crisis period*	*Small*	*Small crisis period*
$\alpha_p^{CAR} i, t-1$	0.0166	0.0684	0.0835*	−0.0043
	(0.0362)	(0.0726)	(0.0495)	(0.1391)
AGE	0.0004	−0.0078	−0.0005	0.0064
	(0.0009)	(0.0060)	(0.0007)	(0.0050)
EXPENSE	−0.0010	−0.0009	−0.0011*	−0.0002
	(0.0007)	(0.0010)	(0.0006)	(0.0016)
FLOWS	−0.0192	−0.0370	0.0392**	−0.0012
	(0.0166)	(0.0343)	(0.0181)	(0.0515)
SIZE	0.0002***	0.0002	−0.0001	−0.0005
	(0.0001)	(0.0002)	(0.0001)	(0.0003)
CONS	−0.0020*	−0.0000	0.0046***	0.0071*
	(0.0011)	(0.0027)	(0.0015)	(0.0035)
N	11,931	2254	3511	553

Standard errors in parentheses $^{*}p < 0.10$, $^{**}p < 0.05$, $^{***}p < 0.01$

On December each month from 2006 to 2019, we perform a cross-sectional regression of current alpha on past alpha. In the equity mutual fund setting, the dependent variable in each regression, $\alpha_p^{CAR} i, t$, is the intercept in a four-factor model, and is calculated using the monthly returns on an equal weighted portfolio of mutual funds. Past $\alpha_p^{CAR} i, t-1$ is the intercept in a four-factor model and is calculated using the monthly returns on an equal weighted portfolio of mutual funds during the previous year. AGE is defined as the number of months from the fund's inception. $\text{Flow}_{i,t-1}$ is the normalized monthly net flow of fund i in month $t-1$. SIZE is the logarithm of the total net assets of fund i in period $t-1$ $\log(\text{TNA})_{i,t-1}$. $\text{ExpenseRatio}_{i,t-1}$ is the net expense ratio. The crisis period range between June 2007 to December 2010. The t-statistics are based on standard errors clustered by both fund and time. *, **, and ***, respectively, denote significance at the 10, 5, and 1% levels

follow the approach of Clare et al. (2019).[35] Alphas $\alpha_p^{Bond} i, t$, is the intercept of the following model:

$$r_{p,t} = \alpha_p^{BOND} + \beta_{1,p} MKTRF_t^{Bond} + \beta_{2,t} MKTRF_t^{Equity} + \beta_{3,p} DEFAULT_t + \beta_{4,p} TERM_t + \varepsilon_{p,t} \quad (16)$$

where $r_{p,t}$ is the monthly return on a portfolio of funds in excess of the one-month T-bill rate; $MKTRF_t^{Bond}$ is the Local (European or US) Total Bond Market Index return in excess of the one-month T-bill rate. $MKTRF_t^{Equity}$ is the (European) U.S. equity market returns in excess

[35] Clare, A., O'Sullivan, N., Sherman, M., & Zhu, S. (2019). The performance of US bond mutual funds. *International Review of Financial Analysis, 61*, 1–8.

Table 5 Annual regressions of multifactor alpha on past alpha—EUROPE EQUITY

	Large	*Large crisis period*	*Small*	*Small crisis period*
$\alpha_p^{CAR}i, t-1$	-0.0744^{**}	-0.0605	0.0053	-0.0454
	(0.0302)	(0.0598)	(0.0333)	(0.0478)
AGE	0.0001	0.0095^{**}	-0.0007	0.0015
	(0.0004)	(0.0048)	(0.0008)	(0.0048)
EXPENSE	-0.0016^{***}	-0.0021^{***}	-0.0001	-0.0006
	(0.0002)	(0.0005)	(0.0007)	(0.0014)
FLOWS	0.0051^{*}	0.0086	-0.0050	0.0270
	(0.0027)	(0.0053)	(0.0055)	(0.0170)
SIZE	0.0000	0.0000	-0.0001	-0.0001
	(0.0001)	(0.0001)	(0.0001)	(0.0003)
CONS	0.0031^{***}	0.0055^{**}	0.0051^{***}	0.0097^{**}
	(0.0011)	(0.0027)	(0.0019)	(0.0044)
N	16,719	3415	7180	1490

Standard errors in parentheses $^{*}p < 0.10$, $^{**}p < 0.05$, $^{***}p < 0.01$

On December each month from 2006 to 2019, we perform a cross-sectional regression of current alpha on past alpha. In the equity mutual fund setting, the dependent variable in each regression, $\alpha_p^{CAR}i, t$ is the intercept in a four-factor model, and is calculated using the monthly returns on an equal weighted portfolio of mutual funds. Past $\alpha_p^{CAR}i, t-1$ is the intercept in a four-factor model and is calculated using the monthly returns on an equal weighted portfolio of mutual funds during previous year. AGE is defined as the number of months from the fund's inception. $\text{Flow}_{i,t-1}$ is the normalized monthly net flow of fund i in month $t-1$. SIZE is the logarithm of the total net assets of fund i in period $t-1$ $\log(\text{TNA})_{i,t-1}$. $\text{ExpenseRatio}_{i,t-1}$ is the net expense ratio. The crisis period range between June 2007 to December 2010. The t-statistics are based on standard errors clustered by both fund and time. *, **, and ***, respectively, denote significance at the 10, 5, and 1% levels

of the one-month T-bill rate and is included to control for potential equity market bias $DEFAULT$ is the difference in return between investment grade corporate bonds and government bonds (10-year Treasury Constant Maturity Yield); $TERM_t$ is the difference in return between long-term (30-year Treasury Constant Maturity Yield) and short-term government bonds (one-year Treasury Constant Maturity Yield). Consistently with what we performed for the equity side (Eq. 14), we run here a similar regression:

$$\alpha_{i,t}^{Bond} = a_m + b_m \alpha_{i,t-1}^{Bond} + \gamma_1 X_{i,t-1} + e_{i,t} \tag{17}$$

The dependent variable $\alpha_{i,t-1}^{Bond}$ is similarly defined to $Perf_{i,m-1}$ in Eq. (14). We include in the regressions a host of other observable fund characteristics. To be specific we consider $X_{i,t-1}$ representing a set of control variables (in month $t-1$) that includes: fund size (as measured by the log of total net assets under management), Age, Expense ratio, past-month fund flows.

Table 6 presents results for the US Fixed Income Sample and Table 7

Table 6 Annual regressions of multifactor alpha on past alpha—US BOND

	Corporate	*Corporate crisis period*	*Government*	*Government crisis period*
$\alpha_p^{Bond}i, t-1$	0.0712***	0.0163	−0.0172	−0.1623
	(0.0264)	(0.0982)	(0.0337)	(0.0973)
AGE	−0.0071	−0.0025	0.0160**	0.0408
	(0.0062)	(0.0719)	(0.0065)	(0.0657)
EXPENSE	0.0130**	0.0182	0.0016	−0.0065
	(0.0062)	(0.0286)	(0.0057)	(0.0116)
FLOWS	0.3910*	0.2491	−0.2210	−0.4762
	(0.2112)	(0.7205)	(0.3444)	(0.5577)
SIZE	0.0015	0.0061	0.0018*	0.0046
	(0.0013)	(0.0039)	(0.0011)	(0.0028)
CONS	0.0081	−0.0560	−0.0173	−0.0398
	(0.0212)	(0.0612)	(0.0182)	(0.0421)
N	7283	956	7000	1480

Standard errors in parentheses $^{*}p < 0.10$, $^{**}p < 0.05$, $^{***}p < 0.01$

On December each month from 2006 to 2019, we perform a cross-sectional regression of current alpha on past alpha. In the fixed income (Bond) mutual fund setting, the dependent variable in each regression, $\alpha_p^{CAR}i, t$, is the intercept of the following model: $r_{p,t} = \alpha_p^{BOND} + \beta_{1,p} MKTRF_t^{Bond} + \beta_{2,t} MKTRF_t^{Equity} + \beta_{3,p} DEFAULT_t + \beta_{4,p} TERM_t + \varepsilon_{p,t}$; where $r_{p,t}$ is the monthly return on a portfolio of funds in excess of the one-month T-bill rate; $MKTRF_t^{Bond}$ is the Local (European or US) Total Bond Market Index return in excess of the one-month T-bill rate. $MKTRF_t^{Equity}$ is the (European) U.S. equity market returns in excess of the one-month T-bill rate and is included to control for potential equity market bias $DEFAULT$ is the difference in return between investment grade corporate bonds and government bonds (10-year Treasury Constant Maturity Yield); $TERM_t$ is the difference in return between long-term (30-year Treasury Constant Maturity Yield) and short-term government bonds (one-year Treasury Constant Maturity Yield). AGE is defined as the number of months from the fund's inception. $\text{Flow}_{i,t-1}$ is the normalized monthly net flow of fund i in month $t-1$. SIZE is the logarithm of the total net assets of fund i in period $t-1$. $\text{ExpenseRatio}_{i,t-1}$, is the net expense ratio. The crisis period range between June 2007 to December 2010. The t-statistics are based on standard errors clustered by both fund and time. *, **, and ***, respectively, denote significance at the 10, 5, and 1% levels

Table 7 Annual regressions of multifactor alpha on past alpha—EUROPE BOND

	Corporate	*Corporate crisis period*	*Government*	*Government crisis period*
$\alpha_p^{Bond} i, t-1$	−2.2749	−2.1909	−0.0276	−0.9425
	(3.5044)	(8.3792)	(1.9844)	(4.0542)
AGE	−0.0005	−0.0916	0.0006	0.0428
	(0.0046)	(0.2510)	(0.0030)	(0.0821)
EXPENSE	−1.0003***	−3.8481	0.0401	−0.1833
	(0.3309)	(2.3404)	(0.5309)	(2.2302)
FLOWS	−0.0000*	−0.0000*	0.0000	0.0000
	(0.0000)	(0.0000)	(0.0000)	(0.0000)
SIZE	0.0043	0.2087	0.0082	0.0240
	(0.0639)	(0.4421)	(0.0656)	(0.3104)
CONS	0.5806	0.7319	−0.7099	−3.4605
	(0.9784)	(7.1867)	(1.1597)	(5.7767)
N	15,327	2892	8501	1819

Standard errors in parentheses $^{*}p < 0.10$, $^{**}p < 0.05$, $^{***}p < 0.01$

On December each month from 2006 to 2019, we perform a cross-sectional regression of current alpha on past alpha. In the equity mutual fund setting, the dependent variable in each regression, $\alpha_p^{CAR} i, t$, is the intercept in a four-factor model, and is calculated using the monthly returns on an equal weighted portfolio of mutual funds. In the fixed income (Bond) mutual fund setting, the dependent variable in each regression, $\alpha_p^{Bond} i, t$, is the intercept of the following model: $r_{p,t} = \alpha_p^{BOND} + \beta_{1,p} MKTRF_t^{Bond} + \beta_{2,t} MKTRF_t^{Equity} + \beta_{3,p} DEFAULT_t + \beta_{4,p} TERM_t + \varepsilon_{p,t}$; where $r_{p,t}$ is the monthly return on a portfolio of funds in excess of the one-month T-bill rate; $MKTRF_t^{Bond}$ is the Local (European or US) Total Bond Market Index return in excess of the one-month T-bill rate. $MKTRF_t^{Equity}$ is the (European) U.S. equity market returns in excess of the one-month T-bill rate and is included to control for potential equity market bias $DEFAULT$ is the difference in return between investment grade corporate bonds and government bonds (10-year Treasury Constant Maturity Yield); $TERM_t$ is the difference in return between long-term (30-year Treasury Constant Maturity Yield) and short-term government bonds (one-year Treasury Constant Maturity Yield). AGE is defined as the number of months from the fund's inception. $Flow_{i,t-1}$ is the normalized monthly net flow of fund i in month $t - 1$. SIZE is the logarithm of the total net assets of fund i in period $t - 1$. $Flow_{i,t-1}$, is the net expense ratio. The crisis period range between June 2007 to December 2010. The t-statistics are based on standard errors clustered by both fund and time. *, **, and ***, respectively, denote significance at the 10, 5, and 1% levels

reports results for the European Fixed Income Sample. Clearly, performance over the past year is informative about future relative performance only in the case of mutual funds with investment style focused over Corporate Bond in the US market. However, note that these tests check the persistence in relative performance and do not necessarily indicate that the winners provide abnormal positive returns (Huij & Verbeek, 2007).[36] Indeed, a significant positive loading on the slope coefficient would be consistent with persistence in underperformance of a group of funds.

3.6 Performance Persistence Over Different Holding Periods

We repeat this approach for a holding period of three months, and mostly by considering as dependent variables the monthly returns on the quintile portfolios created by the recursive portfolio construction technique described in Sect. 3.1.

Economic significance may be inferred from the sign, the magnitude and t-statistics of the forward-looking alphas. The tables show the alpha and t-statistic of alpha of the coefficients coupled to forward-looking quintile returns for one-month and three-month holding periods as indicated. Table 8 present results for the US Equity mutual funds sample while in Table 9 we report results for the European Equity mutual funds sample. Panel A reports the results of this procedure for one-month holding period while Panel B reports results for three-month holding period. From Table 8 we see that for one-month holding periods, the forward-looking alphas respond generally in a positive meaning to past performance ($\alpha_p^{CAR}i, t-1$), with statistically significant at the 1% significance level according to the t-statistic. This indicates that over the sample period, following a strategy of investing in the past top performing funds would have yielded a positive holding period abnormal performance. This is the case for both the fund manager and for the fund investor. The persistence findings could be strictly sensitive to the length of the holding period in the procedure. When we extend the holding period from one month to three months it is very evident that the persistence declines. It is indeed interesting to observe how the magnitude of the estimation coefficient related to the past performance are declining according to the increasing of the Holding period (e.g., in Panel A, the coefficient $\alpha_p^{CAR}i, t-1$ coupled to the Quintile 1, 1.67 is higher than corresponding measure, 1.28, in Panel B. the same holds for Quintile 5, 1.27 in Panel A, and Panel B 0.93). This evidence holds irrespective to the portfolio formation Ranking Quantile. It is also interesting to observe how persistence has a different intensity depending on the portfolio formation

[36] Huij, J., & Verbeek, M. (2007). Cross-sectional learning and short-run persistence in mutual fund performance. *Journal of Banking & Finance, 31*(3), 973–997.

Table 8 Performance persistence among US Equity mutual funds

Panel A: Holding period 1 Month

	Quintile 1	*Quintile 2*	*Quintile 3*	*Quintile 4*	*Quintile 5*
$\alpha_p^{CAR}i, t-1$	1.6779***	0.8862***	0.7132***	0.7312***	1.2793***
	(0.2977)	(0.0183)	(0.0384)	(0.0392)	(0.0788)
AGE	0.0031	0.0001	0.0001	−0.0004***	−0.0000
	(0.0021)	(0.0001)	(0.0001)	(0.0001)	(0.0003)
EXPENSE	−0.0018	−0.0000	−0.0002***	−0.0003***	−0.0004*
	(0.0011)	(0.0001)	(0.0001)	(0.0001)	(0.0002)
FLOWS	0.0012	0.0049	0.0219*	0.0229***	0.0093
	(0.0075)	(0.0035)	(0.0114)	(0.0064)	(0.0081)
SIZE	−0.0004	0.0000	0.0000*	0.0000*	0.0000
	(0.0004)	(0.0000)	(0.0000)	(0.0000)	(0.0000)
CONS	0.0043	-0.0003	-0.0003	0.0000	0.0013*
	(0.0063)	(0.0003)	(0.0002)	(0.0004)	(0.0007)
N	17,837	16,473	7681	6761	15,364

Panel B: Holding period 3 Months

	Quintile 1	*Quintile 2*	*Quintile 3*	*Quintile 4*	*Quintile 5*
$\alpha_p^{CAR}i, t-1$	1.2803***	0.7090***	0.5452***	0.4251***	0.9341***
	(0.2608)	(0.0346)	(0.0463)	(0.0593)	(0.0839)
AGE	0.0028	−0.0000	−0.0001	−0.0004**	−0.0001
	(0.0020)	(0.0001)	(0.0002)	(0.0002)	(0.0004)
EXPENSE	−0.0018*	−0.0001	−0.0001	−0.0005***	−0.0008***
	(0.0011)	(0.0001)	(0.0001)	(0.0001)	(0.0003)
FLOWS	−0.0008	0.0077	0.0151	0.0199**	0.0231**
	(0.0112)	(0.0054)	(0.0153)	(0.0084)	(0.0091)
SIZE	−0.0004	0.0000*	0.0000	0.0000	0.0001**
	(0.0004)	(0.0000)	(0.0000)	(0.0000)	(0.0000)
CONS	0.0054	−0.0007	−0.0002	0.0004	0.0009
	(0.0066)	(0.0005)	(0.0006)	(0.0006)	(0.0008)
N	17,584	16,221	17,141	16,727	15,209

Standard errors in parentheses $^{*}p < 0.10$, $^{**}p < 0.05$, $^{***}p < 0.01$

This table presents results of performance persistence tests. The dependent variables are the monthly returns on the quintile portfolios created by the recursive portfolio construction technique described in Sect. 3.1. Funds are sorted into quintile portfolios based on fund four factor alphas estimated over a backward-looking formation period of 1 month. We consider holding periods of both one month and three months. Past $\alpha_p^{CAR}i, t-1$ is the intercept in a four-factor model and is calculated using the monthly returns on an equal weighted portfolio of mutual funds during the previous year. AGE is defined as the number of months from the fund's inception. $\text{Flow}_{i,t-1}$ is the normalized monthly net flow of fund i in month $t-1$. SIZE is the logarithm of the total net assets of fund i in period $t-1$ $\log(\text{TNA})_{i,t-1}$. $\text{ExpenseRatio}_{i,t-1}$, is the net expense ratio. The sample period range between June 2006 to December 2019. The t-statistics are based on standard errors clustered by both fund and time. *, **, and ***, respectively, denote significance at the 10, 5, and 1% levels

Table 9 Performance persistence among Europe Equity mutual funds

Panel A: Holding period 1 Month

	Quintile 1	*Quintile 2*	*Quintile 3*	*Quintile 4*	*Quintile 5*
$\alpha_p^{CAR}i, t-1$	1.3245***	0.8757***	0.8233***	0.7549***	1.2966***
	(0.2665)	(0.0244)	(0.0188)	(0.0259)	(0.2108)
AGE	0.0014	−0.0002*	0.0000	−0.0002	−0.0012
	(0.0014)	(0.0001)	(0.0001)	(0.0002)	(0.0008)
EXPENSE	−0.0004	−0.0002***	−0.0002***	−0.0001	−0.0000
	(0.0003)	(0.0001)	(0.0001)	(0.0001)	(0.0004)
FLOWS	0.0020	0.0032**	−0.0003	0.0032	0.0144
	(0.0025)	(0.0013)	(0.0013)	(0.0020)	(0.0163)
SIZE	−0.0001	−0.0000	0.0000	−0.0000	0.0001
	(0.0001)	(0.0000)	(0.0000)	(0.0000)	(0.0001)
CONS	−0.0023	0.0004	0.0001	0.0003	0.0021**
	(0.0016)	(0.0003)	(0.0002)	(0.0003)	(0.0009)
N	12,384	11,013	9956	9045	10,252

Panel B: Holding period 3 Months

	Quintile 1	*Quintile 2*	*Quintile 3*	*Quintile 4*	*Quintile 5*
$\alpha_p^{CAR}i, t-1$	0.9222***	0.5628***	0.5604***	0.5371***	0.7361***
	(0.1931)	(0.0356)	(0.0336)	(0.0409)	(0.0824)
Age	0.0012	−0.0006***	−0.0005	−0.0004	0.0000
	(0.0013)	(0.0002)	(0.0003)	(0.0003)	(0.0003)
EXPENSE	−0.0003	−0.0005***	−0.0005***	−0.0006***	−0.0008***
	(0.0004)	(0.0001)	(0.0001)	(0.0002)	(0.0002)
FLOWS	0.0042	0.0024	0.0024	0.0069***	0.0138
	(0.0033)	(0.0020)	(0.0022)	(0.0026)	(0.0118)
SIZE	−0.0001	−0.0000	−0.0000	0.0001**	0.0001
	(0.0001)	(0.0000)	(0.0000)	(0.0000)	(0.0000)
CONS	−0.0008	0.0012**	0.0018***	0.0009*	0.0016
	(0.0012)	(0.0005)	(0.0005)	(0.0005)	(0.0010)
N	12,182	10,813	9753	8850	10,054

Standard errors in parentheses $^{*}p < 0.10$, $^{**}p < 0.05$, $^{***}p < 0.01$

This table presents results of performance persistence tests. The dependent variables are the monthly returns on the quintile portfolios created by the recursive portfolio construction technique described in Sect. 3.1. Funds are sorted into quintile portfolios based on fund four factor alphas estimated over a backward-looking formation period of 1 month. We consider holding periods of both one month and three months. Past $\alpha_p^{CAR}i, t-1$ is the intercept in a four-factor model and is calculated using the monthly returns on an equal weighted portfolio of mutual funds during the previous year. AGE is defined as the number of months from the fund's inception. $\text{Flow}_{i,t-1}$ is the normalized monthly net flow of fund i in month $t-1$. SIZE is the logarithm of the total net assets of fund i in period $t-1$ $\log(\text{TNA})_{i,t-1}$. $\text{ExpenseRatio}_{i,t-1}$, is the net expense ratio. The sample period range between June 2006 to December 2019. The t-statistics are based on standard errors clustered by both fund and time. *, **, and ***, respectively, denote significance at the 10, 5, and 1% levels

Ranking Quantile. In particular, as we observed in the analysis of performance persistence performed by portfolio ranking approach (Tables 1 and 2), the persistence of alpha is particularly relevant for the extreme quintiles of the distribution (First quintile, corresponding to the highest quintile and Last or Fifth Quintile corresponding to the lowest quintile, e.g., in Panel A, the coefficient $\alpha_p^{CAR}i, t-1$ coupled to the Quintile 1, 1.67 is lower than Quintile 5, 1.27 while in Panel B, the coefficient $\alpha_p^{CAR}i, t-1$ coupled to the Quintile 1, 1.28 is lower than Quintile 5, 0.93). Past top-performing bond funds go on to perform relatively in a good manner in the following period while there is also positive persistence at the bottom end of the performance distribution—past poor performing funds remain relatively poor performing in the future.

Overall, our results provide some evidence in support of the proposition that economically significant performance persistence exists among US Equity mutual funds.

Table 9 reports results for the European Equity mutual funds sample. Economic significance may be inferred from the sign, the magnitude and *t*-statistics of the forward-looking alphas for one-month and three-month holding periods. Panel A reports the results of this procedure for one-month holding period while Panel B reports results for three-month holding period. From Table 9, in a similar fashion of previous findings (Table 8), we see that for one-month holding periods, the forward-looking alphas respond generally in a positive meaning to past performance ($\alpha_p^{CAR}i, t-1$), with statistically significant at the 1% significance level according to the *t*-statistic. The persistence findings are not strictly sensitive to the length of the holding period in the procedure. When we extend the holding period from one month to three months it is very evident that the persistence declines. It is indeed interesting to note, similarly to what observed above for the US equity Sample, how the magnitude of the estimation coefficient related to the past performance are declining according to the increasing of the Holding period, that is the time horizon of the investment (e.g. in Panel A, the coefficient $\alpha_p^{CAR}i, t-1$ coupled to the Quintile 1, 1.32 is higher than corresponding measure, 0.92, in Panel B. The same holds for Quintile 5, 1.29 in Panel A, and 0.73 in Panel B). This evidence holds irrespective to the portfolio formation Ranking Quantile. It is also interesting to observe how persistence has a different intensity depending on the portfolio formation Ranking Quantile. In particular, as we observed in the analysis of performance persistence performed by portfolio ranking approach (Tables 1 and 2), the persistence of alpha is particularly relevant for the extreme quintiles of the distribution (First quintile, corresponding to the highest quintile and Last or Fifth Quintile corresponding to the lowest quintile. In Panel A, the coefficient $\alpha_p^{CAR} i, t-1$ coupled to the Quintile 1, 1.32 is lower than Quintile 5, 1.29 while in Panel B, the coefficient $\alpha_p^{CAR} i, t-1$ coupled to the Quintile 1, 0.92 is lower than Quintile 5, 0.73). Past top-performing bond funds go on to perform relatively well in the following period while when considering the bottom end of the performance distribution, we observe that past poor performing funds remain relatively poor performing in the future.

In summary, whatever measure of performance used, Portfolio Rank Based Approach or by considering regression analysis and contingency tables methodology, evidences of persistence in performance is found, on average, for the majority of fund portfolios in our sample.

References

Abdelsalam, O., Duygun, M., Matallín-Sáez, J. C., & Tortosa-Ausina, E. (2017). Is ethical money sensitive to past returns? The case of portfolio constraints and persistence in Islamic funds. *Journal of Financial Services Research, 51*(3), 363–384.

Abdelsalam, O., Duygun, M., Matallín-Sáez, J. C., & Tortosa-Ausina, E. (2014). Do ethics imply persistence? The case of Islamic and socially responsible funds. *Journal of Banking & Finance, 40*, 182–194.

Agarwal, V., & Naik, N. Y. (2000). Multi-period performance persistence analysis of hedge funds. *Journal of Financial and quantitative Analysis*, 327–342.

Agudo, L. F., & Magallón, M. V. (2005). Empirical evidence of performance persistence in a relatively unexplored market: The case of Spanish investment funds. *Applied Financial Economics Letters, 1*(2), 85–88.

Akbas, F., Armstrong, W. J., Sorescu, S., & Subrahmanyam, A. (2015). Smart money, dumb money, and capital market anomalies. *Journal of Financial Economics, 118*(2), 355–382.

Amihud, Y., & Goyenko, R. (2013). Mutual fund's R 2 as predictor of performance. *The Review of Financial Studies, 26*(3), 667–694.

Babalos, V., Caporale, G. M., Kostakis, A., & Philippas, N. (2008). Testing for persistence in mutual fund performance and the ex-post verification problem: Evidence from the Greek market. *The European Journal of Finance, 14*(8), 735–753.

Baks, K. P. (2004). *On the performance of mutual fund managers.* Manuscript, Emory University. https://repository.upenn.edu/dissertations/AAI3072967/.

Banegas, A., Gillen, B., Timmermann, A., & Wermers, R. (2013). The cross section of conditional mutual fund performance in European stock markets. *Journal of Financial Economics, 108*(3), 699–726.

Barras, L., Scaillet, O., & Wermers, R. (2010). False discoveries in mutual fund performance: Measuring luck in estimated alphas. *The Journal of Finance, 65*(1), 179–216.

Bauer, R., Koedijk, K., & Otten, R. (2005). International evidence on ethical mutual fund performance and investment style. *Journal of Banking & Finance, 29*(7), 1751–1767.

Benos, E., & Jochec, M. (2011). Short term persistence in mutual fund market timing and stock selection abilities. *Annals of Finance, 7*(2), 221–246.

Berk, J. B., & Green, R. (2004). Mutual fund flows and performance in rational markets. *Journal of Political Economy, 112,* 1269–1295.

Bessler, W., Blake, D., Lückoff, P., & Tonks, I. (2018). Fund flows, manager changes, and performance persistence. *Review of Finance, 22*(5), 1911–1947.

Blake, D., & Timmermann, A. (1998). Mutual fund performance: Evidence from the UK. *Review of Finance, 2*(1), 57–77.

Blake, D., Lehmann, B. N., & Timmermann, A. (1999). Asset allocation dynamics and pension fund performance. *The Journal of Business, 72*(4), 429–461.

Blake, C. R., & Morey, M. R. (2000). Morningstar ratings and mutual fund performance. *Journal of financial and Quantitative Analysis*, 451–483.

Bollen, N. P., & Busse, J. A. (2001). On the timing ability of mutual fund managers. *The Journal of Finance, 56*(3), 1075–1094.

Bollen, N. P. B., & Busse, J. A. (2005). Short-term persistence in mutual fund performance. *Review of Financial Studies, 18,* 569–597.

Brown, S., & Goetzmann, W. (1995). Attrition and mutual fund performance. *Journal of Finance, 50,* 679–698.

Brown, S. J., & Goetzmann, W. N. (1997). Mutual fund styles. *Journal of Financial Economics, 43*(3), 373–399.

Busse, J. A., & Irvine, P. J. (2006). Bayesian alphas and mutual fund persistence. *The Journal of Finance, 61*(5), 2251–2288.

Busse, J. A., Goyal, A., & Wahal, S. (2010). Performance and persistence in institutional investment management. *The Journal of Finance, 65*(2), 765–790.

Carhart, M. (1997). On persistence in mutual fund performance. *Journal of Finance, 52*(1), 57–82.

Carhart, M. M., Kaniel, R., Musto, D. K., & Reed, A. V. (2002). Leaning for the tape: Evidence of gaming behavior in equity mutual funds. *The Journal of Finance, 57*(2), 661–693.
Carpenter, J. N., & Lynch, A. W. (1999). Survivorship bias and attrition effects in measures of performance persistence. *Journal of Financial Economics, 54*(3), 337–374.
Casarin, R., Pelizzon, L., & Piva, A. (2002). *Italian equity funds: Efficiency and Performance persistence* (Working paper).
Chen, Y., Ferson, W., & Peters, H. (2010). Measuring the timing ability and performance of bond mutual funds. *Journal of Financial Economics, 98*(1), 72–89.
Chevalier, J., & Ellison, G. (1999). Are some mutual fund managers better than others? Cross-sectional patterns in behavior and performance. *The Journal of Finance, 54*(3), 875–899.
Christensen, M. (2005). *Danish mutual fund performance, selectivity, market timing and persistence* (Working paper).
Clare, A., O'Sullivan, N., Sherman, M., & Zhu, S. (2019). The performance of US bond mutual funds. *International Review of Financial Analysis, 61,* 1–8.
Cohen, R. B., Coval, J. D., & Pástor, Ľ. (2005). Judging fund managers by the company they keep. *The Journal of Finance, 60*(3), 1057–1096.
Coles, J. L., Daniel, N. D., & Nardari, F. (2006). Does the choice of model or benchmark affect inference in measuring mutual fund performance? In *EFA 2006 Zurich Meetings.*
Cortez, M. D. C. R., Paxson, D. A., & Armada, M. J. D. R. (1999). Persistence in Portuguese mutual fund performance. *The European Journal of Finance, 5*(4), 342–365.
Cremers, K. M., & Petajisto, A. (2009). How active is your fund manager? A new measure that predicts performance. *The Review of Financial Studies, 22*(9), 3329–3365.
Cuthbertson, K., Nitzsche, D., & O'Sullivan, N. (2008). UK mutual fund performance: Skill or luck? *Journal of Empirical Finance, 15*(4), 613–634.
Cuthbertson, K., Nitzsche, D., & O'Sullivan, N. (2010). Mutual fund performance: Measurement and Evidence 1. *Financial Markets, Institutions & Instruments, 19*(2), 95–187.
Dahlquist, M., Engström, S., & Söderlind, P. (2000). Performance and characteristics of Swedish mutual funds. *Journal of Financial and quantitative Analysis*, 409–423.
Daniel, K., Grinblatt, M., Titman, S., & Wermers, R. (1997). Measuring mutual fund performance with characteristic-based benchmarks. *The Journal of Finance, 52*(3), 1035–1058.

Deaves, R. (2004). Data-conditioning biases, performance, persistence and flows: The case of Canadian equity funds. *Journal of Banking & Finance, 28*(3), 673–694.
Droms, W. G. (2006). Hot hands, cold hands: Does past performance predict future returns. *Journal of Financial Planning, 19*(5), 60–69.
Droms, W. G., & Walker, D. A. (2001). Persistence of mutual fund operating characteristics: Returns, turnover rates, and expense ratios. *Applied Financial Economics, 11*(4), 457–466.
Dumitrescu, A., & Gil-Bazo, J. (2018). Market frictions, investor sophistication, and persistence in mutual fund performance. *Journal of Financial Markets, 40*, 40–59.
Elton, E. J., Gruber, M., Blake, C., Krasny, Y., & Ozelge, S. (2010). The effect of holdings data frequency on conclusions about mutual fund behavior. *Journal of Banking & Finance, 34*(5), 912–922.
Elton, E. J., Gruber, M. J., & Blake, C. R. (2012). Does mutual fund size matter? The relationship between size and performance. *The Review of Asset Pricing Studies, 2*(1), 31–55.
Elyasiani, E., & Jia, J. (2011). Performance persistence of closed-end funds. *Review of Quantitative Finance and Accounting, 37*(3), 381–408.
Fama, E. F., & French, K. R. (1993). Common risk factors in the returns on stocks and bonds. *Journal of financial economics, 33*(1), 3–56.
Fama, E. F., & French, K. R. (1996). Multifactor explanations of asset pricing anomalies. *The Journal of Finance, 51*(1), 55–84.
Fama, E. F., & French, K. R. (2010). Luck versus skill in the cross-section of mutual fund returns. *The Journal of Finance, 65*(5), 1915–1947.
Ferreira, M. A., Keswani, A., Miguel, A. F., & Ramos, S. B. (2012). The flow-performance relationship around the world. *Journal of Banking & Finance, 36*(6), 1759–1780.
Fletcher, J., & Forbes, D. (2002). An exploration of the persistence of UK unit trust performance. *Journal of Empirical Finance, 9*(5), 475–493.
Fong, T. P. W., Sze, A. K. W., & Ho, E. H. C. (2018). Determinants of equity mutual fund flows–Evidence from the fund flow dynamics between Hong Kong and global markets. *Journal of International Financial Markets, Institutions and Money, 57*, 231–247.
Glode, V. (2011). Why mutual funds "underperform". *Journal of Financial Economics, 99*(3), 546–559.
Goetzmann, W., Ingersoll, J., Spiegel, M., & Welch, I. (2007). Portfolio performance manipulation and manipulation-proof performance measures. *The Review of Financial Studies, 20*(5), 1503–1546.
Gregory, A., & Whittaker, J. (2007). Performance and performance persistence of 'ethical' unit trusts in the UK. *Journal of Business Finance & Accounting, 34*(7–8), 1327–1344.

Grinblatt, M., & Titman, S. (1992). The persistence of mutual fund performance. *The Journal of Finance, 47*(5), 1977–1984.
Grinblatt, M., & Titman, S. (1993). Performance measurement without benchmarks: An examination of mutual fund returns. *Journal of Business*, 47–68.
Grinblatt, M., Titman, S., & Wermers, R. (1995). Momentum investment strategies, portfolio performance, and herding: A study of mutual fund behavior. *The American Economic Review*, 1088–1105.
Gruber, M. (1996). Another puzzle: The growth in actively managed mutual funds. *Journal of Finance, 51,* 783–810.
He, J., Ng, L., & Wang, Q. (2004). Quarterly trading patterns of financial institutions. *The Journal of Business, 77*(3), 493–509.
Hendricks, D., Patel, J., & Zeckhauser, R. (1993). Hot hands in mutual funds: Short-run persistence of relative performance, 1974–1988. *The Journal of Finance, 48*(1), 93–130.
Henriksson, R. D., & Merton, R. C. (1981). On market timing and investment performance. II. Statistical procedures for evaluating forecasting skills. *Journal of Business*, 513–533.
Herrmann, U., & Scholz, H. (2013). Short-term persistence in hybrid mutual fund performance: The role of style-shifting abilities. *Journal of Banking & Finance, 37*(7), 2314–2328.
Hoberg, G., Kumar, N., & Prabhala, N. (2018). Mutual fund competition, managerial skill, and alpha persistence. *The Review of Financial Studies, 31*(5), 1896–1929.
Ibbotson, R. G., & Patel, A. K. (2002). *Do winners repeat with style?* Available at SSRN 292866.
Jegadeesh, N., & Titman, S. (1993). Returns to buying winners and selling losers: Implications for stock market efficiency. *The Journal of Finance, 48*(1), 65–91.
Jensen, M. C. (1968). The performance of mutual funds in the period 1945–1964. *The Journal of Finance, 23*(2), 389–416.
Jeon, H., Kang, J., & Lee, C. (2017). Precision about manager skill, mutual fund flows, and performance persistence. *The North American Journal of Economics and Finance, 40,* 222–237.
Jiang, G. J., & Yuksel, H. Z. (2017). What drives the "Smart-Money" effect? Evidence from investors' money flow to mutual fund classes. *Journal of Empirical Finance, 40,* 39–58.
Jiang, G. J., Yao, T., & Yu, T. (2007). Do mutual funds time the market? Evidence from portfolio holdings. *Journal of Financial Economics, 86*(3), 724–758.
Jones, R. C., & Wermers, R. (2011). Active management in mostly efficient markets. *Financial Analysts Journal, 67*(6), 29–45.

Kacperczyk, M., Nieuwerburgh, S. V., & Veldkamp, L. (2014). Time-varying fund manager skill. *The Journal of Finance, 69*(4), 1455–1484.

Kacperczyk, M., Sialm, C., & Zheng, L. (2008). Unobserved actions of mutual funds. *The Review of Financial Studies, 21*(6), 2379–2416.

Kahn, R. N., & Rudd, A. (1995). Does historical performance predict future performance? *Financial Analysts Journal, 51*(6), 43–52.

Kosowski, R., Timmermann, A., Wermers, R., & White, H. (2006). Can mutual fund "stars" really pick stocks? New evidence from a bootstrap analysis. *The Journal of Finance, 61*(6), 2551–2595.

Kosowski, R. (2011). Do mutual funds perform when it matters most to investors? US mutual fund performance and risk in recessions and expansions. *The Quarterly Journal of Finance, 1*(03), 607–664.

Krimm, S., Scholz, H., & Wilkens, M. (2011). *Selection, timing and total performance of equity funds: Wasting time measuring timing* (Working paper). Catholic University of Eichstätt-Ingolstadt.

Lakonishok, J., Shleifer, A., & Vishny, R. W. (1992). *Study of US equity money manager performance*. Brookings Institute Study.

Lynch, A. W., & Musto, D. K. (2003). How investors interpret past fund returns. *The Journal of Finance, 58*(5), 2033–2058.

Malkiel, B. G. (1995). Returns from investing in equity mutual funds 1971 to 1991. *The Journal of Finance, 50*(2), 549–572.

Mamaysky, H., Spiegel, M., & Zhang, H. (2004). *Improved forecasting of mutual fund alphas and betas, Yale School of Management* (ICF Working Paper 04–23).

Massa, M., & Patgiri, R. (2009). Incentives and mutual fund performance: Higher performance or just higher risk taking? *The Review of Financial Studies, 22*(5), 1777–1815.

Matallín-Sáez, J. C., Soler-Domínguez, A., & Tortosa-Ausina, E. (2016). On the robustness of persistence in mutual fund performance. *The North American Journal of Economics and Finance, 36*, 192–231.

Matallín-Sáez, J. C., Soler-Domínguez, A., Tortosa-Ausina, E., & de Mingo-López, D. V. (2019). Ethical strategy focus and mutual fund management: Performance and persistence. *Journal of Cleaner Production, 213*, 618–633.

Meier, I., & Rombouts, J. V. (2009). *Style rotation and performance persistence of mutual funds*. Available at SSRN 1313242.

Morey, M. R., & O'Neal, E. S. (2006). Window dressing in bond mutual funds. *Journal of Financial Research, 29*(3), 325–347.

Nain, A., & Yao, T. (2013). Mutual fund skill and the performance of corporate acquirers. *Journal of Financial Economics, 110*(2), 437–456.

Ortiz, C., Sarto, J. L., & Vicente, L. (2012). Portfolios in disguise? Window dressing in bond fund holdings. *Journal of Banking & Finance, 36*(2), 418–427.

Otten, R., & Bams, D. (2002). European mutual fund performance. *European Financial Management, 8*(1), 75–101.

Pástor, Ľ., & Stambaugh, R. F. (2002). Mutual fund performance and seemingly unrelated assets. *Journal of Financial Economics, 63*(3), 315–349.

Pástor, L., & Stambaugh, R. F. (2012). On the size of the active management industry. *Journal of Political Economy, 120*(4), 740–781.

Pástor, Ľ., Stambaugh, R. F., & Taylor, L. A. (2015). Scale and skill in active management. *Journal of Financial Economics, 116*(1), 23–45.

Quigley, G., & Sinquefield, R. A. (2000). Performance of UK equity unit trusts. *Journal of Asset Management, 1*(1), 72–92.

Rakowski, D., & Wang, X. (2009). The dynamics of short-term mutual fund flows and returns: A time-series and cross-sectional investigation. *Journal of Banking & Finance, 33*(11), 2102–2109.

Renneboog, L., Ter Horst, J., & Zhang, C. (2011). Is ethical money financially smart? Nonfinancial attributes and money flows of socially responsible investment funds. *Journal of Financial Intermediation, 20*(4), 562–588.

Sias, R. (2007). Causes and seasonality of momentum profits. *Financial Analysts Journal, 63*(2), 48–54.

Silva, F., Cortez, M. C., & Rocha Armada, M. J. (2005). The persistence of European bond fund performance: Does conditioning information matter? *International Journal of Business, 10*(4).

Teo, M., & Woo, S. J. (2001). *Persistence in style-adjusted mutual fund returns.* Available at SSRN 291372.

Thomas, A., & Tonks, I. (2001). Equity performance of segregated pension funds in the UK. *Journal of Asset Management, 1*(4), 321–343.

Treynor, J., & Mazuy, K. (1966). Can mutual funds outguess the market. *Harvard Business Review, 44*(4), 131–136.

US Securities and Exchange Commission. (2004). *Disclosure regarding market timing and selective disclosure of portfolio holdings.* https://www.sec.gov/rules/final/33-8408.htm.

Vidal-García, J. (2013). The persistence of European mutual fund performance. *Research in International Business and Finance, 28,* 45–67.

Vidal-García, J., Vidal, M., & Nguyen, D. K. (2016a). Do liquidity and idiosyncratic risk matter? Evidence from the European mutual fund market. *Review of Quantitative Finance and Accounting, 47*(2), 213–247.

Vidal-García, J., Vidal, M., Boubaker, S., & Uddin, G. S. (2016b). The short-term persistence of international mutual fund performance. *Economic Modelling, 52,* 926–938.

Wermers, R. (2000). Mutual fund performance: An empirical decomposition into stock-picking talent, style, transactions costs, and expenses. *The Journal of Finance, 55*(4), 1655–1695.

Wermers, R. (2003). *Are mutual fund shareholders compensated for active management "bets"?*. Working Study: University of Maryland.
Wermers, R. (2012). *Matter of style: The causes and consequences of style drift in institutional portfolios*. Available at SSRN 2024259.

CHAPTER 7

Volatility

1 Introduction

Past return volatility is a powerful determinant of future mutual fund performance. When thinking about the relationship between volatility and mutual fund returns, our mind goes directly to what is defined as volatility anomaly. A dollar invested in a portfolio of mutual funds with low past return volatility at the beginning of 2000 is worth about $4.00 at the end of 2019 both in US and European Equity Mutual Fund Markets. In the same fashion, Baker et al. (2011) show that one dollar invested in portfolio of low volatility stocks in 1968 is worth $59.55 in 2008. The matching high volatility portfolio is worth only $0.58.[1]

Haugen and Heins (1972, 1975) first showed that stocks with low volatility past returns subsequently outperformed those with high volatility, a result that has come to be known as the "vol anomaly."[2]

[1] Jordan, B. D., & Riley, T. B. (2015). Volatility and mutual fund manager skill. *Journal of Financial Economics, 118*(2), 289–298.

[2] See Hou and Loh (2012) for a thorough review and analysis of potential explanations for the vol anomaly.

G. Galloppo, *Asset Allocation Strategies for Mutual Funds*,
https://doi.org/10.1007/978-3-030-76128-8_7

According to Huang et al. (2011),[3] mutual funds might change their risk levels for several reasons. On the one hand, agency issues in delegated portfolio management might induce fund managers to strategically change their risk levels to manage the expected money inflows to the fund (e.g., Chevalier & Ellison, 1997) or to control their performance figures (e.g., Goetzmann et al., 2007). On the opposite hand, fund managers might change their risk levels to require advantage of their stock selection and timing abilities (e.g., Daniel et al., 1997). Although, changes in portfolio risk are designed for agent-induced transactions or transactions motivated by timing, the change of the risk portfolio could also occur, when managers change the composition of their portfolio to take advantage of their stock selection ability. To understand the sources of the poor performance of risk shifters, Huang et al. (2011) study the various mechanisms through which funds can change risk. First, funds can shift risk by changing the composition between equity holdings and cash holdings. Second, among the stocks it holds, the fund can transfer risk by changing its exposure to systemic risk (for example, by switching between low-beta stocks and high-beta stocks). Third, the fund can transfer risk by changing its exposure to specific risks (for example, by concentrating its holdings in a few positions or industries). Huang et al. (2011) found that all these mechanisms are important for explaining the risk transfer behavior of mutual funds. However, the inferior performance is mainly due to the fact that the fund has increased its idiosyncratic risk exposure, while the decrease in cash holdings and the increase in systemic risk will only lead to a slight decline in fund performance.

2 Previous Findings in Literature

Pioneer theoretical work (e.g., Aggarwal & Rao, 1990; Daigler & Wiley, 1999; Kaniel et al., 2008) suggests that sophisticated institutional investors respond rationally to the stock market volatility and are less likely to get affected.[4] They are called "smart investors", who can offset

[3] Huang, J., Sialm, C., & Zhang, H. (2011). Risk shifting and mutual fund performance. *The Review of Financial Studies, 24*(8), 2575–2616.

[4] Qureshi, F., Kutan, A. M., Ismail, I., & Gee, C. S. (2017). Mutual funds and stock market volatility: An empirical analysis Empirical analysis of Asian emerging markets. *Emerging Markets Review, 31,* 176–192.

personal irrational investments and reduce market noise (Ormos & Timotity, 2016). Friedman (1953) pointed out that rational investors can stabilize the price of securities. Fama (1965) also confirmed that institutional investors can alleviate huge deviations in asset prices. On the contrary, it was pointed out that the prudential behavior of institutional investors should lead to market stability (Bohl et al., 2009). Previous studies (Brown et al., 1996; Dennis & Strickland, 2002; Sias, 1996) found a positive correlation between mutual funds and market volatility.

According to Jordan and Riley (2015), the vol anomaly is large, persistent, and ubiquitous in security returns. Amihud (2002) and Ang et al. (2006, 2009) show past volatility is a strong cross-sectional predictor of future stock returns.

Baker and Haugen (2012) found volatility anomalies in all 21 developed countries they studied. Blitz and Vliet (2007) proved that global portfolios of low-volatility stocks are better than matched high-volatility portfolios about 12% a year. Frazzini et al. (2013) found that stocks, bonds and other asset classes in many different countries fluctuate abnormally.

Fu (2009) finds the vol anomaly is only strong among very small stocks. Li et al. (2012) pointed out that in order to trade under abnormal trading volume, frequent rebalancing between fewer liquid stocks is required. Han and Lesmond (2011) claimed that vol anomaly disappeared after adjusting for microstructure effects (such as a rebound in prices). Baker et al. (2011) argue that leverage constraints make it difficult for institutional investors to invest in abnormal volatility.

Huang et al. (2011) classify mutual funds into portfolios based on recent risk transfer measures and compare their subsequent performance. The authors found that funds that change risk tend to perform worse than funds that maintain a stable level of risk. The performance consequences are particularly severe for funds that increase their risk levels. For example, using the Carhart model, a fund whose volatility has increased by more than 2.5 percentage points relative to the average volatility of the past three years has an annual abnormal return rate of −2.6%. The results are robust using alternative performance measures and risk shifting proxies.

A recent study by Qureshi et al. (2017) examines the relationship among mutual funds, market returns and market volatility in ASEAN-5. Qureshi et al. (2017) used the PVAR method to conclude that as the flow of stock funds increases, market volatility will increase, and vice versa. They found that stock mutual funds are risky investors involved in speculation, which intensifies the volatility of stock prices. However, market volatility reduces as a result of increase in balanced mutual fund flows. This finding indicates that balanced fund flows follow more rational investment strategies. Reasonable explanations for this relationship are explained by their strategies, a balanced fund indeed tend to diversify risks.

When analyzing the relationship between volatility and capital flow, earlier studies recorded two relationships between market volatility and fund flow. First, fund flows follow the markets' past performance. Obviously, fund managers will envision future returns based on past performance and usually follow a positive feedback strategy by buying from rising markets and selling in falling markets. Other fund managers may take the opposite approach (may follow a contrarian/negative feedback strategy), which may reduce market volatility by increasing investment. Increase in market volatility reduces the fund flows, and vice versa (Cao et al., 2008). Since different strategies of mutual fund portfolio allocation may cancel each other out, the overall impact of flows on stock market return volatility is an important empirical question, which is studied also here, in our research. Second, the noise trader/investor sentiment is the main reason for the market to deviate from its basic value (Black, 1986; Lee et al., 1991). This is true considering mutual fund flows are used as proxy for investors' sentiments. Therefore, positive or negative flows will affect market returns and market volatility (Cao et al., 2008). Busse's research (1999) is one of the pioneering studies to assess whether fund managers respond to financial market turmoil. Busse (1999) concluded that mutual funds do influence and capture market fluctuations. This work is extended by Cao et al. (2008). They determined the connection between the total flow of mutual funds and the volatility of market returns, and found that there is a negative correlation between the flow and the previous day's volatility, which shows the timing of mutual fund investors. They concluded that positive flow is associated with lower market volatility, while negative flow is associated with higher market volatility. In addition, flow fluctuations will have a negative impact on market volatility, that is, inflow forecasts will reduce market volatility, and outflow forecasts will increase market volatility. Atilgan et al. (2015) provide a recent review of literature on equity markets in emerging markets with respect to the volatility. Thomas et al. (2014)

investigated the empirical relationship between pension fund investment in the OECD market and stock market volatility. They find negative relationship between pension funds and stock market volatility. This negative relationship is due to the fact that pension funds are very long-term investments and help control price deviations from fundamentals.

Consistent with some other studies, Jordan and Riley (2015) find that a mutual fund's past return volatility is a powerful determinant of future performance. In the context of the Fama-French four-factor model, the annual alpha value of the portfolio of low-volatility funds is 5.4% higher than that of the portfolio of high-volatility funds. One standard deviation reduction in fund volatility in the previous year is expected to increase the alpha value of the second year by about 2.5%, so its impact will be ten times greater. The authors also show that the overall fund return volatility is driving this effect, not the idiosyncratic volatility. They also explored whether the outstanding performance of low-volatility funds reflects the skills of managers.

By using a patterned test according to Kosowski et al. (2006) and Fama and French (2010), they found that low-volatility fund managers seem to have important skills. However, they also found that there is a similar performance gap between low-volatility funds and high-volatility funds, as well as between funds that deviate from the benchmark and funds that do not (if the difference in performance is skill, it should not exist among funds that are "closet indexers").

Jordan and Riley (2015) next consider whether the "vol" anomaly can explain their results. In particular, they added a new pricing factor LVH (low volatility vs. high volatility) to the four-factor model and repeated the analysis. The LVH factor is equal to the return of a low-volatility stock portfolio minus the return of a high-volatility stock portfolio. Similar to the factors that illustrate the impact of size (SMB), value (HML) and momentum (UMD), LVH can prevent managers from generating obvious abnormal performance by simply exposing them to known pricing anomalies. Including LVH, the alpha values of low-volatility funds and high-volatility funds are statistically and economically indistinguishable from zero. Said differently, while in a standard four-factor framework, mutual fund return volatility is a reliable, persistent, and powerful predictor of future abnormal returns, the abnormal returns are eliminated by the addition of a "vol" anomaly factor contrasting returns on portfolios of low and high volatility stocks.[5] Failure to account for the vol anomaly, either directly or indirectly, can lead to substantial mismeasurement of fund manager skill.[6] Fama and French (2015) use a five-factor model to capture the cross-correlation of stock returns, and they find that this model returns a better performance measure than the three-factor model of Fama and French (1993). They concluded that profitability and investment factors are equally effective in eliminating abnormal returns.

Among other things, Jordan and Riley (2015) simulated low-volatility and high-volatility mutual funds. These funds invest by randomly selecting stocks based on the return volatility. The return ratio of these stocks is proportional to the actual low and high volatility. The same for volatility funds. They found similar return patterns in simulated funds to actual low-volatility and high-volatility mutual funds. For example, the Sharpe and Treynor ratio of the average simulated low volatility fund is 2–4 times that of the average simulated high volatility fund.

When accounting for expense ratios, that could also be an evidence of active management, Livingston et al.[7] (2019) show that higher expense ratios and turnover ratio have had greater volatility of performance as well as lower mean performance, a doubly adverse pattern.[8]

Che (2018) investigates the impact on stock return volatility of different trading styles (momentum and contrarian) and types of investors (foreign, individual or institutional). He finds that foreign investors actually increase volatility of stock returns, while individual and financial institutional investors' decrease it.

[5] A similar approach is investigated by Fama and French (2015). They use a five-factor model directed at capturing the size, value, profitability, and investment patterns in average stock returns performs better than the three-factor model of Fama and French (FF, 1993). They conclude that profitability and investment factors are equally effective at eliminating the abnormal returns.

[6] Jordan, B. D., & Riley, T. B. (2015). Volatility and mutual fund manager skill. *Journal of Financial Economics, 118*(2), 289–298.

[7] Authors use data for equity mutual funds from 1991–2012.

[8] Livingston, M., Yao, P., & Zhou, L. (2019). The volatility of mutual fund performance. *Journal of Economics and Business, 104*, 105835.

3 Methodology and Empirical Results

3.1 *The Performance of Low and High Volatility Mutual Funds*

We first classify funds into portfolios based on past return volatility to explore the performance of low-volatility and high-volatility mutual funds. At the beginning of each calendar year, we categorize funds into deciles based on the standard deviation of the daily funds return of the previous calendar year. The low-volatility portfolio holding 20% of the mutual funds in the sample has the lowest standard deviation in the previous calendar year. The high volatility portfolio holds 20% of the mutual funds in the sample, which has the highest standard deviation in the previous calendar year. Each portfolio is equal weighted and has the same number of funds at the start of the year. A fund remains in the same portfolio for the entire year.

Figure 1 shows the value of one dollar invested in mutual funds sorted on past return volatility for EU bond sample. We observe decreasing returns with rise of the volatility. High volatility portfolio is worth around $100 in the observed period. The low volatility portfolio is characterized by increasing value of $100 invested in 2006 to up to $140 of return in the end of the observed period.

Figure 2 shows the value of one dollar invested in mutual funds sorted

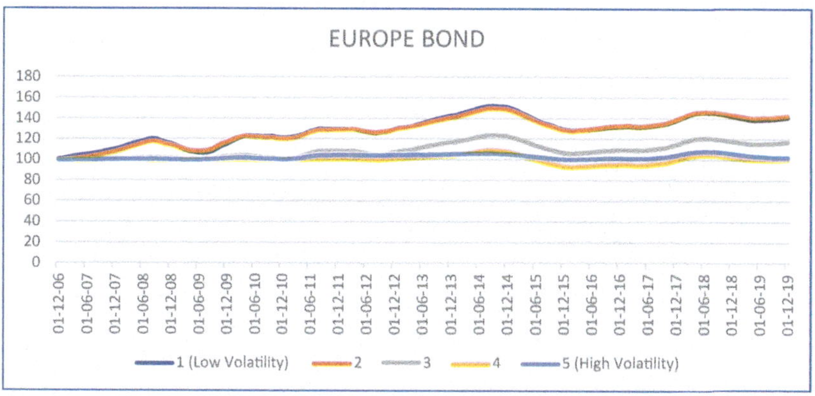

Fig. 1 The return on one dollar invested in mutual funds sorted on past return volatility

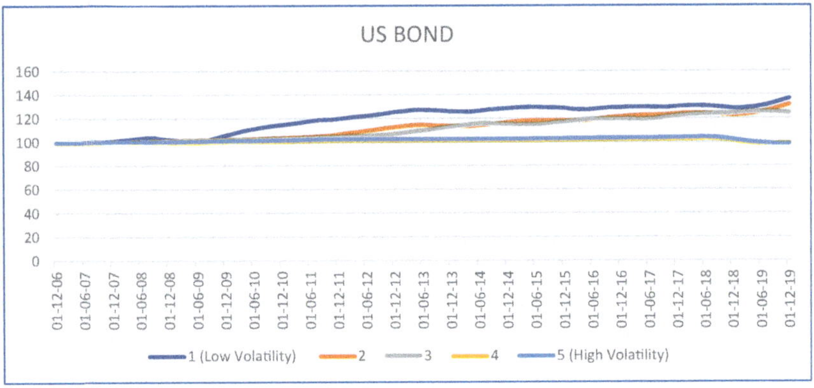

Fig. 2 The return on one dollar invested in mutual funds sorted on past return volatility

on past return volatility for US bond sample. We observe decrease of returns with rise of volatility. When volatility is high, returns tend to remain almost at the same $100 value. In low volatility portfolio returns are systematically increasing from $100 invested in the beginning of the period analyzed up to almost $140 in the end of the period.

Figure 3 shows the value of one dollar invested in mutual funds sorted

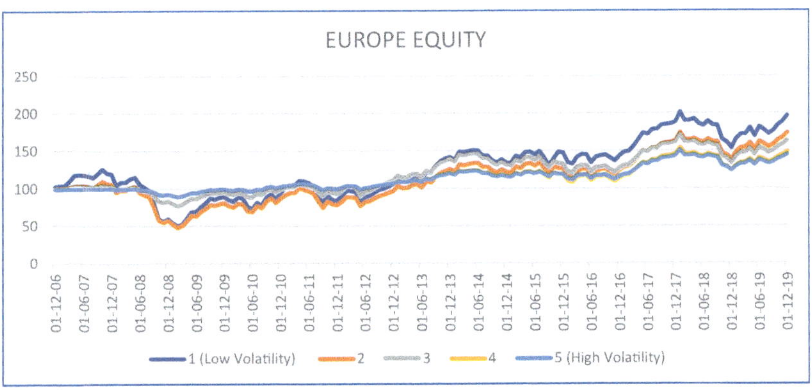

Fig. 3 The return on one dollar invested in mutual funds sorted on past return volatility

on past return volatility for EU equity sample. In low volatility portfolio returns drop sharply from 2008 to 2009, and afterwards they increase up to the end of the period. Therefore, the value of $100 invested in 2006 equals $200 in 2019 in low volatility portfolio. Returns of high volatility portfolio tend to remain almost at the same level of $100 from 2006 to 2012, then they start increasing up to $150 in 2019.

Figure 4 shows the value of one dollar invested in mutual funds sorted on past return volatility for US equity sample. In general, the evidence shows decrease of returns with increase of volatility, except the period from 2008 to 2009, when lower volatility portfolios were characterized by lower returns. In low volatility portfolio we observe the increase of value of $100 invested up to almost $250 by 2019. High volatility portfolio demonstrates the increasing value of $100 invested up to $150 by 2019.

EUROPE BOND SAMPLE

This figure shows the changing value of $100 invested in December 2006 through December 2019 in five equal weighted portfolios of mutual funds. The low (high) volatility portfolio buys the 20% of mutual funds in the sample with the lowest (highest) standard deviation of monthly returns in the prior calendar year.

US BOND SAMPLE

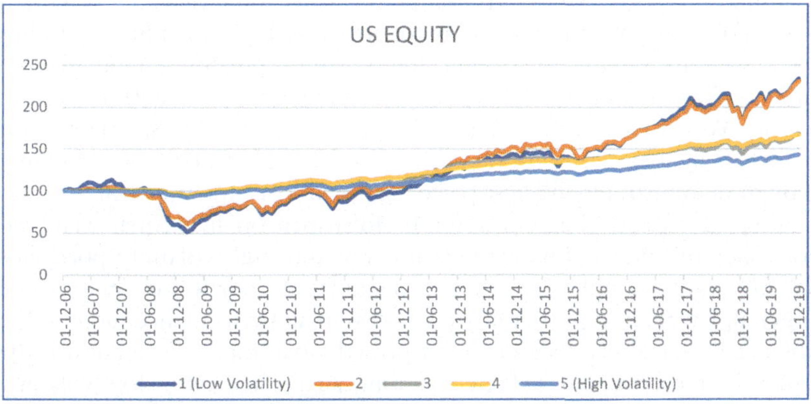

Fig. 4 The return on one dollar invested in mutual funds sorted on past return volatility

This figure shows the changing value of $100 invested in December 2006 through December 2019 in five equal weighted portfolios of mutual funds. The low (high) volatility portfolio buys the 20% of mutual funds in the sample with the lowest (highest) standard deviation of monthly returns in the prior calendar year.

EUROPE EQUITY SAMPLE

This figure shows the changing value of $100 invested in December 2006 through December 2019 in five equal weighted portfolios of mutual funds. The low (high) volatility portfolio buys the 20% of mutual funds in the sample with the lowest (highest) standard deviation of monthly returns in the prior calendar year.

US EQUITY SAMPLE

This figure shows the changing value of $100 invested in December 2006 through December 2019 in five equal weighted portfolios of mutual funds. The low (high) volatility portfolio buys the 20% of mutual funds in the sample with the lowest (highest) standard deviation of monthly returns in the prior calendar year.

In order to assess the impact of the low volatility portfolio in terms of performance, we consider simple return and several multifactor alphas together with Fama-French four-factor factor exposures for the low and high volatility portfolios.

Table 1 reports the results for performance on five equal weighted portfolios of equity mutual funds for low and high volatility portfolios for US equity sample. In overall, low volatility portfolios tend to hold larger alphas than high volatility portfolios regardless the method of evaluation. We observe the best performance measured by Simple Return model in all types of equities, where low volatility portfolio of equity growth demonstrates the best performance all over the funds (0.90%).

Table 2 reports the results for performance on five equal weighted portfolios of equity mutual funds for low and high volatility portfolios for EU equity sample. In general, low volatility portfolios demonstrate larger alphas than high volatility portfolios in all performance models. We observe better alpha coefficients in growth style funds. In addition, the highest value of alpha coefficient among all the results in low volatility portfolios is seen in Simple Return model (1.22%) and CAPM model (1.16%) of equity growth style.

This table shows the performance on five equal weighted portfolios of equity mutual funds. The low (high) volatility portfolio buys the 20% of

Table 1 US EQUITY SAMPLE

EQUITY LARGE				
Volatility Quintile	*Simple Return*	*Alpha CAPM*	*Alpha Fama—French*	*Alpha Carhart*
1 (Low Volatility)	0.75%	0.16%	0.18%	0.20%
2	0.53%	0.00%	−0.06%	−0.05%
3	0.48%	0.00%	−0.02%	−0.01%
4	0.07%	−0.03%	−0.04%	−0.03%
5 (High Volatility)	0.43%	0.02%	0.01%	0.02%
EQUITY BLEND				
1 (Low Volatility)	0.60%	0.00%	−0.08%	−0.07%
2	0.58%	0.01%	−0.02%	−0.01%
3	0.22%	−0.04%	−0.06%	−0.05%
4	0.02%	−0.09%	−0.09%	−0.09%
5 (High Volatility)	0.35%	−0.03%	−0.06%	−0.05%
EQUITY SMALL				
1 (Low Volatility)	0.76%	0.13%	0.20%	0.23%
2	0.45%	−0.04%	0.00%	−0.02%
3	0.48%	0.03%	0.11%	0.12%
4	0.43%	0.04%	0.14%	0.13%
5 (High Volatility)	0.60%	0.06%	0.12%	0.09%
EQUITY VALUE				
1 (Low Volatility)	0.51%	−0.13%	−0.04%	−0.05%
2	0.56%	−0.02%	0.02%	0.03%
3	0.40%	−0.08%	−0.04%	−0.04%
4	0.44%	0.01%	0.05%	0.05%
5 (High Volatility)	0.25%	−0.02%	−0.05%	−0.01%
EQUITY GROWTH				
1 (Low Volatility)	0.90%	0.36%	0.43%	0.49%
2	0.57%	0.05%	−0.06%	−0.07%

(continued)

Table 1 (continued)

EQUITY LARGE				
Volatility Quintile	*Simple Return*	*Alpha CAPM*	*Alpha Fama—French*	*Alpha Carhart*
3	0.36%	−0.01%	−0.07%	−0.05%
4	0.10%	0.01%	−0.01%	0.00%
5 (High Volatility)	0.46%	0.08%	0.05%	0.06%

Table 2 EUROPE EQUITY SAMPLE

Volatility Quintile	*Simple Return*	*Alpha CAPM*	*Alpha Fama—French*	*Alpha Carhart*
EQUITY LARGE				
1 (Low Volatility)	0.32%	0.19%	0.45%	0.27%
2	0.30%	0.12%	0.29%	0.15%
3	0.26%	0.05%	0.14%	0.10%
4	0.24%	0.05%	0.10%	0.02%
5 (High Volatility)	0.21%	0.12%	0.09%	0.02%
EQUITY BLEND				
1 (Low Volatility)	0.30%	0.15%	0.41%	0.21%
2	0.27%	0.11%	0.27%	0.14%
3	0.26%	0.04%	0.13%	0.09%
4	0.20%	0.05%	0.09%	0.01%
5 (High Volatility)	0.24%	0.13%	0.12%	0.04%
EQUITY SMALL				
1 (Low Volatility)	0.62%	0.51%	0.61%	0.34%
2	0.48%	0.39%	0.46%	0.27%
3	0.44%	0.26%	0.30%	0.20%
4	0.28%	0.12%	0.13%	0.05%
5 (High Volatility)	0.17%	0.09%	0.10%	0.04%
EQUITY VALUE				
1 (Low Volatility)	0.21%	−0.01%	0.34%	0.20%
2	0.22%	0.05%	0.29%	0.18%
3	0.25%	−0.01%	0.16%	0.13%
4	0.26%	−0.04%	0.06%	0.02%
5 (High Volatility)	0.14%	0.08%	0.09%	0.00%
EQUITY GROWTH				
1 (Low Volatility)	1.22%	1.16%	0.71%	0.29%
2	0.44%	0.35%	0.44%	0.23%

(continued)

Table 2 (continued)

Volatility Quintile	*Simple Return*	*Alpha CAPM*	*Alpha Fama—French*	*Alpha Carhart*
EQUITY LARGE				
3	0.36%	0.10%	0.14%	0.08%
4	0.40%	0.11%	0.17%	0.09%
5 (High Volatility)	0.50%	0.22%	0.23%	0.14%

mutual funds in the sample with the lowest (highest) standard deviation of daily returns in the prior calendar year. We show the performance of each portfolio from December 2006 through December 2019.

This table shows the performance on five equal weighted portfolios of equity mutual funds. The low (high) volatility portfolio buys the 20% of mutual funds in the sample with the lowest (highest) standard deviation of daily returns in the prior calendar year. We show the performance of each portfolio from December 2006 through December 2019.

EUROPE EQUITY SAMPLE

Table 3 shows Carhart model risk factor loadings according to fund volatility for US equity sample. Beta market is the highest in low volatility portfolios for all types of equities. However, between large and small asset types, low volatility portfolios tend to have smaller beta in large cap funds (0.925) than in small caps (0.984), however, high volatility portfolios show larger beta coefficients in large cap funds sample (0.515) rather than in small caps (0.417). Among other investment styles, the largest beta coefficient is observed for low volatility portfolios (0.987) of value style funds sample. For momentum loading, the sign of alpha coefficient is negative in all equity type samples and shows the worst value of the coefficient in low volatility portfolio of value style funds (−0.138).

Table 4 shows Carhart model risk factor loadings according to fund volatility for EU equity sample. Beta market is the highest in low volatility portfolios for all types of equities. Low volatility portfolios of small caps demonstrate higher value of beta (1.191) than of large caps (1.044). The same is also true for high volatility portfolios of large and small caps funds. Low volatility portfolios of growth style demonstrate the highest beta coefficient (1.187) among growth, blend and value styles.

3.2 *How Long Does Volatility Persist as a Predictor of Future Fund Performance?*

Then, we test the persistence of fund volatility as a predictor of future fund performance. We used fund volatilities measured in calendar year t-1 to form portfolios in the calendar year t.

Figure 5 shows our analysis for EU equity sample. We observe quite notable difference in performance between low (from 0.41% in t to 0.35% in $t + 4$) and high volatility portfolios (from 0.24% in t to 0.35% in $t + 4$), however they get the same return 0.35% in $t + 4$. The difference in

Table 3 Carhart model risk factor loadings according to fund volatility

EQUITY LARGE				
Volatility Quintile	*Beta Market*	*SMB*	*HML*	*Momentum*
1 (Low Volatility)	0.925	0.072	−0.161	−0.080
2	0.780	0.035	−0.132	−0.065
3	0.455	0.010	−0.044	−0.037
4	0.067	0.000	−0.003	−0.004
5 (High Volatility)	0.515	0.025	−0.076	−0.043
EQUITY BLEND				
1 (Low Volatility)	0.976	−0.029	−0.057	−0.074
2	0.904	−0.013	−0.070	−0.045
3	0.208	−0.011	−0.015	−0.009
4	0.004	0.001	0.002	0.001
5 (High Volatility)	0.482	−0.014	−0.033	−0.028
EQUITY SMALL				
1 (Low Volatility)	0.984	0.851	−0.080	−0.057
2	0.469	0.312	−0.020	−0.023
3	0.409	0.239	−0.021	−0.027
4	0.355	0.223	0.009	0.008
5 (High Volatility)	0.417	0.254	0.014	0.043
EQUITY VALUE				
1 (Low Volatility)	0.987	0.104	0.113	−0.138
2	0.925	0.032	0.082	−0.076
3	0.424	−0.001	0.048	−0.029
4	0.422	−0.008	0.025	−0.029
5 (High Volatility)	0.314	−0.028	−0.032	−0.043
EQUITY GROWTH				
1 (Low Volatility)	0.848	−0.100	−0.220	−0.049
2	0.664	0.002	−0.243	−0.037
3	0.352	0.012	−0.077	−0.025
4	0.056	−0.004	−0.012	−0.007
5 (High Volatility)	0.461	−0.016	−0.132	−0.029

performance is the largest from t to $t + 1$. However, in each measurement period the low volatility portfolio has the best performance, and the worst is seen for the fourth quintile volatility portfolio. The effect of fund volatility on future fund performance is highly persistence.

Figure 6 shows the results for US equity sample. The difference in performance between low and high volatility portfolios is very large. However, in each measurement period low volatility portfolio has the best performance (from 0.65% in t to 0.60% in $t + 4$) over the high volatility

Table 4 Carhart model risk factor loadings according to fund volatility

Volatility Quintile	*Beta Market*	*SMB*	*HML*	*Momentum*
EQUITY LARGE				
1 (Low Volatility)	1.044	0.286	0.328	0.072
2	0.857	0.199	0.230	0.021
3	0.472	0.120	0.066	−0.015
4	0.408	0.133	0.024	0.006
5 (High Volatility)	0.336	0.024	0.045	0.122
EQUITY BLEND				
1 (Low Volatility)	1.041	0.271	0.311	0.051
2	0.851	0.196	0.220	0.011
3	0.447	0.115	0.063	−0.016
4	0.367	0.126	0.015	0.005
5 (High Volatility)	0.367	0.038	0.044	0.127
EQUITY SMALL				
1 (Low Volatility)	1.191	1.179	0.267	0.129
2	0.967	0.910	0.220	0.079
3	0.664	0.608	0.059	0.012
4	0.389	0.398	0.014	0.019
5 (High Volatility)	0.307	0.302	0.042	0.104
EQUITY VALUE				
1 (Low Volatility)	1.115	0.303	0.654	−0.050
2	1.026	0.233	0.503	−0.049
3	0.654	0.145	0.271	−0.046
4	0.501	0.147	0.179	−0.013
5 (High Volatility)	0.399	0.119	0.123	0.031
EQUITY GROWTH				
1 (Low Volatility)	1.187	0.720	−0.843	−0.228
2	0.947	0.297	0.144	0.087
3	0.555	0.169	−0.066	0.018
4	0.484	0.165	−0.122	−0.007
5 (High Volatility)	0.486	0.184	−0.121	0.035

portfolio (from 0.05% in t to 0.09% in $t + 4$), where high volatility portfolio shows the worst performance among all quintiles in all measurement periods.

Figure 7 shows our analysis for EU bond sample. The difference in performance between low and high volatility portfolio is large in all measurement periods, where low volatility portfolio demonstrates the best returns (from 0.17% in t to 0.25% in $t + 4$) and the high one—the worst returns (from −0.02% into to −0.02% in $t + 4$).

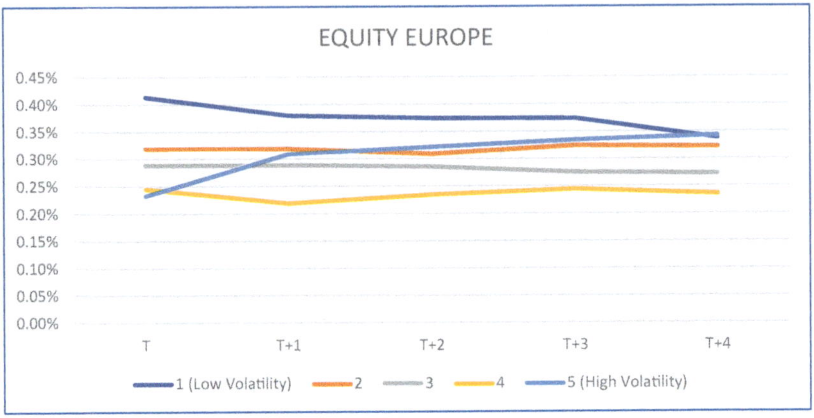

Fig. 5 How long does volatility persist as a predictor of future fund performance?

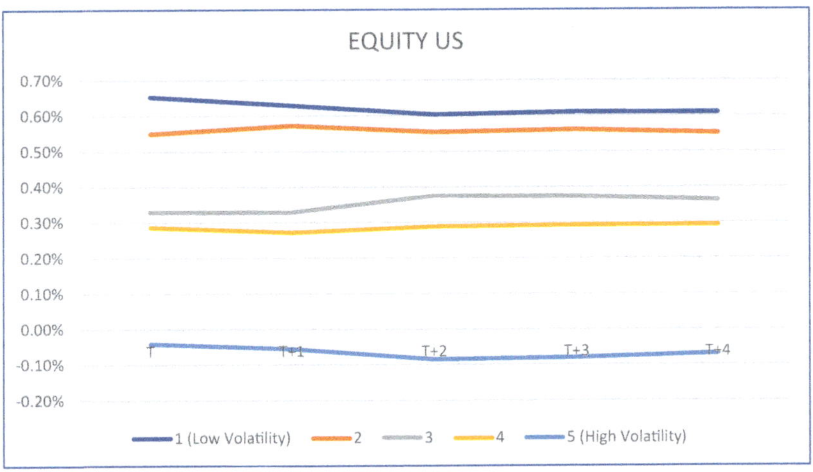

Fig. 6 How long does volatility persist as a predictor of future fund performance?

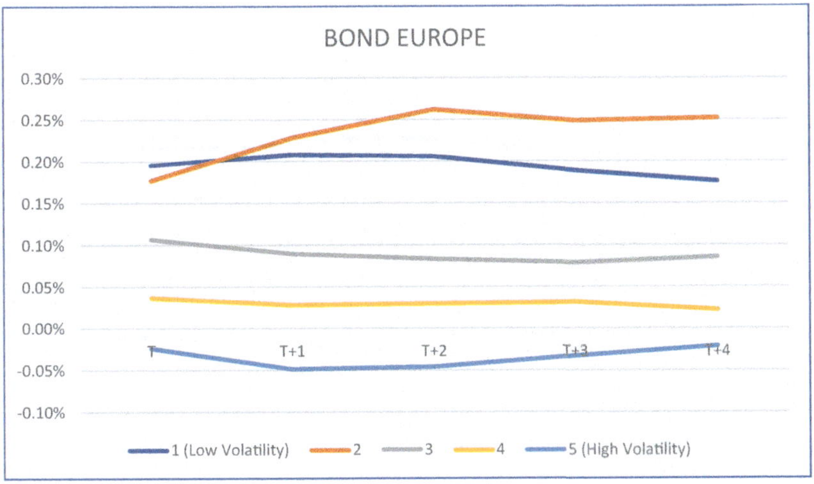

Fig. 7 How long does volatility persist as a predictor of future fund performance?

Figure 8 shows our results for US bond sample. We do not observe any significant fluctuations in volatility portfolios with increasing measurement periods. The low volatility portfolio demonstrates the best performance (from 0.17% in t to 0.19% in $t + 4$), while the fourth quintile volatility portfolio shows the worst returns. Performance of high volatility portfolio remains almost at the same level (0.12%) in all measurement periods.

This figure shows the monthly percentage alpha from a Fama-French four-factor regression on the monthly returns on portfolios of low and high volatility mutual funds for Equity Mutual Fund and for Alpha BOND factor from Eq. 4 for Bond Mutual funds. The low (high) volatility portfolio is an equal weighted portfolio of funds with the lowest (highest) 20% of standard deviation of daily returns in previous calendar years. We measure volatility in calendar year $t-1$ and use that measure to form portfolios in calendar years t through $t + 4$.

This figure shows the monthly percentage alpha from a Fama-French four-factor regression on the monthly returns on portfolios of low and high volatility mutual funds for Equity Mutual Fund and for Alpha BOND factor from Eq. 4 for Bond Mutual funds. The low (high) volatility portfolio is an equal weighted portfolio of funds with the lowest

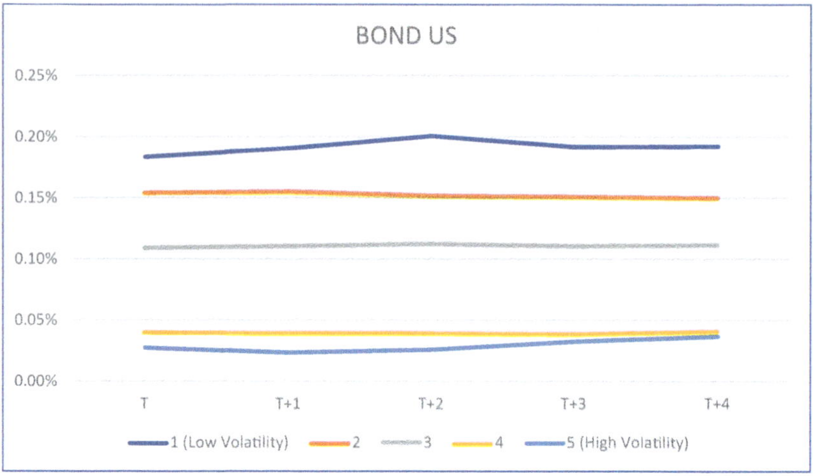

Fig. 8 How long does volatility persist as a predictor of future fund performance?

(highest) 20% of standard deviation of daily returns in previous calendar years. We measure volatility in calendar year $t-1$ and use that measure to form portfolios in calendar years t through $t + 4$.

This figure shows the monthly percentage alpha from a Fama-French four-factor regression on the monthly returns on portfolios of low and high volatility mutual funds for Equity Mutual Fund and for Alpha BOND factor from Eq. 4 for Bond Mutual funds. The low (high) volatility portfolio is an equal weighted portfolio of funds with the lowest (highest) 20% of standard deviation of daily returns in previous calendar years. We measure volatility in calendar year $t-1$ and use that measure to form portfolios in calendar years t through $t + 4$.

This figure shows the monthly percentage alpha from a Fama-French four-factor regression on the monthly returns on portfolios of low and high volatility mutual funds for Equity Mutual Fund and for Alpha BOND factor from Eq. 4 for Bond Mutual funds. The low (high) volatility portfolio is an equal weighted portfolio of funds with the lowest (highest) 20% of standard deviation of daily returns in previous calendar years. We measure volatility in calendar year $t-1$ and use that measure to form portfolios in calendar years t through $t + 4$.

Overall, the low volatility portfolio has the best performance regardless of the period of evaluation.

Figures from 5 to 8 shows that, on average, there is a large difference in performance between the low and high volatility portfolios.

3.3 Past Volatility Predicts Future Performance?

We test whether past volatility and other fund characteristics predict future performance using the following panel model:

$$\alpha_{i,t+1} = \alpha_{i,t} + SD_{i,t} + Idio_{i,t} + Fund\,Controls_{i,t} + Time\,FE + \varepsilon_{i,t} \quad (1)$$

where $\alpha_{i,t+1}$ is the annualized percentage α for fund i in calendar year $t + 1$ calculated with Carhart Model. According to Huang et al. (2011) notation[9] the Carhart model is specified as follows:

$$\begin{aligned} RF_{k,t} - R_{TB,t} &= \alpha_k + \beta_k^{M}(R_{M,t} - R_{TB,t}) + \beta_k^{SMB}(R_{S,t} - R_{B,t}) \\ &+ \beta_k^{HML}(R_{H,t} - R_{L,t}) + \beta_k^{UMD}(R_{U,t} - R_{D,t}) + \varepsilon_{k,t} \end{aligned} \quad (2)$$

The return of portfolio k during time period t is denoted by $RF_{k,t}$. The index M corresponds to the market portfolio and the index TB to the risk-free Treasury bill rate. Portfolios of small and large stocks (SMB) are denoted by S and B; portfolios of stocks (HML) with high and low ratios between their book values and their market values are denoted by H and L; and portfolios of stocks (UMD) with relatively high and low returns during the previous year are denoted by U and D. In table we define *UMD* as *MOM*. The Carhart model nests the CAPM model (which includes only the market factor) and the Fama-French model (which includes the size and the book-to-market factors in addition to the market factor). In tables we report Carhart alpha, as $\alpha_{p\ \ i,t+1}^{CAR}$.

$Fund\,Controls_{i,t}$ include the natural log of assets, natural log of age, and expense ratio all measured as of the end of calendar year t and the Carhart four-factor exposures calculated from monthly returns during calendar year t. We cluster the standard errors on year and fund. All continuous variables are winsorized at the .5% and 99.5% levels. All control variables are one-period lagged.

[9] Huang, J., Sialm, C., & Zhang, H. (2011). Risk shifting and mutual fund performance. *The Review of Financial Studies, 24*(8), 2575–2616.

We present results from estimating Eq. (1) in Tables 5 and 6. The standard deviation of past returns reveals to be a strong predictor (economically) of future fund performance.

Table 5 shows that standard deviation of past returns has an impact on future fund performance of EU equity funds. Alpha and standard deviation are positive with strong statistically significant reaction at 1% level. Idiosyncratic standard deviation, Age, size, SMB, HML, *MOM* are not

Table 5 Does fund volatility predict future performance?

	(1)	*(2)*	*(3)*	*(4)*
$\alpha_p^{CAR}i,t$	78.5389***			78.0703***
	(0.4729)			(0.4883)
$SD_{i,t}$		10.5595***		1.5844***
		(1.1550)		(0.2560)
$Idio_{i,t}$			−0.0349**	
			(0.0144)	
AGE	−0.0060	−0.0152	0.0017	−0.0073
	(0.0050)	(0.0234)	(0.0241)	(0.0050)
EXPENSE	−0.0248***	−0.1028***	−0.1071***	−0.0246***
	(0.0031)	(0.0136)	(0.0143)	(0.0030)
SIZE	0.0007	0.0083**	0.0084**	0.0006
	(0.0008)	(0.0034)	(0.0036)	(0.0008)
BETA	−0.0046	−0.4278***	−0.2225***	−0.0438***
	(0.0099)	(0.0437)	(0.0404)	(0.0133)
SMB	−0.0023	0.0187	0.0320*	−0.0022
	(0.0047)	(0.0178)	(0.0183)	(0.0047)
HML	0.0127**	0.1381***	0.2030***	0.0030
	(0.0055)	(0.0254)	(0.0219)	(0.0058)
MOM	0.0040	−0.3537***	−0.3949***	0.0072
	(0.0071)	(0.0236)	(0.0241)	(0.0070)
CONS	0.0515***	0.0236	0.2445***	0.0210
	(0.0158)	(0.0638)	(0.0661)	(0.0162)
N	52662	52662	52483	52483

Standard errors in parentheses
$^{*}p < 0.10$, $^{**}p < 0.05$, $^{***}p < 0.01$

Table 6 Does fund volatility predict future performance?

	(1)	(2)	(3)	(4)
$\alpha_p^{CAR}i,t$	80.0979***			80.3230***
	(0.3720)			(0.3743)
$SD_{i,t}$		4.5685***		−0.5061**
		(0.7422)		(0.2001)
$Idio_{i,t}$			−0.0244***	0.0022**
			(0.0043)	(0.0010)
AGE	−0.0069*	−0.0258	−0.0353*	−0.0073*
	(0.0039)	(0.0189)	(0.0194)	(0.0040)
EXPENSE	−0.0117***	−0.0601***	−0.0578***	−0.0118***
	(0.0021)	(0.0098)	(0.0099)	(0.0021)
SIZE	0.0016***	0.0154***	0.0153***	0.0017***
	(0.0004)	(0.0021)	(0.0022)	(0.0004)
BETA	0.0180***	−0.2183***	−0.1649***	0.0420***
	(0.0030)	(0.0276)	(0.0220)	(0.0078)
SMB	0.0324***	0.0685***	0.0886***	0.0355***
	(0.0046)	(0.0190)	(0.0193)	(0.0046)
HML	−0.0195***	0.1162***	0.0961***	−0.0210***
	(0.0046)	(0.0172)	(0.0181)	(0.0047)
MOM	0.0029	−0.2189***	−0.2318***	−0.0013
	(0.0058)	(0.0234)	(0.0248)	(0.0059)
CONS	−0.0254***	−0.1706***	−0.1017***	−0.0233***
	(0.0073)	(0.0378)	(0.0376)	(0.0081)
N	64117	64117	64117	64117

Standard errors in parentheses
*$p < 0.10$, **$p < 0.05$, ***$p < 0.01$

predictive of alpha in $t + 1$. Net expense ratio and Beta have a negative effect on alpha with statistically significant reaction at 1% in $t + 1$.

Table 6 shows the impact of standard deviation of past returns on future fund performance of US equity funds. With decrease of standard deviation of past returns, next year's alpha decreases. However, in $t + 1$ alpha is positive and statistically significant at 1% level, while volatility is negative and statistically significant at 5%. Idiosyncratic standard deviation is predictive of alpha at 5% statistically significant level with positive sign. Age, net expense ratio, and HML are negative and statistically significant.

Size, SMB and Beta at positive at 1% statistically significant level. *MOM* shows no effect on alpha for US equity funds.

EUROPE EQUITY SAMPLE

This table presents results from the following panel model:

$$\alpha_{P\ \ i,t+1}^{CAR} = \alpha_{i,t} + SD_{i,t} + Idio_{i,t} + Fund\,Controls_{i,t} + Time\,FE + \varepsilon_{i,t}$$

The dependent variable is the annualized percentage alpha for fund i in calendar year $t + 1$ calculated from the Carhart four-factor model using monthly returns. $SD_{i,t}$ is the standard deviation of monthly returns during calendar year t. $Idio_{i,t}$ is the idiosyncratic standard deviation of monthly returns during calendar year t. Fund Controls include the natural log of assets, natural log of age, and expense ratio all measured as of the end of calendar year t and the Carhart four-factor exposures calculated from monthly returns during calendar year t. We include year fixed effects. All variables are winsorized at the .5% and 99.5% levels standard errors clustered at fund level are reported in brackets *, **, and *** represent statistical significance at the 10%, 5%, and 1% levels.

US EQUITY SAMPLE

This table presents results from the following panel model:

$$\alpha_{P\ \ i,t+1}^{CAR} = \alpha_{i,t} + SD_{i,t} + Idio_{i,t} + Fund\,Controls_{i,t} + Time\,FE + \varepsilon_{i,t}$$

The dependent variable is the annualized percentage alpha for fund i in calendar year $t + 1$ calculated from the Carhart four-factor model using monthly returns. $SD_{i,t}$ is the standard deviation of monthly returns during calendar year t. $Idio_{i,t}$ is the idiosyncratic standard deviation of monthly returns during calendar year t. Fund Controls include the natural log of assets, natural log of age, and expense ratio all measured as of the end of calendar year t and the Carhart four-factor exposures calculated from monthly returns during calendar year t. We include year fixed effects. All variables are winsorized at the .5% and 99.5% levels standard errors clustered at fund level are reported in brackets *, **, and *** represent statistical significance at the 10%, 5%, and 1% levels.

3.4 *Persistence in Fund Volatility*

Using panel regressions, we test the hypothesis of persistence in fund volatility. Results are from the following panel model:

$$SD_{i,t+1} = \alpha_{i,t} + SD_{i,t} + \alpha_p^{CAR} i, t + FundControls_{i,t} + TimeFE + \varepsilon_{i,t} \quad (3)$$

The dependent variable, $SD_{i,t+1}$ is the standard deviation of monthly returns for fund i in calendar year $t + 1$. $SD_{i,t}$ is the standard deviation of monthly returns during calendar year t. Fund Controls include the natural log of assets, natural log of age, and expense ratio, all measured as of the end of calendar year t and the Carhart alpha is calculated from monthly returns during calendar year t. We include year fixed effects. All variables are winsorized at the .5% and 99.5% levels. All control variables are one-period lagged.

We present results from estimating Eq. (3) in Tables 7 and 8. As shown, past standard deviation of past returns has an impact on future Fund Volatility. We note that the coefficient on Lagged Volatility is positive and highly significant in all regression models, indicating strong persistence in performance volatility.

Table 7 demonstrates results for monthly fund performance volatility for US and EU equities. Past volatility ($SD_{i,t}$) demonstrates strong statistically significant effect on volatility in $t + 1$ at 1% level for all equity funds. Then, we observe positive statistically significant effect of Carhart alpha on volatility in US blend (1%), US value (5%) and EU small (5%) samples. Age is negative and highly statistically significant at 1% level in the majority of fund samples analyzed. Net expense ratio shows negative statistically significant reaction for US small sample (1%), EU large (1%), EU small (5%) and EU blend (5%) samples. There is no effect of size in EU sample, while the reaction is positive and statistically significant at 1% level for US large and blend style equites and negative and statistically significant for US small (10%) and US value (1%) equities.

Table 8 shows analysis of monthly fund performance volatility for EU and US bond sample. Portfolio alpha is according to the following model:

$$r_{p,t} = \alpha_p^{BOND} + \beta_{1,p} MKTRF_t^{Bond} + \beta_{2,t} MKTRF_t^{Equity} + \beta_{3,p} DEFAULT_t + \beta_{4,p} TERM_t + \varepsilon_{p,t} \quad (4)$$

Table 7 Analyses of monthly fund performance volatility—EQUITY SAMPLE

PANEL A: US	*US_LARGE*	*US_SMALL*	*US_BLEND*	*US_VALUE*	*US_GROWTH*
$SD_{i,t}$	96.5819***	90.7188***	97.3294***	91.0449***	96.2736***
	(0.4693)	(1.8625)	(0.2505)	(1.6785)	(0.6878)
$\alpha_p^{CAR}i, t$	1.4617	2.2349	3.5361***	3.2761**	1.3444
	(1.2162)	(1.3548)	(0.6590)	(1.4927)	(2.2980)
AGE	−0.0938***	−0.0289	−0.0777***	−0.0076	−0.1135***
	(0.0138)	(0.0262)	(0.0089)	(0.0172)	(0.0346)
EXPENSE	0.0022	−0.0449***	−0.0033	0.0129	0.0090
	(0.0085)	(0.0137)	(0.0033)	(0.0119)	(0.0145)
SIZE	0.0046***	−0.0070*	0.0037***	−0.0070***	0.0054*
	(0.0016)	(0.0038)	(0.0010)	(0.0020)	(0.0028)
CONS	0.1063***	0.6219***	0.0882***	0.4608***	0.0961**
	(0.0248)	(0.1175)	(0.0213)	(0.0747)	(0.0453)
N	13350	3973	37815	4271	4708
PANEL B: EUROPE	*EU_LARGE*	*EU_SMALL*	*EU_BLEND*	*EU_VALUE*	*EU_GROWTH*
$SD_{i,t}$	94.0007***	92.2474***	91.2152***	94.4953***	94.6519***
	(1.5790)	(1.5861)	(1.7347)	(1.5918)	(1.0088)
$\alpha_p^{CAR}i, t$	0.8923	2.2496**	0.5579	1.8439	−1.1661
	(0.6546)	(0.9052)	(0.6442)	(1.3777)	(2.2845)
AGE	−0.0331***	−0.0508***	−0.0421***	−0.0616***	−0.0728***
	(0.0097)	(0.0148)	(0.0103)	(0.0217)	(0.0203)
EXPENSE	−0.0217***	−0.0265**	−0.0127**	−0.0179	−0.0009
	(0.0065)	(0.0113)	(0.0063)	(0.0121)	(0.0135)
SIZE	0.0004	−0.0007	−0.0022	−0.0039	0.0002
	(0.0017)	(0.0024)	(0.0024)	(0.0027)	(0.0033)
CONS	0.3149***	0.4699***	0.4862***	0.4068***	0.2815***
	(0.0856)	(0.0836)	(0.0808)	(0.0755)	(0.0758)
N	18673	8005	18124	4008	3852

Standard errors in parentheses
$^{*}p < 0.10$, $^{**}p < 0.05$, $^{***}p < 0.01$

where $r_{p,t}$ is the monthly return on a portfolio of funds in excess of the one-month (Us or European) T-bill rate; $MKTRF_t^{Bond}$ is the Local (European or US) Total Bond Market Index return in excess of the one-month T-bill rate. $MKTRF_t^{Equity}$ is the (European) U.S. equity market returns in excess of the one-month T-bill rate and is included to control

Table 8 Analyses of monthly fund performance volatility—BOND SAMPLE

PANEL A: EUROPE	*CORPORATE*	*CORPORATE CRISIS*	*GOVERNMENT*	*GOVERNMENT CRISIS*
$SD_{i,t}$	89.2485***	90.0782***	87.4930***	80.4889***
	(2.1651)	(3.0235)	(1.0564)	(2.4632)
$\alpha_p^{BOND}i,t$	0.1673***	0.2197***	0.0206	0.1882***
	(0.0505)	(0.0688)	(0.0448)	(0.0512)
AGE	−3.0440***	−25.2611	−3.1210***	−13.1855*
	(0.7085)	(15.3562)	(0.8992)	(7.1363)
EXPENSE	0.0281	−0.4097	0.6731	0.4096
	(0.8305)	(2.2432)	(0.6566)	(1.6531)
SIZE	−0.2290*	−0.6223	−0.0142	0.2005
	(0.1207)	(0.5098)	(0.0926)	(0.2050)
CONS	33.7091***	60.2979***	35.5321***	74.1481***
	(4.3585)	(10.5666)	(2.9470)	(7.4512)
N	17087	2574	9359	1619

PANEL B: US	*CORPORATE*	*CORPORATE CRISIS*	*GOVERNMENT*	*GOVERNMENT CRISIS*
$SD_{i,t}$	96.8362***	94.5331***	98.7462***	98.2050***
	(0.3726)	(1.8575)	(0.2572)	(0.7821)
$\alpha_p^{BOND}i,t$	0.0315	0.1421**	−0.0486**	0.0000
	(0.0289)	(0.0627)	(0.0242)	(0.0679)
AGE	−3.5250***	−13.9653	−1.3320***	−14.2068**
	(0.5306)	(8.6203)	(0.4196)	(6.0424)
EXPENSE	1.0790**	0.3173	−0.4256	−0.9964
	(0.4870)	(2.2126)	(0.3232)	(0.9289)
SIZE	0.1219*	−0.8505**	0.0559	0.1470
	(0.0650)	(0.3265)	(0.0645)	(0.3078)
CONS	2.5084**	28.0367***	1.3806	4.8430
	(1.1140)	(5.6025)	(1.2031)	(4.7418)
N	8394	846	7785	1328

Standard errors in parentheses
$^{*}p < 0.10$, $^{**}p < 0.05$, $^{***}p < 0.01$

for potential equity market bias $DEFAULT$ is the difference in return between investment grade corporate bonds and government bonds (10-year Treasury Constant Maturity Yield); $TERM_t$ is the difference in return between long-term (30-year Treasury Constant Maturity Yield) and short-term goverment bonds (one-year Treasury Constant Maturity

Yield). Past volatility ($SD_{i,t}$) demonstrates strong statistically significant effect on volatility in $t + 1$ at 1% level for all bond funds. Panel A describes our results for Europe bond sample. We see positive 1% statistically significant effect of Carhart alpha on volatility for EU corporate bonds in all periods and for EU government bonds in crisis. Age has negative statistically significant effect on volatility in all EU bonds except corporates during the crisis. There is no effect of net expense ratio. Size has a negative impact on volatility only for EU corporate bonds in no crisis time and at 10% statistically significant level. Panel B shows our analysis for US bond sample. Carhart alpha positively impacts volatility of corporate bonds during the crisis at 5% statistically significant level and this relation is negative at 5% statistically significant level for government bonds in no crisis period. Age is negative and statistically significant for government bonds in all periods and for corporate bonds in no crisis. The net expense ratio is positive and statistically significant at 5% level in corporate bond no crisis sample. Size has positive effect of volatility at 10% statistically significant level in corporate bonds sample no crisis and negative impact at 5% statistically significant level in corporate bonds sample during the crisis.

This Table presents regression analyses of the volatility in monthly fund performance.

Results are from the following panel model:

$$SD_{i,t+1} = \alpha_{i,t} + SD_{i,t} + \alpha_p^{CAR} i, t + Fund\,Controls_{i,t} \\ + Time\,FE + \varepsilon_{i,t}$$

The dependent variable, $SD_{i,t+1}$ is the standard deviation of monthly returns for fund i in calendar year $t + 1$. $SD_{i,t}$ is the standard deviation of monthly returns during calendar year t. Fund Controls include the natural log of assets, natural log of age, and expense ratio, all measured as of the end of calendar year t and the Carhart alpha calculated from monthly returns during calendar year t. We include year fixed effects. All variables are winsorized at the .5% and 99.5% levels standard errors clustered at fund level are reported in brackets *, **, and *** represent statistical significance at the 10%, 5%, and 1% levels.

This Table presents regression analyses of the volatility in monthly fund performance.

Results are from the following panel model:

$$SD_{i,t+1} = \alpha_{i,t} + SD_{i,t} + \alpha_p^{BOND} i, t + FundControls_{i,t} + TimeFE + \varepsilon_{i,t}$$

The dependent variable, $SD_{i,t+1}$ is the standard deviation of monthly returns for fund i in calendar year $t + 1$. $SD_{i,t}$ is the standard deviation of monthly returns during calendar year t. Fund Controls include the natural log of assets, natural log of age, and expense ratio, all measured as of the end of calendar year t and the Bond alpha calculated from monthly returns during calendar year t according to Eq. 4. We include year fixed effects. All variables are winsorized at the .5% and 99.5% levels standard errors clustered at fund level are reported in brackets *, **, and *** represent statistical significance at the 10%, 5%, and 1% levels. The crisis period range between June 2007–December 2010.

References

Aggarwal, R., & Rao, R. P. (1990). Institutional ownership and distribution of equity returns. *Financial Review, 25*(2), 211–229.

Amihud, Y. (2002). Illiquidity and stock returns: Cross-section and time-series effects. *Journal of Financial Markets, 5*(1), 31–56.

Ang, A., Hodrick, R. J., Xing, Y., & Zhang, X. (2006). The cross-section of volatility and expected returns. *The Journal of Finance, 61*(1), 259–299.

Ang, A., Hodrick, R. J., Xing, Y., & Zhang, X. (2009). High idiosyncratic volatility and low returns: International and further US evidence. *Journal of Financial Economics, 91*(1), 1–23.

Atilgan, Y., Demirtas, K. O., & Simsek, K. D. (2015). Studies of equity returns in emerging markets: A literature review. *Emerging Markets Finance and Trade, 51*(4), 757–773.

Baker, N. L., & Haugen, R. A. (2012). *Low risk stocks outperform within all observable markets of the world.* Available at SSRN 2055431.

Baker, M., Bradley, B., & Wurgler, J. (2011). Benchmarks as limits to arbitrage: Understanding the low-volatility anomaly. *Financial Analysts Journal, 67*(1), 40–54.

Black, F. (1986). Noise. *The Journal of Finance, 41*(3), 528–543.

Blitz, D. C., & Van Vliet, P. (2007). The volatility effect. *The Journal of Portfolio Management, 34*(1), 102–113.

Bohl, M. T., Brzeszczyński, J., & Wilfling, B. (2009). Institutional investors and stock returns volatility: Empirical evidence from a natural experiment. *Journal of Financial Stability, 5*(2), 170–182.

Brown, K. C., Harlow, W. V., & Starks, L. T. (1996). Of tournaments and temptations: An analysis of managerial incentives in the mutual fund industry. *The Journal of Finance, 51*(1), 85–110.

Busse, J. A. (1999). Volatility timing in mutual funds: Evidence from daily returns. *The Review of Financial Studies, 12*(5), 1009–1041.

Cao, C., Chang, E. C., & Wang, Y. (2008). An empirical analysis of the dynamic relationship between mutual fund flow and market return volatility. *Journal of Banking & Finance, 32*(10), 2111–2123.

Che, L. (2018). Investor types and stock return volatility. *Journal of Empirical Finance, 47,* 139–161.

Chevalier, J., & Ellison, G. (1997). Risk taking by mutual funds as a response to incentives. *Journal of Political Economy, 105*(6), 1167–1200.

Daigler, R. T., & Wiley, M. K. (1999). The impact of trader type on the futures volatility-volume relation. *The Journal of Finance, 54*(6), 2297–2316.

Daniel, K., Grinblatt, M., Titman, S., & Wermers, R. (1997). Measuring mutual fund performance with characteristic-based benchmarks. *The Journal of Finance, 52*(3), 1035–1058.

Dennis, P. J., & Strickland, D. (2002). Who blinks in volatile markets, individuals or institutions? *The Journal of Finance, 57*(5), 1923–1949.

Fama, E. F. (1965). The behavior of stock-market prices. *The Journal of Business, 38*(1), 34–105.

Fama, E. F., & French, K. R. (1993). Common risk factors in the returns on stocks and bonds. *Journal of Financial Economics, 33*(1), 3–56.

Fama, E. F., & French, K. R. (2010). Luck versus skill in the cross-section of mutual fund returns. *The Journal of Finance, 65*(5), 1915–1947.

Fama, E. F., & French, K. R. (2015). A five-factor asset pricing model. *Journal of Financial Economics, 116*(1), 1–22.

Frazzini, A., Kabiller, D., & Pedersen, L. H. (2013). *Buffett's alpha* (No. w19681). National Bureau of Economic Research.

Friedman, M. (1953). The case for flexible exchange rates. *Essays in Positive Economics, 157*(203), 33.

Fu, F. (2009). Idiosyncratic risk and the cross-section of expected stock returns. *Journal of Financial Economics, 91,* 24–37.

Goetzmann, W., Ingersoll, J., Spiegel, M., & Welch, I. (2007). Portfolio performance manipulation and manipulation-proof performance measures. *The Review of Financial Studies, 20*(5), 1503–1546.

Han, Y., & Lesmond, D. (2011). Liquidity biases and the pricing of cross-sectional idiosyncratic volatility. *The Review of Financial Studies, 24*(5), 1590–1629.

Haugen, R. A., & Heins, A. J. (1972). *On the evidence supporting the existence of risk premiums in the capital market.* Available at SSRN 1783797.

Haugen, R. A., & Heins, A. J. (1975). Risk and the rate of return on financial assets: Some old wine in new bottles. *Journal of Financial and Quantitative Analysis*, 775–784.

Hou, K., & Loh, R. (2012). *Have We Solved the Idiosyncratic Volatility Puzzle?* Working Paper Series, Ohio State University, Charles A. Dice Center for Research in Financial Economics.

Huang, J., Sialm, C., & Zhang, H. (2011). Risk shifting and mutual fund performance. *The Review of Financial Studies, 24*(8), 2575–2616.

Jordan, B. D., & Riley, T. B. (2015). Volatility and mutual fund manager skill. *Journal of Financial Economics, 118*(2), 289–298.

Kaniel, R., Saar, G., & Titman, S. (2008). Individual investor trading and stock returns. *The Journal of Finance, 63*(1), 273–310.

Kosowski, R., Timmermann, A., Wermers, R., & White, H. (2006). Can mutual fund "stars" really pick stocks? New evidence from a bootstrap analysis. *The Journal of Finance, 61*(6), 2551–2595.

Lee, C. M., Shleifer, A., & Thaler, R. H. (1991). Investor sentiment and the closed-end fund puzzle. *The Journal of Finance, 46*(1), 75–109.

Li, X., Sullivan, R., & García-Feijóo, L. (2012). The limits to arbitrage revisited: The low-risk anomaly. *Financial Analysts Journal*.

Livingston, M., Yao, P., & Zhou, L. (2019). The volatility of mutual fund performance. *Journal of Economics and Business, 104,* 105835.

Ormos, M., & Timotity, D. (2016). Market microstructure during financial crisis: Dynamics of informed and heuristic-driven trading. *Finance Research Letters, 19,* 60–66.

Qureshi, F., Kutan, A. M., Ismail, I., & Gee, C. S. (2017). Mutual funds and stock market volatility: An empirical analysis of Asian emerging markets. *Emerging Markets Review, 31,* 176–192.

Sias, R. W. (1996). Volatility and the institutional investor. *Financial Analysts Journal, 52*(2), 13–20.

Thomas, A., Spataro, L., & Mathew, N. (2014). Pension funds and stock market volatility: An empirical analysis of OECD countries. *Journal of Financial Stability, 11,* 92–103.

CHAPTER 8

Diversification

1 Introduction

The diversification of Portfolio—a practice of diversifying funds among many different investments—is a common-sense concept with many similarities in popular language and culture.

Its theoretical foundations were introduced in the normative work of Harry Markowitz (1952a, 1959), and later confirmed by the work of William Sharpe (1964).[1]

For more than 30 years, the issue of how many assets should be included in a diversified portfolio has been widely discussed in the financial literature. Nevertheless, the definitive answer to that question has not yet been found. Even worse, there are several studies that contradict with each other.[2]

Traditional portfolio theory believes that high transaction costs (e.g., Brennan, 1975), high search costs (e.g., Merton, 1972), small portfolio size and the inability of investors to implement on average profitable

[1] Chan, K., Covrig, V., & Ng, L. (2005). What determines the domestic bias and foreign bias? Evidence from mutual fund equity allocations worldwide. *The Journal of Finance, 60*(3), 1495–1534.

[2] For example, Evans and Archer (1968) observed that most of the impact of diversification is generated by the sum of eight to ten securities while Statman (1987) concluded that to achieve sufficient portfolio diversification, at least thirty to forty stocks are needed.

G. Galloppo, *Asset Allocation Strategies for Mutual Funds*,
https://doi.org/10.1007/978-3-030-76128-8_8

investment decisions may prevent investors from making appropriate asset purchases (Goetzmann & Kumar, 2008). The lack of diversification can also be attributed to the belief that any multi-stock portfolio, regardless of its covariance structure, will be fully dispersed. Similarly, investors may adopt the "wrong" diversification strategy, which is just to hold low-volatility stocks and ignore the correlation between them.

The attractiveness of investors to certain types of stocks may be related to the level of portfolio diversification. For example, investors with insufficient diversification may assume more than benchmark weight over certain categories or styles (such as small stocks, growth stocks, etc.) or certain industries (such as technology stocks), or they may prefer larger variance and positive skewness (e.g., Barberis & Huang, 2007; Polkovnichenko, 2005). In addition, the lack of diversity may be related to various psychological factors and behavioral biases. Investors could ignore correlations (e.g., Barberis et al., 2006; Kahneman & Lovallo, 1993; Kumar & Lim, 2008). Therefore, the average correlation among stocks in investor portfolios could be high because investors do not fully understand why diversification reduces portfolio risk. This could arise because investors, as we just said before, might adopt an "erroneous" diversification strategy, where they hold stocks with lower volatility while ignoring correlations among them.

Moreover, they might misestimate the strength of correlations or follow price trends (e.g., Dhar & Kumar, 2001).

Another concern that greatly affects the level of portfolio diversification is the issue of overconfidence. Investors who are overconfident in the accuracy of private information or the ability to interpret private information (such as Odean, 1999) will deliberately choose to hold a focused and under-diversified investment portfolio. They might choose not to diversify their investments if they mistakenly believe that they will achieve outstanding performance through active trading (Goetzmann & Kumar, 2008). Investors holding under-diversified portfolios due to a sense of over-confidence in their investment abilities tend to invest in familiar stocks (such as local stocks, employer stocks, etc.). Such preference for familiar stocks (Grinblatt & Keloharju, 2001; Huberman, 2001; Zhu, 2002) can be related to the diversification level of the investment portfolio. As for the issue of familiar stocks, previous scholars (e.g., Huberman, 2001; Ivković & Weisbenner, 2005; Zhu, 2002) show that individual investors exhibit a preference for local stocks. Due to this misleading familiarity, investors might perceive local stocks to be relatively less risky without realizing that more knowledge of selected stocks does not necessarily mean control over the outcome (that is, the return on the portfolio). Chan et al. (2005)[3] examine how mutual funds from 26 developed and developing countries allocate their investment between domestic and foreign equity markets and what factors determine their asset allocations worldwide. Authors find robust evidence that these funds, in aggregate, allocate a disproportionately larger fraction of investment to domestic stocks. Familiarity variables act in an asymmetric way. From one side, the domestic bias (domestic investors overweighting the local markets) comes out. From the other side, a foreign bias (foreign investors under or overweighting the overseas markets) takes place.

Some investors might hold under-diversified portfolios for informational reasons. Christoffersen and Simutin (2017) show that managers must trade-off beating their benchmark with limiting tracking error. The optimal concentration for a fund is a function of the fund manager's information set. If the manager does not have information about the prices of securities, it is best to hold a fully diversified portfolio. An increase in concentration does not bring the expected increase in alpha, but will result in an increase in the expected volatility. Conversely, if managers have valuable information about security prices, they want to increase the concentration of their portfolio until the expected marginal benefit of alpha growth becomes equal to the expected marginal cost of volatility (Fulkerson & Riley, 2019).

When investors have useful, time-sensitive information about several stocks, they will try their best to choose to hold a low-diversity portfolio that contains only those stocks. In addition, according to Goetzmann and Kumar (2008), due to limitations of investors' information processing capabilities, they can choose to collect only information about a subset of assets or asset classes (Merton, 1972). In this case, the costs associated with knowing the asset or asset class may result in insufficient diversification.

[3] Chan, K., Covrig, V., & Ng, L. (2005). What determines the domestic bias and foreign bias? Evidence from mutual fund equity allocations worldwide. *The Journal of Finance*, *60*(3), 1495–1534.

On the contrary, some fund managers apply other approaches than increased portfolio concentration to take advantage of valuable information[4] Under this rationale, the manager makes a good use of information about expected future returns to construct an active portfolio. When a mutual fund manager increases the concentration of their portfolio, they can give additional weight to their best investment ideas and increase the expected alpha of their fund (Fulkerson & Riley, 2019). However, when they recognize that their own information about expected future returns is of low quality, they tend to hold a less concentrated portfolio and closely track the market portfolio.

The attitudes of investors towards risk may affect their diversification decisions. Investors with high (low) risk tolerance may hold fewer (more) number of mutual funds in their portfolio. Previous scholars (e.g., Blume & Friend, 1975; Morin & Suarez, 1983) show that risk aversion increases with age and wealth, which indicates that the diversification of the portfolio will increase with age and income (wealth). The diversification of the investment portfolio may also increase with age, because as experience accumulates, investors will gain more information about the market (for example, King & Leape, 1987). At the same time, young investors may reduce their diversification due to overconfidence. In addition to age and wealth, the level of education and financial level may also affect investors' diversification decisions. Under this perspective, experimental studies indicate that the insensitivity to correlations is greater among people who are financially less sophisticated (e.g., Kroll et al., 1988).

The diversification portfolio level does influence on the realized performance, indeed when increasing portfolio concentration is expected to increase the fund's idiosyncratic volatility.

If investors with poor diversification are bearing greater idiosyncratic risks and cannot obtain appropriate compensation, the risk-adjusted performance of their investment portfolio will be lower.

Academic studies underline the fact that individual investors tend to hold very less diversified portfolios. Goetzmann and Kumar (2008), in a study of more than 40,000 stock accounts at a brokerage firm, found that the mean number of stocks in a portfolio was four and the median number was three. Similar evidence is found by Polkovnichenko (2005), in a survey of 14 million households he discovers that investors were

[4] Fulkerson, J. A., & Riley, T. B. (2019). Portfolio concentration and mutual fund performance. *Journal of Empirical Finance, 51*, 1–16.

holding portfolios of one to five stocks. According to Statman (2004), another piece of the puzzle is the concentration of portfolios in particular styles (such as large capitalization stock) or locations (such as a preference of U.S. investors for U.S. stocks). Such concentrated portfolios forgo the benefits of broad diversification.

2 Previous Findings in Literature

Mutual fund managers should choose to increase their portfolio concentration when their information set is valuable enough that the benefits of the expected increase in alpha more than offsets the costs of the expected increase in idiosyncratic volatility.[5] Consistent with that idea, Fulkerson and Riley (2019) find that fund performance improves after concentration increases. Since the expected cost of increasing concentration will change over time between different funds, the expected return required before managers choose to increase concentration should also change. Among other results, authors show that the concentration-performance relationship is stronger for funds with fewer institutional ownership.

Prior evidence on the relation between fund portfolio concentration and performance is mixed. On the one hand, Sapp and Yan (2008) found that mutual funds with a higher level of security concentration underperform compared to less concentrated funds. On the other hand, Kacperczyk et al. (2005) found that mutual funds with higher industry concentration performed better than funds with lower concentration. Cui and He (2017) found a positive correlation between concentration at the national level and the performance of institutional investors; and Ivković et al. (2008) shows that households with more concentrated investment portfolios are better than households with fewer concentrated investment portfolios (Fulkerson & Riley, 2019). Kacperczyk et al. (2005) provided two potential reasons why mutual fund managers would increase portfolio concentration. First, if the cost of poor performance is small relatively to the benefit of good performance, the volatility that can be expected from increased concentration can actually benefit fund managers. Secondly, Kacperczyk et al. (2005) pointed out that if the information set of mutual fund managers is improved, it may increase the concentration of the investment portfolio.

[5] Fulkerson, J. A., & Riley, T. B. (2019). Portfolio concentration and mutual fund performance. *Journal of Empirical Finance, 51*, 1–16.

This behavior is consistent with the portfolio selection model of Treynor and Black (1973). In this model, managers without information should hold market portfolios, but managers with strong beliefs in specific securities should increase portfolio concentration by giving those securities a disproportionate weight. In the same fashion, Kacperczyk et al. (2005) found that fund managers focusing on a few industries outperform other fund managers. Van Nieuwerburgh and Veldkamp (2010) considered the cost of information acquisition and found that managers who are unwilling to bear a large amount of search costs can also reasonably hold a concentrated portfolio. Cohen et al. (2010) found that the largest position in the fund's portfolio (i.e., the "best idea" of fund manager) performed significantly better than benchmark. These results indicate that certain funds benefit from a portfolio of securities concentrated, where fund managers may have the most valuable information.

Goetzmann and Kumar (2008)[6] study shows that U.S. individual investors hold under-diversified portfolios, where the level of under-diversification is greater among younger, low-income, less-educated, and less sophisticated investors. In a similar fashion of previous scholars, authors find that the level of under-diversification is also correlated with investment choices that are consistent with over-confidence, trend-following behavior, and local bias. In addition, investors who overweight stocks with higher volatility and skewness are also less diversified. In contrast, there is little evidence that portfolio size or transaction costs limit diversification. Insufficient diversification is costly for most investors, but a small number of investors could prefer a lower level of diversification due to superior information.

Eun et al. (2008), while investigating for the effect of the international diversification, find that the return-generating mechanisms for large- and small-cap stocks are quite different. Authors discover that while returns on large-cap stocks are substantially driven by common global factors, returns on small-cap stocks are primarily driven by local and idiosyncratic factors. Indeed, large cap stocks tend to be those of multinational companies with a substantial foreign customer and investor base, whereas small-cap companies are likely to be more locally oriented with a limited

[6] Goetzmann, W. N., & Kumar, A. (2008). Equity portfolio diversification. *Review of Finance, 12*(3), 433–463.

international exposure.[7] As a result, the gains from the international diversification of large stocks may be insignificant, because their gains are largely driven by common global factors, while small-cap stocks may become an effective tool for international diversification due to the fact that small cap returns are mainly generated by local and special factors.

According to Statman (2004)[8] the diversification puzzle can be solved, however, in the context of behavioral portfolio theory, where investors construct their portfolios as layered pyramids in which the bottom layers are designed for downside protection and the top layers are designed for upside potential. What motivates this behavior is the aspirations of investors, not their attitudes toward risk.[9]

Statman (2002) states that the view of investors in behavioral portfolio theory is different from the view of investors in mean–variance portfolio theory.[10] "Mean variance investors" treat their portfolio as a whole and are always reluctant to take risks, while "behavioral investors" do not treat their portfolio as a whole, nor do they always avoid risks. In the simple version of the behavioral portfolio theory, investors divide their funds into two tiers of the portfolio pyramid, a downward protection layer designed to protect them from poverty, and an upward potential layer designed to make them rich. In the full version of the theory, investors divide their funds into multiple levels, each level corresponding to a goal or expectation.

An explanation of why investors hold sub-optimally diversified portfolios, in line with behavioral portfolio theory, relies on the fact that investors consider the individual stocks they hold as part of the upside-potential layer of their portfolios and are willing to forgo the benefits of diversification in an attempt to reach their aspirations. The desire of investors to attain their upside-potential aspirations leads them to take

[7] Eun, C. S., Huang, W., & Lai, S. (2008). International diversification with large-and small-cap stocks. *Journal of Financial and Quantitative Analysis,* 489–523.

[8] Statman, M. (2004). The diversification puzzle. *Financial Analysts Journal, 60*(4), 44–53.

[9] Statman, M. (2004) with this respect affirms: "Some investors fill the uppermost layer with the few stocks of an undiversified portfolio; others fill it with lottery tickets. Neither lottery buying nor undiversified portfolios are consistent with mean–variance portfolio theory, but both are consistent with behavioral portfolio theory".

[10] Statman, M. (2002, January/February). Lottery players/stock traders. *Financial Analysts Journal, 58*(1), 14–21.

higher risks in these layers than they take in the downside-protection layers.

Statman (2004) gives a significative example of this behavior affirming that personal aspirations lead investors to buy aggressive growth funds, individual stocks, and call options, all of which have positive expected returns accompanying their high risks. Moreover, at the extreme, the desire of investors to reach their aspirations leads them to buy lottery tickets and participate in other gambles that have negative expected returns. Investors do not gamble because they seek risk. Rather, they gamble because they badly want to reach their aspirations. In the world of gambling, gamblers believe that their expected return is positive, but they incorrectly estimated the odds of the bet, but other gamblers still know the odds and the bet, because bets with a negative expected return provide them with the only chance to achieve their wishes. In a parallel framework, Dubins and Savage (1976) talk about an investor who is in a casino with $1000 and desperately aspires to have $10,000 by morning. The best bet for him, so to maximize its utility and correspond to his "optimal portfolio", is concentrated in a single gamble, one that offers a chance, however small, of winning $10,000.

In a milestone paper, Friedman and Savage (1948) noted that risk aversion and risk seeking share roles in investor behavior; that is, people who buy insurance policies often also buy lottery tickets. Under the behavioral finance framework, Friedman and Savage theorized that people buy lottery tickets because they aspire to reach the riches of higher social classes whereas they buy insurance as protection against a fall into the poverty of lower social classes Four years later, Markowitz (1952a, 1952b) wrote two scientific work, in one he extended Friedman and Savage's insurance–lottery framework and in the other, he created the mean–variance framework. The big difference between the mean—variance framework and the insurance—lottery framework, stay in the aspect that investors in the mean–variance framework are always risk averse, never risk seeking and they never buy lottery tickets.

3 Methodology and Empirical Results

3.1 The Art and Science of Diversification

The art and science of diversification in the context of financial assets is based, in its simplest conception, on two approaches: the naive diversification and the optimized diversification a la Markowitz. Naïve diversification refers to the "1/N heuristics" method, which essentially entails evenly dividing the total allocation among the available assets (Chan et al., 2005). Naïve diversification attributes no importance to the relationship between assets. That is to say the correlation between the assets is not utilized in the allocation decision. This method of diversification does, indeed, reduce volatility, and it is simple to use when there is a lack of knowledge about the assets and interrelationships among these.[11] In contrast, Markowitz proposed optimized diversification in a paper published in 1952. His mathematical method considers the correlation between assets in order to maximize returns and minimize overlap, in terms of risk portfolio contribution. Therefore, assets with high volatility but negative correlation are good combinations in the investment portfolio, while assets with high volatility and high correlation have lower weights in the final portfolio (Lhabitant & Vicin, 2004).

3.2 Diversification in Practice: Naive Diversification

Although diversification has become the unquestioned bedrock of investment allocation decisions, in practice, it is frequently the case that asset allocation does not just blindly apply the diversification principles set forth by Markowitz (Lhabitant & Learned, 2002). By way of illustration, when making complex portfolio decisions, few investors effectively consider correlations (that is, the non-linearity of risks). Instead, they prefer to use simpler rules to allocate assets, such as evenly distributing the distribution among available assets. This method is also called "naive diversification" or "1/N heuristic" and has a long history in asset allocation. In fact, it was even recommended in the Talmud. Writing in about the fourth century, a certain Rabbi Issac bar Aha gave the following asset allocation advice: "A man should always place his money, a third

[11] Lhabitant, F. S., & Vicin, M. L. D. P. (2004). Finding the sweet spot of hedge fund diversification. *Journal of Financial Transformation, 10*, 31–39.

into land, a third into merchandise, and keep a third on hand".[12] Harry Markowitz reported that he used this rule himself and justified his choice on psychological grounds: "My intention was to minimize my future regret. So, I split my contributions fifty-fifty between bonds and equities".[13] In short, the naïve diversification approach is the protection of ignorance. It aims to distribute assets evenly in the portfolio to reduce overall risk while ignoring the mathematical complexity on which modern portfolio theory is based. According to the latter, naïve diversification does not give proper consideration to the correlations among the assets and should therefore result in sub-optimal portfolios (Lhabitant & Learned, 2002). However, in practice, it may happen that naïve diversification results in reasonably diversified portfolios that are surprisingly even close to some portfolio on the efficient frontier. In contrast, in terms of false benefits, the consequences of fueling the optimizer can be very significant, as demonstrated by Michaud terming this situation the "Markowitz optimization enigma" portfolio relying on the fact that performance may fall sharply in periods outside the sample period used for the optimization.[14] In fact, the mean-variance optimizer needs to make accurate predictions of risk, return and correlation to combine the best forward-looking investment.

In the spirit of Lhabitant and Learned (2002),[15] we create equally weighted portfolios of increasing size ($N = 1, 2, \ldots, 50$) by randomly selecting mutual funds from our data set. For each portfolio, we build a time series of returns and use it to generate various statistics measures: average return, volatility, skewness and kurtosis, downside risk and correlation. To catch the inter-temporal variation of benefits due to such diversification, we split our sample intro three periods and ran different statistical tests on each sample, which cover pre-crisis (29/12/2006), during crisis (28/11/2008) and end of our sample period (31/12/2019) for Europe and US bonds (Corporate and Government types), and

[12] Guerard, J. B. Jr. (Ed.). (2009). *Handbook of portfolio construction: Contemporary applications of Markowitz techniques*. Springer Science & Business Media.

[13] Benartzi, S., & Thaler, R. H. (2001). Naive diversification strategies in defined contribution saving plans. *American Economic Review, 91*(1), 79–98.

[14] Jorion, P. (1992). Portfolio optimization in practice. *Financial Analysts Journal, 48*(1), 68–74.

[15] Lhabitant, F. S., & Learned, M. (2002). Hedge fund diversification: How much is enough? *The Journal of Alternative Investments, 5*(3), 23–49.

Europe and US Equity (Large and Small Cap size, and Blend, Value, Growth asset styles).

In general, naïve diversification of mutual funds provides benefits for the investor. However, our study finds that a minimum number of funds are needed to maximize the potential benefits while this minimum number varies depending on the strategy.

3.3 Return and Volatility

Table 1 and Fig. 1a–c show the evolution of the mean return of mutual fund portfolios as a function of the underlying mutual funds. Not surprisingly, the return on the portfolio is not greatly affected by the number of funds. This result is due to the linearity of the average operator. It is evident that the mean return varies widely across strategies and over time. In general, we do not observe mean portfolio returns to be significantly affected by the number of mutual funds, which goes in line with Amin and Kat (2002). However, we observe that mean returns differ strongly across strategies and time period. During the pre-crisis period, for Europe Bond group both corporate and government types, we observe no significant difference in mean returns with increasing number of funds. US bond remain positive and low in the pre-crisis period with increase of funds, while during the crisis mean returns of corporate bonds drop sharply and, on the contrary, those of government bond raise almost double. At the end of period mean return values are positive and corporate bond group demonstrates mostly higher values than those of government group when increasing number of funds in portfolio. We observe significant drop for EU equity group in end of period, especially in equally-weighted portfolios for the size of 2, 5 and 10 mutual funds, with the lowest value of the coefficient for 2 mutual funds in Europe Equity Large Cap (−5.84%), Europe Equity Small (−3.97%), Europe Equity Value (−4.00%) and for 10 mutual funds group in Europe Equity Large Cap (−4.28%). US Equities drop with increasing number of funds in all time periods analyze, however, at the end of the period there is a tendency for slight increase of US Equity Large Cap (from 1.02 to 1.42%), US Equity Small (from 1.88 to 2.01%).

Table 2 and Fig. 2a–c report the evolution of the Standard Deviation of mutual fund portfolios as a function of the number of its underlying mutual funds. The number of funds required to reduce the volatility is quite small. We find that approximately ten mutual funds are enough to

Table 1 Impact of diversification—Evolution of the mean return of a mutual fund portfolio as a function of the underlying mutual funds (Monthly Observations—Estimation Window 12 months)

Panel A—EUROPE BOND

	Number of Mutual Fund in Portfolio						
	Initial	*2*	*5*	*10*	*20*	*30*	*50*
29/12/2006							
Europe Corporate Bond	0.96%	0.38%	0.27%	0.32%	0.32%	0.38%	0.35%
Europe Government Bond	0.56%	0.35%	0.29%	0.27%	0.35%	0.41%	0.37%
28/11/2008							
Europe Corporate Bond	−0.91%	−0.53%	−0.48%	−0.53%	−0.63%	−0.72%	−0.69%
Europe Government Bond	−1.41%	−0.38%	−0.48%	−0.52%	−0.47%	−0.48%	−0.42%
31/12/2019							
Europe Corporate Bond	0.25%	0.36%	0.22%	0.24%	0.26%	0.24%	0.28%
Europe Government Bond	0.02%	0.30%	0.38%	0.33%	0.32%	0.30%	0.23%

Panel B—US BOND

	Number of Mutual Fund in Portfolio						
	Initial	*2*	*5*	*10*	*20*	*30*	*50*
29/12/2006							
US Corporate Bond	1.30%	0.55%	0.22%	0.12%	0.09%	0.05%	0.05%
US Government Bond	−0.03%	0.07%	0.03%	0.07%	0.08%	0.22%	0.28%
28/11/2008							
US Corporate Bond	−3.24%	−1.56%	−0.65%	−0.44%	−0.31%	−0.21%	−0.25%
US Government Bond	−0.54%	0.40%	0.22%	0.14%	0.16%	0.31%	0.35%
31/12/2019							
US Corporate Bond	1.30%	0.38%	0.38%	0.57%	0.56%	0.61%	0.60%
US Government Bond	0.49%	0.35%	0.43%	0.28%	0.22%	0.34%	0.38%

(continued)

Table 1 (continued)

Panel C—EUROPE EQUITY

	Number of Mutual Fund in Portfolio						
	Initial	*2*	*5*	*10*	*20*	*30*	*50*
29/12/2006							
Europe Equity Large Cap	2.11%	1.06%	1.10%	1.39%	1.23%	0.90%	0.68%
Europe Equity Blend	0.92%	1.26%	1.36%	1.55%	1.20%	1.17%	1.14%
Europe Equity Small	2.88%	0.96%	1.23%	0.96%	1.14%	1.15%	1.05%
Europe Equity Value	2.72%	1.47%	0.88%	0.90%	0.93%	0.84%	1.01%
Europe Equity Growth	1.01%	0.90%	1.79%	1.27%	1.12%	0.99%	0.83%
28/11/2008							
Europe Equity Large Cap	−5.84%	−5.84%	−3.92%	−4.28%	−3.34%	−2.77%	−2.28%
Europe Equity Blend	−1.74%	−2.65%	−3.46%	−3.79%	−2.94%	−2.81%	−2.76%
Europe Equity Small	−5.80%	−3.97%	−3.42%	−2.28%	−2.98%	−3.47%	−3.15%
Europe Equity Value	−5.85%	−4.00%	−2.40%	−2.95%	−2.81%	−2.56%	−2.93%
Europe Equity Growth	−1.72%	−1.83%	−3.14%	−3.10%	−2.95%	−2.56%	−2.39%
31/12/2019							
Europe Equity Large Cap	2.13%	2.06%	1.91%	1.78%	1.74%	1.71%	1.55%
Europe Equity Blend	1.63%	1.59%	1.33%	1.29%	1.53%	1.48%	1.48%
Europe Equity Small	2.17%	1.44%	1.50%	1.65%	1.79%	1.79%	1.71%
Europe Equity Value	1.02%	1.08%	1.01%	1.11%	1.01%	1.06%	1.12%
Europe Equity Growth	2.00%	1.62%	1.75%	1.98%	1.83%	1.88%	1.91%

Panel D—US EQUITY

	Number of Mutual Fund in Portfolio						
	Initial	*2*	*5*	*10*	*20*	*30*	*50*
29/12/2006							
US Equity Large Cap	0.94%	0.43%	0.34%	0.31%	0.23%	0.25%	0.27%
US Equity Blend	1.15%	0.62%	0.47%	0.65%	0.54%	0.52%	0.44%
US Equity Small	1.05%	0.68%	0.39%	0.21%	0.26%	0.29%	0.35%
US Equity Value	1.41%	0.31%	0.24%	0.27%	0.44%	0.45%	0.53%
US Equity Growth	0.60%	0.15%	0.20%	0.20%	0.22%	0.20%	0.17%
28/11/2008							
US Equity Large Cap	−1.41%	−1.96%	−2.11%	−2.36%	−1.75%	−1.81%	−1.86%
US Equity Blend	−3.83%	−3.23%	−2.36%	−2.80%	−2.37%	−2.36%	−2.20%
US Equity Small	−4.36%	−2.61%	−2.95%	−1.28%	−1.39%	−1.36%	−1.47%
US Equity Value	−3.48%	−0.47%	−0.35%	−1.41%	−1.78%	−1.76%	−1.95%
US Equity Growth	−3.69%	−2.16%	−2.24%	−1.93%	−2.14%	−1.95%	−1.93%
31/12/2019							
US Equity Large Cap	1.02%	1.71%	2.05%	1.88%	1.54%	1.50%	1.42%
US Equity Blend	2.06%	0.88%	0.88%	0.84%	1.09%	1.11%	1.12%
US Equity Small	1.88%	2.02%	2.13%	2.27%	2.06%	2.01%	2.01%
US Equity Value	2.16%	1.99%	1.80%	1.36%	1.37%	1.40%	1.43%
US Equity Growth	2.99%	1.41%	1.30%	1.30%	1.33%	1.25%	1.27%

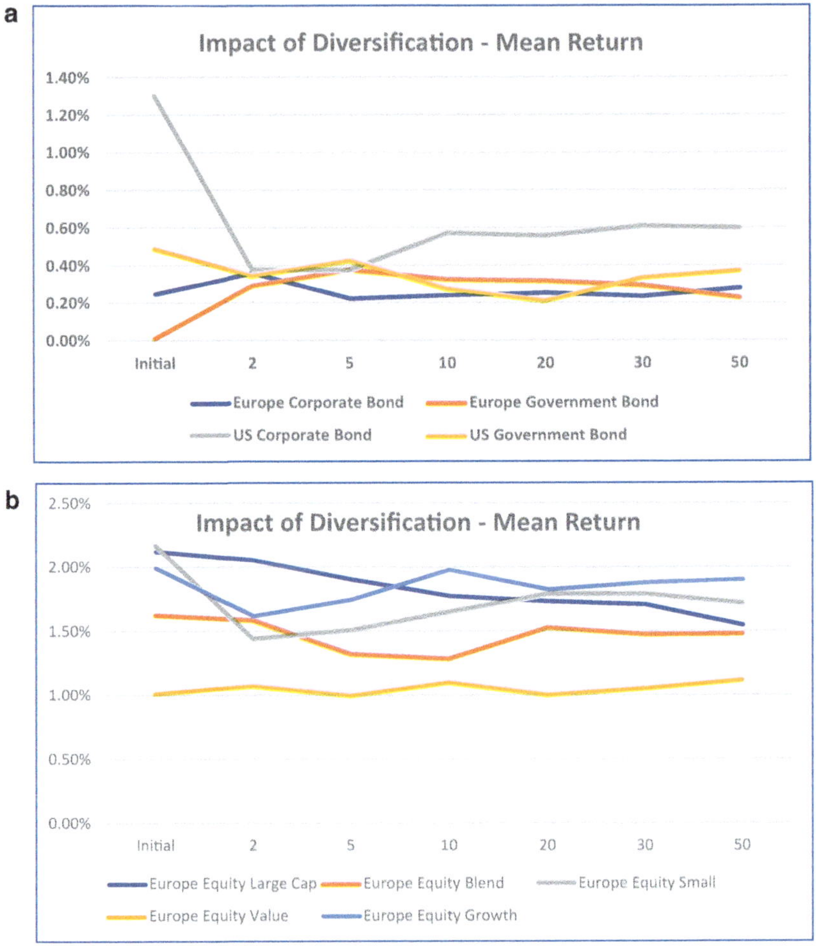

Fig. 1 Impact of diversification on the mean return of a fund of funds portfolio (Monthly Observations—Estimation Window 12 months—Last Observation 31-12-2019). **a** FIXED INCOME. **b** EQUITY EUROPE. **c** EQUITY US

c

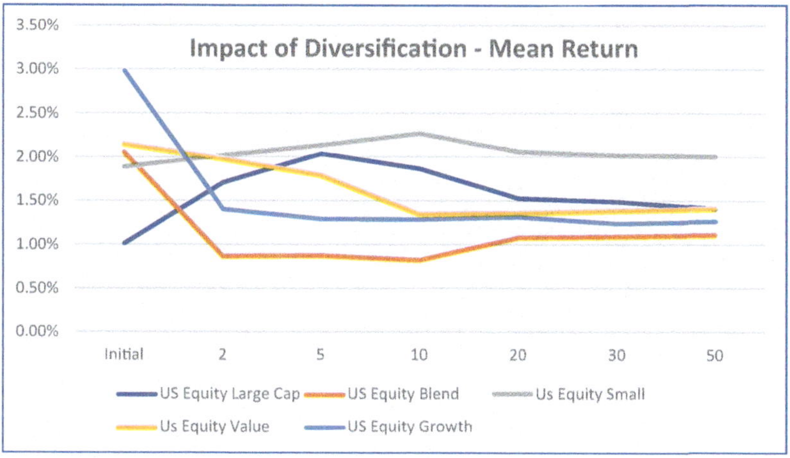

Fig. 1 (continued)

reduce most of the volatility. Adding more funds thereafter produces only marginal gains. This result stands whatever the period and the investment style.

For Europe Bond in all the periods, together with increase of number of mutual funds in portfolio we observe decrease of volatility and then its raise again, but the picture is the oppositive for government bonds in crisis and end of period. For US bonds, volatility tends to be much less than its initial value with more funds in portfolio, and it has a tendency to raise slow when we test for 50 mutual funds. For EU equities in general, we observe decrease of volatility from its initial value in all types of funds with increase of mutual funds in a portfolio, with exception of raise of volatility for Europe Equity Blend in pre-crisis period, Europe Equity Blend and Europe Equity Growth during the crisis, and Europe Equity Large Cap and Europe Equity Growth in end of period. For US equities we also observe mostly decrease of volatility from its initial value in all types together with increase of mutual funds in portfolio, with exception of US Equity Large during crisis period.

Table 2 Impact of diversification—evolution of the standard deviation of a mutual fund portfolio as a function of the underlying mutual funds (Monthly Observations—Estimation Window 12 months)

Panel A—EUROPE	*Number of Mutual Fund in Portfolio*						
	Initial	*2*	*5*	*10*	*20*	*30*	*50*
29/12/2006							
Europe Corporate Bond	1.96%	0.79%	0.59%	0.65%	0.69%	0.80%	0.73%
Europe Government Bond	2.22%	0.82%	0.66%	0.58%	0.77%	0.90%	0.87%
28/11/2008							
Europe Corporate Bond	4.01%	1.82%	1.51%	1.84%	1.91%	2.11%	2.04%
Europe Government Bond	5.66%	2.26%	2.59%	2.36%	2.26%	2.41%	2.15%
31/12/2019							
Europe Corporate Bond	1.58%	1.74%	1.38%	1.44%	1.55%	1.55%	1.60%
Europe Government Bond	0.53%	1.76%	1.80%	1.82%	1.80%	1.78%	1.70%

Panel B—US BOND

	Number of Mutual Fund in Portfolio						
	Initial	*2*	*5*	*10*	*20*	*30*	*50*
29/12/2006							
US Corporate Bond	2.06%	0.99%	0.43%	0.29%	0.22%	0.16%	0.19%
US Government Bond	1.47%	0.29%	0.28%	0.31%	0.29%	0.43%	0.49%
28/11/2008							
US Corporate Bond	7.09%	3.45%	1.51%	1.07%	0.88%	0.66%	0.75%
US Government Bond	2.27%	1.27%	0.78%	0.88%	0.87%	0.91%	0.88%
31/12/2019							
US Corporate Bond	1.21%	0.39%	0.38%	0.63%	0.65%	0.69%	0.70%
US Government Bond	1.38%	0.96%	0.93%	0.71%	0.57%	0.65%	0.67%

(continued)

Table 2 (continued)

Panel C—EUROPE EQUITY

	Number of Mutual Fund in Portfolio						
	Initial	*2*	*5*	*10*	*20*	*30*	*50*
29/12/2006							
Europe Equity Large Cap	2.69%	1.34%	1.64%	1.86%	1.48%	1.08%	0.82%
Europe Equity Blend	0.84%	1.24%	1.62%	1.81%	1.41%	1.51%	1.45%
Europe Equity Small	4.75%	1.58%	1.74%	1.35%	1.64%	1.62%	1.47%
Europe Equity Value	2.80%	1.84%	1.10%	1.18%	1.20%	1.07%	1.24%
Europe Equity Growth	1.30%	1.19%	2.36%	1.77%	1.58%	1.39%	1.15%
28/11/2008							
Europe Equity Large Cap	8.27%	8.27%	5.78%	6.20%	4.99%	4.18%	3.51%
Europe Equity Blend	2.76%	3.75%	4.94%	5.50%	4.28%	4.06%	3.99%
Europe Equity Small	9.44%	6.38%	5.94%	3.97%	4.88%	6.02%	5.36%
Europe Equity Value	9.41%	6.35%	3.81%	4.44%	4.18%	3.85%	4.43%
Europe Equity Growth	2.57%	2.46%	4.73%	4.90%	4.59%	4.13%	3.87%
31/12/2019							
Europe Equity Large Cap	2.93%	3.24%	3.42%	3.43%	3.54%	3.55%	3.39%
Europe Equity Blend	4.15%	4.34%	3.90%	3.89%	3.78%	3.67%	3.60%
Europe Equity Small	4.69%	2.84%	3.40%	3.68%	4.18%	4.10%	4.03%
Europe Equity Value	4.52%	4.35%	4.24%	4.42%	3.57%	3.70%	3.79%
Europe Equity Growth	2.79%	1.90%	2.54%	2.96%	2.98%	3.26%	3.35%

Panel D—US EQUITY

	Number of Mutual Fund in Portfolio						
	Initial	2	5	*10*	*20*	*30*	*50*
29/12/2006							
US Equity Large Cap	2.40%	1.54%	1.49%	1.32%	0.78%	0.77%	0.69%
US Equity Blend	1.74%	1.01%	0.73%	1.18%	1.02%	0.99%	0.88%
Us Equity Small	4.09%	2.45%	2.67%	1.01%	1.04%	1.03%	1.08%
Us Equity Value	1.52%	0.80%	0.60%	0.43%	0.71%	0.67%	0.79%
US Equity Growth	3.57%	0.59%	0.92%	0.79%	0.75%	0.67%	0.70%
28/11/2008							
US Equity Large Cap	2.66%	3.97%	4.42%	4.47%	3.15%	3.24%	3.29%
US Equity Blend	5.38%	5.27%	3.76%	4.51%	3.90%	3.89%	3.68%
Us Equity Small	7.53%	5.21%	5.55%	2.45%	2.63%	2.66%	2.86%
Us Equity Value	5.93%	0.89%	0.67%	2.22%	2.83%	2.88%	3.24%
US Equity Growth	6.22%	3.22%	3.79%	4.06%	3.63%	3.55%	3.53%
31/12/2019							
US Equity Large Cap	3.13%	3.17%	3.67%	3.37%	3.16%	3.06%	2.90%
US Equity Blend	4.54%	1.58%	1.76%	1.83%	2.22%	2.31%	2.27%
Us Equity Small	4.83%	5.11%	4.81%	5.02%	4.57%	4.58%	4.70%
Us Equity Value	3.98%	4.23%	4.38%	3.68%	3.67%	3.61%	3.83%
US Equity Growth	3.68%	1.94%	2.10%	2.14%	2.15%	2.04%	2.15%

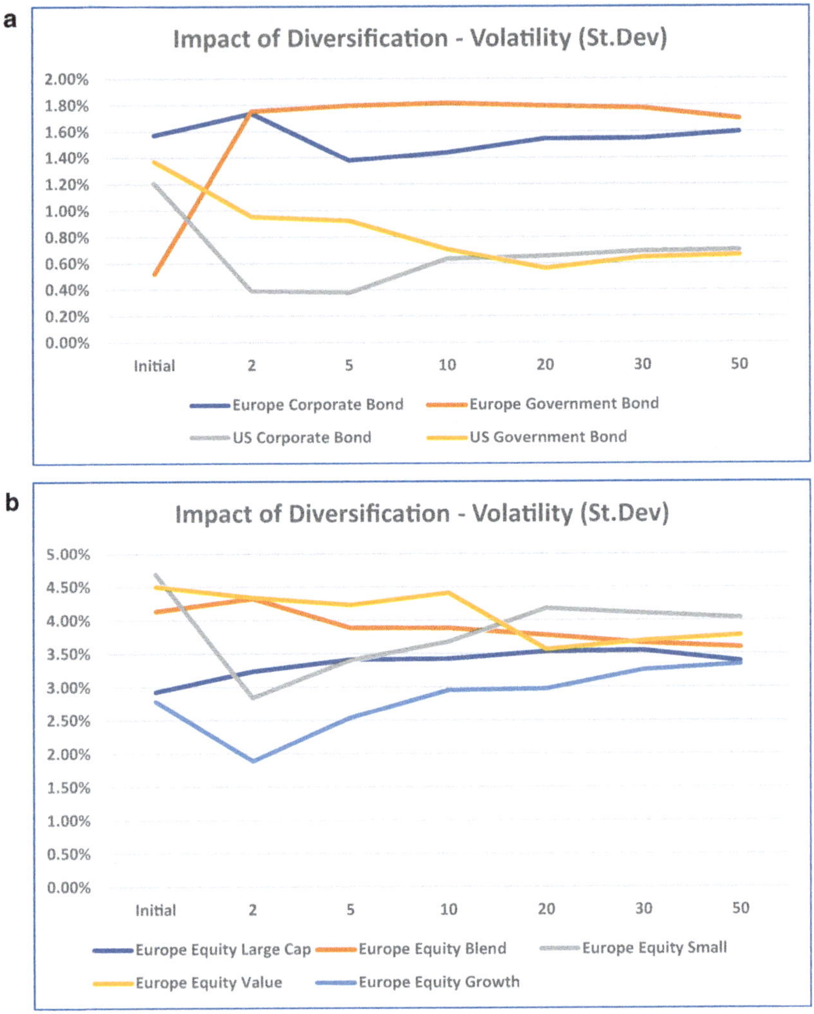

Fig. 2 Impact of diversification on the volatility of a fund of funds portfolio (Monthly Observations—Estimation Window 12 months—Last Observation 31-12-2019). **a** FIXED INCOME. **b** EQUITY EUROPE. **c** EQUITY US

c

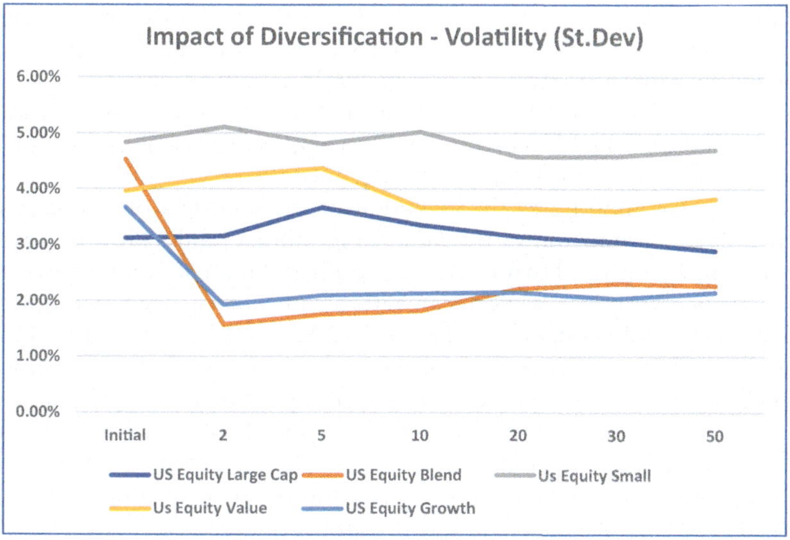

Fig. 2 (continued)

3.4 *Skewness and Kurtosis*

Mutual fund returns are generally not normally distributed. Asymmetry and fat tails in return distribution are a result of complexity of their strategies. If fund returns are positively skewed, the investor is probably quite happy. If the tails are fat, the investor can expect a more thrilling investment ride (Lhabitant & Vicin, 2004). The characteristics of a mutual fund past performance do not determine its future performance, as all disclosure statements continuously remind us.[16]

Previous results indicate that increasing the number of mutual funds in the portfolio can reduce volatility while maintaining expected returns. However, the characteristic of the time series of mutual funds may have properties that go beyond these two parameters (Lhabitant & Learned, 2002). To be specific, their returns do not follow a normal distribution (bell curve), but tend to show an asymmetric distribution with fat

[16]Lhabitant, F. S., & Vicin, M. L. D. P. (2004). Finding the sweet spot of hedge fund diversification. *Journal of Financial Transformation, 10,* 31–39.

tails. Therefore, we should also consider in the analysis higher distribution moments, such as skewness and kurtosis. Skewness is expected to disappear with diversification as funds with negative skewness are mixed with positively skewed ones so that, at the aggregate level, these individual effects are cancelled.[17] For the same reason, we expect diversification to reduce over-peak return and this way reduce the excess kurtosis.

Table 3 demonstrates the evolution of the skewness of mutual fund portfolios as a function of the underlying mutual funds. Previous results of our analysis proved that increasing number of mutual funds in portfolio can reduce volatility, while mean returns are not changed significantly. According to Lhabitant and Learned (2002) returns of mutual funds do not follow a normal distribution in time series and tend to demonstrate asymmetry. That is why, it is also important to analyze skewness and kurtosis. We expect skewness to be reduced and equal to zero with diversification, because funds with negative skewness are mixed with funds with positive skewness, and this expectation is true for Europe corporate bond and US corporate bond at the end of period. With respect to its initial value, we do not observe any significant change in skewness with increasing number of mutual funds in pre-crisis period for Europe Bonds, except Europe Government bond at the end of period that increases from negative (−0.11) to positive (0.81) when adding more funds in portfolio. We note change of sign of the skewness value from positive to negative and then vice-versa and then again, when adding more mutual funds in portfolios of US bonds in pre-crisis period. During the crisis, the coefficient is negative for US corporate bond and positive for US government bonds, however it drops systemically along with adding more funds in a portfolio. Skewness drops and is positive for US government bonds at the end of period. It is clearly seen that skewness variations are not uniform across different Equity styles. In majority of observations, when number of funds increases, the skewness increases and then drops again and then vice-versa. The sign is negative in all portfolio sizes in pre-crisis period for Europe Equity Small, Europe Equity Value, Europe Equity Growth, all crisis period and all post-crisis. We observe systematic negative increase of the skewness coefficient along with increasing number of funds only for Europe Equity Growth in crisis. We observe quite the same picture for

[17] Lhabitant, F. S., & Learned, M. (2002). Hedge fund diversification: How much is enough? *The Journal of Alternative Investments*, 5(3), 23–49.

Table 3 Impact of diversification—evolution of the skewness of a mutual fund portfolio as a function of the underlying mutual funds (Monthly Observations—Estimation Window 12 months)

Panel A—EUROPE BOND

	Number of Mutual Fund in Portfolio						
	Initial	*2*	*5*	*10*	*20*	*30*	*50*
29/12/2006							
Europe Corporate Bond	0.26	0.25	0.77	0.60	0.40	0.37	0.25
Europe Government Bond	0.11	0.41	0.36	0.34	0.30	0.25	0.27
28/11/2008							
Europe Corporate Bond	−0.80	−1.13	−1.14	−1.06	−1.23	−1.14	−1.05
Europe Government Bond	−1.60	−0.50	−0.59	−0.74	−0.72	−0.71	−0.67
31/12/2019							
Europe Corporate Bond	0.00	0.00	0.00	0.00	0.00	0.00	0.00
Europe Government Bond	−0.11	0.81	0.79	0.70	0.73	0.75	0.79

(continued)

Table 3 (continued)

Panel B—US BOND

	Number of Mutual Fund in Portfolio						
	Initial	*2*	*5*	*10*	*20*	*30*	*50*
29/12/2006							
US Corporate Bond	0.31	0.12	0.19	−0.14	−0.11	−0.36	−0.33
US Government Bond	0.25	−0.07	0.07	0.05	−0.07	0.02	0.04
28/11/2008							
US Corporate Bond	−2.21	−1.98	−1.92	−1.76	−1.55	−1.20	−1.34
US Government Bond	0.06	1.26	0.99	0.70	0.69	0.53	0.44
31/12/2019							
US Corporate Bond	0.00	0.00	0.00	0.00	0.00	0.00	0.00
US Government Bond	0.91	1.04	0.81	0.72	0.59	0.44	0.37

Panel C—EUROPE EQUITY

	Number of Mutual Fund in Portfolio						
	Initial	*2*	*5*	*10*	*20*	*30*	*50*
29/12/2006							
Europe Equity Large Cap	−0.08	−0.08	0.64	0.28	−0.08	−0.08	−0.09
Europe Equity Blend	−0.39	−0.70	0.28	0.15	0.15	0.42	0.15
Europe Equity Small	−0.61	−0.39	−0.15	−0.15	−0.22	−0.27	−0.29
Europe Equity Value	−0.54	−0.67	−0.53	−0.57	−0.48	−0.44	−0.48
Europe Equity Growth	−0.37	−0.34	−0.13	−0.28	−0.31	−0.30	−0.33
28/11/2008							
Europe Equity Large Cap	−0.94	−0.94	−0.89	−0.90	−0.92	−0.93	−0.94
Europe Equity Blend	−0.86	−0.88	−0.83	−0.83	−0.83	−0.82	−0.81
Europe Equity Small	−0.87	−0.77	−0.78	−0.80	−0.77	−0.83	−0.84
Europe Equity Value	−0.63	−0.79	−0.79	−0.85	−1.09	−1.11	−1.06
Europe Equity Growth	−0.73	−0.73	−0.75	−0.78	−0.85	−0.85	−1.03
31/12/2019							
Europe Equity Large Cap	−0.54	−0.54	−0.48	−0.49	−0.37	−0.36	−0.38
Europe Equity Blend	−0.66	−0.73	−0.41	−0.42	−0.40	−0.43	−0.34
Europe Equity Small	−0.61	−0.39	−0.15	−0.15	−0.22	−0.27	−0.29
Europe Equity Value	−0.54	−0.67	−0.53	−0.57	−0.48	−0.44	−0.48
Europe Equity Growth	−0.37	−0.34	−0.13	−0.28	−0.31	−0.30	−0.33

(continued)

Table 3 (continued)

Panel D—US EQUITY	*Number of Mutual Fund in Portfolio*						
	Initial	*2*	*5*	*10*	*20*	*30*	*50*
29/12/2006							
US Equity Large Cap	0.79	−0.04	−0.04	0.17	0.13	0.01	−0.02
US Equity Blend	−0.57	−0.69	−0.34	−0.66	−0.66	−0.65	−0.64
US Equity Small	−0.18	0.10	0.01	−0.04	−0.08	−0.10	−0.11
US Equity Value	−0.69	−0.32	−0.40	−0.44	−0.43	−0.46	−0.48
US Equity Growth	−0.90	−0.71	−0.44	−0.06	−0.10	−0.13	−0.09
28/11/2008							
US Equity Large Cap	−1.41	−0.74	−1.07	−0.76	−0.71	−0.69	−0.83
US Equity Blend	−0.44	−0.90	−0.94	−0.78	−0.85	−0.83	−0.87
US Equity Small	−0.65	−0.67	−0.43	−0.55	−0.59	−0.64	−0.66
US Equity Value	−0.80	−1.41	−1.41	−0.74	−0.70	−0.77	−0.72
US Equity Growth	−0.85	−0.99	−0.83	−0.94	−0.87	−0.89	−0.88
31/12/2019							
US Equity Large Cap	0.65	0.23	0.31	−0.01	−0.19	−0.18	−0.28
US Equity Blend	−0.78	0.50	0.04	−0.19	−0.28	−0.29	−0.37
US Equity Small	−0.18	0.10	0.01	−0.04	−0.08	−0.10	−0.11
US Equity Value	−0.69	−0.32	−0.40	−0.44	−0.43	−0.46	−0.48
US Equity Growth	−0.90	−0.71	−0.44	−0.06	−0.10	−0.13	−0.09

US Equities. The sign of skewness is negative in all portfolio sizes in pre-crises period for US Equity Blend, US Equity Value, US Equity Growth, all crisis period for all styles, and for US Equity Value and Growth styles in post-crisis. Systemic drop in skewness is seen US Equity Small (from 2 to 50 mutual funds) and US Equity Value with negative sign in pre-crisis period, US Equity Small and US Equity Value (negative sign) at the end of the period.

Table 4 shows the evolution of the Kurtosis of mutual fund portfolio as a function of the underlying mutual funds. We note changes of kurtosis to differ widely over time and across investment strategies and styles. We observe constant raise of the coefficient with increasing number of mutual funds in portfolio in Europe Government bond (pre-crisis). For other observations, kurtosis seem to raise up to 5 mutual funds in portfolio and then drop again, in all time periods. For US bonds, we observe high rise of coefficients in crisis times up to 6.10 b.p for US Corporate bond and 4.90 b.p for US Government bond. Interestingly, kurtosis demonstrates a tendency to increase when comparing with initial value and adding more funds in portfolio for US Corporate Bond (pre-crisis) from 1.96 b.p. to 2.60 b.p., for US Government bond (crisis) from 1.70 b.p. to 3.29 b.p., while there is a tendency to drop when comparing with initial value for US Corporate bond (crisis) from 6.89 b.p. to 4.94 b.p. For EU Equity pre-crisis, kurtosis remains almost at the same level with change of funds number, however, we observe a tendency for a little increase in Europe Equity Small. The values of coefficients are not changed dramatically when analysis for crisis time and end of period. Kurtosis systematically grows for Europe Equity Growth in crisis time, Europe Equity Large Cap and Europe Equity Value and has a tendency to drop for Europe Equity Growth at the end of period and when adding more mutual funds in portfolio. For US Equity group we do not see any dramatic change in values, however, in general, we observe kurtosis to grow slightly with increase number of funds in pre-crisis period.

3.5 *Downside Risk Statistics*

Since downside risk is of great concern to many investors, we have also examined the impact of mutual fund diversification on two commonly accepted downside risk measures, namely, the largest monthly loss and the value at risk (VaR). The largest monthly loss is the greatest decline in net asset value for a particular mutual fund for any one-month period over the

Table 4 Impact of diversification—Evolution of the kurtosis of a mutual fund portfolio as a function of the underlying mutual funds (Monthly Observations—Estimation Window 12 months)

Panel A—EUROPE BOND

	Number of Mutual Fund in Portfolio						
	Initial	*2*	*5*	*10*	*20*	*30*	*50*
29/12/2006							
Europe Corporate Bond	1.99	2.02	3.14	2.72	2.55	2.37	2.63
Europe Government Bond	2.05	1.91	2.03	2.04	2.09	2.14	2.31
28/11/2008							
Europe Corporate Bond	2.76	3.48	3.62	3.35	3.65	3.49	3.81
Europe Government Bond	5.26	2.35	2.57	2.87	2.82	2.87	2.79
31/12/2019							
Europe Corporate Bond	2.88	2.34	2.92	2.67	2.54	2.48	2.49
Europe Government Bond	5.43	3.48	3.45	3.13	3.27	3.20	3.17

Panel B—US BOND

	Number of Mutual Fund in Portfolio						
	Initial	*2*	*5*	*10*	*20*	*30*	*50*
29/12/2006							
US Corporate Bond	1.96	1.97	1.87	2.30	2.20	2.68	2.60
US Government Bond	2.20	1.89	2.11	2.21	2.31	2.25	2.20
28/11/2008							
US Corporate Bond	6.89	6.10	5.89	5.18	4.99	4.76	4.94
US Government Bond	1.70	4.90	4.27	4.22	4.36	3.60	3.29
31/12/2019							
US Corporate Bond	2.05	1.80	2.04	2.59	2.49	2.30	2.26
US Government Bond	2.65	2.87	2.39	2.33	2.65	2.59	2.48

Panel C—EUROPE EQUITY							
	Number of Mutual Fund in Portfolio						
	Initial	*2*	*5*	*10*	*20*	*30*	*50*
29/12/2006							
Europe Equity Large Cap	2.88	2.88	3.02	2.90	2.70	2.70	2.67
Europe Equity Blend	3.11	3.14	4.80	4.37	4.37	4.59	3.84
Europe Equity Small	2.11	2.11	2.16	2.14	2.37	2.39	2.38
Europe Equity Value	3.57	3.53	3.53	3.00	3.50	3.20	3.15
Europe Equity Growth	3.39	3.38	3.54	4.06	3.31	3.38	3.38
28/11/2008							
Europe Equity Large Cap	2.92	2.92	2.78	2.92	2.95	2.98	3.04
Europe Equity Blend	2.69	2.90	2.87	2.83	2.83	2.75	2.77
Europe Equity Small	2.76	2.57	2.60	2.69	2.76	2.83	2.89
Europe Equity Value	2.22	2.54	2.54	2.79	3.61	3.61	3.42
Europe Equity Growth	2.43	2.43	2.80	2.82	2.92	2.91	3.36
31/12/2019							
Europe Equity Large Cap	2.08	2.23	2.33	2.52	2.53	2.46	2.46
Europe Equity Blend	2.50	2.58	2.65	2.66	2.56	2.60	2.51
Europe Equity Small	2.58	2.56	2.19	2.09	2.21	2.20	2.17
Europe Equity Value	2.15	2.36	2.40	2.43	2.36	2.60	2.63
Europe Equity Growth	2.91	2.54	2.52	2.34	2.41	2.44	2.47

(continued)

Table 4 (continued)

Panel D—US EQUITY	*Number of Mutual Fund in Portfolio*						
	Initial	*2*	*5*	*10*	*20*	*30*	*50*
29/12/2006							
US Equity Large Cap	2.73	3.42	3.96	4.12	3.61	3.79	3.70
US Equity Blend	3.76	3.72	3.27	3.44	3.49	3.46	3.77
US Equity Small	2.81	2.53	2.72	2.79	3.23	3.15	3.07
US Equity Value	3.81	2.73	2.73	3.62	3.74	3.72	3.81
US Equity Growth	3.52	3.52	2.79	4.81	4.55	4.33	4.09
28/11/2008							
US Equity Large Cap	3.21	2.76	3.86	3.17	3.01	2.94	3.17
US Equity Blend	2.28	3.16	3.25	2.99	3.22	3.21	3.22
US Equity Small	2.83	3.14	2.79	2.74	2.81	2.89	2.85
US Equity Value	3.75	3.21	3.21	2.73	2.73	2.96	2.83
US Equity Growth	3.08	3.48	3.07	3.73	3.56	3.55	3.44
31/12/2019							
US Equity Large Cap	2.57	3.31	3.95	3.42	3.30	3.28	3.19
US Equity Blend	3.37	4.69	4.22	3.98	3.72	3.63	3.53
US Equity Small	2.93	3.13	3.24	2.97	2.90	2.94	2.87
US Equity Value	3.19	2.91	3.01	3.44	3.23	3.17	3.16
US Equity Growth	3.38	3.23	2.87	3.65	3.52	3.42	3.30

period considered. Value at Risk (VaR) has become the standard measure that financial analysts use to quantify market risk. VaR is defined as the maximum potential change in value of a portfolio of financial instruments with a given probability over a certain horizon[18] A standard value of probability, corresponding to so called "normal market conditions" may correspond, for example, to 95%.

Table 5 and Fig. 3a–c show evolution of the Worst Monthly Returns of a Mutual Fund Portfolio as a function of the underlying mutual funds. The worst returns and the lowest benefits from diversification are observed in financial crisis time for all assets. There is seen an obvious benefit from increasing number of funds in portfolio for Europe Bonds in pre-crisis and crisis periods, while there is not much change of the coefficient at the end of period. For US bonds, increasing number of funds in portfolio demonstrates a tendency to reduce worst monthly return in pre-crisis time, and it is very beneficial in crisis times especially for US Corporate bonds (from −23.63% initial value to −2.13% when 50 mutual funds in portfolio), while the coefficients are not affected dramatically at the end of period. For EU Equity, we also note significant improvements when increasing number of funds up to 50, especially for Europe Equity Small in pre-crisis (from −6.13 to −1.53%); Europe Equity Large Cap (from −23.85 to −9.97%), Europe Equity Small (from −25.57 to −14.42%), Europe Equity Value (from −23.92 to −12.61%) during the crisis. We do not see some dramatic changes in the end of period, however, there is a tendency for drop in worst returns. For US Equity in pre-crisis, we observe decrease in worst returns when increasing number of funds. The same is also true for crisis time with significant benefits for US Equity Small (from −20.69 to −7.56%), US Equity Value (from −17.37 to −8.61%), US Equity Growth (from −17.72 to −9.51%) and at the end of period.

Table 6 and Fig. 4 report the evolution of the empirical Value at Risk (VAR) of a Mutual Fund Portfolio as a function of the underlying mutual funds. For this measure for Europe Bond and US Bond, it seems like diversification works well in terms of downside risk reduction in pre-crisis and especially during the crisis (for EU Corporate Bonds VAR drops from −10.26 to −5.45%, for EU Government Bonds—from −14.60 to −5.43% and for US Corporate Bond from −19.76 to −1.99% in portfolio

[18] https://www.ecb.europa.eu/pub/pdf/scpwps/ecbwp075.pdf.

Table 5 Impact of diversification—evolution of the worst monthly return of a mutual fund portfolio as a function of the underlying mutual funds (Monthly Observations—Estimation Window 12 months)

Panel A—EUROPE BOND

	Number of Mutual Fund in Portfolio						
	Initial	*2*	*5*	*10*	*20*	*30*	*50*
29/12/2006							
Europe Corporate Bond	−1.75%	−0.71%	−0.48%	−0.55%	−0.69%	−0.78%	−0.72%
Europe Government Bond	−3.04%	−0.73%	−0.60%	−0.52%	−0.73%	−0.91%	−0.95%
28/11/2008							
Europe Corporate Bond	−9.53%	−4.77%	−4.05%	−4.74%	−5.04%	−5.53%	−5.37%
Europe Government Bond	−16.50%	−4.84%	−5.80%	−5.54%	−5.29%	−5.63%	−4.99%
31/12/2019							
Europe Corporate Bond	−1.75%	−1.86%	−1.66%	−1.69%	−1.76%	−1.74%	−1.75%
Europe Government Bond	−1.21%	−2.28%	−2.23%	−2.36%	−2.34%	−2.27%	−2.11%

Panel B—US BOND

	Number of Mutual Fund in Portfolio						
	Initial	*2*	*5*	*10*	*20*	*30*	*50*
29/12/2006							
US Corporate Bond	−1.73%	−0.99%	−0.43%	−0.39%	−0.28%	−0.26%	−0.32%
US Government Bond	−2.14%	−0.39%	−0.43%	−0.45%	−0.44%	−0.51%	−0.53%
28/11/2008							
US Corporate Bond	−23.63%	−11.25%	−4.85%	−3.25%	−2.59%	−1.83%	−2.13%
US Government Bond	−3.91%	−1.31%	−0.95%	−1.36%	−1.26%	−1.15%	−1.06%
31/12/2019							
US Corporate Bond	−0.69%	−0.21%	−0.17%	−0.39%	−0.45%	−0.46%	−0.49%
US Government Bond	−0.99%	−0.67%	−0.64%	−0.58%	−0.51%	−0.53%	−0.55%

(continued)

Table 5 (continued)

Panel C—EUROPE EQUITY

	Number of Mutual Fund in Portfolio						
	Initial	*2*	*5*	*10*	*20*	*30*	*50*
29/12/2006							
Europe Equity Large Cap	−3.12%	−1.56%	−1.04%	−1.51%	−1.44%	−1.06%	−0.81%
Europe Equity Blend	−0.81%	−1.44%	−1.47%	−1.74%	−1.35%	−1.23%	−1.33%
Europe Equity Small	−6.13%	−2.04%	−1.81%	−1.41%	−1.82%	−1.80%	−1.53%
Europe Equity Value	−3.40%	−2.71%	−1.63%	−1.51%	−1.45%	−1.26%	−1.45%
Europe Equity Growth	−1.47%	−1.58%	−2.38%	−1.81%	−1.66%	−1.25%	−1.04%
28/11/2008							
Europe Equity Large Cap	−23.85%	−23.85%	−16.08%	−17.56%	−14.15%	−11.84%	−9.97%
Europe Equity Blend	−7.48%	−10.73%	−14.09%	−15.52%	−12.07%	−11.39%	−11.20%
Europe Equity Small	−25.57%	−16.85%	−15.31%	−10.32%	−13.07%	−16.08%	−14.42%
Europe Equity Value	−23.92%	−16.99%	−10.19%	−12.42%	−12.03%	−11.04%	−12.61%
Europe Equity Growth	−6.53%	−6.64%	−13.09%	−13.42%	−12.82%	−11.39%	−10.76%
31/12/2019							
Europe Equity Large Cap	−3.20%	−4.08%	−4.59%	−4.96%	−5.09%	−5.01%	−4.89%
Europe Equity Blend	−6.70%	−7.32%	−6.24%	−6.34%	−5.79%	−5.67%	−5.33%
Europe Equity Small	−7.33%	−4.02%	−4.27%	−4.23%	−5.33%	−5.29%	−5.23%
Europe Equity Value	−7.26%	−7.45%	−7.27%	−7.62%	−5.81%	−6.02%	−6.23%
Europe Equity Growth	−3.86%	−2.11%	−2.71%	−3.35%	−3.63%	−4.08%	−4.31%

Panel D—US EQUITY

	Number of Mutual Fund in Portfolio						
	Initial	*2*	*5*	*10*	*20*	*30*	*50*
29/12/2006							
US Equity Large Cap	−2.22%	−2.67%	−2.76%	−2.33%	−1.26%	−1.25%	−1.05%
US Equity Blend	−2.80%	−1.71%	−1.02%	−1.90%	−1.68%	−1.64%	−1.43%
US Equity Small	−5.57%	−3.55%	−4.56%	−1.66%	−1.71%	−1.64%	−1.66%
US Equity Value	−2.23%	−0.74%	−0.55%	−0.61%	−1.15%	−1.06%	−1.23%
US Equity Growth	−7.64%	−1.27%	−1.68%	−1.44%	−1.41%	−1.24%	−1.30%
28/11/2008							
US Equity Large Cap	−7.01%	−9.83%	−11.95%	−11.45%	−8.09%	−8.25%	−8.64%
US Equity Blend	−13.99%	−14.92%	−10.82%	−12.42%	−10.71%	−10.68%	−10.04%
US Equity Small	−20.69%	−14.18%	−14.11%	−6.33%	−6.89%	−7.03%	−7.56%
US Equity Value	−17.37%	−2.34%	−1.75%	−5.86%	−7.56%	−7.71%	−8.61%
US Equity Growth	−17.72%	−9.43%	−10.40%	−11.21%	−9.84%	−9.57%	−9.51%
31/12/2019							
US Equity Large Cap	−2.88%	−3.93%	−3.95%	−4.06%	−4.48%	−4.32%	−4.22%
US Equity Blend	−8.20%	−1.93%	−2.62%	−2.97%	−3.49%	−3.64%	−3.63%
US Equity Small	−7.20%	−7.16%	−6.79%	−6.85%	−6.28%	−6.49%	−6.71%
US Equity Value	−6.58%	−6.17%	−6.97%	−6.43%	−6.22%	−6.07%	−6.45%
US Equity Growth	−5.51%	−3.05%	−2.83%	−2.60%	−2.74%	−2.61%	−2.67%

a

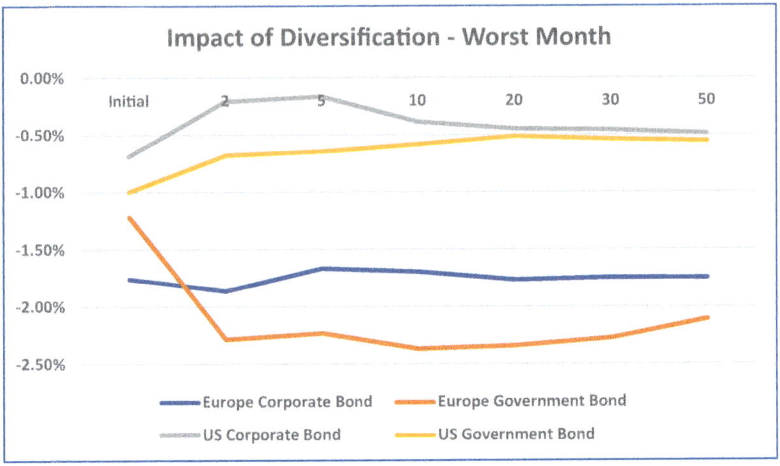

b

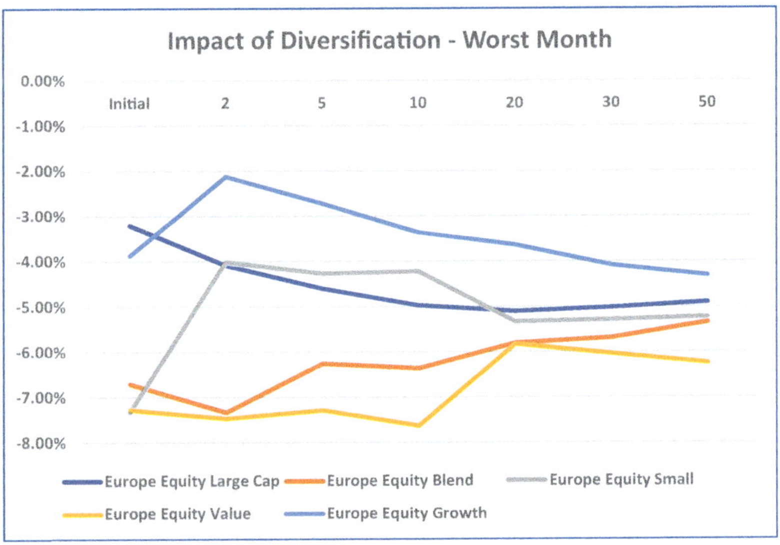

Fig. 3 Impact of diversification on the worst month of a fund of funds portfolio (Monthly Observations—Estimation Window 12 months—Last Observation 31-12-2019). **a** FIXED INCOME. **b** EQUITY EUROPE. **c** EQUITY US

c

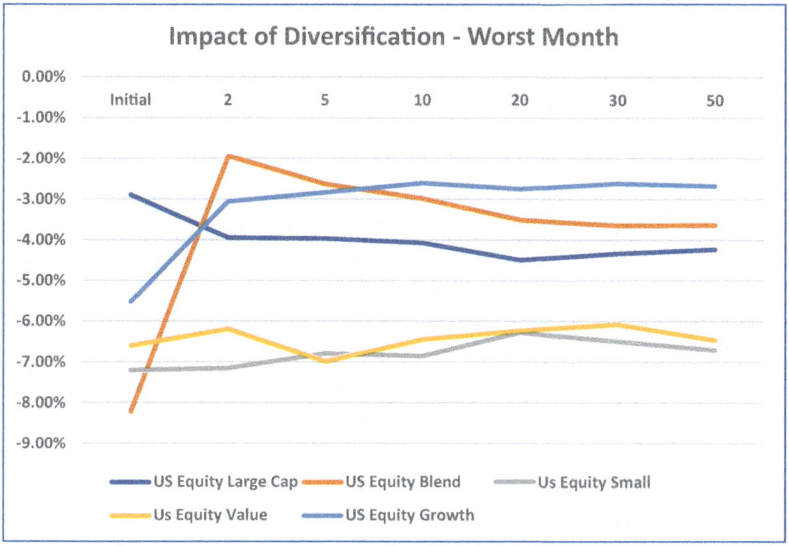

Fig. 3 (continued)

with 50 mutual funds). At the end of period there is only slight reduction of risk when testing for diversification for Europe Corporate Bond and US Corporate Bond, while value of risk tends to rise for Europe Government Bond. We observe benefits from diversification also when analyzing EU and US Equities, especially during the crisis, where for EU equities diversification is more beneficial in terms of size of assets and for US equities it is mostly true when considering investment style (value at risk drops for Europe Equity Large Cap from −25.11 to −10.45%, Europe Equity Small from −27.79 to −15.64%, Europe Equity Value from −27.77 to −13.25%, US Equity Small from −21.91 to −8.14%, US Equity Blend from −16.37 to −10.77%, US Equity Value from −17.29 to −9.50%, US Equity Growth from −18.18 to −10.15%). On the contrary, there are some groups of assets that demonstrate a tendency of VAR to rise along with increase of mutual funds in portfolio, mainly for EU Equities in terms of asset styles blend and growth in pre-crisis and during the crisis and at the end of period (Europe Equity Growth), while for US Equities we observe this slight reaction mainly for Large cap during the crisis.

Table 7 and Fig. 4a–c demonstrates the evolution of the Drawdown of

Table 6 Impact of diversification—evolution of the value at risk (VAR) of a mutual fund portfolio as a function of the underlying mutual funds (Monthly Observations—Estimation Window 12 months)

Panel A—EUROPE BOND

	Number of Mutual Fund in Portfolio						
	Initial	*2*	*5*	*10*	*20*	*30*	*50*
29/12/2006							
Europe Corporate Bond	−3.61%	−1.45%	−1.11%	−1.19%	−1.29%	−1.48%	−1.36%
Europe Government Bond	−4.62%	−1.56%	−1.26%	−1.07%	−1.44%	−1.69%	−1.66%
28/11/2008							
Europe Corporate Bond	−10.26%	−4.76%	−4.00%	−4.81%	−5.07%	−5.64%	−5.45%
Europe Government Bond	−14.60%	−5.65%	−6.50%	−6.01%	−5.75%	−6.09%	−5.43%
31/12/2019							
Europe Corporate Bond	−3.42%	−3.69%	−3.00%	−3.12%	−3.35%	−3.37%	−3.45%
Europe Government Bond	−1.21%	−3.80%	−3.81%	−3.91%	−3.87%	−3.85%	−3.73%

Panel B—US BOND

	Number of Mutual Fund in Portfolio						
	Initial	*2*	*5*	*10*	*20*	*30*	*50*
29/12/2006							
US Corporate Bond	−3.49%	−1.76%	−0.78%	−0.55%	−0.41%	−0.33%	−0.40%
US Government Bond	−3.45%	−0.61%	−0.61%	−0.64%	−0.60%	−0.78%	−0.85%
28/11/2008							
US Corporate Bond	−19.76%	−9.60%	−4.17%	−2.93%	−2.37%	−1.75%	−1.99%
US Government Bond	−5.83%	−2.56%	−1.60%	−1.93%	−1.87%	−1.81%	−1.71%
31/12/2019							
US Corporate Bond	−1.51%	−0.53%	−0.50%	−0.91%	−0.96%	−1.00%	−1.04%
US Government Bond	−2.71%	−1.88%	−1.73%	−1.37%	−1.11%	−1.17%	−1.18%

(continued)

Table 6 (continued)

Panel C—EUROPE EQUITY	*Number of Mutual Fund in Portfolio*						
	Initial	*2*	*5*	*10*	*20*	*30*	*50*
29/12/2006							
Europe Equity Large Cap	−4.15%	−2.07%	−2.71%	−2.94%	−2.21%	−1.62%	−1.23%
Europe Equity Blend	−1.04%	−1.62%	−2.41%	−2.67%	−2.08%	−2.35%	−2.23%
Europe Equity Small	−8.18%	−2.73%	−2.82%	−2.19%	−2.69%	−2.63%	−2.37%
Europe Equity Value	−3.80%	−2.82%	−1.69%	−1.85%	−1.87%	−1.66%	−1.87%
Europe Equity Growth	−1.76%	−1.87%	−3.71%	−2.86%	−2.56%	−2.23%	−1.86%
28/11/2008							
Europe Equity Large Cap	−25.11%	−25.11%	−17.39%	−18.71%	−14.97%	−12.52%	−10.45%
Europe Equity Blend	−8.16%	−11.40%	−14.97%	−16.60%	−12.91%	−12.28%	−12.07%
Europe Equity Small	−27.79%	−18.84%	−17.25%	−11.54%	−14.34%	−17.50%	−15.64%
Europe Equity Value	−27.77%	−18.79%	−11.27%	−13.30%	−12.55%	−11.53%	−13.25%
Europe Equity Growth	−7.44%	−7.55%	−14.16%	−14.51%	−13.64%	−12.17%	−11.41%
31/12/2019							
Europe Equity Large Cap	−4.71%	−5.50%	−6.06%	−6.21%	−6.51%	−6.57%	−6.36%
Europe Equity Blend	−8.03%	−8.51%	−7.75%	−7.78%	−7.29%	−7.07%	−6.91%
Europe Equity Small	−8.77%	−5.18%	−6.42%	−6.92%	−7.95%	−7.77%	−7.68%
Europe Equity Value	−9.50%	−9.05%	−8.88%	−9.19%	−7.31%	−7.57%	−7.70%
Europe Equity Growth	−4.50%	−2.80%	−4.18%	−4.91%	−5.12%	−5.72%	−5.89%

Panel D—US EQUITY

	Number of Mutual Fund in Portfolio						
	Initial	*2*	*5*	*10*	*20*	*30*	*50*
29/12/2006							
US Equity Large Cap	−4.64%	−3.16%	−3.13%	−2.75%	−1.59%	−1.55%	−1.35%
US Equity Blend	−2.90%	−1.73%	−1.24%	−2.11%	−1.83%	−1.79%	−1.61%
US Equity Small	−8.49%	−5.03%	−5.83%	−2.14%	−2.16%	−2.10%	−2.18%
US Equity Value	−2.14%	−1.55%	−1.16%	−0.73%	−1.21%	−1.11%	−1.30%
US Equity Growth	−7.71%	−1.29%	−1.99%	−1.62%	−1.55%	−1.39%	−1.46%
28/11/2008							
US Equity Large Cap	−7.61%	−11.23%	−12.41%	−12.77%	−9.10%	−9.35%	−9.53%
US Equity Blend	−16.37%	−15.51%	−11.13%	−13.31%	−11.45%	−11.43%	−10.77%
US Equity Small	−21.91%	−14.74%	−15.89%	−6.99%	−7.51%	−7.57%	−8.14%
US Equity Value	−17.29%	−2.54%	−1.90%	−6.58%	−8.38%	−8.47%	−9.50%
US Equity Growth	−18.18%	−9.38%	−10.99%	−11.64%	−10.40%	−10.16%	−10.15%
31/12/2019							
US Equity Large Cap	−6.28%	−5.66%	−6.51%	−5.97%	−5.82%	−5.63%	−5.34%
US Equity Blend	−8.53%	−2.80%	−3.22%	−3.43%	−4.09%	−4.29%	−4.17%
US Equity Small	−9.38%	−9.88%	−9.07%	−9.43%	−8.59%	−8.66%	−8.94%
US Equity Value	−7.11%	−7.87%	−8.40%	−7.21%	−7.17%	−7.02%	−7.50%
US Equity Growth	−5.59%	−3.26%	−3.49%	−3.72%	−3.76%	−3.57%	−3.74%

a

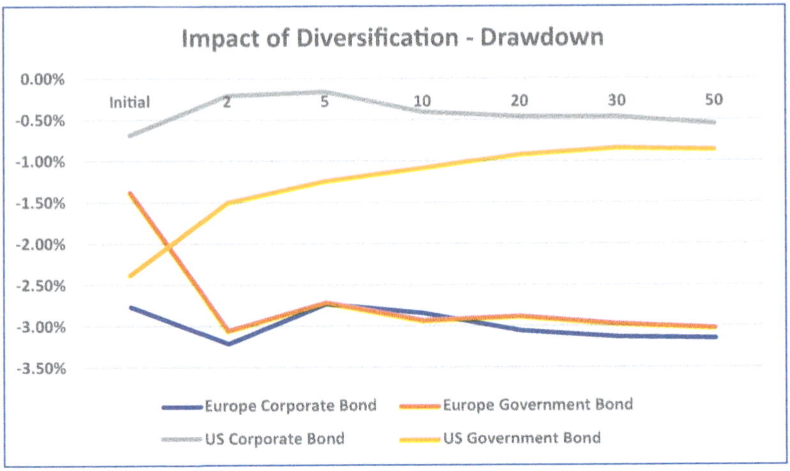

b

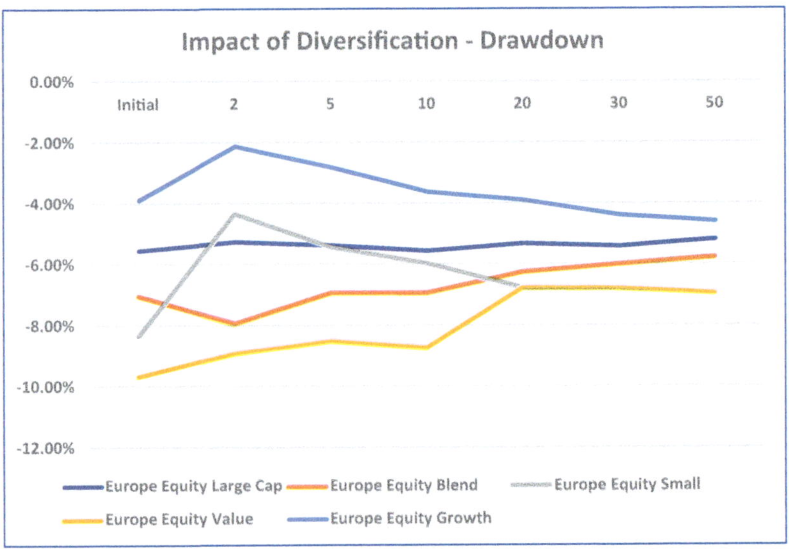

Fig. 4 Impact of diversification on the drawdown of a fund of funds portfolio (Monthly Observations—Estimation Window 12 months—Last Observation 31-12-2019). **a** FIXED INCOME. **b** EQUITY EUROPE. **c** EQUITY US

c

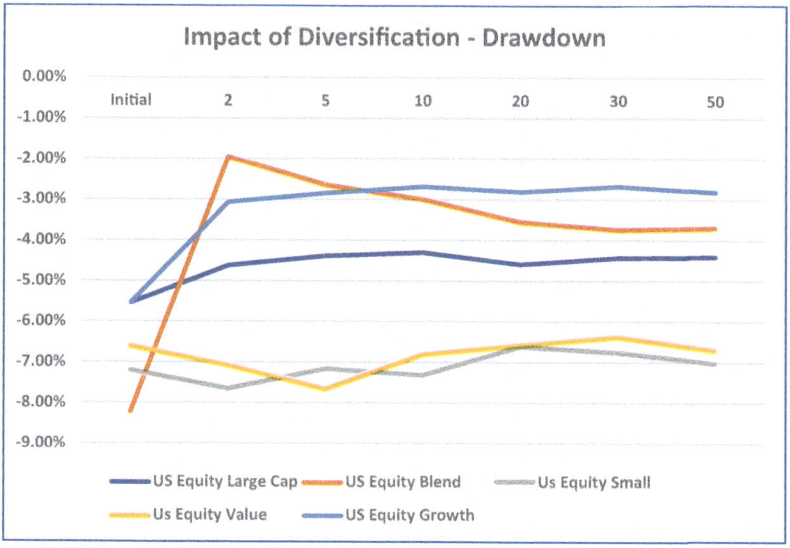

Fig. 4 (continued)

a Mutual Fund Portfolio as a function of the underlying mutual funds. The maximum drawdown is the biggest percentage- losing period ("peak to valley") experienced by a particular fund, regardless of whether or not the drawdown consisted of consecutive months of negative performance. It corresponds to the loss that an investor would experience buying shares at the highest net asset value and selling them at the lowest net asset value over a period. It looks like the effect of diversification is very beneficial for EU and US bond asset class with notable effect during the crisis (Drawdown for EU corporate bonds is from −22.20 to −11.80%, for EU government bond—from −29.61 to −11.28%, for US corporate bond—from −42.30 to −3.88%, and for US government bond—from −10.68 to −1.65%). However, the loss measure even slightly increases with diversification for EU corporate Bond and EU government Bond. We also observe positive benefits from diversification for drawdown of mutual fund portfolio for both EU and US equities in all time periods, except opposite results for EU Equity Blend in pre-crisis, both EU Equity Blend and EU Equity Growth during the crisis, and EU Equity Growth at the

Table 7 Impact of diversification—evolution of the drawdown of a mutual fund portfolio as a function of the underlying mutual funds (Monthly Observations—Estimation Window 12 months)

Panel A—EUROPE BOND

	Number of Mutual Fund in Portfolio						
	Initial	*2*	*5*	*10*	*20*	*30*	*50*
29/12/2006							
Europe Corporate Bond	−1.75%	−1.71%	−0.48%	−0.55%	−0.69%	−0.79%	−0.72%
Europe Government Bond	−3.46%	−1.52%	−0.76%	−0.61%	−0.80%	−0.96%	−0.98%
28/11/2008							
Europe Corporate Bond	−22.20%	−10.24%	−8.76%	−10.41%	−10.88%	−12.32%	−11.80%
Europe Government Bond	−29.61%	−11.85%	−13.65%	−12.67%	−12.16%	−12.70%	−11.28%
31/12/2019							
Europe Corporate Bond	−2.76%	−3.21%	−2.73%	−2.84%	−3.05%	−3.13%	−2.15%
Europe Government Bond	−1.37%	−3.05%	−2.71%	−2.92%	−2.88%	−2.97%	−2.02%

Panel B—US BOND

	Number of Mutual Fund in Portfolio						
	Initial	*2*	*5*	*10*	*20*	*30*	*50*
29/12/2006							
US Corporate Bond	−1.73%	−0.99%	−0.52%	−0.45%	−0.34%	−0.35%	−0.43%
US Government Bond	−2.19%	−0.65%	−0.86%	−0.74%	−0.67%	−0.69%	−0.74%
28/11/2008							
US Corporate Bond	−42.30%	−20.41%	−8.72%	−5.98%	−4.58%	−3.40%	−3.88%
US Government Bond	−10.68%	−2.10%	−1.52%	−2.37%	−2.06%	−1.80%	−1.65%
31/12/2019							
US Corporate Bond	−0.69%	−0.21%	−0.17%	−0.41%	−0.47%	−0.47%	−0.35%
US Government Bond	−2.37%	−1.48%	−1.23%	−1.07%	−0.91%	−0.83%	−0.85%

(continued)

Table 7 (continued)

Panel C—EUROPE EQUITY

	Number of Mutual Fund in Portfolio						
	Initial	*2*	*5*	*10*	*20*	*30*	*50*
29/12/2006							
Europe Equity Large Cap	−3.34%	−1.67%	−1.11%	−1.57%	−1.47%	−1.08%	−0.83%
Europe Equity Blend	−0.96%	−1.55%	−1.54%	−1.83%	−1.42%	−1.27%	−1.44%
Europe Equity Small	−11.15%	−3.72%	−3.05%	−2.48%	−3.14%	−2.90%	−2.48%
Europe Equity Value	−3.40%	−2.85%	−1.71%	−1.88%	−1.67%	−1.42%	−1.65%
Europe Equity Growth	−2.10%	−2.21%	−2.85%	−2.23%	−2.11%	−1.55%	−1.29%
28/11/2008							
Europe Equity Large Cap	−70.06%	−70.06%	−47.00%	−51.33%	−40.70%	−33.63%	−27.62%
Europe Equity Blend	−20.84%	−31.84%	−41.49%	−45.43%	−35.34%	−33.75%	−33.15%
Europe Equity Small	−69.64%	−47.67%	−42.75%	−28.58%	−36.44%	−43.25%	−38.96%
Europe Equity Value	−70.14%	−47.95%	−28.77%	−35.42%	−33.69%	−30.95%	−35.37%
Europe Equity Growth	−21.82%	−21.93%	−38.09%	−37.40%	−35.63%	−31.11%	−29.01%
31/12/2019							
Europe Equity Large Cap	−5.53%	−5.25%	−5.37%	−5.55%	−5.31%	−5.40%	−5.17%
Europe Equity Blend	−7.01%	−7.90%	−6.90%	−6.91%	−6.23%	−5.98%	−5.75%
Europe Equity Small	−8.35%	−4.36%	−5.45%	−5.98%	−6.78%	−6.79%	−6.90%
Europe Equity Value	−9.65%	−8.88%	−8.47%	−8.69%	−6.74%	−6.76%	−6.91%
Europe Equity Growth	−3.86%	−2.11%	−2.80%	−3.61%	−3.88%	−4.37%	−4.58%

Panel D—US EQUITY

	Number of Mutual Fund in Portfolio						
	Initial	*2*	*5*	*10*	*20*	*30*	*50*
29/12/2006							
US Equity Large Cap	−3.83%	−3.36%	−3.38%	−3.44%	−1.88%	−1.83%	−1.53%
US Equity Blend	−2.92%	−1.96%	−1.18%	−2.19%	−1.88%	−1.85%	−1.74%
US Equity Small	−10.93%	−6.76%	−9.00%	−3.16%	−2.99%	−2.82%	−2.91%
US Equity Value	−2.23%	−1.28%	−0.96%	−0.72%	−1.33%	−1.20%	−1.37%
US Equity Growth	−9.65%	−1.61%	−2.82%	−1.83%	−1.82%	−1.62%	−1.70%
28/11/2008							
US Equity Large Cap	−36.89%	−34.48%	−25.89%	−28.97%	−21.36%	−22.07%	−22.75%
US Equity Blend	−45.99%	−39.08%	−28.46%	−33.94%	−28.81%	−28.67%	−26.85%
US Equity Small	−52.31%	−32.92%	−36.82%	−15.68%	−16.86%	−16.80%	−18.08%
US Equity Value	−42.13%	−5.63%	−4.22%	−16.93%	−21.47%	−21.18%	−23.56%
US Equity Growth	−44.23%	−22.47%	−25.88%	−26.86%	−23.96%	−23.06%	−23.55%
31/12/2019							
US Equity Large Cap	−5.52%	−4.60%	−4.36%	−4.28%	−4.56%	−4.40%	−4.38%
US Equity Blend	−8.20%	−1.93%	−2.62%	−2.97%	−3.52%	−3.71%	−3.66%
US Equity Small	−7.20%	−7.66%	−7.17%	−7.32%	−6.62%	−6.77%	−7.02%
US Equity Value	−6.58%	−7.05%	−7.63%	−6.78%	−6.55%	−6.34%	−6.67%
US Equity Growth	−5.51%	−3.05%	−2.83%	−2.66%	−2.79%	−2.65%	−2.80%

end of period. However, we observe that most of the diversification benefits are obtained with a number of funds that varies between 5 and 10, depending on the strategy.

All in all, these Downside risk measures give similar answer: diversification seems to work well in terms of downside-risk reduction, but most of the diversification benefits are obtained with about 10 or 20 funds. Adding more funds still provides benefits, but the gains could seem marginal compared to the drawbacks of managing the enlarged portfolio.

3.6 Correlation Statistics

Finally, the last statistics we examined is correlation. We should question any conclusion drawn from an asset allocation that would assume constant correlations or rely on the stability of historical estimates of correlation coefficients. According to the same approach performed for the previous statistical measures, we estimate our correlation patterns by considering different financial market cycles. On the one hand, the mutual fund industry provides a wide range of strategies based on different risk factors both in terms of asset class, geographic focus and management style. On the other hand, these investors prefer to take a diversified approach and allocate their capital in more than one mutual fund even when they invest in a certain asset type. It is, therefore, essential to examine the impact of number of funds in portfolio on its correlation attributes with two very common stock indices, represented, hereafter, by the S&P 500 (for US geographical focus) and Eurostoxx 600 (for European geographical focus).

Table 8 summarizes our findings for evolution of correlation with Bond and Equity Sector of a Mutual Fund Portfolio as a function of the underlying mutual funds. For EU Bonds, it appears that in its absolute value, negative correlation in pre-crisis period tends to decrease, while positive correlation rises with increase of number of funds for EU bonds during the crisis and at the end of period, except for EU Government bonds during the crisis (the coefficient drops from 50.21 to 32.56% when having 50 funds in portfolio). For US bonds, in general, there is a tendency of correlation to grow together with number of funds except for US Corporate and US Government Bonds during the crisis and US Government Bond at the end of period. We observe positive coefficient of correlation almost across all time periods and different portfolio sizes for EU and US Equities. In general, diversification within styles leads to slight decrease in

Table 8 Impact of diversification—evolution of the correlation with the equity sector (S&P500 or Eurostoxx 600) of a mutual fund portfolio as a function of the underlying mutual funds (Monthly Observations—Estimation Window 12 months)

Panel A—EUROPE BOND

	Number of Mutual Fund in Portfolio						
	Initial	*2*	*5*	*10*	*20*	*30*	*50*
29/12/2006							
Europe Corporate Bond	−7.89%	−5.43%	−7.97%	−5.95%	−5.22%	−5.54%	−5.98%
Europe Government Bond	−26.23%	−13.16%	−10.42%	−8.84%	−8.09%	−7.33%	−8.30%
28/11/2008							
Europe Corporate Bond	38.05%	47.98%	51.87%	48.03%	53.07%	52.72%	50.66%
Europe Government Bond	50.21%	27.98%	31.62%	35.17%	34.23%	34.10%	32.56%
31/12/2019							
Europe Corporate Bond	46.78%	55.59%	50.33%	53.05%	53.68%	53.39%	53.49%
Europe Government Bond	10.77%	28.50%	27.47%	32.54%	31.86%	34.43%	35.58%

(continued)

Table 8 (continued)

Panel B—US BOND

	Number of Mutual Fund in Portfolio						
	Initial	*2*	*5*	*10*	*20*	*30*	*50*
29/12/2006							
US Corporate Bond	−2.36%	16.04%	19.23%	25.36%	30.50%	31.47%	29.81%
US Government Bond	12.18%	24.01%	30.54%	24.09%	26.76%	18.19%	17.49%
28/11/2008							
US Corporate Bond	70.38%	50.97%	50.69%	59.15%	55.29%	47.54%	50.67%
US Government Bond	−18.40%	−23.19%	−16.65%	−4.05%	−6.05%	−4.98%	−0.92%
31/12/2019							
US Corporate Bond	14.67%	5.01%	4.44%	15.52%	13.27%	11.42%	12.11%
US Government Bond	−52.93%	−54.07%	−48.35%	−36.38%	−38.68%	−23.01%	−15.47%

Panel C—EUROPE EQUITY

	Number of Mutual Fund in Portfolio						
	Initial	*2*	*5*	*10*	*20*	*30*	*50*
29/12/2006							
Europe Equity Large Cap	53.62%	53.62%	50.41%	53.02%	56.07%	56.07%	55.62%
Europe Equity Blend	56.12%	63.26%	50.47%	51.72%	51.72%	45.63%	50.89%
Europe Equity Small	54.63%	54.63%	27.37%	38.18%	43.52%	41.50%	43.57%
Europe Equity Value	58.73%	70.45%	70.45%	63.38%	55.91%	56.65%	57.14%
Europe Equity Growth	60.34%	60.23%	47.83%	43.27%	48.22%	44.56%	44.56%
28/11/2008							
Europe Equity Large Cap	90.22%	90.22%	88.90%	89.82%	89.17%	89.06%	88.76%
Europe Equity Blend	88.28%	91.55%	90.01%	89.59%	89.59%	88.34%	88.38%
Europe Equity Small	81.82%	82.38%	80.73%	81.49%	81.60%	82.41%	82.51%
Europe Equity Value	86.15%	86.65%	86.65%	89.36%	83.82%	80.09%	82.03%
Europe Equity Growth	83.78%	83.67%	85.33%	86.50%	86.53%	82.72%	78.38%
31/12/2019							
Europe Equity Large Cap	54.36%	71.42%	78.21%	82.14%	86.78%	87.49%	86.86%
Europe Equity Blend	91.23%	90.61%	86.60%	85.80%	86.42%	86.58%	86.54%
Europe Equity Small	90.47%	91.44%	86.38%	82.64%	82.76%	84.57%	83.63%
Europe Equity Value	86.52%	84.37%	80.91%	82.60%	83.23%	81.05%	82.52%
Europe Equity Growth	92.95%	90.10%	88.82%	87.71%	87.00%	83.71%	83.99%

(continued)

Table 8 (continued)

Panel D—US EQUITY

	Number of Mutual Fund in Portfolio						
	Initial	*2*	*5*	*10*	*20*	*30*	*50*
29/12/2006							
US Equity Large Cap	35.60%	48.98%	51.80%	55.58%	59.92%	61.43%	64.81%
US Equity Blend	89.98%	78.71%	77.61%	76.90%	76.04%	76.63%	76.76%
US Equity Small	49.21%	57.12%	62.47%	58.55%	56.27%	57.88%	58.16%
US Equity Value	71.95%	35.60%	35.60%	59.49%	70.33%	71.96%	74.41%
US Equity Growth	70.42%	70.42%	74.99%	55.63%	61.34%	64.08%	64.21%
28/11/2008							
US Equity Large Cap	−14.85%	66.02%	69.20%	78.97%	84.75%	85.10%	86.35%
US Equity Blend	97.79%	85.24%	87.41%	90.97%	89.76%	89.99%	89.57%
US Equity Small	97.35%	96.57%	95.47%	94.82%	94.48%	94.48%	94.80%
US Equity Value	97.94%	−14.85%	−14.85%	77.76%	85.25%	85.48%	87.87%
US Equity Growth	99.25%	97.72%	95.79%	86.30%	87.37%	87.02%	88.16%
31/12/2019							
US Equity Large Cap	87.69%	87.10%	79.49%	82.41%	86.31%	86.48%	87.75%
US Equity Blend	95.97%	77.68%	80.70%	82.47%	85.96%	84.80%	85.48%
US Equity Small	93.95%	88.95%	91.25%	88.21%	87.94%	88.73%	88.95%
US Equity Value	98.14%	92.77%	88.05%	89.99%	88.76%	88.94%	89.25%
US Equity Growth	94.54%	96.30%	90.77%	80.46%	82.56%	83.35%	84.18%

absolute values of correlation for Europe Equities in most of the period, except of some increase of values for EU Equity Large Caps in pre-crisis, EU Equity Blend during the crisis, EU Equity Large Caps at the end of period. Correlation when diversifying across all styles of US Equities tend to decrease during the crisis (except the opposite behavior for US Equity Large with drastic increase of correlation value from −14.85 to 86.35%) and in the end of period. However, diversification benefits to increase of correlation in pre-crisis period for majority of asset styles of US Equities.

According to previous literature, our empirical findings tend to demonstrate that diversification works well in a mean variance space. That is, increasing the number of mutual funds in a mutual fund portfolio decreases the portfolio's volatility, while not dramatically lowering its average return level. Downside risk statistics (such as maximum monthly loss, maximum drawdown or value at risk) are also on average reduced in larger-size[19] mutual fund portfolios. This seems to validate the existence of funds of funds as useful investment vehicles. However, when one goes beyond the mean–variance framework and considers additional factors such as skewness and kurtosis, diversification is far from being a free lunch considering that diversification may even generate negative skewness.

Furthermore, from the graphs and tables we note that the reduction of the portfolio statistics is not exactly linear since, due to the random choice of funds that make up the portfolio, it may happen that the first fund selected, which also corresponds to the first portfolio (Initial or $N = 1$ in the charts and tables) may have better performance measures than subsequent portfolio combinations. Nevertheless, on average, except for the correlation, there is on average a linear reduction in portfolio statistics.

3.7 Measures of Concentration[20]

We introduce alternative measures of concentration to capture the extent of diversification in individual investors' portfolios. The first is a "crude" measure of diversification and it corresponds to a simple count of the

[19] We remember that here larger-size is intended for larger number of funds in portfolio.

[20] In this section, we report alternative measures of concentration with respect to what we introduce in the chapter of ACTIVE MANAGEMENT.

number of fund or stock holdings in the portfolio as:

$$N\ Stocks = N \tag{1}$$

This diversification measure is commonly used but it often overstates the level of diversification (Blume et al., 1974). This measure has also been used in prior work including Ivković et al. (2008). The second is the Security Concentration Index (SCI) from Sapp and Yan (2008):

$$SCI = \sum_{i=1}^{N} (w_{f,i} - w_{m,i})^2 \tag{2}$$

where $w_{f,i}$ is the weight on stock i in the portfolio of fund f, $w_{m,i}$ is weight on stock i in the market portfolio, and N is the number of stocks held by the fund. The third is the industry Concentration Index (ICI) from Kacperczyk et al. (2005):

$$ICI = \sum_{j=1}^{N} (x_{f,j} - x_{m,j})^2 \tag{3}$$

where $x_{f,j}$ is the proportion of the portfolio of fund f invested in industry j, $x_{m,j}$ is industry j's proportion in the market portfolio, and the industries are usually grouped into ten general categories (according to the GICS Sector Definition).[21] As ICI and SCI increase and the number of holdings decreases, fund concentration increases.

The fourth measure is the normalized portfolio variance (NV), which is obtained by dividing the portfolio variance by the average variance of stocks in the portfolio (Goetzmann & Kumar, 2008):

$$NV = \frac{\sigma_p^2}{\bar{\sigma}^2} \tag{4}$$

The covariance matrix is estimated using the past five years of monthly returns data. The NV measure indicates that portfolio variance can be reduced by increasing the number of stocks in the portfolio or by a

[21] https://www.msci.com/gics.

proper selection of stocks such that the average covariance (or correlation) among stocks in the portfolio is lower.[22] Variance reduction through active and specific stock picking activity reflects "management skill" in portfolio composition, while addition of stocks in the portfolio without lowering the average portfolio correlation is likely to act just according to the "portfolio breadth" dimension, without stimulating a positive effect on the overall portfolio riskiness (Goetzmann et al., 2005).

In the spirit of the Active share measure, the diversification level of a portfolio can also be measured as its deviation from the market portfolio (Blume & Friend, 1975). The weight of each security in the market portfolio could be very small. Thus, the diversification measure can be approximated as the sum of squared portfolio weights (SSPW):

$$SSPW = \sum_{i=1}^{N} (\omega_i - \omega_m)^2 = \sum_{i=1}^{N} \left(\omega_i - \frac{1}{N_m} \right)^2 \approx \sum_{i=1}^{N} \omega_i^2 \tag{5}$$

where N is the number of securities held by the investor, N_m is the number of stocks in the market portfolio, ω_i is the portfolio weight assigned to stock t in the investor portfolio, and ω_m is the weight assigned to a stock in the market portfolio ($\omega_m = 1/N_m$). A lower value of SSPW reflects a higher level of diversification.

Overall, when considering these metrics, it is important to note that U.S. Securities and Exchange Commission (SEC) rules allow mutual funds to disclose their holdings with a 60-day delay. As a result, there is a significant lag between when a concentration increase occurs and when investors observe that increase (Fulkerson & Riley, 2019).[23]

A difference does exist between diversification by investment style and diversification by fund managers. The first is based on choosing different asset types (e.g., Equity vs. Fixed Income Mutual funds) within a broad-spectrum investable universe. The latter is based on the choice within the same category (e.g., European Equity large-cap), with respect to different fund managers. Clearly, the benefit of increasing managers within a strategy is a function of the homogeneity or heterogeneity of the sample from which the managers are drawn. Style diversification (diversification

[22] Goetzmann, W. N., & Kumar, A. (2008). Equity portfolio diversification. *Review of Finance, 12*(3), 433–463.

[23] See Final Rule: Shareholder Reports and Quarterly Portfolio Disclosure of Registered Management Investment Companies https://www.sec.gov/rules/final/33-8393.htm.

by investment style) obviously provides better opportunities for diversification than just diversification by fund managers. In this regard, it seems that information on investment methods reported by fund managers should also be used in the process of portfolio construction, to increase the overall portfolio diversification.

In terms of level of diversification of optimal portfolios,[24] the graph of the efficient frontier does not reveal at first sight the level of potential risk reduction offered by a specific optimal portfolio on the frontier. This helpful information can be obtained by calculating two closely interrelated measures. The first is the diversification ratio proposed by Choueifaty and Coignard (2008).[25] The diversification ratio (DIVR),[26] is given by the ratio between the weighted average of the volatilities of the assets in a portfolio and the actual standard deviation of the overall portfolio as follows:

$$DIVR = \frac{\sum_{i=1}^{n} \sigma_i w_i}{\sigma_p} = \frac{\sum_{i=1}^{n} \sigma_i w_i}{\sqrt{\sum_{i=1}^{n} \sigma_i^2 w_i^2 + \sum_{i=1}^{n} \sum_{j=1}^{n} w_i w_j \sigma_{ij}}} \quad (6)$$

where:
σ_p = portfolio risk;
w_i = weight of asset i in the portfolio;
σ_{ij} = covariance between asset i and asset j.

The second useful metric is the ($DIVB$) benefit of diversification (Basile & Ferrari, 2016)[27] representing a percentage expressing by how much the overall portfolio risk is lower than the weighted average of the volatilities of the N asset in the portfolio:

$$DIVB = \frac{\sum_{i=1}^{n} \sigma_i w_i - \sigma_p}{\sum_{i=1}^{n} \sigma_i w_i}$$

[24] For an extensive literature on portfolio risk contribution please see: Basile, I., & Ferrari, P. (Eds.). (2016). *Asset management and institutional investors*. Springer International Publishing.

[25] Choueifaty, Y., & Coignard, Y. (2008). Toward maximum diversification. *The Journal of Portfolio Management, 35*(1), 40–51.

[26] The diversification ratio is a value which, when applied to long only portfolios must always be strictly greater than 1, except in the case of a single-asset class portfolio.

[27] See Footnote Number 310.

$$= \frac{\sum_{i=1}^{n} \sigma_i w_i - \sqrt{\sum_{i=1}^{n} \sigma_i^2 w_i^2 + \sum_{i=1}^{n} \sum_{j=1}^{n} w_i w_j \sigma_{ij}}}{\sum_{i=1}^{n} \sigma_i w_i} \quad (7)$$

Even if the expressions are different, the benefits of diversification and diversification ratios can be explained in a similar way, because in both cases, a higher/lower value indicates that a given portfolio allocation will lead to a more/less efficient diversification among assets.

If we then wanted to know what proportion of the total portfolio risk can be attributed to each of its components, we should consider that each asset contribution is surely influenced by the weight associated to asset *i* in the portfolio, but it is also directly related to both its volatility and its correlation pattern with other asset classes. To this end, it gets very useful to take the inspiration from the so-called risk decomposition tools, as proposed in Scherer (2015)[28] and in Qian (2006).[29] Authors offered several metrics. One is called marginal risk MR_i, or marginal risk contribution. It represents the change in total portfolio risk caused by infinitely small changes in the weight of asset *i*. This value is obtained by calculating the first-order partial derivative of the risk function with respect to a single asset w_i,[30] as follows:

$$MR_i = \frac{\partial \sigma_p}{\partial w_i} = \frac{\partial_i^2 w_i^2 + \sum_{i=1}^{n} \sigma_{ij} w_i}{\sigma_p} \quad (8)$$

Another measure of risk contribution is the total risk contribution (TRC_i) or component risk, which represents the portion of total portfolio risk that can be assigned to *i*. The total risk contribution (TRC_i) is obtained by multiplying straight away the weight assigned to *i* (w_i) by its marginal risk (MR_i), as shown below in (9):

$$TRC_i = w_i \,.\, MR_i = w_i \,.\frac{\partial \sigma_p}{\partial w_i} = w_i \,.\frac{\partial_i^2 w_i^2 + \sum_{i=1}^{n} \sigma_{ij} w_i}{\sigma_p} \quad (9)$$

[28] Scherer, B. (2015). *Portfolio construction and risk budgeting* (5th ed.). London: Risk Books.

[29] Qian, E. (2006). On the financial interpretation of risk contributions: Risk budgets do add up. On the Financial Interpretation of Risk Contribution: Risk Budgets Do Add Up. *Journal of Investment Management, 4*(4).

[30] We should note that the number of first order partial derivatives that can be calculated by 8 is equal to the number, N, of asset classes.

Interestingly enough, by summing the TRC_i over all the assets, the overall portfolio risk is obtained:

$$\sigma_p = \sum_{i=1}^{n} TRC_i = \sum_{i=1}^{n} w_i \cdot \frac{\partial \sigma_p}{\partial w_i} \tag{10}$$

3.8 *Mean–Variance Diversification*[31]

To get a precise answer to the question of how many assets should be included in a diversified portfolio, investors should conduct a marginal analysis of costs and benefits associated with diversified development. This is exactly what Markowitz did, when he developed modern portfolio theory. Albeit intuitive for us all, Harry Markowitz (1952b, 1959) wrote the first paper on the benefits of diversification for an investor.[32] Under the assumption that investors are primarily concerned with two elements in their portfolios—risk and return—Markowitz suggested a quadratic programming algorithm to optimize the combination of assets based on their mean rates of return and standard deviations (Lhabitant & Vicin, 2004). The purpose is to summarize the risk assets based on the correlation between the risk assets to minimize the overall risk. The key to this process is that the risk of portfolio is less than the sum of risks of its individual assets.

Markowitz's initial assumption was that risk-averse, mean-variance utility agents were concerned with only two elements of their portfolios—the expected return, as measured by the mean rate of return, and the risk, as quantified by the standard deviation or variance of the mean rate of return (Lhabitant & Learned, 2002). When risky assets are aggregated, their correlation often determines the majority of the total risk rather than individual volatilities.[33] Therefore, the total risk of a carefully constructed investment portfolio should be less than the sum of the risks

[31] Statman, M. (2004). The diversification puzzle. *Financial Analysts Journal, 60*(4), 44–53.

[32] Lhabitant, F. S., & Vicin, M. L. D. P. (2004). Finding the sweet spot of hedge fund diversification. *Journal of Financial Transformation, 10*, 31–39.

[33] Lhabitant, F. S., & Learned, M. (2002). Hedge fund diversification: How much is enough? *The Journal of Alternative Investments*, 5(3), 23–49.

of the various components in the investment portfolio. Markowitz, therefore, proposed a quadratic programming algorithm to calculate the best combination of assets.

Considering the lack of computing power in the 1950s, Markowitz's method was considered a hard but useless exercise. However, his statement directly contributed to the later Capital Asset Pricing Model (CAPM) of Sharpe (1964), Lintner (1965) and Mossin (1966). Their respective work clearly divides the risk into two parts. The systematic part is the part that is inevitable once investors invest in a specific asset class, while the non-systematic or specific part can be reduced by creating a mixed asset portfolio, or even eliminated at the portfolio level.

In mean–variance portfolio theory, the optimal level of diversification is determined by marginal analysis; that is, diversification should be increased as long as its marginal benefits exceed its marginal costs (Statman, 2004). The benefits of diversification in mean–variance portfolio theory is in the reduction of risk; the costs are transaction and holding costs.[34] Risk is measured by the standard deviation of portfolio returns. Declining correlations increase the marginal benefits of diversification.

Table 9 reports the average inter- and intra-category correlations among sample of Mutual funds, both equity and bond type, computed from the full correlation matrix over the period 2006–2019. We consider the influence of Global Financial Crisis, and we split the overall period in two samples, corresponding to Non-Crisis period and Crisis Period. In Panel A, average inter- and intra-category correlations are provided for the NON-CRISIS PERIOD, ranging from December 2006 to June 2007, and from January 2011 to December 2019. Panel B reports average correlations for the CRISIS PERIOD, ranging from June 2007 to December 2010. Overall, correlations among mutual funds are strongly influenced by both the country and investment style classifications. Panel C reports the difference between average correlations reported in Panel A and Panel B. What is the most striking when observing the results especially in Panel C, is the change in intensity between the intra-category correlations, while some pairwise correlations remain substantially unchanged (eg EU CORP vs. EU GOV and US LARGE and US GOV). The EU GROWTH category reduces the intensity of the

[34] Statman, M. (2004). The diversification puzzle. *Financial Analysts Journal, 60*(4), 44–53.

Table 9 Inter- and intra-category average correlations

Panel A: NO CRISIS PERIOD

	EU CORP	*EU GOV*	*US COR*	*US GOV*	*EU LARGE*	*EU BLEND*	*EU SMALL*	*EU VALUE*	*EU GROWTH*	*US LARGE*	*US BLEND*	*US SMALL*	*US VALUE*	*US GROWTH*
EU COR	1.00													
EU GOV	0.96	1.00												
US CORE	0.55	0.50	1.00											
US GOV	0.22	0.34	0.58	1.00										
EU LARGE	0.74	0.64	0.52	−0.04	1.00									
EU BLEND	0.74	0.63	0.51	−0.05	1.00	1.00								
EU SMALL	0.73	0.61	0.49	−0.09	0.96	0.96	1.00							
EU VALUE	0.73	0.63	0.46	−0.10	0.98	0.98	0.94	1.00						
EU GROWTH	0.59	0.49	0.45	−0.04	0.86	0.86	0.84	0.83	1.00					
US LARGE	0.55	0.42	0.40	−0.20	0.86	0.86	0.84	0.84	0.75	1.00				

Panel A: NO CRISIS PERIOD

	EU CORP	*EU GOV*	*US COR*	*US GOV*	*EU LARGE*	*EU BLEND*	*EU SMALL*	*EU VALUE*	*EU GROWTH*	*US LARGE*	*US BLEND*	*US SMALL*	*US VALUE*	*US GROWTH*
US BLEND	0.59	0.47	0.41	−0.16	0.87	0.86	0.84	0.85	0.75	0.98	1.00			
US SMALL	0.39	0.26	0.30	−0.24	0.73	0.73	0.74	0.70	0.67	0.91	0.87	1.00		
US VALUE	0.51	0.38	0.35	−0.23	0.83	0.83	0.79	0.82	0.71	0.97	0.95	0.92	1.00	
US GROWTH	0.56	0.44	0.43	−0.16	0.85	0.84	0.84	0.82	0.74	0.98	0.97	0.85	0.91	1.00

Panel B: CRISIS PERIOD

	EU COR	*EU GOV*	*US COR*	*US GOV*	*EU LARGE*	*EU BLEND*	*EU SMALL*	*EU VALUE*	*EU GROWTH*	*US LARGE*	*US BLEND*	*US SMALL*	*US VALUE*	*US GROWTH*
EU COR	1.00													
EU GOV	0.95	1.00												
US COR	0.76	0.65	1.00											
US GOV	0.30	0.45	0.43	1.00										
EU LARGE	0.83	0.69	0.70	−0.01	1.00									
EU BLEND	0.83	0.69	0.70	−0.01	1.00	1.00								
EU SMALL	0.81	0.66	0.70	−0.05	0.97	0.97	1.00							
EU VALUE	0.83	0.69	0.66	−0.04	0.99	0.99	0.95	1.00						
EU GROWTH	0.85	0.71	0.70	−0.01	0.99	0.99	0.98	0.98	1.00					

(continued)

Table 9 (continued)

Panel B: CRISIS PERIOD

	EU COR	*EU GOV*	*US COR*	*US GOV*	*EU LARGE*	*EU BLEND*	*EU SMALL*	*EU VALUE*	*EU GROWTH*	*US LARGE*	*US BLEND*	*US SMALL*	*US VALUE*	*US GROWTH*
US LARGE	0.65	0.48	0.56	−0.18	0.91	0.90	0.89	0.90	0.89	1.00				
US BLEND	0.69	0.53	0.59	−0.14	0.93	0.93	0.91	0.93	0.91	0.99	1.00			
US SMALL	0.57	0.40	0.49	−0.26	0.85	0.85	0.85	0.84	0.84	0.97	0.95	1.00		
US VALUE	0.62	0.46	0.53	−0.19	0.90	0.90	0.87	0.90	0.87	0.99	0.99	0.96	1.00	
US GROWTH	0.66	0.49	0.56	−0.19	0.90	0.90	0.88	0.89	0.88	0.99	0.99	0.96	0.97	1.00

Panel C: DIFFERENCE (NO CRISIS PERIOD—CRISIS PERIOD)

	EU COR	*EU GOV*	*US COR*	*US GOV*	*EU LARGE*	*EU BLEND*	*EU SMALL*	*EU VALUE*	*EU GROWTH*	*US LARGE*	*US BLEND*	*US SMALL*	*US VALUE*	*US GROWTH*
EU COR	1.00													
EU GOV	0.01	1.00												
US COR	−0.21	−0.15	1.00											
US GOV	−0.08	−0.11	0.15	1.00										

Panel C: DIFFERENCE (NO CRISIS PERIOD—CRISIS PERIOD)

	EU COR	*EU GOV*	*US COR*	*US GOV*	*EU LARGE*	*EU BLEND*	*EU SMALL*	*EU VALUE*	*EU GROWTH*	*US LARGE*	*US BLEND*	*US SMALL*	*US VALUE*	*US GROWTH*
EU LARGE	−0.09	−0.06	−0.18	−0.03	1.00									
EU BLEND	−0.09	−0.06	−0.18	−0.03	0.00	1.00								
EU SMALL	−0.08	−0.05	−0.21	−0.03	−0.01	−0.01	1.00							
EU VALUE	−0.09	−0.07	−0.20	−0.06	−0.01	−0.01	−0.02	1.00						
EU GROWTH	−0.26	−0.21	−0.25	−0.03	−0.13	−0.13	−0.13	−0.15	1.00					
US LARGE	−0.10	−0.06	−0.16	−0.01	−0.05	−0.05	−0.05	−0.06	−0.14	1.00				
US BLEND	−0.11	−0.06	−0.17	−0.02	−0.07	−0.07	−0.07	−0.08	−0.16	−0.01	1.00			
US SMALL	−0.18	−0.13	−0.18	0.03	−0.12	−0.12	−0.10	−0.14	−0.17	−0.07	−0.09	1.00		
US VALUE	−0.11	−0.07	−0.18	−0.04	−0.07	−0.07	−0.08	−0.08	−0.16	−0.02	−0.04	−0.04	1.00	
US GROWTH	−0.09	−0.05	−0.13	0.02	−0.05	−0.05	−0.05	−0.07	−0.14	−0.01	−0.02	−0.11	−0.07	1.00

Note This table reports the inter- and intra-category average correlations EU CORP is the European Bond Corporate group; EU GOV is the European Bond Government group; US CORP represents the US Bond Corporate group; US GOV stands for the US Bond Government group; EU LARGE is the LARGE European Equity Group; EU BLEND is the BLEND European Equity Group; EU SMALL is the SMALL European Equity Group; EU VALUE is the VALUE European Equity Group; EU GROWTH represents is the GROWTH European Equity Group. Same applies for identifying the US Group Investment Styles Panel A reports average correlations for the NON-CRISIS PERIOD, ranging from to December 2006 and June 2007, and from January 2011 and December 2019. Panel B reports average correlations for the CRISIS PERIOD, ranging from June 2007 and December 2010. Panel C reports the difference between average correlations reported in Panel A and Panel B.

linear relationship with the entire US equity universe quite a bit. The reduction ranging between 0.14 and 0.17. while the greatest intensity of changes regards the asset, classes linked to European equity investment styles, namely EU LARGE, EU BLEND, EU SMALL, EU VALUE and EU GROQTH in relation to the US CORP asset type. This evidence is very interesting in light of the construction of the right portfolio mix and makes it clear that the financial market stage must be taken into account very carefully in the strategic asset allocation of the portfolio.

3.9 Investor Portfolios Relative to Benchmark Portfolios[35]

To further quantify the level of under-diversification, we compare investors' portfolios with two benchmark portfolios: (i) the market portfolio and (ii) a large number of randomly constructed portfolios. The market portfolio represents the risk-return trade-off investors could have achieved by following the prescriptions of the CAPM, and the set of random portfolios represent the risk return trade-off achieved by a "naive" investor, who might randomly select stocks. The market portfolio represents a "minimum" level of risk-return trade-off an investor portfolio should achieve.

Figures 5, 6, 7 and 8, show the positions of investor portfolios relative to the market portfolio and the capital market line (CML) in the mean-standard deviation (μ-σ) plane. We arbitrarily choose four monthly time-periods (December 2006, November 2008, January 2013 and December 2019). We use the past year of monthly returns data to estimate the means and the standard deviations of the market portfolio and investor portfolios. The risk-free rate corresponds to the 90-day Treasury rate. We find that on average only a small fraction of investor portfolios is above the capital market line. For instance, in December 2006 regardless the asset type, not more than 25.2% of the portfolios are above the CML, and in January 2013, not more than 19.1% of the portfolios are above the CML.

Even in other months, only a small fraction of investor portfolios is above the CML. The only exception is related to the period November 2008, (corresponding to mid of the Global Financial Crisis) where instead there is evidence to the contrary, both for the Equity and Fixed

[35] Goetzmann, W. N., & Kumar, A. (2008). Equity portfolio diversification. *Review of Finance, 12*(3), 433–463.

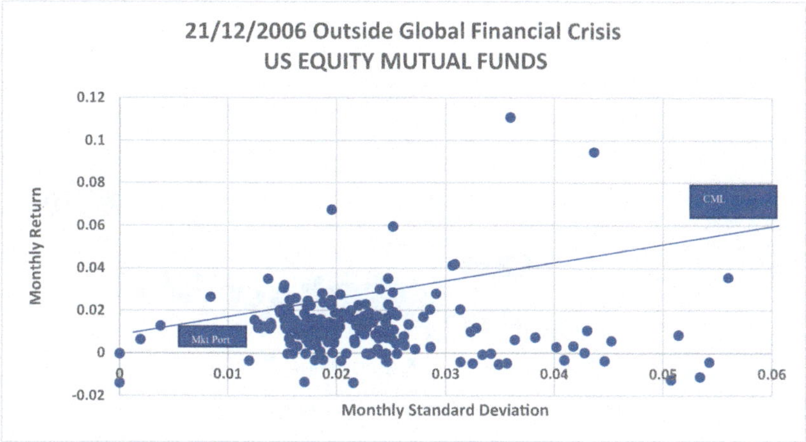

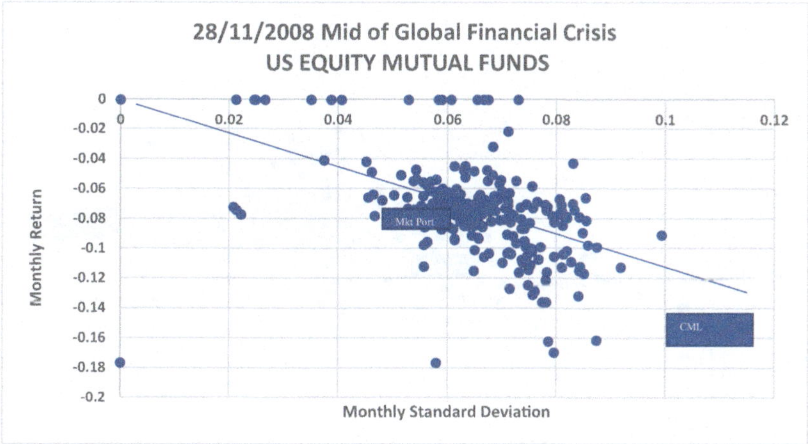

Fig. 5 US EQUITY. Mutual Fund portfolios relative to the market portfolio. This figure shows the positions of Mutual Fund portfolios relative to the market portfolio (and the Capital Market Line). The past years of monthly returns data are used to estimate the means and the standard deviations of the market portfolio and Mutual Fund portfolios. The risk-free rate corresponds to the 90-day treasury rate

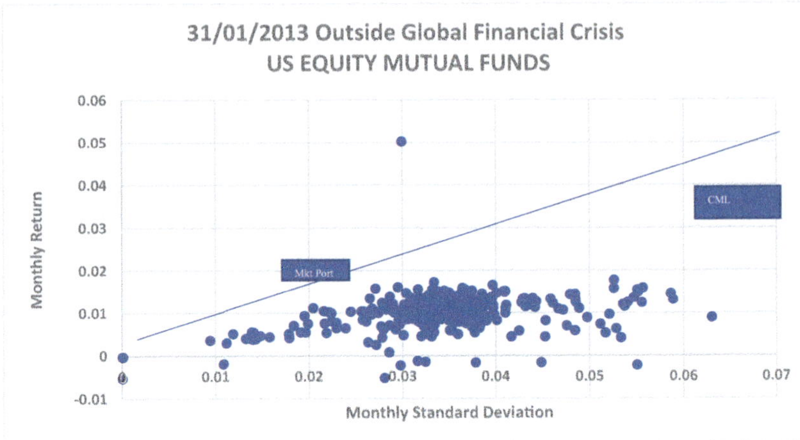

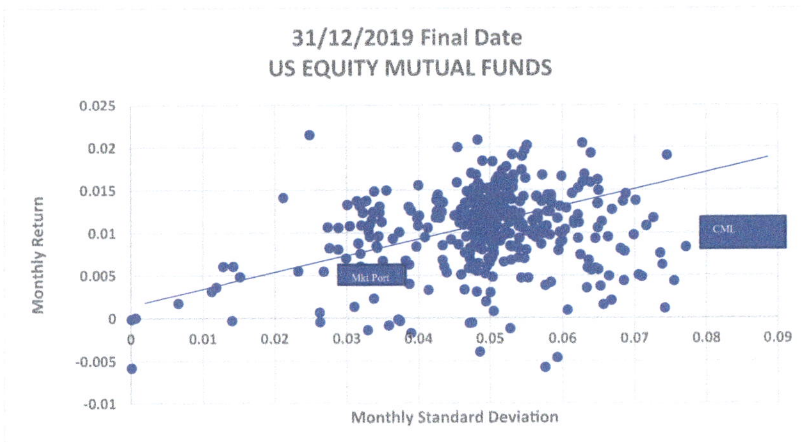

Fig. 5 (continued)

Income investment side. Overall, the graphical evidence indicates that most portfolios have significantly higher volatility levels relative to the market portfolio, and investors are not compensated for their higher risk exposures.

For a more accurate comparison between the volatilities of the mutual fund portfolios and the market portfolio, in Figs. 9, 10, 11 and 12, we

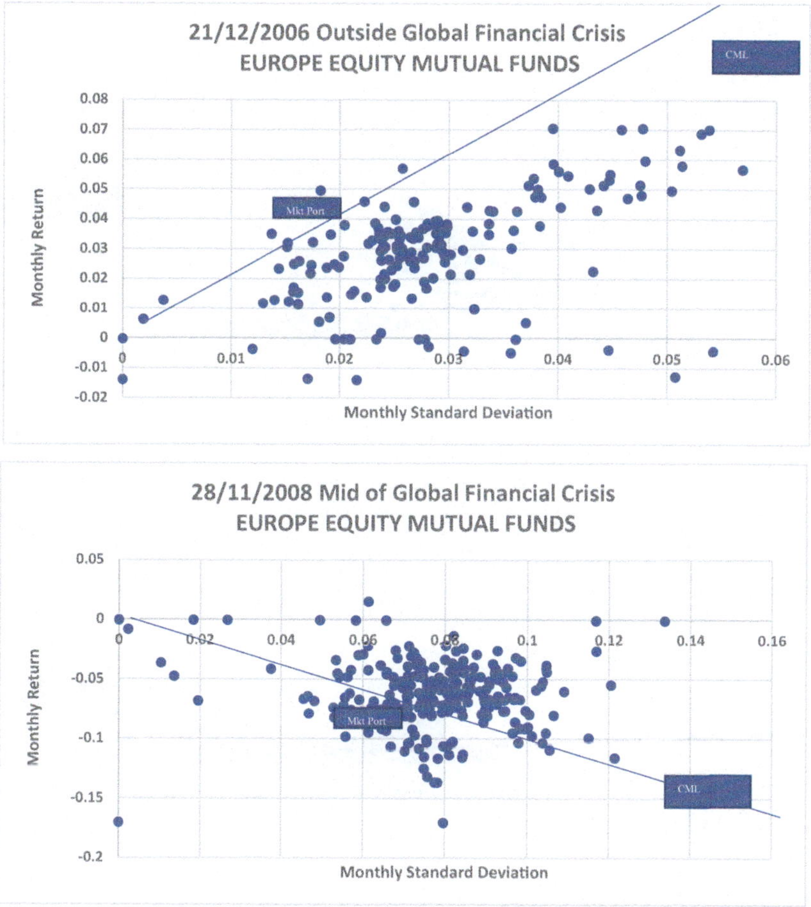

Fig. 6 EUROPE EQUITY. Mutual Fund portfolios relative to the market portfolio. This figure shows the positions of Mutual Fund portfolios relative to the market portfolio (and the Capital Market Line). The past years of monthly returns data are used to estimate the means and the standard deviations of the market portfolio and Mutual Fund portfolios. The risk-free rate corresponds to the 90-day treasury rate

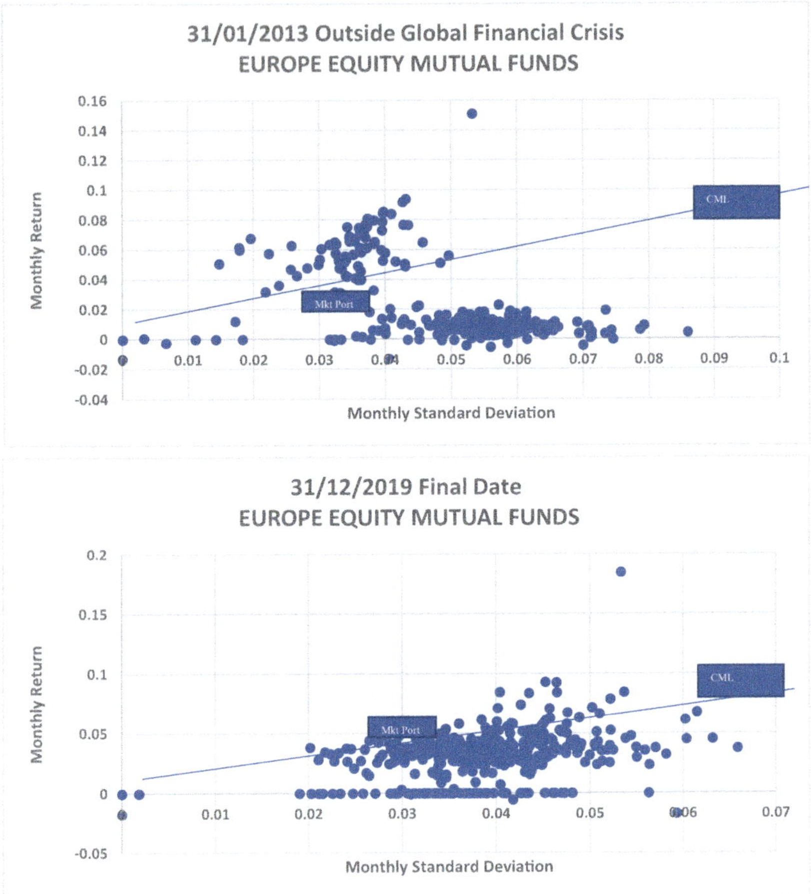

Fig. 6 (continued)

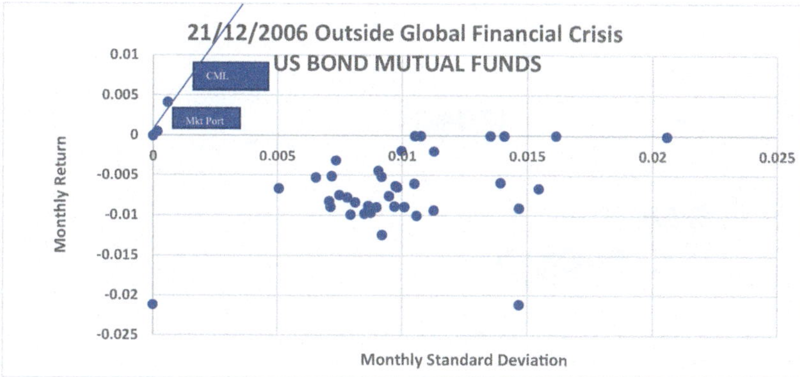

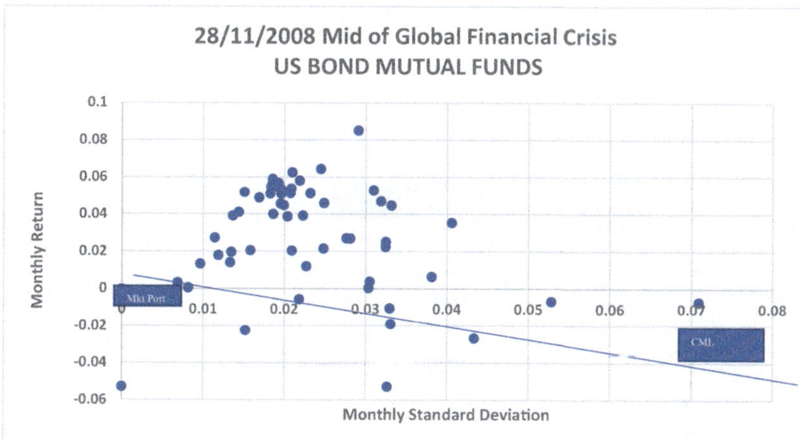

Fig. 7 US FIXED INCOME. Mutual Fund portfolios relative to the market portfolio. This figure shows the positions of Mutual Fund portfolios relative to the market portfolio (and the Capital Market Line). The past years of monthly returns data are used to estimate the means and the standard deviations of the market portfolio and Mutual Fund portfolios. The risk-free rate corresponds to the 90-day treasury rate

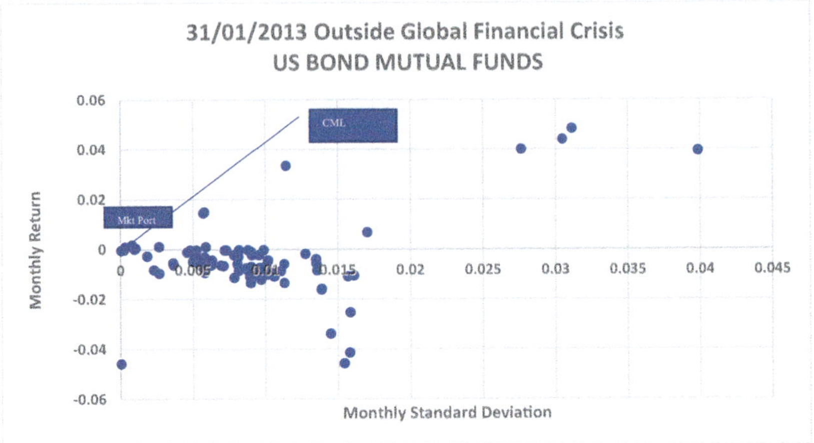

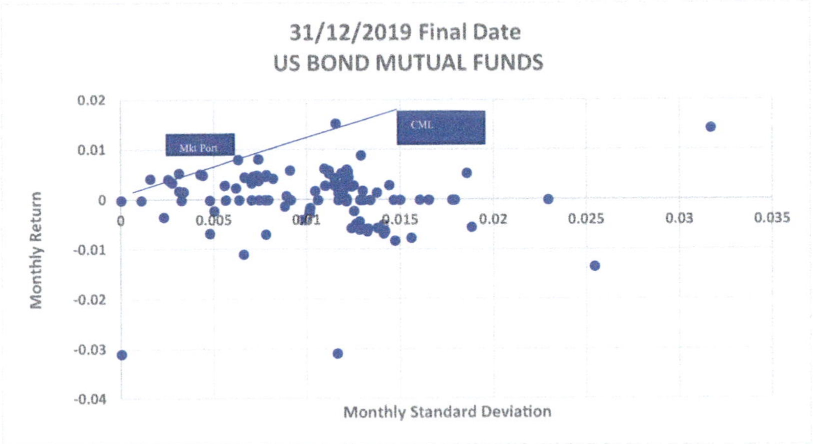

Fig. 7 (continued)

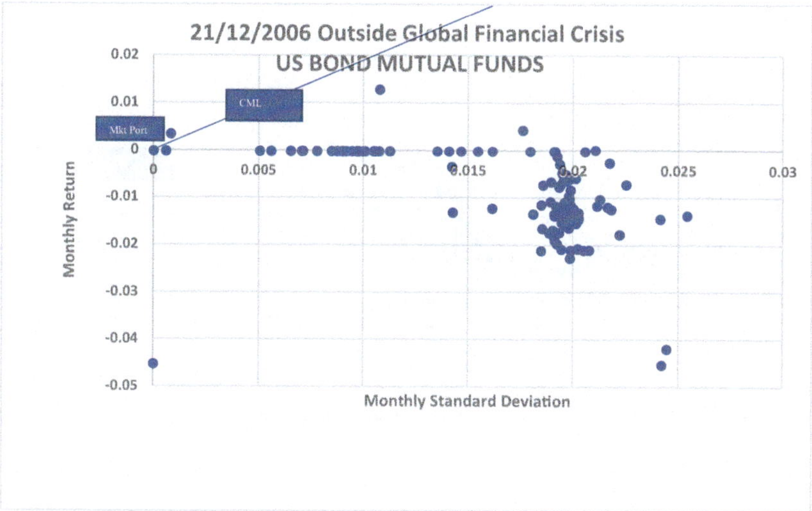

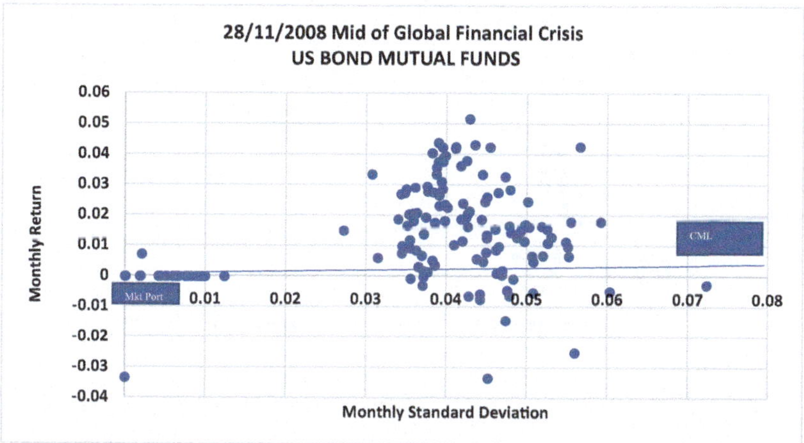

Fig. 8 EUROPE FIXED INCOME. Mutual Fund portfolios relative to the market portfolio. This figure shows the positions of Mutual Fund portfolios relative to the market portfolio (and the Capital Market Line). The past years of monthly returns data are used to estimate the means and the standard deviations of the market portfolio and Mutual Fund portfolios. The risk-free rate corresponds to the 90-day treasury rate

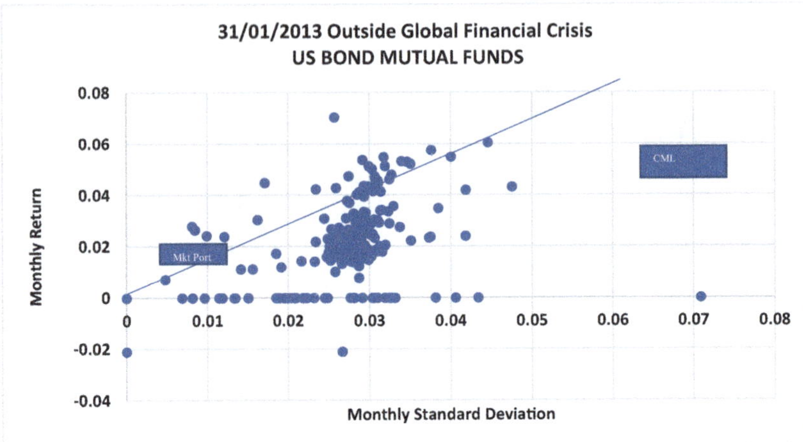

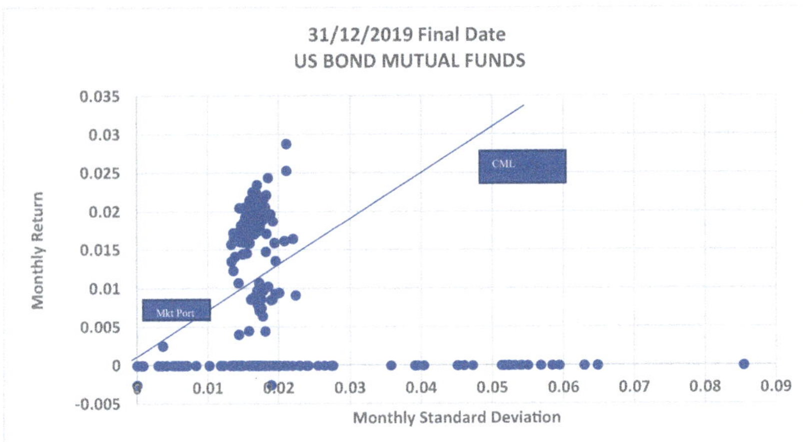

Fig. 8 (continued)

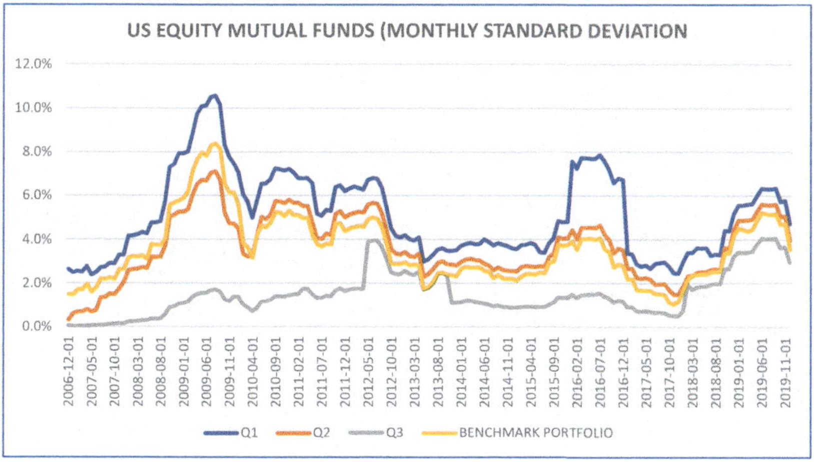

Fig. 9 Diversification level relative to benchmark portfolio. Figure shows selected volatility statistics of mutual fund portfolios and the volatility of the market portfolio using a 12-month rolling window. The mutual fund portfolios data are for US Equity Asset Type for the period from 2006 to 2019

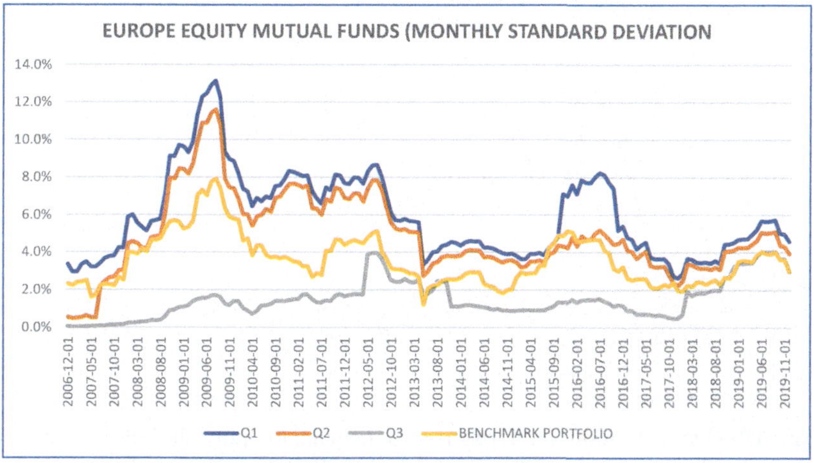

Fig. 10 Diversification level relative to benchmark portfolio. Figure shows selected volatility statistics of mutual fund portfolios and the volatility of the market portfolio using a 12-month rolling window. The mutual fund portfolios data are for European Equity Asset Type for the period from 2006 to 2019

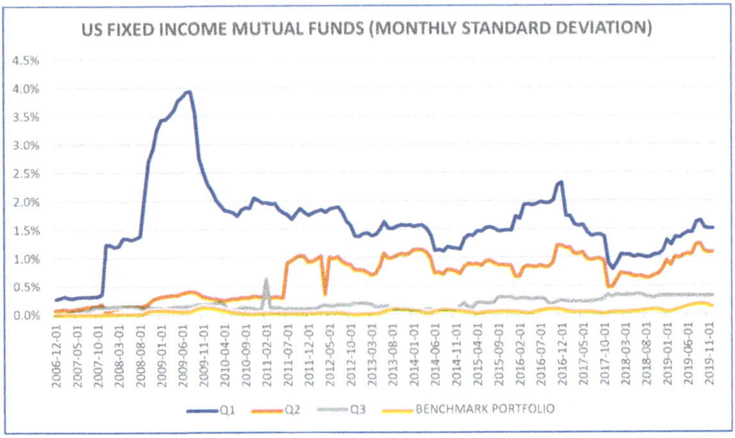

Fig. 11 Diversification level relative to benchmark portfolio. Figure shows selected volatility statistics of mutual fund portfolios and the volatility of the market portfolio using a 12-month rolling window. The mutual fund portfolios data are for US Fixed Income Asset Type for the period from 2006 to 2019

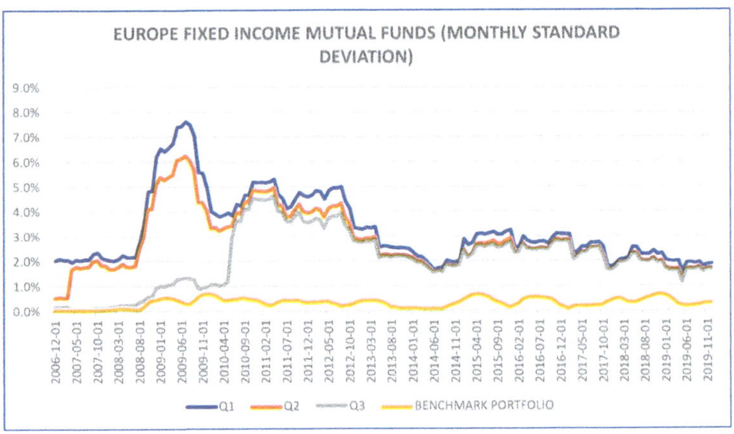

Fig. 12 Diversification level relative to benchmark portfolio. Figure shows selected volatility statistics of mutual fund portfolios and the volatility of the market portfolio using a 12-month rolling window. The mutual fund portfolios data are for Europe Fixed Income Type for the period from 2006 to 2019

plot the rolling volatility (using a 12-month window) of the market portfolio along with the rolling volatility statistics 25th percentile, median, and 75th percentile corresponding to the first (Q1), the second (Q2) and the third (Q3) quartile of mutual fund portfolios' standard deviations (Q1 corresponds to the highest volatility values). The plot shows that, regardless of the asset type considered, in any given time period, more than 50% of mutual fund portfolios have greater volatility than the market portfolio, while when considering Europe and US Fixed Income asset class, more than 75% of mutual fund portfolios have greater volatility than the market portfolio.

References

Amin, G. S., & Kat, H. M. (2002). *Portfolios of hedge funds: What investors really invest in*. Cass Business School Research Paper.

Barberis, N., & Huang, M. (2007, February). *Stocks as lotteries: The implications of probability weighting for security prices* (Working paper). Yale International Center for Finance.

Barberis, N., Huang, M., & Thaler, R. H. (2006). Individual preferences, monetary gambles, and stock market participation: A case for narrow framing. *American Economic Review, 96*, 1069–1090.

Basile, I., & Ferrari, P. (Eds.). (2016). *Asset management and institutional investors*. Springer International Publishing.

Benartzi, S., & Thaler, R. H. (2001). Naive diversification strategies in defined contribution saving plans. *American Economic Review, 91*(1), 79–98.

Blume, M. E., Crockett, J., & Friend, I. (1974). Stockholders in the United States: Characteristics and trends. *Survey of Current Business, 54*, 16–40.

Blume, M. E., & Friend, I. (1975). The asset structure of individual portfolios and some implications for utility functions. *Journal of Finance, 30*, 585–603.

Brennan, M. J. (1975). The optimal number of securities in a risky asset portfolio when there are fixed costs of transacting: Theory and some empirical results. *Journal of Financial and Quantitative Analysis, 10*, 483–496.

Chan, K., Covrig, V., & Ng, L. (2005). What determines the domestic bias and foreign bias? Evidence from mutual fund equity allocations worldwide. *The Journal of Finance, 60*(3), 1495–1534.

Christoffersen, S., & Simutin, M. (2017). On the demand for high-beta stocks: Evidence from mutual funds. *The Review of Financial Studies, 30*, 2596–2620.

Cohen, R., Polk, C., & Silli, B. (2010). *Best ideas* (Working paper).

Cui, L., & He, X. (2017). Expanding near the home base or venture far? The influence of home country state on the economic distance of foreign direct investments. *Journal of Business Research, 75*, 95–107.

Dhar, R., & Kumar, A. (2001). *A non-random walk down the main street: Impact of price trends on trading decisions of individual investors*. Yale International Center for Finance (Working paper).

Dubins, L. E., & Savage, L. J. (1976). *Inequalities for stochastic processes: How to gamble if you must*. Dover Publications.

Eun, C. S., Huang, W., & Lai, S. (2008). International diversification with large- and small-cap stocks. *Journal of Financial and Quantitative Analysis, 43*(2), 489–523.

Friedman, M., & Savage, L. J. (1948, August). The utility analysis of choices involving risk. *Journal of Political Economy, 56*(4), 279–304.

Fulkerson, J. A., & Riley, T. B. (2019). Portfolio concentration and mutual fund performance. *Journal of Empirical Finance, 51,* 1–16.

Goetzmann, W. N., Li, L., & Rouwenhorst, K. G. (2005). Long-term global market correlations. *Journal of Business, 78,* 1–38.

Goetzmann, W. N., & Kumar, A. (2008). Equity portfolio diversification. *Review of Finance, 12*(3), 433–463.

Grinblatt, M., & Keloharju, M. (2001). How distance, language, and culture influence stockholdings and trades. *Journal of Finance, 56,* 1053–1073.

Guerard, J. B. Jr. (Ed.). (2009). *Handbook of portfolio construction: Contemporary applications of Markowitz techniques*. Springer Science & Business Media.

Huberman, G. (2001). Familiarity breeds investment. *Review of Financial Studies, 14,* 659–680.

Ivković, Z., & Weisbenner, S. (2005). Local does as local is: Information content of the geography of individual investors' common stock investments. *Journal of Finance, 60,* 267–306.

Ivković, Z., Sialm, C., & Weisbenner, S. (2008). Portfolio concentration and the performance of individual investors. *Journal of Financial and Quantitative Analysis, 43,* 613–655.

Jorion, P. (1992). Portfolio optimization in practice. *Financial Analysts Journal, 48*(1), 68–74.

Kacperczyk, M. T., Sialm, C., & Zheng, L. (2005). On industry concentration of actively managed equity mutual funds. *Journal of Finance, 60,* 1983–2011.

Kahneman, D., & Lovallo, D. (1993). Timid choices and bold forecasts: A cognitive perspective on risk taking. *Management Science, 39,* 17–31.

King, M., & Leape, J. (1987). Asset accumulation, information and life cycle. *Journal of Financial Economics, 29,* 97–112.

Kroll, Y., Levy, H., & Rapoport, A. (1988). Experimental tests of the separation theorem and the Capital Asset Pricing Model. *American Economic Review, 78,* 500–519.

Kumar, A., & Lim, S. S. (2008). How do decision frames influence the stock investment choices of individual investors? *Management Science, 54*(6), 1052–1064.

Lhabitant, F. S., & Learned, M. (2002). Hedge fund diversification: How much is enough? *The Journal of Alternative Investments, 5*(3), 23–49.

Lhabitant, F. S., & Vicin, M. L. D. P. (2004). Finding the sweet spot of hedge fund diversification. *Journal of Financial Transformation, 10,* 31–39.

Lintner, J. (1965). The valuation of risk assets and the selection of risky investments in stock portfolios and capital budgets. *Review of Economics and Statistics, 47*(1), 13–37.

Markowitz, H. (1952a, March). Portfolio selection. *Journal of Finance, 7*(1), 77–91.

Markowitz, H. (1952b). The utility of wealth. *Journal of Political Economy, 60*(2), 151–158.

Markowitz, H. M. (1959). *Portfolio selection: Efficient diversification of investment*. Wiley.

Merton, R. C. (1972). An analytical derivation of the efficient portfolio. *Journal of Financial and Quantitative Analysis, 7,* 1851–1872.

Morin, R. A., & Suarez, A. F. (1983). Risk aversion revisited. *Journal of Finance, 38,* 1201–1216.

Mossin, J. (1966). Equilibrium in a capital asset market. *Econometrica, 34*(4), 768–783.

Odean, T. (1999). Do investors trade too much? *American Economic Review, 89,* 1279–1298.

Polkovnichenko, V. (2005). Household portfolio diversification: A case for rank-dependent preferences. *Review of Financial Studies, 18,* 1467–1502.

Sapp, T., & Yan, X. (2008). Security concentration and active fund management: Do focused funds offer superior performance. *Financial Review, 43,* 27–49.

Sharpe, W. F. (1964). Capital asset prices: A theory of market equilibrium under conditions of risk. *Journal of Finance, 19*(3), 425–442.

Statman, M. (1987). How many stocks make a diversified portfolio? *Journal of Financial and Quantitative Analysis, 22*(3), 353–363.

Statman, M. (2002). Lottery players/stock traders. *Financial Analysts Journal, 58*(1), 14–21.

Statman, M. (2004, August). What do investors want? *Journal of Portfolio Management, 30,* 153–161.

Treynor, J. L., & Black, F. (1973). How to use security analysis to improve portfolio selection. *Journal of Business, 46,* 66–86.

Van Nieuwerburgh, S., & Veldkamp, L. (2010). Information acquisition and under-diversification. *Review of Economic Studies, 77,* 779–805.

Zhu, N. (2002). *The local bias of individual investors* (Working Paper). University of California.

CHAPTER 9

Rating

1 Introduction—Background on Morningstar's Star Rating

Talking about ratings in the mutual fund field means talking about Morningstar.

A casual reading of the business press and mutual fund advertisements gives the impression that Morningstar, Inc., the Chicago-based rating agency, is highly influential with investors.[1]

Several academic studies motivate their analysis with the argument that Morningstar is the "most popular" and "best-known" ranking service among investors (Guercio & Tkac, 2008).

Morningstar star rating represents very specific and observable information about the quality of the fund, which is received every month.

Morningstar's one-star to five-star ranking system is discrete, and investors can obtain this rating at a low cost, which shows that the change in rating is a clear and easy-to-observe quality signal to provide investors with funds.

According to Reuter and Zitzewitz (2010), Morningstar first offered its star ratings in 1986 by subscription to its print product *Morningstar Mutual Funds* and currently offers them free on its website. Morningstar

[1] Guercio, D. D., & Tkac, P. A. (2008). Star power: The effect of Morningstar ratings on mutual fund flow. *Journal of Financial and Quantitative Analysis*, 907–936.

G. Galloppo, *Asset Allocation Strategies for Mutual Funds*,
https://doi.org/10.1007/978-3-030-76128-8_9

covers almost all existing funds and calculates the star ratings of all funds established for at least three years. Specifically, Morningstar uses 36-month load-adjusted returns to calculate a three-year risk-adjusted rating for each fund.

The star rating will be recalculated once a month, and the updated star rating will reflect the performance of the most recent month, and will be used at the beginning of the next month (approximately three working days after the end of the month).

Investments must have at least 36 continuous months of total returns in order to receive a rating.[2] For each time period (three, five, and 10 years), Morningstar ranks all funds in a category using Morningstar Risk-Adjusted Return, and the funds with the highest scores receive the most stars. A fund's peer group for the three-, five-, and 10-year ratings is based on the fund's current category. That is, there is no adjustment for historical category changes in the three-, five-, and 10-year ratings.

Morningstar rates each share class of a portfolio separately, because each share class has different fees and total return time periods available. The fund's Morningstar star rating is based on its historical performance in terms of returns and risks relative to peer groups. Morningstar rates mutual fund share classes on a scale that ranges from one star (the lowest possible rating) to five stars (the highest possible rating).[3] The rating assigned to each mutual fund share class depends on its relative performance within its Morningstar-determined investment category over the prior 3 years, 5 years, and 10 years, "after adjusting for risk and accounting for all sales charges."[4] Morningstar does not rate mutual fund

[2] Morningstar_Rating_for_Funds_Methodology pag. 12 see https://www.morningstar.com/content/dam/marketing/shared/research/methodology/771945_Morningstar_Rating_for_Funds_Methodology.pdf.

[3] Reuter, J., & Zitzewitz, E. (2010). How much does size erode mutual fund performance? A regression discontinuity approach (No. w16329). National Bureau of Economic Research.

[4] Morningstar changed various detailed of its ratings process in June 2002. See Blume (1998) for a description of the rating system used from 1996 to 2002 and (last accessed 22/11/2020). https://www.morningstar.com/content/dam/marketing/shared/research/methodology/771945_Morningstar_Rating_for_Funds_Methodology.pdf for Morningstar's description of their current ratings process. Reuter and Zitzewitz (2010) state that the most significant change was that the number of Morningstar Categories used for ratings increased from four on May 2002 (Domestic Equity, International Equity, Taxable Bonds, and Municipal Bonds) to 48 on June 2002, eventually growing to 81 in August 2009. In the opinion of the Scholars, the new Morningstar Categories

share classes that are less than three years old. For mutual fund stocks between the ages of three and five, Morningstar's rating depends entirely on its relative performance over the past 36 months.

For each of the four mutually exclusive peer groups (domestic stocks, international stocks, taxable bonds, and municipal bonds), and "Within each Morningstar Category, the top 10% of funds receive five stars, the next 22.5% four stars, the middle 35% three stars, the next 22.5% two stars, and the bottom 10% receive one star".[5] Therefore, small differences in past returns (for example, from the 10th to the 11th percentile, or from the 89th to the 90th percentile) will cause discrete changes in Morningstar's ratings.

Morningstar calculates 5-year and 10-year star ratings[6] in the same way, the only difference is the number of months of load adjustment returns used in the calculation. The overall star rating is computed as a weighted average of these ratings.[7] For funds too young to have a five- and ten-year rating, its overall rating is equal to its three- year rating.

Morningstar calculates a fund's overall rating as a 60–40 average of the 5-year and 3-year integer ratings, causing it to "round up" when the better performance is over the longer horizon.[8] For example, a share class with a 36 month return that puts it at the 89th percentile (four stars) and a 60-month return that puts it at the 90th percentile (five stars), receives an overall rating of five stars.

better reflect actual investment styles (e.g., distinguishing domestic equity funds that focus on large-cap growth from those that focus on small-cap value).

[5] https://www.morningstar.com/content/dam/marketing/shared/research/methodology/771945_Morningstar_Rating_for_Funds_Methodology.pdf.

[6] According to Reuter and Zitzewitz (2010) Morningstar also changed the method used to risk-adjusting returns, and made the relative importance of 5 and 10-year returns depend on whether a fund had experienced style drift.

[7] 4 For example, as it could be noted in Guercio and Tkac (2008), for a fund at least 10 years old, its overall star rating equals 0.2 times its three-year rating, plus 0.3 times its five-year rating, plus 0.5 times its ten-year rating.

[8] As mentioned in Reuter and Zitzewitz (2010), after June 2002, Morningstar began giving older history less weight when funds had experienced style drift. Depending on how much style drift was experienced and when it was experienced, a fund's 3-year history can receive more than 50% of the weight, causing the rounding to occur in the other direction.

For stock categories, Morningstar treats each stock category independently to assign star ratings. In fact, the star ratings are different between the same basic fund category.

2 Previous Findings in Academic Literature

Blake and Morey (2003) examine[9] the degree to which the Morningstar rating system is a predictor of out-of-sample mutual fund performance, an important issue given that high-rated funds receive the lion's share of investor cash inflow. Authors use a data set based on growth mutual funds adjusted for expenses to check the forecasting quality of the rating system. In addition, the scholars use various performance indicators in different time frames and sampling periods. They also compared the forecast quality of the Morningstar rating system with a "naive" predictor: a simple historical average monthly rate of return. The results indicate six main findings. First, low ratings from Morningstar generally indicate relatively poor future performance. Second, in most cases, there is little statistical evidence that Morningstar's highest-rated funds perform better than the second-to-last and median-rated funds. Third, Morningstar ratings do no better than the "naïve" predictor for predicting fund performance. Fourth, in terms of mutual fund flows, empirical results show that the strong positive flow response is unique to funds earning an initial 5-star rating (among previously unrated funds, the initiation of a 5-star rating delivers $26 million, or 53% above normal expected flow, to the average fund achieving such a status). The fact that the 1-to-4-star startup does not produce a positive flow response indicates that the Morningstar rating itself does not have a "subtitle" value. Indeed, this might reflect the unique ability of a 5-star rating to attract new assets to a fund.

Fifth, with respect to the rating change authors find significant positive responses to rating upgrades, and negative responses to rating downgrades, typically ranging from 15 to 35% of normal flow. In the empirical work of Del Guercio and Tkac (2008) the upgrading from 4 stars to 5 stars will have the greatest impact on the flows within 6 months after the upgrade, resulting in an abnormal flow of US$44 million, which is 35%

[9] Blake, C. R., & Morey, M. R. (2003). Morningstar ratings and mutual fund performance. *Journal of Financial and Quantitative Analysis*, 451–483.

higher than the normal expected flows. In contrast, the impact of downgrading from 5 stars to 4 stars on abnormal flows is much smaller, only-8 million US dollars, which shows that the flow response from downgrading from 5 stars is not symmetrical to upgrading to 5 stars. Sixth there is some differences in terms of the response to changes and initiations, this inconsistency could be the case that the presence of a previous rating materially affects aggregate investor reallocation decisions.

Reuter and Zitzewitz (2010) find that one-star funds underperform other funds over the next 24 months, but find little difference in the future performance of other funds. 5-star and 2-star funds perform approximately as well in the future despite 5-star funds experiencing greater inflows.

3 Methodology and Empirical Results

3.1 *Morningstar Stars Attribution*

From the empirical work by Hereil et al. (2010),[10] we extract a formal representation framework of Morningstar stars attribution to mutual funds. Authors argue that a time-series approach provides new insights into investor decision making, because one can observe and isolate investor response to a change in the "quality" of the fund.

$$U(W) = -\frac{W - \gamma}{\gamma} \tag{1}$$

where W is the investor's wealth and $\gamma > 0$ a parameter that describes the intensity of the investor's risk aversion. We denote by R the monthly excess return of the fund over the risk-free rate. The certainty equivalent excess return R^{CE} is defined as follows:

$$U\left(1 + R^{CE}\right) = \mathbb{E}[U(1 + R)] \tag{2}$$

Solving the previous equation gives us:

$$R^{CE} = \mathbb{E}\left[(1 + R)^{-\gamma}\right]^{-1/\gamma} - 1 \tag{3}$$

[10] Hereil, P., Mitaine, P., Moussavi, N., & Roncalli, T. (2010). Mutual fund ratings and performance persistence. Available at SSRN 1749414.

In order to illustrate that R^{CE} is effectively a risk-adjusted performance measure, we consider a Taylor expansion of the previous equation:

$$R^{CE} \simeq \mathbb{E}[R] - \gamma(\gamma + 1)\mathbb{E}\left[R^2\right] + \ldots \tag{4}$$

We verify that R^{CE} is an increasing function of the mean, but a decreasing function of the volatility. The risk-adjusted performance measure, called the Morningstar risk-adjusted return (MRAR), is then the estimate of the certainty equivalent excess return R^{CE}:

$$MRAR = \left[\frac{1}{T}\sum_{t=1}^{T}(1 + R_t)^{-\gamma}\right]^{-\frac{12}{\gamma}} - 1 \tag{5}$$

where T is the number of observations and R_t is the excess return of the fund at month t. Morningstar's analysts have concluded that when γ is set to 2 results in fund rankings that are consistent with the risk tolerances of typical retail investors.[11] The fund is then ranked within its category peer group and a rating is assigned using a percentile rule. The breakdown of stars is as follows: the top 10% funds are five stars, the next 22.5% funds are four stars, the next 35% funds are 3 stars the next 22.5% funds are 2 stars and the bottom 10% funds are 1 star.

3.2 *Measuring the Persistence of Ratings*

According to Hereil et al. (2010) an approach to measure the persistence of ratings is to consider the discrepancy between the probability to stay at the initial state, or a certain specific level, and the probability to go in another state:

$$d_k(t) = \Pr\{R(t) = \mathcal{R}_k | R(0) = \mathcal{R}_k\} - \Pr\{R(t) \neq \mathcal{R}_k | R(0) = \mathcal{R}_k\} \tag{6}$$

By construction, the function $d_k(t)$ is a decreasing function of t and takes its value in the range $[-1.1]$. It is equal to 1 if $t = 0$ and it is equal to $2\Pr\{R(t) = \mathcal{R}_k\} - 1$ when t tends to infinity.

[11] https://www.morningstar.com/content/dam/marketing/apac/au/pdfs/Legal/RatingMethodology_Factsheet.pdf?#:~:text=The%20Morningstar%20Rating%20is%20a,%2C%20five%2C%20and%2010%20years.&text=This%20also%20increases%20the%20universe,of%20their%20funds'%20track%20records.

We then define the persistence time as the maturity such that the probabilities to stay in the state or outside the state are equal. More formally, we have:

$$\tau_k = \inf\{t > 0 : d_k(t) \leq 0\} \tag{7}$$

3.3 *The Europerformance/Edhec Rating Methodology*[12]

Although the Morningstar rating system is certainly dominant in the quality classification of mutual funds, the approach of The Europerformance/Edhec rating is also interesting. The ratings are constructed by combining three criteria. First, one measures extreme risks using a Corner-Fisher Value-at-Risk at a 99% confidence level. If the VaR of the fund is too high, the fund is not rated. Second, the alpha of the fund is estimated. It is done in two steps. In a first step, the style analysis of Sharpe is considered to build the implied benchmark of the fund. When this benchmark is selected, one deduces alpha by a regression analysis:

$$R_{i,t} - R_f = \alpha + \sum_{j=1}^{n} \beta_j \left(R_{j,t} - R_f\right) + \varepsilon_t \tag{8}$$

The alpha criterion allows us to distinguish funds rated below and above 3 stars. For example, the 4 and 5 stars correspond to funds which have a strictly positive alpha. The distinction between 4 and 5 stars is done using a gain frequency measure. It corresponds to the number of times in percent that the fund has delivered performance that was better than that of its benchmark. This approach is similar to the logic of downside measures. If the gain frequency measure is less than 50%, the fund is rated 4 stars, otherwise it is rated 5 stars. Finally, a super rating is attributed to funds rated 5 stars and which have a Hurst exponent H larger than $1/2$.

3.4 *Dummy Variable Regression Analysis*

According to Blake and Morey (2003), one of the methods to examine out-of-sample predictive performance is a cross sectional dummy variable

[12] Here we follow Hereil, P., Mitaine, P., Moussavi, N., & Roncalli, T. (2010). Mutual fund ratings and performance persistence. Available at SSRN 1749414.

regression analysis. This approach allows us to examine the Morningstar star ranking group differences in performance predictability.

For the dummy variable regression analysis, we estimate the following equation when using the Sharpe ratio or mean monthly excess return as performance metric:

$$S_{i,t} = \gamma_0 + \gamma_1 D4_{i,t} + \gamma_2 D3_{i,t} + \gamma_3 D2_{i,t} + \gamma_4 D1_{i,t} + u_{i,t} \tag{9}$$

where:

$S_{i,t}$= performance metric for fund i,
$D4$ = 1 if a 4-star fund or if in "naïve" predictor group 4, 0 if not,
$D3$ = 1 if a 3-star fund or if in "naïve" predictor group 3, 0 if not,
$D2$ = 1 if a 2-star fund or if in "naïve" predictor group 2, 0 if not,
$D1$ = 1 if a 1-star fund or if in "naïve" predictor group 1, 0 if not,
i =1 through N, where N is the total number of funds in the subsample.

In the above equation, the 5-star fund group or the "naïve" predictor group 5 is the reference group for the dummy variable regression.

We could use the 5-star funds or "naïve" predictor group 5 as a reference group because they provide a ceiling from which we can compare the performance of the lower group funds.[13]

In this econometric approach, it is a common practice to consider as residual categories the groups in which the intensity of the variable being analyzed is minimum or maximum. Therefore, as peer group for comparison, the groups to which, the extremes of the variable distribution under examination belong, are usually used.

If the star ratings or "naïve" predictors accurately predict out-of-sample performance, we should see increasingly negative (and significant) coefficients as we move from γ_1 to γ_4.

Sharpe ratio, when all the dummy variables are equal to 0, and the coefficients γ_1 through γ_4 represent the differences between the dummy variables and the reference group. For example, a negative γ_4 implies the group of 4-star funds performs worse than the group of 5-star funds; a positive γ_1 implies the group of 1-star funds outperforms the 5-star fund group. The t-statistics on the coefficients provide a test of the significance

[13] Blake, C. R., & Morey, M. R. (2003). Morningstar ratings and mutual fund performance. *Journal of Financial and Quantitative Analysis*, 451–483.

of the difference between an individual dummy group and the reference group.

3.5 Timing and Measurement of Fund Flows

In line with the approach of Guercio and Tkac (2008), we analyze monthly net dollar flows in or out of a fund, using the standard definition in the literature of the change in total net assets minus appreciation:

$$Flow_{it} = TNA_{it} - TNA_{it-1}(1 + R_{it}) \tag{10}$$

This definition of fund flow assumes that flow occurs at the end of the month. Updated star ratings reflect the most recent month's performance and are available to investors at the beginning of the following month. Thus, if a star change occurs using return data through September 2008, we record October 2008 as the month of the star change and designate the flow in October as the first possible flow that could be due to the change.

Table 1 provides summary statistics on mutual fund flows by Morningstar rating category for bond and equity sample. In line with numerous findings on the popularity of four and five-star funds, such funds collectively attract the largest flows in total \$5.51 bln for bond sample and \$5.26 bln for equity sample, however, in both asset classes funds with ratings from three to one star experience outflows of \$3.99 bln for bonds sample and \$1.5 bln for equities.

Figure 1 illustrates average monthly dollar flows in five Morningstar rating categories over the sample period and is consistent with Table 1. For bond sample, the typical funds with ratings from one to three stars experience outflows from \$0.5 to \$2 bln, while typical four and five-star funds receive inflows up to \$5 bln. For equity sample, there is an evidence

Table 1 Summary statistics on mutual fund flow by Morningstar star rating category

RATING	*BOND SAMPLE*	*EQUITY SAMPLE*
1	−0.48	−0.45
2	−1.69	−0.53
3	−1.82	−0.52
4	0.42	0.29
5	5.09	4.97

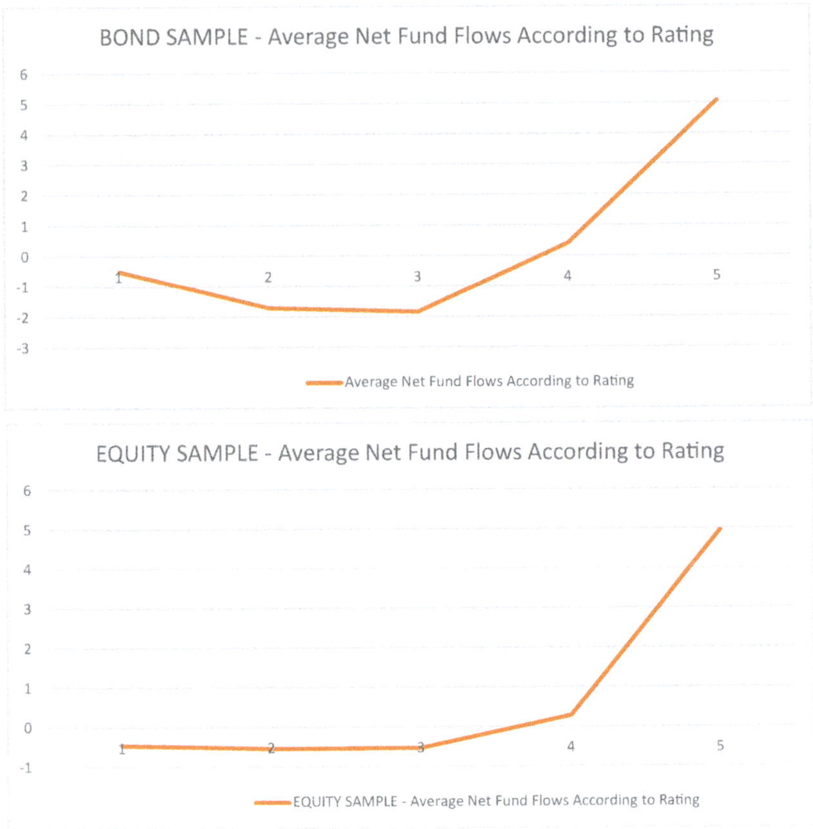

Fig. 1 Average monthly dollar flow in five Morningstar star rating categories

of outflows in mutual funds with ratings from one to three at the level around $0.5 bln, while higher ratings benefit the increase of inflows to funds. This evidence on relationship between fund flows and Morningstar ratings is consistent with previous findings of Sirri and Tufano (1998) on non-linear relation between flows and past performance.

This panel contains the total dollar flow to mutual funds in five Morningstar star rating categories. The sample includes all funds in Morningstar's domestic equity and bond rating category over the period from

December 2006 through December 2019. Fund-months appear in the not rated category if they are rated by Morningstar.

Bond & equity sample

To create this plot, we average monthly dollar fund net flow for funds with a one through five-star rating from December 2006 through December 2019.

3.6 *Frequency of Star Rating Change Events*

Table 2 provides estimated transition matrix for frequency of star rating changes in overall, bond and equity sample. The majority of these changes are upgrades or downgrades of one star, however, we also analyze changes greater than one star. For overall sample we observe the highest 17% change when upgrading from three to four stars rating and 17.38% when downgrading from four to three stars rating. For bonds sample, we note the highest change when upgrading from three to four stars (4.14%) and from four to five stars (2.41%), and downgrading from four to three stars (4.10%).

For equity sample we observe the highest change when upgrading from three to four stars (12.86%), from two to three stars (9.93%), and from four to five stars (8.01%), while downgrading from four to three stars (13.28%) and from three to two stars (10.38%).

3.7 *Summary Statistics for Funds Characteristics and Star Ratings*

The most interesting differences between funds with higher and lower ratings involve future flows and future returns. Consistent with investors responding to Morningstar ratings (or to the return histories underlying them), in the overall sample (Table 3) we observe that funds with higher ratings receive higher net flows over the whole period. Funds with ratings from three to five tend to outperform other funds, however, the difference in their future performance is very little across all performance measures. Returns tend to grow very little when upgrading the star rating but performance of all-star funds tends to reduce over the next months. Five-star funds experience greater inflows than others that is explained by Berk-Green model, where five-star funds attract more inflows due to more sophisticated manager skills, however, the amount of these inflows is getting less over the next months.

Table 2 Estimated transition matrix

PANEL A: ALL SAMPLE				
Star Rating Changes				
From	*to*			
	5	*4*	*3*	*2*
4	10.42%			
3	0.41%	17.00%		
2	0.06%	0.30%	12.19%	
1	0.03%	0.02%	0.10%	4.15%
From	*to*			
	4	3	2	1
5	11.06%	0.21%	0.02%	0.00%
4		17.38%	0.16%	0.02%
3			12.62%	0.14%
2				4.26%

PANEL B: BOND SAMPLE				
Star Rating Changes				
From	*to*			
	5	*4*	*3*	*2*
4	2.41%			
3	0.06%	4.14%		
2	0.04%	0.04%	2.25%	
1	0.03%	0.03%	0.03%	0.60%
From	*to*			
	4	3	2	1
5	2.50%	0.04%	0.02%	0.00%
4		4.10%	0.09%	0.00%
3			2.25%	0.06%
2				0.63%

(continued)

Table 2 (continued)

PANEL C: EQUITY SAMPLE				
Star Rating Changes				
From	*to*			
	5	*4*	*3*	*2*
4	8.01%			
3	0.36%	12.86%		
2	0.02%	0.26%	9.93%	
1	0.00%	0.02%	0.07%	3.55%
From	*to*			
	4	3	2	1
5	8.56%	0.17%	0.00%	0.00%
4		13.28%	0.07%	0.02%
3			10.38%	0.09%
2				3.63%

Table 3 Fund characteristics and star rating. Summary statistics. ALL SAMPLE

Star Rating	*Age*	*Fee*	*Tot.Assets*	*Flows*	
1	84.8	1.5	112828595	−451221	
2	86.8	1.3	155335155	−783704	
3	85.3	1.0	210083128	−894020	
4	87.9	0.8	309310193	332810	
5	83.2	0.7	364441007	4999244	
Star Rating	*Return*	*Alpha CAPM*	*Alpha Fama_French*	*Alpha Carhart*	*Standard Deviation*
1	0.0037	−0.0024	−0.0014	−0.0016	0.0368
2	0.0048	−0.0013	−0.0002	−0.0003	0.0392
3	0.0061	0.0004	0.0016	0.0013	0.0375
4	0.0068	0.0013	0.0025	0.0020	0.0369
5	0.0081	0.0028	0.0037	0.0029	0.0378
Star Rating	*Return (t+1)*	*Return (t+2)*	*Return (t+3)*	*Return (t+4)*	*Return (t+12)*
1	0.0051	0.0040	0.0043	0.0038	0.0050
2	0.0058	0.0055	0.0051	0.0048	0.0055
3	0.0062	0.0056	0.0057	0.0057	0.0058
4	0.0064	0.0063	0.0059	0.0055	0.0059
5	0.0065	0.0061	0.0062	0.0059	0.0062
Star Rating	*Flows (t+1)*	*Flows (t+2)*	*Flows (t+3)*	*Flows (t+4)*	*Flows (t+12)*
1	310507	−498104	175264	612923	−43133
2	−883525	−521941	−607512	−827892	150467
3	−965443	69592	274298	454594	1080176
4	−643409	−632505	−771814	−820972	−969289
5	3297184	3095186	2462907	1738301	396565

Fund Characteristics and Fund Performance are the average characteristics of the fund share.

In Europe Bond Sample (Table 4) funds with rating from four to five receive inflows while others experience outflows, and they tend to outperform across all our performance measures. Returns tend to grow when upgrading the star rating, and in general the performance tends to be slightly higher over 12 months period, and it does not change much across all other time-windows for all ratings. Four- and five-star funds experience inflows over all next periods, however with a tendency for lower inflows for larger holding period. Interestingly, one-star rating funds tend to outperform two-star rating funds, starting from the 3-month period.

Fund Characteristics and Fund Performance are the average characteristics of the fund share.

In US Bond Sample (Table 5), we mainly observe outflows for all ratings except the inflows for two-star funds. Returns tend to be positive from three to five-star rating funds in all our measures of performance. We observe drop in returns for one, two and three-star ratings funds over the next periods, while returns for four- and five-star rating funds remain almost at the same level even in 12 months' time. Five-star funds experience significant outflows in all time windows, while one- and two-star funds receive mainly inflows over time.

Fund Characteristics and Fund Performance are the average characteristics of the fund share.

In Europe Equity Sample (Table 6), there are inflows only in four- and five-star rating funds. Funds tend to outperform when upgrading their star rating, however, we observe positive performance in all our models for three-, four- and five-star funds. Returns tend to reduce in two-month time, and remain more or less at the same level for five-star funds in the next periods. Five-star funds experience inflows in all time windows, except outflows in 12-month time, however, three-star funds get inflows starting from the two-month windows. Other rating funds experience mostly outflows in the majority of time windows.

Fund Characteristics and Fund Performance are the average characteristics of the fund share.

Funds from US Equity sample (Table 7) experience inflows in all star ratings except the two-star group, and inflows in three-star funds are significantly less than those into one star. Funds of three-, four- and five-star ratings tend to outperform across all our models of performance

Table 4 Fund characteristics and star rating. Summary statistics. EUROPE BOND SAMPLE

Star Rating	*Age*	*Fee*	*Tot.Assets*	*Flows*	
1	89.0	0.9	131702726	−1015711	
2	87.2	0.7	325160233	−2203460	
3	86.7	0.6	344737718	−2347217	
4	90.2	0.5	427244207	793294	
5	85.0	0.4	536032310	7897626	
Star Rating	*Return*	*Alpha CAPM*	*Alpha Fama_French*	*Alpha Carhart*	*Standard Deviation*
1	−0.0008	−0.0015	0.0014	0.0008	0.0274
2	0.0004	−0.0008	0.0022	0.0019	0.0274
3	0.0010	−0.0001	0.0032	0.0027	0.0268
4	0.0016	0.0005	0.0035	0.0027	0.0258
5	0.0030	0.0019	0.0047	0.0042	0.0270
Star Rating	*Return (t+1)*	*Return (t+2)*	*Return (t+3)*	*Return (t+4)*	*Return (t+12)*
1	0.0012	0.0002	0.0000	−0.0011	0.0023
2	0.0004	0.0002	−0.0001	−0.0003	0.0012
3	0.0012	0.0010	0.0010	0.0008	0.0012
4	0.0014	0.0013	0.0012	0.0012	0.0015
5	0.0019	0.0015	0.0015	0.0014	0.0026
Star Rating	*Flows (t+1)*	*Flows (t+2)*	*Flows (t+3)*	*Flows (t+4)*	*Flows (t+12)*
1	−829670	144162	519885	401136	−90751
2	−2114220	−2575706	−2346380	−2403396	−905587
3	−2017195	−2068838	−1792046	−563137	−258537
4	343297	181451	165744	−691036	−462325
5	7249955	6753016	5327879	5272490	2949567

Table 5 Fund characteristics and star rating. Summary statistics. US BOND SAMPLE

Star Rating	*Age*	*Fee*	*Tot.Assets*	*Flows*	
1	78.8	1.0	32824589	−5339	
2	80.2	0.8	41416934	125826	
3	82.4	0.7	136537825	−437013	
4	84.3	0.5	284876394	−691043	
5	73.7	0.5	245116633	−1964399	
Star Rating	*Return*	*Alpha CAPM*	*Alpha Fama_French*	*Alpha Carhart*	*Standard Deviation*
1	0.0006	−0.0008	−0.0010	−0.0007	0.0109
2	0.0003	0.0001	−0.0005	−0.0004	0.0086
3	0.0020	0.0012	0.0008	0.0008	0.0116
4	0.0028	0.0022	0.0017	0.0018	0.0119
5	0.0034	0.0024	0.0020	0.0020	0.0139
Star Rating	*Return (t+1)*	*Return (t+2)*	*Return (t+3)*	*Return (t+4)*	*Return (t+12)*
1	0.0011	0.0006	0.0008	0.0007	0.0008
2	0.0010	0.0011	0.0013	0.0012	0.0006
3	0.0020	0.0019	0.0019	0.0017	0.0013
4	0.0025	0.0021	0.0020	0.0021	0.0025
5	0.0028	0.0032	0.0028	0.0028	0.0030
Star Rating	*Flows (t+1)*	*Flows (t+2)*	*Flows (t+3)*	*Flows (t+4)*	*Flows (t+12)*
1	357407	201041	246334	−117099	157287
2	189888	−58642	−175375	209458	121837
3	70949	−513205	−64413	−107178	396739
4	−888789	−164648	−334339	−27984	64331
5	−3673955	−3901079	−4261480	−5111572	−2112973

Table 6 Fund characteristics and star rating. Summary statistics. EUROPE EQUITY SAMPLE

Star Rating	*Age*	*Fee*	*Tot.Assets*	*Flows*	
1	84.1	1.7	197751924	−1155972	
2	88.9	1.4	166199419	−1060701	
3	87.0	1.1	241388395	−1140255	
4	90.3	0.9	311685250	40631	
5	86.9	0.9	361256536	5244376	
Star Rating	*Return*	*Alpha CAPM*	*Alpha Fama_French*	*Alpha Carhart*	*Standard Deviation*
1	0.0040	−0.0021	−0.0003	−0.0012	0.0431
2	0.0037	−0.0015	0.0006	−0.0002	0.0484
3	0.0062	0.0005	0.0021	0.0012	0.0477
4	0.0067	0.0014	0.0032	0.0020	0.0455
5	0.0079	0.0031	0.0042	0.0028	0.0430
Star Rating	*Return (t+1)*	*Return (t+2)*	*Return (t+3)*	*Return (t+4)*	*Return (t+12)*
1	0.0042	0.0034	0.0037	0.0028	0.0037
2	0.0057	0.0051	0.0044	0.0040	0.0064
3	0.0062	0.0057	0.0058	0.0061	0.0066
4	0.0065	0.0062	0.0057	0.0047	0.0058
5	0.0066	0.0061	0.0062	0.0061	0.0059
Star Rating	*Flows (t+1)*	*Flows (t+2)*	*Flows (t+3)*	*Flows (t+4)*	*Flows (t+12)*
1	−584344	−2258490	−1486312	234843	−745462
2	−1186854	−187781	−545924	−1143404	617024
3	−1665012	1797781	2157341	1792316	3614103
4	−1794214	−1714880	−1992185	−1788728	−2201798
5	3278667	3063995	2504858	1695360	−382862

Table 7 Fund characteristics and star rating. Summary statistics. US EQUITY SAMPLE

Star Rating	*Age*	*Fee*	*Tot.Assets*	*Flows*	
1	85.8	1.7	63691927	74520	
2	85.8	1.4	94578632	−133003	
3	83.6	1.1	121996858	44173	
4	84.1	0.9	228103105	596889	
5	76.6	0.7	286703428	4400296	
Star Rating	*Return*	*Alpha CAPM*	*Alpha Fama_French*	*Alpha Carhart*	*Standard Deviation*
1	0.0049	−0.0031	−0.0028	−0.0025	0.0392
2	0.0078	−0.0016	−0.0016	−0.0012	0.0403
3	0.0097	0.0003	0.0004	0.0007	0.0396
4	0.0115	0.0015	0.0013	0.0016	0.0405
5	0.0130	0.0029	0.0023	0.0026	0.0405
Star Rating	*Return (t+1)*	*Return (t+2)*	*Return (t+3)*	*Return (t+4)*	*Return (t+12)*
1	0.0072	0.0059	0.0062	0.0060	0.0072
2	0.0085	0.0083	0.0080	0.0078	0.0071
3	0.0099	0.0088	0.0091	0.0089	0.0085
4	0.0107	0.0111	0.0102	0.0104	0.0097
5	0.0103	0.0099	0.0105	0.0094	0.0102
Star Rating	*Flows (t+1)*	*Flows (t+2)*	*Flows (t+3)*	*Flows (t+4)*	*Flows (t+12)*
1	1159949	529517	1311316	1075431	432124
2	−303242	−33778	−34438	−104201	218413
3	38565	−179179	−201785	−64124	−262676
4	82083	−38500	−97418	43317	−139721
5	2533511	2565122	2246109	1276889	9375583

measures. Returns tend to increase when upgrading the star rating in all time windows. Returns of one- and five-star funds tend to remain almost the same in 12-month time. One and five-star funds experience inflows in all time windows, however, their amount is reducing in the next months' time. Two-star funds experience inflows only in a longer period of 12 months.

Fund Characteristics and Fund Performance are the average characteristics of the fund share.

3.8 Event Study Method for Calculating Abnormal Flow

This section describes the details of event study methods to the context of mutual fund flows as performed by Del Guercio and Tkac (2008).

An event-study allows us to isolate the incremental flow due to the rating change as separate from "normal" flow to that fund. To compute expected, or normal flow, we estimate the following benchmark regression for each fund *i*:

$$F_t^i = \alpha^i + \beta_1^i SF_t^i + \beta_2^i RET_{t-1}^i + \beta_3^i F_{t-1}^i + \varepsilon_t^i \tag{11}$$

where:

F_t^i is the net dollar flow to fund *i* at month *t*.

SF_t^i is the aggregate net flow to all funds in the same style category as fund *i* at month *t*, *i*.

RET_{t-1}^i is fund *i*'s return at *t*–1, and F_{t-1}^i is the net flow to fund *i* at *t*–1.

Authors use nineteen Morningstar-defined style categories to identify each fund's style and to compute aggregate style flows.

We define the first month, an investor having information available about a new Morningstar rating as event time 0. This time correspond to the beginning of the new month after the change rating event may occur. To estimate the coefficients for the benchmark flow regressions we use 12 months of data, ending 3 months before time 0 (i.e., event month –5 to –15).

Using the analogy to a market model for stock returns, appropriate regressors for the benchmark model are those expected both to affect all funds and to vary over time. For example, the aggregate net flow to a particular style category (SF_t^i) is a common factor for all funds in that category, and flows to various styles differ substantially over time. We estimate the sensitivity of each fund to the popularity of its style (β_1^i) to account for this component of a fund's flow around the event of a rating change.

We also include fund-specific measures of lagged returns and lagged flow because they have been found to influence flow in the cross-section.[14]

Del Guercio and Tkac (2008) measure of abnormal flow around a change in Morningstar star rating is therefore:

$$AF_t^i = F_t^i \hat{\alpha}^i - \hat{\beta}_1^i SF_t^i - \hat{\beta}_2^i RET_{t-1}^i - \hat{\beta}_3^i F_{t-1}^i \tag{13}$$

In words, the abnormal flow to fund i at time t equals the actual flow at time t minus the expected flow due to aggregate style flow, its lagged return, and lagged flow, minus the average abnormal flow to fund i ($\hat{\alpha}^i$). This average abnormal flow captures fund-specific determinants of flow that do not vary over time. Note, that the sign of abnormal flow does not have the same interpretation as net flow. For example, a positive abnormal flow does not necessarily imply that the fund is experiencing inflows. Rather, it implies that the fund is receiving more flows than expected. Expected, or normal, flow may also be either positive or negative. For example, a fund may also have a high positive normal flow because its style is very popular this month, or it has a good track record but has negative abnormal flow due to a recent drop in ratings.

To test for statistical significance, Guercio and Tkac (2008)[15] apply an event study method to the context of fund flows. Basically, the test methodology mimic same approach used by previous scholars in the context of stock market reaction. Authors focus on standardized abnormal flows, where event period abnormal flows are standardized by the estimated forecast variance of the normal flow. They also compute cumulative standardized abnormal flows by summing the standardized abnormal flows for each fund from event time 0 to t, and then dividing by the square root of the number of months used in the cumulation. Following standard practice, at each event date t Guercio and Tkac (2008) compute average standardized abnormal flows (ASTAFt) and average cumulative

[14] According to Guercio and Tkac (2008), although cross sectional studies also find a relation between flow and fund size, the relative fund size (versus other funds) does not vary much over time suggesting it has limited applicability as a cross-sectional factor.

[15] Authors apply Dodd and Warner (1983) approach.

standardized abnormal flows (ACSTAFt) by averaging across *N* events (funds). Similar to what happens in the context of stock market reaction, an advantage of analyzing standardized abnormal flows is that it prevents funds with large forecast variances (noisy flows) from dominating the statistical tests. Under this method of calculating ASTAF, funds with more precisely measured abnormal flows are implicitly weighted more heavily.

ASTAFt and ACSTAFt over the event window month 0 to +6 are then computed. Due to the Morningstar star rating approach, the length of the event window is somewhat arbitrary.[16]

Unlike event study on returns, where market efficiency means that stock prices immediately respond to new information, in mutual fund flows context it is not obvious how quickly it is expected to see the impact of changes in ratings on capital flows. The immediate flow response to the star changes is probably due to the watchful investors monitoring funds on a monthly basis.

The delayed fund flow response is also reasonable. This may be because more casual investors took some time to respond to the new rating, or because most of these investors mainly made advertisements for funds touting the new ratings. Response, and these ads will take some time to publish.

By grouping funds according to their pre-change star rating, it calculates the flow response due to a change from three to four stars, from four to five stars, etc. and assess these measures for statistical significance. Similar to the event study approach catching for stock market reaction, the standardized cross-sectional test of Boehmer et al. (1991) to assess the statistical significance of event period is used, by testing both $ASTAF_t$ and $ACSTAF_t$. $ASTAF_t$ and $ACSTAF_t$ are divided by its contemporaneous cross-sectional standard error. The cross-section of events used to compute the mean of the standardized abnormal flows is also used to compute the standard error. This approach assume that standardized abnormal flows are independently and identically distributed. Because this measure uses event-period abnormal flows to calculate the standard errors, it adjusts for any change in the variance of the standardized abnormal

[16] According to Guercio and Tkac (2008), given that Morningstar releases ratings within a few business days of month end, for example event month 5 is technically more than five months after a rating change (i.e., five months plus a fractional month). Nonetheless, authors refer to the month when they observe the rating change as the correct month (e.g. Month 5) so they get for simplicity, five months after a rating change.

flow from the estimation period to the event-window (Guercio & Tkac, 2008). According to the rationale of the test, if funds differ widely in their response to a change, for example, from 5- to 4-stars, and this will also result in a large cross-sectional standard error reducing the t-statistic, making it more difficult to reject the null hypothesis of no abnormal flow response.

3.9 *Assessment of the Economic Significance of Flow Response to Star Rating Changes*

Figure 2 shows average monthly dollar flows for star rating changes. In all sample, we observe large outflows on average for downgraded funds from five to four-star rating changes and from four to three-star rating changes, while inflows to best performing five-star rating changes funds are very low. In bond sample, five-star rating changes funds receive significant inflows when upgrading, while there are large outflows when downgrading from one to two-star rating changes funds and from three to four-star rating changes funds. In the equity sector we observe tendency for large outflows when downgrading from three to four-star rating changes and from four to five-star rating changes, while the inflows when upgrading the rating are very low comparing to downgrading, however, the inflows of five-star rating changes funds are still the largest (that is from a not rated Fund to a five-star rating) (Figs. 3 and 4).

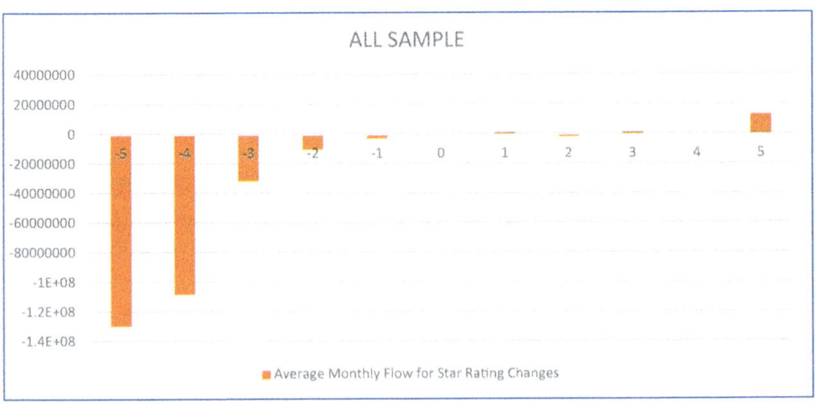

Fig. 2 Average monthly dollar flow for star rating changes—ALL SAMPLE

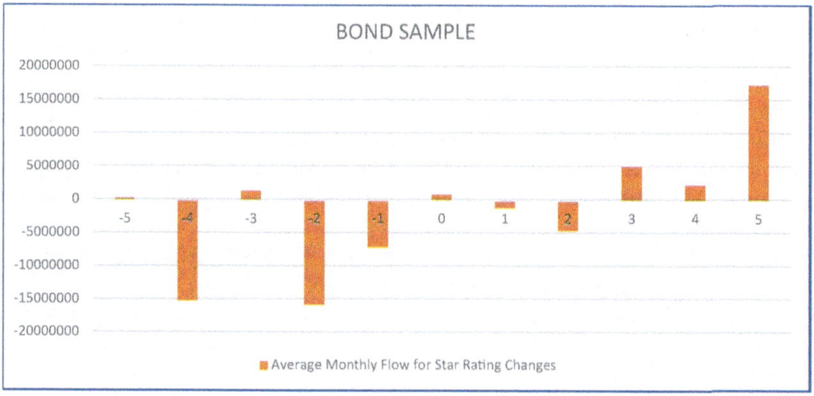

Fig. 3 Average monthly dollar flow for star rating changes—BOND SAMPLE

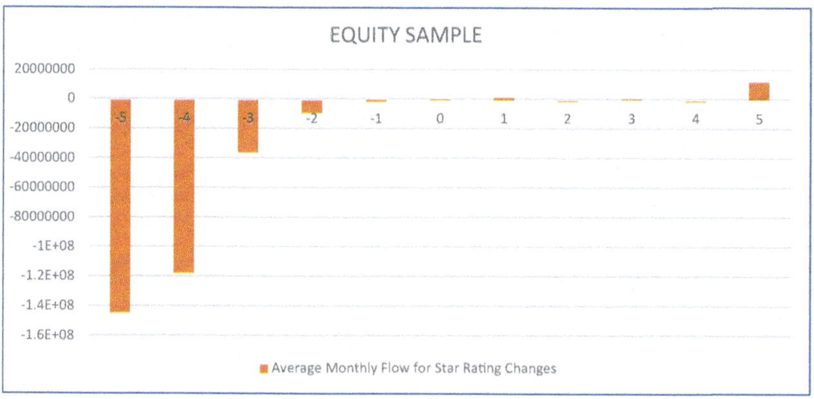

Fig. 4 Average monthly dollar flow for star rating changes—EQUITY SAMPLE

References

Blake, C. R., & Morey, M. R. (2003). Morningstar ratings and mutual fund performance. *Journal of Financial and Quantitative Analysis*, 451–483.

Blume, M. E. (1998). An anatomy of Morningstar ratings. *Financial Analysts Journal, 54*(2), 19–27.

Boehmer, E., Masumeci, J., & Poulsen, A. B. (1991). Event-study methodology under conditions of event-induced variance. *Journal of Financial Economics, 30*(2), 253–272.

Dodd, P., & Warner, J. B. (1983). On corporate governance: A study of proxy contests. *Journal of Financial Economics, 11,* 401–438.

Guercio, D. D., & Tkac, P. A. (2008). Star power: The effect of Morningstar ratings on mutual fund flow. *Journal of Financial and Quantitative Analysis,* 907–936.

Hereil, P., Mitaine, P., Moussavi, N., & Roncalli, T. (2010). *Mutual fund ratings and performance persistence.* Available at SSRN 1749414.

Reuter, J., & Zitzewitz, E. (2010). *How much does size erode mutual fund performance? A regression discontinuity approach* (No. w16329). National Bureau of Economic Research.

Sirri, E. R., & Tufano, P. (1998). Costly search and mutual fund flows. *The Journal of Finance, 53*(5), 1589–1622.

Index

G. Galloppo, *Asset Allocation Strategies for Mutual Funds*,
https://doi.org/10.1007/978-3-030-76128-8

D

J

K

L

The manufacturer's authorised representative in the EU is Springer Nature Customer Service Centre GmbH, Europaplatz 3, 69115 Heidelberg, Germany. If you have any concerns regarding our products, please contact ProductSafety@springernature.com

Printed and bound by CPI Group (UK) Ltd, Croydon, CR0 4YY
30/09/2026
02225321-0014